THE YORUBA DIASPORA IN THE ATLANTIC WORLD

The Yoruba Diaspora
in the
Atlantic World

edited by
Toyin Falola and Matt D. Childs

Indiana University Press
Bloomington and Indianapolis

Publication of this book is made possible in part with the assistance of a Challenge Grant
from the National Endowment for the Humanities, a federal agency that supports
research, education, and public programming in the humanities.

This book is a publication of

Indiana University Press
601 North Morton Street
Bloomington, IN 47404-3797 USA

http://iupress.indiana.edu

Telephone orders   800-842-6796
Fax orders   812-855-7931
Orders by e-mail   iuporder@indiana.edu

The paper used in this publication meets the minimum requirements
of American National Standard for Information Sciences—
Permanence of Paper for Printed Library Materials, ANSI Z39.48-1984.

Manufactured in the United States of America

Library of Congress Cataloging-in-Publication Data

The Yoruba diaspora in the Atlantic world / edited by Toyin Falola and Matt D. Childs.
    p. cm. — (Blacks in the diaspora)
    Includes bibliographical references and index.
    ISBN 0-253-34458-1 (cloth : alk. paper) – ISBN 0-253-21716-4 (pbk. : alk. paper)
    1. Yoruba (African people)—America—History.   2. Slavery—America—History.
3. Return migration—Africa, West.   4. African diaspora.   I. Falola, Toyin.   II. Childs,
Matt D., date   III. Series.
    E29. Y67Y67   2004
    970'.00496333—dc22

2004013528

1 2 3 4 5   10 09 08 07 06 05

For Oduduwa's Children Scattered Throughout the Diaspora

For Timothy and Dotty Childs

For Dr. A. Olusegun Fayemi,
pathologist, photographer, and social activist

Ori lo mo ibi ti ese nre.
One's destiny guides one's journeys in life.

Contents

IV. The Return to Yorubaland

Acknowledgments

In David Eltis's *Rise of African Slavery in the Americas* (2000) a particular statement stood out strongly, which called for extra attention. Drawing upon the massive trans-Atlantic slave trade database, Eltis remarked that although the Yoruba did not constitute a majority of the forced African captives shipped across the Atlantic, they have "had an impact out of all proportion to [their] relative demographic weight" on diasporic culture in the Americas (253). Having read Eltis's book after defending my dissertation in the spring of 2001 at the University of Texas at Austin, I talked with Toyin Falola about why the Yoruba have had (and continue to have) such a large influence on defining diasporic culture in the New World. When I asked Falola the question raised by Eltis's data, he smiled and laughed with unrestrained Yoruba pride, commenting, "I know the answer, but it would not pass for scholarly rigor." Knowing that my work centered on the diaspora in the Americas, he suggested that we co-edit a book to examine the Yoruba diaspora in the Atlantic world that would bring together Africanists and Americanists (meaning scholars of all the Americas). Little did I know that Falola had been contemplating a volume for some time, which allowed the project to develop rapidly.

Drawing upon our respective areas of expertise, we have endeavored to provide detailed coverage of Yoruba origins, dispersion in the Americas, cultural influences, and then the return migration to West Africa. Co-editing a volume of this size and one that attempts to speak to both African and American literatures could not have been done on our own. Scholars who were spread across North America, South America, Africa, and Europe promptly answered our call for chapters. We were disappointed on one issue, however. Despite contacting several scholars of U.S. African American history, no historian answered our call for a chapter. In many ways this is indicative of a historiographical phenomenon particular to American history. U.S. historiography has focused almost exclusively on issues of race, racism, and an overarching racial consciousness among the enslaved and their descendants, while largely ignoring the specific cultural, social, and historical legacies of specific African cultural groups.

In the process of co-editing a volume of nineteen chapters we have incurred numerous debts, only a small portion of which we have the space to recognize. As the list of contributors reveals, the authors of this volume represent an "Atlantic" perspective on the Yoruba with scholars drawn from Europe, Latin America, the United States, Canada, and Africa. Over the course of contacting authors, receiving various drafts of chapters through e-mail attachments, and getting rapid responses to stylistic and bibliographic queries, we must thank Al Gore or whoever invented the Internet. Without the communicative power of the Internet, this book could not have brought so many scholars together in such an efficient and timely manner.

In regard to the specific acknowledgments of the co-editors, Matt Childs thanks the Department of History at Florida State University for research leave, the "First Year Assistant Professor Award" to begin reading, studying, and researching in fields far removed from my dissertation, and a special *gracias* to *el jefe* Neil Jumonville for all his support. In particular, Childs thanks the history department for supporting Jennifer McCarley and most especially Amy Carney for their long hours of work on the bibliography. Toyin Falola would like to thank Ashley Rothrock who helped with some aspects of the bibliography. He remains indebted to those who continue to pressure him to contribute to the literature on slavery, most notably Paul Lovejoy. This is offered as a sacrifice to placate the spirit of those who seek Falola's intervention, and as gratitude to the ancestor-slaves who refuse to leave us alone.

Matt D. Childs and Toyin Falola

THE YORUBA DIASPORA IN THE ATLANTIC WORLD

CHAPTER ONE

The Yoruba Diaspora in the Atlantic World: Methodology and Research

Matt D. Childs and Toyin Falola

The African diaspora as a field of scholarly investigation has been studied for more than one hundred years, and that interest shows no sign of waning as the world becomes increasingly integrated.[1] As contemporary ethnic and racial conflicts dot the globe, the lessons of racial and ethnic oppression and the strategies of resistance to exploitation that have characterized the African diaspora for more than five centuries seem all the more relevant. Indeed, as the racial theorist Howard Winant has remarked, "World history has arguably been racialized at least since the rise of the modern world system; racial hierarchy remains global even in the postcolonial present; and popular concepts of race, however variegated, remain in general everyday use almost everywhere."[2] The twentieth century witnessed the emergence, and finally accepted legitimization of the diaspora for historical study that, along with African history, have been the most marginalized fields in the historical profession. Recently more attention has been focused on the role of Africans and their descendants throughout the world at institutions of higher learning on both sides of the Atlantic. This volume represents an addition to the growing literature that seeks to understand how the largest forced migration in human history fundamentally shaped all four continents bordering the Atlantic world. To examine the legacy of the African diaspora in detail, this book focuses specifically on the Yoruba experience in Africa and the Americas, primarily during the seventeenth to twentieth centuries.

The pioneering work of African Americans such as W.E.B. Du Bois and Carter G. Woodson laid the foundation for the study of the African diaspora. As Linda Heywood and Kristin Mann have recently emphasized, Du Bois and Woodson have been insufficiently recognized in the profession for catalyzing scholarly investigations of the African diaspora in academic debates on the subject outside African and African American studies.[3] Du Bois's publications, such as *The Suppression of the African Slave Trade to the United States of America, 1638–1870* (1896) and *The Negro* (1915), among others, placed African American history within a diasporic framework that extended far beyond the United States.[4] Carter G. Woodson founded the Association of Negro Life and History in 1915 and, through the *Journal of Negro History*, published a wide range of topics on the culture and history of Africans throughout the diaspora. Beginning in the 1920s anthropologist Melville Herskovits began a long career of studying what he argued were African survivals in the Americas that shaped both religious and secular life. Therefore he advocated that much could be gained about the present condition of the population of African descent in the Americas by studying African history and culture.[5] Outside the United States, scholars such as Nina Rodrigues and Gilberto Freyre in Brazil and Fernando Ortiz in Cuba, among others, explored Afro-Brazilian and Afro-Cuban culture through a diasporic framework during the first half of the century.[6] Collectively these works demonstrated the importance of the diaspora as a field of study, but they were marred by imprecision and failed to show how cultural traits on both sides of the Atlantic changed and became more complex over time.

A new direction in the study of the African diaspora began with Philip Curtin's *The Slave Trade: A Census* (1969). Curtin's pathbreaking work was the first extensive census of the trans-Atlantic slave trade to map out the major routes and total volume over four centuries.[7] In recent years scholars have turned their attention away from elaborating and revising Curtin's figures to focus, instead, on tracing the African origins and American destinations of slaves. As a result of collaborative efforts, computer assistance, and the construction of data sets, it has become easier for scholars to eschew the generic nondescriptive terms "Africa" and "African," and identify more precisely the origins of slaves and their New World destinations. David Eltis, David Richardson, Stephen D. Behrendt, and Herbert S. Klein have compiled an easily accessible database of more than twenty-seven thousand slaving voyages that now make it possible to trace the Old World origins and American destination of Africans with greater precision than ever before.[8] Complementing the demographic databases assembled on the slave trade is the team of scholars brought together by Paul Lovejoy's Nigerian Hinterland Slave Trade Project at York University, Canada, that are gathering biographic source material on the lives and experiences of slaves in the African diaspora.[9] As demographic and biographic knowledge of the slave trade has expanded markedly over the last thirty years, historians of Africa and the Americas are currently engaged in a productive dialogue that has greatly expanded the study of the African diaspora on both sides of the Atlantic.

While our knowledge of the diaspora and the connections between Africa and the Americas has increased markedly since the 1960s, scholars have yet to reach a consensus on which paradigm provides the best analytical framework.

As historians continue to study and flesh out the historical, cultural, and social consequences of the trans-Atlantic slave trade for those who experienced the horrors of the middle passage, and for their ancestors, two modes of inquiry can be broadly identified. In a widely influential essay first authored in 1976, Sidney Mintz and Richard Price argued that the random nature of the slave trade was such that Africans imported into the Americas "did not compose at the outset, groups" that could be identified with a single specific and unifying culture traced to an Old World homeland. Rather, these authors contended that African slaves who were brought to the New World represented "crowds" of disparate groups and cultures, "and very heterogeneous crowds at that." Mintz and Price did not ignore the cultural traditions that Africans brought with them, but they forcefully suggested that scholarship should examine the creation of Creole cultures and innovations in the New World in response to the fact that "what they [slaves] undeniably shared at the outset was their enslavement." Mintz and Price cautioned scholars against looking for similarities between Old World and New World African traditions, encouraging them instead to focus their analysis on the ways in which diverse African cultures came together and began to form and invent new bonds of association and identity born out of slavery through the process of Creolization. In brief, these authors argued for scholars to center their studies on the "organizational task of enslaved Africans in the New World and that of creating institutions—institutions that would prove responsive to the needs of everyday life under the limiting conditions that slavery imposed upon them."[10] Since the 1970s the literature on slavery in the Americas, especially slavery in the United States, has largely followed the Mintz and Price Creolization model with its emphasis on New World innovations and its minimizing of African cultural origins.

Beginning in the 1990s a new direction in the field of diasporic studies emerged to challenge the Creolization model by employing the Atlantic Ocean as one unit of study. John Thornton's *Africa and Africans in the Making of the Atlantic World, 1400–1680* (1st ed., 1992; 2nd ed., 1998) and Paul Gilroy's *The Black Atlantic* (1993) urged scholars to view the African diaspora as a process shaped by events and experiences on both sides of the Atlantic.[11] At the same time historians of Africa such as Joseph Miller, Paul Lovejoy, Michael Gomez, Robin Law, John Thornton, David Eltis, and others took an increasing interest in slavery in the Americas.[12] Embracing an Atlantic model for diaspora studies, scholars emphasized that slaves who were forcefully transported to the Americas carried with them their own history, culture, and identity that decisively shaped their experience in the Americas. Challenging the suggestion made by Mintz and Price that the slave trade was random in nature which resulted in a "crowd" of different cultures, historians have begun to identify specific migration patterns from quantitative and qualitative sources that link slave-exporting regions in Africa with specific destinations in the Americas.[13] Increasingly scholars are focusing on a single exporting region in Africa and a single destination in the Americas to trace out in detail how both sides were intimately connected through the slave trade.[14] Those who favor an Atlantic approach to diasporic studies do not deny (and many even study) the cultural changes and innovations that were fundamental aspects of the experience of Africans in the Americas, but they do contend that in order to understand the history and struggles of Africans in the Americas it is indeed necessary to study both sides of the Atlantic.

The contributors to this volume identify with the Atlantic approach to studying the diaspora, but also emphasize the important changes and innovations in African culture and history produced by New World enslavement that are part of the Creolization model. In order to create a dialogue between the two approaches, rather than cast them as alternative interpretive models, the authors have focused on the Yoruba diaspora in the Atlantic world from roughly the seventeenth to the twentieth century. Few could disagree with Paul Lovejoy's obvious (but overwhelmingly neglected) point for scholars to recognize that the enslaved "interpreted their lived experiences in terms of their personal histories, as anyone would, and in that sense the African side of the Atlantic continued to have meaning."[15] The focus on the Atlantic dimension of the diaspora "is important because it places the 'middle passage' in the middle" of the slaves' experiences.[16]

The meaning of "Africa" for Africans in the Americas, as with all historical topics related to identity, varied over time and place. The Yoruba are no exception. For Cuba and northeastern Brazil in the nineteenth century, with the huge influx of Yoruba slaves (as several chapters in this volume detail) Havana and Bahia could be regarded as Yoruba cities in the Americas. But it should be emphasized that the Yoruba were in the Americas and thus had to adapt and be creative in adjusting to their new surroundings even as they consciously strove to continue their African cultural traditions. In other regions such as the United States or Central America, where the overall numbers of Yoruba slaves were much smaller, the cultural forces of Creolization played a much more prominent role after the first and second generations had been established. In these locations, New World innovations seem more prominent in the processes that resulted in identity transformation. However, since Creolization is defined as creating new cultures, one cannot understand the process without studying what has been changed. This makes the Atlantic component a necessary part of understanding Creolization for Africans and their descendants. The Yoruba diaspora demonstrates that scholars must be cognizant of both the Atlantic and Creolization models, as they provide different analytical insights into the cultural, fraternal, political, social, and religious institutions utilized by Africans and their descendants in the Americas to give concrete meaning to their everyday lives.

As the various contributors to this volume reveal, the Yoruba defy precise classification. Despite the various names used to identify them throughout the diaspora, such as Lucumí in Cuba and Nagô in Brazil, the Yoruba, in contrast to other Africans, were often singled out as a separate cultural group, which allows scholars to focus on their experiences in detail. One origin of their common identity and culture is the region of Yorubaland, the homeland that connects the Yoruba who are spread throughout the Atlantic world. As with efforts to classify the Yoruba identity, Yorubaland has also been difficult to define with precision. Samuel Johnson, in his classic study, delimited the area of Yorubaland as being to the "immediate West of the River Niger (below the confluence) and South of the Quorra (i.e. the Western Branch of the Same River above the confluence) having Dahomey on the West and the Bight of Benin to the South. It is roughly speaking between latitude 6° and 9° north and longitude 2° 30' and 6° 30' East."[17] Although Yorubaland can be geographically defined, this does not mask the political and ethnic diversity within the region both in the past and the present but only delimits the area where the Yoruba language is most commonly spoken.

Examining the origins and dispersal of the Yoruba throughout the diaspora will contribute to the larger literature about the emergence and transformations of Yoruba identity from the seventeenth century on. Over the last twenty years several scholars have argued that the experiences in the diaspora made the common elements of Yoruba culture stand out in sharp relief against other Africans they encountered in the New World. It was through the process of seeking out fellow slaves and free persons of color in the Americas from Yorubaland that they began to recognize a common Yoruba identity, whereas in Africa, differences tied to region, political culture, and customs were more likely to emphasize their disparities. Historian Biodun Adediran suggests that the term "Lucumí" was used in the Americas to refer to all Yoruba subgroups under a single heading. Because they were so broadly identified under one name and, more important, came to identify themselves as Lucumí, Adediran argues that most likely a pan-Yoruba identity already existed in Africa but became more pronounced in the Americas.[18] In explaining how the Yoruba from diverse regions became known as Nagô in Brazil, João José Reis writes: "The Yoruba of the Oyo, Ehba, Ijebu, Ilesha and Ketu kingdoms became Nagôs in Bahia through complex exchanges and convergences of cultural signs with the help of a common language, similar divinities (Orishas), the unification of many under Islam, long experience as subjects of the Oyo *alafins* (kings), Yoruba urban traditions and, obviously a life of slavery in Bahia."[19] This more inclusive identity thrived where Yoruba speakers encountered members of other African ethnic and linguistic cultures in the Americas, and consequently they became all the more cognizant of shared cultural elements that bound them with other Yoruba.

Historian Robin Law, a contributor to this volume, has argued that a pan-Yoruba identify did not form so quickly in the Americas as the inclusive terms "Lucumí" or "Nagô" might indicate. He contends that the appearance of these terms as ethnic designators reflects shifts in the slave trade rather than "alternative names for a same entity," which other scholars have argued testify to a pan-Yoruba identity. Law points to the fact that prior to 1720 most Yoruba slaves came from the southern region of Yorubaland known as Lucumí. Yet during the eighteenth century Yoruba slaves, captured by the states of Dahomey and Oyo, increasingly became identified as Nagô. Therefore, Law reasons, the terms "Lucumí" and "Nagô," rather than indicating a pan-Yoruba identity realized in the diaspora, reflect the persistence of local identifications from Yorubaland carried over to the diaspora.[20]

In examining the late nineteenth and early twentieth centuries J. Lorand Matory argues that the crystallization of a recognizable and mutually understood Yoruba identity came about when Africans from Cuba, Brazil, Jamaica, North America, the Virgin Islands, and Sierra Leone returned to Lagos. Going back to their "ancestral" homeland, and well connected economically and politically through British officials, several traders, travelers, writers, and priests drew on their experiences in the diaspora to create foundational myths and a belief system that crafted a common Yoruba identity. Matory's pioneering essay demonstrates how diasporic identities were formed through a dialogue on both sides of the Atlantic that was constantly reformulated. As with all identities that are socially constructed and rooted in their own historical and cultural moments, what it meant to be Lucumí, Nagô, or Yoruba varied widely from region to region and over time.[21]

In its examination of the historical, cultural, demographic, political, social, and economic aspects of the Yoruba diaspora in the Atlantic world this volume is divided into four sections. Part I, "The Yoruba Homeland and Diaspora," examines the different processes that resulted in the enslavement of the Yoruba in Africa and their dispersion throughout the Americas. Part II, "The Yoruba Diaspora in the Americas," explores in detail the New World experiences of the Yoruba, with individual chapters focusing on the British Caribbean, Central America, Cuba, Haiti, and Brazil. Part III, "The Cultural Foundations of the Yoruba Diaspora," which offers a multidisciplinary perspective, employs contributions from literature, anthropology, ethnomusicology, and other disciplines to explore the religious, linguistic, social, literary, familial, musical, and material influences and legacies of Yoruba culture in the New World. And Part IV, the final section entitled "The Return to Yorubaland," examines the unique feature of the Yoruba diaspora that distinguishes it from other African diasporas: the return of ex-slaves to their ancestral homeland. Taken together the chapters provide a most detailed discussion of the Yoruba, from their origins in Africa to their experiences in the Americas and ultimately their return to Africa.

David Eltis's chapter maps out the origins and conditions that gave rise to the process that funneled the Yoruba into the trans-Atlantic slave trade. The Yoruba entered the slave trade on a large scale only at the end of the eighteenth century. Thus, in the overall history of the trans-Atlantic slave trade, the Yoruba figured prominently only when the trade was coming to an end. This has served to assist scholars tracing ethnicity, because as one gets closer to the present the amount of documentation tends to increase. One example is the use of the

British Mixed Commission court records for the "liberated" Africans, which provides extraordinary details on identity for the examination of ethnicity. The Yoruba became concentrated in three major areas by the end of the eighteenth and during the nineteenth centuries: Cuba; Bahia, Brazil; and Saint Domingue. Yet despite the concentration of the Yoruba in these main areas, it is important to note that no European migrant group that migrated between 1651 and 1840 was spread over such a broad territory of the New World from the United States to Argentina or approached the Yoruba in total numbers. Eltis identifies a crucial issue explored throughout this volume, namely, that the Yoruba cultural influence on the diaspora was disproportionate to their numbers.

The Yoruba have been known and identified, and have identified themselves, as Lucumí and Nagô since at least the sixteenth century. As with other societies and nations, a common language was crucial to fostering a collective Yoruba identity out of disparate roots. Paul Lovejoy examines how the shared "umbrella of language" contributed to the making of a common Yoruba ethnicity, even though Yoruba might not have been their first or primary language. Following the work of John Peel, Lovejoy regards religion and especially Islam as central to contributing to a collective identity both in West Africa and the Americas because the term "Yoruba" has Muslim origins and was later adopted by Christians.[22] Examining the political, social, and economic relations that connected the Nigerian hinterland with the coast and then to the slave societies of the New World, Lovejoy demonstrates the direct relationship between political instability in Africa often caused by the jihad and the destinations of the Yoruba in the New World. These relations were particularly pronounced when the tensions within the Oyo Empire began to surface in the 1790s, eventually leading to collapse and the exportation of slaves most notably to Bahia, Brazil, and Cuba. Lovejoy also provides a profile of the enslaved through a demographic analysis of the age and sex ratios of slaves, noting that if enslavement occurred one hundred to two hundred kilometers from the coast then the trade was overwhelmingly male, whereas enslavement that occurred near the coast was extensively trade in women and children. Complementing Eltis's chapter, the reader is presented with a concise interpretation of the important role of the Yoruba in the trans-Atlantic slave trade.

Ann O'Hear's selection brings a detailed analysis to one of the most defining demographic aspects of the Yoruba in the trans-Atlantic slave trade addressed by Eltis and Lovejoy. Compared to other African ethnic and cultural groups, the Yoruba only entered the slave trade in large numbers in the nineteenth century. Similar to the processes that resulted in a large Kongo diaspora of the eighteenth century, incessant warfare ensnared the Yoruba in the slave trade. Explaining the rise of such important city-states as Ilorin after the collapse of Oyo, O'Hear offers a close examination of the internal politics and military warfare that caused shifts and changes in Yoruba enslavement. Drawing on European and Nigerian archival sources, she is able to flesh out and clarify the Byzantine power struggles that contributed to the processes of Yoruba enslavement. Especially important in understanding the diversity of the Yoruba diasporic experience is O'Hear's analysis of the continued process of enslavement within Yorubaland that thrived in response to local circumstances long after the closing of the Atlantic trade.

Brazilian historians João José Reis and Beatriz Galloti Mamigonian analyze the important role of the Yoruba known under the broad categories of "Nagô" in Bahia and "Mina" in Rio de Janeiro. Exploring their lived experiences and the continuance of such practices as scarification known as abaja, religious beliefs such as Islam and Candomblé, and their own forms of social organization in marketing goods, they show how traditions derived from Yorubaland were transformed and refashioned in Brazil. In the nineteenth century Nagô ethnic identity became well known and feared in Brazil, especially in Bahia, because of Yoruba participation and leadership in numerous slave rebellions, most notably the 1835 Malê Revolt. While more prominent in Bahia, the Yoruba could be found throughout Brazil. Elsewhere, and especially in Rio de Janeiro, they were known as "Mina." Although surrounded by a slave population overwhelmingly of Central African origin, an identity tied to the Bight of Benin continued to inform how slaves and freed persons defined themselves. Minas actively sought out other Minas in creating social relations and devising strategies of resistance. The experience of the Yoruba in Brazil demonstrates the benefits of examining the diaspora from the perspective of how Africans defined themselves through ethnic categories, a perspective that complicates the interpretations focusing largely on racial categories.

Michele Reid turns her attention to an examination of the Yoruba in Cuba, with particular emphasis on their cultural and religious influence on society. Although Cuba was colonized by Spain in the 1490s and the first Yoruba arrived in the 1500s, the importation of larger numbers of slaves only began during the eighteenth and nineteenth centuries. Cuba and Yorubaland were intimately connected through warfare, the trans-Atlantic slave trade, and plantation agriculture worked by slave labor. As Lovejoy, Eltis, and O'Hear demonstrate in their chapters, the enslavement of Yoruba accelerated as political turmoil occurred in Oyo, fueling both the trans-Atlantic slave trade and enslavement in Yorubaland. In brief, the decline of the Oyo Empire presented conditions that resulted in the rise of Cuba as one of the most important plantation societies in the nineteenth-century Caribbean. Reid explores how the Lucumí, as the Yoruba were known in Cuba, continued to distinguish themselves culturally as a separate African group among many through the formation of fraternal associations organized around lines of ethnicity, and religiously through the practice of Santería. Finally, Reid highlights the cycle of repression and resurgence of Yoruba-derived themes in twentieth-century Cuba. As in other parts of the Americas explored and discussed in this volume, the Yoruba in Cuba were able to exert a marked impression on the broader diasporic culture.

The trade currents of the Atlantic resulted in the Yoruba extending their cultural influence throughout the New World. Russ Lohse provides a fascinating account of how even when their numbers were small, as was the case until the late eighteenth century, much can be gained by focusing on the Yoruba enslavement in the Americas. Tucked far away on the frontiers of Central America, eighteenth-century colonial Costa Rica had neither large urban populations of Africans nor a plantation society where Yoruba culture tended to flourish. Nevertheless, with the benefits of particularly rich judicial, notarial, and parish records, Lohse is able to suggest how Yoruba identity may have shaped the slave experience, causing us to consider that similar processes must have occurred elsewhere. The tantalizing albeit sparse sources Lohse uses to examine the Yoruba in Costa Rica should prompt other scholars to reexamine the presence of the Yoruba on the fringes of empire throughout the Americas. Through a close reading of sources grounded in the cultural practices of the Yoruba, Lohse is able to suggest how Old World experiences may have structured the interpretive framework slaves used to make sense of their lived realities in the Americas.

Rosalyn Howard provides a telling comparison of two islands colonized by the British, and the different and common experiences of the Yoruba in the Caribbean. The British Caribbean displays the general processes that brought the Yoruba to the New World through the well-known and horrific trans-Atlantic slave trade, which also included indentured servants after abolition and "liberated" Africans by the British who intercepted slave-trading ships. Drawing on her anthropological training grounded in primary and secondary sources, Howard structures her analysis of the Yoruba around the ongoing debate about the presence of African cultural traits, or "Africanisms," in the New World. Recognizing the dangers of how the terms "Africa," "Africans," and "Africanisms" represent general notions of culture, she problematizes the concepts by exploring the origins and ongoing changes of the Orisha religion in Trinidad to assess specific Yoruba cultural influences. For the Bahamas, Howard provides an examination of the trials endured by the "emancipated" Africans when they first arrived in the Bahamas and of their settlement in what became known as three "African Villages." On both islands, the Yoruba influenced the cultural and social relations by continuing to identify with their African past, indicated eloquently in an article in the newspaper *The Freeman* published by the black Bahamian community celebrating the fiftieth anniversary of their arrival.

One of the longest and currently most vibrant legacies of the Yoruba diaspora in the Americas has been religion. Whether known as Santeria in Cuba, Candomblé in Brazil, or more generically as the worship of the orishas, Yoruba religious practices extended across the Atlantic and practitioners can be found in ever-growing numbers from New York to Buenos Aires and in many areas in between. Christine Ayorinde examines the important role of Santería as the dominant Afro-Cuban religion that is still widely practiced today and gaining ever more adherents. The ritualistic aspects of Santería and the locations of worship offer a crucial space where Yoruba culture has continued to thrive and become refashioned over the centuries.

The process by which Candomblé became intimately associated with the Yoruba and their descendants in Brazil began from a much more heterogeneous origin than scholars have often acknowledged. Luis Nicolau Parés avoids the pitfalls that often plague diasporic studies that focus on similarities in Africa and the Americas without accounting for their unique evolution and transformation. Parés argues that the origins of Candomblé in Bahia were influenced by other ethnic groups that could not be traced to Yorubaland. These non-Yoruba groups played a decisive role in shaping the belief system and even the language of religion. Throughout the nineteenth and into the twentieth centuries, however, the Yoruba in Brazil, known as Nagôs, began to exhibit greater influence over the religion that Parés describes as the "Nagôization" of Candomblé. An interesting note is that Creoles and the population of African descent that are not of Yoruba ancestry often choose to define themselves as Nagô, as this identity connotes religious affiliation and is not exclusively an ethnic identity. Parés's observations on the cultural constructions of identities and their malleability over time and place demonstrate the need for scholars to examine questions of ethnicity through cultural and social frameworks grounded in their own histories.

Brazilian historian Mariza de Carvalho Soares examines the diversity of the Yoruba through an examination of their experience in Rio de Janeiro. Two dominant streams of the Atlantic slave trade connected Brazil firmly to the African coast. One of those examined by various authors in this volume focuses on the Yoruba from the Bight of Benin to Bahia, while the other current was from West-Central Africa to Rio de Janeiro. Scholars have tended to neglect the fact that slaves and free people of color from Yorubaland could be found in Rio de Janeiro as part of the internal Brazilian slave trade from Bahia or as a result of a minor route from the Bight of Benin, even if they were a minority among the more numerous West-Central Africans as explained by João José Reis and Beatriz Gallotti Mamigonian. Drawing on rich and detailed primary sources including an account authored by an African in the 1780s, Soares is able to trace out the lives and experiences of the Gbe- and Yoruba-speaking people that came to be known as the "Mina" in Rio de Janeiro from the eighteenth to the early twentieth centuries.

The Yoruba diaspora to the Americas was rooted in the experiences of the slave trade, but the ongoing process of making and establishing connections with an ancestral homeland continued long after the abolition of slavery. People of Yoruba descent made an ongoing and conscious effort to define themselves in both local and global terms born of diasporic connections.

Historians, anthropologists, and sociologists have long recognized the important role of the family as a crucial institution in creating and passing on cultural traits. The Yoruba in the diaspora are no exception. Kevin Roberts examines how kinship, family, and gender roles were preserved and transformed in the Atlantic world during slavery. By surveying the major destinations of the Yoruba explored by other authors in this volume, namely, Brazil, the Caribbean, and Sierra Leone, Roberts demonstrates how the Yoruba were able to continue in altered form their central practices of extended family, fictive kinship, and even gender roles. The Yoruba family thus served as an essential institution for cultural transfer and creation in developing strategies to survive New World enslavement.

The role of music in shaping diasporic identities and culture has long been recognized by scholars. Robin Moore provides a provocative account of the role of music in Santería and other popular African-derived religions in Cuba after the triumph of Fidel Castro's Cuban Revolution in 1959. Initially the revolutionary government allowed Santería to flourish, regarding it as a religion of the "popular classes" that chipped away at the institutional power of the Catholic Church. This political scenario of the 1959 revolution provided an opportunity for a profusion of Afro-Cuban religious performances and a new freedom in public performances based on African aesthetics. However, as with most aspects of social life in revolutionary Cuba, there were limits to which these cultural avenues could be pursued independent of government influence. As the Cuban Revolution became fully aligned with Marxist ideology, religion and African culture came to be regarded as an obstacle to the development of a communist society. Consequently the central role of music in Santería and other Afro-Cuban religious ceremonies and practices was suppressed and restricted. Beginning in the 1970s, however, with Cuba's participation in revolutionary struggles in Angola, Mozambique, Ethiopia, and South Africa, there was a new opening to embrace solidarity with Africa through a shared cultural heritage. With the collapse of the Soviet Union in 1991 and the economy focused on tourism, Afro-Cuban culture became an attraction that brought foreigners to the island and created an opening for the expression of Cuban religious beliefs that previously had never existed. Moore's chapter pointedly illustrates how the expression and practice of Afro-Cuban culture and music as part of a diasporic identity has always been conditioned by larger and ever-changing political events.

Similar to the pioneering scholarship of Robert F. Thompson and his investigation of Kongo art in Africa and the Americas, the artwork of the Yoruba in the Americas can also be used as an analytical category to study different dimensions of the diaspora. As Babatunde Lawal demonstrates, art is used by the Yoruba not only to mediate between the human and spirit worlds but also to enrich the quality of life and celebrate the joy of living. The Yoruba have influenced the visual and performance arts of the diaspora through the cultural legacies they brought with them during the middle passage such as sculpture, dance, and architecture. More recently, however, the population of African ancestry that might not trace its direct lineage to Yorubaland has embraced Yoruba aesthetics to reclaim an African ancestral legacy. Thus the visual arts provide a particularly poignant example of how the real and the imag-

11

ined Yoruba pasts in the Americas continue to decisively shape identity in the diaspora today.

One of the singular and unique features of the Yoruba diaspora in the Atlantic world that distinguishes it from other diasporas of African cultural and ethnic groups was the large return migration from Cuba, Brazil, Sierra Leone, and other regions of the Americas. The pattern was especially strong in the nineteenth century, but Robin Law points to examples from the seventeenth and eighteenth centuries that reveal an elaborate network of trade and political relations which allowed for trans-Atlantic migration in both directions. Historians have traditionally minimized the return migration in the overall scope of the diaspora, focusing instead on African origins and American destinations. Important insights into the Yoruba experience in the Americas and Africa can be learned from studying those who desired to return to an ancestral homeland after emancipation. As a result of their experience in the diaspora, many of the returnees maintained a separate identity, such as the Krio whom C. Magbaily Fyle examines in his chapter. On their return to West Africa many of the former slaves employed their broad diasporic identity rather than a firmly rooted local identity to facilitate their role as merchants and traders. Agreeing with Lorand Matory's call that the Yoruba must be conceptualized as a "trans-Atlantic nation," both Law and Fyle demonstrate that the liberated slaves who returned to West Africa decisively contributed to the fashioning of Yoruba national identity.

Scholars focusing on the "liberated" or "recaptive" Africans who returned to Sierra Leone and other regions of West Africa have long emphasized the important role of Christianity and missionaries in the resettlement process. Similar to issues discussed in the chapter by Robin Law, in which he emphasized the importance of the Catholic beliefs that Brazilian returnees brought with them in the return diaspora, Gibril Cole argues that Islam also deserves special mention among the "recaptives." Islamic wars in Yorubaland resulted in slaves being funneled into the trans-Atlantic slave trade. Not surprisingly many of the "liberated" Africans were Muslims and retained their Islamic faith despite the efforts of Christian missionaries. The British colonial government in Sierra Leone, similar to the Brazilian government, began to single out the Muslims for prosecution as their religious faith provided a unifying identity to resist their subordinate position in society. Despite British efforts, the Yoruba Muslims thrived in Sierra Leone society since they played a crucial role as traders with the interior. Amazingly, many purchased condemned slave ships and transformed the vessels from symbols of their enslavement into vehicles at their command to transport and market goods along the West African coast and interior.

The actions of the Muslim traders transforming the condemned slave ships into vessels to ship goods eloquently capture the experience of the Yoruba diaspora. By focusing on the Yoruba diaspora, from the trans-Atlantic slave trade that shipped Africans throughout the Atlantic world to their experiences in the Americas to their return to West Africa, we gain a detailed perspective of the social, cultural, political, economic, and historical processes that represented the largest forced migration in human history and decisively shaped the modern world.

Notes

1. For recent and concise historiographical treatments of the diaspora as a field of study, see Michael J. C. Echeruo, "An African Diaspora: The Ontological Project," in *The African Diaspora: African Origins and New World Identities*, ed. Isidore Okpewho, Carole Boyce Davies, and Ali A. Mazuri (Bloomington: Indiana University Press, 1999), 3–18; Kristin Mann, "Shifting Paradigms in the Study of the African Diaspora and of Atlantic History and Culture," *Slavery and Abolition* 22, no. 1 (April 2001): 3–21; and Linda M. Heywood, introduction to *Central Africans and Cultural Transformations in the American Diaspora*, ed. Linda M. Heywood (Cambridge: Cambridge University Press, 2002), 2–8.

2. Howard Winant, "Race and Race Theory," *Annual Review of Sociology* 26 (2000): 170.

3. Mann, "Shifting Paradigms," 3–4; and Heywood, Introduction, 3.

4. W.E.B. Du Bois, *The Suppression of the African Slave Trade to the United States of America, 1638–1870* (1896; reprint, Baton Rouge: Louisiana State University Press, 1969); idem, *The Negro* (1915; reprint, New York: Oxford University Press, 1970).

5. See Herskovits's most widely known work, *The Myth of a Negro Past* (Boston: Beacon, 1958).

6. Nina Rodrigues, *Os Africanos no Brasil* (São Paulo: Editora Nacional, 1932); Gilberto Freyre, *The Masters and the Slaves: A Study in the Development of Brazilian Civilization*, trans. Samuel Putnam (New York: Knopf, 1946); Fernando Ortiz, *Los negros brujos* (Havana: Editorial de Ciencias Sociales, 1995 [1906]); idem, *Los negros esclavos* (Havana: Editorial de Ciencias Sociales, 1975 [1916]).

7. Philip D. Curtin, *The Atlantic Slave Trade: A Census* (Madison: University of Wisconsin Press, 1969).

8. David Eltis et al., eds., *The Trans-Atlantic Slave Trade: A Database on CD-ROM* (Cambridge: Cambridge University Press, 1999).

9. For an overview of the Nigerian Hinterland Slave Trade Project, including a list of members, publications, and conferences, see http://www.yorku.ca/nhp/index.htm. Accessed 20 June 2003.

10. Sidney W. Mintz and Richard Price, *The Birth of African-American Culture: An Anthropological Perspective* (Boston: Beacon, 1992 [1976]), 18–19.

11. John Thornton, *Africa and Africans in the Making of the Atlantic World, 1400–1800*, 2nd ed. (Cambridge: Cambridge University Press, 1998); Paul Gilroy, *The Black Atlantic: Modernity and Double Consciousness* (Cambridge, Mass.: Harvard University Press, 1993).

12. See, for example, Joseph Miller, *The Way of Death: Merchant Capitalism and the Angolan Slave Trade, 1730–1830* (Madison: University of Wisconsin Press, 1988); Paul Lovejoy, *Transformations in Slavery: A History of Slavery in Africa*, 2nd ed. (Cambridge: Cambridge University Press, 2000); Michael A. Gomez, *Exchanging Our Country Marks: The Transformation of African Identities in the Colonial and Antebellum South* (Chapel Hill: University of North Carolina Press, 1998); Robin Law, "The Evolution

of the Brazilian Community in Ouidah," *Slavery and Abolition* 22, no. 1 (April 2001): 22–41; Thornton, *Africa and Africans*; and David Eltis, *The Rise of African Slavery in the Americas* (Cambridge: Cambridge University Press, 2000).

13. See, for example, Eltis, *The Rise of African Slavery*, esp. 245; and Thornton, *Africa and Africans*, esp. 192.

14. See, for example, Heywood, *Central Africans and Cultural Transformations in the American Diaspora*; and Kristin Mann and Edna G. Bay, eds., *Rethinking the African Diaspora: The Making of the Black Atlantic World in the Bight of Benin and Brazil* (London: Frank Cass, 2001).

15. Paul E. Lovejoy, "The African Diaspora: Revisionist Interpretations of Ethnicity, Culture, and Religion under Slavery," *Studies in the World History of Slavery, Abolition, and Emancipation* 2, no. 1 (1997), available at http://www2.h-net.msu.edu/~slavery/essays/esy9701love.html.

16. Paul E. Lovejoy, "Identifying Enslaved Africans in the African Diaspora," in *Identity in the Shadow of Slavery*, ed. Paul E. Lovejoy (London: Continuum, 2000), 2.

17. Quoted in Toyin Falola and Akanmu Adebayo, *Culture, Politics, and Money among the Yoruba* (New Brunswick, N.J.: Transaction, 2000), 6.

18. Biodun Adediran, "Yoruba Ethnic Groups or a Yoruba Ethnic Group? A Review of the Problem of Ethnic Identification," *África: Revista do Centro de Estudos Africanos da Universidade de São Paulo, Brazil* 7 (1984): 57–70.

19. João José Reis, "'The Revolution of the *Ganhadores*': Urban Labour, Ethnicity and the African Strike of 1857 in Bahia, Brazil," *Journal of Latin American Studies* 29, no. 2 (May 1997): 355–93; quote at 361.

20. Robin Law, "Ethnicity and the Slave Trade: 'Lucumi' and 'Nago' as Ethnonyms in West Africa," *History in Africa* 24 (1997): 205–19.

21. J. Lorand Matory, "The English Professors of Brazil: On the Diasporic Roots of the Yorùbá Nation," *Comparative Studies in Society and History* 41, no. 1 (January 1999): 72–103.

22. J. D. Y. Peel, *Religious Encounter and the Making of the Yoruba* (Bloomington: Indiana University Press, 2000).

I
THE YORUBA HOMELAND
AND DIASPORA

CHAPTER TWO

The Diaspora of Yoruba Speakers, 1650–1865: Dimensions and Implications

David Eltis

The study of slavery, and more broadly of the repopulation of the Americas, has been shaped by those scholars who are prepared to engage with data as well as text. For example, common sense suggests that any evaluation of the process of Creolization requires some basic information on how many immigrants came from where and over what period. The Yoruba have such a high profile in the forced movement of peoples from Africa to the Americas that it is surprising so little quantitative analysis has been done, and if this is the situation for such a well-known group, then it is certainly no better for others. The literature on the African diaspora contains much more on coastal regions of origin than on the way those caught up in the slave trade identified themselves. Our current knowledge is largely limited to broad geographic trends. For the Bight of Benin, the eastward drift in the origin of slaves entering the trans-Atlantic traffic from the region's hinterland is well established, but the extent and timing of that shift remain obscure. As the Yoruba resided in the East, it is assumed that they became increasingly caught up in the trade. Africanists have begun to carry out preliminary systematic assessments of the position of African nations in co-erced migration, but these assessments still fall well short of what has been achieved for their free-migrant European counterparts. In this chapter I attempt a more systematic assessment of their involvement and explore the implications of the findings for some broader issues in the re-peopling of the Americas.

Like many migrant groups, the Yoruba did not exist initially as a cohesive self-conscious people. In the sense of self-identification the emergence of Yoruba, or "Lucumí" in Spanish or "Nagô" in Portuguese, may not have oc-curred until the Yoruba diaspora was well advanced—perhaps well into the nine-teenth century. No single political unit ever encompassed Yoruba speakers, and no one embarkation point in West Africa funneled the Yoruba into the Atlantic slave traffic. Some scholars have argued that Yoruba speakers came to see themselves as Yoruba only as a result of their experiences in the New World,[1] although it seems more likely that identification with the term developed on both sides of the Atlantic at the same time in response to similar pressures. The collapse of Oyo in the Old World triggered widespread flight and migration and threw fragments of many different Yoruba-speaking groups together in new environments that included many non–Yoruba speakers. Such Old World disruption must have closely replicated the conditions in the New World created by the slave trade. Such circumstances tend to accelerate the constant renewal of identity formation that is a characteristic of all cultures. The initial impact of the social trauma of migration was probably the seeking out of like groups and a redefinition of social identity on the basis of shared elements, especially language or religion. The best-documented analogy lies perhaps in Europe rather than Africa in the situation of eighteenth-century German-speaking emigrants to both the Americas and Eastern Europe. With no political unity in their homeland, migrants did not conceive of themselves as Germans but rather as Rhinelanders or Swiss or Prussians. Emigration radically reshaped the migrant group's perceptions of itself and its descendants, but not, initially, as that of British or American or Russian citizens. Rather, migration initially made them German in their own eyes and in the eyes of others.[2]

Evaluation of such a process does require some idea of the dimension and direction of the movement of peoples. As David Richardson, Stephen Behrendt, and I have developed more fully elsewhere, the basic method of deriving estimates of slave departures for the African coast is to take five-year estimates (or at longer intervals where quinquennial data are not available) of the national participation of the trade and distribute these over eight African coastal regions according to the evidence of slaving activity revealed in *The Transatlantic Slave Trade: A Database on CD-ROM* recording more than twenty-seven thousand voyages.[3] Some Yoruba speakers left Africa via western Bight of Biafra ports such as the Brass River and Bonny, but the great majority embarked in ports located in the Bight of Benin. The Bight of Benin is taken here to span the coast from the Rio Volta to Rio Nun.[4] The slave trade on the coasts of West and West-Central Africa was always dominated by a few embarkation points. Except on the Windward Coast, the slave traffic did not evolve by means of trans-Atlantic slavers carrying on an extensive coasting trade prior to setting out on the middle passage. Vessels and African traders seem to have concentrated their activities on a few ports in each region from the outset, though the identity of these ports changed slowly over time. The Congo, Old Calabar, Ouidah, and the Gambia River seem to have dominated their respective regions from the start. The traffic expanded by the addition of new ports or the replacement of old ones.

Trading patterns within Africa are much less well documented than are ship-borne activities, but all the evidence suggests that slaves generally came to the coast by the most direct route. In the hinterlands of the Gold Coast, and in the Bights of Benin and Biafra, extensive east-west trading or movement of slaves destined for Atlantic markets, especially across major ethnic boundaries, was unusual, at least in the absence of a convenient water route such as the Upper Niger. Trade routes within Africa proved flexible and adaptive in the face of wars and political shifts, but it is not unreasonable to look for major language groups leaving ports closest to the point where they became destined for the trans-Atlantic traffic.

The point is illustrated by a remarkable document series in the records of the Anglo-Spanish Court of Mixed Commission that met in Havana between 1821 and 1845. Like its counterparts located around the Atlantic basins, the Court adjudicated slave vessels captured by signatories (of which Great Britain was always one) of bilateral treaties. In the final stage of their evolution, the treaties authorized courts to condemn and destroy slave vessels and their contents and formally liberate any slaves found onboard. At British insistence, great care was taken to identify such liberated slaves because they were to be turned loose in societies in which black skin was enough to make re-enslavement a great risk. To ensure a permanent basis for identifying freed slaves, each court kept two copies of a register of liberated individuals, one of which was sent to London.[5] As with the records kept by the Sierra Leone mixed commission courts (most of which are also extant), the registers noted the name, age, and place of habitation of every African falling within the jurisdiction of the court. The court added the person's height and sex, a description of the most obvious cicatrization, and, of course, the name of the vessel that carried the recaptives from Africa.[6] In over 99 percent of the cases, the name of the recaptive in the ledger is clearly African and forms one of the very few extant precolonial sources for African names.[7] All information appears to have been mediated by African interpreters from the same part of the coast from which the captured vessel had embarked slaves, the identities of whom were added to the ledger. Unlike in the Sierra Leone case, where the practice of recording place of habitation was discontinued within a few years, the country column was completed throughout the period of the court's operation. The ledgers contain the African name and country of 10,390 individuals, both of which provide a basis for identifying region of origin of each recaptive without traversing the minefield of European-inspired identifications of African ethnicity that have plagued attempts to pin down the homelands of Africans in the Americas.[8] Moreover, the information in the ledgers may be compared to what is known about the African port of embarkation for each of the forty-one vessels that the court adjudicated. Every one of these vessels may be found in the recently published database on the trans-Atlantic slave trade, and in all cases the African coastal origin of the slave ships is clear.[9]

Table 2.1 shows a preliminary breakdown of the ethnic designations that the court assigned to 3,663 men, women, and children from the Bight of Benin in these years. These designations are grouped initially by broad geographic regions in the hinterland—western, northern, and eastern—and, in the case of the eastern region, a subdivision is created separating Yoruba from non-Yoruba. The overall dominance of the Yoruba is immediately obvious. For the Spanish at this time it would seem that the term "Lucumí" was not a synonym for Yoruba, despite an assumption some have made. The extensions to the term "Lucumí" in the table indicate that Cubans assigned many non-Yoruba this general sobriquet. Further, some liberated Africans who left from ports outside though adjacent to the Bight of Benin are also described as Lucumí, and others leaving from the most easterly ports in the Bight of Benin are identified as Carabalí. Thus, by the term "Lucumí," Cubans could not have meant someone who entered the middle passage from a port in the Bight of Benin or an individual who identified him- or herself as Yoruba. The best definition of the broad country terms such as "Lucumí" and "Carabalí," as well as "Congo" and "Ganga" that fill the court records is geographic. Lucumí are those that live in the hinterland of the Bight of Benin; Carabalí are their counterparts behind the major Bight of Biafra ports; Congo are those in West Central Africa; and Ganga are in the broad hinterland of Sierra Leone.

Such broad designations are clearly not very helpful to modern researchers interested in the nations or ethnicities of those forced into the middle passage, but Table 2.1 also shows that most such designations were qualified by an extension that was much more specific and, for the majority of slaves, may be linked with nations known to modern researchers. Tentative identification of these terms suggests that 62.5 percent, or the overwhelming majority of those leaving the Bight of Benin, saw themselves as Yoruba. Those countries that cannot be identified had few adherents.[10] As there appears no particular reason why the British navy should have captured more slaves of one ethnicity than another,[11] there is no known bias in the sample shown in Table 2.1, and the ratios of country names shown in the table might be taken as indicative of the years 1826 to 1839 as a whole. Applying the ratios to the volume of forced migration from the Bight of Benin in these same years leads to an estimate of Yoruba slave departures over this fourteen-year period of 101,750, or 7,200 per year.[12]

For the pre-1826 era a very different tack is necessary that hinges on broad historical trends within Africa and detailed data on departures from individual ports. A preliminary step in the analysis is to establish the general proposition, already made, that coerced migrants from a particular African nation would tend to depart from the port closest to where that nation was located. Table 2.2 shows the Spanish data on ethnicity distributed by ports within the Bight of Benin where individuals claiming to belong to that nation embarked. The panels broadly correspond to the western coastal region, Popo; the central coastal region, Ouidah; and the eastern region, Badagri and Lagos. As we might expect, the share of Yoruba who embarked increased as we survey the ports from west to east. In the east the overwhelming majority of recaptive Africans designated themselves as Yoruba. There is no reason why this pattern would not

Table 2.1. African Peoples Carried from Ports in the Bight of Benin as Identified in the Registers of the Havana Court of Mixed Commission, 1826–1839

	Modern Name	Number	Share of Known Nations
Western Region			
Lucumí Arara	Allada	142	.05
Mina Popo	Popo	317	.10
Mina	?	307	.10
Mina Janti	Fanti	88	.03
Arara	Allada	41	.01
Magin	Mahi*	62	.02
Mago Arara	Allada	77	.03
Regional Total		1,034	.34
Northern Region			
Mandinga Fula	Fulani	2	.00
Lucumí Jausa	Hausa	6	.00
Lucumí Tapa	Nupe	22	.01
Lucumí Bogu	Borgu	1	.00
Lucumí Cacanda	Kakanda	1	.00
Lucumí Chamba	Konkomba or Gurma	61	.02
Regional Total		93	.03
Eastern Region 1.			
Yoruba			
Lucumí Ello	Oyo	1,236	.41
Lucumí Aguia	?	23	.01
Lucumí Efu	Efon/Ekiti	1	.00
Lucumí Eba	Egba	58	.02
Lucumí Llabu	Yagba or Ijebu?	74	.02
Lucumí Ecumacho	Ikumeso or Ekun Eso	470	.15
Lucumí Ota	Ota (Awori)	49	.02
Lucumí Yesa	Ijesha	3	.00
Lucumí Sabe	Sabe	1	.00
Regional Total		1,915	.63

continued

Table 2.1. *(continued)*

	Modern Name	Number	Share of Known Nations
Eastern Region 2.			
Non-Yoruba			
Carabali Oru	Oron	3	.00
Regional Total		3	.00
Total Identified		3,045	
Unidentified			
Lucumí		582	
All Others (16 groups)		36	
Grand Total		3,663	

*Curtin, *Census*, 183, does not link "Magin" with "Mahi" and leaves the former unidentified.
Source: Calculated from Public Record Office, Foreign Office, series 313 (FO 313), vols. 56–62.
The basic sources used for the identifications of ethnic terms are D. H. Crozier and R. M. Blench, *An Index of Nigerian Languages*, 2nd ed. (Dallas: Summer Institute of Linguistics, 1992); Philip D. Curtin, *The Atlantic Slave Trade: A Census* (Madison: University of Wisconsin Press, 1969); and Robert S. Smith, *Kingdoms of the Yoruba*, 3rd ed. (London: James Currey, 1988). Oscar Grandio, Paul Lovejoy, and Ojo Olatunji, all of York University, Canada, guided me through unfamiliar territory.

have been established well before the 1820s. In the absence of any known enduring political or military impediment to embarking slaves in Lagos or Badagri it is reasonable to assume that Yoruba speakers would have formed at best a minority of those taken onboard in western ports in the earlier period. Put differently, if large numbers of Yoruba speakers had been dispatched to the Americas before, say, the collapse of the Oyo Empire in the late eighteenth century, then one would have expected Lagos and Badagri to emerge as major conduits for such a movement. For slave owners in Africa and the Americas, as well as in a revolt-ridden middle passage, male adult slaves, however valuable, were potential trouble and an expense, particularly when in transit. A direct route between initial sale or capture and embarkation was essential to sustaining profits. Most of the slave narratives that indicate a slow and circuitous route to the coast are based on the experiences of children easy to control.

The second step in estimating a Yoruba-speaking presence in the pre-1820s era is to distribute slave departures over time within the Bight of Benin. Fortunately both the data on slave departures and the patterns of precolonial history of the Slave Coast—essentially the Bight of Benin—are the best documented of any region that supplied large numbers of slaves to the Americas. Table 2.3 provides port distribution estimated directly from an updated version of the CD-ROM database. It shows first the heavy preponderance of western

Table 2.2. African Peoples Carried from the Bight of Benin: Yoruba/ Non-Yoruba Status (columns) by Major Port of Embarkation (rows) as Identified in the Havana Court of Mixed Commission Registers, 1826–1839

Embarkation Points	Western, Non-Yoruba		Northern, Non-Yoruba		Eastern, Non-Yoruba		Yoruba Only		Total	
	No.	%	No.	%	No.	%	No.	%	No.	%
Popo	777	79.7	81	8.3	0	0	117	12.0	975	100
Ouidah	269	18.2	12	0.8	1	0.1	1,194	80.9	1,476	100
Lagos	5	0.8	0	0	2	0.3	604	98.9	611	100
Total	1,051		93		3		1,915		3,062	100

Source: Calculated from Table 2.1. The ports of embarkation for the vessels listed in FO 313, vols. 56–62, have been identified from TSTD.

and central Slave Coast ports in the dispatch of slaves to the Americas in the seventeenth and early eighteenth centuries. Above all, of course, it shows the extraordinary preeminence of Ouidah in the first quarter of the eighteenth century just prior to the Dahomean conquest. This preeminence was not just in the Bight of Benin but likely held for the whole African coast where for a time Ouidah was the highest-volume single embarkation point. In the aftermath of the conquest, ports immediately east of Ouidah—first Epe and then Badagri— entered the traffic, but so too did the Popoes to the west, though prior to this point there had certainly been some coastal traffic in slaves from these ports to Ouidah. Direct slave departures from Epe began about 1737, but for the second and third quarters of the eighteenth century this initial eastward shift away from Ouidah was modest, serving to fill the gap left by Dahomean destruction of Jakin in 1732, rather than displacing Ouidah. Epe and Badagri together dispatched less than one-third of the number of slaves that left Ouidah between 1726 and 1750, and Popo departures amounted to just one-fifth of Ouidah's.

Table 2.4 provides five-year estimates of slave departures for the critical transition period from 1751 to 1800 during which Port Novo took over from Ouidah as the leading slave trade port. The defining feature of this half-century was the struggle between Dahomey and the eastern ports for slaves originating in the interior east of Dahomey, as far east, in fact, as Benin. Epe was the leading eastern port at the outset. Like Badagri, it traded somewhat more heavily with the French and was susceptible to the depressive effects on slave departures of European wars. Benin was less affected by wars in the Atlantic because it catered more to the generally victorious English, sporadically from the 1720s and steadily from the mid-1750s, though many of these captives came not from Benin proper but from other adjacent Edo-speaking and Itsekiri polities.[13] For

Table 2.3. Estimated Departures of Slaves (in thousands) from Ports
in the Bight of Benin by Quarter Century, 1650–1865

	Popo*	Ouidah	Offra/ Jakin	Epe	Porto Novo	Badagri/ Apa	Lagos/ Onim	Benin	All Other	Total
1651–75	0	1.0	20.9	0	0	0	0	0	0	21.9
1676–1700	2.7	133.4	85.9	0	0	0	0	0	0.9	222.9
1701–25	1.8	374.4	28.6	0	0	0	0	1.2	1.6	407.5
1726–50	43.8	177.9	21.2	36.0	0	15.3	0	10.9	1.0	306.2
1751–75	20.1	130.4	0.6	17.2	11.7	32.8	3.6	36.2	0.3	253.0
1776–1800	15.0	78.3	5.6	0.5	96.8	18.1	24.0	25.1	0.9	264.4
1801–25	7.2	72.5	0.9	0	19.2	14.1	114.2	4.6	4.7	236.6
1826–50	11.9	82.9	1.9	0	7.7	5.2	170.6	1.2	6.8	288.4
1851–65	1.1	24.7	0	0	0	0	4.9	0	7.0	37.7
1651–1865	103.6	1,075.5	165.6	53.7	135.4	85.5	317.3	79.2	23.2	2,039

*As the point of embarkation was often termed "Popo," this column combines Little Popo and Great Popo, even though these ports were fifteen miles apart. For those voyages where the prefix was supplied, 95 percent embarked their slaves at Little Popo.

Source: Eltis, Richardson, Behrendt, New Census, forthcoming.

fifteen years after 1755 Benin was the leading departure point in the eastern Bight of Benin. This does not necessarily indicate an upsurge in the slave trade, because some of these slaves would undoubtedly in an earlier period have left via Ouidah, Epe, or Badagri. Moreover, even without slaves from Benin (and fewer from Oyo), Ouidah still dispatched between two and three times more slaves to the Americas in these years than did Benin. Badagri overtook Benin for a brief period after 1770 as a point of direct contact with Europeans, perhaps aided by lower customs for both African and European traders. Political instability within the Badagri ward system soon interfered with trade, however, and when Oyo withdrew its protection of Badagri, Dahomey formed an alliance with other eastern ports and launched a series of attacks culminating in the destruction of both Epe and Badagri.[14] But Porto Novo rather than Dahomey emerged as the chief beneficiary of the alliance, dispatching more slaves than any other Slave Coast port in the last quarter of the eighteenth century. It is striking how well the five-year estimates of slave departures accord with what is known of the political and military activity of this period—derived from both African oral traditions and European reports.

Porto Novo dominance did not last. Departures from Lagos expanded between four- and fivefold in the period between the last quarter of the eighteenth and the first quarter of the nineteenth centuries. There was little in the late eighteenth century to point to Lagos's role as the leading Slave Coast embarkation point of the nineteenth century.[15] About one thousand slaves left each

Table 2.4. Estimated Departures of Slaves from Ports in the Bight of Benin by Five-Year Periods, 1751–1800 (in thousands)

	Popo*	Ouidah	Offra/ Jakin	Porto Novo	Badagri/ Apa	Lagos/ Onim	Benin	Epe	Total
1751–55	4.0	28.1	0	0	8.4	0	1.8	8.6	51.0
1756–60	9.0	21.7	0	0	0	0	7.2	0	37.8
1761–65	4.8	30.0	0.6	1.6	4.1	0.6	10.1	0.9	52.7
1766–70	3.7	21.7	0	5.6	2.7	1.0	11.3	4.5	50.5
1771–75	2.2	29.8	0.6	4.4	13.1	2.0	9.4	0	60.9
1776–80	3.2	18.8	1.6	17.8	6.8	1.8	3.2	0	53.2
1781–85	1.0	21.7	2.5	8.0	2.7	3.2	5.0	0	44.2
1786–90	0	12.1	0.9	33.9	3.3	8.4	7.4	0.3	66.3
1791–95	11.5	16.5	0	11.8	1.9	6.6	2.2	0	50.4
1796–1800	4.6	15.5	0	15.3	1.4	3.3	0	0	50.3
1751–1800									2,039

*As the point of embarkation was often termed "Popo," this column combines Little Popo and Great Popo, even though these ports were fifteen miles apart. For those voyages where the prefix was supplied, 95 percent embarked their slaves at Little Popo.

Source: Eltis, Richardson, Behrendt, New Census, forthcoming.

year in the 1790s, and British slave traders almost doubled this annual average in the few years prior to 1807. But most of the quadrupling of annual departures between 1801 and 1825 occurred because of the activities of Portuguese slavers, mainly carrying slaves to Bahia. The sample size on which the estimates for 1801–25 in Table 2.3 are based is small by the standards of the data set but adequate (the precise port of embarkation is known for only one-fifth of the slaves estimated to have left), and it is possible that the estimate for Lagos is too high, but nevertheless the increase in slave departures at the beginning of the nineteenth century must have been substantial. As the trans-Atlantic slave trade came to a close, together Lagos and Ouidah sent 90 percent of all people entering the trans-Atlantic slave trade from the Slave Coast, with Lagos alone accounting for 60 percent prior to the British attacking and occupying the island in 1851, sixteen years before the rest of the trans-Atlantic traffic ended. Lagos's sudden withdrawal from the traffic as a result of the British attack restored Ouidah to its old position as the major — indeed at times the only — Slave Coast embarkation point.

The late preeminence of Lagos in the slave traffic was shaped partly by politics and partly by its location. As in the previous century Ouidah offered a less attractive market for slave traders from outside Dahomey than did Lagos and Porto Novo. The evolution of the Dahomean slave merchant community separate from the king is now well established. Fewer Ouidah deportees were captured by Dahomey forces or enslaved within Dahomey in the 1840s than a century earlier. Yet state control remained, and the city-states of the east not only bought almost all the slaves they sold, they offered the opportunity to outsiders to trade on their own account. Many representatives of Brazilian-based firms, drawn from the Afro-Portuguese community, carried on business in Lagos.[16] Lagos was also closer to the major source of slaves than other ports at this time, given that the collapse of the Oyo Empire probably generated most of the slaves that embarked for the Americas from the Slave Coast after 1825. Yet Lagos was also more susceptible to direct attack from the sea than was any other major port. The lagoon system allowed slaves to be moved quickly to points of embarkation beyond the knowledge of patrolling cruisers, which is one reason why the slave trade lasted longer here than elsewhere. But in sharp contrast to Ouidah and Porto Novo, naval vessels could bombard the slave traders' facilities at Lagos, and maintain an occupation at a lower cost than similar action against almost any other major slaving center on the West African coast would have incurred. Two British attacks were needed before Lagos was occupied, but occupation was possible and ended the slave trade immediately.

The third step in the derivation of an estimate of Yoruba departures is to link particular ports with African nations. We have nothing like the Spanish material for estimating numbers of Yoruba before the 1820s. Indeed, as noted, it may be that what is being measured is Yoruba speakers rather than a self-conscious Yoruba group. A first approach is to build on the earlier discussion of the relationship between the location of major African nations and ports of embarkation. Table 2.2 shows the Yoruba embarking at ports located closest to their homeland. Given that this appears to have been a universal phenomenon for Old World peoples moving to the New World, whether the migrants were forced onboard ship or embarked voluntarily, might we not apply the port-ethnicity ratios in Table 2.2 to the whole pre-1820 era? To do this it is necessary first to group the embarkation points shown in Table 2.3 into western regions (Popo, Great and Little), central regions (Ouidah, Offra, Epe, Porto Novo), and eastern regions (Badagri, Lagos, Benin). The share of slaves who were Yoruba shown in column 8 of Table 2.2 are assigned to these three groups for the whole period. These ratios are then used to convert the estimates of gross departures from the sum of ports making up each group in Table 2.3 into estimates of Yoruba departures only. The resulting estimate of the size of the Yoruba-speaking diaspora is thus a function of, first, a detailed sample of ethnicity from a fourteen-year period in the nineteenth century and, second, a distribution of slave departures from groupings of Slave Coast ports for twenty-five-year periods between 1651 and 1867. This procedure yields a total for the Yoruba-speaking diaspora extending over 217 years of 1.67 million.[17]

It will strike most historians as overly mechanical to leave the estimate at this first-pass stage dependent as it is on a distribution from the nineteenth century. What do sources that cannot be reduced to a database have to offer on the subject? The ethnicity of captives leaving the Bight of Benin is less well known than the military and political struggles among coastal communities that shaped the departure of those captives, and the overview of slave provenance in the Bight of Benin offered here summarizes rather than adds to what is already known. Three broad phases may be discerned in the two centuries after 1650: the first running to c. 1725, the second from the conquest of Ouidah to the emergence of Lagos as the dominant port around 1800, and the third from 1800 to the close of the slave trade.

An extremely rapid expansion of the slave trade occurred in the first period carrying volumes to the highest ever reached (in the Bight of Benin, at least) in 1701–25. The traffic funneled though Ouidah, Popo, and Offra, ports that, if not "free" in the current European usage, certainly attracted sellers of slaves from eighty miles or more inland. Lucumí (including both Yoruba and non-Yoruba) slaves appear in early-eighteenth-century Cuba (a very minor market for slaves at this period), but there is no evidence of a strong Yoruba-speaking component in this first phase of the traffic. The British Caribbean was the major market for Slave Coast slaves between 1670 and 1714, as the slave trade rose to its regional peak. The extensive primary sources on the British slave trade for these years mention many African peoples, but I am aware of none that identify slaves as Yoruba or the peoples who were eventually encompassed by this term. The very occasional references to groups termed as Lucumí in records in the Americas, and the low ratios of this same group among Slave Coast slaves that observers on the African coast offered, suggest that they constituted no more than 12 percent of departures from the Bight of Benin. As not all Lucumí were Yoruba speakers, the Yoruba share would have been smaller again.[18] Dahomey activities generated a large proportion of the slaves leaving the Bight of Benin at this time, but the absence of Yoruba suggests that Dahomey military expansion was to the north, rather than the east, with unrest arising from the fall of the Akwamu Empire in the west. Oyo activities in the east must have provided much smaller numbers. The great majority of slaves dispatched to the Americas must have been Ewe, Adja, Huea, or Fon.[19]

The second phase spanned the relative decline of Ouidah from the late 1720s to its ultimate replacement by Lagos as the premier Atlantic export center in the early nineteenth century. Dahomey actions against lagoon-based rivals in the slave export business generated captives and shifted slave provenance southward—closer to the coast, but the attempt by Dahomey to assume a middleman role and obtain slaves from outside Dahomey commercially would have in part offset this southward shift in provenance. The eastern ports that emerged in this phase drew slaves primarily from Yoruba speakers in the east affected by Oyo activities rather than their chief rival to the west, Dahomey. Most of the Epe/Badagri slaves originated in Oyo, far to the north and east, and constituted a diversion of a flow that had previously passed through Ouidah and likely were mainly Yoruba speakers.[20] But Badagri and Lagos together accounted for only 15 percent of all Bight of Benin deportees in the second half of the eighteenth century. One might hypothesize a mix of Ewe-, Fon-, and Gbe-speaking

27

and Yoruba peoples with a smaller stream of captives drawn from the ethnically diverse Delta region and passing through Benin.

In the third phase of slave departures, the balance between Yoruba speakers and Ewe-Fon-Gbe captives shifted strongly toward the former. As already noted, Ouidah's middleman role increased in the nineteenth century, with more slaves originating beyond Dahomey borders. That these slaves came mostly from the northeast is suggested by the fact that after 1810 more than half the slaves taken from the Slave Coast to the Americas landed in Bahia. Here Yoruba and, to a much lesser extent, Hausa, not Ewe-Fon, traditions dominated nineteenth-century slave communities in Bahia. In the late eighteenth century, by contrast, St. Domingue—also drawing heavily on Ouidah—Yoruba were almost as numerous as Ewe-Fon. On the basis of 221 inventories of slaves in the Bahia area between 1737 and 1841, Verger noted "the almost total absence of the Nagô-Yoruba until the beginning of the nineteenth century, and their presence en masse around 1830. . . . Dahomeans are present from the very beginning."[21] After 1851 and the suppression of the slave trade to Brazil and Lagos, Ouidah paradoxically appeared to widen its catchment area, as slaves who would have passed through Bonny were now embarked on the Slave Coast, but the volumes in these last years were only two thousand a year on average compared to eleven thousand in the 1826–50 period.

A lower-bound estimate of Yoruba-speaking departures is derived by breaking the whole slave trade era at 1800. Before 1800 we might assume that only 10 percent of all those forced to leave the Bight of Benin were Yoruba, and for the nineteenth century we could accept the Havana evidence reinforced by Verger's assessment of Bahian plantation inventories that posits a massive increase in Yoruba arrivals after 1800 from very low levels before that year. Ten percent of the pre-1800 totals in the last column of Table 2.3 is 147.6 thousand, and the post-1800 portion of the Yoruba-speakers total, estimated earlier (see n. 17), is 499.4 thousand. The total estimate for Yoruba departures for the whole period is thus 647,000.

The distance between the upper- and lower-bound estimates, 1.67 million and 0.65 million, respectively, is uncomfortably wide, but the foregoing discussion and the new estimates of slave departures from within the Bight of Benin at least allow us to focus on what we need to know and what further assumptions might be called for. To summarize, we know that relatively few Yoruba (or those who later came to be designated as Yoruba) left for the Americas before the conquest of Ouidah—probably no more than 10 percent of all those leaving from the Bight of Benin. The upper-bound estimate is certainly wrong in its assumption that four out of five deportees from Ouidah and Offra were Yoruba speakers prior to 1726. At the other end of the time spectrum, we have the Havana sample suggesting that almost nine out of ten of those forced to embark in the Bight of Benin after 1800 were Yoruba in the broader sense. Between 1725 and 1800, and indeed for any period before 1800, we can assume that almost none of those leaving western Bight of Benin ports were Yoruba speakers. Eastern embarkation points such as Badagri and Lagos, by contrast, must have dispatched mainly Yoruba speakers, but between 1726 and 1800 these ports sent only an estimated ninety-three thousand slaves into the traffic—or just over one thousand a year—and none at all before 1726.[22] The major problem area, and a major source of the wide gap between upper- and lower-bound estimates, lies with the central Bight of Benin ports, particularly Ouidah, during the last seventy-five years of the eighteenth century. There can be no certainty at present on how the nearly six hundred thousand people who embarked in these ports at this time identified themselves.

Nevertheless, some additional assumptions, broadly consistent with trends established in the literature, allow the construction of a third estimate of departures. For the central ports it seems reasonable to project a gradual if accelerating increase in Yoruba-speaking deportees over time from the 1720s to the beginning of the nineteenth century, with most of the acceleration coming late in the period as a result of the disorder stemming from the decline of the Oyo Empire. Thus we assume an increase from 10 percent Yoruba in the first quarter of the eighteenth century, by 16-percentage-point increments over each of the next three-quarters of the century—to 26 percent in 1726–50, 42 percent in 1751–75, and 58 percent in 1776–1800. After 1800 we assume a more substantial increase, occasioned by the decline of Oyo, to the 81 percent supported by the Havana data. For the relatively small numbers leaving from western ports before 1800, 5 percent Yoruba might be assumed, and for the western ports the ratio used in the first set of estimates of 98.9 percent Yoruba is retained. These assumptions generate the estimates shown in column 1 of Table 2.5 and constitute the preferred series. A total Yoruba-speaking migration of 968,000 is derived, two-thirds of whom left for the Americas between 1776 and 1850—with the peak years occurring between 1826 and 1850.[23]

Table 2.5 also shows an estimated distribution of these quarter-century totals across destinations in the Americas. The method used to derive this series is described more fully elsewhere. Briefly, the revised trans-Atlantic database provides an American destination for 849,000 slaves leaving the Bight of Benin between 1651 and 1865 out of a projected total of just over two million departures. This large number provides a basis for estimating the missing destinations, though readers should note that at this stage we have not attempted to separate Yoruba from non-Yoruba destinations.[24] With an average middle passage mortality of about 13.4 percent (based on 756 voyages leaving the Bight of Benin), the data in Table 2.5 should not be confused with arrivals. Perhaps only 838,000 survivors disembarked in the Americas and Sierra Leone. It is unnecessary to stress the roughness of this exercise. The proportion of Yoruba speakers among deportees between 1726 and 1800 may well have followed a more dramatic curve than the one used to derive Table 2.5. There is little doubt

Table 2.5. Preferred Series of Departures of Yoruba-Speaking Captives from Africa and Their Destinations in the Americas by Quarter Century, 1651–1867 (in thousands)

	Estimated Nos. Yoruba	British Mainland, N. America	British Leewards	British Windwards + Trinidad	Jamaica	Barbados	Guianas	French Windwards
1651–75	2.2							2.2
1676–1700	22.2		0.6		4.4	7.6	0.7	0.7
1701–25	41.7	0.5	0.8		6.7	3.6	4.6	5.1
1726–50	89.5	0.4	2.4		4.1	2.2	9.8	25.2
1751–75	140.1	2.6	1.6	2.2	20.0	2.0	2.1	8.0
1776–1800	172.9		0.4	10.9	18.7	1.3	1.7	2.4
1801–25	211.4	1.4		3.6	5.9	1.5	7.1	1.0
1826–50	257.4			2.8		1.5	0.4	1.2
1851–67	30.7							
All years	968.2	4.9	5.7	19.5	59.9	19.7	26.5	45.7

Table 2.5 (continued)
Preferred Series of Departures of Yoruba-Speaking Captives from Africa
and Their Destinations in the Americas by Quarter Century, 1651–1867 (in thousands)

	St. Domingue	Spanish American	Spanish Caribbean	Dutch Caribbean	N.E. Brazil	Bahia	S.E. Brazil	Other Americas	Africa
1651–75									
1676–1700		0.3		1.4		4.8		1.6	
1701–25	6.3	1.5	0.1	3.0	0.1	9.1	0.1	0.1	
1726–50	39.0		0.3	0.9	0.7	4.7		0.5	
1751–75	49.8		0.3	0.4	0.7	50.6		0.3	
1776–1800	54.7		2.9			79.3		0.2	
1801–25		0.7	5.6		3.8	175.2	977		7.8
1826–50			65.6		1.7	116.2	28.4	5.4	32.4
1851–67			25.0				2.2		1.8
All Years	149.9	2.5	99.8	5.7	6.9	439.8	31.7	8.1	41.9

Source: Eltis, Richardson, Behrendt, New Census, forthcoming; and see text.

that this first attempt to reconstruct a diaspora for an African language (and eventually an ethnic) group will be refined in the future as more information becomes available.

The table shows a remarkably scattered diaspora. Yoruba speakers made up less than 9 percent of Africans carried to the New World, but they were taken to most parts of the Americas between the Chesapeake in the north to Rio de la Plata in the south. No European migrant group ranged over so much of the Americas, or approached the number of Yoruba speakers, in the century prior to 1850.[25] Yet despite this range, well over two-thirds of the Yoruba were intended for just three destinations—St. Domingue, Cuba (accounting for almost the entire Spanish Caribbean column in Table 2.5), and Bahia. Remarkably few Yoruba speakers reached the British Caribbean, except for the British Windwards and Trinidad, in the short interlude from 1792 to 1807, the period between the wartime ending of the French traffic and British abolition of the slave trade. Twenty thousand embarked for Jamaica in the third quarter of the eighteenth century, but both here and in the British Windwards and Trinidad, they made up less than 7 percent of all Africans taken to these islands at this time. It is very likely that Yoruba speakers were not the largest African language group carried to the Americas in the slave trade era and, while they came to form the large majority of peoples leaving the Bight of Benin, in only one area—Bahia— did Yoruba peoples constitute as much as two-fifths of slave arrivals in any American receiving region.[26] As Table 2.5 shows, Yoruba speakers came late into the slave trade and generally entered the traffic in peak numbers just as the strong links between specific locations in Africa and the Americas apparent earlier in the trade began to break down. Cuba in particular, receiving over 95 percent of its slaves after 1790, drew significant numbers of Africans from all parts of sub-Saharan Africa except Senegambia and the northeast coast. Yoruba speakers cannot have accounted for more than 12 percent of Cuban arrivals and certainly made up less than 20 percent of those taken to St. Domingue. In Bahia, by contrast, it is possible that they comprised nearly 40 percent and were the largest single group.[27]

The above discussion of the direction of the Yoruba diaspora takes no account of the secondary migrations that occurred as the slave trade came to an end. The movement of several thousand Yoruba back to their homelands from Sierra Leone, from Brazil, and from Cuba is now well known.[28] While the Yoruba appear to have been particularly prominent in such efforts to return to Africa, this repatriation is not likely to have been large relative to the outflow—perhaps no more than several thousand. More important numerically were the shifts from one part of the diaspora to another. Close to forty thousand Africans were carried to the British Caribbean after 1834, mainly to Jamaica, British Guiana, and Trinidad, with likely no more than one-fifth being Yoruba speakers. They came mainly from Sierra Leone where recaptives had been first indentured and then resettled within the colony, but British vessels also carried them from St. Helena, Rio de Janeiro, and Cuba.[29] The largest, if least measurable, relocation within the diaspora occurred before slavery ended, as planters moved with or sent their slaves to other parts of the Americas. The French Caribbean, as we have seen, received the second-largest contingent of Yoruba-speaking slaves in the Americas. French planters left the French Lesser Antilles with their slaves in the late eighteenth century for Trinidad before it became British. Others left St. Domingue for Louisiana and Cuba both before and after the onset of the most successful slave revolt in history. Such secondary and return migration is often dramatic, but we should nevertheless keep it in proportion to the whole diaspora. Certainly far less than 10 percent of those enumerated in column 1 of Table 2.5 moved to completely new regions whether in the Old or New Worlds after their initial forced migration. The return migration to Africa points to the aspirations of the Yoruba rather than, for most, the reality of their experience.

Finally, it is worth noting that languages and, more broadly, cultures of some groups appear to migrate more easily and successfully than others. Thus while German speakers were the largest European group to migrate to eighteenth-century North America (and, indeed, outnumbered Yoruba speakers prior to 1808) and were followed by far more migrants again in the mid-nineteenth century, they appear to have integrated into the host society with remarkable speed as well as adding less that is easily distinguished as "German" to the culture of that society. Within coerced African migration, the Yoruba were among the latest to arrive but were neither the most numerous nor the least scattered over the Americas. Reasonably precise estimates for other groups will eventually become available, but it is probable that Igbo and some West-Central African peoples were larger and more heavily concentrated than the Yoruba—the Igbo in parts of the British Caribbean and some of what have been termed Congo groups in southeast Brazil. Yet the impact of the Yoruba speakers on Creole societies that emerged in many parts of the Americas appears to modern scholars to have been strong and, in the light of the evidence presented here, out of proportion to the relative size of Yoruba arrivals. While Igbo "survivals" in the Chesapeake have recently received much attention, comparisons with the Yoruba in the broader Americas point instead to the relative weakness of Igbo oral traditions, especially as represented in songs, religious rituals, stories, proverbs, and so on.

In Cuba, in any given year in the nineteenth century, the Yoruba had no choice but to mingle on the plantations of western Cuba with large numbers of Susu from Sierra Leone / Guinea-Conakry, with Igbo from throughout what is now southeast Nigeria, Yao from southeast Africa, and Lunda from the Kasai Valley in Angola, with no single group numerically dominant. The island, in fact, received the greatest mix of African peoples of any large region in the Americas. The cabildos of Havana and the rituals of the polytheistic Santería religion observed by large numbers of African-Cubans may or may not have been instantly recognizable to, say, Egba, Ijeba, or Ijesha peoples in West Africa, but it would be difficult to find many of its roots in non-Yoruba Africa.

In Trinidad a similar situation existed on a much smaller scale. Yoruba speakers were no doubt represented among the holdings of the French planters who arrived at the invitation of the Spanish colonial government before the British takeover. British slave traders brought in more Yoruba speakers immediately after British annexation, as they returned in force to the old Slave Coast in the wake of the collapse of the French slave trade, and a third influx came in the form of indentured workers from Sierra Leone. Yet far greater inflows arrived from other parts of West and West-Central Africa, and the numbers of Yoruba among the 13,984 African-born slaves identified in the first Trinidad slave registration in 1813 can only be described as tiny.[30] This contrasts oddly with the large Yoruba presence detected in language, in religion, and, indeed, in the communities, both urban and rural, that were identified as Yoruba as late as the late nineteenth and early twentieth centuries.[31] Once more it is hard to avoid the assessment that the Yoruba influence was disproportionate to their numbers. One can find almost any comment that one wishes about any African nation in the European records, but the opinion of de Verteuil in 1858 was echoed by many others in the nineteenth century as well as by their modern neighbors in Africa. The Yoruba, he said, "were guided in marked degree by the sense of association; and . . . the principle of combination for the common weal has been fully sustained where-ever they have settled in any numbers; in fact the whole Yoruba race may be said to form a social sort of social league for mutual support and protection."[32]

In Bahia, as already noted, Yoruba speakers formed a larger share of African arrivals than in either Cuba or Trinidad, but they were still a minority. Quite apart from spectacular incidents, such as the 1835 Bahia slave rebellion where the Yoruba constituted more than three-quarters of those taken before the courts, the Yoruba presence here is the strongest and best documented of any African people in any American region.[33] Of all trans-Atlantic links established between Africa and the Americas during the slave trade era, the one between Bahia and the Bight of Benin was likely the only one that continued on the basis of commodities, albeit at hugely reduced levels of value, when the slave trade itself was suppressed. A market for Yoruba textiles in Bahia continued into the second half of the nineteenth century despite the textile manufacturing revolution of the North Atlantic.

The environment of the Americas, of course, was ultimately critical in the shaping of all New World societies—European or African. But the case of the Yoruba suggests that not all incoming cultures had roles proportionate to the numbers of migrants in the interaction between migrants, and between migrants and the environment, that produced Creole societies. In evaluating Creolization, one cannot simply rely on the relative numbers of different peoples—whether African or European—any more than one can ignore the origin of migrants altogether. Historians should perhaps pay more attention to where migrants, or at least coerced African migrants, came from, but ultimately—and perhaps ironically, given the nature of this essay—the size of a group is not necessarily a reliable indicator of the impact of that group.

Notes

I am indebted to Stanley L. Engerman, Paul Lovejoy, Ugo Nwokeji, Philip Morgan, and David Richardson, as well as participants in The Johns Hopkins History Seminar, November 2002, and the Columbia Seminar on Atlantic History held at the State University of New York at Stony Brook, February 2003, for comments on earlier versions of this essay.

1. Robin Law, "Ethnicity and the Slave Trade: 'Lucumi' and 'Nago' as Ethonyms in West Africa," *History in Africa* 24 (1997): 205–19.

2. See Marianne Wokeck, "Irish and German Migration to Eighteenth Century North America," in *Coerced and Free Migration: Global Perspectives*, ed. David Eltis (Stanford, Calif.: Stanford University Press, 2002), 176–203; and the literature cited there.

3. This procedure is based on estimates of the distribution of slaves carried on national groupings of ships from Europe and the Americas over the eight African coastal regions. The estimates are not presented here, but are easy to derive for almost any period after 1675 from David Eltis et al., *The Transatlantic Slave Trade: A Database on CD-ROM* (Cambridge: Cambridge University Press, 1999); henceforth, *TSTD*.

4. Not all slave ships made it to the Americas or even to Africa. Fortunately the set is quite rich in information on the outcome of the voyage in that for almost 90 percent of the voyages we know if the ship obtained slaves, and for just over 90 percent we know if the ship reached Africa prior to initiating trade. Overall, almost one slave voyage in ten included in the present set did not deliver slaves to the Americas, and only 82 percent of all ships did so while still under the control of the original owners.

5. The Havana registers are in the British Public Record Office, FO 313, vols. 56–62. For what are likely the only uses of this material, see Roseanne Marion Adderley, "'New Negroes from Africa': Culture and Community among Liberated Africans in the Bahamas and Trinidad, 1810–1900" (Ph.D. dissertation, University of Pennsylvania, 1996). The Sierra Leone registers (in the FO 84 series) have been used in Richard Meyer-Heiselberg, *Notes from the Liberated African Department in the Archives at Fourah Bay College, Freetown, Sierra Leone* (Uppsala: Scandinavian Institute of African Studies, 1967); David Northrup, *Trade without Rulers: Precolonial Economic Development in Southeastern Nigeria* (Oxford: Clarendon, 1978), 58–65, 231; David Eltis, "Welfare Trends among the Yoruba at the Beginning of the Nineteenth Century: The Anthropometric Evidence," *Journal of Economic History* 50 (1990): 521–40; and idem, "Nutritional Trends in Africa and the Americas: Heights of Africans, 1819–1839," *Journal of Interdisciplinary History* 12 (1982): 453–75. See also G. Ugo Nwokeji and David Eltis, "The Roots of the African Diaspora: Methodological Considerations in the Analysis of Names in the Liberated African Registers of Sierra Leone and Havana," *History in Africa* 29 (2002): 365–79; and idem, "Characteristics of Captives Leaving the

Cameroons for the Americas, 1822–1837," *Journal of African History* 43 (2002): 191–210.

6. The registers distinguish between "scores," "cuts," "marks," and "tattoos," on the one hand, which we take to be evidence of voluntary cicatrization procedures, and "scars," on the other. Scars are more likely to be the result of involuntary activity. Most of the latter would have little cultural significance.

7. A smaller example is the defendants' names in court proceedings following from the 1835 Bahia revolt. See João José Reis, *Slave Rebellion in Brazil: The Muslim Uprising of 1835 in Bahia*, trans. Arthur Brakel (Baltimore: The Johns Hopkins University Press, 1993), 155–56.

8. It should be stressed that the linking of names and ethnicity carries no necessary implications for the definition of ethnicity itself. For a discussion of this issue, see Nwokeji and Eltis, "Characteristics," 191–92.

9. *TSTD.*

10. The second-largest of the Yoruba group in Table 2.1 is Ecumacho, which has no modern counterpart. Ojo Olatunji (personal communication) of York University has suggested that this is Ikumeso or Ekun Eso—in Yoruba, "the valiant's province." Eso is the title for Oyo military elite, which was drawn from the Eastern Province of the kingdom. In any event, the personal names of the individuals in this group are mainly Yoruba.

11. Most of the captured vessels were taken in the Americas rather than off Africa so that the location of African ports, and therefore, arguably, the ethnicity of the captives, should have been close to random.

12. Derived by multiplying the 162,800 slaves leaving the Bight of Benin between 1826 and 1840 (David Eltis, David Richardson, and Stephen Behrendt, *The Atlantic Slave Trade: A New Census* [Cambridge: Cambridge University Press, forthcoming]) by .625 (the share of all identified recaptives that were Yoruba from Table 2.1). While the overall estimate of the Bight of Benin volume used here is for fifteen years, a few Yoruba left from ports in the Bight of Biafra and are therefore not included in the Bight of Benin estimate. The upward bias from including the extra year is offset by the downward bias of omitting Yoruba leaving through non–Bight of Benin ports.

13. A. F. C. Ryder, *Benin and the Europeans, 1485–1897* (London: Humanities, 1969), 197–98.

14. Robin Law, "A Lagoonside Port on the Eighteenth Century Slave Coast: The Early History of Badagri," *Canadian Journal of African Studies* 28 (1994): 32–59; Caroline Sorensen-Gilmour, "Slave-Trading along the Lagoons of South-West Nigeria: The Case of Badagry," in *Ports of the Slave Trade (Bights of Benin and Biafra)*, ed. Robin Law and Silke Strickrodt, 85–86 (Stirling, U.K.: Centre of Commonwealth Studies, University of Stirling, 1999).

15. This paragraph and the next are based on David Eltis, *Economic Growth and the Ending of the Transatlantic Slave Trade* (New York: Oxford University Press, 1987), 168–69.

16. For the slave trade in Lagos in the 1840s, see Kristin Mann, *The Birth of an African City: Trade, State and Emancipation in Nineteenth Century Lagos*, forthcoming, chaps. 1 and 2. The correspondence of King Kosoko captured by the British and published verbatim in the House of Lords *Sessional Papers*, 1852–53, 22:327–66 shows the king selling slaves on commission in Bahia but accounting for less than 10 percent of all

slaves sold in 1848 and 1849. Kosoko also had his own slave vessel built in Bahia. See also the enclosures in H. Wise to Calhoun, 1 November 1844, U.S. Congress, H. Exec. Doc. no. 148, 28 –29, 44– 47. For Ouidah, see Robin Law, "Royal Monopoly and Private Enterprise: The Case of Dahomey," *The Journal of African History* 18 (1977): 559 –71; and idem, "Slave-Raiders and Middlemen, Monopolists and Free Traders: The Supply of Slaves for the Atlantic Trade in Dahomey, c. 1715–1850," *The Journal of African History* 30 (1989): 45– 68.

17. The derivation is shown in the following table:

	Total Benin Slaves in Thousands	Estimated Numbers of Slaves Leaving from Groupings of Embarkation Points Shown in Table 2.3 in Thousands			Estimated Percentage of Yoruba Leaving from Major Embarkation Points Shown in Column 8 of Table 2.2			Estimated Yoruba Departures in Thousands
		Western	Central	Eastern	Popo	Oiudah	Lagos	
1651–75	21.9	0	21.9	0	12.0	80.9	98.9	17.7
1676–1700	222.9	2.7	220.2	0	12.0	80.9	98.9	178.5
1701–25	407.5	1.8	404.6	1.2	12.0	80.9	98.9	328.7
1726–50	306.2	43.9	235.9	26.3	12.0	80.9	98.9	222.1
1751–75	253.0	20.1	160.1	72.7	12.0	80.9	98.9	203.8
1776–1800	264.4	15.1	181.8	67.4	12.0	80.9	98.9	215.6
1801–25	236.6	7.3	94.5	135.6	12.0	80.9	98.9	211.4
1826–50	288.4	12.2	94.7	181.3	12.0	80.9	98.9	257.4
1851–65	37.7	1.4	30.3	6.0	12.0	80.9	98.9	30.7

18. The evidence is summarized and discussed in Robin Law, *The Slave Coast of West Africa, 1550–1750: The Impact of the Atlantic Slave Trade on an African Society* (Oxford: Clarendon, 1991), 186 – 91; and idem, "Ethnicity and the Slave Trade," 205–19, esp. 207.

19. Law, "Ethnicity and the Slave Trade," 207; idem, *The Kingdom of Allada* (Leiden: Research School CNWS, School of Asian, African, and Amerindian Studies, 1997), 101–104; Paul E. Lovejoy and David Richardson, "The Yoruba Factor in the Atlantic Slave Trade," unpublished paper.

20. Law, *The Slave Coast*, 309 –14; idem, "A Lagoonside Port on the Eighteenth Century Slave Coast," 32–59.

21. Pierre Verger, *Trade Relations between the Bight of Benin and Bahia, 17th to 19th Centuries*, trans. Evelyn Crawford (Ibadan, Nigeria: Ibadan University Press, 1976), 1–7, quote at 7. For St. Domingue, see David Geggus, "Sex Ratio, Age and Ethnicity in the Atlantic Slave Trade: Data from French Shipping and Plantation Records," *Journal of African History* 30 (1989): 23– 44; Eltis, *Economic Growth*, 169 –70.

22. A case could be made for including Porto Novo in the eastern group for this assessment. Any bias resulting from the decision to keep Porto Novo in the central grouping of ports, however, is offset by the inclusion of Benin in the eastern group. Benin,

the principal eastern slave-trading port between 1726 and 1775, would have sent high proportions of Edo, western Delta peoples, and other non–Yoruba speakers into the traffic, although hard evidence of the ethnicity of captives leaving Benin before the 1770s is lacking.

23. The revised derivation—reflected in columns 5 to 8—is shown in the following table:

	Total Benin Slaves in Thousands	Estimated Numbers of Slaves Leaving from Groupings of Embarkation Points Shown in Table 2.3 in Thousands			Revised Estimated Percentage of Yoruba Leaving from Major Embarkation Points Shown in Column 8 of Table 2.2			Estimated Yoruba Departures in Thousands
		Western	Central	Eastern	Popo	Oiudah	Lagos	
1651–75	21.9	0	21.9	0	5.0	10.0	98.9	2.2
1676–1700	222.9	2.7	220.2	0	5.0	10.0	98.9	22.2
1701–25	407.5	1.8	404.6	1.2	5.0	10.0	98.9	41.7
1726–50	306.2	43.9	235.9	26.3	5.0	26.0	98.9	89.5
1751–75	253	20.1	160.1	72.7	5.0	42.0	98.9	140.1
1776–1800	264.4	15.1	181.8	67.4	5.0	58.0	98.9	172.9
1801–25	236.6	7.3	94.5	135.6	12.0	80.9	98.9	211.4
1826–50	288.4	12.2	94.7	181.3	12.0	80.9	98.9	257.4
1851–65	37.7	1.4	30.3	6.0	12.0	80.9	98.9	30.7

24. See Eltis, Richardson, and Behrendt, *New Census*, forthcoming, chap. 3.

25. The Portuguese and British came closest, before 1850, but each of these countries sent out perhaps only two-thirds of the total number of Yoruba (see David Eltis, "Free and Coerced Migrations from the Old World to the New," in Eltis, *Coerced and Free Migration*, 62–63).

26. Even here, evidence taken from probate records for Salvador, the largest city in the province of Bahia, indicates a much smaller ratio of Yoruba—only one-fifth. See Reis, *Slave Rebellion in Brazil*, 140.

27. These ratios are derived by comparing column 1 of Table 2.5 with estimates of total departures from different regions in the Americas in Eltis, Richardson, and Behrendt, *New Census*, forthcoming. For confirmation of the small numbers of Yoruba in the British Caribbean, see Barry Higman's breakdown of the slave registration data in his *Slave Populations of the British Caribbean, 1807–1834* (Baltimore: The Johns Hopkins University Press, 1984), 442–58. An alternative estimate based on probate records for Salvador, the largest city in the province of Bahia, indicates a much smaller ratio of Yoruba than suggested here—only one-fifth. See Reis, *Slave Rebellion in Brazil*, 140.

28. Jean Herskovits Kopytoff, *A Preface to Modern Nigeria: The "Sierra Leonians" in Yoruba, 1830–1890* (Madison: University of Wisconsin Press, 1965), esp. 44–60; Rudolfo Sarracino, *Los que Volvieron a África* (Havana: Editorial de Ciencias Sociales, 1988), 47–124. British sources, especially FO 84 in the Public Record Office, contain much material on this that has yet to be exploited—including the remarkable case of

the "San Antonio" (voyage id 3456 in *TSTD*) which, in 1844, carried fare-paying free Africans wishing to return to the Lagos vicinity on its outbound voyage before attempting to return to Cuba with slaves.

29. Johnson U. J. Asiegbu, *Slavery and the Politics of Liberation, 1787–1861: A Study of Liberated African Emigration and British Anti-Slavery Policy* (New York: Africana, 1969); David Northrup, *Indentured Labor in the Age of Imperialism, 1834–1922* (Cambridge: Cambridge University Press, 1995); Monica Schuler, *"Alas, Alas, Kongo": A Social History of Indentured African Immigration into Jamaica, 1841–1865* (Baltimore: The Johns Hopkins University Press, 1980).

30. Higman, *Slave Populations*, 449.

31. Maureen Warner-Lewis, "Trinidad Yoruba: A Language of Exile," *International Journal of the Sociology of Language* 83 (1990): 9–20; idem, *Trinidad Yoruba: From Mother Tongue to Memory* (Tuscaloosa: University of Alabama Press, 1996). For similar patterns in Guyana and Belize, see James Adeyinka Olawaiye, "Yoruba Religious and Social Traditions in Ekiti, Nigeria, and Three Caribbean Countries: Trinidad-Tobago, Guyana, and Belize" (Ph.D. dissertation, University of Missouri, Kansas City, 1980).

32. Louis Antoine Aimé de Verteuil, *Three Essays on the Cultivation of Sugar Cane in Trinidad* . . . (Port of Spain: Printed at the Standard's Office, 1858), 175; cited in Warner-Lewis, *Trinidad Yoruba*, 44.

33. Reis, *Slave Rebellion in Brazil*, 140; Verger, *Trade Relations between the Bight of Benin and Bahia*.

CHAPTER THREE

The Yoruba Factor
in the Trans-Atlantic Slave Trade

Paul E. Lovejoy

Using demographic data, this chapter attempts to account for the strong Yoruba influence in the African diaspora in the Americas, as well as in West Africa, since the late eighteenth century. According to the previous chapter by David Eltis, almost half the enslaved who left the ports of the Bight of Benin were Yoruba, representing close to one million people.[1] The scale of the migration, heavily concentrated in the period from 1780 to 1850, makes the movement of Yoruba into the diaspora one of the largest migrations across the Atlantic up to that time, rivaling all other African, and indeed European, ethnic groups in scale of resettlement. This attempt to estimate how many Yoruba were forcibly moved, including when and where they went, raises questions of which Yoruba are in question, and what the concept "Yoruba" and related terms have meant.

Yoruba were present in the Americas from at least the early seventeenth century, known under the designations of "Lucumí" and "Nagô." The number of Yoruba increased during the eighteenth century, becoming particularly significant in the last several decades of that century, and especially in the nineteenth century, when they represented the single most important ethno-linguistic grouping in the trade from the Bight of Benin. In the eighteenth century many Yoruba were taken to the French Caribbean, as well as to Bahia, whereas in the nineteenth century they went mainly to Bahia and then to Cuba, and, in accordance with British anti–slave trade measures, to Sierra Leone and Trinidad. In determining the broad outlines of the population displacement from the interior of the Bight of Benin, my purpose is, first, to estimate ethnic origins and, second, to provide the context for biographical data on individual slaves that have been assembled.

The question of who are to be identified as Yoruba raises the complicated issue of defining ethnicity and the relative importance of a recognizable nomenclature for such an identification. Robin Law has demonstrated that the various terms ("Lucumí," "Nagô," "Aku," "Yoruba") have their own history, and the use of the term "Yoruba" was more than a convenience. Yoruba Christians consciously adopted the term in the mid-nineteenth century to describe the pan-ethnic and linguistic grouping that had become cohesive in the Americas and Sierra Leone, and where, it was hoped, a similar consciousness would be developed in "Yorubaland" itself.[2] As Adediran has demonstrated, the various terms for the sub-ethnicities of Yoruba are complex and closely tied to historical developments and specific localities.[3] The choice of the term "Yoruba" is perhaps curious, specifically because it has Muslim origins and was adopted by Christians. The emergent intellectuals among the repatriates were committed to a national agenda that required a specific pan-Yoruba identity, as Matory has demonstrated in his discussion of the influence of "Yoruba intellectuals" in the development of ethnic consciousness in Bahia in the last part of the nineteenth century, although it is not clear why they used a Muslim term to describe themselves as a community.[4] Neither Law nor Matory addresses this question; yet I would suggest that, both symbolically and figuratively, the term is significant. Its use emphasizes the importance of Islam in helping to shape ethnic cohesion among those who came to see themselves as "Yoruba." Indeed, the use of a Muslim term serves to correct the underrepresentation of Islam in the discussion of the genesis of the Yoruba as an ethnic group, and thereby reinforces the analysis of John Peel in his discussion of the role of religion in "the making of the Yoruba."[5] In examining Yoruba ethnicity, it is necessary to understand the role of the umbrella of language, the similarity in culture as expressed through divination and worldview, and the interrelated historical tradition of common origins from Ife. The role of Christianity and Islam in shaping ethnicity was profound, as Peel has argued in addressing its meaning and how this changed over time.

"Yoruba" has been a descriptive category for people speaking a common language in the interior of the Bight of Benin since at least the sixteenth century, and likely earlier still.[6] The first reference to the term is in the writings of Ahmed Baba in 1613, but by implication Baba was describing an ethnicity that had existed for some time. Moreover, the reference almost certainly was not restricted to a particular section of the Yoruba, such as Oyo, which at the time was only a minor polity. Yarabawa, in Hausa, refers to people, not a place, meaning the people of Yoruba, which suggests a country, not necessarily a political state. Again, the use of the term among the Hausa seems to predate the rise of Oyo, and hence appears to have had a wider connotation than any particular state.[7] Similarly the earliest term used in the Americas ("Lucumí") appears to have had a generic connotation and probably did not specifically refer to a particular state or section of the Yoruba, although, like "Yoruba," the term "Lucumí" is sometimes thought to refer to Oyo, Ife, or perhaps Ijebu.[8] However, the term appears in the Americas at the time when Oyo entered its imperial phase. The term, as used by Alonso de Sandoval in the early seventeenth century, clearly referred to a broad category of people or a region that may have included others than those who spoke Yoruba, perhaps reflecting areas where Yoruba was nonetheless understood as a language. Lucumí were therefore a significant factor in the early trade of the Bight of Benin. The association of the term with other identifications, such as Lucumí Kakanda and Lucumí Arara, suggests that the term has a meaning that was inclusive of other designations not Yoruba in origin.[9]

The term "Nagô" as used in Brazil and French colonies does not appear before the early eighteenth century.[10] The term is derived from "Anago," a subsection of the Yoruba who lived east of the Weme River, but in the Americas it was a generic concept that was derived from Fon and Allada terminology for all Yoruba. The equation of Anago with a general term for Yoruba probably reflects the historical situation that squeezed the Anago homeland between the expansive activities of first Allada and then Dahomey, on the one hand, and Oyo, on the other. The Anago country was vulnerable to invasion from Allada and Dahomey to the west, and hence, among the Gbe languages, "Nagô" became the term for all Yoruba. The adoption of the term in Brazil may well reflect the fact that many of the earliest Yoruba to arrive there were indeed Anago, who seem to have been decimated in the struggle for power among Allada, Dahomey, and Oyo. Neither Lucumí nor Nagô were used in Sierra Leone, where large numbers of Yoruba recaptives were settled in the nineteenth century, which is understandable because these recaptives did not come through the filter of Gbe terminology and were not identified according to Spanish usage in Cuba or Brazilian nomenclature. Instead, the term "Aku" was used as an ethnic designation, apparently reflecting a common Yoruba greeting.[11]

The issue of Yoruba ethnicity is further complicated because many slaves are associated directly or indirectly with Oyo, which was not only a source of enslaved Yoruba but also was involved in a transit trade in slaves, some of whom became acculturated as Yoruba. These Yoruba-speaking slaves entered the trade in the eighteenth century through Oyo, especially in the period under Alafin Abiodun and the development of the route through Egbado to Porto Novo as a means of bypassing Dahomey.[12] Even though the origins of many of these slaves are unknown, they were nonetheless designated as being "Oyo." Other Yoruba may have been included in the general name used by the Portuguese for this section of the coast, "Mina," although the term was more generally used for the Gbe language groups. It can be assumed that many people who were designated "Nagô," "Lucumí," "Aku," or "Yoruba" probably did not speak Yoruba as their first language, and certainly some individuals had multiple ethnic identities and spoke more than one language. However, with the disintegration of Oyo in the early nineteenth century, slaves who were actually to be identified as people of Oyo became numerous. Moreover, as religion also became an indicator of ethnic origins in the nineteenth century, those identified

42

as Yoruba included Muslims and Christians, as well as those who consulted the *orisha*.

Scale of Exports of Yoruba-Speaking Peoples

The number of enslaved Africans leaving from the ports of the Bight of Benin from 1650 to 1865 has been variously estimated at just over two million people.[13] According to Eltis, Yoruba constituted the largest proportion of the deported population, perhaps numbering as many as 968,200 of the total number of deportees. Historical evidence indicates a Yoruba presence in the Americas for the seventeenth century, although the numbers were small in this period. The number of Yoruba increased over time, especially after 1715, as Law has noted,[14] and reached a peak only in the nineteenth century. As Manning first demonstrated, the early trade of the Bight of Benin was heavily concentrated along the western lagoon, with the various Gbe groups (Ewe / Fon / Allada) suffering the most in terms of population loss.[15] These people were known in the Americas variously as "Gege," "Allada," "Fon," "Mahi," and sometimes only as "Mina."[16] Yoruba came largely in the century after 1750, when the total number of slaves exported from the Bight of Benin was over one million individuals, divided almost equally between 1751 and 1800 and between 1801 and 1865. The number of slaves being deported fell substantially during the European wars from the 1790s through 1815. Although British abolition in 1807 was a complicating factor, the elimination of Dutch and French ships from the high seas was the major reason for the collapse of trade after 1793. The British had been heavily involved in purchasing slaves in the Bight of Benin only in the 1770s and 1780s, and hence their withdrawal after 1807 had little direct effect on the Bight of Benin. Export volume rebounded after 1815, and especially from the late 1820s to the 1840s, with trade directed primarily toward Cuba and Bahia.[17]

The demographic data reveal that the origins of the deported population changed over time. Initially the trade flowed from Oyo to the coast, via Allada or Dahomey and Ouidah. By the last third of the eighteenth century, the principal ports of the trade had shifted eastward, first to Epe and Porto Novo, then to Badagry, and finally to Lagos.[18] This eastward shift was mirrored by a shift in the relative numbers of Yoruba among the enslaved population that was deported, and also coincided with the great migration of Yoruba to Bahia, Cuba, and Sierra Leone. Before the 1760s the overwhelming majority of slaves left from Ouidah, and to a lesser extent from Keta, Little and Grand Popo, to the west of Ouidah, and the ports of Allada on Lake Nokué (Offra and Jaquin).[19] The ports to the east of Ouidah became important in the 1760s, as a result of the development of alternate ports to Dahomey-controlled Ouidah. Despite this competition, the records of slave departures reveal the continued importance of Ouidah, with its competitors only gaining a significant portion of the market in the late 1780s. A large number of ships that traded to the Bight of

Benin are only identified as leaving from "Costa da Mina," but it seems that in many cases this referred to Ouidah.[20] As Eltis demonstrates, half the slaves whose port of departure from the Bight of Benin is known left from Ouidah. Between 1662 and 1863, 272,500 slaves are known to have left Ouidah, whereas 189,100 are known to have departed from Epe and Porto Novo, another 85,500 from Badagry, and 317,300 from Lagos, which became the principal port in the nineteenth century.[21] These eastern ports together accounted for 591,000 slaves, in comparison with the million who left from Ouidah. In the 1790s and the first decade of the nineteenth century, Ouidah's trade virtually collapsed when only twenty-one ships are reported to have departed. Undoubtedly other ships stopped at Ouidah, but the decline was still dramatic. Slave exports from Ouidah rebounded in the second decade of the nineteenth century, but the number of slaves being shipped never attained the levels of the previous century.

This eastward shift responded to the sources of supply for slave shipments— the Yoruba interior. Whereas Ouidah connected to Yoruba markets via routes along the west of the Weme River and then to the northeast, Porto Novo, Badagry, and Lagos were directly south of the Yoruba heartland and hence the closest outlets for most of Yoruba country. Before 1762 only 5,700 slaves are known to have come from this area, in sharp contrast to the extensive trade at Ouidah. Slave exports grew in the quarter century from 1762 to 1786 to levels that were largely maintained until the 1850s. During this period it appears that the vast majority of those who were deported were either Yoruba or people from the Central Sudan, many of whom were Muslims. The relative proportion of these two categories can be roughly determined, thereby isolating the Yoruba factor for analysis.[22]

Eltis has conservatively and with acknowledged reservations estimated that almost one million Yoruba were deported between 1650 and 1865.[23] In the last quarter of the seventeenth century, an estimated 22,000 appear to have been among those deported. The number of Yoruba doubled in the first quarter of the eighteenth century, rising to 41,700, before doubling again in the second quarter to 89,500, and continued to increase at a rapid rate (140,100 in the third quarter of the eighteenth century and 172,900 in the fourth quarter), increasing even more in the nineteenth century (211,400 in the first quarter and 257,400 in the second). These are, of course, rough estimates that minimize the blurring of ethnicity and multiple identities. The early nineteenth century was also the period in which exports from the Central Sudan became a noticeable feature of the trade; Central Sudan slaves were probably sometimes represented as Yoruba, especially if they had been retained in Yoruba country before being exported.

Ethnic Patterns of the Slave Trade in the Bight of Benin

Ethnic categories for people from the Bight of Benin can be distinguished between the various Gbe groups, who have been known in at least parts of the diaspora as "Mina" and sometimes "Gege," although the use of these terms has varied, and Yoruba, who have been variously known as Nagô and Lucumí. There is also a distinction between the southern "Mina," Yoruba, or Nagô and people from the savanna to the north, including those identified as Hausa, Nupe, Borno, Borgu, and "Chamba" or more generally Gurma. Those often referred to as "Mina" and representing Allada, Hueda, Fon, Ewe, and Mahi were particularly numerous in the early period, through at least the conquest of Allada and Hueda, in which Ouidah was located, in the 1720s.[24] The estimates of slave exports based on shipping data do not immediately distinguish among such categories, but the correlation of export figures with political history can provide one gauge of when Yoruba were taken into the trade, and hence implicitly where they went in the Americas, although much of the information on ethnicity has to be inferred, as do the destinations of people in the Americas. The voyage database, for example, only identifies the destination of a portion of those leaving the Bight of Benin.[25] Instead, Eltis's estimate can be used as a rough figure for the possible number of people who in some way can be identified as "Yoruba." This calculation can be compared to research on the ethnicity of slaves in the Americas, particularly in St. Domingue and Bahia, colonies that received disproportionate numbers of slaves from the Bight of Benin in the eighteenth century, in the first case, and in the eighteenth and nineteenth centuries, in the second.[26] As might be expected, an assessment of the ethnic patterns of the trade from the Bight of Benin reveals a heavy concentration of Yoruba. Plantation records for St. Domingue reveal that Yoruba constituted an identifiable component of the slave population.[27] The study of Geggus covers 4,552 slaves, including each decade from the 1720s through the 1790s, but is heavily weighted toward the end of the eighteenth century. For the purpose of the current exercise, we assume that the Geggus sample reflects export patterns weighted toward the period after 1750.[28] In fact, Yoruba were found throughout the francophone Caribbean, including Louisiana and Trinidad, where French planters moved after the uprising in St. Domingue in the 1790s. Yoruba also arrived in considerable numbers in Trinidad after 1807 because of the settlement of recaptives by the British navy. According to Higman's study, Yoruba were also concentrated in Trinidad in the 1830s, many of them having been settled as recaptives off slave ships.[29]

The concentration of Yoruba in Bahia can be traced to the second half of the eighteenth century. Côrtes de Oliveira provides data on the ethnicity of 537 slaves in Bahia between 1775 and 1815 as recorded in inventories, emancipation documents, and census data. The data indicate the proportions of different ethnic groups from the interior of the Bight of Benin; of 267 slaves from the Bight, 104 were Jeje (38.9 percent), 100 were Nagô (37.4 percent), and the remaining 63 were Hausa (50), Tapa (12), and Barba (1), who together constituted 23.6 percent of slaves whose ethnic identity was indicated in the records. The great influx of Yoruba is reflected in the inventories and other documents, as recorded by Côrtes de Oliveira, which show the following ethnic identification of slaves: previously a substantial population came from Angola and other parts of West-Central Africa; the population now contained a preponderance of Yoruba. In the documents dating from 1816 to 1850 Yoruba constituted 69.1 percent of all slaves whose ethnic or regional identity is known (sample: 2,593 slaves). Those identifying with West-Central Africa declined from 50.2 percent to only 14.7 percent, whereas Yoruba increased from 18.6 percent to 69.1 percent.[30] Within the Bight of Benin, the proportion of Yoruba increased from 37.4 percent to 82.3 percent. The sample used here is based on probate records and covers 1,612 free urban blacks and manumitted slaves at Bahia in 1819–35 studied by Brazilian historian João Reis.[31] Reis also provides evidence for the ethnicity of the slaves and free blacks charged after the Muslim revolt in Bahia in 1835. Of the 250 defendants, 196 (78.4 percent) were Nagô (Yoruba); 32, Hausa (12.4 percent); 10, Jeje (Ewe-Fon) (4.0 percent); 7, Borno (2.8 percent); and 6, Tapa (Nupe) (2.4 percent). Similarly Mieko Nashida has demonstrated that Yoruba were numerous in the Bahian slave population of the nineteenth century. According to Nishida, the proportion of Yoruba in the population of Bahia increased in the nineteenth century, reflecting what is known about the trade. The registries of freed persons for 1808–42 include records on 662 individuals, 318 men and 344 women. Of these, 31.3 percent were Yoruba, 24.5 percent "Gege" or Gbe-speakers, and 17.2 percent "Mina," which may be identified with Mahi and others in the Bight of Benin interior. Between 1851 and 1884 the registries record 410 individuals, of whom Yoruba were the overwhelming majority (73.9 percent). Nishida also analyzes the records of individuals who were listed as "Nagô" in emancipation papers between 1838 and 1888. Of those listed as "Nagô" or Yoruba between 1838 and 1848, Yoruba constituted 53.6 percent of those freed, while from 1852 to 1888 Yoruba constituted 79.3 percent. Of these, 58.5 percent were women.[32]

The gender and age composition of the enslaved Yoruba population that was exported changed from the eighteenth to the nineteenth century. The most striking feature arises from distance from the coast, which seems to have a correlation with gender, age, religion, and, of course, ethnicity. There appears to have been conscious attempts to discriminate among the enslaved population being deported. Specifically Muslim Yoruba may have been subjected to expulsion from some places, although Muslims also ended up as slaves in Ibadan, Lagos, Abeokuta, Ijebu, and other Yoruba cities. There were many enslaved Muslims, often from the Central Sudan, whose presence was considered a threat, but the extent to which Islam was a factor in the selection of those to be deported is still to be determined. The proportion of males in the deported population increased, especially after 1810, when the numbers of political prisoners of the jihad that revolutionized the Nigerian hinterland were sold to European merchants. Especially after 1817 Muslims, including Muslim Yoruba, were prominent among these prisoners. The revolt of the Oyo army in 1817 produced a wave of exports, most of whom appear to have gone to Bahia. The Owu war in 1822–23 and the collapse of Oyo in the early 1830s accounted for additional waves of deportation, although many of these were not Muslims. The consolidation of Ilorin and the Nupe emirates was directly related to the enslavement of Yoruba, including Yagba, Igbomina, and other northeast "Okun" Yoruba,[33] and retaliation by Ibadan and other non-Muslim states resulted in the enslavement of many others, whether or not Muslim. Distinguishing among Yoruba who were Muslims and Muslims from further north who had become recognized as Yoruba is often impossible, but men tended to come from the interior and were more likely to be Muslim of whatever background, whereas women and children tended to come from near the coast and were not usually Muslim.

The age and sex ratios of the deported population suggest that women and children were initially a relatively important part of the deported population from the Bight of Benin, but the proportion of men increased over time, as Eltis and Engerman have demonstrated.[34] There was considerable variation over time and among the different regions for which ratios have been calculated. Based on a sample of 41,121 slaves shipped by the French from the Bight of Benin in 1715–92, Geggus has calculated that 48 percent of the deported population were men, 30 percent were women, 13.8 percent were boys, and 8.6 percent were girls — that is, 61.8 percent of the enslaved were males and 22.4 percent were children.[35] According to Eltis and Engerman, 61.1 percent of slaves leaving the Bight of Benin between 1750 and 1799 were males, of whom 61.1 percent were adults, while children comprised 16.9 percent of the deported population.[36]

The ratios of males and females and adults and children shifted between the end of the eighteenth century and the height of the trade in the nineteenth century; generally the trade involved more males and especially more boys, while the number of women declined. This shift in the gender and age composition of the exported population toward more males and a younger population was a general phenomenon of the whole slave trade, not just that from the Bight of Benin, but the reasons in the Bight of Benin were unique to that region. In 1811– 67 the proportion of males had increased to 68 percent of the total number of people deported. According to Eltis and Engerman, 46 percent were men, 21 percent were women, with an additional 22 percent boys and 12 percent girls. In effect, the proportion of adult females declined from 30 percent in the last part of the eighteenth century to 21 percent after British abolition, while the proportion of children increased from 22.4 percent to 34 percent.[37] The proportion of adult males remained largely the same. This pattern can be explained by developments in the interior, changes in transport costs, and the reduction of risks associated with moving slaves great distances.[38] The ratios of adult males seem to have been sustained through deportation of men, mostly Muslims, from the interior. The figures for those ports through which slaves were deported from Yoruba country and the Central Sudan suggest that the decline in females, especially women, meant that fewer Yoruba women were leaving. According to Eltis, males comprised 63.4 percent of the slaves leaving the ports of Porto Novo, Badagry, and Lagos before British abolition, but the proportion rose to 67.4 percent thereafter. The population, moreover, was increasingly younger. Adult males comprised 57.5 percent of cargoes before abolition, with women making up most of the remainder—33.8 percent. After British abolition, adult males declined to 44.0 percent of the departing population, while women declined to 20.2 percent. Children, especially boys, became more common. There were more boys than adult women on most ships after 1810, with boys comprising 23.3 percent of cargoes. It is not clear why this should be the case, except, perhaps, the intention to remove the younger generation that might have lived to fight another day. It is also possible that as the male slave trade reached farther into the interior that male children near the coast became more prized because of the increased cost of moving slaves from the interior.

Many of the males came from the far interior, including those classified as Hausa, Nupe, and Borno males, as well as Yoruba. The women and children from the coastal zone were entirely Yoruba. It has been estimated that 95 percent of slaves who were identified as Hausa, Nupe, or Borno were adult males. Although the interior trade was much smaller than Yoruba exports, the numbers were still large enough to influence the overall pattern. In the period after British abolition, the total has been estimated at between 43,000 and 108,000 slaves from the Central Sudan. The other deportees appear to have been Yoruba, comprised of about 120,000 women, 77,000 girls, 144,000 boys, and 168,000–230,000 men (Table 3.1). I postulate that many of the deported slaves who had come from northern Yoruba areas were also largely adult males, and most likely political prisoners of the jihad and related wars and raids. The profile that emerges after estimates are adjusted for the Central Sudan factor and enslavement of Yoruba in the interior suggests a demographic picture that highlights the rising importance of children who were taken from near the coast. It seems that the majority of the deported population from areas immediately adjacent to the coast were not only children but also included those women who were deported. This pattern is reflected in the biographical materials that have survived.

Those Yoruba, Hausa, and other people who clearly came from the interior included relatively few females, either girls or women, and very few boys. In this respect, this analysis supports those who have claimed that the ratio of males among exports to the Americas tended to increase with distance from the coast. The identification of Muslim slaves among the deported population from the Bight of Benin during the century after 1750 should also be noted. Not only was there a correlation between gender and distance from the coast, but males from the interior of the Bight of Benin tended to be Muslims, some of whom were Yoruba. I have estimated the relative proportions of males and females, suggesting the significance of these ratios in calculating the relative number of males and females shipped from the Bight of Benin, and therefore the proportion of males and females in the Yoruba population. Table 3.1 is based on the conclusion that about 95 percent of slaves from the Central Sudan were males, and since the gender ratio for the deported population has been calculated, it is possible to demonstrate that the enslaved population from the Yoruba areas near the coast had a higher proportion of females than the export figures as a whole. Although the period was one of adjustment to the Napoleonic wars and British abolition, Yoruba nonetheless still formed an important proportion of the total trade, perhaps as many as half of all exports from the 1790s through the mid-1820s, and more after that.

Two patterns of trade existed: one was overwhelmingly adult male from distances of 100 to 200 kilometers from the coastal ports, and the other was extensively a trade in women and children from the zone near the coast. Far fewer adult men were purchased in local slave markets than from the interior. They were a specialty export, and hence a price markup from the interior. The paradox of differential prices between the interior and the coast has to be explained; in the interior women cost more than men, often by a third, and yet European factors were willing to pay more for men at the coast. This paradox seems to overlook the importance of ransoming in determining slave prices; freeborn men often commanded ransoms that were double their market price as slaves.[39] There appears to have been three categories of slaves for sale to Europeans—girls and women obtained from markets near the coast; high-priced men, often political prisoners, from the interior; and males, especially boys, from near the coast.

Significant proportions of Muslims were part of the deported population by the early nineteenth century. In a sample of slaves from the far interior whose religious identity seems certain, about 56 percent can be identified as Muslims through their names, although neither the use nor the nonuse of Muslim names is a clear indicator of religious affiliation.[40] The prevalence of such identifications does reflect that Muslims dominated the commercial system of the interior. Evidence from Bahia suggests there were significant numbers of Muslims among enslaved Yoruba in the early nineteenth century. It is possible that northern Yoruba included large proportions of males and sizeable numbers of Muslims, thereby extending the argument about the importance of Muslim males in the enslaved population from the Central Sudan. By contrast, the deported population from southern Yoruba country had much higher proportions of children and women. In this sense, there appears to have been two patterns in the deportation of Yoruba in the nineteenth century that were correlated with age, sex, and religion, one for the interior extending into the Central Sudan and the other in the Yoruba areas near the coast that were subjected to periodic wars and population displacement.

It may seem surprising that women and children were most likely to come from near the coast and were not otherwise retained within West Africa, where it appears that the market price for female slaves was generally higher, often a third higher, than that of their male counterparts of the same age, whether they were children or in their prime. The prices for males and females became relatively equal only at an advanced age when neither had many productive laboring years remaining. It seems clear that there were internal, structural reasons why women and children ended up in the trade near the coast but were not brought south from the far interior. These reasons are related to the interconnection between the local market for slaves in Yorubaland and the articulation of local debt

Table 3.1. Proportions of Males and Females in the Eastern Bight of Benin Export Trade, 1810–1865

Gender	Total	%	Yoruba Region	%	Central Sudan	%
Males	415,000		310,000–372,000		41,000–103,000	
Men	271,000	44.0	168,000–230,000	33–40	41,000–103,000	95
Boys	144,000	23.3	144,000		—	
Females	202,000		199,000–202,000		2,000–5,000	
Women	125,000	20.2	120,000–123,000	21–24	2,000–5,000	5
Girls	77,000	12.5	77,000		—	
Total	617,000		509,000–574,000		43,000–108,000	

Source: David Eltis and Stanley Engerman, "Fluctuations in the Age and Sex Ratios of Slaves in the Nineteenth-Century Transatlantic Slave Traffic," Slavery and Abolition 7 (1986): 259, 264. I estimate exports from the Central Sudan as being 10–25 percent of the total number deported; see Paul E. Lovejoy, "The Central Sudan and the Atlantic Slave Trade," in Paths toward the Past: African Historical Essays in Honor of Jan Vansina, ed. Robert W. Harms et al. (Atlanta: African Studies Association Press, 1994).

enforcement mechanisms with the slave trade. Some females and children, at least, became slaves because of default on debts for which they were being held as pawns. Females tended to be held as pawns more often than males, and hence defaults on pawning arrangements tended to be on females, whose value could most profitably be realized through a sale to slave buyers, which increased the possibility of a sale to European merchants. Prime male slaves, by contrast, were more likely to be political prisoners and "criminals" being deported from the far interior; because of the price differential that held females at a premium, women were less likely to be sold to the Bight of Benin coast.[41]

The demographic data on the export of enslaved Africans from the Bight of Benin demonstrate that we have a relatively clear picture of the importance of the Yoruba migration under the conditions of trans-Atlantic slavery. In order to identify the "Yoruba" population further, it is necessary to examine the specific sub-ethnic identities of the Yoruba, and the specific wars and military campaigns that account for the majority of slaves leaving the Bight of Benin in the eighteenth and nineteenth centuries. The registers of liberated Africans in Havana between 1826 and 1839 provide a window in the determination of Yoruba ethnicity for this period, which can be correlated with the aftermath of the Owu wars and overlapping the period of disintegration for Oyo.[42] The distinctions among the "Lukumí" population include Oyo, Egba, Ijebu, Ota, Ijesha, Sabe, and other designations. The term encompassed people who also passed through Yoruba country to reach the coast, such as Hausa, Nupe, and Bariba. In this sample of 3,663 individuals, 68 percent (2,497) were classified as Yoruba, 26 percent (946) were classified as one of the Gbe groups, and only 1 percent (32) are clearly identified with the Central Sudan. It may well be that those classified as

Lucumí without further identification may have included individuals from the Central Sudan; otherwise the sample seems to underrepresent the far interior.

Biographical accounts of enslaved Yoruba, of which many hundreds have survived,[43] confirm the major findings presented here: first, the dichotomy between coast and interior in the gender and age composition of the deported population and, second, the importance of the jihad as a factor in enslavement, especially in northern Yorubaland, and the corresponding increase in the incidence of enslavement in southern Yorubaland that was an indirect result of the jihad through the movement of refugees south and the establishment of the new political order of the nineteenth century in the wake of Oyo. The available biographical data allow identification of specific Yoruba subgroups, as well as other categories identified by Yoruba (Gambari for Hausa and Imale for Muslims). The biographical data demonstrate that there was a high proportion of enslavement and sale arising from the jihad and the succession struggle in its wake. This relationship with jihad presents difficulties in examining the Yoruba factor, because various ethnic backgrounds are disguised in the identifications used in the sources. It is possible to isolate some features, such as Muslim names, references to Fulani, and the correlation with specific wars, including the 1817 Ilorin uprising, the Owu wars of the early 1820s, the destruction of Egbado and Nupe, and the campaigns against the Okun Yoruba of the Northeast. Moreover, in most cases certain acts of enslavement, including enslavement for debt or adultery and kidnapping in southern Yorubaland, were probably unrelated to the Muslim factor, unless a Muslim merchant purchased such a victim. Nonetheless, the personal profiles of the enslaved reinforce the image that Islam contributed to the evolution of Yoruba identity. It appears that the choice of the term to describe pan-ethnic allegiance and to reflect ethnic consciousness may well have related to perceptions arising from the Muslim factor. The recently converted Christians who embraced the term "Yoruba" may well have chosen to express their ethnic identity in a manner that conformed to Muslim perceptions.

Notes

I wish to thank the Social Sciences and Humanities Research Council of Canada and the Canada Research Chair in African Diaspora History for support of this research. David Eltis generously provided data on which part of this study is based, and Mariza de Carvalho Soares commented on a draft, and I thank both.

1. David Eltis, "The Diaspora of Yoruba Speakers, 1650–1865: Dimensions and Implications," chapter 2 in this volume.

2. Robin Law, "Ethnicity and the Slave Trade: 'Lucumi' and 'Nago' as Ethnonyms in West Africa," *History in Africa* 24 (1997): 205–19. Law provides a useful summary of the adoption of the term "Yoruba" among the Christian elite from Sierra Leone in the nineteenth century.

3. See Biodun Adediran, "Yoruba Ethnic Groups or a Yoruba Ethnic Group? A Review of the Problem of Ethnic Identification," *África: Revista do Centro de Estudos*

Africanos da Universidade de São Paulo, Brazil 7 (1984): 57–70. Adediran argues that there was a conscious sense of a common heritage and ethnicity well before the adoption of a common term.

4. See J. Lorand Matory, "The English Professors of Brazil: On the Diasporic Roots of the Yorùbá Nation," *Comparative Studies in Society and History* 41, no. 1 (January 1999): 72–103.

5. The important exception in recognizing a strong "Islamic" factor among the Yoruba is J. D. Y. Peel, *Religious Encounter and the Making of the Yoruba* (Bloomington: Indiana University Press, 2000).

6. John Hunwick and Fatima Harrak, *Mi'raj al-Su'ud: Ahmad Baba's Replies on Slavery* (Rabat: Institute of African Studies, 2000).

7. For a different interpretation that equates "Yoruba" with Oyo, see Robin Law, *The Oyo Empire c. 1600–c. 1836: A West African Imperialism in the Era of the Atlantic Slave Trade* (Oxford: Clarendon, 1977), 5. Law bases his conclusion on the observations of H. Clapperton, *Journal of a Second Expedition into the Interior of Africa* (London: Murray, 1829), 4.

8. Law, "Ethnicity and the Slave Trade," 207. See also John Thornton, *Africa and Africans in the Making of the Atlantic World, 1400–1800* (Cambridge: Cambridge University Press, 1998), 112, citing documents dating to 1547. On the rise of Oyo, see Law, *The Oyo Empire*, 37–44, 56–60.

9. Alonso de Sandoval, *Un tratado sobre la esclavitud* (Madrid: Alianza, 1987), 104–26. For a different interpretation, see Eltis, "The Diaspora of Yoruba Speakers." See also Thornton, *Africa and Africans*, xxii–xxiii, 112.

10. Law, "Ethnicity and the Slave Trade," 208.

11. Christopher Fyfe, *A History of Sierra Leone* (London: Oxford University Press, 1962), 170.

12. Peter Morton-Williams, "The Oyo Yoruba and the Atlantic Slave Trade, 1670–1830," *Journal of the Historical Society of Nigeria* 3, no. 1 (1964): 25–45.

13. The number of enslaved Africans leaving the Bight of Benin has been previously estimated at 2,019,300; see Paul E. Lovejoy, *Transformations in Slavery: A History of Slavery in Africa*, 2nd ed. (Cambridge: Cambridge University Press, 2000 [1983]), 51, 56, 146. The preferred series is derived from the analysis of David Eltis; based on David Eltis et al., *The Trans-Atlantic Slave Trade: A Database on CD-ROM* (Cambridge: Cambridge University Press, 1999). An initial query of the database does not produce this estimate, but rather a figure considerably lower (1,130,765), apparently because of the number of individuals who are listed as "unspecified" in regional origins (2,244,809).

14. Robin Law, *The Slave Coast of West Africa, 1550–1750: The Impact of the Atlantic Slave Trade on an African Society* (Oxford: Clarendon, 1991), 187.

15. Patrick Manning, "The Slave Trade in the Bight of Benin, 1640–1890," in *The Uncommon Market: Essays in the Economic History of the Atlantic Slave Trade*, ed. Henry A. Gemery and Jan S. Hogendorn (New York: Academic Press, 1979), 125–29.

16. See Mariza de Carvalho Soares, *Devotos da cor: Identidade étnica, religiosidade e escravidão no Rio de Janeiro, século XVIII* (Rio de Janeiro: Civilização Brasileira, 2000); Soares, "The Mahi-Mina in Rio de Janeiro in the 18th Century," Harriet Tubman Seminar, York University, Canada, 2001 (unpublished); and Gwendolyn Midlo Hall, "African Ethnicities and the Meanings of Mina," in *Trans-Atlantic Dimensions of African Ethnicity*, ed. Paul E. Lovejoy and David V. Trotman (London: Continuum, 2002).

17. Kristin Mann, "Slave Exports from Lagos, c. 1760–1851," Canadian Association of African Studies, Montreal, 1996; David Eltis, *Economic Growth and the Ending of the Transatlantic Slave Trade* (New York: Oxford University Press, 1987).

18. Patrick Manning first recognized the significance of the shift eastward; see his "Slave Trade in the Bight of Benin," 107–41; and idem, *Slavery, Colonialism, and Economic Growth in Dahomey, 1640–1960* (Cambridge: Cambridge University Press, 1982).

19. See Law, *The Slave Coast of West Africa*.

20. On the relative importance of Ouidah in the Bight of Benin trade, see David Eltis, Paul Lovejoy, and David Richardson, "Ports of the Slave Trade: An Atlantic-Wide Perspective, 1676–1832," in *The Ports of the Slave Trade (Bights of Benin and Biafra)*, ed. Robin Law and Silke Strikrodt (Stirling, U.K.: Centre of Commonwealth Studies, University of Stirling, 1999); and Robin Law, *Ouidah: The Social History of a West African Slaving "Port," 1727–1892* (Oxford: James Currey, 2004).

21. Eltis, "The Diaspora of Yoruba Speakers," chapter 2 of this volume; and Mann, "Slave Exports from Lagos."

22. Paul E. Lovejoy, "Jihad e escravidão: As origens dos escravos Muçulmanos de Bahia." *Topoi* (Rio de Janeiro) 1 (2000): 11–44.

23. See Eltis, "Diaspora of Yoruba Speakers," chapter 2 of this volume.

24. Locally the port is known as Glehue, while the name of the small kingdom of Hueda in which Glehue was located is the source of the name Ouidah or Whydah; see Law, *Ouidah*.

25. It should be noted that the voyage database (Eltis et al., *TSTD*) is particularly weak with respect to the population movement from the Bight of Benin. The unknown portion of this movement is so large as to severely limit the use of the database. There were large numbers of individuals whose region of departure in Africa is not known, calculated here as 349,033 arrivals, and the number of those from the Bight of Benin who went to unknown destinations included 405,976 individuals. Hence there was an additional pool of 756,009 individuals who might have gone to either Cuba or Brazil.

Bight of Benin Origins of the Enslaved in Cuba and Bahia:
Consideration of the Unknown Factor

	Arrivals	Percent of Those Disembarked
Cuba—total disembarked	563,551	100
Cuba—Benin	30,741	5.4
Cuba—unknown	407,908	72.3
Bahia—total disembarked	223,699	100
Bahia—Benin	40,357	18.0
Bahia—unknown	47,115	21.0
Unspecified destination from Bight of Benin	405,976	
Unspecified origins	349,033	

In addition, the origins of almost three-quarters of those known to have arrived in Cuba are not known, and only 5.4 percent are credited with coming from the Bight of Benin, representing only 30,741 people. For Bahia, only 40,357 are recorded as arriving from the Bight of Benin, and a much smaller proportion of individuals are listed as being of unknown origin (47,115), although both figures are seriously distorted because of the large unspecified categories discussed above which particularly affect the Bahian data.

26. David Geggus, "The Demographic Composition of the French Caribbean Slave Trade," in *Proceedings of the Thirteenth and Fourteenth Meetings of the French Colonial History Society*, ed. P. Boucher (Lanham, Md.: University Press of America, 1990), 14–29; David Geggus, "Sugar and Coffee Cultivation in Saint Domingue and the Shaping of the Slave Labor Force," in *Cultivation and Culture: Labor and the Shaping of Slave Life in the Americas*, ed. Ira Berlin and Philip D. Morgan (Charlottesville: University of Virginia Press, 1993), 73–98, 314–18; Nina Rodrigues, *Os Africanos no Brasil* (São Paulo: Companhia Editora Nacional, 1977 [1906]), 90–97, 178–79, 218–26, 334–65; Pierre Verger, *Trade Relations between the Bight of Benin and Bahia, 17th to 19th Centuries* (Ibadan, Nigeria: Ibadan University Press, 1976); Mieko Nishida, "Manumission and Ethnicity in Urban Slavery: Salvador, Brazil, 1808–1888," *Hispanic American Historical Review* 73, no. 3 (1993): 361–91.

27. Gabriel Debien, "Les origines des esclaves aux Antilles," *Bulletin de l'Institut d'Afrique Noire*, sèr. B, 23 (1961): 363–87; 24 (1962): 1–41; 25 (1963): 1–38, 215–66.

28. David Geggus, "Sex Ratio, Age, and Ethnicity in the Atlantic Slave Trade: Data from French Shipping and Plantation Records," *Journal of African History* 30, no. 1 (1989): 32. Also see Geggus, "Sugar and Coffee Cultivation in Saint Domingue."

29. B. W. Higman, "African and Creole Slave Family Patterns in Trinidad," *Journal of Family History* 3 (1978): 163–80; appendix, 178–80. Also see Maureen Warner-Lewis, "Trinidad Yoruba: Notes on Survivals," *Caribbean Quarterly* 17, no. 2 (1971): 40–49; and Warner-Lewis, *Trinidad Yoruba: From Mother Tongue to Memory* (Tuscaloosa: University of Alabama Press, 1996). Verene Shepherd and David V. Trotman are in the process of analyzing the slave registrations of the post-1807 period in which enslaved individuals are listed by ethnicity.

30. Maria Inês Côrtes de Oliveira, "Retrouver une identité: Jeux sociaux des Africains de Bahia (vers 1750–vers 1890)" (Ph.D. dissertation, Université de Paris—Sorbonne, 1992), 98; citing Testament et inventaires après décès: Chartes de Liberté; Enquête du Calundu de Cachoera; Liste des Africains résidant dans la Paroisse da Penha.

31. João José Reis, *Slave Rebellion in Brazil: The Muslim Uprising of 1835 in Bahia*, trans. Arthur Brakel (Baltimore: The Johns Hopkins University Press, 1993), 140.

32. Nishida, "Manumission and Ethnicity in Salvador," 370, 378, relying on letters of liberty, Arquivo Público do Estado da Bahia (APB), Seção histórica, and APB, Seção Judiciára, Livros de registro de testamentos da capital.

33. Ade Obeyemi, "The Sokoto *Jihad* and the *O-kun* Yoruba: A Review," *Journal of the Historical Society of Nigeria* 9, no. 2 (1978): 61–87; and Femi James Kolapo, "Military Turbulence, Population Displacement, and Commerce on a Slaving Frontier of the Sokoto Caliphate: Nupe c. 1810–1857" (Ph.D. dissertation, York University, Canada, 1999).

34. David Eltis and Stanley Engerman, "Was the Slave Trade Dominated by Men?" *Journal of Interdisciplinary History* 23 (1992): 237–57; and David Eltis, "Fluctuations in Sex and Age Ratios in the Transatlantic Slave Trade, 1663–1864," *Economic History Review* 46 (1993): 308–23.

35. Geggus, "Sex Ratio, Age, and Ethnicity," 23– 44.

36. Eltis, "Sex and Age Ratios," 308 –23.

37. David Eltis, "Fluctuations in the Age and Sex Ratios of Slaves in the Nineteenth-Century Transatlantic Slave Traffic," *Slavery and Abolition* 7, no. 3 (1986): 259, 264. The gender sample is based on 29,504 slaves, as reported in 114 observations; the age/gender sample is derived from 23,326 slaves in 96 observations.

38. David Eltis, *The Rise of African Slavery in the Americas* (Cambridge: Cambridge University Press, 2000).

39. Paul E. Lovejoy, "Islam, Slavery, and Political Transformation in West Africa: Constraints on the Trans-Atlantic Slave Trade," *Revue française d'histoire d'outre-mer* 89 (2002): 247–82.

40. Lovejoy, "Jihad e Escravidão," 27.

41. Ibid., 22.

42. Eltis, "Diaspora of Yoruba Speakers."

43. Source material for biographical information is scattered, but includes Church Missionary Society Archives, Yoruba Mission, Niger Mission, and Sierra Leone. See Francine Shields, "Biographical Data on Enslaved Yoruba" (1997), unpublished; Kolapo, "Military Turbulence," Appendix 4, "All Incidents of Slavery and the Slave Trade for Area of Study, 1820– 67," 297–317. These materials have been incorporated in *Biographical Database of Enslaved Africans* (Harriet Tubman Resource Centre on the African Diaspora, York University). For a preliminary discussion, see Paul E. Lovejoy, "Biography as Source Material: Towards a Biographical Archive of Enslaved Africans," in *Source Material for Studying the Slave Trade and the African Diaspora*, ed. Robin Law (Centre of Commonwealth Studies, University of Stirling, U.K., 1997).

CHAPTER FOUR

The Enslavement of Yoruba

Ann O'Hear

The collapse of the Oyo Empire in the early nineteenth century and the prolonged Yoruba wars led to the enslavement of a great many Yoruba people and a sharp increase in the numbers of Yoruba slaves who were transported across the Atlantic to the New World, as demonstrated by David Eltis and Paul E. Lovejoy. The nineteenth century is also the period for which detailed information is available on specific activities of enslavement. This chapter concentrates on the enslavement of Yoruba speakers in the nineteenth century through an examination of the processes of enslavement (including warfare, raiding, and kidnapping); surveys the states, groups, and individuals who were involved in these processes; and studies the people who were enslaved, including their areas of origin and their individual stories.[1] In addition, the chapter examines the destinations of enslaved Yoruba, whether the slaves ended their journey within Yorubaland itself or were sent toward the New World through the ports of the Bights of Benin and Biafra. It discusses the internal demand for slaves (which long outlived the external trade) and internal slaveholders. The chapter ends with a brief account of the decline of enslavement in Yorubaland at the end of the nineteenth century, as the British gradually, in piecemeal fashion, established their control over the Yoruba speakers of what is now Nigeria.

The Process of Enslavement

Well before the nineteenth century the Oyo Empire exported significant numbers of slaves who passed through the ports of the Slave Coast on their way to the Americas. These included enslaved criminals, of whom a majority are likely to have been Yoruba speakers from the state of Oyo itself. Certainly some of the exported slaves were Yoruba from Oyo and from other Yoruba-speaking groups. Yoruba speakers were also captured in slave raids by Dahomey and then exported. But criminals very probably constituted only a small proportion of the total number of slaves exported south from Oyo, while large numbers of the exported slaves came originally from Oyo's non-Yoruba-speaking western and northern neighbors. Many Mahi and Bariba were captured in war, and many slaves were obtained by trade from Nupe, Borgu, and elsewhere. Even the greatly increased export of slaves from Oyo in the late eighteenth century may have been fed in large part through trade from the north.[2] Thus Yoruba speakers are likely to have been a minority among the slaves who were exported from the Slave Coast in the pre-nineteenth-century period.

From the early nineteenth century, however, Yoruba speakers came to dominate the exodus of slaves from the Slave Coast, including the rising port of Lagos and elsewhere, although Hausa slaves brought from further north in the Nigerian hinterland were also important in the Atlantic trade.[3] Thousands of Yoruba and other slaves were also absorbed into slavery internally, within various Yoruba and other states, a process that continued well after the demise of the external trade.

The most common methods of enslavement of Yoruba speakers in the nineteenth century included warfare, raids, kidnapping expeditions, and brigandage. The nineteenth century was a period of almost continuous warfare and lawlessness in Yorubaland. Warfare was associated with the fall of Oyo and the rise of Ilorin. The city of Ilorin, which was situated in the northeast part of the Oyo Empire, was largely Yoruba in population.[4] It became the center of an emirate of the Sokoto / Gwandu Caliphate, and made determined (and strongly resisted) efforts to carry the jihad (which had led to the setting up of the caliphate in the early nineteenth century) further south. The Nupe-Fulani emirate of Bida, also part of the caliphate, raided the small-scale northeastern Yoruba polities south of the Niger. Oyo provincial rulers and other chiefs seized the opportunity to carve out independent territories for themselves and to raid and control their neighbors. Warfare spread to the south and east in the Owu wars. The kingdom of Owu and the old Egba settlements were destroyed; the Egba founded a new settlement at Abeokuta and fought to obtain a safe trade route to the coast. The successor states to Old Oyo struggled among themselves. The rising city-state of Ibadan, which became the most successful of the successor states, eventually succeeded in destroying Kurunmi's city-state of Ijaye. Ibadan also embarked on wars of territorial expansion in the Ekiti, Akoko, and Ijesha areas. To the south, the Egba and Ijebu fought to keep Ibadan from achieving direct contact with the coast. And the Ekiti and Ijesha, aided by Ilorin, sought to regain their independence from Ibadan in the Ekitiparapo wars.[5] All these wars, raids, expeditions, and attendant forms of lawlessness resulted in the "production" of large numbers of Yoruba slaves.

The city-state of Ilorin took over some of Oyo's role as a slave supplier, both by capture and by trade. Ilorin's pre-emirate ruler and rebellious Oyo general, Afonja, captured and enslaved people in the area immediately around the city of Ilorin and in the Igbomina, Igbolo, and Epo areas of the Oyo Empire, re-settling them around Ilorin, absorbing male slaves into his army, and selling women and children to obtain arms.[6] Afonja's Muslim allies moved west and carried out raids in the Ibarapa Province of the empire from a base at Iseyin. Among the slaves captured in these raids was a boy from the town of Osogun, who was sold into the Atlantic trade, freed by the British antislavery squadron, and landed in Freetown. This was Samuel Ajayi Crowther, who became famous as an Anglican bishop and a scholar.[7] Afonja's Muslim successors in Ilorin raided the Igbomina and Ekiti to the east, thus continuing Ilorin's role as slave supplier.[8]

As the century wore on, Ilorin found itself competing with Ibadan and the Nupe-Fulani emirate of Bida in raiding the small-scale Yoruba polities stretch-ing to the area of the Niger-Benue confluence, but also raiding in cooperation with its competitor states. The Akoko area suffered from the competition be-tween the three raiding states, being, in the words of Hogben and Kirk-Greene, "one of those unhappy districts alternatively raided by Nupe, Ibadan, and Ilorin."[9] In an example of cooperative raiding, in 1875–76 Ilorin and Ibadan joined forces in the Wokuti campaign, which Samuel Johnson, the eminent Yoruba historian, described as an "expedition for slave-hunting" in the Ekiti, Yagba, and Akoko country.[10]

In later years, Ilorin, in alliance with the Ekitiparapo, who were fighting for the independence of Ekiti, engaged in a prolonged conflict with Ibadan that also provided opportunities for Ilorin forces to seize slaves. In the course of Ilorin's long siege of its rebellious vassal town of Offa, for example, a cer-tain Nathaniel Popoola Olawoyin was seized and sold to an Abeokuta man. He became a Christian, returned to Offa in 1907, and helped to found the Church Missionary Society (CMS) church there.[11] Although Ilorin's activi-ties had been to an extent circumscribed by competition with its powerful neighbors, it was still reported to have "started on a kidnapping expedition" as late as 1894, far to the east in "the Akoko country, distant about twenty days travel from Ilorin."[12]

Nupe raids south of the Niger on the northeastern Yoruba may have begun even before the founding of Bida Emirate. According to a British official, the raids had already started before the Fulani took over the Nupe kingdom: "It is largely owing to . . . Majia's raids that the tribes in the Kabba Division are so mixed. The Yagba, Bunu, [and] Aworo [Oworo] . . . seem to have paid the Nupe tribute unless left sufficiently long without a visit."[13] Raids and demands for tribute continued through the nineteenth century and slave seizures intensified for the last time in the final years before the defeat of Bida Emirate by the Royal

Niger Company in 1897. For example, according to the account given by British official C. K. Meek in 1918,

> Towards the end of Maliki's and the beginning of Abubakr's reign the Bida Fi-lanis, fully appreciating the Niger Company's preparations for war, made a final raid on Aworo [Oworo] and it is safe to say that in the Aworo district today there isn't a single male or female over the age of 30 who has not been a slave at Bida.[14]

Another non-Yoruba state responsible for enslaving Yoruba was Dahomey to the west, which attacked the Egba regularly. During the siege of Ijaye by Ibadan, for example, an invading Dahomean army attacked an Egba town near Abeokuta and captured all the slaves they could.[15]

Of all the successor states to Old Oyo, Ibadan became the most powerful and the most successful in obtaining and profiting from slaves. Soon after the founding of the new Egba town of Abeokuta (dated by Saburi Biobaku to 1830), for example, Ibadan and Ijebu bands were overrunning its farms and kidnap-ping "in broad daylight anyone who ventured beyond the town wall."[16] Ibadan's most successful slave-raiding period, however, appears to have come in the 1850s and 1860s, during the decline of the Atlantic slave trade and after its de-mise, while Ibadan was fighting for control over the Ekiti and Ijesha countries. CMS missionary David Hinderer, for example, reported in 1855 on the cap-tives the Ibadan soldiers had brought from Ekiti towns:

> The Ibadan war has at last terminated, and the warriors have come home with great riches, alas! I say, with hosts of slaves. Though not many are sold down to the coast except to Porto Novo by way of Abeokuta, yet is the price high. Their farms are filled with them, and many of the rich warriors make new farms with them.[17]

Consul Campbell at Lagos estimated that about ten thousand captives were brought to Ibadan as a result of the 1855 Ekiti campaigns.[18] In 1877 CMS mis-sionary James Johnson asserted that the Ijesha predominated among slaves in Ibadan. In 1882 the Ijesha ruler, Owa Agunloye, reported that,

> I myself was taking [sic] captive . . . but I managed to escape; there is scarcely any man or woman in all the one thousand four hundred and sixty towns and villages that I rule over that were not three or four times slaves to the Ibadans.[19]

Other Yoruba states also participated in slave-taking, including states which at other times were themselves the victims of slave raids. At the beginning of the 1830s the Egba of Abeokuta were victims of slave raiding. A few years later their war chiefs were bringing back "Oyo, Ife, or Ijebu captives whom they absorbed into their households, when not sold abroad, as domestic slaves."[20] In 1862 Governor Freeman of Lagos asserted that the Egba had sold a larger number of Ijaye people, whom they were supposed to be protecting, into slav-ery than Ibadan, Ijaye's enemy, had done.[21] The Ijesha, preyed on by Ibadan, in turn raided weaker eastern Yoruba groups. Ijesha warriors, including the famed Ogedemgbe, conducted private military campaigns from which they returned with many slaves.[22] The olupo (king) of Ajasse, in Igbomina, joined the Nupe in raiding Oworo to the east.[23] The Ekiti warriors Aduloju of Ado and Eshu (Esugbayi) of Aiyede also raided the northeastern Yoruba for slaves.[24]

Ambitious warriors, competing for power as the Oyo Empire collapsed, captured slaves to serve as members of their armies, to feed their households, and to be sold in order to buy weaponry. Afonja of Ilorin was one such warrior. Others included the Timi of Ede, who asserted his independence of Oyo and proceeded to attack his neighbors; Ojo Amepo, who left Ilorin, set himself up at Amese in the Epo Province, and raided widely from there; and Atiba, a son of Alafin (King) Abiodun of Oyo, who joined Oja, a raider operating from Ago Oja. Later Abiodun himself became *alafin*, successor to the rulers of the old empire, and set up his court at Ago Oja, which became known as New Oyo.[25] Another warrior, Kurunmi, migrated to Ijaye with many slaves and then continued to expand his following:

> [As] a young man, he was a notorious freebooter and slave-hunter. With a number of followers, who had attached themselves to his fortunes, he would go out from [Ijaye] into some distant province on predatory excursions. By kidnapping in the farms and plundering caravans he became rich and powerful and the leader of a party which favoured his ambition to become the ruler of the city.[26]

Similarly the warrior Oluyole used his many slaves to establish his base at Ibadan. Ogedemgbe, other Ijesha warriors, and Ekiti warriors in later years imitated their Ibadan mentors.[27]

Less prominent warriors and even slave soldiers also joined in the process of enslavement. In Ilorin an informant asserts that a slave who caught slaves for his master although "still a slave . . . was given different treatment."[28] Elsewhere in Yorubaland a slave who caught slaves might retain some of them, to use for his own purposes, or be given a monetary reward. A war chief might also reward a soldier slave by freeing him.[29]

In addition to acquiring slaves by warfare, powerful states might obtain slaves as tributary payments from vassal groups. Among the northeastern Yoruba, for example, who became tributary to Bida, tribute payment in the form of slaves rather than cowries (currency) seems to have increased from the reign of Masaba (d. 1873) on, as cowries became increasingly devalued.[30] Those who were given as tribute may already have been slaves before they were handed over, but this was not always the case. The Reverend C. E. Wating, who traveled in the northeastern Yoruba country with Bishops Tugwell and Phillips in 1894, reported on Ayeri, a town near Kabba, where

> the king came to call on us . . . and told us the English king was the ruler of the world, and he besought us white men to come and help him. He said that four

years ago, on his coming to the throne, the Nupes came and took away 300 of his people. He told us that oppression has been the rule here for forty years; that at first the Nupes only demanded couriers [cowries?], then farm produce, and that now they will have slaves as well. As all their own slaves are gone as tribute, they have to give their own children, and many, after giving their wives and children for tribute, have left the town and not come back—among others his own brother and cousin; that there are hardly any young people in the country, and that their nation is becoming extinct.[31]

Slaves given as tribute to overlord states might include those who had been enslaved as punishment for a crime. As punishment for murder in Ibadan, Hinderer reported, "the headmen . . . are not satisfied to take life for life only, but in addition catch and sell all the family of the offender."[32] In 1879 the Egba decreed that anyone breaking their embargo on trade with Ibadan should be sold as a slave.[33] And in most of Yorubaland, it was said, "a thief or burglar or anyone who was unable to pay his debt or fines inflicted on him was sold together with his wife and children."[34] In addition, according to Samuel Johnson, there were "well attested cases where a member of a family would be condemned to slavery by a unanimous vote of all the relatives when he has brought disgrace on the family."[35]

Although individuals might be sold into slavery as punishment for crimes, however, the majority of slaves entered the slave trade, whether external or internal, after they had been acquired as tribute, and, even more especially, as a result of warfare and raids carried out by states vying for importance as successors to the Oyo Empire, by non-Yoruba states, and by ambitious warriors.

The Enslaved

Members of many Yoruba-speaking groups were enslaved at various times in the nineteenth century, along a moving and fluctuating enslavement frontier. As David Eltis points out, large areas of what is now called Yorubaland were "unaffected at first," and there were "few hints of disruption in the western Yoruba societies through which Clapperton and the Landers passed in the 1820s."[36] In the 1850s and 1860s, the Ekiti and Ijesha were heavily preyed on. But in the end it seems likely that the groups that lost the greatest number of people were the small polities of the northeastern Yoruba, including the Yagba, Ijumu, Bunu, Oworo, Akoko, and Owe, who were attacked by Ibadan, Ilorin, Nupe, and even their own Ekiti and Ijesha neighbors.[37]

At the time these small northeastern Yoruba polities were not considered to be "Yoruba." In the nineteenth and early twentieth centuries a distinction was made, both by Western-educated Nigerians and by colonial officers, between the more central Yoruba and the peripheral groups to the northeast who spoke dialects of the Yoruba language. At the same time, it is highly unlikely that the northeastern Yoruba had any idea of a "pan-Yoruba" identity that would embrace them. Even the Bunu ex-slave James Thomas, who returned to the confluence as a CMS missionary in the mid-nineteenth century, differentiated between his people and the "Yoruba," although he allowed that their languages were "almost alike."[38] It is possible that such a differentiation made it more acceptable for the groups called "Yoruba" to enslave the peoples of the northeast, although their powerlessness to resist the city-states and their war leaders must have been the deciding factor. And in the fluid and perilous conditions of the nineteenth century even close cultural and linguistic ties did not necessarily prevent mutual enslavement.

There does seem, however, to have been general disapproval among Yoruba of those who attempted to enslave people from their own towns (other than criminals or those who had caused disgrace), especially, Oroge argues, after Oluyole and Kurunmi led an expedition against the town of Abemo, following a civil war in which members of the losing side were captured by the winners.[39] A report from mid-century Abeokuta testifies to the severe punishment meted out to those found guilty of enslaving their own townspeople, although it also confirms that this practice still continued:

> Strict watch is kept over those suspected of stealing men. . . . the house of one individual who was executed for this crime in Abbeokuta, was razed to the ground. It . . . was found to contain rooms within rooms, doors opposite doors, to facilitate the capture and concealment of the victims. The practice is to decoy some unwary person and there confine him until some opportunity offers for shipping him.[40]

Reports from Ondo and Ibadan also attest to the seriousness with which the crime of enslaving one's own townspeople was regarded.[41] At the very end of the nineteenth century enslavement of people from one's own area may well have briefly increased, in a last desperate attempt to obtain slaves before the British took control.

Some accounts are available of individuals' experiences of enslavement. One such individual was Samuel Ajayi Crowther, who was captured when Osogun was attacked by a force of "Oyo Mahomedans" (another version of Crowther's narrative has "Yorriba Mahommedans"), accompanied by Fulani, in 1821. He was about fifteen years old at the time. Initially he was taken to Iseyin, the headquarters of his attackers. After being sold several times, he eventually reached Lagos, where he was sold to the Portuguese:

> Being a veteran in slavery . . . and having no more hope of ever going to my country again, I patiently took whatever came; although it was not without a great fear and trembling that I received, for the first time, the touch of a White Man, who examined me whether I was sound or not. Men and boys were at first chained together, with a chain of about six fathoms in length, thrust through an iron fetter on the neck of every individual, and fastened at both ends with padlocks. In this situation the boys suffered the most. . . . At last we boys [were] separated from

the men . . . we were corded together, by ourselves. Thus we were going in and out, bathing together, and so on. The female sex fared not much better. Thus we were for nearly the space of four months.[42]

Finally Crowther and the other slaves were embarked on a Portuguese ship bound for Brazil. The ship was intercepted, and Crowther was landed in Free-town, Sierra Leone, in 1822.[43]

Another Yoruba slave who has left a record of his experiences was Osife-kunde, an Ijebu trader. He was a young man when he was captured in 1820 in the lagoons along the Nigerian coast, on his way east by boat from Lagos, where he had bought European goods, to a town that has been identified as Mahin. He was ambushed by Ijo pirates who took him to the Niger Delta port of Warri where he was sold and sent to Brazil. In the 1830s his owner brought him to Paris, where he described his early life, his enslavement, and his homeland to a French scholar, D'Avezac-Macaya.[44]

Somewhat later, but before Abeokuta was founded in 1830, an Egba boy who later took the name of Joseph Wright was enslaved when his town was cap-tured in the course of the attacks on the Egba after the fall of Owu. Years later he still vividly remembered his experience, and the fate of those who were even less fortunate than he:

> The enemies satisfied themselves with little children, little girls, young men, and young women; and so they did not care about the aged and old people. They killed them without mercy.[45]

> I was brought [to their camp] the same day the city was taken. . . . When I came to that place, the man who took me in the city took me and made a present to the chief man of war who commanded the band which he belonged to; for the custom was when any of their company went with bands of war, if he catch slaves, half of the slaves he would give to his Captain.[46]

> While I was with these enemies in the camp . . . I saw a child of about eighteen months old cast out of the camp because the child was so young that nobody would buy him. That poor orphan was there crying at the point of death for about two days, and none [took] pity to pick him up.[47]

Wright's account illustrates the types of slaves that were valued, and the brutal treatment that might be meted out to captives who were not considered sal-able, capable of transporting themselves, or able to work. While the enslavers were said to prefer young people, including "little children," this obviously did not extend to children so young that they could not walk or carry loads. And although older slaves might have their uses in a more settled economy, they were largely a hindrance in the mobile world of the raiders.

Like Crowther, Wright was eventually sent south and sold to the Portuguese in Lagos. The slave ship on which he was embarked was intercepted by the British, and Wright was landed in Sierra Leone, received an education, and became a clergyman. But unlike Crowther and a number of other "recaptives" (slaves freed by the antislavery squadron) who eventually returned to Nigeria, Wright remained in Sierra Leone and engaged in Christian missionary work there.[48]

Directions and Demands
in the Internal and External Slave Trade

Some Yoruba slaves were sent northward, including the many northeastern Yoruba who found themselves in Bida as a result of tribute exactions or raids. There was also some trade in slaves from Ilorin to the north, and slaves were sent north from that city as tribute to its overlords in Gwandu or Sokoto.[49] However, the slaves who were put on the market in Ilorin entered a trade that flowed overwhelmingly from north to south, to Ibadan, Abeokuta, Ijebu Ode, Lagos, and beyond. Even after the Atlantic slave trade from Lagos declined and finally died out, the north-south flow continued unabated through the nineteenth century, as slaves continued to be incorporated into both large- and smaller-scale households in the Yoruba states.[50]

Various towns and cities became slave marts in this north-south trade, either temporarily or over the long term, and the Egba and Ijebu developed their position as powerful middlemen through the century.[51] In the 1820s the Ijebu were the principal suppliers of slaves to Lagos.[52] Abeokuta established itself as another major supplier of Lagos in the early 1830s, soon after its foundation.[53]

A variety of traders became involved. Chiefly families often sold slaves from their private houses, as in Ibadan and Ilorin.[54] By the 1870s, in Ibadan, chiefs and others were able to use commission agents. According to missionary James Johnson in 1877,

> There [were] several private slave markets in [Ibadan] supplying its demands and those of Abeokuta, Ijebu, Porto Novo and other places. . . . I called at one of these markets owned by a Mohammedan Commission Agent. . . . He mistook me for one of his English speaking customers from Abeokuta.[55]

Even many of the "Saro," ex-slaves themselves, who had been landed in Sierra Leone and later returned to Yorubaland, were involved in slave ownership and trading.[56]

Many of the slaves brought south were exported through the Slave Coast ports. Of these, by far the most important overall was Ouidah, but in the early nineteenth century the port of Lagos rose to importance, and from 1837 it exported more slaves than Ouidah.[57] In the first half of the nineteenth century Yoruba slaves dominated departures from both these ports.[58] In the 1850s the export slave trade from Lagos declined precipitously, as a result of British activities with regard to both Lagos and the Brazilian trade, and finally came to an end after Britain's annexation of Lagos in 1861. British efforts to close the

Brazilian trade succeeded by 1851, but the Cuban trade continued until 1867, with many Yoruba leaving for Cuba from Ouidah.[59] There is even evidence that slaves from as far away as north of Aboh, on the lower Niger, were taken to Ouidah in the late 1850s.[60] These slaves may well have included some north-eastern Yoruba who had been sent down the Niger.

Until the end of the 1830s most of these northeastern Yoruba slaves would have been exported into the Atlantic trade through Bight of Biafra ports, headed especially for Cuba and, for a time, to the French Caribbean.[61] In 1834 James Thomas was a kidnap victim in his native Bunu area. He was brought to the Niger, taken south to Aboh and from there to Bonny, sold into the Atlantic trade, rescued, and landed in Sierra Leone. He became a Christian, and served as a CMS missionary in Gbebe and Lokoja at the Niger-Benue confluence between 1858 and 1878. Visiting Aboh in 1858, he met Bunu slaves employed on Aboh war canoes, as well as the son of the man who had sold him to Bonny.[62]

The slave trade continued through Aboh, though presumably largely for the internal market.[63] Samuel Crowther remarked on the "accumulation of slaves" by the wealthy in the towns of Aboh, Idah, and Igbegbe on the Niger, explaining that "since the slave-trade has been abolished in the Bight of Biafra, slaves have become very cheap; and . . . they have the means of purchasing a great many slaves."[64]

The internal demand for slaves was particularly marked in nineteenth-century Yorubaland itself. As many scholars have noted, the Yoruba states and individuals vying for power needed slaves to fill their armies; to feed their armies, followers, and households; to engage in craft industries; and to act as carriers and trading agents. All of this long predated the end of the Atlantic slave trade, but the rise of "legitimate" trade in palm oil added to the demand for labor.[65] Although they were not shipped across the Atlantic, slaves who remained in Yorubaland were integrated to a degree into the Atlantic world through the items they produced.

Slaves were regarded as a good investment. According to James Johnson,

> The Egbas . . . have an inveterate attachment to slave labour as do others also and are often investing money in it saying it is absolutely necessary for their work and accounting it a better investment of cowries than investments upon cloths and beads . . . which may be easily consumed by fire.[66]

The classic example of the internal use of slaves is Ibadan, described here by Samuel Johnson with reference, perhaps, to the period around 1860:

> Ibadan had . . . been greatly augmented, not only by immigrants . . . but also by the thousands of slaves brought in annually . . . .
>
> Except under especially pressing circumstances the chiefs do not now sell their slaves or rather captives of war excepting the old and infirm and that chiefly to procure arms and ammunition. The able-bodied men are kept and trained as sol-diers, and it has become the law and custom that soldier-slaves are never to be

sold under any circumstances; they are to remain permanently as members of
the house. The fair young women are added to the harems by the great, and young
men save themselves the expenses of a dowry by making wives of any that come
into their hands. . . . All the rest are sent into the farms, each to be employed in
his or her own line of work. The chiefs had large farms and farm houses containing from a hundred to over a thousand souls. The men are engaged in clearing the bush, cultivating the soil, cutting palm nuts and doing other male work;
the women in making palm oil, nut oil, soap, weaving mats, rearing poultry and
the smaller cattle, cultivating kitchen vegetables of all kinds for the weekly markets and the fairs; older women in preparing and spinning cotton, shelling palm
nuts, etc. All are engaged as "hands" in time of harvest.

These extensive plantations not only support their huge establishments but
also supply the markets, so that a military state though Ibadan was, food was actually cheaper there than in many other towns.[67]

This account illustrates the numerous uses to which slaves were put, and the
scale and complexity of the economy that grew up around the major war leaders and other large-scale slaveholders. Female slaves could be used for repro-
ductive as well as other uses. Males might capture other slaves in war. Both,
however, were extensively used in agricultural and other production, not only
for household purposes but for the market. Both males and females played their
part in the production of palm oil for the new "legitimate" trade that replaced
the external slave trade.

Many Yoruba were slave owners on a large scale. For example, Kurunmi of
Ijaye was said to have three hundred wives and one thousand slaves. One of
his farms was reported to be more than one hundred acres in size, worked by
an army of slaves.[68] At Epe in the 1850s, Kosoko, the exiled king of Lagos, and
his henchman, Tapa Osodi, each had more than five thousand slaves working
on their "various plantations."[69] In Abeokuta, in the 1850s, the large-scale
owners included Saro, who were "considerable holders of slaves on their
farms."[70] In later years in the same city there were "large individual producers
with from 100–500 slaves working for them."[71] At the same time, the Balogun
of Ikorodu in Ijebu reportedly held more than four hundred slaves.[72] In Ondo
in the second half of the nineteenth century a large slaveholding probably meant
about one hundred slaves on average, but Edun, the Lisa of Ondo, had more
than eight hundred, "with a seraglio [harem] of about three to four hundred
women."[73] In Ilorin the Balogun Ajikobi, one of the senior Yoruba war chiefs,
had "many" plantations, with "at least twenty-five slaves working on each."[74]
Women were also counted among the large-scale owners. In 1854 Madam
Tinubu was reported to possess "some hundreds of armed slaves."[75] Samuel
Johnson noted Efusetan of Ibadan as "owning some 2,000 slaves in her farms
alone exclusive of those at home. She also had her own captains of war and
warboys."[76]

In Ilorin small-scale holdings were apparently common, because a master like the Balogun Ajikobi might divide up his slaves among several scattered farms, and because "most slave-holders had mere handfuls" of slaves. The Ilorin warrior Ojibara, said to have had "about four" plantations with "not less than ten slaves" working on each of them, may represent the middle rank of owner.[77] In Ibadan, in 1868, an Ifa priest had "about 12 men slaves" working in his farm. E. Adeniyi Oroge, who provides this example, points out that there were many slaveholdings of varying sizes in nineteenth-century Yorubaland.[78]

Not all the slaves of Yoruba slaveholders were Yoruba themselves. Certain specialist tasks were performed by Fulani and Hausa slaves.[79] Basorun Oluyole of Ibadan is said to have had thousands of mainly Hausa-speaking slaves.[80] According to missionary James Johnson, the slaves in Abeokuta were "drawn chiefly from the tribe known as Gambari," that is, Hausa, in 1880. The same informant reports that Hausa speakers were predominant among slaves in Ijebu at the end of the century.[81] These reports may reflect the use of significant numbers of slaves who were Hausa speakers (though not necessarily Hausa by ethnicity), but they are likely to be considerably exaggerated.

Enslavement: Final Intensification and Decline

The enslavement of Yoruba continued until the end of the nineteenth century. Bida Emirate intensified its slave-taking among the northeastern Yoruba in the last years before the emirate was defeated by the British in 1897.[82] Ilorin is said to have joined Etsu Maliki (who died in 1895) and his successor, Etsu Abubakar, in "extensive slave-raiding of Kabba . . . and Oworo lands."[83] Between 1897 and 1900 there was a period of escalated slave seizure in and around Ilorin, no doubt in reaction to the exodus of a large number of slaves after the city was defeated by the Royal Niger Company in 1897 and also owing to a perceived need to recoup as many slave losses as possible before the British returned to take control of the area. The Ilorin reaction to slave loss and the threat of losing the possibility of "producing" slaves in the future was epitomized in its emir's pleading letter to Goldie, leader of the Royal Niger Company's 1897 expedition against Ilorin, begging him to return the slaves who had fled when the city was defeated by the forces of the Royal Niger Company. This illustrates the importance of slavery even for a state that had no crop to sell in the "legitimate" trade.[84] Ilorin was not alone in its fears, as "many warriors" elsewhere "turned inward, raiding around their own neighbourhoods," although this was quickly stopped by the British authorities.[85]

The British takeover ended the enslavement of Yoruba by capture in war, raiding, kidnapping, and tribute collection. Open slave trading disappeared, although a clandestine trade in children from the German Cameroons and the "pagan" peoples of northern Nigeria continued, through Ilorin, for a number of years. Slavery itself, however, persisted in Yorubaland as elsewhere, though

67

it began to decline as conditions continued to change, and by the 1930s it was nearing its end.[86]

Yoruba-speaking slaves were sent to the Americas long before the nineteenth century. However, the early nineteenth century saw a great increase in the trade in Yoruba slaves to the New World, fed by the collapse of the old Oyo Empire and the prolonged Yoruba wars. Yoruba speakers were enslaved in the nineteenth century through warfare, raids, kidnapping, and brigandage, and also as tribute. Major states and war leaders were prominent in the process of enslavement, ownership, and trade, and even slave soldiers and freed slaves joined in the process. People from various Yoruba-speaking groups were enslaved along a moving frontier, but it seems likely that the northeast Yoruba were, overall, the most severely affected. The trans-Atlantic trade continued until mid-century, sending Yoruba speakers into the New World diaspora, as is illustrated by a number of firsthand accounts. But an internal movement of slaves outlived the trans-Atlantic trade by many years, as slaves were highly valued in the nineteenth-century economy. Even those slaves who remained in Yorubaland might be regarded, in some sense, as integrated into the Atlantic world through their involvement in production for the "legitimate" trade.

Notes

1. Some of the material in this chapter previously appeared in Ann O'Hear, *Power Relations in Nigeria: Ilorin Slaves and Their Successors* (Rochester, N.Y.: University of Rochester Press, 1997), and is reproduced here by permission of the University of Rochester Press. See also Ann O'Hear, "Ilorin as a Slaving and Slave-Trading State," in *Slavery on the Frontiers of Islam*, ed. Paul E. Lovejoy (Princeton, N.J.: Markus Wiener, 2003); and Ann O'Hear, "The Yoruba and the Peoples of the Niger-Benue Confluence," in *Yoruba Frontiers*, ed. Toyin Falola and Funso S. Afolayan, forthcoming.

2. David Eltis, "The Slave Trade in Nineteenth-Century Nigeria," in *Studies in the Nineteenth-Century Economic History of Nigeria*, ed. Toyin Falola and Ann O'Hear (Madison: African Studies Program, University of Wisconsin, 1998), 86; Robin Law, *The Oyo Empire c. 1600–c. 1836: A West African Imperialism in the Era of the Atlantic Slave Trade* (Oxford: Clarendon, 1977), 225–27, 306–308; Robin Law, *The Slave Coast of West Africa, 1550–1750: The Impact of the Atlantic Slave Trade on an African Society* (Oxford: Clarendon, 1991), 190–91; Philip D. Morgan, "The Cultural Implications of the Atlantic Slave Trade: African Regional Origins, American Destinations, and New World Developments," in *Routes to Slavery: Direction, Ethnicity, and Mortality in the Transatlantic Slave Trade*, ed. David Eltis and David Richardson (London: Frank Cass, 1997), 129.

3. Eltis, "Slave Trade in Nineteenth-Century Nigeria," 86; David Eltis and David Richardson, "West Africa and the Transatlantic Slave Trade: New Evidence of Long-Run Trends," in Eltis and Richardson, *Routes to Slavery*, 27; Law, *Oyo Empire*, 308; Paul E. Lovejoy, "The Central Sudan and the Atlantic Slave Trade," in *Paths Toward the Past: African Historical Essays in Honor of Jan Vansina*, ed. Robert W. Harms et al. (Atlanta: African Studies Association Press, 1994), 354; Paul E. Lovejoy and David

Richardson, "The Initial 'Crisis of Adaptation': The Impact of British Abolition on the Atlantic Slave Trade in West Africa, 1808–1820," in *From Slave Trade to "Legitimate" Commerce*, ed. Robin Law (Cambridge: Cambridge University Press, 1995), 40; Kristin Mann, "Shifting Paradigms in the Study of the African Diaspora and of Atlantic History and Culture," *Slavery and Abolition* 22, no. 1 (April 2001): 9; Morgan, "Cultural Implications," 129.

4. In 1929, according to Ilorin Resident H. B. Hermon-Hodge, in the city of Ilorin,

Ajikobi and Alanamu are definitely Yoruba wards, as are the Ibagan [*sic*] and Okaka sub-wards of the Gambari and Fulani wards respectively. The emir's ward and two of the sub-wards of the Fulani ward possess Fulani rulers, and three sub-wards of the Gambari ward a Hausa administration; but in none save Zongo and Karuma in the Gambari ward, essentially Hausa quarters, does any but the Yoruba predominate among the ordinary population.

H. B. Hermon-Hodge, *Gazetteer of Ilorin Province* (London: Allen and Unwin, 1929), 272.

5. For an overview of the Yoruba wars of the nineteenth century, see Toyin Falola and G. O. Oguntomisin, *Yoruba Warlords of the Nineteenth Century* (Trenton, N.J.: Africa World Press, 2001), 3–8. See also Eltis, "Slave Trade in Nineteenth-Century Nigeria," 88; Law, *Oyo Empire*, 258, 274–76, 280, 284–85; Lovejoy, "Central Sudan," 354.

6. Law, *Oyo Empire*, 278; Samuel Johnson, *The History of the Yorubas* (Lagos: C.S.S. Bookshops, 1976 [1921]), 200. The Epo Province included the area south and southwest of Old Oyo, plus the areas of New Oyo and Iwo (Law, *Oyo Empire*, 105; Johnson, *History*, 13).

7. J. F. Ade Ajayi, "Samuel Ajayi Crowther of Oyo," in *Africa Remembered: Narratives by West Africans from the Era of the Slave Trade*, ed. Philip D. Curtin, chap. 9 (Prospect Heights, Ill.: Waveland, 1997 [1967]), including 296, 302–304, on his capture. Chapter 9 includes an introduction by J. F. Ade Ajayi and "The Narrative of Samuel Ajayi Crowther."

8. In the reign of Emir Abdusalami of Ilorin, "many slaves" were taken during campaigns to the south of Omu, in the Igbomina area (Nigerian National Archives Kaduna [NNAK] SNP 7/13 4703/1912, Omu District—Offa Division—Assessment Report, June 1912 [by C. S. Burnett], para. 9; same file, Omu Isanlu District Assessment Report by V. F. Biscoe, 1912, para. 6). In the 1840s slaves were captured during Ilorin raids on Ekiti towns (Rhodes House [RH] Mss. Afr. s.1210; C. W. Michie, Political Situation Northern Provinces and History of Ilorin, Report on Local Government Reform in the Bala and Afon Districts of Ilorin Emirate, 1954, para. 11; NNAK SNP 10/4 304p/1916, District Assessment Report Osi by G. O. Whitely).

9. S. J. Hogben and A. H. M. Kirk-Greene, *The Emirates of Northern Nigeria* (London: Oxford University Press, 1966), 300.

10. Johnson, *History*, 403.

11. J. S. Olawoyin, *My Political Reminiscences* (Ikeja, Nigeria: John West, 1993), 10. J. S. Olawoyin, a prominent Offa politician of the middle to late twentieth century, was the grandson of Nathaniel Popoola Olawoyin. On Ilorin's slave-capturing activities during its siege of Offa, see also O'Hear, *Power Relations*, 24.

12. *Lagos Weekly Record*, 29 September 1894. On the circumscribing of Ilorin's slave-capturing opportunities over time, see also O'Hear, *Power Relations*, 24.

13. K. V. Elphinstone, *Gazetteer of Ilorin Province* (London: Waterlow, 1921), 30.

14. NNAK SNP 10 393p/1918, An Assessment Report on the Aworo (Oworraw) District of the Kabba Division, by Mr. C. K. Meek, Assistant District Officer, para. 45. For Nupe-Fulani raids on northeastern Yoruba groups in Emir Maliki's reign, see also Michael Mason, "The Jihad in the South: An Outline of the Nineteenth Century Nupe Hegemony in North-Eastern Yorubaland and Afenmai," *Journal of the Historical Society of Nigeria* 5, no. 2 (1970): 201; E. G. M. Dupigny, *Gazetteer of Nupe Province* (London: Waterlow, 1920), 20.

15. J. F. Ade Ayaji and Robert Smith, *Yoruba Warfare in the Nineteenth Century*, 2nd ed. (Ibadan, Nigeria: Ibadan University Press, 1971), 108.

16. Saburi O. Biobaku, *The Egba and Their Neighbours, 1842–1872* (Ibadan, Nigeria: Ibadan University Press, 1991 [1957]), 17 (including n. 2), 18; see also 22 for 1834 marauders.

17. Church Missionary Society Archives, University of Birmingham, U.K. (CMS) CA2/049(a), Hinderer to Venn, 26 October 1855, quoted in E. Adeniyi Oroge, "The Institution of Slavery in Yorubaland with Particular Reference to the Nineteenth Century," (Ph.D. thesis, Centre of West African Studies, University of Birmingham, U.K., 1971), 161–62.

18. PRO FO 84/976, Campbell to Clarendon, 7 December 1855, cited in Oroge, "Institution of Slavery," 162.

19. Public Record Office, London (PRO) CO 147/48, Statements . . . made by His Majesty King Owa Agunloye-bi-Oyibo . . . , 12 January 1882, enclosure 10 in Rowe to Kimberley, 14 March 1882, quoted in Oroge, "Institution of Slavery," 176.

20. Biobaku, *The Egba*, 24–25.

21. PRO CO 147/1, Freeman to Newcastle, 4 June 1862, quoted in Falola and Oguntimisin, *Yoruba Warlords*, 221. See also Ajayi and Smith, *Yoruba Warfare*, 98–99.

22. Oroge, "Institution of Slavery," 176, quoting Bolanle Awe, "Ogedemgbe of Ilesha: An Introductory Note," unpublished seminar paper, Lagos, 1969, 4.

23. Elphinstone, *Gazetteer*, 19.

24. Oroge, "Institution of Slavery," 177, citing S. A. Akintoye. On Aduloju, see also Falola and Oguntomisin, *Yoruba Warlords*, 84–88.

25. Law, *Old Oyo*, 280, 295–96, 298. On Atiba's career, see also S. O. Babayemi, *The Fall and Rise of Oyo c. 1706–1905: A Study in the Traditional Culture of an African Polity* (Lagos: Lichfield Nigeria, 1990), chap. 3.

26. R. H. Stone, *In Africa's Forest and Jungle; or, Six Years among the Yorubans* (London: Anderson and Fernier, 1900), 53–54; quoted in Oroge, "Institution of Slavery," 92.

27. Toyin Falola, "Slavery and Pawnship in the Yoruba Economy of the Nineteenth Century," in *Unfree Labour in the Development of the Atlantic World*, ed. Paul E. Lovejoy and Nicholas Rogers (London: Frank Cass, 1994), 225. For the activities of various warriors, see Falola and Oguntomisin, *Yoruba Warlords*, chaps. 2–9.

28. Interviews with Salumanu, Magaji Yaba, Ilorin, 29 and 30 September 1988.

29. Johnson, *History*, 325–26; and PRO CO 520/92, "The Laws and Customs of the Yoruba," in Egerton to Crewe, 11 April 1910 (section 8), both cited in Oroge, "Institution of Slavery," 131–32.

30. Michael Mason, *Foundations of the Bida Kingdom* (Zaria, Nigeria: Ahmadu Bello University Press, 1981), 77; idem, "Jihad in the South," 205; NNAK SNP 10 393p/1918, Assessment Report on Aworo District, by C. K. Meek, paras. 29–30.

31. Rev. C. E. Wating, quoted in Seymour Vandeleur, *Campaigning on the Upper Nile and Niger* (London: Methuen, 1898), 189–90.

32. CMS CA2/049(b), David Hinderer, Journal for the Quarter Ending 25 September 1851, quoted in Oroge, "Institution of Slavery," 132.

33. CMS CA2/056, Johnson to Wright, 9 May 1879, cited in Oroge, "Institution of Slavery," 132–33.

34. PRO CO 520/92, "The Laws and Customs of the Yoruba," in Egerton to Crewe, 11 April 1910 (section 10), quoted in Oroge, "Institution of Slavery," 133.

35. Johnson, *History*, 102.

36. Eltis, "Slave Trade in Nineteenth-Century Nigeria," 88–89.

37. Oroge, "Institution of Slavery," 176–77. For the northeastern Yoruba, see also O'Hear, "The Yoruba and the Peoples of the Niger-Benue Confluence."

38. Femi J. Kolapo, "The 1858–59 Gbebe CMS Journal of Missionary James Thomas," *History in Africa* 27 (2000): 190, entry for 17 July 1859. During the twentieth century, the northeastern Yoruba came to claim a connection with the Yoruba world, very likely as a counterbalance to their precarious and isolated position as largely non-Muslim Yoruba speakers in what was, until 1967, the Northern Region of Nigeria. See Eva K. Askari, "The Social Organization of the Owe," *African Notes* 2, no. 3 (1964–65): 9; and P. C. Lloyd, "Political and Social Structure," in *Sources of Yoruba History*, ed. S. O. Biobaku (Oxford: Clarendon, 1973), 209.

39. Oroge, "Institution of Slavery," 124–25; Johnson, *History*, 270–72.

40. Miss S. Tucker, *Abbeokuta; or, Sunrise within the Tropics: An Outline of the Origin and Progress of the Yoruba Mission* (London: James Nisbet, 1853), xvi–xvii.

41. See Oroge, "Institution of Slavery," 125–26.

42. "Narrative of Samuel Ajayi Crowther," in Curtin, *Africa Remembered*, 310–11. For Crowther's statement that the conquerors of Osogun were "Oyo Mahomedans," see 302. For "Yorriba Mahommedans," see 302 n. 29.

43. Ibid., 311–14.

44. "Osifekunde of Ijebu," in Curtin, *Africa Remembered*, chap. 8. Chapter 8 includes an introduction by P. C. Lloyd and an account by d'Avezac-Macaya, "The Land and People of Ijebu," written on the basis of information from Osifekunde, translated by Philip D. Curtin. See the introduction to chapter 8, 236–37.

45. "Joseph Wright of the Egba," in Curtin, *Africa Remembered*, chap. 10. Chapter 10 includes an introduction by Philip D. Curtin and "The Narrative of Joseph Wright," which was found in a notebook in the box labeled "Sierra Leone, 1835–1840" in the Archives of the Methodist Missionary Society, London. For the quotation, see "Narrative," 326.

46. "Narrative of Joseph Wright," 327.

47. Ibid., 328.

48. "Joseph Wright of the Egba," introduction by Philip D. Curtin, in Curtin, *Africa Remembered*, 320–22.

49. See, for example, CMS CA2/066/88, Rev. A. C. Mann, Journal for the Quarter Ending September 1855, 2 August; O'Hear, *Power Relations*, 25.

50. O'Hear, *Power Relations*, 26–27, and references, esp. 207–208 n. 56.

51. Falola, "Slavery and Pawnship," 230, and references.

52. Law, *Oyo Empire*, 281–82; see also 274.

53. Biobaku, *The Egba*, 19–20. The Egba had also played a middleman role in the slave trade before the disruption of their old settlements and the founding of Abeokuta.

See "Narrative of Samuel Crowther," in Curtin, *Africa Remembered*, 305–306 (including n. 46).

54. Oroge, "Institution of Slavery," 164; O'Hear, *Power Relations*, 28.

55. CMS CA2/056, Report from Rev. J. Johnson, Abeokuta, August 1877, quoted in Oroge, "Institution of Slavery," 164.

56. Oroge, "Institution of Slavery," 217–19.

57. Eltis and Richardson, "West Africa," 22, 27; Law, *Oyo Empire*, 274.

58. Eltis, "Slave Trade in Nineteenth-Century Nigeria," 86.

59. Ibid., 91; Laird W. Bergad, Fe Iglésias García, and María del Carmen Barcia, *The Cuban Slave Market, 1790–1880* (Cambridge: Cambridge University Press, 1995), 57–59; Kristin Mann, "Owners, Slaves, and the Struggle for Labour in the Commercial Transition at Lagos," in Law, *From Slave Trade to "Legitimate" Commerce*, 145.

60. Eltis, "Slave Trade in Nineteenth-Century Nigeria," 91, 96 n. 22.

61. Eltis and Richardson, "West Africa," 21; Lovejoy and Richardson, "Initial 'Crisis of Adaptation,'" in Law, *From Slave Trade to "Legitimate" Commerce*, 38.

62. Femi James Kolapo, "Military Turbulence, Population Displacement, and Commerce on a Slaving Frontier of the Sokoto Caliphate: Nupe c. 1830–1857" (Ph.D. dissertation, York University, North York, Ontario, Canada, May 1999), 135–36, 138–39; Kolapo, "1858–59 Gbebe Journal," 170, entry for 2 August 1858.

63. Femi J. Kolapo, "Nineteenth-Century Niger River Trade and the 1844–1862 Aboh Interregnum," *African Economic History*, forthcoming, on the trade in slaves carried on by Okeyea, one of the sons of Obi Osai, in Aboh. Presumably the "Brass traders" who are mentioned here were buying slaves for use as canoemen or for other tasks in Brass, or for sale to towns on the lower Niger and in the delta.

64. In Samuel Crowther and John Taylor, *The Gospel on the Banks of the Niger: Journals and Notices of the Native Missionaries Accompanying the Niger Expedition of 1857–1859* (London: Dawsons, 1859), 438, quoted by Law, introduction to idem, *From Slave Trade to "Legitimate" Commerce*, 7.

65. See Ajayi and Smith, *Yoruba Warfare*, 124–25; Toyin Falola, "The End of Slavery among the Yoruba," *Slavery and Abolition* 19, no. 2 (1998): 232–33; Toyin Falola, "Power Relations and Social Interactions among Ibadan Slaves, 1850–1900," *African Economic History* 16 (1987): 96–97; Falola, "Slavery and Pawnship," 223, 225, 242; Oroge, "Institution of Slavery," 90, 183, 185–86. British Consul William Baikie noted in 1862 that the growth of "legitimate" trade in Yorubaland had led to "an increased demand and price for slaves." Quoted in Robin Law, "'Legitimate' Trade and Gender Relations in Yorubaland and Dahomey," in Law, *From Slave Trade to "Legitimate" Commerce*, 198.

66. CMS CA2/056, Johnson to Wright, 21 June 1878, quoted in Oroge, "Institution of Slavery," 179.

67. Johnson, *History*, 324–25. For the various types of work done by slaves in nineteenth-century Yorubaland, see, for example, Falola, "Slavery and Pawnship"; O'Hear, *Power Relations*, chap. 2; Oroge, "Institution of Slavery."

68. Falola, "Slavery and Pawnship," 226.

69. PRO FO 84/1175, Beddingfield to McCoskry, 26 January 1862, enclosed in McCoskry to Russell, 8 February 1862, cited in Falola, "Slavery and Pawnship," 228.

70. PRO FO 84/1031, Campbell to Clarendon, 2 July 1857, quoted in Oroge, "Institution of Slavery," 216.

71. PRO CO, evidence of J. P. L. Davies enclosed in CO 147/133, Denton to Chamberlain, 4 June 1898, quoted in Oroge, "Institution of Slavery," 166–67.

72. PRO CO 147/134, Denton to Chamberlain, 3 August 1898, cited in Falola, "Slavery and Pawnship," 228.

73. See Oroge, "Institution of Slavery," 169; Falola, "Slavery and Pawnship," 228, and sources quoted there.

74. O'Hear, *Power Relations*, 30.

75. PRO FO 84/950, Campbell to Clarendon, 11 August 1854, quoted by Oroge, "Institution of Slavery," 182.

76. Johnson, *History*, 393.

77. O'Hear, *Power Relations*, 30.

78. Oroge, "Institution of Slavery," 180, including CMS CA2/075, Journal Extracts of D. Olubi for the Half Year Ending June 1868.

79. Oroge, "Institution of Slavery," 196–97.

80. I. B. Akinyele, *Iwe Itan Ibadan, Iwo, Ikirun ati Osogbo* (Ibadan, Nigeria: Ibadan University Press, 1911?), 47, cited in Oroge, "Institution of Slavery," 159.

81. CMS CA2/056, Johnson to Wright, Annual Report, January 1880, quoted in Oroge, "Institution of Slavery," 167; PRO CO 147/133, Evidence of Rev. James Johnson, enclosed in Denton to Chamberlain (confidential), 4 June 1898, cited in Oroge, "Institution of Slavery," 168.

82. See 56 above, and note 14.

83. L. A. K. Jimoh, *Ilorin: The Journey So Far* (Ilorin, Nigeria: L. A. K. Jimoh, 1994), 167–68. Jimoh does not give any source for the information that Ilorin joined Nupe in these raids. Hogben and Kirk-Greene, whose work Jimoh utilizes, do not mention Ilorin-Nupe cooperation. See their *Emirates of Northern Nigeria*, 300–301.

84. O'Hear, *Power Relations*, 63–68. For Emir Suleiman's letter to Goldie, see 64.

85. Falola, "End of Slavery," 236.

86. Oroge, "Institution of Slavery," chap. 6; Falola, "End of Slavery." For the clandestine trade, see Oroge, "Institution of Slavery," 366, 410, 418; and O'Hear, *Power Relations*, 79.

II
THE YORUBA DIASPORA
IN THE AMERICAS

CHAPTER FIVE

Nagô and Mina: The Yoruba Diaspora in Brazil

João José Reis and Beatriz Gallotti Mamigonian

The extension and volume of the Brazilian slave trade, and the special connection between Bahia and the Bight of Benin made Brazil, along with Cuba, home to one of the largest concentrations of Yoruba-speaking peoples in the Americas. This chapter addresses the distribution of the Yoruba diaspora throughout Brazil, focusing primarily on Bahia and Rio de Janeiro in the nineteenth century. In those two areas, because of the particular conditions of the slave system and the different ethnic composition of their African population, Yoruba identity took distinct forms under the local terms "Nagô" (mainly in Bahia) and "Mina" (in southern Brazil).

The slave trade to Brazil, which spanned from the mid-1500s to the 1850s, brought approximately three and a half million enslaved Africans to the Portuguese territories in South America that became, after 1822, independent Brazil. Although Central and Eastern Africa contributed more than three-quarters of this total, the trade from West Africa constituted an important branch of the Brazilian slave trade. While most slave trading was conducted from the ports in and around the Portuguese colony of Angola, merchants in Bahia established in the eighteenth century a direct exchange with the Bight of Benin that would change the profile of the slave population in the colony.[1]

The forced migration of Yoruba-speaking peoples to Brazil can be traced to the slave trade conducted in the "Mina Coast" during the first three-quarters of the eighteenth century, and mainly to business with the Bight of Benin from the 1770s through the 1850s. During the latter period Bahian merchants consolidated their existing network in the region and concentrated their trade east of Ouidah in the ports of Porto Novo, Badagry, and Onim (later, Lagos). They defied a ban on the Portuguese slave trade north of the equator imposed by

Britain in 1810, and continued importing "new Africans" into Brazil after the slave trade was prohibited by the Anglo-Brazilian treaty in 1830 and by national law in 1831.[2] Recorded figures of the volume of the Brazilian slave trade are unsatisfactory, particularly for the eighteenth century. For the best-documented period, 1801 to 1856, it is estimated that West Africa supplied just under 10 percent of the total number of slaves imported by Brazil. More certain is the peculiar geographic concentration of this diaspora: 88 percent of slaves leaving the Bight of Benin for Brazil landed in Bahia.[3]

The mission to follow the Yoruba on the Brazilian side of the Atlantic takes us along the slave routes within the country and poses an additional question of identifying them among the other African slaves. In Brazil, West African slaves were identified by the general term "Mina," after the name the Portuguese slave traders gave to the coast where they had embarked. Originally from various ethnic groups in the hinterland or on the coast, they left Africa from Grand Popo, Ouidah, Porto Novo, Jakin, Badagry, or Onim, and all became "Minas" in the eyes of the traders and masters once they were in Brazil. Distributed from Bahia, and, on a smaller scale, from Rio de Janeiro and other ports that entertained trade with the West African coast, Mina slaves could be found everywhere in Brazil in the mid-eighteenth century. A very important flow supplied slaves to the mining boom in the interior captaincies of Minas Gerais, Goiás, and Mato Grosso. Africans would travel from Bahia to the mining regions in Central Brazil, or by sea to Rio de Janeiro and from there to Minas Gerais and Goiás. In the eighteenth century the trip from Rio de Janeiro to Goiás through Minas Gerais took at least three months for armed convoys; the trip surely lasted longer for the caravans of trade goods, cargo beasts, and new Africans.

The presence of Yoruba speakers is positively documented for Bahia and Minas in the first half of the eighteenth century. Many "Courana" (Kuramu) slaves are listed in a census taken in 1748–49 in the Bahian mining region of Rio de Contas, which also registered the presence of just one "Nagô" slave. These slaves were also described as "born on the Mina coast," their more specific ethnonym—in this case Courana and Nagô—being registered as part of their names: Joana Courana and Francisco Nagô, for instance. In the small village of Paracatu, in Minas Gerais, a group of women of the Courá (another variation of Kuramu) nation were arrested in 1747 by officials of the Inquisition for their involvement in African religious rituals. Finally, Nagôs are mentioned among the African groups found in Goiás in the late eighteenth century.[4]

Although they probably were among the "Minas" imported during the eighteenth century and scattered throughout Brazil, it was over the course of the nineteenth century that Yoruba slaves were identified as a separate group, coinciding with their arrival in great numbers. In Bahia they came to be known as "Nagô," while those elsewhere in the country continued to be identified as "Mina," spelling out their specific origins and identities only on particular occasions and in particular circumstances.

Table 5.1. African Regions of Embarkation of Slaves Exported to Brazil (1801–1856)

	Northeast	%	Pernam-buco	%	Bahia	%	Southeast	%	% of Total
West-Central Africa	8,046	56.7	22,107	80.0	56,161	42.5	682,040	76.1	71.8
Southeast Africa	221	1.6	3,251	11.8	3,152	2.4	190,366	21.3	18.4
Bight of Benin	484	3.4	1,022	3.7	45,102	34.1	5,247	0.6	4.8
Bight of Biafra	1,008	7.1	800	2.9	8,076	6.1	11,094	1.2	2.0
Senegambia	4,433	31.2	306	1.1	294	0.2	0	0.0	0.5
Sierra Leone	0	0.0	0	0.0	1,779	1.3	1,412	0.2	0.3
Gold Coast	0	0.0	156	0.6	17,535	13.3	5,654	0.6	2.2
West Africa	5,925	41.7	2,284	8.3	72,786	55.1	23,407	2.6	9.8
Africa									
Unspecified	1,730	(10.87)	3,573	(11.4)	52,623	(28.49)	108,081	(10.77)	(13.4)
Total	15,922	100.0	31,215	100.0	184,722	100.0	1,003,894	100.0	100.0

Source: David Eltis et al., *The Trans-Atlantic Slave Trade: A Database on CD-ROM* (Cambridge: Cambridge University Press, 1999). Records from 2,757 Atlantic voyages. Percentile columns exclude number of slaves imported from unspecified regions. The actual volume of the slave trade is estimated to have been much higher.

Nagôs: The Yorubas of Bahia

Africans of Yoruba origin came to represent the vast majority of slaves in Bahia, which was one of the most important sugar plantation areas of Brazil between the turn of the sixteenth and the mid-nineteenth centuries. Sugar was grown in the humid lands of soft, muddy soil that surrounded the Bay of All Saints, a region known as Recôncavo, in the western extreme of which was Salvador, the capital city of Bahia. Other crops grown in the region included tobacco and manioc, the former largely used in the trade with the Bight of Benin, the latter representing the main local staple food. Sugar, however, was the king, even when the crop experienced difficult times. From the late seventeenth century, competition with the Caribbean led the region into serious difficulties until the Haitian revolution and the consequent destruction of slavery and the plantation economy in the island opened the market once again for the Brazilian product. At the turn of the nineteenth century Bahia's export economy was booming. The number of sugar plantations—called *engenhos* in Brazil—expanded significantly and was followed by an intensification of African slave trade to the region.[5]

During the first half of the nineteenth century the African ethnic profile of Bahia changed substantially. It has been estimated that at least 318,200 slaves were imported into Bahia between the early and the mid-1800s, at least 70 percent of them from the Bight of Benin region and its hinterland.[6] Slaves from West-Central Africa, namely, from present-day Angola, who had represented the bulk of imports until the last quarter of the eighteenth century, continued to arrive although in dwindling numbers. Data from probate records in the Recôncavo, including Salvador, indicate that in 1805–6 captives imported from West Africa represented 63 percent of African-born slaves; the number grew to 75 percent five years later; and it reached close to 90 percent at the closing of the slave trade in 1850. But the most impressive change took place within the West African group, as observed in the city of Salvador, an important center of servile labor, where the proportion of slaves in the population varied in the vicinity of 40 percent, only 30 percent of them born in Brazil. In 1820, 67 percent of African-born slaves had come from West Africa, and only 16 percent were Yoruba speakers. Fifteen years later the Yoruba increased their representation to 31 percent, and in the 1850s they comprised 76 percent of the African-born and 86 percent of the West African slaves in the city. For Bahia in general, considering the whole second half of the nineteenth century, Nagôs represented 79 percent of African-born slaves and 54 percent of the freed persons.[7]

These numbers resulted from the almost exclusive concentration of Bahia's slave trade in Yoruba areas in the three decades prior to the final abolition of the Brazilian slave trade. On the other side of the Atlantic, this phenomenon was connected to the decline and fall of the Oyo Empire, the civil wars that followed, and the Muslim expansion in Yorubaland. These events were interconnected, and they all fed the production of thousands of victims for the slave trade.

Even though West Africans could also be known as Mina in Bahia, by the second decade of the century more specific denominations, which were already available, became more common. As the century progressed the Gbe speakers, for instance, would become known as Jeje, although more specific ethnonyms such as Daomé, Ardra (for Allada), Maki or Mahi, and Savalu sometimes appear in the record, as well as composite ethnonyms such as Jeje-Mahi. There were also the Nupe, known in Bahia by the Yoruba term "Tapa," and the Hausa, who were called Uçá or Hauçá, the closest identification—phonetically at least—to an original, self-ascriptive appellation. Finally, the Yoruba came to be known as Nagô. This ethnonym was not invented in Bahia but at the other end of the slave trade circuit. Yoruba slaves exported through the ports in Gbe-speaking areas, namely, those under Dahomean influence or control such as Ouidah and Porto Novo, were called Nagô after Anagô, the designation of Dahomey's immediate eastern neighbors in Yorubaland.[8] However, slaves who became Nagô in Bahia originally did not consider themselves members of a unified people. As is well known, such an identity was only formed in the course of the second half of the nineteenth century under the term "Yoruba," which derives from "Yarriba," the term the Hausas used in reference to the Oyo. Actually, by the mid-nineteenth century, Yoruba, Yorubani, and variations around this expression had already been adopted in the European missionary literature.[9] The term "Yoruba" itself is not known to have been used in Brazil to refer to Nagô slaves, the latter being adopted by Yoruba-speaking Africans to identify themselves in Bahia. In sum, Yoruba speakers became Nagôs in Bahia before becoming Yorubas in Africa.

If the *term* "Nagô" emerged in the African end of the slave trade circuit, a Nagô *identity* was a Brazilian, more specifically a Bahian creation. Slaves in Bahia used a good part of their common African background to recognize themselves as *parentes*. The Portuguese word for relative was thus adopted to signify ethnic bond. In the case of the Nagôs, the most salient element unifying them was precisely the language, but there were others. They had a common mythic origin as descendants of Oduduwa, and Ile Ife was considered a sacred city for all Yorubas. Although regional Orisa cults were important, many gods had expanded their influence across frontiers. The belief in a higher god known as Olorun, master of the Sky, and the Ifa divination system were largely disseminated. The long Oyo hegemony in Yorubaland favored the expansion of the cult of Sango—typical of Oyo, and a truly imperial deity linked to the ruling dynasties—just as Ogun, the god of iron and war, became very popular during the military conflicts that followed the fall of Oyo. The very existence of an imperial power in the region helped to create some sense of belonging, albeit a subordinate one, to a larger polity. The Yorubas were cosmopolitan peoples, engaged in long-distance trade, and were all highly urbanized, living in small, medium, and large villages, around which they established agricultural endeavors. All these previous, common experiences contributed to the formation of a Nagô identity in the New World. It should be added that the majority of the Yoruba-speaking slaves of Bahia had come from the Oyo kingdom, and therefore they were the most important Yoruba subgroup in creating a local Nagô identity.[10]

Nevertheless, much of the former more specific and older African identities continued to make sense in the new Brazilian context. The Nagôs knew one another by names given by their families in their homeland, which contrasted with what they called their "whiteman's land [or Christian] names," used to interact with Brazilian masters and other free people, except African freedmen and women. African names rarely appear in the Bahian documents. One of the few sources to mention them are the trial records related to the 1835 uprising in Salvador. There we find names such as Ajayi, Alade, Dada, and Ojo, as well as Muslim names they had also brought from Africa such as Sule, Bilāl and Ahuna.[11]

Another important sign of identity, one that could link individuals to specific Yoruba ethnic groups, was the *abaja* or facial scarifications. When the person was still a child, these marks were inscribed on the body, particularly the face, with very sharp metal instruments manipulated by specialists, usually a devotee of Ogun. Among the Ijebu the operation was conducted when children reached the age of six or seven and was performed by a priest known as the *alakila*, meaning the master of scarification. The imprint of the *abaja* represented an essential stage in the process of the child's socialization in the family and his or her further integration within a particular ethnic group. The mark had so much importance as a sign of belonging to a group that, according to the 1820s testimony of Richard Lander, when someone was expelled from the group—he was probably referring to the Oyo—for a serious crime, the *abaja* was mutilated using the same method employed to create it. Whoever was thus punished would become a renegade in his or her own group.[12]

Nagôs arrested in 1835 often had their *abaja* described in the police records, and advertisements of fugitive slaves published in newspapers also offered this information. The majority, however, were only vaguely mentioned as having "signs of his or her nation," or "signs of his or her homeland on the face." Accused of conspiracy in 1835, the freed woman by the name of Agostinha carried "many long signs" on her face, and on hers Tereza displayed "many signs from her homeland and some on the forehead." Sometimes the description could be more detailed. The Nagô freedman named Jorge da Cruz Barbosa had been marked with "three signs from his homeland on each side of his face," and Licutan, a slave probably from Oyo and one of the leaders in 1835, displayed "perpendicular signs, others transversal on his face."[13] Apparently also from Oyo, a Nagô young woman by the name of Raquel was advertised in 1859 as a fugitive, and described as having "five signs on each side of the face, and one across it." These marks resemble the *keke* or *gombo* with the *ibamu* line.[14] Not all Nagôs, on the other hand, were *alabaja*, a person marked with the *abaja,* several having been described without it in the documents. One newspaper ad in 1847 stated that Vitoria was "a Nagô but has no signs on his face, only a few scratches on the belly." The owner of this slave knew that Bahians were more familiar with Nagôs who had facial marks, and thus he wished to emphasize that this one did not carry them. Another evidence that masters could, to some extent, decipher the cultural code inscribed in the facial marks is given by an ad about twenty-year-old Luiza, who was said to be "a Nagô with signs of the Jeje." One possible explanation for this woman's marks, which are not described, is that she was taken to Dahomey when still a child and ended up being marked according to the local custom, but for some reason retained her Nagô identity.[15]

Osifekunde, an Ijebu enslaved in Rio de Janeiro for many years and liberated in France in the 1820s, told his French interviewer, ethnologue Marie Armand d'Avezac, that in Yorubaland only individuals from Kuramo and Itsekiri did not use scarifications. The Bahian data are not detailed enough to confirm this information. We doubt that among Bahian Nagôs only individuals from these two areas had bare faces. Eastern Yoruba groups such as Ijesa, Efon, Igbomina, Yagba, and Ondo apparently only adopted the *abaja* when the civil wars associated with the collapse of Oyo engulfed the whole region, and they did so because an old, pre-1820s treaty engineered by Oyo protected the *alabaja* from enslavement. Clearly facial scarification was a typical though not exclusive Oyo trait. That so many *alabaja* ended up as slaves in Bahia confirms the role of the Oyos in the invention of the Nagô nation.[16]

It can be said that the Nagô nation was a confederation of different Yoruba-speaking ethnic subgroups living in Bahia, but the notion of nation could sometimes be expanded to include non-Yorubas or, conversely, could be reduced to specify Yoruba subgroups. Identity in this case was highly fluid and strategically employed, according to the situation. Individuals belonging to non-Yoruba groups could participate in Nagô networks and become Nagôs by association. For example, when interrogated by the police in 1835, a Nupe man said that his nation was Nagô-Tapa, and an African woman declared that "she was Jeje but only spoke Nagô."[17] Jejes, Tapas, and Nagôs, for example, were neighbors in Africa in a proximity that allowed for cultural exchanges and circulation of individuals from one place to the other as merchants, soldiers, or slaves. In the Bahian records consulted, not one of the numerous Angolans had a relationship with Nagôs similar to that of the Tapa man and the Jeje woman just mentioned.

On the other hand, even for the Yoruba speakers, "Nagô" could be too large a term to define ethnic affiliation. A slave by the name of Antônio interrogated by the police in 1835 said that "although we are all Nagôs, each one has his own homeland."[18] The man who pronounced these words was trying to tell the police that he did not belong to the Nagô faction that had produced the rebellion. He was from Egba, whereas the majority of the rebellious Nagôs were probably natives of Oyo. Nevertheless, in spite of Antônio's strategy to save his skin, Nagô identity functioned as a powerful mechanism of solidarity within

Yoruba groups, and as a tool of communication and negotiation between them and other nations in the Bahian African community and in society generally, including whites. His own words suggest that to be a Nagô was something meaningful to him, although he did not—actually he could not afford to—always operate under such an identity. In trying to say he was not rebellious, Antônio denied his "Nagô-ness" to the police.

The creation of a Nagô identity in Bahia was, above all, a result of the Yoruba experience under slavery. Africans, after all, were brought to Brazil to work as slaves in the plantations, villages, and larger cities such as Salvador. There is evidence of the formation of a Nagô ethnicity both in the rural and urban areas since the early nineteenth century. For instance, one day in late December 1808, in the village of Santo Amaro at the heart of Bahia's sugar plantation region, a group of rural slaves that was said by a local authority to be of the Nagô nation met during a Christmas holiday to celebrate to the sound of drums, wearing golden adornments on their semi-nude bodies, and feasting on lavish food. Other African groups also gathered to enjoy the day free from work, namely, the Angolans, Jejes, and Hausas. On that occasion, according to a police report, the Nagôs formed an alliance with the Hausas in a noisy drumming and vigorous dancing session that lasted beyond sunset, against police orders and ecclesiastical rules, while the other two groups celebrated quietly, separately from each other, and returned home within the established hour. Extraordinary rituals such as these consolidated ethnic identities but also helped to promote interethnic alliances that had flourished and were nurtured in the everyday life of cane fields, sugar mills, and slave quarters of the plantation districts. Four decades later, in the district of Nazaré where both sugar and especially manioc were grown, a Nagô slave by the name of Bernardo was accused of detracting other ethnic *parentes* from work to play the drums. Bernardo was known in the village as "prince of the Nagôs," a title that could perhaps be explained by his affiliation with a ruling family in Africa but which was reenacted in Bahia probably because of his genuine leadership within the local Nagô slave community. He was, by the way, a slave that moved freely about the village, where he had built a house for himself, signs that he had struck a good deal with his mistress. These two episodes suggest that work, rituals—including work rituals— and ethnic identity were interconnected in the consolidation of a Nagô community in the plantation region of Bahia.[19]

There is considerably more information on the ethnic organization and ritualization of labor in the capital city of Salvador. Here, Africans worked primarily as domestics and slaves-for-hire; they were also cooks, washerwomen, seamstresses, tailors, bricklayers, merchants, porters, and so on. Those who worked in the streets, be they slaves or freed, were called *ganhadeiras* (women) or *ganhadores* (men). Following a well-established West African tradition, the majority of African women who worked outside did so as merchants, going from one extreme of the city to the other selling all kinds of cooked and raw food, such as vegetables, fruits, fish, whale meat, African delicacies, and so on. They often sold fabric brought from the West Coast of Africa—including Yorubaland—by freedmen who traveled across the South Atlantic in slave ships as international petty merchants. Many African freedmen operated as itinerant merchants between Salvador and the Recôncavo, across the Bay of All Saints, selling fabric to rural slaves and freedmen and bringing chicken, pigs, fruits, and other produce to sell in the capital. But the majority of the *ganhadores* worked as porters, loading and unloading boats in the port, carrying heavy loads and barrels in groups of four and six to and from the port, and going up and down the hills of Salvador delivering goods to stores and wealthy households. Many also worked as sedan chair porters, in which capacity they carried passengers who thus avoided the muddy and dusty streets of the city and at the same time enjoyed one of the most symbolic features of white supremacy and African subalternity in Bahia. For the Nagô, it must have been particularly humiliating to carry people on their shoulders, if we believe in Hugh Clapperton's 1825 report of his visit in Yorubaland, where he could not find anyone who would agree to carry him and other members of his expedition, not even the sick, aboard hammocks. He heard from an Oba in Oyo that the local people would not carry another man for "a man is not a horse." But now in Bahia the Yorubas, be they slave or freed, were forced to put aside their self-esteem to earn the daily wage carrying sedan chairs.[20]

Slavery in the city was based on the hire-out or *ganho* system (thus *ganhador* and *ganhadeira*), according to which slaves contracted with masters to bring in a certain daily or more often weekly sum, the excess of which they could keep for themselves. Slaves moved about freely in the streets selling or carrying goods and offering other kinds of services. It was common although not general practice for slave owners to allow them to live in rented rooms, often with former slaves as landlords. They returned to their masters to "pay for the week." Slaves who worked hard in favorable market conditions managed to save enough money to purchase their freedom after years of toil. Freed slaves frequently plied the same trades they had when in captivity, although some prospered to such an extent that they themselves became masters of other Africans. This is an important point: the Nagô community was not egalitarian, for there were slaves and freed, and, among the latter, rich and poor. A small sample of African slave owners from Santana parish in Salvador in 1849 illustrates a mixture of ethnicity across class lines: of seventy-eight slaves owned by African freedmen and women, forty-nine (60 percent) belonged to the same ethnic group as that of their masters. Among the Nagôs this proportion jumps to 76 percent; that is, of the forty-one Nagô slaves whose African masters' nations could be positively identified, thirty-one were owned by other Nagôs.[21]

The same census indicates that 60 percent of the *ganhadores* were born in Africa, among whom 78 percent were Nagôs. This nation also prevailed among former slaves employed as street workers, acounting for 70 percent of the group. Forty percent of the men were listed as domestic servants, but this should not lead us to believe that they worked exclusively in their masters' households.

One well-known aspect of urban slavery was that slaves could work both in the house and in the street. Besides, many masters declared that their slaves were domestic so that they could avoid taxation imposed by the government on those employed in the streets in certain trades. Of the Nagôs explicitly registered as slaves-for-hire, 50 percent worked as bearers of cargoes and people, and aboard the boats that crisscrossed the bay or carried loads to and from ships. The others worked as cobblers, tailors, bricklayers, bakers, barbers, and carpenters. As for the Nagô freedmen, 30 percent declared that they were sedan-chair bearers. Almost ten years later, in 1857, a citywide registration counted 77 percent Nagôs among slaves-for-hire without specifying their occupations.[22] These numbers reflected the intensive importation of captives from Yorubaland in the last two decades before the final abolition of the slave trade to Brazil in 1850.

The *ganhadores* were organized in groups called *cantos*, which, for most of the nineteenth century, gathered enslaved and freed workers belonging to the same ethnic groups. The *canto*, literally "corner" or "song," introduced peculiar rhythms and rituals to African urban labor. While slaves and freedmen waited for clients, Muslims sewed Islamic clothes, studied Arabic, practiced writing, or read Islamic texts; African healers applied leeches and cupping glasses, prescribed herbs, and divined for their workers or outsiders. When the *ganhadores* carried bulky merchandise in groups of four or six, they kept step rhythmically to the sound of African work songs sung in a typical call-and-answer style.

We do not know when the first *cantos* were formed in Bahia, but they were already there in the early nineteenth century before the massive importation of Yorubas. They were probably modeled after different West African traditions of collective, voluntary work. The Yorubas had their own, known as *òwe* or *aró*, whose members were usually devoted to certain gods such as Oke, Oko, and Aja Saluga, related, respectively, to the hills, to agriculture, and to wealth. The *cantos* had their leaders or *capitães* (captains) whose function was to contract services with clients, allocate tasks, and receive and redistribute payments. Just as the *canto* may have been inspired in the *aró* societies, captains could be modeled after the Yoruba *aláàro bò*, meaning intermediary, or, more specifically, the *àró bó*, which means mediator in a business. The Nagôs may not have invented the *cantos*, but they certainly put their cultural imprint on them. Just as leaders and officials in Africa carried a baton as a symbol of authority, so did the African *canto* captains in Bahia. However, we should not reify details such as this as purely an African signifier, for in Bahia municipal and judicial officers used similar objects as well to represent the established state power. The two traditions may have converged.

The inauguration ceremony of *canto* captains is a good example of African ritualization of ethnic identity in the workplace, and here the Yoruba participation is clear because the information comes from a late-nineteenth-century testimony, a time when the Nagôs represented no less then 80 percent of the African street workers in Salvador. Members of the *canto* filled a barrel with seawater and lifted it with the help of ropes and a long pole, the same method they used to carry barrels of the local rum or *cachaça*. The newly elected captain mounted the barrel, carrying a bottle of rum in one hand and a tree branch (probably sacred leaves) in the other. The cortege marched through the streets of the port district singing and returned to the *canto* site, where the captain poured a libation of *cachaça* on the floor. The barrel full of salt water may have symbolized the ocean—itself replete with water spirits—that brought the Nagôs from home to the Bahian diaspora. The libation was characteristic in saluting their gods and is a gesture common in Bahia to this day. The leaves may have symbolized an aspect of African sacred nature. In this way, ethnically organized, *canto* workers apparently produced ceremonies that dramatized rupture with homeland and ritual return to origins. Rituals such as this one reinforced ethnic identity in the realm of labor.[23]

African ethnic networks also existed in the marketing of goods from the Recôncavo. We have offered the Christmas slave celebration in 1808 as evidence of Nagô ethnic identity in this region. Those slaves worked primarily on cane fields or in the sugar-making process, but many also dedicated part of their time to growing foodstuffs, primarily manioc, which, made into a flour, represented the main staple food of slaves and poor people in Bahia and other parts of Brazil. The excess production of slave gardens was sold in local markets, but manioc flour was also produced and commercialized by small farmers, including freed Africans. The latter usually chose to sell their produce to other Africans rather than to Brazilian-born buyers, which indicates that a sort of ethnic commercial network was in operation in Bahia. When the Nagôs became the predominant group within the African community in the 1850s, they probably managed to control much of this network. In 1855, for instance, established Bahian merchants of Salvador accused Africans and, in some cases, African slaves of Portuguese merchants of monopolizing the supply and distribution of manioc flour in the city. According to the complaint, manioc producers were "almost all of them Africans and slaves [who] only sell to their fellow [Africans], leaving the undersigned [merchants] inhibited from competing in the flour market with severe loss to their interests." To the dismay of Bahian merchants, organizational schemes similar to the *canto* seemed to bind African food growers and street vendors together, probably Nagô in their majority. There is indirect evidence of that. Going back to the 1849 parish census, fifty-five out of ninety-one freed Africans employed in commerce were Nagôs, and these merchants represented 52 percent of all freed Nagôs registered in the parish of Santana.[24]

The formation of a sizeable freed African group in Bahia resulted from Africans' extensive use of individual manumissions as an avenue of social mobility, even if, in the race toward freedom, masters favored Creole (i.e., Brazilian-born blacks) and Mulatto slaves over African-born slaves. Unpaid manumissions usually rewarded long years of good service and loyalty, recorded in wills as instructions with which to comply after masters died. Many Nagôs obtained their freedom in this way. In 1809 Antônia Maria da Conceição promised she would free João after her death as long as he cared for her in her old age; in 1815 Antônio Carvalho manumitted Ana for her good services during twenty years; and in 1819 Maria Matos freed Antônia after twenty-five years of good service. Women and children were favored in this process for their greater proximity and sometimes affective relations with masters and mistresses. Rarely, however, was a slave freed for the reason evoked in the case of another Nagô female slave by the name of Ana. In 1836 her Creole master, Bernardo de Jesus Monteiro, discovered that she was his mother, having become his slave as part of a heritage received from his deceased father-in-law, probably an African-born freedman, perhaps a Nagô himself. Also manumitted free of charge in 1836 was the little Creole slave by the name of Maria, only six months old. According to her master, João Maciel de Souza, he freed her "for the love I have for her, and her innocence, and the good services [received] from her mother," Prudência, a Nagô who remained in captivity. Most free manumissions were conditional, the most common condition being to serve masters until they died. But there were others. In Christmas of 1848 Jacob, for example, was given his freedom gratuitously as long as he taught another of his master's slaves to perform his work as street cleaner. In the event he did not fulfill this condition he would have to pay a certain sum to his master.[25]

All these Nagôs obtained their freedom free of charge, but the majority of slaves, and the Nagôs were no exception, had to pay for it. The purchase of freedom was not unknown in Yorubaland, where the term *owo irara* defined the money used in such transactions, which means that the Bahian Nagôs were familiar with them.[26] A random sample of thirty-six manumissions obtained in Bahia by Nagô slaves revealed that only eight were given for free, seven women and one man. Women actually represented 67 percent of the sample, an inversion of the male/female ratio in the population, but seventeen out of twenty-four women had to pay for their freedom. There were different forms of paid manumission. Just as free manumission could be conditional, so could an onerous one. José Thomas de Aquino received 450,000 réis from Tibério, who would enjoy his freedom only if he remained in the company of his master in exchange for food and "other needs." Slaves could pay a lump sum or in installments. Martiniana de Santana, a *ganhadeira*, gave her mistress Rita Maria da Silva 500,000 réis and was allowed to pay gradually the remaining 100,000 for which they had contracted. The sum of 600,000 was below the market value for a slave like Martiniana in 1856, which is why her mistress added one condition to the deal: the now freed woman would have to perform unspecified domestic services for Rita until Rita died. Finally, the contract between the unnamed Nagô mother of João and her mistress was unique. In 1836 the slave woman bought her child's freedom for 50,000 réis while he was still in her womb so that he would not be born into slavery.[27]

At the same time that manumissions reflected the slaves' struggle to obtain freedom through personal effort, the decision to grant individual manumissions rested with masters until a law was passed in 1871 which forced the latter to free slaves who offered their "fair" market value. Before this law, the conquest of freedom depended only on direct negotiation between the sides involved and functioned as a means of slave control.[28] Actually the law gave masters the right to revoke their slaves' freedom for acts of disloyalty. Many paid manumissions included clauses forcing freed slaves to obey former masters. José da Costa found an original method to punish the rebelliousness of his Nagô slave Domingos. He charged 350,000 réis for his freedom and declared on his freedom papers that, "because the slave possessed a very insolent disposition, I impose the following conditions: He will always be very obedient to both myself and any other free persons, in particular to my relatives and vassals, and in case he does not behave in such a way he will again be subject to captivity, and I will return the sum I received from him."[29] Domingos was not the only Nagô slave to go free because their masters felt that they could not control them under slavery. Antônio Baptista Correia freed one of his slaves in 1844, because, he wrote, "I want peace of mind for I cannot suffer any longer the insolence of my slave, Eliseu of the Nagô nation, and for having received from him 800,000 réis for his freedom."[30] One can guess what occurred: Eliseu had the money to buy his freedom, his master was too slow in selling him freedom, and the slave became a troublemaker in order to force his master to act. Instead of facilitating slave control, the possibility of obtaining manumission could promote daily resistance when masters did not act according to their promises or their expected roles.

Escaping slavery through this method was not always an individual effort exclusively. Besides the help of relatives and friends, there were manumission societies called *juntas de alforria*, also organized along ethnic lines. They were credit organizations which, in a rotational system, helped slaves to purchase their freedom. After borrowing from the group either the total amount or, more often, enough money to complement their savings and pay the master, the now freed African continued to contribute until he repaid in full the sum he or she had borrowed. The *junta* was run similarly to a Yoruba *esusu* society, and we believe the latter served as a model for Nagô slaves in Bahia. The *esusu* is thus described by Samuel Johnson: "A fixed sum agreed upon is given by each at a fixed time (usually every week) and place, under a president; the total amount is paid over to each member in rotation. This enables a poor man to do something worth while where a lump sum is required."[31] Alfred Ellis called these associations "*esu* societies" and noted that they were widely disseminated among the Yoruba in the late nineteenth century. Their members, according to him, met every fifth market day to collect dues and to give away credit.[32]

The Nagôs of Bahia also tried to obtain freedom through less conventional methods. Slave resistance was part of slavery. Besides the daily challenges to which they subjected their masters, as we have seen in the case of Domingos and Eliseu above, the Nagôs attempted individual flights and also organized collective rebellions and other forms of resistance movements. Table 5.2 dis-

plays the weight of these flights in the slave and fugitive populations throughout the nineteenth century. They did not run away more often than slaves from
other African nations or Brazilian-born slaves. Actually if we exclude the latter
and leave only those Africans with greater presence in Bahia—Nagôs, Hausas,
Jejes, Angola, Cabinda, and Mina—we find that the Nagôs lagged 4 percent
behind their potential for flight, that is, they comprised 50 percent of the
Africans in the slave population and only 46 percent among the fugitives. The
Angolans, Hausas, and Cabindas ran away proportionally more than the Nagôs,
and the Jejes ran away less than all the other groups positively identified.

The newspaper ads for runaway slaves announced some of the circumstances
surrounding the flight of Nagôs. Many women, for instance, escaped with their
children. In July 1824 Luiza ran away with her six- to seven-month-old son.
She was described as tall, thin, with a bullet scar on her leg, maybe a reminder
from a previous flight. Because she was well acculturated or *ladina*, which
meant she could speak good Portuguese, she was able to pass as a freed slave,
according to her master. Gertrudes, on the other hand, fled when she was four
to five months pregnant. She had been bought at the beginning of her preg-
nancy, and her new master, a prosperous tailor but also a slave merchant, may
have decided to sell her once again, perhaps outside Bahia, away from friends
and loved ones, maybe away from the father of her unborn child. Those were
days—the early 1840s—of intense southward slave trade inside Brazil.[33]

Like Luiza, many other Nagôs said to be *ladinos* used their knowledge of
the land and its language to escape slavery, even if momentarily. Efigênia, for
instance, was a *ganhadeira* who circulated through the streets of Salvador every
day, until one day she decided not to return to her master. He advertised two
of her most notable characteristics: she always dressed in black and "speaks [Por-
tuguese] very well." Who among the good Bahian Catholic folks would harass
a mourning woman who spoke the white man's language so well? Efigênia knew
how to manipulate the local cultural codes to her own benefit. Another slave
who was given the (unfit) name of Fiel—which means "loyal" in Portuguese—
was also said to be a "good talker" ("*prosista bastante*"). He had a story on the
tip of his tongue according to which he had been manumitted in a will by a
deceased master. To take on his new persona more convincingly, he had also
changed his name to Jacob and had been living a new life in freedom as Jacob
for almost three years when his distressed master published one more ad in 1857.
After such a long time, his master still missed a slave he described as "hand-
some and joyful, with the front teeth a bit open, three small signs on each side
of the face, [who] always has his hair high and well combed."[34]

However, Nagô slaves who dared to run away did not necessarily have to be
familiar with Bahia. Many recently arrived Nagôs could also be found in ads
reporting fugitive slaves, such as sixteen- to eighteen-year-old Frederico, who,
in November 1847, had been astray for three days in spite of being, according
to his master, "little experienced with the streets of this city." Three other cases
from the same year illustrate the intensity of the illegal trade in the 1840s. João,

Table 5.2. Slaves Advertised as Fugitives in Newspapers and the
Distribution of the Slave Population in Nineteenth-Century Bahia

Nation	Fugitives (sample)	%	Slaves in Salvador (sample)	%
Nagô	432	19.7	1,601	22.9
Hausa	96	4.4	276	3.9
Jeje	75	3.4	520	7.4
Angola	201	9.1	425	6.1
Cabinda	73	3.3	172	2.5
Mina	61	2.8	210	3.0
Other and non-identified Africans	328	14.9	657	9.4
Crioulos	533	24.3	2,319	33.1
Other Brazilians	398	18.1	815	11.6
Total	2,197	100	6,998	100

Source: Authors' Fugitive Slaves Databank; Andrade, A mão-de-obra escrava, 189–90.

a young fellow, ran away from Firmino Rodrigues, a slave trader who operated a warehouse on the port. According to an ad, João was tall, thin, had three marks on each side of the forehead—an unusual Nagô scarification—and "speaks little Portuguese because he is very brute." A Nagô boy who also had fled from the port area a couple of months earlier, whose Christian name was not even mentioned—he probably did not have one yet—"did not carry the signs of his homeland, and understands little Portuguese" but had "big and lively eyes." In 1825, before the prohibition of the trans-Atlantic slave trade, José's owner could clearly say that his fugitive slave was "a new negro [negro novo]," the expression used in Brazil for recently arrived Africans. These Nagôs fresh on the land would certainly not dare to escape if they did not find people who understood their language and were ready to help and hide them—in other words, other Nagôs familiar with the new environment. This kind of solidarity can also be found in situations not necessarily involving negros novos. A Nagô slave woman by the name of Thereza used to undertake temporary flights from her master and to hide herself in the quarters of other urban slaves. Aware of the situation, her master asked other slave owners to help him find Thereza in their houses, adding that this behavior was very common among local slaves. We have little doubt that ethnic networks were behind this kind of slave experience in Salvador as well as in the plantation districts.[35]

Ethnic identity and solidarity were behind bolder forms of resistance. The Nagôs were greatly responsible for the reputation for rebelliousness that slaves in Bahia had all over Brazil. The large numbers of Nagôs imported to Bahia is only a partial explanation for their rebelliousness. Their numbers, of course, facilitated the formation of a strong, local Nagô identity but was not sufficient to feed collective resistance. The vast majority of Yorubas imported in the first three decades of the nineteenth century were young male adults, and many had had experience as warriors. Religious ideology also played an important role, both the devotion to warlike Orisas such as Sango and Ogun and the presence in Bahia of a brand of militant Islam closely associated with the expansion of this religion in Yorubaland, particularly within Oyo territory.[36]

The Nagôs to be sure did not always act alone. The Hausas shared with them the reputation for carrying on organized, violent movements of protest against enslavement. The Hausas prevailed in revolts during the first two decades of the nineteenth century, and were followed by the Nagôs in the next two decades, when slave imports from Yorubaland drastically increased. There is evidence, however, that Nagôs joined Hausas and other Africans on at least two occasions, in 1814 and 1816. The February 1814 movement began as a massive flight of slaves from Salvador to a nearby *quilombo* or runaway community, from where they proceeded to the coast and attacked whale fishing stations on the northern shores of the capital's rural districts. They also assaulted the village of Itapuã before heading inland toward the plantation zone, which they never reached, for they were barred by troops sent to control the situation. Fifty-eight rebels were killed; others committed suicide rather than submit. Later in the same year a vast conspiracy was discovered, also led by the Hausas, and was said to have included nearly all other African nations as well as Indians. But this conspiracy never materialized. Two years later an uprising occurred in the heart of the Recôncavo, following a slave celebration in the village of São Francisco do Conde. The rebels set fire to several plantations before they were completely subdued three days later. There is no indication of which African group prevailed in this uprising, but probably both Nagôs and Hausas were among them.

Of the more than one dozen slave uprisings in the 1820s, the one in December 1826 provides more information than the others. Like the 1814 revolt, this one involved the convergence of fugitive slaves to a runaway community on the outskirts of Salvador, a place called Urubu—or "Vulture" in Portuguese. Armed with bows and arrows, knives, pitchforks, hatchets, and spears, the rebels successfully resisted the first combat with slave hunters, killing three and wounding three. But with the arrival of reinforcements they were defeated in a brief yet violent battle, and thus were unable to proceed with their plan to attack Salvador on Christmas Eve. Only one African woman by the name of Zeferina was arrested at Urubu. She was a Nagô, and she confessed that the majority of the rebels belonged to that same nation. Other indirect evidence also points in this direction. The runaway hideout served as a site for a Candomblé, an African religious group dedicated to the Orisas. Most of the religious paraphernalia confiscated by the police bore the color red, which is the color of Orisa Sango, the god of thunder, worshiped with special intensity by the Oyo people and revered among the Nagôs in Bahia.

Between 1827 and 1830 a series of revolts shook the plantation districts. Some were restricted to one or two plantations, but others involved slaves from several. The most serious uprising was in September 1827, in São Francisco do Conde, where rebels burned ten plantations before being subdued. In March of the following year the slaves belonging to whale fishing stations again rose up in arms, burned several houses, fishing nets, and cane fields, and were only defeated when marching toward the Recôncavo. At least twenty slaves lost their lives, and others took refuge in the woods. The majority seemed to be newly arrived Nagôs, including the four rebels arrested, of whom only one, named Joaquim, was punished with 150 lashes. Bahian authorities showed some restraint precisely because they considered *negros novos* to be less liable to punishment than seasoned ones. Two other uprisings—one in September, the other in November of the same year—also involved recently arrived slaves. Both rebellions occurred in the heart of the sugar-producing region. In the first incident rebels burned the slave quarters and sacked the house of the plantation chaplain, who doubled as a cane farmer. Slaves from other plantations joined in, and those who refused to participate, including freed African artisans, were either killed or wounded. The November episode included an attack on the plantation headquarters, and the killing of a foreman and a few Creole slaves. The foreman's wife was also severely beaten. Flames would consume other cane fields between the end of 1828 and early 1830, when the government finally conceived of a military plan, with financial support from planters, involving the military occupation of key plantations. This plan apparently calmed down the Nagô rebels in the region, until 10 April 1830, when they moved their action to the city of Salvador.

Early in the morning of that day about twenty *ganhadores* assaulted three hardware stores, supplied themselves with swords and long knives imported from Germany called *parnaíbas* in Bahia, and attacked a warehouse that displayed slaves for sale. More than one hundred Yoruba *negros novos* joined the insurgents, and eighteen others—perhaps those who were non-Yoruba—refused to do so and were killed on the spot. Strengthened in their numbers, they tried to invade a police station, killing a soldier in the process. The garrison resisted the attack until more soldiers arrived to help, putting down the revolt. Once defeated, the Africans were brutally lynched by policemen and the crowd.

This movement was an unsuccessful rehearsal for the most serious rebellion of the period, which occurred five years later, also in Salvador. In the late evening of 24 January 1835 a forewarned group of militiamen, led by a justice of the peace, burst into a house in the heart of the city, only a few yards from the government palace, the town council house, and the cathedral. Inside, a group of approximately sixty Nagôs had been making the last preparations for an uprising early in the morning of the following day, a Sunday dedicated to the celebration of Our Lady of Guidance (Nossa Senhora da Guia). Despite being surprised at the house, rented by two Nagô freedmen, the rebels easily overcame their attackers and pushed the fight into the streets, where their num-

93

bers increased as other Africans, responding to their calls, joined them. They attacked the palace guard, the municipal prison, and several police stations and military barracks in different parts of the city. Unable to conquer or occupy any one of these bastions and symbols of local power, and exposed to heavy fire, they tried to leave Salvador and reach the Recôncavo, where previous contacts had been made with plantation slaves. On their way, however, stood the cavalry barracks, whose men fought and badly defeated the rebels. The five hundred to six hundred insurgents, who fought for nearly four hours, had very few firearms at their disposal, their main weapon being *parnaíba* knives. At least seventy Africans died in the fight, which claimed only nine lives in the adversary's camp, including passersby.

The majority of rebels were urban workers, but they counted on the help of a few plantation slaves as well. The uprising was led by Muslim preachers, and their followers formed the core of the rebels, although non-Muslim Nagôs also joined in. Some historians have suggested that it was a continuation in Bahia of the Fulani-led jihad in Hausaland.[37] Although jihadic ideology may have inspired some of its leaders, that alone does not make the movement itself a jihad, much less one inspired by the Fulani. There were actually very few Fulani among the Bahian slaves, and none were involved in this movement. The majority of Muslims in 1835, including their most important leaders, were Yoruba. Enslaved and freed Hausas, a group particularly devoted to Islam, were also involved but very modestly. The near monopoly of the movement by the Nagôs is shown in numerous evidence. The rebels were known as *Malês* and the insurrection a *Malê* revolt, terms derived from the Yoruba *Imale* for Muslim. With one exception, of the half dozen Muslim conspiratorial groups identified by the police, five were formed exclusively by Nagôs. One group, however, was led by a Nupe *alufa* or priest by the name of Luís Sanin, whose followers, however, were all Nagôs; another group was led by a Hausa malām, known by the Christian name of Elesbão do Carmo and the African name of Dandará, who said he only "taught his *parentes*," that is, other Hausas. Muslims in Bahia seemed to have ethnically segregated lives. No Hausa could be found in Nagô prayer groups that also served as conspiratorial cells, groups led by Manoel Calafate (Manuel the Caulker), Pacífico Licutan (probably Lakitan or Olakiitan, "wealth never ends"), Sule (who bore the Christian name of Nicobé), and Dassalu (or Mama), all of them Nagô slaves except Manuel who was a freedman. Also Nagô was a slave named Ahuna, whom several witnesses pointed to as the higher leader in 1835 but who was never arrested to tell his story.

The 73 percent Nagô slaves and freedmen among those arrested vastly overrepresented the 30 percent of Nagôs in the African community of Salvador. In the meantime, the Hausas accounted for 10.5 percent of those arrested and 9.4 percent of the Africans in the city. The police, however, were overzealous in arresting Hausas, particularly Hausa freedmen, because of their publicly known familiarity with Arabic writing; written Muslim prayers and passages from the Koran used as amulets were one of the most important pieces of evidence in court, because the rebels carried them as protective devices during the fighting. But in contrast to dozens of Nagôs who confessed or were implicated by other rebels during the police inquiry, only one Hausa actually confessed to being a rebel, and of the thirty-one arrested only three were found guilty.[38]

The evidence thus suggests that the Nagôs fought this war practically alone, Islamic ideology not being enough to unite, under the banner of Allah, all African Muslims living in Salvador in 1835. Just as they avoided participation in prayer groups led by Nagô *alufas*, the vast majority of Hausas refused to join a rebellion dominated by the Nagôs. The Hausas were proud, perhaps, to belong to a group with a much stronger Islamic background than the Yorubas, but it was the latter that had become the majority and the most militant in the local Muslim community. Most Yorubas, perhaps all, were from Oyo, and in this period more specifically from Ilorin, the Yoruba Muslim bastion whose pagan *baálè* Afonjá had rebelled against the Alafin with the help of Oyo Hausa slaves and free Muslim Yorubas (c. 1817). Afonjá was later killed by their non-Yoruba Muslim allies (c. 1823–24). The Nagô Muslims in Bahia had been victims of Oyo forces, but many of those captured in the mid-1820s were probably followers of a man known as Solagberu, the leader of the Yoruba Muslims, who was eliminated by the Fulani leader Abdul Salami, the first Emir of Ilorin, who feared political competition from a native leader. In this Yoruba city itself Fulani, Hausa, and Yoruba Muslims lived segregated in their own quarters, although they could fight together against Ilorin's enemies. The ethnic equilibrium they enjoyed back home probably collapsed in the Bahian context, and political power certainly was reversed. Whereas the Hausa and above all the Fulani controlled Ilorin, it was the Yoruba Muslims or malês that posed the real threat to control Bahia, and with it the Hausas and other Africans. In 1835 the Hausas, who had been the Muslim militants of the past, had given up their revolutionary path.[39]

Of course, not everyone who was indicted had actually participated in the revolt or was Muslim. The evidence suggests that at least this particular revolt was largely an ethnic movement of the Nagô. During the uprising the war cry heard in the streets of Salvador was "*Viva Nagô*" or "Long live the Nagôs." The role of Islam in 1835 is often said to have been that of creating a multiethnic alliance, but the revolt actually failed to mobilize the largest Muslim ethnic group, the Hausas. The Nagôs prevailed both numerically and politically, but they managed to recruit only a few individuals from other ethnic groups, including Hausa, Tapa, Borno, Gurma, and Jeje. On the other hand, a number of non-Muslim Nagôs, recently and poorly converted, joined the uprising. To borrow an expression used in another, more recent context, it is possible that, among the Nagô of 1835 Bahia, "Muslim-ness and Yoruba-ness" largely converged.[40]

More than 62 percent of the African defendants were slaves. This is an important finding even if we keep in mind that the proportion of the freed among the defendants (close to 38 percent) outnumbered by 17 percent their estimated proportion within the African community of Salvador. Some authors have rejected the notion that the struggle against slavery was a major issue or that it was an issue at all in the rebellion, pointing to the fact that there were so many freedmen involved.[41] But to accept their views one would have to take for granted that revolutions are made only by the totally dispossessed. What can be said in this respect is that if Islam failed to promote a consistent multiethnic front, it facilitated the convergence between slave and free. However, the majority of the defendants were slaves, and among the Nagô defendants, slaves constituted a large majority, namely, 73 percent. In addition, of the seven Muslim leaders that we have been able to positively identify, five were slaves, including the most revered *alufas* Ahuna and Pacífico Licutan, whose Muslim name was Bilāl—after Muhammad's black *muezzin*—a name often treated as a synonym for *muezzin* in West Africa. Under interrogation Bilāl affirmed that he and his fellow Nagô companions—his *parentes* was the expression he used— suffered *"mau cativeiro"* ("bad captivity"), a clear reference to the plight of urban slaves, and of Muslim Nagô slaves in particular.[42] Although we have no clear idea of the rebel leaders' long-term plans, there is no doubt that they fought against the enslavement of Africans in Bahia, and that they counted on the occurrence of a general African slave rebellion as a follow-up to the actions carried on by the men who started the fight. That, of course, did not happen, and the rebels were defeated.

Four defendants—three slaves and one freedman, all of them Nagôs—were executed. We only know the Yoruba name of the freedman: Ajayi, written Ajahi in the police papers. Hundreds were whipped and imprisoned; most of the freedmen were deported back to Africa where, ironically, they became known as "Brazilians." Numerous slaves were sold outside Bahia, mainly to Rio de Janeiro and Rio Grande do Sul, both important traditional markets targeted by Bahian slave traders. Anywhere in Brazil, and particularly in Bahia, of course, blacks found with Muslim writings were immediately arrested. The *Malê* rebellion had tremendous repercussions throughout the country: local and national laws were passed to improve slave control, including the death penalty for slaves accused of killing or seriously injuring masters, overseers, or members of their families. Though the repression against Muslims and the hardening of slave laws were mild when compared to the way other countries and colonies in the Americas treated their slave rebels, it happened at a time when the liberal discourse, including the first sprouts of abolitionism, abounded in Brazilian society and government.

The *Malê* revolt was the last violent movement in which the Nagôs played a major, almost exclusive role. It was, in fact, the last notable slave revolt in Bahia. However, the Nagôs and other Bahian slaves did not cease to resist. From 1836 through 1837 an attempt by the provincial government to abolish the *cantos* faced a systematic opposition from the *ganhadores*, who refused to join work groups created and controlled by government officials. When masters and merchants, dismayed with the disruption of business, sided with slaves and freedmen against the new rules, the government was forced to retreat. Another twenty years passed before a new attempt was made at controlling the *ganhadores*.[43]

In 1857 the municipal council issued a law imposing a registration scheme for African slave and free workers employed as porters in the streets of Salvador. From then on the *ganhadores* were to register with the municipality, pay an annual tax of ten thousand réis—the equivalent to about one week's earnings—and carry a metal plaque suspended from the neck. The workers stopped working for a week, bringing the city to a halt, thus producing the first urban general strike in a specific labor sector in the history of Brazil. The movement was organized by the *cantos*, and these groups, in 1857, were largely Nagô. Of the 241 slave *ganhadores*—out of 477 that could be found—whose nations could be positively identified, 77 percent were Nagôs. As for the freedmen, only eleven Nagôs and one Jeje declared their nations, the remaining seventeen simply saying that they were "Africans." This does not mean that the strike was organized by the Nagôs alone, but their superior numbers certainly made it easier for them to mobilize for the strike. In other words, ethnic identity played a big role in this relatively successful movement. Within three days of the strike, under pressure from businessmen who badly needed workers to carry their merchandise from port to store and around the city, the provincial government forced the municipal council members to abolish the fee, but the wearing of the plaque was maintained. The Africans remained on strike for a few more days but then gradually returned to work. One by one they would refuse to wear the plaque, which they considered humiliating.[44]

The 1857 strike was a peaceful movement, and yet it happened at a time when the Nagôs were strongest numerically. Something had happened between the 1820s and the 1850s that radically changed the style of collective resistance among them. First, we should consider changes on the side of the adversaries. In the 1820s and 1830s not only the African slaves but also the free, Brazilian-born population were rebellious, even though their movements never converged, except when Africans joined the free rebels as individuals. In these two decades Bahia had experienced a war against the Portuguese garrison in 1822–23, followed by popular, military, and federalist revolts and conspiracies in 1824, 1828, 1831, 1832, 1833, and 1837. Divisions among the free classes diminished their capacity to control the slave class effectively. When government and planters took serious steps to control the slave rebels by setting up troops in the plantations in 1828, the number of revolts declined. Despite serious revolts of the free people, only two slave rebellions took place in the 1830s, both in Salvador. After 1837 the free rebels went home, and Bahian ruling classes could be more vigilant with slaves.

Things had also changed with regard to the slaves. Among the Nagôs now being imported the number of trained warriors and militant Muslims declined considerably. As the Yoruba civil wars moved south in the late 1830s and the 1840s more and more of the "civilian" population fell victim to slave traders, which is reflected in the unprecedented numbers of women and children among the captives sold to Bahia.[45] What was happening to the Yoruba-speaking community on this side of the Atlantic was equally important. The repression that followed the 1835 uprising disrupted and dispersed the Nagôs, particularly their Muslim sector. Numerous slaves were sold to southern Brazil, and hundreds of freedmen and women were either deported to Africa or decided themselves to return so as to escape police persecution.

Those who remained, on the other hand, adopted forms of resistance other than outright collective rebellion. Most Nagôs actually had not been involved in the revolts of the period, having decided to follow the path of negotiation for more breathing space within slavery itself. That was the case of those who worked their way out of slavery through manumission, for example. But there were other mechanisms of adaptation. Religion was one of the most important. We have already seen that militant Islam was behind the 1835 uprising and probably other revolts of the period. But there was also a more accommodating brand of Islam in which alufas and malāms, instead of proselytism, directed their activists toward divination, amulet-making, witchcraft healing, and similar practices. Many Muslims of this kind became victims of police prosecution in 1835 without having contributed to the revolt.

These Nagô Muslims adhered to the predominantly pragmatic local religious ways dominated by Catholicism, on the one hand, and, on the other, by Candomblé, the term of Angolan extraction used to define African religion in general in nineteenth-century Bahia. Like other Africans, the Nagôs could belong to both religious systems. African Catholicism developed around lay brotherhoods dedicated to patron saints, the most popular among them being Our Lady of the Rosary, and the black saints Benedito, Ifigênia, and Antônio de Catageró. Although the tendency was toward ethnic-based brotherhoods, Nagôs actually belonged to several different ones. In 1825 Gertrudes Maria do Espírito Santo, for instance, wrote in her will that she wanted to be accompanied to her grave by five brotherhoods: the Brotherhood of Jesus, Mary, and Joseph, her favorite; two brotherhoods dedicated to Our Lady of the Rosary; one brotherhood dedicated to Saint Benedito; and one devoted to Our Lord Jesus of Redemption. In 1832 Custódia Machado de Barros left instructions that she wanted to be buried in a grave inside the Saint Francis conventual church that housed her brotherhood of Saint Benedito. But she also wanted the company of brothers and sisters from the brotherhoods of Saint Ifigênia, Our Lord of Redemption, and Our Lady of the Rosary in the central parish of Sé. This last brotherhood, on the other hand, was the only one that another Nagô freed woman, Maria da Conceição, mentioned in her will dated 1828. Finally, as a gesture of devotion, Maria Agostinha de Brito Machado willed, in 1836, that ten thousand réis from her modest belongings should be given to the same Brotherhood of Our Lady of the Rosary and another ten to the altar of Santana.[46]

Devotion to these saints was not expressed only when death approached. The relationship between saint and devotee had the character of a contract according to which "promises" were made to the saint in exchange for help usually in the domain of health, money, and love. The payment could be made in the form of prayer, masses, and alms. Brothers and sisters also organized lavish annual festivals to celebrate their patron saints, with a lot of music, fireworks, food, and drinks, which followed more conventional processions led by Catholic priests. During these festivals black kings and queens were often crowned and new brotherhood officials elected.[47]

There was what could be called a structural similarity between this kind of Catholicism and Candomblé, in the sense that the latter's devotees also negotiated with spiritual beings by offering sacrifices in exchange for help. This may be one of the reasons why Africans and their descendants circulated so easily between the two religious systems. The Nagôs, in particular, may have been inspired at least in part by their experience with Catholicism to adapt the religion of the Orisas to Bahia. Just as Catholic churches venerated several saints under the same roof, the Nagô Candomblé inaugurated a tradition of gathering Orisas from different regions and ethnic groups in Yorubaland under the same ceiling. Thus the convergence of all Yorubas into a unified Nagô identity had a ritualistic dimension in the way the Orisas were to be honored in Brazil. In this way Candomblé played a key role in the constitution of a Nagô identity in the Brazilian, primarily Bahian, diaspora and, with the decline of both the brotherhoods and the Muslim groups in the second half of the nineteenth century, Candomblé would become the main religious expression of the Nagô nation. To be fair, the Nagôs were not alone in this process, for both the Angolans with their Nkisi and the Jejes with their Vodun also contributed considerably to the Afro-Bahian religious landscape. But there is no doubt that the Nagô contribution became increasingly dominant as the century progressed.[48]

The Mina in Rio de Janeiro and Elsewhere

Outside Bahia, where the slave population was overwhelmingly Central African in origin, West Africans developed a single, widely encompassing identity around the term "Mina." A significant portion of them were of Yoruba origin, and they spread throughout the country. After 1835, as mentioned, an important flow of the internal slave trade took Nagôs to the southeast, particularly to Rio de Janeiro and Rio Grande do Sul. There they became Minas or, when they needed to be specific, "Mina-Nagô," and played an important role in the formation of the local culture.

The presence of Minas was also significant in the mining regions in the interior of the country. Their proportion among the African slaves is particularly well documented for Goiás in the nineteenth century where, between

1810 and 1824, West Africans comprised 66.7 percent of those sold in the north of the province, and 37.6 percent of those sold in the south. Goiás was situated at the end of the two major slave routes for West Africans into the interior of Brazil—one leaving from Bahia and the other from Rio de Janeiro—and the regional variation in the ethnic composition of the population reflected that fact.[49] Mina slaves had the reputation of being good miners, possibly earned on the basis of skills acquired in their regions of origin in Africa. Mina women, especially, were believed to bring luck and prosperity to their masters.[50]

It is in the city of Rio de Janeiro that the lives of Mina Africans, and particularly of Nagôs, are better documented outside Bahia. Being a "Mina" in nineteenth-century Rio de Janeiro, as Mary Karasch has noted, had taken on several meanings.[51] Under Mina there could be identified people belonging to Fanti, Ashanti, Gbe, Hausa, or Nupe groups, as well as Yoruba. Their minority status in a population that was overwhelmingly Central African helped to collate this distinct group to the point that Mina became their form of self-identification before other groups within the slave society. This in no way meant, however, that Mina formed a homogeneous community. That people from the different Mina subgroups were affiliated to separate religious devotions attests to this phenomenon.[52]

Being Mina also meant, especially after 1835, a potential inclination toward rebellion. This reputation was earned by the Muslims among them, by Hausas, and particularly by Nagôs, many of whom had been sold to Rio de Janeiro after the uprising in Salvador. Muslim Minas, who were often literate, were seen as proud, courageous, and hard-working people who accumulated their savings toward manumission. Rio police took the potential threat represented by the Mina, and particularly the Malês, very seriously, and tried hard to follow their activities closely in the hope of avoiding a repetition of the events in Bahia. The discovery, on two separate occasions, of Arabic writings in possession of Africans only fed the public concern that slaves were plotting in secret codes. In 1849 Rio's chief of police reported that,

> some Mina blacks resident in this city gathered in secret associations where, under impenetrable mystery, there were practices and rites that became suspect; they communicated among themselves through ciphered writings, and it also came to my knowledge that the blacks of the same nation existing in Bahia corresponded with them, and so did those from São Paulo and Minas [Gerais].[53]

The police raid at one such gathering place yielded "an infinity of papers written with different inks and in unknown characters, some books also in manuscript" that, "translated, interpreted, and deciphered" by experts revealed their contents: "prayers taken from the Koran, in spurious Arabic, to which were grafted words in the Mina and Malê languages." However, the chief of police, admitting that the Malês had the right to private worship, found no reason to keep them in prison. He decided, nevertheless, to keep an eye on them, for

> it is natural that the spirit of religious association will take them further, and that the followers it will gather, fanatic by its principles, will use this religion to justify and convey the ideas against slavery, for I see, in all that has been apprehended in the recent searches, exactly what had also been found in Bahia at the time of the slave uprising in 1835.[54]

The size of the Muslim community in Rio de Janeiro, otherwise shrouded in secrecy, can be estimated by the demand for Korans: the French Minister in Brazil, the Count of Gobineau, reported in 1869 that the French booksellers Fauchon and Dupont sold one hundred copies of the Koran each year in Rio de Janeiro.[55]

Scattered evidence suggests that there were African Muslim communities, or at least individuals, in other provinces as well. Besides those from São Paulo and Minas Gerais mentioned in the above police report, other news arrived in Rio of an apprehension of a Koran and many written papers, and the arrest of a Yoruba *alufa* by the name of Rufino, in the capital of Pernambuco in 1853. Under interrogation, this man said that he was from Oyo, that his father had also been an *alufa* there, and that he had been captured in a raid by Hausas and embarked to Bahia. From Bahia, before the 1835 uprising, he was sold to Rio Grande do Sul, the southernmost province of Brazil, where he obtained his freedom, and later went to Rio de Janeiro and embarked as a cook in a slave ship that was eventually captured by the English and taken to Sierra Leone. Here Rufino attended a Koranic school for a few months, returned to Brazil for a while, and then went back to Sierra Leone where he spent almost two years receiving more Islamic training. He finally returned to Recife, Pernambuco's capital, where he devoted his life to divination, curing witchcraft, and amulet-making. Rufino was a typical pragmatic Muslim, but a devout one nonetheless. Although he was no social rebel, during his interrogation he gave ample proof of his faith, which he defended with great dignity to the amazement of the police officers and other white men present at the police station.[56]

As a Nagô, Rufino probably did not feel lonely during the years he spent in Rio Grande do Sul, where a large Nagô community existed. For instance, he was not the only Nagô who bought his freedom there. Out of a sample of 419 manumissions obtained in that province in the second half of the nineteenth century by Africans whose specific ethnonyms could be identified—Minas excluded—61 percent were Nagôs. At the same time Rufino, as a Muslim, was not isolated. In 1840 a beautiful leather-covered manuscript book written in Arabic was confiscated from a "Mina club" in Porto Alegre, the capital of the province, and was later donated to the Brazilian Historical Institute in Rio de Janeiro, where it is presently held. It is possible that Rufino himself belonged to that club, for he apparently left Porto Alegre in that very year perhaps fearing persecution.[57]

Yet most Yorubas were not Muslims, and instead of keeping to themselves they reached out and became quite visible among the Africans in cities like Rio de Janeiro and Porto Alegre. In the latter city manumission records suggest that West Africans represented the vast majority (67 percent of the manumitted) of the freed African community. In contrast, in Rio de Janeiro they never represented more than 7 percent of the African population before 1850 in the samples compiled by Mary Karasch. She noted that most of them did not come to Rio directly from Africa but rather from Bahia, which most likely was also true of those living in Rio Grande do Sul.[58] This southward flow of Bahian-acculturated Yorubas increased significantly after 1835, fed by the fear of their participation in another slave uprising and by the pressures on the slave market after the abolition of the trans-Atlantic slave trade in 1850, which created a vigorous internal slave trade to the more prosperous provinces of the country. This is reflected in data from probate records, where West African slaves represented 19 percent and 15 percent of the Africans in rural and urban Rio de Janeiro, respectively, between 1860 and 1864.[59] This does not mean that the Minas doubled their presence in the city in a few decades; the slave population of Rio de Janeiro had reached its peak in 1849, at 78,800 slaves (38.3 percent of the city's population), and steadily declined, in both number and proportion, in the following decades.[60] It does mean, however, that the Minas had doubled their weight and importance within the African population of the city.

As in Bahia, Mina slaves in Rio could be found in the usual urban slave occupations under the self-hire system. Minas were well placed in the labor market, performing well-paid activities that facilitated the purchase of freedom. Porters in Rio's harbor, particularly coffee carriers, were the elite among *ganhadores*, and there are indications of many Minas among them. The selling of foodstuffs was notoriously controlled by African women, and scattered evidence suggests the Minas were numerous among those who actually owned *quitandas* or market stalls. Bringing produce to be sold in the city and selling prepared food in the streets made a living and earned the manumission of many slave women. Similar to what occurred in Bahia, owning a produce stall or owning a food stall or *casa de angu* placed these women at the confluence of the rural and urban slave communities, and at the center of the vibrant African and Creole urban daily life.

The Minas were closely monitored by the police for their potential threat to the social order. A few examples demonstrate that in Rio de Janeiro they mastered the codes of the slave system and employed this knowledge to their benefit in various ways. The case of Henrique José, known as "Riscadinho," a Mina freedman responsible for a *zungu*, a meeting place and temporary shelter for slaves living away from masters, is emblematic.[61] Riscadinho—"the striped one," an allusion to his facial scarifications—was involved in a network dedicated to the "seduction" of slaves in the 1840s and, more than once, while passing as a police informant, furnished misleading information to police officers. In 1845 the city chief of police detailed the workings of "seduction" and identified those responsible:

> It is the freedmen, mainly the Minas, who through an insignificant business they call *"pombear"* or *"casa de vender angu"* attract the slaves and seduce them, promising them a smiling future. Lured, the pieces are delivered to the conductors who take them, and the seducing agents take on new tasks.[62]

Riscadinho was identified as the great seducer of slaves in the city in 1845, a task he accomplished thanks to his privileged position as the owner of a small establishment where slaves and freedpersons converged to eat *angu*, a typical Central African dish adopted by all slaves in Rio.[63] *Casas de angu* by day, they turned into *zungus* by night. *Zungus* often housed illegal divination or game sessions. *Casas de angu* served as the urban connection to the runaway communities in the interior. Petty traders (*pombeiros*) served as go-betweens and agents in this network of "seduction," the workings of which implied the participation of both the seduced slave and their seducers. In a city where the majority of slaves were either Central Africans or their descendants, that Riscadinho, his foreignness stamped on his face and conveyed in his nickname, had acquired such a prominent position, and earned the trust of slaves and freedpersons of other origins—convincing them of the possibility of a "smiling future"—speaks to the open attitude of the Minas to participate in the Afro-Cariocan society. Recognizing his potential danger, the imperial government deported him to Angola, and thus very far from his probable original native country in Yorubaland.

Despite their perceived potential danger, the Minas were rarely prominent in acts of open resistance recorded in the southeast, which is probably owing to their small number in the slave population. Of course, Mina slaves ran away; yet they did so in a proportion smaller or equal to their weight in the population: in the police raids against runaway communities in the rural town of Itaguaí, province of Rio de Janeiro, between 1816 and 1877, only 1 Mina among 41 Africans of identified origins was arrested. In a sample of 203 fugitives advertised in a newspaper in the city of Rio between 1809 and 1821, only 9 West Africans were listed as follows: 4 Minas, 1 Mina-hausa, 2 Hausas, and 2 Calabars. These numbers are roughly comparable with the proportion of Mina slaves in Rio at the time, and also reproduce the pattern among Nagô fugitives in Bahia. The small size of the Mina community in the capital of Brazil did not restrain them from exercising this style of resistance.[64]

The Minas distinguished themselves from other Africans when it came to earning manumission and fighting for freedom from within the system. In Rio de Janeiro, West Africans seem to have constituted the group with the highest capacity to accumulate savings: they were responsible for 50 percent of the paid manumissions between 1840 and 1859, while representing only between 9 per-cent and 15 percent of the slave population.[65] Their high rate of manumissions fed a growing group of emancipated persons who represented almost one-third of the freed African population in the city. Work groups and savings associa-tions, most probably ethnically based and mirrored after the *juntas* existing in Bahia, were behind their success. Gobineau reported the existence of such or-ganizations among the Minas in Rio de Janeiro in 1869.[66]

One last example suggests that the Mina identity, coupled with the reputa-tion for rebelliousness that they earned in Bahia, was used to foster legal strug-gles for freedom in the southeast. Ethnic solidarity was clearly used as a weapon by a unique group of liberated Africans of Yoruba origin who first landed in Bahia after the 1831 prohibition of the slave trade and were thus emancipated, and then transferred to Rio de Janeiro where, twenty years after their arrival, they petitioned for emancipation.[67] The group of Nagô men were initially eman-cipated in the fateful year of 1835, served their fourteen-year apprenticeship at the Navy Arsenal in Bahia and, upon demanding their right to "full freedom" in 1848 or 1849, were sent to Rio de Janeiro and forced to continue serving their terms. Some of them, sent to the Iron Foundry of Ipanema in the interior of the province of São Paulo, staged an unusual episode of resistance: they sub-mitted a written petition to the local judge reaffirming their request for final and effective emancipation. The document demonstrated their firm decision to fight collectively but peacefully—just like the 1857 Bahian strikers—within the established system. Considered dangerous to the order in the factory, they were sent back to Rio de Janeiro, where they joined former companions and, in the 1850s, resumed their legal quest for freedom, now under separate, indi-vidual petitions. All of them identified themselves interchangeably as Mina and Nagô, often using their Bahian connection to claim different rights from those conferred to other liberated Africans.

The most compelling use of their ethnic identity came from a liberated African by the name of Cyro, in his struggle against the individual for whom he had worked, and who wanted to prevent him from receiving his letter of emancipation. Dionísio Peçanha, the hirer of his services, managed to have the African arrested and placed in a hard-labor prison while he negotiated Cyro's transfer to the distant northern province of Amazonas. Meanwhile, Cyro's two sons, who had lost their mother, had no one but their father to care for them. The African wrote a note to Peçanha requesting that he go to the House of Cor-rection the next day to release his sons and insisted that Peçanha should ob-tain his immediate release. Cyro threatened that if his demands were not met in three days, Peçanha "would find out what a Mina is capable of."[68] While he did not refrain from negotiating, he powerfully combined the reputation of rebelliousness and fierceness of the Mina in his favor, and managed to have his wishes fulfilled.

The Minas in Rio de Janeiro, although a minority within the African pop-ulation which gradually shrank and aged after 1850, came to occupy a distinctive place among Afro-Cariocans. Joined in Rio by more freed persons, ex-slaves, and their families from Bahia even after abolition, they carved out a singular place in the city. At the turn of the twentieth century the "Bahians" were concentrated in an area of the city of Rio known as Little Africa. Their lively cultural life is credited for providing decisive influence on the practice of Candomblé, and for being at the root of Rio de Janeiro's samba culture. This phenomenon was not unique to this region of southern Brazil. Again in Rio Grande do Sul, in the early 1880s, a group called Nagô Carnival Club paraded in the streets of the city of Pelotas, the second in importance in the province, demanding the abolition of slavery. The scribe of this club was a Candomblé priest, and its allegoric leader was a character named King Oba. In Rio Grande *Batuque* is the term used for Candomblé, and the Yoruba branch of the religion is divided into Oyo, Ijexá, and Nagô.[69]

One of the largest groups in the Yoruba diaspora, the Yorubas in Brazil played a singular role within the Brazilian slave society. Initially known as "Minas," the term that identified all Africans brought from West Africa through the Portuguese slave trade, in the first decades of the nineteenth century Yorubas came to construct a separate identity for themselves, that of "Nagôs." The close trading connection between the Bight of Benin and Bahia favored their concentration in that Brazilian province; the wars surrounding the fall of the Oyo Empire explain their dramatic presence in the Bahian slave trade. Yoruba speakers came to represent the majority among African-born slaves and freedpersons in Bahia in the course of the nineteenth century. As such, they deeply imprinted their manners, rituals, organizations, and beliefs on Bahian slave culture.

The inclination of Yorubas to defy slavery—whether through institutional mechanisms, manumission, or the courts, or through daily resistance, individual flight, or collective rebellion—led to the series of revolts and plots by Hausas and Yorubas that have no parallel in New World slavery and earned them the reputation of being "rebellious" while also somehow determining their dispersion throughout the country. Sold in great numbers away from Bahia after 1835, Nagôs joined existing groups of "Mina" slaves in southern Brazilian cities such as Rio de Janeiro and Porto Alegre. In small numbers amid a slave population mainly of West-Central African origin, they stood out from the rest of the slaves and freedpersons for their strong ethnic links and ethnic-based organizations, which facilitated their control over portions of the labor market and promoted the social mobility of their members. However, Yorubas also demonstrated their ability to integrate with and often lead Africans of other ethnic groups and Creoles in the everyday life under slavery or nominal freedom. The history of Nagô religion and its dissemination in Brazil is perhaps the best example of the way Yorubas exercised the politics of inclusion in, and expansion of, their culture, inclusion in this case being the key to expansion. From the north to the south of Brazil the Yoruba diaspora left an enduring imprint on the cultural landscape of the country.

Notes

1. Philip D. Curtin, *The Atlantic Slave Trade: A Census* (Madison: University of Wisconsin Press, 1969); David Eltis et al., *The Trans-Atlantic Slave Trade: A Database on CD-ROM* (Cambridge: Cambridge University Press, 1999); Pierre Verger, *Flux et reflux de la traite des nègres entre le golfe de Bénin et Bahia de Todos os Santos du XVIIe au XIXe siècle* (The Hague: Mouton, 1968).

2. Leslie Bethell, *The Abolition of the Brazilian Slave Trade: Britain, Brazil, and the Slave Trade Question, 1807–1869* (Cambridge: Cambridge University Press, 1970); Pierre Verger, "Bahia, 1810–1835. Relations économico-philanthropiques Anglo-Portugaises et leur influence sur la traite brésilienne des esclaves," in idem, *Flux et reflux*, 287–323; Luis Henrique Dias Tavares, *Comércio proibido de escravos* (São Paulo: Ática, CNPq, 1988).

3. New data collection focusing on the South Atlantic will likely provide a better picture of the slave trade to Brazil than we have now. According to David Eltis, part of the trade from West Africa to Bahia between 1816 and 1830 has been recorded as if it had left from West-Central Africa by ship masters looking to escape persecution. Consequently, not only the volume but also the proportion of slaves from West Africa in Bahia will be revised upward in the second edition of the data set.

4. On Goiás, see Mary Karasch, "Central Africans in Central Brazil, 1780–1835," in *Central Africans and Cultural Transformations in the African Diaspora*, ed. Linda Heywood (Cambridge: Cambridge University Press, 2002), 117–51; and idem, "Os quilombos do ouro na capitania de Goiás," in *Liberdade por um fio: história dos quilombos no Brasil*, ed. João José Reis and Flávio dos Santos Gomes (São Paulo: Companhia das Letras, 1996), 240– 62; on the group of Courana women in Minas Gerais, see Luiz R. B. Mott, *Escravidão, homossexualidade e demonologia* (São Paulo: Ícone, 1988), 87–118; on Rio de Contas, see "Matrícula Seg. do Anno de 1848," Arquivo Municipal de Rio de Contas, uncatalogued.

5. On the plantation system of Bahia, see Stuart B. Schwartz, *Sugar Plantations in the Formation of Brazilian Society: Bahia, 1550–1835* (Cambridge: Cambridge University Press, 1985); B. J. Barickman, *A Bahian Counterpoint: Sugar, Tobacco, Cassava, and Slavery in the Recôncavo, 1780–1860* (Stanford, Calif.: Stanford University Press, 1998).

6. David Eltis, *Economic Growth and the Ending of the Transatlantic Slave Trade* (New York: Oxford University Press, 1987), 243– 44. This figure differs from the one presented in Table 5.1 because it reflects an estimate by Eltis of the possible "true" number of slave imports to Bahia.

7. These calculations are based on the following sources: lists of slaves in probate records, part of a project in collaboration with Paul Lovejoy; Maria José de Silva Andrade, *A mão-de-obra escrava em Salvador de 1811 a 1860* (São Paulo: Corrupio, 1988), 189 – 90; João J. Reis, "'The Revolution of the *Ganhadores*': Urban Labour, Ethnicity, and the African Strike of 1857 in Bahia, Brazil," *Journal of Latin American Studies* 29, no. 2 (May 1997): 390–91; and Maria Inês Côrtes de Oliveira, "Retrouver une identité: jeux sociaux des Africains de Bahia (vers 1750–vers 1890)" (Ph.D. dissertation, Université de Paris–Sorbonne, 1992), 107, 109.

8. Robin Law, "Ethnicity and the Slave Trade: 'Lucumi' and 'Nago' as Ethnonyms in West Africa," *History in Africa* 24 (1997): 205–19. For a general discussion of African

ethnonyms in Bahia during the slave trade era, see Maria Inês Côrtes de Oliveira, "Quem eram os 'negros da guiné'? A origem dos africanos na Bahia," *Afro-Ásia* 19/20 (1997): 53–63.

9. J. D. Y. Peel, "The Cultural Work of Yoruba Ethnogenesis," in *History and Ethnicity*, ed. E. Tonkin, M. McDonald, and M. Chapman (London: Routledge and Kegan Paul, 1989), 198–216. See also Michael R. Doortmont, "The Invention of the Yorubas: Regional and Pan-African Nationalism versus Ethnic Provincialism," in *Self-Assertion and Brokerage: Early Cultural Nationalism in West Africa*, ed. P. F. de Moraes Farias and K. Barber (Birmingham, U.K.: Center for West African Studies, University of Birmingham, 1990), 101–108.

10. Robin Law, "The Heritage of Oduduwa: Traditional History and Political Propaganda among the Yoruba," *Journal of African History* 14, no. 2 (1973): 207–22; J. F. A. Ajayi writes explicitly about the dissemination of Sango's cult with the expansion of Oyo in "The Aftermath of the Fall of Òyó," in *History of West Africa*, ed. J. F. Ade Ajayi and Michael Crowder (London: Longman, 1974), 133. On the dissemination of Ogun, see Sandra T. Barnes and Paula Girshick Ben-Amos, "Ogun, the Empire Builder," and J. D. Y. Peel, "A Comparative Analysis of Ogun in Precolonial Yorubaland," both in *Africa's Ogun: Old World and New*, ed. Sandra T. Barnes (Bloomington: Indiana University Press, 1997), 39–64, 263–89, respectively. Another discussion on this theme is J. Lorand Matory, *Sex and the Empire That Is No More: Gender and the Politics of Metaphor in Oyo Yoruba Religion* (Minneapolis: University of Minnesota Press, 1994), 13–22. Oba Olorun, Ogun, Obatala, and Elegba were mentioned by Osifekunde, of Ijebu, and Obatala by Crowther, of Osogun (southern Òyó). See P. C. Lloyd, "Osifekunde of Ijebu," in *Africa Remembered: Narratives by West Africans from the Era of the Slave Trade*, ed. Philip D. Curtin (Madison: University of Wisconsin Press, 1967), 274–75; and J. F. Ade Ajayi, "Samuel Ajayi Crowther of Oyo," in Curtin, *Africa Remembered*, 294.

11. See the trial records of the 1835 rebellion deposited at the Arquivo Público do Estado da Bahia (hereafter, APEBa); and João José Reis, *Slave Rebellion in Brazil: The Muslim Uprising of 1835 in Bahia*, trans. Arthur Brakel (Baltimore: The Johns Hopkins University Press, 1993), 156.

12. Richard Lander, ed., *Records of Captain Clapperton's Last Expedition to Africa*, 2 vols. (London: Cass, 1967 [1830]), 217–18; Lloyd, "Osifekunde of Ijebu," 255–56. On the specialists of scarification and their relationship with Ogun, see Henry John Drewal, "Art or Accident: Yoruba Body Artists and Their Deity Ogún," in Barnes, *Africa's Ogun*, 235–60.

13. "Devassa do Levante de Escravos Ocorrido em Salvador em 1835," *Anais do Arquivo Público do Estado da Bahia* 38 (1968): 131–35.

14. *Jornal da Bahia*, 24 May 1859. The Yoruba facial marks are discussed by Samuel Johnson, *The History of the Yorubas: From the Earliest Times to the Beginning of the British Protectorate* (London: Routledge and Kegan Paul, 1966 [1921]), 104–109.

15. *Correio Mercantil*, 29 March 1847.

16. E. Adeniyi Oroge, "The Institution of Slavery in Yorubaland with Particular Reference to the Nineteenth Century" (Ph.D. dissertation, Center of West African Studies, University of Birmingham, U.K., 1971), 114. According to Oroge, devotees of Orisa Oko, an agricultural god, were also protected from being enslaved (Oroge, "The Institution of Slavery in Yorubaland," 130). Samuel Johnson, writing in the late nineteenth century, noted facial marks used by natives of Yagba, Ijesa, Ondo, Efon e Igbomina, all

of them members of groups which, according to Oroge, did not wear them. It is possible, however, that these groups developed this custom at a later date, which is why Johnson could identify their ethnic marks (Johnson, *The History of the Yorubas*, 104–109).

17. "A Justiça de Pedro Pinto, Nagô, forro," APEBa, Insurreições, maço 2849, fl. 9v.

18. "Devassa do Levante," 7.

19. On the Santo Amaro celebration, see João J. Reis, "Tambores e tremores: a festa negra na Bahia na primeira metade do século XIX," in *Carnaval e outras f(r)estas: Ensaios de história social da cultura*, ed. Maria Clementina P. da Cunha (Campinas: Unicamp, 2002), 104–14; and, on Prince Bernardo, see Reis, "Recôncavo rebelde: revoltas escravas nos engenhos baianos," *Afro-Ásia* 15 (1992): 121–26.

20. Hugh Clapperton, *Journal of a Second Expedition into the Interior of Africa, from the Bight of Benin to Soccatoo* (London: Cass, 1966 [1829]), 11, 15. Throughout his narrative Clapperton mentions cloth manufactories and dye houses in the Yoruba country.

21. "Relação dos africanos libertos e escravos residentes na Freguesia de Santana [1849]," APEBa, Escravos (assuntos), no. 2898. On Bahian slaves' and freedmen's urban labor market, see Andrade, *A mão-de-obra*; and Katia Mattoso, *Bahia século XIX: Uma província no Império* (Rio de Janeiro: Nova Fronteira, 1992), 527–43; João J. Reis, "De olho no canto: trabalho de rua na Bahia na véspera da abolição," *Afro-Ásia* 24 (2001): 199–242; and Reis, "'The Revolution of the *Ganhadores*,'" 355–93.

22. Reis, "'The Revolution of the *Ganhadores*'," 391.

23. Description of this ceremony can be found in Manuel Querino, *A raça africana no Brasil e seus costumes* (Salvador: Progresso, 1955), 88–89.

24. APEBa, Legislativa. Abaixo-assinados, vols. 983 and 984.

25. APEBa, Livros de Registros do Tabelião, vol. 162, João (1 December 1809); vol. 200, Ana (11 March 1815); vol. 197, Antônia (3 March 1819); vol. 249, Ana (7 August 1836), Maria (3 October 1836); vol. 288, Jacob (25 December 1848).

26. Oroge, "The Institution of Slavery in Yorubaland," 142.

27. APEBa, Livro de Registros do Tabelião, vol. 268, Tibério (27 October 1839); vol. 326, Martiniana (8 August 1856); vol. 255, João (4 August 1836).

28. See Manuela Carneiro da Cunha, *Negros, estrangeiros: Os escravos libertos e a sua volta à África* (São Paulo, Brasiliense, 1985), 17–61.

29. APEBa, Livro de Registros do Tabelião, vol. 207, Domingos (4 July 1840).

30. Ibid., vol. 288, Eliseu (22 April 1844).

31. Johnson, *History of the Yorubas*, 119.

32. Alfred Ellis, *The Yoruba-Speaking Peoples* (Oosterhout: Anthropological Publications, 1966 [1894]), 150.

33. *Grito da Razão*, 27 July 1824; *Correio Mercantil*, 18 January 1840. On slave family flights in Bahia, see Isabel Cristina F. dos Reis, *Histórias de vida familiar e afetiva de escravos na Bahia do século XIX* (Salvador: Centro de Estudos Baianos/UFBA, 2001), chap. 3.

34. *Jornal da Bahia*, 14 January and 28 April 1857.

35. *Correio Mercantil*, 6 November, 21 June, and 8 April 1847; *Grito da Razão*, 2 August 1825.

36. The following paragraphs on the Nagô slave revolts are based on Reis, *Slave Rebellion in Brazil*.

37. This is an interpretive angle that was inaugurated in the early twentieth century by Brazilian anthropologist Nina Rodrigues, *Os africanos no Brasil* (São Paulo: Nacional, 1932), 61–62. See also Roger Bastide, *As religiões africanas no Brasil* (São Paulo: Pio-

neira, 1971), 150–53; Verger, *Flux et reflux*, 325–54; and, more recently, Paul Lovejoy, "Background to Rebellion: The Origins of Muslim Slaves in Bahia," *Slavery and Abolition* 15, no. 2 (1994): 151–80; and Alberto da Costa e Silva, "Sobre a rebelião de 1835 na Bahia," *Revista Brasileira* 8, no. 31 (2002): 9–33; among others.

38. See João J. Reis, "O 'Rol dos Culpados': Notas Sobre um Documento da rebelião de 1835," *Anais do APEBa* 48 (1985): 119–38.

39. On events in Ilorin, see Robin Law, *The Oyo Empire, c. 1600–c. 1836: A West African Imperialism in the Era of the Atlantic Slave Trade* (Oxford: Clarendon, 1977), 255–60; and Hakeem Olumide Danmole, "The Frontier Emirate: A History of Islam in Ilorin" (Ph.D. dissertation, Center of West African Studies, University of Birmingham, U.K., 1980), chaps. 2 and 3.

40. The ethnic dimension of the 1835 rebellion is discussed in detail, and is based on new evidence, in a revised and considerably expanded edition of Reis, *Slave Rebellion*, entitled *Rebelião escrava no Brasil: a história do levante dos malês na Bahia em 1835 (nova edição revista e ampliada)* (São Paulo: Companhia das Letras, 2003). On the construction of Yoruba identity by Muslims, see P. F. de Moraes Farias, "'Yoruba' Origins Revisited by Muslims: An Interview with the *Arókin* of Òyó and a Reading of the *Asl Qaba'il Yuruba* of Al-Hajj Adam al-Iluri," in Farias and Barber, *Self-Assertion and Brokerage*, 109–47.

41. See the works by Nina Rodrigues, Bastide, and Verger mentioned in note 37 above.

42. "Devassa do Levante," 85.

43. Reis, "'The Revolution of the *Ganhadores*,'" 372–39.

44. Ibid., 355–93.

45. Eltis, *Economic Growth*, 257.

46. Testamento-Capital de Gertrudes Maria do Espírito Santo, APEBa, no. 3/1343/1812/62; Inventário de Custódia Machado de Barros, APEBa, no. 5/2023/2494/7; and APEBa, Livro de registro de Testamentos, vol. 17, fls. 44–45; and vol. 26, fls. 90v–91v.

47. On Catholic black brotherhoods, among many other titles, see João J. Reis, "Identidade e Diversidade Étnicas nas Irmandades Negras no Tempo da Escravidão," *Tempo* 3 (1997): 7–33; Kátia Mattoso, *Être Esclave au Brésil* (Paris: Hachette, 1979): 169–71; A. J. R. Russell-Wood, "Black and Mulatto Brotherhoods of Colonial Brazil: A History," *Hispanic American Historical Review* 54, no. 4 (1974): 567–602; Patricia Mulvey, "The Black Lay Brotherhoods of Colonial Brazil" (Ph.D. dissertation, City University of New York, 1976). On black coronation ceremonies, see Marina Mello e Souza, *Reis negros no Brasil escravista: História da festa de coroação de Rei Congo* (Belo Horizonte: Ed. UFMG, 2002).

48. See João J. Reis, "Candomblé in Nineteenth-Century Bahia: Priests, Followers, Clients," *Slavery and Abolition* 22, no. 1 (2001): 116–34. On nineteenth-century Candomblé in Bahia, see also Rachel Elizabeth Harding, *A Refuge in Thunder: Candomblé and Alternative Spaces of Blackness* (Bloomington: Indiana University Press, 2000); Renato da Silveira, "Iya Nassô Oka, Babá Axipá e Bamboxê Obiticô: uma narrativa sobre a fundação do Candomblé da Barroquinha, o mais antigo terreiro Ketu na Bahia," unpublished paper, 2001; and Luis Nicolau Parés, "Do lado do Jeje: história e ritual do Vodun na Bahia," unpublished paper, 2002. On building Nagô religious hegemony in nineteenth-century Bahia, see Luis Nicolau Parés, "The 'Nagôization' Process in Bahian Candomblé," chapter 10 in this volume.

49. Karasch, "Central Africans," 136.

50. Mariza de Carvalho Soares, *Devotos da cor: identidade étnica, religiosidade e es-*

cravidão no Rio de Janeiro, século XVIII (Rio de Janeiro: Civilização Brasileira, 2000), 85–86.

51. Mary C. Karasch, *Slave Life in Rio de Janeiro, 1808–1850* (Princeton, N.J.: Princeton University Press, 1987), 25–27.

52. The case of the Maki, explored by Mariza Soares, is one example. See her *Devotos da cor* and her chapter 12 in this book.

53. Cited by Carlos Eugênio Líbano Soares, *A capoeira escrava e outras tradições rebeldes no Rio de Janeiro, 1808–1850* (Campinas: Unicamp, 2001), 387, 389.

54. Cited by Carlos Eugênio Líbano Soares, *A capoeira escrava*, 389.

55. Alberto da Costa e Silva, "Buying and Selling Korans in Nineteenth Century Rio de Janeiro," *Slavery and Abolition* 22, no. 1 (2001): 83–90; on the practice of Islam in Rio, see also Karasch, *Slave Life in Rio*, 284–85.

56. Rufino's story is being studied by Flávio dos Santos Gomes, João José Reis, and Marcus Carvalho, "Rufino José Maria: um malê no mundo Atlântico" (work in progress).

57. On manumissions in Rio Grande do Sul, see Paulo Roberto Staudt Moreira, *Faces da liberdade, máscaras do cativeiro* (Porto Alegre: EDIPUCRS, 1996), 90.

58. Karasch, *Slave Life in Rio*, 25.

59. Manolo Florentino, "Alforria e etnicidade no Rio de Janeiro oitocentista: Notas de pesquisa," *Topói* 5 (2002): 9–40.

60. Karasch, *Slave Life in Rio*, 64–65.

61. The case of "Riscadinho" and the discussion on *"casas de angu"* and *"zungus"* are taken from Carlos Eugênio Líbano Soares, *Zungú: Rumor de muitas vozes* (Rio de Janeiro: Arquivo Público do Estado do Rio de Janeiro, 1998).

62. Ibid., 60.

63. *Angu* was a creamlike dish made of manioc flour and water, pieces of meat and vegetables, palm oil, and spices.

64. Minas were 1.5 percent of the Africans in Vassouras between 1837 and 1840. Flávio dos Santos Gomes, *Histórias de Quilombolas: mocambos e comunidades de senzalas no Rio de Janeiro — século XIX* (Rio de Janeiro: Arquivo Nacional, 1995), 146, 217. The data on the ethnic profile of fugitives in the city of Rio are from *Gazeta do Rio de Janeiro* and were kindly provided by Flávio Gomes. See also idem, "Jogando a rede, revendo as malhas: fugas e fugitivos no Brasil escravista," *Tempo* 1, no. 1 (1996): 67–93.

65. Florentino, "Alforrias e etnicidade," 25–40.

66. Karasch, *Slave Life in Rio*, 323.

67. Liberated Africans formed a special category of people, "neither slave nor free," emancipated from the ships caught in the illegal trade. They had to serve apprenticeship terms and during this period remained under the custody of the local government. This case has been discussed in Beatriz G. Mamigonian, "Do que 'o preto mina' é capaz: etnia e resistência entre africanos livres," *Afro-Ásia* 24 (2000): 71–95.

68. The note is attached to Peçanha to Ministério da Justiça, 26 March 1856, in Cyro Mina, Petição de Emancipação, 22 March 1855, Arquivo Nacional, Diversos SDH—cx. 782 pc.2.

69. Roberto Moura, *Tia ciata e a pequena África no Rio de Janeiro* (Rio de Janeiro: Secretaria Municipal da Cultura, 1995); Marco Antônio Lirio de Mello, *Reviras, batuques e carnavais: a cultura de resistência dos escravos em Pelotas* (Pelotas: UFPel, Editora Universitária, 1994), 43–46, 57–71; Ari Oro, "Religiões afro-brasileiras do Rio Grande do Sul: passado e presente," *Estudos Afro-Asiáticos* 24, no. 2 (2002): 345–84.

CHAPTER SIX

The Yoruba in Cuba:
Origins, Identities, and Transformations

Michele Reid

From Havana to Santiago de Cuba and cities in between, the four-hundred-year-old presence of the Yoruba diaspora pulses throughout twenty-first-century Cuba. Yoruba influences in contemporary Cuba can be found in music, dance, and religion, and prime examples include the sounds and sights of son (salsa), rumba, and Santería, on and off the island. More than isolated cultural survivals or retentions, these phenomena and numerous others form a part of the diverse, complex, and continuous trajectories involved in Cuban cultural formation.[1] By synthesizing the historical factors that fostered the development of Yoruba and Yoruba-influenced components so integral to contemporary Cuban culture and national identity, this essay highlights the major contributions and transformations of the Yoruba and their descendants as the means for understanding the transformative impact of the African diaspora in Cuba.

Overall, this chapter explores the West African origins of the Lucumí (as the Yoruba were known in Cuba) in the Spanish colonial period and their struggles during the nineteenth-century Cuban slave regime, and concludes with an overview of the multifaceted contributions their cultural traditions have made in shaping Cuban national identity. The first section presents the Yoruba and Spanish involvement in the Atlantic slave trade, the rise of Cuban slavery, and the active quests of Lucumí captives and freedmen to maintain their identity and struggle for liberty. The next discussion centers on the transformation of Yoruba practices, particularly religious redefinition, under the sphere of sociocultural mutual aid associations. In closing, this essay highlights the acceptance and appropriation of Afro-Cuban themes on a national level.

Origins of the Yoruba in Cuba:
Lucumí, Yoruba, Spain, and the Slave Trade

Using the criteria of common language, religion, geographical continuity, and sociopolitical organization, scholars have reconstructed the historic origins of the Yoruba in West Africa, primarily in Nigeria and Benin. In Nigeria the territory comprises the southwest area, including the states of Lagos, Oyo, Ogun, and Ono, and the Kwara State's Kabba and Ilorin regions. In Benin (formerly Dahomey), Yorubaland falls between the southern Nigerian border and the Weme River, and also extends west into the Atakpame region. This strategic location facilitated local, regional, and ultimately international exchange. Via land routes and tributaries, the Yoruba communicated with other peoples and cultures in West Africa. Access to the sea in the south and linkages to points north of the Sahara Desert increased outside contact with Europeans and other Africans.[2] Interaction with Europeans and the growth of plantation colonies in the New World gave rise to the Atlantic slave trade. In effect, from the sixteenth to the nineteenth centuries the slave trade funneled thousands of Yoruba captives to Cuba and the Americas. The massive influx of slaves with Lucumí or similar cultural origins, particularly in the nineteenth century, would become key in shaping Lucumí identity in Cuba.

The Yoruba and the Slave Trade

The level of involvement of the Yoruba in the Atlantic slave trade varied both regionally and over time. Early-sixteenth-century accounts by Portuguese officials detail the purchase of slaves and ivory from Ijebu, the Yoruba kingdom in the south. The Yorubaland trade in slaves continued from the southern region intermittently into the seventeenth century, shifting its focus to the west in the Allada kingdom of Dahomey, in present-day Benin. Yoruba ethnic groups, however, continued to be an important slave source for sale through Allada. Dahomey's royal monopoly on the sale of captives contributed significantly to state revenues. Dutch descriptions of Allada from the mid-seventeenth century indicate that slaves sold there were from an interior, northeast kingdom known as Ulkuma or Ulkami. A distinguishing characteristic of this region was its large slave trade, mainly as prisoners of war and criminals, to the Portuguese and the Dutch for transport to the New World.[3]

By the beginning of the eighteenth century the main European trade center had shifted to the east in Ouidah, but, as with Allada, slaves continued to be supplied from Yorubaland. French sailors from the first decades of the eighteenth century listed the nationalities of slaves sold via Ouidah, including the Ayois and the Nagô. The Ayois represented Oyo, Yorubaland's most powerful northern state. The Nagô derived from a small population in southwestern

Yoruba and evolved into a generic name used by their western neighbors in reference to the entire Yoruba group.[4] Warfare between Dahomey, Whyday, and Allada disrupted the interior slave trade. In response, the dominant Yoruba state of Oyo attacked and successfully claimed Dahomey. Oyo's defeat of Dahomey restabilized the slave trade in the Ouidah port, and new sea outlets were opened at Porto-Novo and Badagry, rival ports east of Dahomey.[5] By the 1780s the scale and intensity of slave trading from Oyo had accelerated rapidly. The combined Oyo and Dahomey trade systems made the Bight of Benin Africa's second-largest zone for slave trading. Of the total captives leaving West Africa in the eighteenth century, 18 percent (1.2 million) were shipped from this region.[6] The Spanish Empire, directly and indirectly, received thousands of Yoruba captives for its colonies in the Americas.

Spain and the Slave Trade

Spain began introducing slaves into its Caribbean territories in the early sixteenth century, with the first ones arriving in 1518. Initially the Spanish Crown granted individual licenses to transport one or more slaves. By 1528 Spain issued "asientos," or monopoly contracts, to foreign slave traders such as the Portuguese, the English, the Dutch, and the French.[7] Consequently the Spanish colonies in the Americas received slaves from all over the African coasts. In general, early sources for slaves to Cuba were in the Guinea region, between the Senegal River and Cape of Palms. In the second half of the seventeenth century the area extended southward to Angola.[8] By the eighteenth century Spain issued a major asiento to England, granting the British control over the supply of slaves for all Spanish America. Within the first twenty-five years English slave traders imported roughly seventy-five thousand Africans. A steady flow of captives arrived into ports in Cartegena, Upper Peru, Buenos Aires, the Rio de la Plata region, the Panamanian isthmus, and the South American north coast. The burgeoning sugar industry in the Spanish Caribbean, particularly in Cuba, solidified the region as the new center for slave importations.[9]

The British occupation of Cuba in 1763 initiated an unprecedented economic era on the island. A dramatic increase in slave imports accompanied the new administration. Although British control of Cuba lasted less than a year, an estimated four thousand African slaves arrived on the island. This figure represented 8 to 10 percent of all imported slaves in the previous 250 years.[10] After the return of Cuba, the Spanish Crown initiated wide-scale commercial development in its colonies. Furthermore, in 1789, Spain implemented a free slave trade policy to Spanish American colonies for all nations. This resulted in the growth of slavery in present-day Venezuela and Colombia, and in the Caribbean islands of Puerto Rico and Cuba. Ultimately Cuba emerged as the largest slave colony in Spanish America.[11]

The Yoruba in Cuba: The Rise of Cuba and the Fall of Oyo

Warfare in both the Caribbean and Yorubaland proved decisive in the rise of Cuba and the fall of the Oyo Empire. In 1791 revolution engulfed the French colony of Saint Domingue (Haiti), forever changing the balance of power and the distribution of slaves in the Caribbean into the nineteenth century. The Haitian slave rebellion, the only successful one in the Americas, destroyed the largest sugar plantation society and forced the abolition of slavery on the island.[12] In turn, the fall of Saint Domingue, combined with the colonial free trade policy in slaves, initiated Cuba's ascent as the world leader in sugar production. As colonial Cuba advanced via a sugar industry fueled by African slaves, across the Atlantic Ocean the Oyo Empire faced serious decline. Attempts by Owu, the primary force in southern Yorubaland, to suppress the kidnapping of Oyo slave traders by Ijebu raiders provoked a wide-scale conflict with the Ijebu. With the aid of displaced refugees from the Oyo civil wars, Owu was destroyed by 1821. This, however, sparked a series of devastating battles in the southern region.[13] Warfare disrupted trade routes from the interior, causing the European need for slaves to be filled from within the Yoruba territory. Consequently the already weakened Oyo Empire encountered revolt both from within and without. After a series of successful attacks from Dahomey, internal warfare, and Muslim rebellion in the first third of the nineteenth century, the Oyo Empire collapsed completely.[14]

The combined effects of increased European demand for slaves in the Americas, Yoruba warfare, and the eventual collapse of the Oyo Empire yielded unprecedented levels of slave imports from Yorubaland.[15] In the nineteenth century the region became the most active West African slave embarkation point north of the equator, continuing slave shipments until the 1860s. Over the century approximately 421,000 African captives were shipped to the Americas.[16] Although the bulk went to Brazil, Cuba received a significant proportion to meet the labor demand required for the production of sugar and coffee in the rural areas, and to fill the needs of the urban sectors.

Over 85 percent of the slaves that entered Cuba arrived after 1800. In censuses taken from 1817 to 1861 the slave population remained consistently between 36 and 46 percent of the total number of inhabitants. When free people of color were included, the total number of men and women of African descent rose, ranging from 52 to 56 percent of approximately 800,000 people.[17] The increase in the black population fueled colonial Cuban fears of a Haitian-style slave revolt, but they were not enough to quell the economic ambitions of planters and Spanish officials. To maintain its rapidly expanding industry, particularly between 1820 and 1840, Cuba increased its slave imports exponentially. Scholars estimate that 271,659 slaves were introduced legally and illegally from 1820 to 1853.[18] By the end of the 1850s Cuba was the sole slave importer in the Americas, bringing in 121,000 African captives in this decade alone.[19]

Scholars offer several reasons and evidence of why, among the thousands of enslaved Africans who arrived in Cuba, Yoruba traditions and influences persisted, particularly in the nineteenth century. Research indicates that numerous African captives transported to Cuba, and elsewhere in the Americas, were typically captured in groups, as war prisoners, and many may have originated from the same town.[20] Examples among Yoruba-speaking groups include the Oyo, Ife', Iyebu, Egba, Egbado, Iyesa, Ekiti, Onod, Owo, and Akoko.[21] While scribes and slave traders often recorded the ethnic names of African captives haphazardly, records of slaves sold in Cuba from 1790 to 1880 indicate that of the almost seven thousand Africans of known origin, at least 9 percent were Yoruba.[22] In addition, enslaved Yoruba arrived clandestinely to the island, circumventing Spain's treaty with England to abolish the slave trade. For instance, Spanish government correspondence throughout the first half of the nineteenth century reports capturing ships transporting "negros bozales" (African-born blacks) "de nación Lucumí" (from the Lucumí nation or ethnic group).[23] Furthermore, scholars concur that between 1817 and 1860 the Yoruba comprised the single largest proportion, at least 30 percent, of the slaves imported to Cuba.[24] Thus the successive and increasing waves of Yoruba arriving in Cuba contributed to their ability to maintain the cultural integrity of numerous practices. Moreover, the continuous interaction of African slaves, Europeans, and Creoles (persons born in the Americas) added multiple demographic, cultural, and political layers that would reconfigure colonial identities on the island.

The Lucumí in Cuba

In Cuba, and elsewhere in the New World, Yoruba arrivals were known as Lucumí.[25] Historians suggest that the name originated from the northeastern Yoruba kingdom known as Ulkuma or Ulkami. Scholars also speculate that the term "Lucumí" derived from the Yoruba common greeting, "oluku mí" (my friend), and that slaves used this phrase to communicate to the new Yoruba-speaking captives arriving in Cuba to indicate that they were not alone in a foreign land.[26] Sources from the sixteenth to the nineteenth centuries also document the presence of Lucumí in Cuba. For example, data from slave trade licenses issued in Havana from the 1570s through 1699 list Lucumí among more than forty African ethnicities.[27] Nineteenth-century Spanish government correspondence reported capturing Portuguese slave ships illegally transporting slaves "de nación Lucumí."[28] Once in Cuba, Yoruba captives may have initially identified themselves according to their ethnic subgroup, calling themselves Lucumí-Adó, Lucumí-Oyo, Lucumí-Egbá, Lucumí-Yebú, and so on.[29] In addition, colonial records list Lucumí as the ethnicity for Cuban slaves, such as Ramón Montalvo, and free blacks, like Antonio Abad. Some individuals, such as Santiago Lucumí, even carried their ethnicity as a surname. Cabildos de nación (sociocultural mutual aid associations) also pertained to specific African ethnicities, although membership was not limited to those with the same ethnic background. Yoruba associations included Lucumí Ello and Lucumí

Aguzá, and were often attached to a Catholic saint, such as the Lucumí cabildos San Pedro Nolasco, Nuestra Señora del Rosario, and Señora de las Nieves.[30] The documentation of the Lucumí origin of slaves and freedmen, real or imposed, and the categorization of cabildos de nación by ethnic affiliation enabled the Yoruba to reaffirm their cultural roots in a foreign and oppressive setting. Consequently their identity did not, indeed could not, remain static. Rather, in response to and in spite of internal and external social forces of slave society, the Yoruba in Cuba actively took part in recrafting their identity.[31]

Particularly notable were Lucumí efforts challenging the bounds of slavery by their involvement in uprisings in the nineteenth century. In 1812 the government accused José Antonio Aponte, a free black man, of conspiring to overthrow colonial rule and slavery. Aponte was a retired officer of the Cuban militia of color, leader of the Shangó Tedum cabildo, a prominent practitioner of Lucumí religion, and a member of the Ogboni, a powerful secret society of Yorubaland. Using his leadership skills and connections as a carpenter, Aponte united skilled artisans, such as carpenters and furniture, shoe, and saddle makers, along with oxcart drivers and bell ringers, and spread plans for an insurrection to his cabildo members across the island. Officials sentenced Aponte and his collaborators to execution by hanging. In 1835 Hermengildo Jáurequi and Juan Nepomuceno Prieto, the latter a leader of a Lucumí cabildo and a retired militia officer, planned the Lucumí Conspiracy. They, like Aponte, wanted to abolish slavery and overthrow the government. Officials also discovered their plans and thwarted the rebellion. In addition, in 1844, Cuban authorities accused "libres de color" (free people of African descent) of leading a revolt, known as the Conspiracy of La Escalera, in collaboration with slaves, Cuban whites, and British abolitionists, to overthrow slavery and Spanish rule on the island. Lucumís, both slave and free, were included among the hundreds of people, predominantly of African descent, sentenced by the Military Commission.[32] For instance, slave Ramón Montalvo was absolved of his involvement in the conspiracy but was subject to vigilant surveillance for a year. Officials expelled Antonio Abad from the island for his involvement in the conspiracy.[33] These examples signified the struggle of the Lucumí, and the collective efforts of Africans and their descendants in general, to strive for a life without bondage in Cuba. Their ability to organize, maintain traditions, and push the limits of freedom in a slave society illustrated their powerful impact and influence in colonial, and later in postcolonial, Cuba.

New World Identities

The thousands of Africans who arrived in nineteenth-century Cuba may have arrived without material culture, but they carried their personal and group identities with them, and the Yoruba were no exception.[34] Surrounded by foreign languages, customs, and beliefs, in a coercive and brutal environment, the Yoruba forged a new identity. The Yoruba, and other Africans and their descendants in Cuba, were forced to adapt to or shed Old World linguistic, religious, social, creative, and political markers. In doing so, the Lucumí reformulated their beliefs in a Cuban context. The following section addresses two important institutions of cultural maintenance and cohesion: organizations called cabildos de nación and the Yoruba-based religion called Santería.

Cabildos de Nación

To sustain their cultural traditions and improve their conditions, slaves, along with free people of color, participated in cabildos de nación, socioreligious and cultural mutual aid organizations for free and slave men and women of African origin.[35] These organizations conserved the core of African belief systems, dances, ritual practices, languages, instruments, chants, and songs.[36] Cabildos de nación stemmed from "cofradías de negros" (fraternities of Africans) organized in early-sixteenth-century Seville, Spain, and in many ways paralleled socioreligious organizations in West Africa.[37] These associations first appeared in Cuba in the sixteenth century, as slavery emerged on the island. Cabildo membership was typically associated with common ancestry. Thus people with ties to the Lucumí as well as to other ethnic groups such as the Arará, Carabalí, Congo, Gangá, Mandinga, and Mina participated.[38] As the population of African descent grew, Spain established cabildos de nación to provide assistance and cultural activities for slaves and freed women and men.[39] Records indicate that in 1573 the Havana Council authorized cabildos de negros to celebrate a popular Seville festival date.[40] The early and continued establishment of these associations provided the Yoruba and other African groups a space in which to maintain and reinforce cultural expressions and provide for the social and economic needs of cabildo members and their families.

Supervised by the "capataz" (king), "matrona" (queen), and an elected council, cabildos de nación provided a network of mutual aid, recreation, and assistance to the sick and poor, especially for people of African ancestry in urban areas. For instance, cabildos de nación purchased land or houses for organizational use. Havana records from 1691 indicate that the arará magino cabildo was the first to purchase a house.[41] Many cabildo houses were rented out, enabling the association to generate funds for activities such as buying the freedom of loved ones still in bondage.[42] Records document that of the approximately 79 percent (755 out of 954) of the slaves who were manumitted in Havana in 1810 and 1811, many received some assistance from cabildos de nación.[43] The colonial administration attempted to regulate certain aspects of cabildo life, including the formation of cabildos and where and when they could hold meetings, but their oversight proved inconsistent.[44]

As these organizations spread across the island, they enabled their members to foster and transform African traditions, and also to adopt and utilize European practices to the benefit of cabildo constituents. Cabildo leaders served as ambassadors or legal counselors when dealing with colonial and local authorities. If cabildo members wished to file a complaint with Spanish officials, or were arrested or fined, the capataz assumed responsibility for representing each person with membership in the cabildo and for remitting the posted bail.[45] In addition, capataces and matronas protected the property rights of the cabildo. For instance, in the cabildo San Francisco de Paula, nación Carabalí, female and male officers protested when their landlord attempted to condemn and destroy their house.[46] Such responsibilities garnered a high level of social prestige within the sector of color and with colonial authorities.[47] The ability of cabildos to successfully maneuver the colonial legal system is certain to have fostered the desire for equality in a time when more and more African descendants were born in Cuba, and had contact with a growing free sector of color.

In addition, cabildos de nación comprised a key component in sustaining Yoruba musical and dance traditions in colonial Cuba. Recreational and spiritual activities included gathering on festival days to drum, dance, and sing.[48] Records from the late fourteenth century refer to the dances and celebrations of African slaves in Seville, Spain, which continued as African captives arrived in the Americas.[49] Nineteenth-century descriptions depict cabildo de nación members displaying a flag with a picture of their patron saint, and presenting energetic musical performances that included singing and dancing, particularly on festival days, such as "Día de los Reyes" (Day of the Kings) on January 6.[50] Drums, like the dundun, batá, bembé, and iyesa, and gourds, such as chekere or agbe, continued their ritual functions. The instrumentation of the songs and dances of Lucumí origin would eventually represent some of the strongest musical influences of the Yoruba legacy in Cuba and form part of the Cuban national identity.[51]

Located throughout the island, cabildos de nación offered a sense of group identity, ethnic cohesion, and a means for Africans and their descendants in Cuba to preserve the customs of their homeland. However, these organizations were not without ethnic conflict and division. For instance, there were sustained rivalries between the Carabalí and the Congo.[52] Divisions also existed between bozales and criollos (Cuban-born blacks), and slaves and free people of color. For example, the majority of cabildo leaders in the first half of the nineteenth century were free blacks born in Cuba.[53] Despite internal friction, cabildos de nación became a refuge for many. Yoruba displacement into the Americas forced them to reconstruct, adapt, or reinvent their beliefs in a new setting. Although operating in a highly circumscribed world, cabildos de nación supplied them with an autonomous space in which to carry out these activities.

Santería

One of the most important and enduring contributions of Yoruba tradition to Cuban culture has been in the popular religion, Santería. Santería, which means "the way of the saints," is also known as "La Regla de Ocha," the rule or law of the orisha. Emerging from Yoruba- and Catholic-derived forms of religious expression, Santería is a New World, neo-African religion. Forged by syncretism, or a meshing based on adaptation, mutual influence, combination, and representation of the sacred, Santería evolved from polycultural African and European belief systems by worshiping the orishas, the pantheon of Yoruba gods, behind the image of Catholic saints.[54] This was a complex process that continues to the present.

Slaves, particularly those in Spanish colonies, endured varying levels of religious control. For instance, according to seventeenth-century accounts in Venezuela, Catholic orders such as the Jesuits presented enslaved blacks with pictures to instruct them in religious conversion. Common drawings included depictions of Christ on a cross, with a priest collecting the blood and pouring it over his black congregation. A two-sided picture followed. On one side appeared a drawing of happy black women and men who had accepted Catholicism and had been baptized. The reverse side depicted the sad expressions of black slaves who had refused to conform to religious conversion.[55] This "spiritual conquest" enforced on African and indigenous populations in the Americas proved inconsistent and incomplete. In many cases conversion appeared to take hold on the surface, particularly when the belief systems of the colonizer and the colonized shared significant similarities, as Yoruba and Catholic religions did.[56]

As more and more slaves arrived in Cuba, the Catholic Church attempted to stimulate religious conversion and instruction of slaves via cabildos de nación. For instance, prior to the mid-eighteenth century, the Church required cabildo members to gather primarily on Sundays and holidays. However, in 1755, the Roman Catholic Church officially recognized cabildos de nación. In doing so, the Church aimed to enforce Christian religious conversion among the African-born and criollos (Africans born in Cuba). The new bishop of Havana sought to restrict cabildo activities and associate them more directly with Catholic saints. He visited each cabildo house to administer the sacrament and prayer before the image of Mary and assigned them a saint to pray to. In addition, the bishop appointed a specific priest to each cabildo to attend to them on holy days and Sundays, and to instruct them in the Christian doctrine.[57] Despite these and other efforts of the Catholic Church, cabildos only nominally facilitated specific Christian religious goals. Rather, forced into a social structure organized and sanctioned by the Catholic Church, the Yoruba captives adjusted many of their practices to adapt to their new situation. The symbolism available in Catholicism provided a space for Yoruba religious beliefs to be reinterpreted and to reemerge.[58]

Catholicism in colonial Cuba emphasized two major factors that enabled the transformation into Santería: one God and active religious intermediaries.[59] The Yoruba religious tradition is based on the belief in one Supreme Being—called Olodumare, Olorún, Olofi, or Olofín. Specific contexts apply to the usage of each name. For example, *Olodumare* is used in reference to godly creations. Olorún may be used in this context but with heavenly or celestial connotations. Olofín is invoked in reference to godly interactions with humans. Generally, however, these names are interchangeable. In addition, there is a series of divine intermediaries called the orishas, who personify and govern the forces of the universe. For each important activity there is an orisha who wields its power. Traditionally the Yoruba recognized as many as seventeen hundred orishas, each deity being worshiped by a separate community.[60] The dramatic transference of the Yoruba to Cuba disrupted their religious context. The focus of Catholicism on the veneration of the saints facilitated the emergence of orishas in Cuba. The annual calendar celebrated a cycle of saint holy days, and people, cities, towns, neighborhoods, and even sugar mills carried the name of a patron saint. Furthermore, divine images abounded in homes and churches, with shrines set up for the holiest of saints.[61] As a result, the hundreds of orishas known to distinctive Yoruba ethnic groups merged in the New World in Cuba, with only the most important ones surviving to be transformed into Santería.

Central to the Santería belief system is the tenet that each person is guided and protected by a particular deity called an orisha, or saint. This principal applies to everyone, regardless of whether they choose to believe in Santería. The relationship with the orisha is akin to that of parent-child, and followers often refer to themselves as the son or daughter of their orisha.[62] In addition, each deity is associated with a force of nature, a human interest, and a Catholic saint. For instance, Ochún is the orisha of river water. She represents love, fertility, and marriage, and takes the form of the Virgin of Charity. Changó, or Santa Barbara, controls thunder, fire, and lightning. As a warrior he symbolizes power and control over difficulties, but also embodies virility and passion. Another important deity is Yemayá, or the Virgin of Regla, and is the sister of Ochún. She is the orisha of the sea and represents motherhood. Meanwhile, Obatalá, as the oldest of the orishas, is considered the father. He symbolizes purity, peace, education, and enlightenment. He is most often associated with the Virgin of Mercy, but also with Jesus, Saint Joseph, and Saint Michael. Elegguá, the only child orisha, symbolizes balance and destiny, and carries messages between individuals and the other orishas. He is known as a trickster because he opens and closes the road for change—for success or disaster. He has numerous saint affiliations, including Saint Benito, Saint Anthony of Padua, and the Holy Infant of Prague.[63] These, and several other orishas, form the core foci to achieving protection, guidance, and success in the daily lives of thousands of Santería worshipers. Over the centuries of colonial rule, the formation of Santería produced more than a religious conversion. These deities, their images, and their reconstructed meanings over time acknowledge an ethnically and socially broader definition of Cuban national culture.[64] Moreover, the Yoruba and other African captives and their descendants used tools of adaptation and invention to facilitate ideological transformation, to maintain spiritual integrity, and to resist colonial oppression.

The development and practice of Santería in cabildos de nación faced increasing governmental pressures, as well as hostility and fear from the general population during the colonial era and into the twentieth century. It was not until the 1920s and 1930s that Yoruba-influenced cultural traditions became recognized as positive and essential components of Cuban national identity. Although a detailed discussion of these manifestations in areas such as music, dance, and religion in contemporary Cuba is beyond the scope of this paper, the final section highlights the struggle of Afro-Cubans to have their heritage and contributions accepted and validated in the national and revolutionary periods.

Sigue la lucha: Afro-Cuban Cultural Influences in the Twentieth and Twenty-First Centuries

With the legal end of slavery in Cuba in 1886 and Cuban independence in 1902, cabildos de nación were reconfigured for post-abolition society and the new Cuban nation. Reformulated as communities called "reglas," after the regulations of cabildo life, and "socorros mutuos," mutual aid associations, the former cabildos deemphasized ethnicity and religious affiliation; fewer Afro-Cubans could claim birth in Africa, and therefore most members were criollos (Cuban-born).[65] In addition, Cuban authorities and some Afro-Cubans considered cabildos to be vestiges of an old era and obstacles to establishing a modern society. Furthermore, officials considered cabildos de nación and secret African-derived societies a threat to social and political stability. The prior involvement of Lucumí and other cabildo members in the conspiracies of 1812, 1835, and 1844 made the Cuban government uneasy as it embarked on constructing a postcolonial identity. Yet even after Cubans of African ancestry proved their loyalty with broad participation in the island's anticolonialist struggles against Spain, they faced continued discrimination under the new republic.[66]

Consequently the valorization of Yoruba-derived and other African-influenced contributions to Cuban society went unrecognized by the state until the Afrocubanismo movement of the 1920s and 1930s. The defeat of the Machado administration (1924–1933) fostered nationalist sentiment and placed Cuba's African-influenced music and dance in the spotlight.[67] Afrocubanismo, a musical, literary, dramatic, and fine arts movement by Afro-Cubans, influenced virtually every arena of popular and elite art. Artists went in search of firsthand exposure to Afro-Cuban folk and religious culture, uniting a cross section of Cubans of all colors. The movement fostered a level of tolerance and interest in African-influenced traditions, such as Santería, that had not existed in the past.[68] Further, the movement inspired the rapid national and international rise of several different Yoruba-derived musics and dance, including son (salsa) and rumba.[69] Formerly ignored or dismissed by the middle classes, Afro-Cuban artistic expression emerged as symbols of Cuban nationality,[70] and thus demonstrated the simultaneous continuity and change of Yoruba customs in the Cuban colonial and postcolonial context.

Although the Afrocubanismo movement received wide acclaim, not everyone readily embraced the new trend. As the movement began to address the political and social condition of Afro-Cubans, numerous artists were forced into exile or imprisoned.[71] Critics in Cuba initially discredited the movement, claiming that it bastardized national traditions.[72] Still they recognized, albeit grudgingly, that the rumba and son were "characteristic dances" of Cuba, and were "principally" of African origin.[73] Others concurred with its mass appeal, proclaiming that Afro-Cuban themes were "far from weakening." To the contrary, they were finally being recognized as overwhelmingly "essential" elements of Cuban contemporary dance music, and also in other types of entertainment.[74]

The 1940s and 1950s, however, saw a rapid decline in African themes, particularly among Cuban middle-class artists. Initially inspired by the creative catalyst, many now deemed Afro-Cuban expression as aesthetically limiting, overly radical, and no longer representative of contemporary Cuba.[75] Still, Afro-Cubans continued their artistic pursuits. For instance, Jesús "Chucho" Valdés, famed Cuban musical director, composer, and pianist, recalled growing up "surrounded by the distinctive rhythms of Santería" in his Havana neighborhood.[76] Celia Cruz, Obdulio Morales, and Mercedita Valdés, along with white Cubans Celina González and Reutilio Domínguez, featured Yoruba-derived religious themes specifically for commercial release and promoted weekly radio programs spotlighting Afro composition. Cruz and Valdés continued their efforts into the 1950s, recording the sacred Santería chants in Yoruba. Yet even on the fiftieth anniversary of the Cuban republic, critics characterized Afro-Cuban music as unmusical, denying the significance of any African contribution to the national culture of Cuba.[77] In spite of criticism, Cubans of African descent continued their efforts, dominating the field of entertainment, particularly in music and dance, and followers of Santería and other African-based religions continued worshiping, in secret when necessary.[78]

The 1960s and 1970s witnessed another cycle of resurgence and suppression of Afro-Cuban themes, influenced, in part, by the Cuban Revolution in 1959 and the subsequent mass emigration of thousands of primarily white Cubans.[79] Viewing all cultural manifestations as tools to support the revolution, the state took control of the management, sponsorship, and promotion of cultural presentations. The government appropriated specific aspects of Afro-Cuban expression, integrating them into the national heritage and socialist culture. For instance, the founding of the Conjunto Folklórico Nacional was the first government-supported institution to provide courses in traditional Afro-Cuban dance and music. While the state publicly recognized the significance of Afro-Cuban religions to the island's cultural heritage, Castro promoted a scientific and rational socialism that left little room for religious ritual and belief. Consequently the new socialist government took measures to restrict or ignore other forms of African-derived practices. Instruction in Afro-

Cuban themes was virtually nonexistent through the mid-1970s. Students attempting to form private study groups suffered harassment and even imprisonment. Furthermore, the state prohibited all types of religious expression, including Santería.[80]

It was not until the 1980s and 1990s that the Castro regime became more tolerant of African-influenced themes. Partially influenced by better relations with a variety of African nations and visits by African American and African activists in the 1970s, the Cuban government began to discuss racial issues previously considered moot based on the idealized equalizing effects of the revolution. By the 1980s more blacks were appointed to prominent party positions, and Afro-Cuban cultural events were promoted more openly. As a result, numerous institutions, such as the Casa de Africa, and groups like the Muñequitos de Matanzas, in addition to the Conjunto Folklórico Nacional, were established or received greater attention. In addition, the state offered recording contracts to Santería religious leaders and performers. Furthermore, in 1988 the first Congress on Yoruba Culture was held, and the Casa de Américas initiated annual meetings on African influences in Latin America. With the fall of the Soviet Union in 1989, and the need for hard currency at the beginning of the Special Period in 1990, Cuba's tourism industry sought to capitalize on the popularity of Afro-Cuban culture. The government developed "folklore tourism" packages emphasizing African-influenced music and dance, being careful to "desacralize" the religious content.[81]

Since the 1990s and into the twenty-first century, Yoruba-derived creative expressions have reemerged with even greater fervor. They have received widespread acceptance and recognition by the Cuban populace and the state, as well as on the international stage, unseen since the Afrocubanismo movement of the 1920s and 1930s. For instance, popular entertainers commonly incorporated religious lyrics and melodies into secular performances. Artists created music that fused Santería chants and batá drumming rhythms with contemporary electronic instruments, resulting in countless popular releases by groups such as Mezcla, Síntesis, NG y La Banda's, and Los Orishas, and artists including Lázaro Ros and Pachito Alsonso.[82] Events such as those at the Casa de Música or at other venues in historic Havana featuring Afro-Cuban dance, music, and religious presentations have become essential to building the economy through tourism. While, on one hand, these activities herald Afro-Cuban contributions, on the other, the island's scholars have warned of the dangers of "prostituting traditional Cuban religion" and other cultural forms. This "marketing of heritage," while constructing and celebrating cultural markers, often objectifies Afro-Cuban culture as "exotic" and as "sensual and mystical" in an effort to stimulate international consumption of national culture.[83]

Meanwhile, on the everyday level, Santería initiates can be seen dressing openly in sacred white garments, and it is not uncommon for children to bear names such as Ayamey—the orisha Yemaya spelled backward.[84] The popular resurgence and state appropriation of Yoruba-derived practices has signified a new level of cultural and religious tolerance and expression, transforming not only Yoruba-influenced practices but also reshaping the meaning of Cuban national identity, particularly representations crafted for foreign consumption on and off the island. Only future studies may be able to determine how much of this shift has been informed by the harsh realities of economic scarcity and ideological desperation caused by the Special Period.

In spite of countless attempts at suppression under colonial, new republic, and revolutionary regimes, the Yoruba and their descendants have continued to assert individual and group expression on multiple levels of society. For almost four centuries cabildos de nación provided the space for Lucumí to maintain and adapt Yoruba social, political, and cultural expressions in a new context. Through individual resistance, organized struggle, and covert practices, Yoruba-derived traditions fused with European structures, making Afro-Cuban expressions an intrinsic part of Cuban identity. Lucumí and Catholic belief systems meshed into Santería, which today has millions of practitioners throughout the world. Yoruba and Spanish musical traditions also intermingled to create son, forming the basis for internationally popular salsa music. Yoruba roots continue to be asserted in an array of new ways, from tourism to naming practices. This essay has attempted to demonstrate the major ways in which Yoruba traditions and influences shaped and fused with New World identities in Cuba, shifting, intertwining, and recasting these traits to become integral components in contemporary society. The rich and dynamic contributions of the Yoruba and their descendants are testaments to the enduring legacy of the Yoruba in Cuba.

Notes

1. Paul E. Lovejoy, "The African Diaspora: Revisionist Interpretations of Ethnicity, Culture, and Religion under Slavery," *Studies in the World History of Slavery, Abolition, and Emancipation* 2, no. 1 (1997), http://www2.h-net.msu.edu/~slavery/essays/esy9701love .html; Sidney W. Mintz, "Africa of Latin America: An Unguarded Reflection," in *Africa in Latin America: Essays on History, Culture, and Socialization,* ed. Manuel Moreno Fraginals (New York: Holmes and Meier, 1984), 286–305, 299; Rogelio Martínez Furé, "A National Cultural Identity? Homogenizing Monomania and the Plural Heritage," in *Afro-Cuban Voices: On Race and Identity in Contemporary Cuba,* ed. Pedro Pérez Sarduy and Jean Stubbs (Gainesville: University Press of Florida, 2000), 156–67; Marshall Salins, *Historical Metaphors and Mythical Realities: Structure in the Early History of the Sandwich Islands Kingdom* (Ann Arbor: University of Michigan Press, 1981), 7.

2. A. I. Asiwaju, "Dynamics of Yoruba Studies," in *Studies in Yoruba History and Culture: Essays in Honour of Professor S.O.L Biobaku,* ed. G. O. Olusanya (Ibadan, Nigeria: Ibadan University Press, 1983), 28; Robin Law, "The Atlantic Slave Trade in Yoruba Historiography," in *Yoruba Historiography,* ed. Toyin Falola (Madison, Wis.: African Studies Program, 1991), 123–24; Herbert S. Klein, *The Atlantic Slave Trade* (Cambridge: Cambridge University Press, 1999), 63.

3. Law, "The Atlantic Slave Trade," 123–24; Klein, *The Atlantic Slave Trade,* 63;

Jorge Castellanos and Isabel Castellanos, *Cultura Afro-Cubana: El negro en Cuba, 1492–1844*, 2 vols. (Miami: Ediciones Universal, 1988), 1:29; A. F. C. Ryder, "Dutch Trade on the Nigerian Coast during the Seventeenth Century," *Journal of the Historical Society of Nigeria* 3, no. 2 (1965): 196; "Valdes remite copia de varias comunicaciones dando cuenta de la aprehensión por los carabineros del puerto de Cabañas de 413 negros bozales llegados en un bergantín portugués," 31 May to 30 September 1841, Havana, Archivo Histórico Nacional, Madrid, Ultramar Collection, Cuba, Estado, 8037, Exp. 17 (hereafter, AHN-UCE).

4. Law, "The Atlantic Slave Trade," 123.

5. Klein, *The Atlantic Slave Trade*, 63; Law, "The Atlantic Slave Trade," 123.

6. Klein, *The Atlantic Slave Trade*, 63.

7. Fernando Ortiz, *Los negros esclavos* (Havana: Editorial de Ciencias Sociales, 1975 [1916]), 81–82; Castellanos and Castellanos, *Cultura Afro-Cubana: El negro en Cuba*, 42.

8. Castellanos and Castellanos, *Cultura Afro-Cubana: El negro en Cuba*, 42.

9. Klein, *The Atlantic Slave Trade*, 38.

10. José Antonio Saco, *Historia de la esclavitud: Desde los tiempos mas remotos hasta nuestros días* (Havana: "Alfa," 1937 [1879]), 4:318; Hugh Thomas, *Cuba: The Pursuit of Freedom* (New York: Harper and Row, 1971), 49–50; Manuel Moreno Fraginals, *El Ingenio: Complejo económico social cubano del azúcar*, 3 vols. (Havana: Editorial de Ciencias Sociales, 1978), 1:35–36; Pablo Tornero Tinajero, *Crecimiento económico y transformaciones sociales: Esclavos, hacendados y comerciantes en la Cuba colonial (1760–1840)* (Madrid: Ministerio de Trabajo y Seguridad Social, 1996), 35; and David R. Murray, *Odious Commerce: Britain, Spain, and the Abolition of the Cuban Slave Trade* (Cambridge: Cambridge University Press, 1980), 4.

11. Klein, *The Atlantic Slave Trade*, 38.

12. Ibid., 39.

13. Law, "The Atlantic Slave Trade," 123–25, 127, 131; Phillip Curtin, *The Atlantic Slave Trade: A Census* (Madison: University of Wisconsin Press, 1969), 248.

14. Law, "The Atlantic Slave Trade"; Toyin Falola, "The Yoruba Wars of the Nineteenth Century," in *Yoruba Historiography*, ed. Toyin Falola (Madison, Wis.: African Studies Program, 1991), 140.

15. Law, "The Atlantic Slave Trade"; Falola, "Yoruba Wars."

16. Klein, *The Atlantic Slave Trade*, 63.

17. Kenneth F. Kiple, *Blacks in Colonial Cuba, 1774–1899* (Gainesville: University Press of Florida, 1976), 84–86, 88–90; Ramón de la Sagra, *Cuba en 1860, o sea cuadro de sus adelantos en la población, la agricultura, el comercio y las rentas públicas. Suplemento a la primera parte de la historia política y natural de la isla de Cuba* (Paris: L. Hachette, 1863), 42.

18. Fernando Ortiz, *Los negros esclavos* (Havana: Editorial de Ciencias Sociales, 1975 [1916]), 101.

19. Klein, *The Atlantic Slave Trade*, 198.

20. Michael Crowder, *The Story of Nigeria* (London: Faber and Faber, 1973), 77.

21. Asiwaju, "Dynamics of Yoruba Studies," 28–29; Julia Cuervo Hewitt, "Yoruba Presence in Contemporary Cuban Narrative" (in Spanish) (Ph.D. dissertation, Vanderbilt University, 1981), 19; see also Ade Ajayi, "Samuel Ajayi Crowther of Oyo," in *Africa Remembered: Narratives by West Africans from the Era of the Slave Trade*, ed. Phillip D. Curtin, 2nd ed., 289–316 (Prospect Heights, Ill.: Waveland, 1997 [1967]).

22. Laird W. Bergad, Fe Iglesias García, and María del Carmen Barcia, *The Cuban Slave Market, 1790–1880* (Cambridge: Cambridge University Press, 1995), 72.

23. AHN-UCE.

24. Castellanos and Castellanos, *Cultura Afro-Cubana: El negro en Cuba*, 43; Curtin, *Atlantic Slave Trade*, 247; David Eltis, "The Export of Slaves from Africa, 1821–1843," *Journal of Economic History* 37 (1977): 419; Fraginals, *El Ingenio: Complejo económico social cubano del azúcar*, 2:9.

25. The term "Lucumí," with variations in spelling, was also used to denote the Yoruba in Venezuela, the Dominican Republic, and Puerto Rico. See also Rafael L. López Valdés, "Notas para el estudio etno-histórico de los esclavos lucumí de Cuba," *Anales del Caribe* 6 (1986): 54–74.

26. Hewitt, "Yoruba Presence," 19; Law, "The Atlantic Slave Trade," 123.

27. Alejandro de la Fuente García, "Esclavos africanos en la Habana: Zonas de Procedencia y denominaciones étnicas, 1570–1699," *Revista Española de Antropología Americana* 20 (1990): 135–50.

28. AHN-UCE.

29. López Valdés, "Notas para el estudio etno-histórico de los esclavos lucumí de Cuba," 72–73; Castellanos and Castellanos, *Cultura Afro-Cubana: El negro en Cuba*, 30.

30. Pedro Deschamps Chapeaux, *Los cimarrones urbanos* (Havana: Editorial de Ciencias Sociales, 1983), 42; Cabildo San Pedro Nolasco to Gobernador Político, Havana, 5 julio 1862, Archivo Nacional de Cuba, Havana (hereafter, ANC), Gobierno Superior Civil Collection, Leg. 1677, no. 83997; Morell de Santa Cruz, "El Obispo Morell de Santa Cruz oficializa los cabildos africanos donde nació la santería, convirtiéndolos en ermitas," Havana, 6 December 1755, in *Cuba: Economía y sociedad, del monopolio hacia la libertad comercial (1701–1763)*, 14 vols., ed. Levi Marrero, 159–60 (Madrid: Playor, 1980), 8:160.

31. Madan Sarup and Tasneem Raja, *Identity, Culture, and the Postmodern World* (Edinburgh: Edinburgh University Press, 1998), 171; Lovejoy, "The African Diaspora," http://www2.h-net.msu.edu/~slavery/essays/esy97011ove.html

32. Phillip A. Howard, *Changing History: Afro-Cuban Cabildos and Societies of Color in the Nineteenth Century* (Baton Rouge: Louisiana State University Press, 1998), 73–75, 78–79. For a detailed discussion of the conspiracies of 1812, 1835, and 1844, see José Luciano Franco, *La conspiración de Aponte de 1812* (Havana: Publicaciones del Archivo Nacional, 1963); Matt Childs, "The Aponte Rebellion of 1812 and the Transformation of Cuban Society: Race, Slavery, and Freedom in the Atlantic World" (Ph.D. dissertation, University of Texas at Austin, 2001); Robert L. Paquette, *Sugar Is Made with Blood: The Conspiracy of La Escalera and the Conflict between Empires over Slavery in Cuba* (Middleton, Conn.: Wesleyan University Press, 1988).

33. "Expediente seguido por la Sección de la Comissión Miliar residente en esta ciudad para cobran las costas causadas en la causa formada contra Gabriel de la Concepción — Placido," 30 June 1844, Havana, ANC-Asuntos Políticos, Leg. 42, no. 15.

34. Rhett Jones, "Why Pan-Africanism Failed: Blackness and International Relations," *The Griot* 14, no. 1 (1995): 53–70; Harlon Dalton, *Racial Healing: Confronting the Fear between Blacks and Whites* (New York: Doubleday, 1995), 107.

35. Pedro Deschamps Chapeaux, *El negro en la economía habanera del siglo XIX* (Havana: Unión de Escritores y Artistas de Cuba, 1971), 31.

36. Yvonne Daniel, *Rumba, Dance, and Social Change in Contemporary Cuba* (Bloomington: Indiana University Press, 1995), 34.

37. Fernando Ortiz, "Los cabildos afro-cubanos," *Revista Bimestre Cubana* 16 (January–February 1921): 9–15; Paquette, *Sugar Is Made with Blood*, 108; Howard, *Changing History*, 21.

38. Paquette, *Sugar Is Made with Blood*, 108, 127; Deschamps Chapeaux, *El negro en la economía*, 34– 42; Fernando Ortiz, *Los bailes y el teatro de los negros en el folklore de Cuba* (Havana: Letras Cubanas, 1981), 28.

39. Howard, *Changing History*, 20.

40. Ortiz, "Los cabildos afro-cubanos, 14.

41. Deschamps Chapeaux, *El negro en la economía*, 31.

42. Howard, *Changing History*, 21, 28; Franklin W. Knight, "Cuba," in *Neither Slave nor Free: The Freedman of African Descent in the Slave Societies of the New World*, ed. David W. Cohen and Jack P. Greene, 279–308 (Baltimore: The Johns Hopkins University Press, 1972), 301; Paquette, *Sugar Is Made with Blood*, 108; Deschamps Chapeaux, *El negro en la economía*, 31; Verena Martinez-Alier, *Marriage, Class, and Colour in Nineteenth Century Cuba: A Study of Racial Attitudes and Sexual Values in a Slave Society* (Ann Arbor: University of Michigan Press, 1989), 94.

43. José Luciano Franco, *Afroamericana* (Havana: Junta Nacional de Arqueología y Etnología, 1961), 129; Paquette, *Sugar Is Made with Blood*, 64.

44. Deschamps Chapeaux, *El negro en la economía*, 33–34; Howard, *Changing History*, 52, 55.

45. Paquette, *Sugar Is Made with Blood*, 109; Howard, *Changing History*, 39.

46. Howard, *Changing History*, 42.

47. Paquette, *Sugar Is Made with Blood*, 109; Howard, *Changing History*, 39.

48. Howard, *Changing History*, 36; Deschamps Chapeaux, *El negro en la economía*, 31.

49. Ortiz, "Los cabildos afro-cubanos," 9–10.

50. Antonio Bachiller y Morales, *Los Negros* (Barcelona: Gorgas y Compañia, n.d.), 114.

51. Victoria Eli Rodríguez, "Cuban Music and Black Ethnicity: Historical Considerations," in *Music and Black Ethnicity: The Caribbean and South America*, ed. Gerard Béhague, 91–108 (New Brunswick, N.J.: Transaction, 1994), 96.

52. Paquette, *Sugar Is Made with Blood*, 108, 125, 127; Deschamps Chapeaux, *El negro en la economía*, 43.

53. Howard, *Changing History*, 28, 36, 40.

54. George Brandon, *Santería from Africa to the New World: The Dead Sell Memories* (Bloomington: Indiana University Press, 1993), 1–2; Joseph M. Murphy, *Santería: African Spirits in America* (Boston: Beacon, 1993), 32; Castellanos and Castellanos, *Cultura Afro-Cubana: El negro en Cuba*, 11–12; Katherine J. Hagedorn, *Divine Utterances: The Performance of Afro-Cuban Santería* (Washington, D.C.: Smithsonian Institution Press, 2001), 253; Migene González-Wippler, *Santería, the Religion: A Legacy of Faith, Rites, and Magic* (New York: Harmony, 1989), 3, 7, 10; Rómulo Lachatañeré, *El sistema religioso de los Afro-Cubanos* (Havana: Editorial de Ciencias Sociales, 1992), 97; Michael Angelo Gomez, *Exchanging Our Country Marks: The Transformation of African Identities in the Colonial and Antebellum South* (Chapel Hill: University of North Carolina Press, 1998), 10; William Taylor, *Magistrates of the Sacred: Priests and Parishioners in Eighteenth-Century Mexico* (Stanford, Calif.: Stanford University Press, 1996), 5. For further discussion of syncretism of religions in the Americas, see Kenneth Mills, *Idolatry and Its Enemies: Colonial Andean Religion and Extirpation, 1640–1750* (Princeton, N.J.: Princeton University Press, 1997).

55. Edward D. Reynolds, *Jesuits for the Negro* (New York: America, 1949), 122.

56. See Robert Ricard, *The Spiritual Conquest of Mexico: An Essay on the Apostolate and the Evangelizing Methods of the Mendicant Orders in New Spain, 1523–1672* (Berkeley: University of California Press, 1966); Taylor, *Magistrates of the Sacred*, 53.

57. Morell de Santa Cruz, "El Obispo Morell de Santa Cruz," 159–61; Klein, *Slavery in the Americas*, 100.

58. Paquette, *Sugar Is Made with Blood*, 125; Murphy, *Santería*, 8–29, 113–14; Olga Roig Ribas, *Santería Yoruba: Magia, culto y sabiduría afroamericana* (Madrid: Ediciones Karma 7, 2001), 12–13.

59. Murphy, *Santería*, 113–14.

60. Jorge Castellanos and Isabel Castellanos, *Cultura Afro-Cubana: Las religiones y las lenguas*, 3 vols. (Miami: Ediciones Universal, 1998), 3:18; Roger Bastide, *African Civilizations in the New World* (New York: Harper and Row, 1971), 116; Robert Farris Thompson, *Flash of the Spirit: African and Afro-American Art and Philosophy* (New York: Vintage, 1984), xv.

61. Bastide, *African Civilizations*, 116; Thompson, *Flash of the Spirit*, xv.

62. Hagedorn, *Divine Utterances*, 212; González-Wippler, *Santería, the Religion*, 13; Carlos Canet, *Lucumí: Religion de los Yorubas en Cuba* (Miami: A.I.P., 1973), 29; Castellanos and Castellanos, *Cultura Afro-Cubana: Las religiones*, 27–57, 81.

63. Castellanos and Castellanos, *Cultura Afro-Cubana: Las religiones*, 27–57, 81; González-Wippler, *Santería, the Religion*, 4, 28–33, 37–41, 57–60; Nelson Valdés, "Fidel Castro (b. 1926), Charisma and Santería: Max Weber Revisited," in *Caribbean Charisma: Reflections on Leadership, Legitimacy, and Populist Politics*, ed. Anton Allahar, 212–41 (Boulder, Colo.: Lynne Rienner, 2001), 225, 233; Natalia Bolívar Arostegui, *Los Orishas en Cuba* (Havana: Ediciones Unión, 1990), 35–41, 79–80, 91–95, 107–108, 116–17.

64. María Elena Díaz, "Rethinking Tradition and Identity: The Virgin of Charity of El Cobre," in *Cuba, the Elusive Nation: Interpretations of National Identity*, ed. Damián J. Fernández and Madeline Cámara Betancourt (Gainesville: University Press of Florida, 2000), 43–59, 46.

65. Lydia Cabrera, *Anagó: Vocabulario Lucumí (el Yoruba que se habla en Cuba)* (Miami: Cabrera y Rojas, 1970), 15–16; Murphy, *Santería*, 33.

66. For a detailed discussion of Afro-Cuban participation in Cuban independence and quests for political equality, see Franco, *La Conspiración de Aponte*; Paquette, *Sugar Is Made with Blood*; Ada Ferrer, *Insurgent Cuba: Race, Nation, and Revolution, 1868–1898* (Chapel Hill: University of North Carolina Press, 1999); Aline Helg, *Our Rightful Share: The Afro-Cuban Struggle for Equality, 1886–1912* (Chapel Hill: University of North Carolina Press, 1995); Tomás Fernández Robaina, *El Negro en Cuba, 1902–1958: Apuntes para la historia de la lucha contra discriminación racial* (Havana: Editorial de Ciencias Sociales, 1994).

67. Robin D. Moore, *Nationalizing Blackness: Afro-Cubanismo and Artistic Revolution in Havana, 1920–1940* (Pittsburgh: University of Pittsburgh Press, 1997), 2.

68. Brandon, *Santería from Africa to the New World*, 92.

69. Daniel, *Rumba, Dance, and Social Change in Contemporary Cuba*, 118–19; Moore, *Nationalizing Blackness*, 2–3, 284–85.

70. Moore, *Nationalizing Blackness*, 2.

71. Brandon, *Santería from Africa to the New World*, 92–93.

72. Moore, *Nationalizing Blackness*, 134.

73. Eduardo Sánchez de Fuentes, "Bailes y canciones," in *Diario de la Marina. Número centenario* (Havana: Ucar, García y Cía., 1932), 101–102, 102; Emilio Roig de Leuchsenring, "Bailando junto al abismo," *Social* 17 (September 1932): 9, 12.

74. Leuchsenring, "Bailando junto al abismo," 80.

75. Brandon, *Santería from Africa to the New World*, 93.

76. John M. Kirk and Leonardo Padura Fuentes, *Culture and the Cuban Revolution: Conversations in Havana* (Gainesville: University Press of Florida, 2001), 67, 72.

77. Moore, *Nationalizing Blackness*, 221–24.

78. Brandon, *Santería from Africa to the New World*, 94; María Teresa Vélez, *Drumming for the Gods: The Life and Times of Felipe García Villamil, Santero, Palero, and Abakuá* (Philadelphia: Temple University Press, 2000), 71–72.

79. Moore, *Nationalizing Blackness*, 224–25; Carlos Moore, *Castro, the Blacks, and Africa* (Los Angeles: University of California, Center for Afro-American Studies, 1998), 315; Brandon, *Santería from Africa to the New World*, 100; Robin Moore, "Salsa and Socialism: Dance Music in Cuba, 1959–1999," in *Situating Salsa: Global Markets and Local Meanings in Latin Popular Music*, ed. Lise Waxer (New York: Routledge, 2002), 51–74, 63.

80. Brandon, *Santería from Africa to the New World*, 101; Vélez, *Drumming for the Gods*, 76; Moore, *Nationalizing Blackness*, 224–25; C. Moore, *Castro, the Blacks, and Africa*, 315.

81. Moore, *Nationalizing Blackness*, 225–26; Brandon, *Santería from Africa to the New World*, 101.

82. Moore, *Nationalizing Blackness*, 226.

83. Virginia R. Dominguez, "The Marketing of Heritage," *American Ethnologist* 13, no. 3 (1986): 546; Robert J. Foster, "Marketing National Cultures in the Global Ecumene," *Annual Review of Anthropology* 20 (1991): 249; Rogelio Martínez Furé, "A National Cultural Identity? Homogenizing Monomania and the Plural Heritage," in *Afro-Cuban Voices: On Race and Identity in Contemporary Cuba*, ed. Pedro Pérez Sarduy and Jean Stubbs (Gainesville: University Press of Florida, 2000), 154–61, 159; Rosalie Schwartz, *Pleasure Island: Tourism and Temptation in Cuba* (Lincoln: University of Nebraska Press, 1997), 87; Daniel, *Rumba, Dance, and Social Change*, 127.

84. Denise Blum, "Cuban Youth and Revolutionary Values: Alla en la lucha" (Ph.D. dissertation, University of Texas at Austin, 2002), 217.

CHAPTER SEVEN

Africans in a Colony of Creoles:
The Yoruba in Colonial Costa Rica

Russell Lohse

The Yoruba diaspora in Central America differed substantially from better-known examples such as that in Brazil, Cuba, and Trinidad, where Yoruba influence proved particularly strong. Colonial Costa Rica, arguably among the most isolated and neglected of all Spanish American colonies, developed no large-scale plantation economy dedicated to the export of staple crops, nor did large port cities emerge—conditions favoring the growth of African ethnic communities in other places. The slave trade to Central America had ended by the time the largest numbers of Yoruba-speaking slaves arrived elsewhere in the diaspora, and nowhere in the isthmus did the Yoruba become numerically dominant among African slaves.

These conditions ensured that the Yoruba slaves who arrived in Costa Rica constructed identities and cultural practices on lines other than the homelands, languages, or religions they had known in Africa, and in ways different than Yoruba in other periods and other parts of the diaspora. In Costa Rica their small numbers and geographic dispersal prevented Yoruba speakers from forming organizations, marrying endogamously, or otherwise maintaining cultural practices on exclusively Yoruba lines. Yet their origins remained important and formed the basis of an African-derived identity in Costa Rica. Shared understandings of enslavement and the middle passage encouraged bonding between captive Yoruba and natives of the Slave Coast. During the "seasoning" process, the Yoruba continued to reach out to shipmates of different ethnic origins. The shipmate bond, implying broader webs of relationships than either ethnicity or estate could provide in Costa Rica, became a key point of reference for enslaved Yoruba and other Africans. At the same time, sustained and intimate con-

130

tact promoted relationships with Creole blacks, mulattoes, Indians, mestizos, and Spaniards born in Costa Rica.

Unlike those of Cuba or Brazil, Costa Rican archives do not contain abundant documents pertaining to Lucumi or Nagô slaves, whether in shipping records, plantation inventories, criminal investigations of slave rebellions, or membership rolls of religious confraternities. These names rarely occur in Costa Rican documents, in part because few Yoruba arrived in the colony, but also because slave masters and authorities often confused Yoruba with members of other ethnic groups, such as the Popo or Arará of the Slave Coast, or identified them by unfamiliar names, such as Nangu and Aná. In this chapter I examine how the particularities of Costa Rican slavery shaped the experiences of a group of captive Yoruba carried on two specific slave ships. Before doing so, it is necessary to discuss at some length the sources which permit the identification of the Yoruba in Costa Rica.

Negros Bozales de Casta Aná: Identifying the Yoruba in Costa Rica

Although Yoruba-speaking captives, usually known as Lucumí, arrived in Spanish America from the sixteenth century, before about 1750 they could usually be counted in the dozens rather than the hundreds or thousands. In the sixteenth and early seventeenth centuries first Upper Guinea, then West-Central Africa supplied most of the Africans to the New World; few Yoruba speakers were sold into the early Atlantic slave trade.[1] Not until the mid-seventeenth century did the Bight of Benin become a major supplier of slaves to the Americas, earning the name "Slave Coast" and leading all African regions in the export of captives between 1700 and 1730.[2] Yoruba speakers comprised a significant share of these captives, but in the early eighteenth century they remained a minority of the hundreds of thousands of captives exported from the Slave Coast.[3]

As important to consider as trends in the African sources of slave supply are conditions in the American colonies receiving the Africans. For much of the colonial period, the *asiento* system restricted the legal Spanish American slave trade to a handful of authorized ports such as Veracruz, Havana, Cartagena, and Panama City. Before the mid-eighteenth century even Spanish American colonies with regular access to slave imports, such as Mexico, Peru, and Colombia, received scores of Yoruba at most, rather than hundreds or thousands.[4] In their small, isolated, and impoverished province, Costa Rican slave owners enjoyed no direct access to the African slave trade. Captives almost never— and never legally—arrived in large shipments directly from Africa. Masters usually purchased slaves singly or in small groups from the neighboring provinces of Panama and Nicaragua, and, as often as not, these were American-born Creoles. Yet despite their high cost and limited availability, African-born slaves remained in demand and continued to arrive throughout the colonial period, particularly in the late seventeenth and early eighteenth centuries, when the province briefly experienced a boom in cacao production.[5] To circumvent colonial trade restrictions, Costa Rican colonists turned to English and Dutch smugglers; although their proportion will never be known with certainty, "contraband" Africans may easily have surpassed those imported legally.[6] Occasionally shipwrecks of slavers bound elsewhere resulted in Costa Rican slave owners greedily snapping up the survivors.[7] Ironically these unforeseeable accidents provided some of the largest documented infusions of Africans into the colony.

One group of Yoruba-speaking captives reached Costa Rica by such an accident. The captains of the Danish slavers *Christianus Quintus* and *Fredericus Quartus* originally intended to sail not to Spanish Central America but to St. Thomas in the Danish West Indies. Between March and September 1709 the ships assembled their human cargoes on the Gold and Slave Coasts, in modern Ghana, Togo, and Benin. On 15 September some of the captives revolted aboard the ship while it was anchored off the Slave Coast; the crew killed the alleged leader and tortured an unspecified number of rebels as an example to the others before the *Fredericus Quartus* sailed for St. Thomas in October.[8] Because they steered wrong by a full three degrees latitude, the ships never reached the Danish sugar island. After being lost at sea for weeks, they finally arrived at a place on the mainland they called "Punta Carreto," which they believed to be in Nicaragua, on 2 March 1710. In fact, "Punta Carreto" was on the site of Punta Cahuita, now in the province of Limón, Costa Rica.[9] There, the Danish crews mutinied and boarded an English bark for Portobello, Panama, after putting ashore 650 African survivors on 4 March. The Africans immediately disappeared into the bush.[10]

A week later Costa Rican colonists captured a group of twenty-four Africans on the beach near Moín, more than thirty-one miles, or fifty kilometers, north of Cahuita.[11] They identified these Africans as belonging to the "castas" (or "nations") Arará, Mina, and Carabalí—names associated, respectively, with the Slave Coast, the Gold Coast, and the Bight of Biafra.[12] On 23 April a second group of forty-five Africans was captured; these men and women were all identified as of casta Mina.[13] Within the next few days, another contingent of Spanish colonists apprehended a third group of twenty-six Africans. When Captain Don Juan Francisco de Ibarra presented sixteen Africans—four men and twelve women—in Cartago on 11 June 1710, they were all described as members of the same casta, this time the casta Nangu. The rest of the Africans had died, Ibarra claimed: one had succumbed to illness in Matina, and nine drowned when the canoe carrying them capsized in the Reventazón River.[14]

In fact, no such drowning accident ever occurred, as authorities suspected at the time, and these nine Africans remained very much alive in Costa Rica. Despite persistent inquiries backed by threats of torture, no incriminating evidence could be amassed against Ibarra for almost a decade.[15] But in 1719 these

Africans themselves testified to how Ibarra had selected them for his own use or to sell to other interested parties. Their testimonies provide unexpected insight into how Yoruba identity was concealed and revealed in Costa Rica.

The sixteen Nangu Africans whom Ibarra brought to Cartago and the nine he illegally appropriated were two parts of the same original group of twenty-six, captured together.[16] Nangu probably represents an early variant of Nagô, a term first attested in 1725 as referring to a western Yoruba "subgroup," and later more broadly applied to Yoruba speakers generally.[17] Applied by Aja-, Ewe-, and Fon-speaking peoples of the Slave Coast to western Yoruba, the term likely entered the documentary record through Francisco, the Slave Coast native of casta Arará who served as interpreter to the captured Africans.[18] Alternatively the Africans may have identified themselves as Nangu: "Anagô" (probably the origin of the name Nagô) is the self-designation of a southwestern Yoruba subgroup in the Ipokia / Itakete area in the southeast of modern Benin.[19]

The relationship of the names Nagô and Lucumí to Yoruba identity has provoked a lively debate among Africanist scholars. Historian Biodun Adediran contended that the word "Lucumí" was broadly used in the Americas to refer to all Yoruba subgroups, reflecting an existing pan-Yoruba identity in Africa. This identity grew strongest, he argued, in frontier regions where Yoruba speakers continually confronted members of other ethnic and linguistic groups, and, in turn, became more aware of the commonalities that united them with other Yoruba.[20] However, historian Robin Law suggested that, before the 1720s, many Yoruba-speaking captives came from southern Yorubaland, a region he associated with the name "Lucumí." After that time western Yoruba speakers known as Nagô entered the slave trade in increasing numbers, as they fell victim to the raids of the expanding states of Dahomey and Oyo.[21] In the earliest records, Law argued, "Nagô" and "Lucumí" were used distinctively and clearly referred to discrete groups; neither word was yet applied to all Yoruba speakers.[22]

The Costa Rican documentation contributes to the continuing debate on Yoruba ethnicity by providing evidence to link the Nagô with the Lucumí in the early eighteenth century, just as the sources of Yoruba-speaking captives entering the trans-Atlantic slave trade were shifting decisively from south to west. María and Petrona were captured in Matina by Captain Don Juan Francisco de Ibarra, along with the group called Nangu.[23] As Adediran and Law agree, in West Africa "Nagô" designated western Yoruba speakers.[24] When asked their castas in 1719, both María and Petrona replied that "their casta among themselves is called Saná, and among the Spaniards Lucumí."[25] Saná appears to be a variant of Aná, as the same women were so described in a bill of sale in 1710. Another document from the same year specified that María was a *"negra bozal* [a black female recently arrived from Africa] *of casta aná, according to her response."*[26] The name "Aná" may be associated with the Ana, the name of a western Yoruba subgroup in modern Togo and Benin.[27] The Ana would naturally have been called Nagô (Nangu) by speakers of Ewe, Aja, or Fon—such as Francisco, the interpreter of casta Arará—and, as María and Petrona specified, were associated with the Lucumí by the Spaniards. The women also made clear that "Lucumí" was not the name of the Aná for themselves. Both the terms "Nagô" ("Nangu") and "Lucumí," previously thought in this period to refer exclusively to distinct Yoruba subgroups, were used in Costa Rica to refer to members of the same group of Yoruba-speaking individuals.[28]

María and Petrona were almost certainly loaded on the *Christianus Quintus* in 1709, either at Popo on the upper Slave Coast in modern Togo or at Ouidah, in modern Benin.[29] In either case, they surely came from a western frontier Yoruba population, surrounded by Ewe- and Aja-speaking groups. Perhaps, as Adediran has argued, such contacts contributed to the development of an enhanced sense of linguistic and cultural commonality with other Yoruba speakers.[30] This would explain María's and Petrona's identification with the Lucumí, a term which Law contended applied mainly to southern Yoruba, despite the fact that their own origins were surely in the west. But if, in Africa, western Yoruba developed a heightened consciousness of difference from the Ewe and Aja, the experience of enslavement and the middle passage tended to bring the groups together. Despite their differences, the peoples of Yorubaland and the Slave Coast shared cultural ties centuries old, which could be deepened and strengthened through the crucible of the slave trade and slavery.

Thunder Gods in Central America

On 16 April 1710, about a month after they arrived at Punta Cahuita, several of the Africans recaptured near Moín were interviewed in Cartago by Francisco, a Slave Coast native of casta Arará, who served as interpreter.[31] Among the questions Francisco posed was a rare request for an African account of the middle passage. He spoke first to an African man called Juan, who explained that he had been given that name on the beaches of Matina.[32] When found on the beach "the black men and women had no names at all," slave catcher Gaspar de Acosta Arévalo claimed; he and Juan Bautista de Retana had named each of them as they were captured, presumably to tell them apart.[33] Although their captors identified these Africans as of the castas Mina (Gold Coast or upper Slave Coast), Arará (Slave Coast), and Carabalí (Bight of Biafra), at least some of these designations were mistaken. Agustina, a Yoruba who identified herself as of casta Aná, later recalled that she had been brought to Cartago by Retana, establishing that these captives included Yoruba as well as people of Slave Coast and Gold Coast origin.[34] Through the experience they shared and to the extent that they shared understandings of that experience, Juan told Agustina's story as well. His narrative suggests contemporary Slave Coast and Yoruba attitudes toward the morality of the trans-Atlantic slave trade, constituting a rare account of the middle passage from the perspective of the Africans enslaved.

"Juan," described as a black man of casta Arará, explained that he was more than forty years old, a native of "Guinea," and that "they stole him from his country and put him with many others of his casta in one of three ships that were anchored" offshore.[35] One of the ships, he said, burned at sea, killing all onboard; the other two ships wandered at sea for a long time, when one of them was lost. The remaining ship, Juan related, was taken by "the people" and, having sighted land, was making for it when they met with "a great storm, [and] many bolts of lightning struck the ship, killing the captain and many people."[36] Their ship badly damaged, those in command sailed off in two canoes after bringing the Africans ashore. The Africans saw no one else until seven men captured them and took them to a place Juan learned was called Matina, where one of the Africans died.[37] With a few slight differences, two more African men, called Nicolás and Miguel, repeated Juan's testimony almost verbatim.[38]

The narratives of Juan, Nicolás, and Miguel can be confronted with the more detailed accounts of the voyage later offered by Danish sailors. The *Christianus Quintus* and *Fredericus Quartus* each stopped at numerous ports on the Gold and Slave Coasts before sailing for the West Indies. On 15 September 1709 some of the captives revolted aboard the ship while it was anchored off the Slave Coast; the crew responded by killing the alleged leader and torturing an unspecified number of rebels as an example to the others.[39] On 28 September the two ships departed the "Guinea Coast"; by then, 49 Africans on the *Fredericus Quartus* had already died. After months at sea, the ships should have been approaching the eastern Caribbean. By 8 February it was painfully clear that the ships had steered badly off course. Food supplies dwindled to a critical level; by 18 February, 135 Africans and 25 crew members had died.[40]

Desperate, the ships' officers decided to abandon St. Thomas as a destination and instead sell their slave cargoes in Portobello, Panama's Atlantic port. The two ships started for Portobello, but a severe storm blew them off course to Punta Cahuita, where the Danes met two English fishing barks on 2 March 1710. When Captain Diedrich Pfeiff insisted that they again head for Portobello, the crew mutinied, putting the Africans ashore on 4 March to spare what scant provisions remained for themselves. On the night of 7 March 1710 the mutineers burned the *Fredericus Quartus* and then allowed the *Christianus Quintus* to run aground in the surf. After destroying the slave ships, some of the Danes forced the Englishmen to carry them to Portobello in two barks.[41]

Despite some points in common, the narratives of Juan, Nicolás, and Miguel differed strikingly from those offered by the Danish sailors. Juan, Nicolás, and Miguel spoke of three ships "that had anchored, and from there they went to sea."[42] Their claim that a third ship was burned at sea, and that all onboard perished, finds no echo in the Danish account—the Danes mentioned neither a third ship nor such a holocaust. At some point in the crossing, the Africans said, a second ship was "lost"; again, the Danes recalled no such mishap, and, according to their account, the two ships remained together.[43] The most dramatic divergence in the African and Danish accounts emerged in the Africans' description of the fate of the last remaining ship. Juan alleged that it had been struck by "many bolts of lightning, . . . killing the captain and many people." The Danes also recalled a severe storm, which had blown them off their intended course to Cahuita. But, according to the Danes, the ships had been destroyed by mutineers, not by a storm. They mentioned no lightning strikes; those Danish crew members who perished died from starvation and disease; and neither Captain Diedrich Pfeiff of the *Fredericus Quartus* nor Captain Anders Wærøe of the *Christianus Quintus* had been killed or even injured—indeed, both eventually returned to Europe.[44]

Some of these discrepancies may be plausibly explained. The sources make no mention of the specific language in which Francisco conducted his interviews; it is possible that he misunderstood, and very likely that he embellished, some of what was told to him. The translated testimony as it was preserved can only faintly echo what the Africans said, and what they intended by what they said. For example, "Juan" almost certainly never said that he was from "Guinea," and it is unlikely he claimed to be of "casta Arará"—Francisco offered these glosses as a translator seeking to distill and convey the sense of what he heard in terms comprehensible to his Spanish-speaking audience.

In the brief accounts they narrated to Francisco, Juan, Nicolás, and Miguel summarized, edited, and recast the horrific events of the past several months. They conspicuously omitted the shipboard slave rebellion, which the crew had punished with execution and torture; they made no mention of the hundreds of Africans who died of disease and starvation; nor did they refer to the many stops the ships made on their wayward journey to Cahuita. But the Africans not only failed to relate all they had seen but they also related things they had not seen. The captives almost certainly could not have witnessed the destruction of the ships, as they took flight on 4 March, and the ships were not destroyed until three days later. It seems unlikely that they witnessed the burning of a first ship or the "loss" of a second ship at sea, even the existence of which cannot be verified. I suggest that in the accounts they offered to Francisco, these Africans meant to tell another story based on their own cultural values and understandings.

By 1710 Francisco, the slave interpreter, had lived in Costa Rica for at least eight years.[45] As a "*ladino* in our Castilian language," he was beyond doubt conversant in Spanish and understood the connotations of the words he chose in translation.[46] Slaves in Costa Rica, even Africans, almost never used words such as "stolen" (*hurtado*) or "taken" (*cogido*) to describe their enslavement. When they did, it was in specific reference to seizure by force. For example, "Congo" slave Felipe Cubero, a West-Central African, claimed to have been brought to Costa Rica by Spaniards who seized him (*lo cogieron*) on the beach near Cartagena, Colombia, after he ventured outside the city to hunt iguanas.[47] Antonio Civitola, also a "Congo," said he had been captured (*lo cogieron*) by Miskito Indians in Matina, who later sold him to his Costa Rican master.[48] Micaela, a Yoruba of casta Aná, recalled that Don Juan Francisco de Ibarra had captured her with many of her shipmates (*los cogieron*) on the Matina coast.[49] These descriptions all referred to unusual situations in which the Africans had been seized through overpowering force.

The word "stolen" (*hurtado*) was used still more rarely; in fact, apart from its usage by Juan, Nicolás, and Miguel, I have found only one other case in which an African used the word to refer to his enslavement. In 1720 Miguel Largo, probably from the upper Slave Coast, testified in broken Spanish that he had been "stolen [when he was] little in the Mina country" (*lo hurtaron chiquito en la tierra de mina*).[50] Without implying that enslaved Africans were content with their condition in either Africa or America, they came overwhelmingly from societies that recognized the legitimacy and legality of slaveholding in prescribed circumstances.[51] Africans in Costa Rica may have emphasized that they were "stolen" when referring to circumstances in which their enslavement occurred outside the usual mechanisms such as sale or pawnship by kin members, judicial enslavement, or even capture in war, which would have been better translated as "being seized" (*ser cogido*). When Africans claimed to have been "stolen," I suspect that they meant to say something especially pointed by the word: they were free people who had been "stolen" by "thieves" who had no right to hold them as slaves—in this case, the Danes.

Around 1715 an anonymous French observer described the worship of a thunder god by natives of the Slave Coast kingdom of Ouidah, who was said to punish thieves by hurling lightning bolts.[52] This figures among the first documentary references to So, the Slave Coast god (vodun) of thunder and lightning, who is also frequently known as Hevieso because of his original association with the town of Hevié.[53] Among the most powerful and feared of all vodun, Hevieso visits his vengeance on wrongdoers by hurling his double-edged axes in the form of lightning bolts. When lightning flashes, Hevieso strikes down a victim with his unerring axe. Trees felled by lightning were believed to be the gathering places of witches, which Hevieso destroyed in order to deny them cover for their evil workings. Hevieso never missed his target; if lightning was sighted but no victim or damage found, he had simply struck down a guilty party elsewhere.[54]

Hevieso, the thunder vodun of the Ewe, Aja, and Fon pantheons, is explicitly linked to Shango, the thunder god (orisha) of the Yoruba.[55] Indeed, the two share many identical attributes including the double-edged axe, the hurling of lightning bolts as stone fragments which must be retrieved by priests, and the special vengeance visited on thieves.[56] Although the origins of the relationship between the Slave Coast cults of Hevieso and the Yoruba cults of Shango have not yet been established, by the early eighteenth century cultural exchange, including the exchange of religious elements, between the Slave Coast peoples and the Yoruba was well cemented and perhaps many centuries old.[57] The same anonymous Frenchman who described the worship of the thunder god noted the prominence of Yoruba priests in Ouidah around 1715.[58] Although ultimately the most widely celebrated, Shango was only one of the thunder gods revered by Yoruba-speaking peoples. Jakuta, identified with both Shango and

Hevieso by the twentieth century, may once have presided over an older, independent cult. Among western Yoruba in what is now Benin, Ara reigned as the local thunder god before later becoming associated with Shango. Both shared a complex of mythic qualities with Shango and Hevieso, including their punishment of thieves by lightning.[59]

By 1710 thunder gods such as Hevieso, Shango, Jakuta, and Ara were widely venerated and similarly conceived throughout the Slave Coast and western Yorubaland. The thunder god controlled a fearful natural force that he unleashed not at random but instead directed at his enemies who violated earthly laws. I have suggested that Africans in Costa Rica claimed they were "stolen" when they wanted to emphasize that they had been wrongfully enslaved by "thieves" who had no right to their persons. Without any traditionally sanctioned authority, the Danes tore kinspeople from the lineages to which they belonged. Like witches, for their own selfish and greedy motives, they fomented chaos in society, disordering sacred bonds of kinship and community. The malicious ability of the Danes to twist supernatural forces to their own ends became evident in their navigation of the open sea, another world to Slave Coast and Yoruba peoples without seafaring traditions.[60] But other awesome powers existed to meet them. The thunder god avenged such crimes by hurling lightning bolts at thieves and witches who violated the moral order.

In the religious worldview of the Slave Coast and Yorubaland, the Danes who stole the Africans from their country had incurred the predictable result of a violent thunderstorm. Because the lightning of the thunder god never missed its target, the Africans assured their interviewer that the captain and his crew of man stealers had been struck down in a great storm that restored a measure of justice to the earth.[61] Lightning also destroyed their slave ships, as it felled the trees that sheltered witches, and for the same reasons: both harbored evil. The narrative offered by the Ararás Juan, Nicolás, and Miguel would have made perfect sense to the Aná Agustina and other Yoruba onboard. Hidden in its confusing details were traces of the cultural understandings that gave meaning to the shared and particular experiences of enslavement and the middle passage which had brought them to Costa Rica.

Yoruba Lives in a Colony of Creoles

Surely the Yoruba who arrived in Costa Rica on the *Christianus Quintus* and *Fredericus Quartus* "interpreted their lived experiences in terms of their personal histories, as anyone would, and in that sense the African side of the Atlantic continued to have meaning," as Paul Lovejoy has argued of enslaved African immigrants in general.[62] Inevitably they understood the painful new world in which they found themselves in their own cultural terms. At the same time, of necessity, they formed new relationships, confronted new cultures, and were forced into new labor regimes. Africans' first months in America constituted a harrowing "seasoning" process, in which they strengthened bonds with one another even as they forcibly adapted to slavery. Like the barracoons of African slaving factories and the middle passage itself, the first American estates where Africans arrived constituted important sites of cultural exchange.[63]

In 1720 María and Petrona, Yoruba slaves of "casta Aná or Lucumí," recalled how they had been captured on the Matina coast ten years before.[64] After apprehending twenty-six Africans near Moín on 24 April 1710, Captain Don Juan Francisco de Ibarra and his companions drove the blacks to Ibarra's cacao hacienda in Matina, where they held them for several days. Some of the Africans were "very maltreated," and all were "starving to death"; indeed, one man died in Matina. [65] After a few weeks Ibarra transported the Africans to the Central Valley, a perilous journey over scorching plains, winding mountain trails, and torrential rivers that is traditionally overestimated at "fifty leagues" (171 miles, or 275 kilometers), which could last from ten days to a month or more.[66] Petrona recalled traveling "day and night" by an "Indian road where there is a hammock"—a reference to the inland road through the territory of the Talamanca Indians, where a tenuous 32-meter footbridge spanned the Reventazón River.[67] At a chosen point Ibarra separated María and Petrona, three other black females, and four black males from the rest of the group. Concocting a story for official consumption that they had drowned, Ibarra took the nine to his "country house" about one league (3.4 miles, or 5.5 kilometers) outside Cartago, sending the remaining sixteen Africans on to the capital.[68]

Ibarra soon put the nine young Africans to work in a maize field on his property.[69] Undoubtedly they formed close relationships during those difficult first months in Costa Rica, and the Yoruba majority of that small group exercised a strong and lasting influence on their two non-Yoruba companions. Indeed, "María Popo" became so closely identified with the Yoruba that in later years her master and government officials consistently referred to her as of casta Aná, although she herself declared her casta as Popo.[70] As a native of the Slave Coast, María Popo was certainly familiar with elements of Yoruba culture, and very likely had had contact with Yoruba speakers—perhaps even the Aná—while still in Africa; she may even have been able to converse with them. In the context of common enslavement in Costa Rica, such cultural ties deepened and took on intimate dimensions. Despite their different ethnic origins, María Popo later referred to the Yoruba Micaela, her shipmate and companion in Ibarra's country house, as "her sister."[71] The Mina youth later called Manuel de Utrera, probably a native of the Gold Coast or upper Slave Coast, was also adopted by his Yoruba fellow slaves. Despite years of separation, when they saw him again ten years later, María and Petrona unhesitatingly identified Manuel as one of their companions in Ibarra's country house, and said that he was called "in their language, Papa Ligua."[72] Just as he received a new Spanish name from his captors, "Manuel" received a new African name from his enslaved Yoruba companions. And although he claimed his own casta as Mina, more than twenty years later Manuel remained identified with the Yoruba "casta Na."[73]

After this period of "seasoning" near Cartago, the Yoruba were divided and sold to different masters throughout Costa Rica's three major ecological and economic zones—the North Pacific, the Central Valley, and the Atlantic lowlands. In September 1710 María and Petrona were driven about 200 miles, or 323 kilometers, to San Francisco de Tenorio, the hacienda of Doña Cecilia Vázquez de Coronado in the North Pacific Valley of Bagaces.[74] Separated from Costa Rica's Central Valley by a volcanic mountain range and several often-impassable rivers, the region developed strong economic and cultural links to Nicaragua and Panama.[75] Dominated by large landholdings devoted to cattle- and mule-breeding, Bagaces developed a highly mobile, ethnically and culturally diverse population. In 1688, 110 blacks and mulattoes made up about 37 percent of the valley's total population of 297, including 17 slaves (about 5.7 percent).[76] Almost certainly María and Petrona were the only Yoruba speakers in the region; there were no other members of their "nation" to whom they could turn for help in their adjustment.[77] Although they surely encountered blacks and mulattoes in Bagaces, whether free or slave, these were virtually all Creoles. Even the cattle and mules which so dominated the landscape must have seemed strange at first, foreign as they were to most areas of Yorubaland.[78]

The closest relationships María and Petrona formed were, of necessity, with members of other ethnic and cultural groups. Although most Bagaces landowners preferred to live in the more comfortable cities of Cartago or Rivas, Nicaragua, Doña Cecilia Vázquez de Coronado and her husband, Sergeant Major Don Salvador Suárez de Lugo, made the less usual choice to reside at San Francisco de Tenorio year-round.[79] No doubt they played powerful roles in the lives of their slaves. When María and Petrona were baptized in the city of Esparza after sixteen months in Bagaces, their masters stood as their godparents.[80] Nothing is known of the fathers of María's and Petrona's four children, except, perhaps, that they were not Africans: all the children were described as mulattoes.[81] Like virtually all slaves in Bagaces, the other slaves at San Francisco de Tenorio, including María Egipciaca and her two young children, Mónica de la Cruz and José Francisco, were almost certainly all Creoles.[82] Inevitably the relationships María and Petrona formed derived more from their local experiences in Bagaces than from Africa. Although María and Petrona had each other, perhaps continued to speak Yoruba, and shared memories spanning the Atlantic Ocean and a decade in slavery, the geography and demographic structure of the Valley of Bagaces militated powerfully against the preservation of their Yoruba heritage. They lived in a Creole world.

In 1719 Micaela, still a slave of Don Juan Francisco de Ibarra, recalled that soon after María and Petrona were taken away nine years earlier, Ibarra returned and, as compensation for his role in their capture, claimed Micaela, then fourteen; Agustina, twenty; and Manuel, sixteen, all Yoruba of casta Aná.[83] A short time later *Alférez* (Standard-Bearer) Bernardo Pacheco—another of the slave catchers—sold Sebastiana, who was eighteen to twenty years old and also a Yoruba, to Ibarra, her initial captor.[84] Having himself taken a hand in their capture, Ibarra exercised an unusually direct, violent, and personal form of domination over the four Yoruba youths.

As young women, Micaela, Agustina, and Sebastiana probably worked primarily in and around Ibarra's main home in Cartago. In his adobe house, roofed with tiles in a city where most dwellings were made of straw, Ibarra covered his walls with twelve religious paintings and furnished his rooms with tortoiseshell trunks, Chinese silks, and books on Spanish law.[85] As Costa Rican historian Rina Cáceres has argued, Cartago slaves inhabited "the space of the colonial elite, with its goods and values"; beyond doubt, their contact with Spanish society was constant, direct, intimate, sometimes brutal—Ibarra also kept two pairs of shackles.[86] And yet, even for Micaela, Agustina, and Sebastiana—whose master had literally captured them—there were other spaces. Precisely because Cartago's elite families owned the largest numbers of slaves, the city offered daily opportunities for contact with fellow Africans.

Groups of West-Central Africans (Congo and Angola) as well as natives of the Gold Coast (Mina), the Slave Coast (Arará and Popo), and Upper Guinea (Mandinga) could all be found in Cartago among more numerous mulatto and Creole slaves.[87] In the capital it proved possible for Africans to preserve specific ethnic identities and languages. At the same time the small numbers and mixture of Africans of different origins, along with the unabated dominance of Creole culture, worked against this. For example, in 1720 Antonia de Aguilar knew she had been born in Africa but did "not know her casta because she [did] not understand any language" spoken by other Africans.[88] While she made clear that Africans spoke several languages in Cartago, Antonia knew none of them, and she did not identify herself on the basis of any of the major African ethnic groupings recognized in Costa Rica. She was far from unusual in that respect: when asked directly, no fewer than twenty-three of eighty-two (28%) African slaves interviewed replied that they did "not know their casta," while 59 (72%) replied with a specific casta name. Africans who did "not know" their casta outnumbered those who claimed any single ethnic origin.[89] Not surprisingly age at the time of arrival played a crucial role in ethnic memory: one man specified that he did "not remember" his casta; several others explained that they did not know their "nation" because they had arrived in Costa Rica when they were "small."[90]

Yet if identification with specific African ethnicities might fade, the fact of birth in Africa and relationships formed in the course of the middle passage and "seasoning" remained important. In a classic essay, anthropologists Sidney Mintz and Richard Price argued that the relationship between shipmates emerged as one of the earliest and most enduring institutions among enslaved Africans.[91] After years or even decades in slavery in Costa Rica, Africans typically knew the whereabouts of their shipmates despite separation by time and distance. Ties between shipmates sometimes assumed the force of kinship.[92] About thirty years old in 1719, María, a slave of María Calvo, had arrived as a young girl and did "not know her casta," although her face bore the identifying ritual scars common to many West African ethnic groups. Nevertheless she had a "sister," María Victoria, who had arrived on the same ship. María Victoria—also unable to name her casta—did not call María her sister but did state that they were shipmates.[93] María Popo, a native of the Slave Coast, referred to the Yoruba Micaela as "her sister." Although the women claimed different ethnic origins, they had been shipmates and companions during "seasoning" in Ibarra's country house.[94]

Africanist John K. Thornton has argued that because few New World estates were populated by arrivals from the same ships, the shipmate bond could rarely provide a basis for common identity.[95] But in Costa Rica, a colony where the arrival of a shipload of Africans constituted a memorable occasion and where slaveholdings were limited, the shipmate bond transcended boundaries of estate and ethnicity and, for Africans, could mean a broader web of relationships than either of those groupings allowed. In any case, these ties did not exclude each other, as shipmates and slaves on the same estate could help reinforce ethnic identity in those who had arrived too young to remember Africa. If the shipmate bond could help Africans constitute new identities, it could also help them to maintain old ones.[96] Pedro de Rosas, for example, said that "he does not know which one might be" his casta, but that "who will be able to say is Pedro Mina, . . . his shipmate [*carabela*]."[97] Fellow slaves on the same estate could also reinforce ethnic identity. Although Pedro himself could not recall, having arrived twenty years earlier as a young boy, "from what his companions have told him, his mother was of casta Congo."[98]

The Yoruba Micaela, Agustina, Sebastiana, and Manuel found other shipmates not only in Cartago but even in their master's household. By 1719 Don Juan Francisco de Ibarra and his wife, Doña Catalina González del Camino, owned fourteen slaves, including two other shipmates of their Yoruba slaves.[99] Probably at the same time that he purchased Sebastiana, Ibarra bought Juan, a boy of casta Popo from the upper Slave Coast, about ten years old, from the *alférez* Bernardo Pacheco.[100] Paul Lovejoy and David Trotman have stated that African children were often "adopted" by members of their ethnic groups in American slave communities.[101] It is easy to imagine that the Yoruba Agustina, Micaela, Sebastiana, and Manuel similarly took an interest in the welfare of their younger shipmate.

Two young Yoruba men, Felipe and Francisco, slaves of another mistress, also lived with shipmates at the home of Doña Nicolasa Guerrero, just outside the Indian pueblo of Ujarrás, three leagues (10.25 miles, or 16.5 kilometers) east of Cartago. In 1711 Costa Rican governor Don Lorenzo Antonio de la Granda y Balbín presented the young men and two African girls of unknown ethnic origin, Catalina and María Gertrudis, to Guerrero, his longtime mistress and mother of his illegitimate daughter. All four Africans had arrived on the Danish slavers and been captured on the beaches of Matina.[102] Both described as sixteen years old at the time, Felipe and Francisco had been held with other Yoruba in Don Juan Francisco de Ibarra's country house, as had the

Mina Manuel de Utrera, of Gold Coast or upper Slave Coast origin, who lived nearby. Several other Africans also lived in Ujarrás, including shipmate Nicolasa Mina and Josefa Arará, a native of the Slave Coast.[103]

In addition to the relationships they maintained with their shipmates and with slaves of similar cultural background on nearby estates, Felipe and Francisco interacted daily with free workers. Like many Spaniards who lived on the plains around Ujarrás, Doña Nicolasa Guerrero planted and milled sugar cane, and also raised cattle and horses.[104] Costa Rican sugar production remained on a small scale, and, unlike in other parts of the Americas, sugar never became synonymous with slavery. Where slaves grew sugar, they usually toiled alongside free workers.[105] Felipe and Francisco surely shared duties with José Miguel, an orphan Guerrero had raised and whom she designated to oversee her properties after her death.[106] When not clearing land, planting, weeding, cutting, hauling, or processing cane, the men would have tended Guerrero's cattle and horses, and grown food for the household. At the time of the sugar harvest, Catalina and María Gertrudis no doubt joined in the work; other local workers were almost certainly hired as well.

While Felipe and Francisco shared their Aná origins and undoubtedly the Yoruba language, Catalina and María Gertrudis shared their experiences of the middle passage and recapture on the Matina coast. As each adjusted to conditions in Ujarrás, their shipmates and companions formed part of that experience as well. But although Yoruba slaves forged strong relationships among their shipmates and fellow Africans, they could rarely be stable ones. Separation through sale threatened all relationships between slaves. By 1717 Guerrero had sold Francisco to Captain Gabriel Maroto.[107] Although their relationship can only be guessed at, it is suggestive that Catalina named a son Francisco, born around that time.[108] In 1722 Felipe, too, left the household, when Doña Nicolasa Guerrero exchanged him for another slave.[109]

For slaves whose relationships were shadowed by uncertainty, and especially for females, whose sexual lives were often dictated by their masters, marriage sanctioned by the Catholic Church—theoretically precluding separation by sale and limiting a woman's sexual availability to her husband—held important implications. Although the marriage registers of Cartago's parish church, beginning in 1664, are admittedly incomplete, the Yoruba Agustina is the first enslaved woman to appear in them. On 3 May 1733 she married Antonio García of casta Mina, a fellow slave of Don Juan Francisco de Ibarra, and probably a native of the Gold Coast.[110] Twenty-three years after arriving in Costa Rica, Agustina's Yoruba origin constituted only one factor in her relationships. Even if she had wanted to marry a fellow Yoruba, the overlapping shipmate relationship, as important in Costa Rica as ethnic ties, might have precluded it.[111] Other considerations, such as birth in Africa, survival of the middle passage, and ownership by the same master—qualities that could assume importance only in the context of New World slavery—might, by then, have seemed more important to Agustina.

143

In addition to the bonds Yoruba women developed with their fellow slaves, they undeniably—not to say voluntarily—formed intimate relationships with members of their master's family. We cannot know how Micaela felt about caring for Don Juan Francisco de Ibarra's children, especially when at least three of her own children had died by 1719.[112] When Ibarra died in 1737 Micaela passed to the service of his son, Captain Don Miguel Cayetano de Ibarra.[113] After thirty-six years of serving his family, Micaela was freed by the younger Ibarra in 1746, when she was about fifty-two years old. Although he may well have sought to avoid providing for Micaela in her advancing years, he claimed to have done so "attending to how well she has served me, and for having raised me."[114] Micaela was the only one of the Yoruba to win her freedom.

While Micaela and Agustina served in Don Juan Francisco de Ibarra's Cartago home until his death, Ibarra sent the Yoruba Manuel to work on his cacao haciendas in the Atlantic lowlands of the Matina Valley.[115] If slave women lived under the noses of their masters, male slaves on the cacao haciendas of Matina, more than a hundred miles away, enjoyed remarkable autonomy. Cartago hacienda owners generally trusted the cultivation, harvest, transport, and sometimes sale of cacao to their slaves, visiting their Matina landholdings only a few times each year. Much of the rest of the time slaves lived alone or in small groups of two or three in crude houses on the haciendas, largely unsupervised by whites.[116] They found their independence increased by a circumstance particular to Costa Rica, where a chronic silver shortage led to the adoption of cacao as legal currency.[117] The direct access of Matina slaves to the crop gave them a rare bargaining power. They often cultivated cacao groves on their own account, amassing capital that they used to acquire needed goods and, increasingly in the eighteenth century, to purchase their own freedom.[118]

Life and work in Matina brought Manuel into regular contact with other Africans, possibly including Felipe and Francisco, his fellow Yoruba and former companions in his master's "country house" outside Cartago, both of whom Doña Nicolasa Guerrero transferred to owners of Matina haciendas.[119] Manuel certainly knew African men of similar cultural background in Matina, such as Slave Coast natives Carlos García of casta Arará, and Pedro Arará, who had earned his freedom by 1719.[120] By 1718 Manuel was promoted to the position of overseer (*mandador*) of Ibarra's hacienda, supervising the cultivation and collection of the cacao and the work of his fellow slaves, who included his shipmate, the Mina Antonio de la Riva.[121] As in Cartago, African slaves in Matina came from various regions; Manuel knew Minas from the Gold and Slave Coasts, Congos from West-Central Africa, and Mandingas from Upper Guinea.[122] Matina owed its strong African character not to the predominance of any particular "nation" but to its ethnic diversity.

Manuel interacted closely not only with Africans of other ethnicities but also with members of other racial groups, and often on roughly equal terms. Juan Núñez and Benito Hernández were free laborers who, like Manuel, worked Ibarra's cacao hacienda and referred to him as their "master [*amo*]."[123] Free mulattoes, often soldiers and owners of small cacao haciendas, comprised a majority of the free residents of Matina, and often had family ties to slaves as well as to whites. Slave men were even mobilized for military service in the colonial militia: in 1718 the Yoruba Manuel served with twenty other slaves alongside the free mulatto militia, armed with his own gun.[124]

Yet along with the relative independence that African men enjoyed in Matina, they faced serious dangers and hardships, such as the threat of military invasion and a lack of female companionship. The Miskito Zambos of coastal Honduras and Nicaragua frequented the shores of Matina, sometimes trading peacefully but at other times sacking its cacao haciendas and kidnapping its residents.[125] The Miskitos maintained a brisk slave trade in Indians of other ethnicities and, to a lesser extent, in blacks and mulattoes, whom they captured in Spanish Central America and sold to their British allies in Jamaica.[126] Because of these risks, Costa Rican masters rarely if ever sent their female slaves to Matina, and the area suffered from a shortage of women generally; in 1719 there was reportedly "not even a woman to make something to eat" in the entire valley.[127] This de facto gender segregation reinforced the tendency of enslaved men who married to choose free women of other ethnic and racial groups as wives, while slave women rarely married at all.[128]

Before dawn on 17 April 1724 a force of five hundred Miskito Zambos entered the Matina Valley in twenty-two pirogues in a surprise attack. The Yoruba Manuel was one of twelve slaves and twenty-one freemen (nineteen of them mulattoes) taken prisoner when the Miskitos raided Matina to sack the cacao harvest.[129] Aníbel, the Miskito governor, directed operations from the hacienda of Manuel's master.[130] After forcing their prisoners to transport up to 1,000 *zurrones* (107 tons, or 97 metric tons) of cacao to their boats, the Miskitos sailed north with them to their territory in Honduras.[131] There they distributed the prisoners among "different masters, Mosquito Indians and Zambos, who generally gave all of them good treatment."[132] Manuel and his fellow prisoners worked cultivating and preparing food for the Miskitos—consisting mainly of yuca, plantains, sea turtle, and fish; in fact, they doubted that the Miskitos could survive long without them.[133] If the work the Miskitos imposed on the prisoners was not particularly demanding, they exercised closer vigilance and more immediate threats of violence than slaves usually experienced in Matina. The experience of imprisonment surely reinforced the bonds between the Africans of different ethnicities and between slaves and free mulattoes, which already formed a fact of life in Matina. Professing only a desire for improved relations with the Spaniards—but also facing a subsistence crisis after a recent hurricane and, as Manuel and his companions overheard, pressure from the British governor of Jamaica—the Miskitos suddenly returned the prisoners to Matina in March 1725.[134] By then Manuel had been seized, bound, and transported by slavers at least three times in his life: once in Africa, where he had been sold to the Danes in 1709; and twice in Matina, where Don Juan Francisco de Ibarra captured him in 1710, and the Miskitos surprised him at his master's hacienda in 1724. The hacienda to which he now returned was the same one where he had been held fifteen years earlier, with twenty-five Yoruba shipmates of casta Nangu.

The experiences of the Yoruba in Costa Rica differed significantly from the history of the Yoruba diaspora in other regions and periods. The Yoruba speakers, probably members of the Aná subgroup of Togo and Benin, who embarked on two Danish slave ships in 1709 on the Slave Coast of West Africa, formed a minority of a human cargo comprised mainly of people who originated from the Gold and Slave Coasts. As members of a western Yoruba population surrounded by speakers of Ewe and Aja, the Aná may have been especially conscious of the linguistic and cultural differences that divided them from their neighbors. In turn, they may have readily perceived their commonalities with other Yoruba speakers, allowing those who arrived in Costa Rica to identify themselves as Lucumí as well as Nagô. Yet the Yoruba and Slave Coast peoples shared much in common culturally, including a belief in a lightning god who avenged theft and witchcraft. They likely understood their experience of enslavement and the middle passage in much the same way.

The middle passage reinforced existing cultural commonalities between people of Yoruba and Slave Coast origins, and also encouraged them to reach out to shipmates of other ethnic groups. After arriving in Costa Rica, some of the Yoruba brought on the *Christianus Quintus* and *Fredericus Quartus* lived together for several months, forming lasting relationships with one another and their companions of other ethnic origins during the "seasoning" process. With few members of their "nation" to turn to in Costa Rica, the Yoruba came to rely as much on the shipmate bond as on ethnicity or estate in their relationships with other Africans. Arriving in numbers simply too small to form associations on exclusively Yoruba lines, their African origins nevertheless remained important as Yoruba forged new relationships with individuals of Slave Coast and Gold Coast origin. Bonds between shipmates endured even when individuals could "not remember" their casta or "nation."

Separation through sale accelerated the process whereby the Yoruba forged new relationships with members of other ethnic, cultural, and racial groups. Scattered throughout the North Pacific, Central Valley, and Atlantic lowlands of Costa Rica, opportunities for contact with Africans of similar background and experience varied along a continuum. Few slaves on the cattle and mule ranches of Bagaces had been born anywhere in Africa. In the cane fields of Ujarrás, Yoruba found several shipmates and other Slave Coast natives of similar cultural background. Chances to forge and pursue relationships with other Africans were greatest in the urban center of Cartago and on the cacao haciendas of Matina. Mostly separated from other Yoruba, they naturally formed their closest relationships with Africans of other ethnicities, with enslaved and free Creole blacks and mulattoes, and with Indians, mestizos, and Spaniards, becoming part of the Creole culture of Costa Rica. As shipmates, slaves, workers, family members, and friends, ethnicity provided just one of the bases on which Yoruba built their lives in Costa Rica.

If the Yoruba left no lasting cultural legacy in Costa Rica, that outcome was determined as much by patterns in the trans-Atlantic slave trade of the time as by local characteristics of slavery in the colony where they arrived. Future research will help to establish how the experiences of Yoruba in Costa Rica resembled or diverged from those in other American regions of the early and mid-colonial periods, but even those countries reflecting a strong Yoruba presence in the nineteenth century almost certainly looked very different in earlier times. Members of a tiny African minority in the overwhelmingly Creole world of eighteenth-century Costa Rica, these Yoruba of casta Aná nevertheless distinguished themselves. Manuel rose to administer his master's cacao haciendas. As ably as any free soldier, he bore arms for the king of Spain and, unlike most military men, could claim to have survived a year's imprisonment by the Miskito Indians. Agustina won the unheard-of distinction of having her marriage recognized by the Catholic Church while still a slave. After losing at least three children, Micaela gained her freedom at an advanced age. Within the stifling confines of enslavement, all successfully faced the challenge of survival in a new culture, and carved out lives worthy of respect and remembrance.

Notes

I wish to thank Sandra Lauderdale Graham, Mauricio Meléndez Obando, and especially Frances Lourdes Ramos for their readings and suggestions on various drafts of this essay.

1. Paul E. Lovejoy, *Transformations in Slavery: A History of Slavery in Africa*, 2nd ed. (Cambridge: Cambridge University Press, 2000 [1983]), 47–50. For example, Mexico, then Spanish America's largest importer of African slaves, received few if any Lucumí during that period, and only a handful later. See Colin Palmer, *Slaves of the White God: Blacks in Mexico, 1570–1650* (Cambridge, Mass.: Harvard University Press, 1976), 2; Gonzalo Aguirre Beltrán, *La población negra de México, 1519–1810: Estudio etnohistórico*, 2nd ed. (Mexico: Fondo de Cultura Económica, 1972), 133–34, 240–41; Adriana Naveda Chávez-Hita, *Esclavos negros en las haciendas azucareras de Córdoba, Veracruz, 1690–1810* (Xalapa, Ver., Mexico: Universidad Veracruzana, Centro de Investigaciones Históricas, 1987), 27; Patrick J. Carroll, *Blacks in Colonial Veracruz: Race, Ethnicity, and Regional Development* (Austin: University of Texas Press, 1991), 32–33, 158. Similarly an extensive survey of Peruvian notarial documents from 1560 to 1650 turned up just 22 Lucumí slaves among a total of 7,573 Africans. All these Lucumí arrived between 1605 and 1650, spread more or less evenly in groups of one, two, and three over five-year periods. Frederick P. Bowser, *The African Slave in Colonial Peru, 1524–1650* (Stanford, Calif.: Stanford University Press, 1974), 40–43.

2. Lovejoy, *Transformations in Slavery*, 50.

3. Robin Law, *The Slave Coast of West Africa, 1550–1750* (Oxford: Clarendon, 1991), 184–91, esp. 188–89. In Colombia, 47 of 624 Africans imported to Cartagena between 1705 and 1713 were described as Lucumí, or about 7.5 percent; other natives

of the Slave Coast (called Arará, Popo, and Fon) accounted for 210, or a further 33.65 percent (Germán Colmenares, *Popayán: Una sociedad esclavista, 1600–1800* [Medellín, Colombia: La Carreta, 1979], 48).

4. For examples, see notes 1 and 3 above.

5. Rina Cáceres, "Costa Rica, en la frontera del comercio de esclavos africanos," *Reflexiones* (Facultad de Ciencias Sociales, Universidad de Costa Rica), no. 65 (December 1997): 6–7.

6. Oscar Aguilar Bulgarelli, *La esclavitud negra en Costa Rica: Origen de la oligarquía económica y política nacional* (San José: Progreso Editora, 1997), 182–83; Mauricio Meléndez Obando, "Contrabando de esclavos," in Tatiana Lobo Wiehoff and Meléndez Obando, *Negros y blancos: Todo mezclado* (San José: Editorial de la Universidad de Costa Rica, 1997), 102.

7. One such incident occurred in November 1700, when a storm blew the Spanish ship *Nuestra Señora de la Soledad y Santa Isabel*, bound from Panama City to Paita, Peru, off its course to La Caldera on Costa Rica's Pacific coast. Perceiving some irregularities in the ship's papers, Lieutenant Governor Don Gregorio Caamaño confiscated its cargo and auctioned cloth, firearms, and other sundries as well as forty-two Africans to Costa Rican colonists in 1701. See Archivo Nacional de Costa Rica (hereafter, ANCR), Sección Colonial Cartago (hereafter, C) 109 (1700–1701); Archivo General de Indias, Seville, Guatemala 359 (1703–1704), piezas 4–6.

8. Georg Nørregård, "Forliset ved Nicaragua 1710," *Årbog 1948* (Handels-og Søfartsmuseet på Kronborg, Helsingør, Denmark), 71, 72–73, 75; idem, *Danish Settlements,* 89. Erich Lygaard to the Directors, Christiansborg, 19 August 1709, in *Danish Documents concerning the History of Ghana,* ed. and trans. Ole Justesen, forthcoming, Documents V.20, V.23, V.25. I am especially grateful to Professor Justesen for allowing me to cite from his forthcoming volume.

9. Nørregård, "Forliset ved Nicaragua," 81. Although the error of the shipwrecked Danish sailors was repeated by their modern chronicler, Georg Nørregård, in the name of his article, two eighteenth-century maps in the British Museum show "Pt. Carrett" and "Point Carata" on the site of modern Punta Cahuita, Limón Province, Costa Rica (John Alexander Holm, "The Creole English of Nicaragua's Miskito Coast: Its Sociolinguistic History and a Comparative Study of Its Lexicon and Syntax" [Ph.D. dissertation, University of London, 1978], 185).

10. Nørregård, "Forliset ved Nicaragua," 79–84; Holm, "Creole English," 185–86.

11. Auto de noticia de 24 negros, Cartago, 22 March 1710, ANCR, C 187, fols. 9, 10.

12. Inventario de negros, Cartago, 14 April 1710, ANCR, C 187, fols. 12–13v.

13. Declaración del Cap. Antonio de Soto y Barahona, Cartago, 1 May 1710, ANCR, C 187, fols. 73v, 75v–77v; Inventario de negros, Cartago, 11 May 1710, ANCR, C 187, fols. 97–100v.

14. Inventario de 16 negros y negras, Cartago, 11 June 1710, ANCR, C 187, fols. 147–49.

15. Declaración de Matías Trejos, Cartago, 6 November 1719, ANCR, Sección Colonial Guatemala (hereafter, G) 185, fols. 81v–82v.

16. Declaración de María de casta lucumí, Cartago, 25 September 1720, ANCR, G 185, fol. 40; Declaración de Petrona, negra, Cartago, 25 September 1720, ANCR, G 185, fol. 40v.

17. Robin Law, "Ethnicity and the Slave Trade: 'Lucumi' and 'Nago' as Ethnonyms in West Africa," *History in Africa* 24 (1997): 212; idem, *Slave Coast,* 189. A New Granada

census recorded "Nango" slaves in 1759, no doubt another variant of Nagô, which was distinguished from Lucumí. See William F. Sharp, *Slavery on the Spanish Frontier: The Colombian Chocó, 1680–1810* (Norman: University of Oklahoma Press, 1976), 115; Law, "Ethnicity and the Slave Trade," 208.

18. Biodun Adediran, "Yoruba Ethnic Groups or a Yoruba Ethnic Group? A Review of the Problem of Ethnic Identification," *África: Revista do Centro de Estudos Africanos da Universidade de São Paulo, Brazil* 7 (1984): 60; Law, "Ethnicity and the Slave Trade," 208, 212; idem, *Slave Coast*, 189–90; idem, *The Oyo Empire, c. 1600–c. 1836: A West African Imperialism in the Era of the Atlantic Slave Trade* (Oxford: Clarendon, 1977), 154; Nombramiento de Francisco de casta arará, esclavo del Cap. Francisco de la Madriz Linares, como intérprete, Cartago, 14 April 1710, ANCR, C 187, fol. 17v.

19. Biodun Adediran, *The Frontier States of Western Yorubaland circa 1600–1889: State Formation and Political Growth in an Ethnic Frontier Zone* (Ibadan, Nigeria: French Institute for Research in Africa, 1994), 13, 15; Law, "Ethnicity and the Slave Trade," 212; John Igue and Olabiyi Yai, "The Yoruba-Speaking Peoples of Dahomey and Togo," trans. Abiola Irele, *Yoruba* 1, no. 1 (1972): 9. See also Adediran, "Yoruba Ethnic Groups," 58; William Bascom, *The Yoruba of Southwestern Nigeria* (New York: Holt, Rinehart, and Winston, 1969), 5; Peter Morton-Williams, "The Oyo Yoruba and the Atlantic Trade, 1670–1830," *Journal of the Historical Society of Nigeria* 3, no. 1 (December 1964): 30–31.

20. Adediran, "Yoruba Ethnic Groups," 60– 61, 67.

21. Law, "Ethnicity and the Slave Trade," 215.

22. Ibid., 213.

23. Declaración de María, negra de casta lucumí, Cartago, 25 September 1720, ANCR, C 267, fols. 49v–51; Declaración de Petrona, negra de casta lucumí, Cartago, 25 September 1720, ANCR, C 267, fols. 51v–52.

24. Adediran, "Yoruba Ethnic Groups," 60; Law, "Ethnicity and the Slave Trade," 208, 212; idem, *Slave Coast*, 189–90; idem, *Oyo Empire*, 154.

25. Declaración de María, San Francisco de Tenorio, 17 September 1719, ANCR, G 185, fols. 6v–7; Declaración de Petrona, San Francisco de Tenorio, 17 September 1719, ANCR, G 185, fols. 8–8v.

26. Cesión de dos negras, Cartago, 14 July 1710, ANCR, G 185, fols. 25–25v; Cesión de esclava, Cartago, 4 July 1710, ANCR, G 188, fol. 15 (emphasis added).

27. Adediran, *Frontier States*, 15; idem, "Yoruba Ethnic Groups," 58; Bascom, *Yoruba of Southwestern Nigeria*, 5. Gonzalo Aguirre Beltrán included the Aná in his extensive catalogue of African ethnicities represented in Mexican colonial documents, asserting that they began to arrive in Mexico in the late sixteenth century, and precisely described their geographic origin as along the Aná tributary of the Mono River in southern Togo. However, he incorrectly identified the Aná as an Ewe-Fon-speaking group (Aguirre Beltrán, *Población negra*, 131). Costa Rican historian Carlos Meléndez followed Aguirre Beltrán in this misidentification; see "El negro en Costa Rica durante la colonia," in *El negro en Costa Rica*, by Carlos Meléndez and Quince Duncan, 9th ed. (San José: Editorial Costa Rica, 1989), 21. Jorge Castellanos and Isabel Castellanos also found the term "Aná" in Cuban documents, and likewise associated the group with the Ewe-Fon in "The Geographic, Ethnologic, and Linguistic Roots of Cuban Blacks," *Cuban Studies* 17 (1987): 96–98.

28. Law, "Ethnicity and the Slave Trade," 213.

29. Justesen, *Danish Documents*, Documents V.20, V.23, V.25.

149

30. Adediran, "Yoruba Ethnic Groups," 67.

31. Nombramiento de Francisco de casta arará, esclavo del Cap. Francisco de la Madriz Linares, como intérprete, Cartago, 14 April 1710, ANCR, C 187, fol. 17v. My approach in this section owes much to the work of Robert W. Slenes. See, especially, "'Malungu ngoma vem!' África encoberta e descoberta no Brasil," *Revista USP* (Universidade de São Paulo, Brazil), no. 12 (December 1991–February 1992): 48 – 67; "The Great Porpoise-Skull Strike: Central African Water Spirits and Slave Identity in Early Nineteenth-Century Rio de Janeiro," in *Central Africans and Cultural Transformations in the American Diaspora*, ed. Linda Heywood (Cambridge: Cambridge University Press, 2002), 183–208.

32. Declaración de Juan, negro bozal, Cartago, 16 April 1710, ANCR, C 187, fol. 18v.

33. Declaración de Gaspar de Acosta Arévalo, Cartago, 16 April 1710, ANCR, C 187, fol. 29v.

34. Declaración de Agustina, negra de casta aná, Cartago, 5 September 1719, ANCR, G 187, fol. 2v; Inventario de 38 negros, Cartago, 11 May 1710, ANCR, C 187, fols. 97–100v.

35. Declaración de Juan, negro bozal, Cartago, 16 April 1710, ANCR, C 187, fols. 18v–19.

36. Ibid., fol. 19.

37. Ibid., fols. 18v–20v.

38. Compare Declaración de Nicolás, negro bozal de casta arará, Cartago, 16 April 1710, ANCR, C 187, fols. 21–23; Declaración de Miguel, negro bozal de casta arará, Cartago, 16 April 1710, ANCR, C 187, fols. 23v–25v.

39. Nørregård, "Forliset ved Nicaragua," 71, 72–73, 75; idem, *Danish Settlements in West Africa, 1658–1850*, trans. Sigurd Mammen (Boston: Boston University Press, 1966), 89; Commander Erich Lygaard to the Directors of the Danish West India and Guinea Company, Christiansborg, 19 August 1709, in Justesen, *Danish Documents*, Document V.20; Lygaard to Directors, Christiansborg, 14 January 1710, in Justesen, *Danish Documents*, Document V.25.

40. Nørregård, "Forliset ved Nicaragua," 75–79, 97.

41. Ibid., 78 – 84.

42. Declaración de Juan, negro bozal, Cartago, 16 April 1710, ANCR, C 187, fol. 19; Declaración de Nicolás, negro bozal de casta arará, Cartago, 16 April 1710, ANCR, C 187, fol. 21v; Declaración de Miguel, negro bozal de casta arará, Cartago, 16 April 1710, ANCR, C 187, fol. 24.

43. Declaración de Juan, negro bozal, Cartago, 16 April 1710, ANCR, C 187, fol. 19; Declaración de Nicolás, negro bozal de casta arará, Cartago, 16 April 1710, ANCR, C 187, fol. 21v; Declaración de Miguel, negro bozal de casta arará, Cartago, 16 April 1710, ANCR, C 187, fol. 24v.

44. Nørregård, "Forliset ved Nicaragua," 92, 96.

45. Memoria de los bienes del Cap. Pedro de Ibáñez, 16 May 1702, ANCR, Mortuales Coloniales de Cartago (hereafter, MCC) 849, fol. 14; Testamento de Doña Manuela de Quirós, otorgado por su marido el Sarg. Mr. Francisco de la Madriz Linares, 5 June 1716, ANCR, Protocolos Coloniales de Cartago (hereafter, PC) 878, fol. 85.

46. Declaración de Juan, negro bozal, Cartago, 16 April 1710, ANCR, C 187, fol. 19; Declaración de Nicolás, negro bozal de casta arará, Cartago, 16 April 1710, ANCR, C 187, fol. 18v.

47. Declaración de Felipe Cubero, negro de casta congo, Matina, 4 December 1719, ANCR, C 243, fol. 8v.

48. Declaración de Antonio Civitola, negro de casta congo, Cartago, 18 December 1719, ANCR, C 259, fol. 5v.

49. Declaración de Micaela, negra de casta aná, Cartago, 5 September 1719, ANCR, G 187, fol. 2.

50. Declaración de Miguel Largo, negro esclavo, Cartago, 30 June 1720, ANCR, C 240, fol. 21.

51. See Paul E. Lovejoy and David V. Trotman, "Experiencias de vida y expectativas: Nociones africanas sobre la esclavitud y la realidad en América," in *Rutas de la esclavitud en África y América Latina*, ed. Rina Cáceres, 379–404 (San José: Editorial de la Universidad de Costa Rica, 2001).

52. Law, *Slave Coast*, 111.

53. Ibid., 332; Melville J. Herskovits, *Dahomey: An Ancient West African Kingdom*, 2 vols. (New York: J. J. Augustin, 1938), 2:151, 153; Paul Mercier, "The Fon of Dahomey," in *African Worlds: Studies in the Cosmological Ideas and Social Values of African Peoples*, ed. Darryl Forde (London: Oxford University Press, 1954), 213, 214; Geoffrey Parrinder, *West African Religion: A Study of the Beliefs and Practices of Akan, Ewe, Yoruba, Ibo, and Kindred Peoples*, 2nd ed. (New York: Barnes & Noble, 1970), 31.

54. Albert de Surgy, *Le système religieux des Evhé* (Paris: Éditions L'Harmattan, 1988), 111–12; Parrinder, *West African Religion*, 31–32.

55. Herskovits, *Dahomey*, 2:153; Surgy, *Le système religieux*, 118; Parrinder, *West African Religion*, 32.

56. J. Omosade Awolalu, *Yoruba Beliefs and Sacrificial Rites* (London: Longman, 1979), 35–36.

57. Dana Lynn Rush provides examples and an interpretation in "Vodun Vortex: Accumulative Arts, Histories, and Religious Consciousnesses along Coastal Benin" (Ph.D. dissertation, University of Iowa, 1997), chap. 2.

58. Law, "Ethnicity and the Slave Trade," 210.

59. Parrinder, *West African Religion*, 32; Awolalu, *Yoruba Beliefs*, 35, 36, 38; Herskovits, *Dahomey*, 2:164; Marc Schiltz, "Yoruba Thunder Deities and Sovereignty: Ara versus Sango," *Anthropos* 80 (1985): 67–84, esp. 67, 80.

60. Well into the nineteenth century many European observers remarked on the aversion of Slave Coast peoples to the venture on the ocean. See Robin Law, "Between the Sea and the Lagoons: The Interaction of Maritime and Inland Navigation on the Pre-colonial Slave Coast," *Cahiers d'Études Africaines* 29, no. 2 (1989): 209–13.

61. Joan Wescott and Peter Morton-Williams wrote of devotees of Shango in twentieth-century Nigeria: "Although the worshippers conform to the conventions of Yoruba behaviour in avoiding violence and destructiveness . . . , there is good evidence that they have fantasies of them and attribute to themselves the magical control of the destructive force of lightning" ("The Symbolism and Ritual Context of the Yoruba *Laba Shango*," *Journal of the Royal Anthropological Institute* 92 [1962]: 25, 27).

62. Paul E. Lovejoy, "The African Diaspora: Revisionist Interpretations of Ethnicity, Culture, and Religion under Slavery," *Studies in the World History of Slavery, Abolition, and Emancipation* 2, no. 1 (1997), available at: http://h-net2.msu.edu/~slavery/essays/esy9701love.html.

63. Michael A. Gomez, *Exchanging Our Country Marks: The Transformation of African Identities in the Colonial and Antebellum South* (Chapel Hill: University of North Carolina Press, 1998), 13–14.

64. Declaración de María, negra de casta lucumí, Cartago, 25 September 1720,

ANCR, C 267, fols. 49v–51; Declaración de Petrona, negra de casta lucumí, Cartago, 25 September 1720, ANCR, C 267, fols. 51v–52.

65. Carta de Juan Francisco de Ibarra y Calvo, Moín, 27 April 1710, ANCR, C 187, fol. 65 (quoted); Inventario de 16 negros, Cartago, 11 June 1710, ANCR, C 187, fol. 149; Declaración del Cap. Don Juan Francisco de Ibarra y Calvo, Cartago, 11 May 1710, ANCR, C 187, fol. 156v.

66. Juan Carlos Solórzano Fonseca, "Comercio exterior de la provincia de Costa Rica (1690–1760)" (Licenciatura thesis, Universidad de Costa Rica, 1977), 32.

67. Declaración de Petrona, negra de casta lucumí, Cartago, 25 September 1720, ANCR, C 267, fol. 51v; Solórzano Fonseca, "Comercio exterior," 31.

68. Auto en que constan las nueve piezas de esclavos que se dieron por ahogadas, con razón de sus dueños, Cartago, 18 October 1720, ANCR, G 185, fols. 45v– 46; Declaración de María, negra de casta lucumí, Cartago, 25 September 1720, ANCR, C 267, fol. 50; Declaración de Petrona, negra de casta lucumí, Cartago, 25 September 1720, ANCR, C 267, fol. 51v; Inventario de los bienes del Sarg. Mr. Don Juan Francisco de Ibarra y Calvo, Cartago, 7 May 1737, ANCR, MCC 850, fol. 21.

69. Declaración de José Feliciano de Acuña, Cartago, 6 November 1720, ANCR, G 185, fol. 88; Declaración de Matías de Quesada, Cartago, 6 November 1720, G 185, fol. 88v.

70. Careo en el cual las negras María y Petrona identifica a María de casta aná como una de sus carabelas, Cartago, 5 October 1720, ANCR, C 267, fol. 58v; ANCR, G 185, fol. 45; ANCR, G 188, fol. 34v; Declaración de María negra de casta popó, Valle de Barva, 12 November 1719, ANCR, G 188, fol. 7v.

71. Declaración de María, negra de casta popó, Valle de Barva, 12 November 1719, ANCR, G 188, fol. 7v.

72. Careamiento de esclavos, Cartago, 2 October 1720, ANCR, G 185, fol. 44.

73. Declaración de Manuel, negro de casta mina, Cartago, 17 September 1719, ANCR, C 268, fol. 1v; Venta de esclavo, Cartago, 31 April 1731, ANCR, PC 906, fols. 29v–33.

74. Venta de dos esclavas, Esparza, 16 October 1710, ANCR, G 185, fols. 14–16; Claudia Quirós Vargas de Quesada, "Aspectos socioeconómicos de la ciudad del Espíritu Santo de Esparza y su jurisdicción (1574–1878)" (Licenciatura thesis, Universidad de Costa Rica, 1976), 195.

75. Murdo J. MacLeod, *Spanish Central America: A Socioeconomic History, 1520–1720* (Berkeley: University of California Press, 1973), 274; Quirós Vargas de Quesada, "Aspectos socioeconómicos," 260– 61.

76. See the census in "Los vecinos del Valle de Bagases pretenden formar una villa, ciudad o lugar en dicho valle, con independencia del gobierno de la provincia de Costa Rica. Año de 1688," in *Asentamientos, hacienda y gobierno*, ed. León Fernández (San José: Editorial Costa Rica, 1976), 93–111; Quirós, *La era de la encomienda*, 284.

77. John K. Thornton's assertion that Africans "could easily find others who spoke their language and shared their norms in the new environment, especially if they were on a large estate or in an urban area" did not hold true in the Bagaces Valley, nor indeed in Costa Rica generally (*Africa and the Africans in the Making of the Atlantic World, 1400–1680*, 2nd ed. [Cambridge: Cambridge University Press, 1998], 205).

78. Law, *Oyo Empire*, 203.

79. Quirós Vargas de Quesada, "Aspectos socioeconómicos," 165.

80. Registro del bautizo de María y Petrona, negras esclavas de Doña Cecilia Vázquez de Coronado, Esparza, 20 February 1713, Archivo Eclesiástico de la Curia Metropoli-

tana de San José, Costa Rica, Sección Sacramental (hereafter, ACM), Libros de Bautizos de Esparza, 1706–1819 / Family History Library (hereafter, FHL), VAULT INTL Film 1223548. The original manuscripts of the colonial sacramental records at the ACM are no longer loaned to researchers and must be consulted on microfilm rolls copied by the Church of Jesus Christ of Latter-Day Saints.

81. Declaración de María, negra de casta lucumí, Cartago, 25 September 1720, ANCR, C 267, fol. 50v; El Sarg. Mr. Don Salvador Suárez de Lugo hace manifestación de sus esclavos, San Francisco de Tenorio, 20 November 1719, ANCR, C 229, fols. 17v–18; ANCR, G 185, fols. 19v–20.

82. Registro del bautizo de Mónica de la Cruz, hija de María Egipciaca, negra esclava de Doña Cecilia Vázquez de Coronado, Esparza, 19 May 1729, ACM, Libros de Bautizos de Esparza, 1706–1819/FHL, VAULT INTL Film 1223548; Venta de esclavos, Cartago, 8 November 1731, ANCR, PC 906, fols. 160v–164.

83. Careamiento de negros, Cartago, 2 October 1720, ANCR, C 267, fols. 55–56.

84. Memoria de las personas que asistieron en la presa de negros, Cartago, 12 August 1710, ANCR, C 182, fol. 45; Venta de esclava, Cartago, 20 November 1715, ANCR, PC 877, fols. 212–14; Venta de esclava, San Antonio de Curridabat, 4 November 1717, ANCR, PC 883, fols. 43–45.

85. Inventario y avalúo de los bienes del Sarg. Mr. Don Juan Francisco de Ibarra y Calvo, Cartago, March 1737, MCC 850, fols. 3v–14v.

86. Rina Cáceres, *Negros, mulattos, esclavos y libertos en la Costa Rica del siglo XVII* (Mexico: Instituto Panamericano de Geografía e Historia, 2000), 74; Inventario y avalúo de los bienes del Sarg. Mr. Don Juan Francisco de Ibarra y Calvo, Cartago, 15 March 1737, MCC 850, fol. 11v.

87. All these casta names were declared by slaves in 1719–20 (see n. 90 below) and are found in greater numbers in the notarial documents PC 868 (1710)–PC 895 (1722).

88. Declaración de Antonia, negra esclava de Diego de Aguilar, Cartago, 13 June 1720, ANCR, C 276, fol. 1v.

89. These figures are derived from statements by African slaves in ANCR, C 211 (1716–19), C 224 (1719), C 229–46 (1719), C 248–54 (1719), C 256 (1719), C 258–68 (1719), C 273–78 (1720), C 280 (1719), C 283–84 (1721), C 288–89 (1719–20), C 292 (1722); ANCR, G 185–88 (1719).

90. Declaración de Miguel, esclavo de Doña Luisa Calvo, Cartago, 15 November 1719, ANCR, C 267, fol. 7; Declaración de Magdalena, esclava de Doña Josefa de Oses, Cartago, 9 September 1719, ANCR, C 232, fol. 2v; Declaración de María, esclava del Sarg. Mr. Antonio de Soto y Barahona, Cartago, 14 September 1719, ANCR, C 233, fol. 1v; Declaración de Teresa, esclava del Sarg. Mr. Antonio de Soto y Barahona, Cartago, 14 September 1719, ANCR, C 233, fols. 2–2v; Declaración de Manuela, esclava del Cap. Francisco de Flores, Cartago, 28 September 1719, ANCR, C 254, fol. 1v.

91. Sidney W. Mintz and Richard Price, *The Birth of African-American Culture: An Anthropological Perspective* (Boston: Beacon, 1992; first published as *An Anthropological Approach to the Afro-American Past* [Philadelphia: Institute for the Study of Human Issues, 1976]), 43, 44, 48. See also Michael A. Gomez's different perspective in *Exchanging Our Country Marks*, 165–66.

92. Mintz and Price, *Birth of African-American Culture*, 43–44.

93. Declaración de María, esclava de María Calvo, Cartago, 10 September 1719, ANCR, C 242, fols. 1v, 2; Declaración de María Victoria, esclava del Cap. Don José de Mier Cevallos, Cartago, 6 September 1719, ANCR, C 266, fol. 1v.

94. Declaración de María negra de casta popó, Valle de Barva, 12 November 1719, ANCR, G 188, fol. 7v.

95. Thornton, *Africa and Africans*, 168.

96. Contrast with Mintz and Price's contention that the shipmate bond "already announced the birth of new societies founded on new kinds of principles" (*Birth of African-American Culture*, 44).

97. Declaración de Pedro de Rosas, esclavo del Cap. Juan Sancho de Castañeda, Cartago, 26 May 1720, ANCR, C 231, fol. 14v.

98. Declaración de Pedro, esclavo del Sarg. Mr. Don Francisco de Ocampo Golfín, Valle de Barva, 12 November 1719, ANCR, G 188, fol. 4.

99. El Sarg. Mr. Juan Francisco de Ibarra y Calvo acusa recibo de los bienes que trajo su esposa Doña Catalina González Camino a su matrimonio, Cartago, 20 June 1718, ANCR, PC 886, fols. 7–10v; El Sarg. Mr. Don Juan Francisco de Ibarra y Calvo hace inventario de los bienes que aportó a su matrimonio con Doña Catalina González del Camino, Cartago, 21 June 1718, ANCR, PC 886, fols. 10v–14; Escritura de mancomún y obligación del Sarg. Mr. Juan Francisco Ibarra y Calvo y de Doña Catalina González Camino (dos esclavos), Cartago, 27 July 1719, ANCR, PC 887, fols. 52v–54; Venta de esclavo, Cartago, 4 September 1713, ANCR, C 211, fols. 131–133v; Venta de esclavo, Cartago, 25 May 1716, ANCR, G 187, fols. 30v–33.

100. Venta de esclavo, Cartago, 4 September 1713, ANCR, C 211, fols. 131–133v.

101. Lovejoy and Trotman, "Experiencias de vida," 382.

102. Cesión de cinco negros y negras, Cartago, 8 January 1711, ANCR, MCC 774, fols. 82–84; Testamento de Doña Nicolasa Guerrero, Ujarrás, 20 February 1730, ANCR, PC 903, fol. 7; Permuta de esclavos, Cartago, 27 March 1722, ANCR, PC 895 fol. 32v–35; Declaración de Francisco Aná, Cartago, 12 September 1719, ANCR, C 267, fol. 2v.

103. Careamiento en el cual salieron otros esclavos de las nueve piezas ocultadas, Cartago, 3 October 1720, ANCR, C 267, fols. 57v–58; Petición del Sarg. Mr. Don Antonio de Utrera y Medina, Cartago, 4 November 1720, ANCR, C 268, fols. 19v–20v; Auto de deliberación sobre el negro Manuel, Cartago, 14 December 1720, ANCR, C 268, fol. 24; Declaración de Josefa Arará, negra esclava de Doña Gertrudis Guerrero, Cartago, 20 May 1720, ANCR, C 273, fol. 2.

104. Testamento de Doña Nicolasa Guerrero, Ujarrás, 19 September 1717, ANCR, PC 882, fols. 94–97v.

105. Elizabeth C. Fonseca, "El cultivo de la caña de azúcar en el Valle Central de Costa Rica: Época colonial," in *Costa Rica Colonial*, ed. Luis F. Sibaja (San José: Ediciones Guayacán, 1989), 83.

106. Testamento de Doña Nicolasa Guerrero, Ujarrás, 19 September 1717, ANCR, PC 882, fols. 94v, 97.

107. Ibid., fols. 94–97v; Declaración de Francisco de casta aná, Cartago, 12 September 1719, ANCR, C 267, fol. 3; Petición de Doña Luisa Calvo, C 267, fol. 19.

108. Although Guerrero estimated Francisco's age as sixteen in her 1730 testament, he was not mentioned in her will of 1717 (Testamento de Doña Nicolasa Guerrero, Ujarrás, 20 February 1730, ANCR, PC 903, fol. 7).

109. Permuta de esclavos, Cartago, 27 March 1722, ANCR, PC 895, fol. 32v–35.

110. ACM, Libros de Matrimonios de Cartago, no. 3/FHL, VAULT INTL film 1219727, Item 8.

111. See Mintz and Price, *Birth of African-American Culture*, 43.

112. Razón de dos esclavas y los hijos que tienen, Cartago, 5 October 1720, ANCR, G 185, fol. 45.

113. Adjudicación de los bienes del Sarg. Mr. Don Juan Francisco de Ibarra y Calvo, Cartago, 20 August 1737, ANCR, MCC 850, fol. 88.

114. Carta de libertad, Cartago, 4 August 1746, ANCR, PC 934, fol. 59; Declaración de Micaela, negra esclava de casta aná, de 24 años al parecer, Cartago, 5 September 1719, ANCR, G 185, fol. 1v.

115. Inventario y avalúo de los bienes del Sarg. Mr. Don Juan Francisco de Ibarra y Calvo, Cartago, 15 March 1737, ANCR, MCC 850, fols. 12v–13; Notificación al Sarg. Mr. Don Juan Francisco de Ibarra y Calvo y su respuesta, Cartago, 23 September 1719, ANCR, G 187, fol. 8.

116. "Informe sobre la provincia de Costa Rica presentado por el Ingeniero Don Luis Díez Navarro al Capitán General de Guatemala Don Tomás de Rivera y Santa Cruz. Año de 1744," *Revista de los Archivos Nacionales* (Costa Rica) 3, nos. 11–12 (September–October 1939), 583; Visita general de Nicaragua y Costa Rica por el obispo Pedro Agustín Morel de Santa Cruz, 1751–1752, University of Texas, Benson Latin American Collection, Joaquín García Icazbalceta Collection, vol. 20, no. 7, fol. 58.

117. "Pedimento del procurador síndico de Cartago al cabildo para que reciba el cacao como moneda en la compra de toda clases víveres y otros artículos de comercio. Año de 1703," *Revista de los Archivos Nacionales* (Costa Rica) 1, nos. 9–10 (July–August 1937), 590–99; "Se dispone que el cacao corra en la provincia de Costa Rica para la compra de víveres por no haber en ella moneda de plata. Año de 1709," *Revista de los Archivos Nacionales* (Costa Rica) 1, nos. 9–10 (July–August 1937), 600–603.

118. Lowell Gudmundson, "Mecanismos de movilidad social para la población de procedencia africana en Costa Rica colonial: Manumisión y mestizaje," in *Estratificación socio-racial y económica de Costa Rica, 1700–1850* (San José: EUNED, 1978), 17–78, esp. 30.

119. Permuta de esclavos, Cartago, 27 March 1722, ANCR, PC 895, fol. 32v–35; Declaración de Francisco de casta aná, Cartago, 12 September 1719, ANCR, C 267, fol. 3; Petición de Doña Luisa Calvo, ANCR, C 267, fol. 19.

120. Venta de esclavo, Cartago, 22 September 1705, ANCR, PC 861, fols. 49v–52; Negros esclavos asistentes en Matina, Matina, 23 January 1719, ANCR, Sección Complementario Colonial (hereafter, CC) 3797, fol. 27; Lista general de gente y armas del Valle de Matina, Matina, 23 January 1719, ANCR, CC 3797, fol. 25.

121. Sarg. Mr. Don Juan Francisco de Ibarra y Calvo hace inventario de los bienes que aportó a su matrimonio con Doña Catalina González del Camino, Cartago, 21 June 1718, ANCR, PC 886, fol. 12v; Declaración de Antonio de casta mina, esclavo del Sarg. Mr. Don Juan Francisco de Ibarra, Cartago, 7 November 1719, ANCR, G 187, fol. 11.

122. Memoria de los prisioneros libres y esclavos, Matina, 1 May 1724, ANCR, C 303, fols. 66–66v; Declaración de Juan Miguel Barahona, negro esclavo de casta mina, Matina, 4 December 1719, ANCR, C 233, fol. 9v; Declaración de Francisco [alias Diego] Mina, esclavo del Cap. Luis Gutiérrez, Cartago, 7 June 1720, ANCR, C 258, fol. 12v; Declaración de Antonio, negro esclavo de casta congo, Cartago, 8 September 1719, ANCR, C 231, fol. 3; Declaración de Pedro, esclavo de casta congo, Matina, 5 December 1719, ANCR, C 232, fol. 9v; Capital de bienes de Doña Agueda Pérez del Muro en ocasión de su casamiento con el Cap. Don Francisco Garrido Berlanga, Cartago, 16 April 1722, ANCR, PC 895, fol. 51v.

123. Declaración de Juan Núñez, Paraje de Santiago, 2 May 1724, ANCR, C 304, fol. 3v; Declaración de Benito Hernández, Paraje de Santiago, 2 May 1724, ANCR, C 304, fol. 4.

124. Negros esclavos asistentes en Matina, Matina, 23 January 1719, ANCR, CC 3797, fol. 27.

125. Germán Romero Vargas, *Las sociedades del atlántico de Nicaragua en los siglos XVII y XVIII* (Managua: Fondo de Promoción Cultural-BANIC, 1995), 80.

126. See Romero Vargas, *Las sociedades del atlántico,* esp. chap. 11; Mary W. Helms, "Miskito Slaving and Culture Contact: Ethnicity and Opportunity in an Expanding Population," *Journal of Anthropological Research* 39, no. 2 (1983): 179–97.

127. Petición del Sarg. Mr. Don Juan Francisco de Ibarra, Cartago, 28 August 1719, Archivo General de Indias, Seville, Escribanía 353B, fol. 620.

128. Gudmundson, "Mecanismos de movilidad," 17–78.

129. Declaración de Diego Sánchez, pardo libre, Cartago, 8 May 1724, C. 303, fols. 68v–69v; Memoria de los prisioneros libres y esclavos, Matina, 1 May 1724, ANCR, C 303, fols. 66–66v.

130. Declaración de Agustín de la Riva, pardo libre, Cartago, 10 May 1724, ANCR, C 303, fol. 72v.

131. Declaración de Diego Sánchez, pardo libre, Cartago, 8 May 1724, ANCR, C 303, fols. 68v–69.

132. Declaración de los prisioneros que fueron restituidos al Valle de Matina, Cartago, 19 April 1725, ANCR, C 313, fol. 64.

133. Ibid., fol. 65.

134. Carta del Sarg. Mr. Don Pedro de Alvarado y Jirón, Matina, 28 March 1725, ANCR, C 313, fol. 59v; Declaración de Juan Antonio Molina, cabo de la vigía de Matina, Matina, 28 March 1725, ANCR, C 313, fol. 60; Declaración de los prisioneros que fueron restituidos al Valle de Matina, Cartago, 19 April 1725, ANCR, C 313, fol. 64v.

CHAPTER EIGHT

Yoruba in the British Caribbean: A Comparative Perspective on Trinidad and the Bahamas

Rosalyn Howard

Yoruba culture was transplanted to the Caribbean region with its African adherents during the holocaust of the trans-Atlantic slave trade. The region absorbed over 50 percent of the ten to twenty million Africans who involuntarily left the continent and survived the middle passage.[1] Members of the Yoruba state in Africa were not early subjects of the trade, owing largely to their well-developed sociopolitical structure. To some extent they—along with the Dahomey, Ashante, Fulani, Kom, Mandingo, and Hausa—dominated neighboring peoples in a multitude of ways: politically, economically, militarily, and culturally. Circumstances radically changed, however, when, between 1700 and 1867, "west-central Africa and the coastal areas of the Bight of Benin (extending roughly from eastern Ghana to western Nigeria) and the Bight of Biafra (extending roughly from central Nigeria to western Cameroon) accounted for over 75% of the total number of Africans shipped across the Atlantic."[2] The Slave Coast, as the region became known, was partially centered on the area now known as Benin, home of the Yoruba, the Ibo, and other lesser-known groups.[3]

Africans replaced indigenous laborers in the Americas whose populations had been decimated by various measures, including overwork, exposure to epidemic and epizootic diseases, and, at worst, subjected to genocide.[4] They represented the abundant source of captive labor that could satisfy what the Europeans required for their colonization of the New World.[5]

Accurate assessments of the number of Yoruba peoples who were landed in Trinidad and the Bahamas, both former British colonies, are difficult to ascertain because of sparse records. Confirmation of their presence, however, is demonstrated by the remnants of Yoruba culture that persist, transformed by time, repression, and contact with other cultures.

Both Trinidad and the Bahamas represent comparatively anomalous examples of the institution of slavery in most British colonies of the Caribbean. Trinidad was not involved in plantation-style sugar production until the late eighteenth century, when the British gained control of the colony from Spain. Upon arrival in Trinidad, just one decade before ending their involvement in the slave trade in 1807, the British encountered a culturally and linguistically diverse society, one that included a larger percentage of free persons of color than other British colonies did; a significant number of the French Creole plantocracy who had migrated there, attempting to thwart their enslaved Africans' rebellious ideas that were engendered by the principles of the French Revolution of liberty, equality, and fraternity; and Hispanophones from Venezuela who had worked in the cacao industry. In subsequent years Trinidad's population became even more ethnically diverse with the importation of thousands of indentured East Indian laborers.[6]

The British gained nominal control of the Bahamas in 1670, when Woodes Rogers, assigned as governor, ousted the pirates who had long favored this strategically located territory. It was, however, a marginal colony, which, analogous to Trinidad, had a large population of free persons of color and an enslaved population that operated with a large measure of autonomy. Additionally the Bahamas never had a sustained, large-scale plantation economy. For a brief period British Loyalists, refugees from North and Central America, reestablished their cotton plantations. But these did not prosper very long for ecological and economic reasons that are detailed later in this chapter. Although these similarities exist, there are significant differences that caused the manifestation of Yoruba culture and religion to diverge in these two former British colonies. The "retention" of Yoruba culture ultimately leads to the controversial discourse on cultural survivals in the African diaspora.

The African Diaspora

The slave trade engendered the displacement of heterogeneous populations of Africans who demonstrated a wide spectrum of cultural and linguistic variation. The traditional cultures of these Africans were destined to become further diversified by exposure to European and indigenous peoples in the New World, creating a "diasporic ethnogenesis" of African-descended peoples with new identities and cultural practices.[7]

The extent to which elements of these African traditional cultures survived in the diaspora has long been a question of debate and analysis for historians, anthropologists, and other social scientists.[8] Many scholars believe that the integral nature of traditional African cultures in daily life led to the maintenance of "Africanisms" in language, religion, family structure, and institutions.[9]

Indeed, contemporary analyses of the cultural dynamics among African-descended peoples continue to be framed by Africanisms and their concomitant constructions of "survivals," "retentions," and "syncretisms."[10]

Recently, however, some scholars are viewing this perspective as problematic, questioning whether the claim that Africanisms are found in the cultures of the Caribbean and the Americas reflects an essentialist framework that plays into the hands of the European hegemonic project.[11] Okpewho counters that because Africans in the New World persist in inducing their African origins, "surely scholars are quite justified in turning an 'essentialist' light on those aspects of African career and conduct that mirror continental African traditions."[12] Still others consider the concept of Africanisms viable as a tool for examining the past through social memory,[13] although they caution against using the term in its traditionally understood framework that posits "a mechanical and essentialized notion of culture in which culture becomes a reified, thing-like entity that may be 'possessed,' 'maintained' or 'lost,' 'decays,' or is 'resistant' in the face of culture contact."[14]

Despite these ongoing debates, there is a strong consensus that some elements of contemporary cultural practices and belief systems found among peoples of African descent in various areas of the diaspora appear to have evolved from the legacies of African cultures.[15] The oral tradition, integral to Yoruba as well as other African cultures, facilitated the transmission of this cultural system through liturgy, literature, songs, and cultural events such as carnival and festivals. In reference to the African oral tradition, Pradel asserts that "divinities and traditions owe their survival especially to the power of collective memory and speech, which guarantees the perpetuation of ancestral values."[16] Memories of their African cultural roots, and the practices derived from these, served and continue to serve both psychological and pragmatic functions in their adaptation to New World societies.[17] Although these cultural practices frequently had to remain surreptitious, "mimesis and memory, as well as the fear of ancestral sanction, served as bases for the continuation of certain beliefs, strategies and lifestyles."[18]

Fragmented elements of Yoruba culture, for example, are apparent in many New World cultures, modified by particular geopolitical and historical circumstances, and are expressions of deeply entrenched cultural grammars.[19] The collision of cultures resulting from the slave trade, however, also serves to blur distinctions that would enable direct attribution of cultural origin.[20] To speak of the maintenance of "traditional" Yoruba cultural traditions is to conceptualize these in stasis. In fact, Yoruba culture has always been permeable and changing, influenced not only by time but also by intimate contacts with diverse ethnic groups in precolonial Africa.[21] The tradition of heterogeneity, inclusiveness, and accommodation in Yoruba culture within Africa may provide one plausible explanation why Yoruba belief systems were so readily interpolated in New World cultures.

Notwithstanding the rich textures and vital natures of African traditional religions in daily life, some colonizers were "persuaded that the West Africans were 'absolute atheists' or Devil worshipers [and] most of the English settlers expressed bewilderment at their slaves' religious practices and saw little reason to convert them."[22] African culture and religion were "assiduously wrapped in negative bands" by colonizers and missionaries who refused to validate or acknowledge their existence.[23] This was the dominant perspective among British Protestants in particular. Their early orthodoxy did not validate continuous revelations, common in many African belief systems, nor—unlike the Catholics with their cadre of saints who served as intermediaries—could their Protestantism tolerate African cosmologies.[24] Before the middle of the eighteenth century—the time when Protestants began to validate possession by the Holy Spirit (a form of continuous revelation) and evangelization as a viable social control mechanism[25]—it was Catholicism that resonated most with Africans; "the cult of saints may have made it easier for Africans from different national traditions to merge their own versions of the cosmos through the revelations of Christian otherworldly beings."[26]

Prior to their New World exposure, some Africans had already been introduced to Christianity, most notably in the Kongo and Angola regions. What emerged was African Christianity, a modified version of both traditions but one that was regionally specific, adapted to the particular belief system of each ethnic group. The African Christian converts served as catechists, assisting priests and missionaries in converting Africans in the Americas. These New World conversions, however, had to be accomplished among ethnically diverse groups of Africans, a scenario that led to new incarnations of African Christianity. Paradoxically, while Christianity was enlisted as a tool to reinforce the rationale for Africans' enslavement and domination, and appropriate Bible verses were adopted for this express purpose (e.g., Eph. 6:5–9; Phil. 2:5–8; Col. 3:22–25; 1 Peter 2:5–25),[27] the Bible was the only European-derived document that reassured Africans of their membership in the human race.[28]

The persistent practice of African religious beliefs and practices, seeking the intervention of ancestors and other mediators in however modified a manner, enabled Africans to resist total dehumanization.[29] In many instances, while confronted with the physically and psychologically destructive forces of enslavement, Africans demonstrated significant agency by reconciling elements of their African cultural traditions (which, as mentioned, sometimes included Christianity) to those they encountered in the New World. The diverse experiences of New World enslavement, the dominant form of Christianity encountered (Catholic or Protestant), and the amount of contact with it were major factors in the degree of acceptance or rejection of Christian elements within the enslaved Africans' traditional belief systems. What developed was essentially a continuum of cosmological and theological variation that continues to be in a process of renegotiation as African-derived belief systems interact with one another as well as with non-African-derived discourses and power matrices.[30]

Yoruba in Trinidad

Trinidad is a Caribbean island in the southern Lesser Antilles, located just off the coast of Venezuela. Its proximity to this Hispanophone country, an eighteenth-century influx of Francophone immigrants, and the presence of a large number of Africans and East Indians have created what is referred to as a "callaloo culture": a culture at once a "felicitous and mutually transforming mixing of cultural, racial, and religious diversity" and, conversely, "a particularistic and politicized notion, even as it is meant to connote an all-encompassing ideological embrace."[31] Despite the incidence of plantation rebellions and revolts elsewhere in the New World, Trinidad was relatively peaceful; the only incident of note was the 1805 Christmas "plot" that never came to fruition.[32] It has been suggested that the lack of conflict between Europeans and Africans in Trinidad was owing to several factors: a comparatively brief duration of the "peculiar institution," demographics, and the type of plantation economy instituted there:

> Colonists did not begin plantation-style cultivation of sugar until the late 1700s and complete emancipation occurred in 1838. The Spanish, French and British imported approximately 22,000 African slaves into Trinidad, the majority arriving at the end of the eighteenth century. In the 1600s there was a lucrative tobacco industry in Trinidad, followed in the 1700s by a successful cacao industry that gave way to cotton in the 1780s; none of these used slave labor to any great extent. Then the sugar industry began its ascendancy . . . in 1784 by the first wave of French immigration.[33]

After the British abolished the trans-Atlantic slave trade in 1807 they policed the seaways, liberating the "cargoes" of slave ships primarily destined for Spanish and Portuguese plantations in the Americas. The "liberated Africans" were then settled in various British colonies including Trinidad and the Bahamas. The 1834 abolition of slavery in the British colonies—which did not effectively cease until the end of the so-called apprenticeship period in 1838—witnessed the arrival of a significant number of Africans in Trinidad, either as "liberated" Africans or as voluntary migrant indentured laborers.

From 1841 to 1861 more than six thousand African indentured laborers were settled in Trinidad; Yoruba immigration was heavily concentrated during this time.[34] According to Maureen Warner-Lewis, "some of the Trinidad Yoruba immigrants had complex cultural and ethnic backgrounds which reflected ongoing processes of change within Africa itself."[35] Their contact with other African ethnic groups within Africa before their arrival in the New World led to "processes which have worked in complex ways to create African-based cultural configurations in the Caribbean."[36] The Yoruba immigrants initially segregated themselves in a separate village in the capital, Port of Spain,[37] and the already diverse population of Trinidad became augmented by an influx of African-born peoples, primarily Yoruba and Kongolese,[38] who had never suffered the indignities of enslavement in the New World.

Unlike the Yoruba, Kongolese cosmology does not contemplate a complex assemblage of deities, which made it less amenable to a complementary association or symbiosis[39] with the predominant religion the Kongolese encountered in Trinidad, namely, Catholicism.[40] The Yoruba's complex and malleable pantheon facilitated just such an interpolation. James Houk, an anthropologist who conducted extensive research on the Orisha religion and who was "initiated" while conducting his fieldwork, speculates that the addition of a substantial number of African-born to the population of newly emancipated Africans was the foundation of what would eventually become the Orisha religion of Trinidad.[41]

Orisha Religion

The Orisha religion mirrors the callaloo culture of Trinidad through its devotees who represent a collage of Trinidadians. According to one follower:

> It is a religion to which every day, three hundred and sixty-five (365) days of the year, people of all races, all colours, all classes, make their way; the declared devotees and initiates as well as the surreptitious needy, and the closet devotees. They come for exorcisms, for medication, for divination. For help in financial matters, to get their cars blessed . . . they come in a never ending stream; the Hindu pundits, the holder of Kali Pujas, the French Creole businessmen, the bank clerk wanting to trap a man in marriage. They all come.[42]

As a result of its engagement of multiple cultural traditions, the Orisha religion has been characterized as a syncretic religion, as have other New World neo-African religions such as Santería (Cuba), Candomblé (Brazil), and Vodou (Haiti). The term "syncretism," popularized in the 1940s by anthropologist Melville Herskovits, has been defined as a multifaceted (ideology and material culture) and multilevel (deep and surface structure) process of blending elements from one culture with another when they are in a continuous contact situation. As a result, cultural transformation occurs as new domains of cultural knowledge and material culture are created.[43] This definition has been frequently employed as a tool of cultural analysis for New World cultures. African American, Afro-American, and indigenous scholars have increasingly engaged a critique of this multivalent term, arguing for the adoption of new paradigms that reflect a non-Eurocentric conceptualization of the African experience in the New World.[44] Desmangles accepts this challenge, suggesting that we consider what happened to traditional African cultures via temporal and spatial juxtaposition in the New World as "symbiosis," that is, coexistence without fusion, rather than "syncretism," that is, blending or fusion.[45]

The Orisha religion, whose name derives from the Yoruba deities, is actually a complex of five religious or spiritual traditions: Yoruba, Catholic, Hindu, Protestant, and Kabbalistic. The priest (*mongba*) and priestess (*iya*) gain prestige for the breadth of their knowledge. The more comprehensive they can make their practices—that is, the more inclusive their shrines and annual festivals (*ebo*) are—the more respect and followers they gain. The many voices of Yoruba resonate in its differential incorporation of these diverse belief systems. The contribution made by each of these components to Orisha religion varies in scope and substance.

Owing to the early influences of French and Spanish immigrants, Catholicism was the dominant religion in Trinidad. Catholic elements, therefore, were the first to be incorporated into the Orisha religion; its developmental period occurred during slavery, necessitating surreptitious practice. The substitution of Catholic iconography for the orishas was employed as follows: St. Michael was substituted for Ogun, St. John of the Cross for Shango, St. Ann for Yemoja, and Jesus Christ (also St. Benedict) for Obatala.[46]

Laws were enacted to prevent the practice of African religions in Trinidad, and some restrictive legislation remains: "The Orisha religion is still not free to be practised. There are laws on the statute books that make it mandatory for a shrine to obtain a license before holding an *Ebo*. . . . Within the last year [1995] someone has been prosecuted under the law."[47]

Houk notes that Catholicism's "present day influence is practically nil, but Catholic beliefs, practices and paraphernalia are still important components of the Orisha belief system."[48] He further states that in recent years there has been strong movement toward an "Africanization" of the Orisha religion, an effort to disassociate the orisha deities from the Catholic saints. This movement is led by younger devotees and has caused some friction between them and older practitioners who believe that "saying a Hail Mary or two never stops them from doing 'The Orisha Work.'"[49] These emergent religious identities are seen as a means of cultural empowerment as African-descended people generate contemporary narratives of spirituality and religious beliefs.[50]

There exists a very close relationship between devotees of the Orisha religion and the Spiritual Baptists, a popular Protestant Christian sect in Trinidad.[51] In fact, many people are members of both belief systems simultaneously, though often clandestinely.

There is also a moderate affiliation with the East Indians' Hindu religion, although historically the relationship between Afro-Trinidadians and Indo-Trinidadians has been contentious: "for approximately a century and a half Indo-Trinidadians have attempted to strengthen their presence as a group in part by posing cultural contrasts (which get translated into ethnic boundaries) between themselves and Afro-Trinidadians."[52] Despite this, some shrine heads are beginning to include Hindu religious artifacts and images in their compounds.[53] Hindu deities, like those in Catholicism and Yoruba, are highly anthropomorphic, making them appear to be redundant or duplications of the orisha deities and their domains.[54]

The Kabbalah is an eclectic blending of religious philosophies with Jewish origins, imported by the Spanish, French, and British colonists.[55] Its influence on the Orisha religion is not a true integration per se. The Kabbalah's limited inclusion as a philosophical platform serves instead to formulate a more comprehensive belief system that will attract more devotees.

A common ethnic and socioeconomic background among followers of the Orisha religion facilitates the synergy of Orisha devotees, Spiritual Baptists, and the Kabbalists.[56] The Orisha religion in Trinidad expresses the art and process of fragmenting and recombining disparate cosmological and theological mosaics into systems that allow persistent regeneration and transformation.

Trinidadian Carnival

Yoruba cultural influences are evident in the Carnival tradition of Trinidad. Celebrated during the week before Ash Wednesday each year, Carnival invokes the Yoruba traditions of reverence for the ancestors and orisha worship. Carnival revelers "playing *mas*" parade in costumes mirroring those found in West Africa. Bright strips of multilayered fabric are reminiscent of *Egungun* costumes worn in the festivals of Benin and Nigeria. White-chalked faces evince ancestral spirit worship. Netted face coverings represent a boundary between the worlds of the living and the ancestral spirits that is to be breached only at one's personal peril.[57] Yoruba chants are repeated, invoking the powerful orisha Shango. Feathers, considered among the Yoruba to be powerful in invoking positive energy (*ase*) and wealth, are also important elements in costume decoration.[58]

Yoruba in the Bahamas

The Bahamas is an archipelago consisting of seven hundred islands (only thirty of which are inhabited) and twenty-four hundred cays and rocks that stretch from the southeastern coast of Florida eastward toward the Windward Passage north of Cuba and Haiti. During the colonial era the Spanish, French, and British intermittently claimed possession of the Bahamas, but the British ultimately gained nominal control in 1670.

The Bahamas remained a British Crown colony until it achieved independence in 1973, although it is still a member of the British Commonwealth. The Bahamas has suffered from a chronic scarcity of natural resources, a widely dispersed population, epidemics, and vast destruction wrought by hurricanes and wars between European powers who vied for control of the colony, which was attractive primarily because of its strategic proximity to the Gulf Stream, a major shipping route. These exigencies created a scenario wherein all Bahamians regardless of skin color or social status were integral to achieving the colony's viability, and explain to some degree why the institution of slavery there diverged from that which was manifested in other British colonies. The Bahamians' social and economic foundation was not defined by sugar plantations, which, even after the abolition of slavery in the British Caribbean, continued to shape the social and economic contours of many British colonies.[59]

In contrast to most of the British West Indies, many Bahamian plantation owners were residents. They or their overseers demonstrated more concern for preserving their "property" than meeting production quotas.[60] Geography was another distinguishing factor; the lack of topsoil and the rocky terrain on most islands made large-scale plantation agriculture virtually impossible. The attempts of British Loyalists to reestablish their cotton plantations met with initial but short-lived success.[61] Most of the Loyalists were refugees from New York, the Carolinas, Georgia, and Florida, who, along with their enslaved Africans, sought asylum in the Bahamas in 1783 after suffering defeat in the American Revolutionary War. Originally fleeing to east Florida from Savannah, Charleston, and New York after the war, they ultimately left Florida for the Bahamas when Spain regained sovereignty there under the 1783 Treaty of Paris. Between 1783 and 1785 an estimated five thousand to seven thousand Loyalists migrated to the Bahamas from Georgia and the Carolinas.[62]

Additionally there were a large number of Africans in residence who had been "liberated" by the British Royal Navy from slave ships en route to Spanish and Portuguese colonies via the Gulf Stream off the western coast of the Bahamas; among these was an unknown number of Yoruba. From 1811 to 1860 "approximately 6000 Africans were landed in the Bahamas from 26 slave vessels, flying either the Spanish or Portuguese flag, which had been captured by British ships or were wrecked on the rocks and reefs surrounding the islands"[63] which lacked lighthouses at the time. Although technically considered "free persons," arguably these liberated Africans did not experience real freedom upon arriving in this British territory. Most if not all of them were subjected to open-ended indentureships that were tantamount to enslavement.

These African-born women and men, most of whom were Congo, Ibo, Mandingo, and Yoruba,[64] met a mostly Creole community of Africans that was very much assimilated to British culture.[65] The language and demeanor of the Creoles led the then governor Colebrooke to remark that "many of the Black people except for the colour of their skins are as much Englishmen, as if they had been born and brought up in that country and the English expression of their countenances is so marked that one really forgets the African feature in looking at them."[66]

Enslaved Creoles and Africans exercised a substantial amount of control over their own lives because of the limited plantation work in the Bahamas. Slave owners permitted them to seek independent employment in commercial and maritime ventures, requiring them to remit a portion of their remuneration. This self-hire system blurred the distinction between free and enslaved to such an extent that, according to Johnson, "slavery and freedom were not polar opposites. In the years after the collapse of cotton, when the demand for slave labor slackened, both rural and urban slaves exercised considerable autonomy, unparalleled elsewhere in the British Caribbean. It was in that context that both a peasantry and a proto-peasantry emerged before emancipation."[67]

The large influx of liberated Africans, primarily into Nassau, alarmed the white Bahamian population and especially provoked the hostility of Loyalists who had imported their own brand of racist ideology.[68] The Loyalists' displeasure precipitated the enactment of strict laws prohibiting integrated housing, and commanding "that all people of colour be off the streets of the town of Nassau after 9:00 P.M. when the Town Bell rang."[69] Similar laws were enacted on the Out (now called "Family") Islands, although these were not as restrictive owing to the substantial differences in lifestyles and demographics in these remote areas compared to Nassau. These laws had the effect of creating and codifying new racial barriers.

Governor J. Carmichael Smyth, an abolitionist, sought to resolve the matter by creating "African Villages" on New Providence Island, though these were located quite a distance from Nassau. Upon arrival, the liberated Africans were treated at the hospital for injuries or illnesses and were provided clothing, as most of them arrived in what was described as a "deplorable condition." This characterization referred not only to the lack of food and bedding but also the lack of clothing for their naked bodies. This sight was apparently quite an assault to British Victorian sensibilities, as confirmed in an 1831 report in *Argus* stating in part: "It is really offensive to the eyes of a civilized community, to witness the wanderings of the barbarians, to the Custom House and elsewhere, almost in a state of nudity."[70]

In addition to Smyth, other Bahamian colonists were sympathetic to the plight of the apprenticed Africans. This attitude is reflected in the following excerpt from a governor's dispatch:

> [I] am unwilling to believe in the intuition of the Governor again to assign over to Masters those persons who had completed periods of apprenticeship, some of them upwards of 14 years and none of them under seven, and who, as appears in the course of the investigation now proceeding with, had given the most decided proofs of their being able to provide for themselves in the absolute fact that, for many years of their apprenticeship, and some of them for the whole period, they had been left by their holders not only to do this but in addition to pay to the holders considerable weekly or monthly sums [from the self-hire system] . . . it appears to me that after the completion of one period of apprenticeship, industry should be converted to the interest of the African ultimately, and not to that of an individual who had no sort of other regard for him.[71]

This correspondence illustrates a degree of concern for the welfare of Africans in the Bahamas that increasingly resonated throughout the British colonies until the institution of slavery was finally ended by the Abolition Act of 15 February 1834.[72] The additional four-year period of "apprenticeship" imposed by the Abolition Act, however, amounted to four more years of unpaid or substantially unremunerated labor. In 1837 the African Board was established to administer the affairs of these liberated Africans.

Unfortunately very limited information about the African origins of these liberated Africans can be gleaned from documents describing the three African villages: Adelaide, Carmichael, and Gambier. Adelaide's first 157 settlers arrived in 1831. They were "supplied with hatchets and hoes for the purpose of farming and were expected to assist in the building of their own houses."[73] In 1834 the second group arrived there, "after the ships 'Felicidad' and 'Hebe' on which they were traveling had been captured by the Royal Navy. It was not certain from which part of Africa the travellers may have come. It is believed that many originated from the Congo, the Gold Coast, and the East Coast of Africa."[74]

Liberated Africans also settled in the African Villages of Carmichael and Gambier, cultivating vegetables and fruits, and selling these at the main market in Nassau. By the next year, however, many of these original settlers had migrated to an area proximate to the Nassau market, the center of commerce.[75] They settled in one of three areas that are generally known as "Over the Hill": Grant's Town, Bain Town, and Fox Hill. Cleveland Eneas, a Yoruba descendant, wrote a book entitled *Bain Town* that documented the history of that particular settlement, using personal anecdotes and oral history passed down from his father and other community members. His account attributes the origin of Bain Town to the settlement of the Yoruba and Congos who had been liberated from slave ships.[76] We learn from Eneas that there were a number of Yoruba among these new settlers and that Yoruba women, in particular, were noted for their market skills and dominated the Nassau market. According to Eneas,

> It may be a wild claim, but the old ladies . . . firmly believed that it was for them that the City Market . . . was specifically built . . . some selling went on, on that spot, by the Yoruba women of Bain Town and Fox Hill as long as could be remembered.[77]

According to Saunders, "African-Caribbean women also used the market-place for organizing the Yoruba derived 'Asue' (also known as 'sou sou', 'partner' or 'meet and turn') to save and meet financial obligations."[78]

The Yoruba people, or N'ongos[79] as they called themselves, were described as "uppity" and viewed the Congos as inferior, both socially and economically. In fact, Eneas states, "No N'ongo man would associate with a Congo under any circumstance. He regarded him as someone to be shunned and segregation and discrimination was rife. For a N'ongo man to be labeled a 'Congo man' was as raw an epithet as could be imagined."[80] The two groups maintained their distance; Bain Town was divided into two districts, Congo Town (Contabutta) and N'ongo Town (Yoruba). The Yoruba not only segregated themselves from other Africans but also from Creole Blacks, as they had done in Trinidad. Eneas described the Yoruba in the Bahamas as "a proud, progressive people who had a flare for elegance and beauty, [and who] were industrious, crafty and independent."[81] *Bain Town* depicts a settlement of the Yoruba people who were thriving socially and economically, and who were preserving some of their African cultural traditions.

The physical boundaries of Bain Town essentially have been erased by the growth of Nassau where today an estimated 65 to 70 percent of the total population of Bahamians (304,000) reside.[82] Like these physical barriers, the cultural distinctiveness of Yoruba and Congo communities—maintained from the late nineteenth century until the 1960s, as substantiated by the existence of separate Congo and Yoruba Lodges or Friendly Societies[83]—has blurred.

A major thrust for conversion of the liberated Africans was made by some Christian denominations immediately on their arrival. The colonial administration, in fact, ordered that the liberated Africans were to be given religious instruction and taught viable skills. Baptists and Methodists were especially active evangelists among them. In the British Caribbean, Baptist missionaries in particular had gained reputations as "'Negro Lovers' who corrupted the minds of the slave with wrong ideas."[84] Saunders says, "the slaves identified with the early Baptist and Methodist preachers, who were originally black, and probably participated in services which included music foreign to their masters and also in death rites such as wakes, possession rites and, perhaps, they believed in obeah."[85] Anglicans and Presbyterians openly disdained and ignored the Africans, however, claiming that there was not enough space in their churches for them.[86]

The practice of Yoruba religious traditions in the Bahamas was likely to have been extremely restricted owing to the sociopolitical influence of Protestant Christian churches, which was significant then and remains so today. Indeed, it is said that "no [political] party in the Bahamas will ever come to power unless its leaders are seen as Christian in some way or another."[87]

The celebration of the fiftieth anniversary of the 1837 arrival of a number of Yoruba into the Bahamas as liberated Africans was reported in *The Freeman*, a newsletter published for the Black Bahamian community.[88] The 8 May 1888 issue has as its headline story "Jubilee of the Landing of the Yoruba and Egba Tribes on the Free Shores of Nassau, N.P. [New Providence]." The newsletter provides an extensive account of the arrival from their original African homeland, described as "the land of mystery and darkness." They apparently had been the captives in a war fought by the leader of the Yoruba nation, King Odoomawoom, against two of his rebel ethnic groups, the Foulahs and the Baabas. The king, who previously had "held his sway with an iron hand," succumbed in the battle. Many of the captive Yoruba leaders and others, including the Egbas, were sold to two American traders and destined for enslavement on Spanish or Portuguese sugar plantations. Upon entering British-controlled waters off the Bahamas, however, they were "espied by a British man-of-war, who sent a shot across their bows and ordered them immediately to haul to." The ships were intercepted and delivered to a Nassau port, and "in Nature's single garb, which was of the darkest possible colour, the Yorubas and Egbas were released from their filthy holes and landed as free men on British soil."[89]

Eneas's 1976 characterization of the Yoruba peoples and their descendants in the Bain Town and Fox Hill areas of Nassau reads much the same way as they were described in the 1888 newsletter account: "Their descendants seldom marry out of their own tribes; and even their language is preserved. . . . To almost a man, they are an economical and thrifty race, and the neat cottages which are fast taking the place of the thatched huts which they built upon first settling tells a tale of progress and advancement in their taste and condition."[90]

For more than a century the Yoruba in the Bahamas preserved many of their cultural traditions, including endogamous marriage, some elements of language, economic practices,[91] and traces of ancestor reverence that are evident in Junkanoo costuming.[92] The Bahamian festival Junkanoo originated during the time of slavery when the masters would allow the enslaved people several days off from their duties during the Christmas holiday season. Much like the Trinidadians during Carnival, the costumes of Junkanoo participants, assembled from multilayered colorful strips, resemble the West African Egungun costumes.[93]

The status of the Yoruba in the British Caribbean ranged on a continuum from enslaved Africans to indentured "liberated" Africans to free persons. In Trinidad the vitality of their culture remains in evidence today primarily through the Orisha religion, a religion that has provided a forum for Yoruba-derived beliefs and practices both during and after slavery. A Yoruba spiritual leader, the Ooni of Ife, who visited the shrine of a Trinidadian, Iyalorisha, in 1988, acknowledged a close correspondence between the deities of the Orisha religion in Trinidad and the Yoruba religion in southwestern Nigeria.[94] The famous annual Trinidadian Carnival is also a forum for the artistic expression of Yoruba material culture through costuming, dance, and music. Warner-Lewis recorded Yoruba songs in Trinidad, and her analysis of them "indicates an affective and informational range of themes which restore personality to their original singers, reflecting their traumas and religious beliefs."[95]

Yoruba culture and religion in the Bahamas, however, found limited expression. Historically it was primarily evident in the African Villages and in the "Over-the-Hill" areas designated for free and enslaved Africans and Creoles in Nassau.[96] The most salient expressions of Yoruba culture were found in Bain Town and Fox Hill; some of these cultural influences persist today in celebrations such as Emancipation Day and Junkanoo, as well as in foodways, such as explained by Eneas:

> The biggest event of the year was . . . Fox Hill Day. This usually started with a celebration of Emancipation Day. . . . it was celebrated chiefly by the Yoruba people. . . . there were stalls selling *acara, moi-moi* and *agidi.* . . . there was fried fish, okra soup, *foo foo*, peas and rice and stewed fish. . . . Food galore to whet the appetite of any Yoruba gourmet.[97]

A comparative analysis of these two countries reveals that while historical and social similarities exist, there are also substantial differences between them, differences that significantly impacted the manifestation of Yoruba culture and religion. They do share a history of being British Caribbean colonies and of having been rather marginal plantation societies.[98] However, demographic differences (Trinidad being much more ethnically diverse than the Bahamas) and dissimilarity in their predominant religious affiliation (i.e., Catholicism in Trinidad versus Protestantism in the Bahamas) created divergent sociocultural and sociopolitical scenarios, which critically impacted the optimization and persistence of Yoruba cultural and religious beliefs and practices.

Notes

I wish to thank Faye V. Harrison for her insightful critique.

1. Philip D. Curtin, "From Guesses to Calculations," in *The Atlantic Slave Trade,* ed. David Northrup (Lexington, Mass.: D.C. Heath, 1994), 45.

2. Paul E. Lovejoy, ed., *Transformations in Slavery: A History of Slavery in Africa,* 2nd ed. (Cambridge: Cambridge University Press, 2000 [1983]), cited in James T. Houk, *Spirit, Blood, and Drums: The Orisha Religion in Trinidad* (Philadelphia: Temple University Press, 1995), 48. See also John W. Blassingame, *The Slave Community* (New York: Oxford University Press, 1976 [1972]), 3.

3. Lucie Pradel, *African Beliefs in the New World* (Trenton, N.J.: Africa World Press, 2000), 40.

4. William H. Simmons, *Notices of East Florida,* a facsimile reproduction of the 1822 edition. Bicentennial Floridiana Facsimile series (Gainesville: University Press of Florida, 1973), 58. Simmons offers a romanticized explanation for the demise of Native American peoples, stating that "the awful and swift destruction which took place among them after the Spanish conquest, was not the result of the labors imposed on them . . . but it was solely the subjection of their spirit, the bitter cup of humiliation, drugged by servitude, that produced their speedy depopulation."

5. A. Leon Higginbotham, *In the Matter of Color: Race and the American Legal Process* (Oxford: Oxford University Press, 1978), 116.

6. Barry W. Higman, "African and Creole Slave Family Patterns in Trinidad," in *Africa and the Caribbean: The Legacies of a Link,* ed. Margaret E. Crahan and Franklin W. Knight (Baltimore: The Johns Hopkins University Press, 1979), 42.

7. Douglas B. Chambers, "Tracing Igbo into the African Diaspora," in *Identity in the Shadow of Slavery*, ed. Paul E. Lovejoy (London: Continuum, 2000), 55.

8. The Herskovits-Frazier debate about African survivals is legendary. Anthropologist Melville Herskovits, in an effort to refute the negative portrayals of Africans and their cultures (or alleged lack of cultures), sought to uncover Africanisms in the cultures of African descendants in the New World. He also sought to combat racist assumptions about African peoples and to prove that the cultures of Africans in the Americas indeed contained expressions of traditional African cultural forms (although modified and at a deep level). Sociologist E. Franklin Frazier, on the other hand, was from the school of thought that Africans in the United States had been stripped of all vestiges of African culture because of the extreme experiences of slavery. Franklin did allow, however, that because of the different circumstances, Africanisms could be found in the cultures of Afro-Caribbean peoples. See Melville J. Herskovits, *The Myth of the Negro Past* (Boston: Beacon, 1958 [1941]); and E. Franklin Frazier, *The Negro Family in the United States* (Chicago: University of Chicago Press, 1966 [1939]). See also Kevin A. Yelvington, "The Anthropology of Afro–Latin America and the Caribbean: Diasporic Dimensions," *Annual Review of Anthropology* 30 (2001): 227–60, for an excellent critique of this debate.

9. Yelvington, "Diasporic Dimensions," 227.

10. Ibid.; see also Paul C. Johnson, "Migrating Bodies, Circulating Signs: Brazilian Candomblé, the Garifuna of the Caribbean, and the Category of Indigenous Religions," *History of Religions* 41, no. 4 (2002): 301–27. Faye V. Harrison notes that it is non-anthropologists, not well informed about the contemporary critiques of Herskovits within African American anthropology, who most often employ these categories (personal correspondence).

11. Paulin Hountonji, ed., *Les savoirs endogènes: Pistes pour une recherche* (Dakar: Codesria, 1994), cited in Noureini Tidjani-Serpos, "The Postcolonial Condition: The Archaeology of African Knowledge—From the Feat of Ogun and Sango to the Postcolonial Creativity of Obatala," *Research in African Literatures* 27, no. 1 (spring 1996): 3–18.

12. Isidore Okpewho, introduction to *The African Diaspora: African Origins and New World Identities*, ed. Isidore Okpewho, Carole Boyce Davies, and Ali A. Mazrui (Bloomington: Indiana University Press, 1999), xvi.

13. Tidjani-Serpos, *Postcolonial*, 3.

14. Yelvington, "Diasporic Dimensions," 5.

15. Paul E. Lovejoy, "Identifying Enslaved Africans in the African Diaspora," in idem, *Identity*, 3; Maureen Warner-Lewis, "Cultural Reconfigurations in the African Caribbean," in Okpewho, Davies, and Mazrui, *The African Diaspora*, 24.

16. Pradel, *African Beliefs*, 38, 43.

17. Okpewho, introduction, xv.

18. Warner-Lewis, "Cultural Reconfigurations in the African Caribbean," 21.

19. Ibid., 22–23; see also Atsuko Matsuoka and John Sorenson, *Ghosts and Shadows: Construction of Identity and Community in an African Diaspora* (Toronto: University of Toronto Press, 2001), 178.

20. Maureen Warner-Lewis, "Ethnic and Religious Plurality among Yoruba Immigrants in Trinidad in the Nineteenth Century," in *Identity in the Shadow of Slavery*, ed. Paul E. Lovejoy (London: Continuum, 2000), 125.

21. Olu Taiwo, "Music, Art, and Movement among the Yoruba," in *Indigenous Religions: A Companion*, ed. Graham Harvey (London: Cassell, 2000), 188; see also J. D. Y.

Peel, "A Comparative Analysis of Ogun in Precolonial Yorubaland," in *Africa's Ogun: Old World and New*, ed. Sandra T. Barnes (Bloomington: Indiana University Press, 1997).

22. Larry Gragg, "The Pious and the Profane: The Religious Life of Early Barbados Planters," *The Historian* 62 (winter 2000): 272. The Quakers were a notable exception.

23. Mercy A. Oduyoye, foreword to *Decolonizing Theology: A Caribbean Perspective*, ed. Noel L. Erksine (Trenton, N.J.: Africa World Press, 1998), xii.

24. John Thornton, *Africa and Africans in the Making of the Atlantic World, 1400–1800* (Cambridge: Cambridge University Press, 1998 [1992]), 270.

25. David Patrick Geggus, "Slavery, War, and Revolution in the Greater Caribbean, 1789–1815," in *A Turbulent Time: The French Revolution and the Greater Caribbean*, ed. David Barry Gaspar and David Patrick Geggus (Bloomington: Indiana University Press, 1997), 4.

26. Thornton, *Africa*, 269; see also 270–71.

27. Nathaniel Samuel Murrell, "Dangerous Memories, Underdevelopment, and the Bible in Colonial Caribbean Experience," in Hemchand Gossai and Nathaniel Samuel Murrell, *Religion, Culture, and Tradition in the Caribbean* (New York: St. Martin's, 2000), 13.

28. Michael J. C. Echeruo, "An African Diaspora: The Ontological Project," in Okpewho, Davies, and Mazrui, *The African Diaspora*, 5.

29. Oduyoye, foreword, xiii.

30. See Warner-Lewis, "Cultural Reconfigurations in the African Caribbean," 24.

31. Aisha Khan, "Journey to the Center of the Earth: The Caribbean as Master Symbol," *Cultural Anthropology* 16 (2001): 7.

32. Houk, *Spirit, Blood, and Drums*, 49. Michael Craton describes this "plot" as more akin to "playacting than real rebellion, a form of sublimation that might even be turned to the advantage of the ruling class" (*Testing the Chains: Resistance to Slavery in the British West Indies* [Ithaca, N.Y.: Cornell University Press, 1982], 236).

33. Houk, *Spirit, Blood, and Drums*, 50–51. The French immigration was a response to an invitation from the Trinidadian governor Ralph Woodford to plantation owners from neighboring islands. This resulted in the addition of approximately 2,000 enslaved Africans to the existing population of 11,633 Creole and 13,968 African-born enslaved persons.

34. Warner-Lewis, "Ethnic and Religious Plurality," 114.

35. Ibid.

36. Ibid, 125.

37. John W. Nunley and Judith Bettleheim, *Caribbean Festival Arts: Each and Every Bit of Difference* (Seattle: University of Washington Press, 1988).

38. Ibid.

39. See Leslie Gérald Desmangles, *The Faces of the Gods: Vodou and Roman Catholicism in Haiti* (Chapel Hill: University of North Carolina Press, 1992).

40. Ibid., 53. Catholicism's influence was established by Trinidad's French and Spanish immigrants, long before the British took control.

41. Ibid., 52; Orisha religion is also referred to as the "shango cult" by Dale Bisnauth in his book, *History of Religions in the Caribbean* (Trenton, N.J.: Africa World Press, 1996), 172.

42. Pearl E. Springer, "Orisa and the Spiritual Baptist Religion in Trinidad and Tobago," in *At the Crossroads: African Caribbean Religion and Christianity*, ed. Burton

Sankeralli, 85–108 (St. James, Trinidad and Tobago: Caribbean Conference of Churches, 1995), 91.

43. The "original creation" thesis that this analysis inspired has been the subject of decades-long debate between Sidney Mintz and Mervyn Alleyne.

44. See Faye V. Harrison, *Decolonizing Anthropology: Moving Further toward an Anthropology for Liberation* (Washington, D.C.: American Anthropological Association, 1991).

45. Desmangles, *Faces of the Gods*, 8.

46. Ibid., 97; and Bisnauth, *History of Religions*, 173. This alternate designation for Obatala is from Bisnauth.

47. Springer, "Orisa and the Spiritual Baptist Religion," 93.

48. Houk, *Spirit, Blood, and Drums*, 65.

49. Springer, "Orisa and the Spiritual Baptist Religion," 97. See also Maureen Warner-Lewis, *Yoruba Songs of Trinidad with Translations* (London: Karnak House, 1994), for a discussion of the Yoruba influence on the music of the Orisha religion.

50. Fiona Macgowan and John Gordon, "Introduction (Syncretism)," *The Australian Journal of Anthropology* 12, no. 3 (December 2001): 1.

51. Spiritual Baptists, like the Yoruba, are polytheists. See Stephen D. Glazier, *Marchin' the Pilgrims Home: Leadership and Decision-Making in an Afro-Caribbean Faith* (Westport, Conn.: Greenwood, 1983), 24–25.

52. Aisha Khan, "On the 'Right Path': Interpolating Religion in Trinidad," in *Religion, Diaspora, and Cultural Identity: A Reader in the Anglophone Caribbean*, ed. John W. Pulis, 247–76 (Amsterdam: Gordon and Breach, 1999), 254.

53. Houk, *Spirit, Blood, and Drums*, 200.

54. Ibid., 179.

55. Ibid., 36–37.

56. Ibid., 201.

57. Nunley and Bettleheim, *Caribbean Festival Arts*, 26.

58. Ibid., 8–9.

59. Howard Johnson, *The Bahamas in Slavery and Freedom* (Kingston, Jamaica: Ian Randle, 1991), vi.

60. Colin P. Hughes, *Race and Politics in the Bahamas* (New York: St. Martin's, 1981), 6–7.

61. According to the historical record: "The coming of the American Refugees boosted the economic situation in the colony as they introduced cotton cultivation previously grown in Georgia. Later Anguilla cotton, a long staple cotton which grew all year round was cultivated. By 1778 cotton production had become a successful operation with over 8,000 acres of land under cultivation. The best cotton islands proved to be the Turks and Caicos Islands, Long Island, Watlings Island, Cat Island and Exuma" (CO23/30/335, Commonwealth of the Bahamas, "An Account of All Cotton Plantations in the Bahamas," in *The Bahamas in the Age of Revolution, 1775–1848* [Nassau, Bahamas: Department of Archives, Ministry of Education, 1989], 9). Cotton plantations failed by the 1830s, however, primarily because of inadequate soil and pests, for example, the chenille bug.

62. Gail Saunders, *Slavery in the Bahamas, 1648–1838* (Nassau, Bahamas: Nassau Guardian, 1990 [1985]), 11.

63. Johnson, *The Bahamas in Slavery and Freedom*, 31. According to Johnson, "Once liberated, the Africans were, by provisions of an Order in Council of March

1808, employed either in the West India Regiment or in the Navy or were apprenticed to 'prudent and humane masters or mistresses' in the colony by the Customs Office" (31–32). Africans recruited from British territories and liberated Africans comprised the Second West India Regiment in the Bahamas. "The Bahamian white inhabitants were not happy with the fact that hundreds of blacks were being used to garrison these islands and, as far back as 1801, showed their resentment and distaste by illtreating the soldiers, and demanding that the Home Government remove them from New Providence. They were severely afraid that if the freed Negroes, slaves, and troops banded together, the type of Negro slave revolution which occurred in Haiti in the 1790s could happen in the Bahamas" (Commonwealth of the Bahamas, *Aspects of Slavery Part II: A Booklet to Commemorate the 150th Anniversary of the Abolition of Slavery* [Nassau, Bahamas: Department of Archives, Ministry of Education, 1984), 22. Some of these liberated Africans were settled in other British colonies including British Guiana, Jamaica, and Trinidad.

64. H. C. Saunders, *The Other Bahamas* (Nassau, Bahamas: Bodab, 1991), 22–23.

65. The sociopolitical and sociocultural landscapes of the Bahamas had been significantly transformed by the arrival of the British Loyalists and their enslaved Africans, many of whom were Creoles.

66. Colebrooke to James Stephen, 4 October 1835, CO 23/94. In Johnson, *The Bahamas in Slavery and Freedom*, 39.

67. Johnson, *The Bahamas in Slavery and Freedom*, vii. The self-hire system emerged by 1784. Johnson also notes that "they exercised substantial control over their lives and labour and accumulated property while they were themselves chattel" (ibid., 2).

68. Besides their racist beliefs, another concern was that this new labor force had the effect of decreasing the value of the Loyalists' human "property."

69. Gail Saunders, *Bahamian Loyalists and Their Slaves* (London: Macmillan Education, 1983), 45. Before the passage of Loyalist vagrancy and racial separation laws, housing for white and black Bahamians was intermingled throughout Nassau. Laws were passed that forbade the playing of drums and assembly of more than six Africans at a time, unless related to one another.

70. Johnson, *The Bahamas in Slavery and Freedom*, 39.

71. Maj. Gen. Lewis Grant, *Governor's Despatches, 1827–1831*, Bahamas Department of Archives, cited in Rosalyn Howard, *Black Seminoles in the Bahamas* (Gainesville: University Press of Florida, 2002), 63–64.

72. An interesting note is that the first "coloured man" was elected to the House of Assembly on the very same date.

73. Letter sent from Gov. J. Carmichael Smyth to James Walker from C. R. Nesbitt, 19 July 1831, CO23/84/297–99. Cited in Patrice Williams, *A Guide to African Villages in New Providence* (Nassau, Bahamas: Department of Archives, 1991 [1979]), 3.

74. Ibid.

75. Many liberated Africans intermarried or had conjugal relationships with enslaved women and men.

76. Cleveland W. Eneas, *Bain Town* (Nassau, Bahamas: Timpaul, 1976), 22–29.

77. Ibid., 37.

78. Gail Saunders, "Aspects of Traditional African-Bahamian in the late 19th and early 20th Century," *Journal of the Bahamas Historical Society* 17 (October 1995): 2.

79. The term "N'ongo" is a vernacular form of the word " Nagô," an archaic term for the Yoruba (Toyin Falola, personal correspondence).

80. Eneas, *Bain Town*, 29.

81. Ibid., 22.

82. This figure is an estimate from 2003. Nassau has such a large population because practically all wage employment opportunities are in Nassau, with fewer available in the other tourist meccas of Freeport and the Grand Bahamas, and even fewer in most of the Family Islands. Therefore residents of the Family (or Out) Islands migrate to Nassau for employment, especially members of the younger generation. This demographic likely does not contemplate a large number of Haitian immigrants, many of whom are illegal.

83. Saunders, *The Other Bahamas*, 22–23.

84. Murrell, "Dangerous Memories," 17.

85. Saunders, *Slavery in the Bahamas*, 167. The subject of obeah is still discussed, if in hushed tones, among contemporary Bahamians. Rather than calling people "obeahmen" or "obeah women" the term "bush medicine doctor" is often employed.

86. Ibid.

87. Dean W. Collinwood, "The Bahamas in Social Transition," in *Modern Bahamian Society*, ed. Dean W. Collinwood and Steve Dodge, 3–26 (Parkersburg, Iowa: Caribbean Books, 1989), 18–19.

88. *The Freeman*, May 1888. Document at the Bahamas Department of National Archives. With an outstanding sense of humor/humility, an "apology" is printed directly below the masthead stating: "We acknowledge to an apology due the Public for typographical and other errors which often creep out in our columns; but when our readers realize that we are editor, foreman, compositor, proof-reader, corrector, printer, 'devil,' and every other function necessary to a newspaper with the assistance of a couple of boys who have seen the inside of a Printing-office for the first time three months ago, we feel sure they will excuse what would otherwise be deemed carelessness or neglect." Many thanks to Sherriley Strachan of the Bahamas National Archives for bringing this obscure document to my attention.

89. *The Freeman*, 1.

90. Ibid.

91. In 1985 the Bahamian historian Saunders noted that "many African customs, for example the *asue*, have survived over the years" (*Slavery in the Bahamas*, 198). My research in the late 1990s confirms that the *asue* persists as a viable economic alternative for some Bahamians, including those living in the Family Islands.

92. The etymology of the term "Junkanoo" is alternately claimed to derive from the name of a West African tribal chief, John Canoe, who was captured and enslaved in the West Indies, and to the French phrase *gens inconnus* which means "the unknown people," a reference to the masking tradition of festival celebrants (Nunley and Bettelheim, *Caribbean Festival Arts*). Other possible sources of the name include John Cony, an African trader prince from the Gold Coast (Ghana); Jankomo, an Ashanti dancer; and John Kuner/Kooner, a benevolent plantation character dressed in tattered, striped clothing ("Junkanoo," Archives Exhibition 13 February–3 March, Nassau, Bahamas, Department of Archives, 1978).

93. Ibid., 28.

94. E. J. Murray, ed., *Religions of Trinidad and Tobago: A Guide to the History, Beliefs, and Polity of 23 Religious Faiths* (Port of Spain, Trinidad and Tobago: Murray, 1998).

95. Warner-Lewis, "Cultural Reconfigurations in the African Caribbean."

96. This statement is based on the extremely limited historical and anecdotal information available. Narratives from the enslaved themselves are nonexistent in the Baha-

mas. Per historian Saunders: "Unfortunately, because no writings of slaves in the Bahamas has come to light, certain areas of the slaves' lives, especially his [sic] cultural life, is very poorly documented" (*Slavery in the Bahamas*, 162).

97. Eneas, *Bain Town*, cited in Philip Cash, Shirley Gordon, and Gail Saunders, *Sources of Bahamian History* (London: Macmillan, 1991), 231.

98. There were stark contrasts in family structure, however. The Bahamas had a much greater proportion of nuclear family households than did Trinidad (Michael Craton and Gail Saunders, *Islanders in the Stream: A History of the Bahamian People*, vol. 1, *From Aboriginal Times to the End of Slavery* [Athens: University of Georgia Press, 1992], 319).

CHAPTER NINE

The Influential Yoruba Past in Haiti

Kevin Roberts

Among their forced New World destinations, large numbers of Yoruba arrived in Haiti. Even with the comparatively early end to the trans-Atlantic slave trade to the island as a result of the Haitian Revolution, forced migrants from the Bight of Benin, both Yoruba and non-Yoruba, constituted such a large proportion of the slave force in Saint Domingue that their cultural heritage remains an important influence on modern Haitian culture. In fact, in the realms of religion, art, and language, Yoruba culture is fundamental to Haiti's distinctive syncretic culture. In short, this geographically small component of the immense Yoruba diaspora illustrates the cultural influence of the Yoruba, even when enslaved, on the New World. The amalgam of West African cultures present in Saint Domingue during enslavement, although diminishing some elements of Yoruba culture, accentuated those characteristics that other African cultural groups shared. By adopting a broad temporal view from enslavement to post-independence to modern Haitian culture, this essay illustrates the deeply seated nature of Yoruba culture in a unique component of the Yoruba diaspora.

Enslavement

The height of the demand for slaves by Saint Domingue slave owners during the 1780s coincided with the period when the Yoruba constituted a large share of the trans-Atlantic slave trade. As a result, the number of Yoruba slaves present in Haiti, and the influence of Yoruba on the colony's syncretic slave culture, were both higher than if the two processes had not converged in the 1780s. Of the nearly one million slaves from the Bight of Benin who were sold into slavery in the New World, approximately one-third were shipped to Saint Domingue. In fact, the aggregate of slave imports from the Bight of Benin to the next three most common destinations—Jamaica, Martinique, and Barbados—barely equals the number shipped to Saint Domingue alone. The fifth most common destination, the Bahia Province of Brazil, received only one-quarter of the number of Benin peoples who arrived in Saint Domingue, and the eighth most common destination, Cuba, received just one-sixth. Nonetheless, scholarship on the influence of both the Yoruba and other Benin peoples on Bahia and Cuba far outnumbers that on Haiti.[1] Although this essay does not provide the full correction needed, it does highlight the existing opportunities for scholars to rectify that gaping hole in the literature on slave culture in the New World.

Overall the most recent figures indicate that nearly 700,000 Africans were sold into slavery in Saint Domingue. The largest share of this figure came from West-Central Africa, where more than 330,000, or approximately 48 percent, of the total slave imports to Saint Domingue originated. The only other region of Africa whose inhabitants sold to Saint Domingue number more than 100,000 was the Bight of Benin. Nearly 200,000, or 27 percent, of Haiti's total imports originated from the Bight of Benin, with many of them being Yoruba.[2]

Estimates on the number of Yoruba sold into slavery in Haiti vary; the imperfect methodology of corroborating fluidly defined ethnonyms with ports of departure in Africa makes that task even less exact. Historian Philip Curtin estimates that slaves from the Bight of Benin composed the second-highest proportion of slaves in Haiti, ranking behind slaves from West-Central Africa. According to Curtin's figures, approximately 173,000 slaves, or 28 percent of slave imports to Saint Domingue, from the Benin region were sold into enslavement on the island. Of this number, perhaps one-quarter or one-third were ethnic Yoruba, and the largest group from the Benin region were from the coast of Dahomey. Increasing warfare between the Oyo Yoruba state and Dahomey state likely contributed to the large number of persons from each group being present in the trans-Atlantic traffic.[3]

In spite of their political differences and warring, the slaves from Oyo Yoruba and Dahomey had many linguistic and cultural similarities that they accentuated under enslavement in Saint Domingue. As the work of John Thornton has shown convincingly, enslaved Africans had far more linguistic and cultural similarities than differences to accentuate under their common duress of enslavement. The presence in Saint Domingue of Dahomean slaves identified as "Arada" and of Oyo Yoruba slaves identified as "Nagô," as well as the subsequent emergence of Vodou, is evidence of the cultural syncretism which Thornton argues was probable given the cultural and linguistic similarities in western Africa. The similar cosmologies of Allada and Yoruba peoples made the forced and tragic transition to New World enslavement easier than it would have been, at least in cultural terms.[4]

The Yoruba were not the most numerous of the dozens of African cultural groups present in Saint Domingue. However, they constituted one of the three or four largest coteries of slaves on the island, particularly during the late eighteenth century. During the 1760s, when imports from the Bight of Benin represented 28 percent of Saint Domingue's imports, Yoruba accounted for over 6 percent of the total number of imports. As the numbers from Benin increased through the next decade to 42 percent of the decadal traffic, the share of Yoruba rose as well: during the 1770s they constituted 15 percent of imports. In the last decade before the beginning of the Haitian Revolution, the 1780s, Benin imports stabilized at 35 percent of total Africans brought to the island, with Yoruba accounting for just over 7 percent of the totals. Along with slaves identified as Congo, Igbo, and coastal Dahomean, the Yoruba were a significant plurality in a population that had no numerically dominant African culture.[5]

Consequently circumstances in Saint Domingue undergirded the influence of Yoruba on the emerging, pluralized slave culture on the island. Scholarship on Africans in many New World slave societies has demonstrated the influence of African groups whose numbers represented a "critical mass" of cultural memory, transfer, and preservation.[6] Moreover, Yoruba, wherever they constituted a "critical mass," were deeply influential in the formation of slave and post-independence cultures. Historian David Eltis, in noting this phenomenon, argues that the Yoruba culture "in the broad spectrum of Old World influence on the New . . . has had an impact out of all proportion to its relative demographic weight."[7] As an examination of post-independence Haitian culture, particularly religious practice, will demonstrate, that influence in Haiti has stretched well beyond the years of enslavement.

The Nineteenth Century

The Haitian Revolution, aside from its obvious impact of ending slavery, helped to perpetuate the syncretic culture among Africans and African-descended Creoles that the Yoruba had been so integral in forming. In addition, the revolution also triggered a dispersal of Saint Domingue slave owners and their slaves, which in turn, given the large proportion of the island's slaves who were Yoruba or Yoruba descendants, sparked a small enlargement of the Yoruba diaspora. The Yoruba-influenced Haitian slave culture was exported to slave societies throughout the circum-Caribbean. Though slave owners from Saint Domingue fled to many colonies in the circum-Caribbean, the most notable exception of this migration planting a Yoruba presence where it did not exist before was Louisiana. In 1809 nearly ten thousand persons from Saint Domingue — including more than three thousand slaves and an equal number of free people of color — arrived in New Orleans, having spent the previous several years in Cuba.[8] In addition to augmenting the growing slave population in and around New Orleans, this migration provided the only substantive number of Africans who were Yoruba or of Yoruba descent.[9]

In Haiti, where independence became a reality in 1804, Yoruba and other former slaves continued to toil in jobs similar to those they had performed as slaves. With few Africans performing jobs as urban slaves prior to the Haitian Revolution, the freed slaves remained largely agricultural laborers in the decades following the uprising. As a mostly rural populace, with minimal cultural interference from urban elites, the cultural, social, and religious traditions forged by these former slaves continued.[10]

The most significant of those traditions was Vodou, a religious amalgam that the Yoruba, Allada, Congolese, and Igbo had developed as a means of mitigating the rigors of enslavement, and of preserving their own religious traditions while incorporating elements of Roman Catholicism. In those pockets of heavily Africanized populations, social and cultural traditions akin to those of particular West African societies were maintained. Most notably, the religious practice of Vodou not only continued but grew, causing a deep social and political divide within the fledgling republic.[11]

Vodou had its origins in the religions of Dahomean and Yoruba peoples. A corruption of the Dahomean word for spirit, Vodou took on a decidedly Atlantic meaning in Haiti, and in other places where similar African and New World traditions emerged. As early as the mid-eighteenth century in Saint Domingue, Vodou had emerged as an important part of the evolving slave culture. The subsequent high numbers of slaves from the Bight of Benin who arrived between 1760 and 1790 triggered the expansion of Vodou. During the revolution Vodou's role may have been important, although that correlation has recently come under question.[12] Nonetheless, following the revolution, Vodou's centrality to the everyday activities and cosmologies of the mostly African populations of the countryside grew.

Though Vodou did indeed arise out of slaves in Saint Domingue combining the religious traditions of several African cultures with their New World environs, Yoruba religious symbolism came to dominate the iconography of the religion. Yoruba or Dahomean deities, such as Ogun, the lord of fire, constitute important religious as well as social and political meanings within Haiti. With his symbol of the machete, Ogun represented, and still represents, a source of power for Haitians. In addition, Ezili, the water goddess of love in Haitian Vodou, is a powerful example of Yoruba influence and of the attendant cultural symbiosis of West African religions and Roman Catholicism. According to one scholar of Vodou, "Ezili in Haiti derives from diverse African ethnic religious traditions . . . most striking are the resemblances between the personae of Ezili in Haiti and those of Oshun in Nigeria and Ezili in Ouidah, Benin."[13] Though the enslaved population as a whole transformed Catholic iconology to match African religious symbols, the prevalence of Yoruba symbolism in the syncretic religious creations illustrates the cultural power of the Yoruba both during and after enslavement. Likely a result of the Yoruba's rich oral traditions, the influence the Yoruba garnered within the island's pluralized African population indicates the existence of a pidgin Yoruba language serving as the lingua franca among African-descended peoples in Haiti.

By the end of the nineteenth century Vodou faced increasing hostility from the Haitian government and from intellectuals. Seen as an institution that prevented Haiti's development as a "civilized" nation, these late-nineteenth-century intellectuals presented the same challenge to African heritage that enslavement did. In spite of these challenges, Vodou remained an integral part of Haitian society. The pattern that had ensured its survival for decades—the intertwining of African religious practices with the officially established beliefs of Roman Catholicism—prevented the government and intellectuals from undermining the continued growth of Vodou. Deeply rooted among the populace, and nebulous in its form, Vodou, and its attendant African cultural heritage, experienced a revival of sorts during the early twentieth century as a new generation of intellectuals "began to take Vodou seriously as part of the national heritage."[14] Since that time, particularly during the last twenty years, scholars have become increasingly interested in Vodou as an example of enslaved Africans' success in preserving their cultural, social, and religious traditions. Whether exploring that issue in reference to enslaved Africans as a single group, or in reference to important components of that group such as the Yoruba, Vodou remains a compelling example both of Yoruba influence and of the creative, long-lasting ways in which enslaved peoples forged a way to mitigate enslavement.

Though that purpose is no longer necessary, the Yoruba influence on Haitian art, dance, and folklore continues to be significant, in large part because of the intertwined nature of those expressive forms and religious practice. Whereas in many former slave societies in the New World it has become increasingly difficult to locate cultural heritages of particular West African societies, the Yoruba influence in Haiti remains a central element in modern Haitian culture. The amalgam of many cultures, particularly the mixing of Yoruba, Dahomey, and Congolese traditions, has produced a culture that is more recognizable as Haitian than as Yoruba, but the influence of the thousands of Yoruba enslaved on the island during the eighteenth century remains an important element of that Haitian culture.

Notes

1. David Eltis et al., *The Transatlantic Slave Trade: A Database on CD-ROM* (Cambridge: Cambridge University Press, 1999), query: "Full time period and Where slaves embarked = Bight of Benin." For examples of scholarship on Yoruba influences in Bahia and in Cuba, see Juan Gonzalez Diaz, "El cabildo congo de nueva paz o sociedad africana virgen de regal," *Revista de la Biblioteca Nacional José Marti* 2 (1992): 37–54; João José Reis, *Slave Rebellion in Brazil: The Muslim Uprising of 1835 in Bahia*, trans. Arthur Brakel (Baltimore: The Johns Hopkins University Press, 1993); Marta Moreno Vega,

"Interlocking African Diaspora Cultures in the Work of Fernando Ortiz," *Journal of Black Studies* 31 (2000): 39–50; Jim Wafer and Hedimo Rodrigues Santana, "Africa in Brazil: Cultural Politics and the Candomblé Religion," *Folklore Forum* 23 (1990): 98–114.

2. Eltis et al., *Slave Trade Database*, query: "Full time period and Where slaves disembarked = St. Domingue."

3. For an excellent analysis of the methodological obstacle presented by the designation "Yoruba," see Robin Law, "Ethnicity and the Slave Trade: 'Lucumi' and 'Nago' as Ethnonyms in West Africa," *History in Africa* 24 (1997): 205–19; Philip D. Curtin, *The Atlantic Slave Trade: A Census* (Madison: University of Wisconsin Press, 1969), 200, 192–94.

4. John Thornton, *Africa and Africans in the Making of the Atlantic World, 1400–1800*, 2nd ed. (Cambridge: Cambridge University Press, 1998), 252–53; Peter Morton-Williams, "An Outline of the Cosmology and Cult Organization of the Oyo Yoruba," in *Peoples and Cultures of Africa*, ed. Elliot Skinner (Garden City, N.Y.: published for the American Museum of Natural History by Natural History Press, 1973), 654–77.

5. Curtin, *Slave Trade*, 192–94; Eltis et al., *Slave Trade Database*, query: "Full time period and Where slaves disembarked = St. Domingue."

6. For example, see Michael A. Gomez, *Exchanging our Country Marks: The Transformation of African Identities in the Colonial and Antebellum South* (Chapel Hill: University of North Carolina Press, 1998).

7. David Eltis, *The Rise of African Slavery in the Americas* (Cambridge: Cambridge University Press, 2000), 253.

8. Paul F. Lachance, "The 1809 Immigration of Saint-Domingue Refugees from New Orleans: Reception, Integration, and Impact," *Louisiana History* 29 (1988): 109–41.

9. In my research of nearly ten thousand slave baptisms from 1790 to 1811 at St. Louis Cathedral in New Orleans, this is the only period in which slaves identified as "Nagô" appear in the records.

10. On this status of nineteenth-century rural peasants, see David Nicholls, *Haiti in Caribbean Context: Ethnicity, Economy, and Revolt* (New York: St. Martin's, 1985), 167–85.

11. Ibid.

12. Carolyn E. Fick, *The Making of Haiti: The Saint Domingue Revolution from Below* (Knoxville: University of Tennessee Press, 1990), 92–94; David Geggus, "Marronage, Vodou, and the Saint Domingue Slave Revolt of 1791," *Proceedings of the Annual Meeting of the French Colonial Historical Society* 15 (1992): 22–35.

13. Leslie G. Desmangles, *The Faces of the Gods: Vodou and Roman Catholicism in Haiti* (Chapel Hill: University of North Carolina Press, 1992), 143–51.

14. Nicholls, *Haiti in Caribbean Context*, 212–13.

III

THE CULTURAL FOUNDATIONS
OF THE YORUBA DIASPORA

CHAPTER TEN

The "Nagôization" Process in Bahian Candomblé

Luis Nicolau Parés

Candomblé is the name given to the regional development of Afro-Brazilian religion in the state of Bahia. Like other religious practice that originated in African traditions brought into Brazil by slaves, Candomblé involves the worship of a series of spiritual entities, often associated with forces of nature, who receive periodic ritual offerings in their shrines. Candomblé is also a spirit possession cult where some devotees, by different initiation processes, are prepared to embody or to impersonate these deities, who during public ceremonies will dance for hours to the sound of the drums. Regular interaction with the gods is supposed to bring fortune to the religious group and to defend it against misfortune.

Beyond the shared liturgical aspects and conceptual consensus that allow Candomblé to be considered a religious institution (i.e., divination, initiation, sacrifice, spirit possession, healing, celebration, etc.), cult groups often resort to the discourse of "nations" to negotiate, construct, and legitimate their ritual differences and collective identities. Today Candomblé cult houses generally claim to belong to one of the three main nations, Nagô, Jeje, and Angola, which are characterized by the worship of different kinds of spiritual entities. The Nagô worship the orixás, the Jeje the voduns, and the Angola the enkices. There are also the caboclos, although cult houses exclusively worshiping these Brazilian spiritual entities seldom claim to constitute a nation.[1] Each of these groups of African deities is usually praised in the corresponding ritual language (Yoruba, Gbe,[2] and Bantu-derived dialectal forms) and has its own ritual particularities (drum rhythms, dances, food offerings, etc.). Hence, despite the creative eclecticism and movement of values and practices across nation boundaries, certain key ritual features are considered important as diacritical signs of a real or imagined continuity with a distinct African past and religious tradition. However, beneath the inclusiveness inherent in the concept of nation, the basic unit of collective identity and pride is the cult group itself, and congregations belonging to the same nation, despite their possible solidarity and cooperation, are not above engaging in a competitive dynamic.

During fieldwork in Bahia between 1935 and 1937 American sociologist Donald Pierson recorded an often-quoted sentence by Eugênia Ana dos Santos, *mãe* Aninha, founder and leader of the Axé Opô Afonjá and one of the most famous priestesses of Candomblé in Salvador at that time. "My sect is pure Nagô, like the Engenho Velho. I have revived a great part of the African tradition which even the Engenho Velho has forgotten. Do they have there a ceremony for the twelve ministers of Xangô? No! But I do."[3] The quote is significant for two reasons.

First, as Vivaldo da Costa Lima notes, *mãe* Aninha's identification of her "terreiro"[4] with the Nagô nation derives from her religious affiliation to a Nagô cult house—the Engenho Velho where she was initiated—and not from kinship, since Aninha's parents were known to be Grunci, an ethnic group from present-day Ghana with no cultural ties to Yorubaland. Hence, at least since the early twentieth century, Bahian Creoles could identify themselves as Nagô by virtue of their religious initiation, regardless of their ethnic ancestry. Lima remarks how the concept of nation gradually lost its political connotation, becoming an almost exclusively theological concept.[5] In the first part of this chapter I examine the historicity of the expansive-inclusive dynamic of the Nagô ethnonym and whether—once restricted to the area of religion—it ever did in fact lose its political connotation.

Second, Aninha's words also establish an explicit conceptual association between the notion of "purity" and the Nagô religious tradition preserved in her cult house and the Engenho Velho—"the eldest Brazilian candomblé," according to oral tradition. Implicit in her remark is an opposition between "Nagô purity" and other "impure," "mixed," or "syncretic" traditions. Furthermore, Aninha claims to have "revived a great part of the African tradition" which even the Engenho Velho had lost, implying a greater closeness and fidelity to Africa which resulted in a surplus of "traditionalism" and authenticity. As several authors have shown, the institution of the twelve ministers, or "obás," of Xangô (male dignitaries who support the leadership of the high priestess) introduced by Aninha and her close friend, the *babalawo* Martiniano Eliseo do Bomfim, was inspired by the political organization of the Oyo kingdom and the Yoruba logic of left and right division. Yet, as constituted in the Brazilian religious cult, the institution of the obás was a rather creative adaptation that found no counterpart in Yorubaland.[6]

Conceived as legitimizing an imagined African orthodoxy, the institution of the ministers of Xangô could be interpreted as a self-conscious attempt to invest a "disturbed past" (as Sidney Mintz qualifies the past of any Afro-American culture) with continuity and moral significance, and, in that sense, it would provide a good example of the "invention of tradition."[7] Ultimately the initiative served wide political goals of black self-determination and empowerment, but it also served as a marker of difference and of status compared to concurrent religious congregations like the Engenho Velho. The "ideology of prestige" founded on the conceptual triad "Africa–purity–tradition" has been promoted within Candomblé since its beginnings, but in the last decades has become more explicit and widespread. The strong relationship between what is often referred to as the "re-Africanization" movement and the Bahian Nagô-Ketu "traditional" cult houses and the Yoruba cultural complex will constitute the focus of the second part of the chapter.

Outline of the Nagô Ethnogenesis and Its Expansive-Inclusive Dynamic

In Brazil the Yoruba ethnonym was seldom heard until recently, although in Afro-Brazilian studies Nina Rodrigues, influenced by the works of Ellis, used it in 1906, and Manoel Querino in 1916. During the Brazilian slave trade period, and later in Candomblé, the term commonly used to designate Yoruba-speaking peoples was "Nagô"; hence I propose to briefly examine the historicity of this particular denomination and the changes its meaning may have experienced through time.

To my knowledge, the first written reference to Nagô in West Africa appears in 1731 in Labat's report of the journey of Chevalier des Marchais in 1725. At this time "Nagô" was used by European and local slave traders in Ouidah and Allada to label a specific group of slaves that they differentiated from other Yoruba-speaking peoples such as the Ayois (Oyo) or Tebou (Ijebu).[8] The Nagô (Anagô, Nagot, or Nagônu) probably were a particular ethnic group settled around the city of Ifonyin in the Egbado region, west of the Yewa River. As Mercier suggests, Anagô may have been originally the ethnic self-denomination of this group. Yet, with time, their Dahomean neighbors began to use the term— which in Fon may also have been a pejorative nickname, meaning "dirty" or "ragged"—to refer not only to the Nagô proper but to a plurality of other western Yoruba-speaking peoples.[9]

The generic dimension the term acquired among the Dahomeans would explain why in 1846 the Scot John Duncan, when crossing the Dassa Mountains (neighboring the Mahi country north of Abomey), called its people "Annagoos," even though the Dassa (Idassa), whose royal genealogy goes back to 1700, claim origin in Egbaland. The use of the term "anagô" to refer generically to the western Yoruba-speaking peoples seems also to be related to the religious context. By the mid-seventeenth century vodun cults of Yoruba origin, like those of Mawu and Lisa, were well known in the Allada kingdom. In the early eighteenth century the cult of the smallpox vodun Sakpata was also imported into Abomey by King Agadja, according to several versions from the town of Dassa-Zoumé. Interestingly, the devotees of these voduns, like those of the iron vodun Gu, receive the name of "anago" or "anagonu" at the end of their initiation. The Sakpata devotees speak and sing in a ritual language that also includes "archaic" Yoruba words. Since it is difficult to imagine these critical religious features to be recent innovations, and because there is evidence that these cults existed at least as far back as the seventeenth century, one could speculate that not only did these vodun cults have a proto-Yoruba ascendance, but also that religious practice together with the slave trade contributed to the semantic expansion of the term "Anagô" or "Nagô."[10]

Thus an internal ethnic self-designation was increasingly used by neighboring groups as an external label to designate a wider universe of culturally heterogeneous people. In the Dahomean mind, the logic of this semantic inclusive expansion rested on the perception of linguistic similarities shared by their neighbors and the fact that they were under the political influence of the Oyo kingdom. Yet it is questionable whether in West Africa the term "Nagô" had ever had a political or ethnic connotation acknowledged by all the Yoruba-speaking peoples themselves. As Gerhard Kubik argues, terms like "Nagô," "Mina," and others started out in the context of the slave trade as "trademarks for human 'goods' to be sold."[11]

In Bahia the first reference to a "Nagô" slave I was able to find dates from 1734 but the term becomes more commonly used only beginning in 1750, coinciding with the shift of the slave trade from Ouidah to the eastern ports of Porto Novo, Badagry, and Onim (Lagos). Nevertheless, during the second half of the eighteenth century, the Jeje (Gbe area) and Angola (Central Africa) were the most demographically predominant African groups in Bahia, while the Nagô only reached a modest 4 percent among the evaluated slave population.[12] As is already well documented by historians, the massive importation of Nagô slaves occurred over the first half of the nineteenth century, coinciding with the gradual disintegration of the Oyo Empire which was initiated by the revolt of Afonja (c. 1797) and the jihad launched by the Fulanis in 1804. As the century progressed and the Oyo's disintegration accelerated amid civil wars, the Nagô captives became more and more numerous, and by 1820 they were already the largest African-born group in Bahia. Between 1840 and 1860 their presence became overwhelming: in Salvador, reaching from 56 percent to 69 percent (according to different sources) of the African slave population.[13]

Initially the term "Nagô" may have been used primarily by slave traders, slave owners, and Catholic Church officials in the service of advertisement and administration, helping to categorize the ethnic plurality of the slave population. However, recently arrived Yoruba-speaking slaves—through linguistic ability to communicate and then by realizing cultural and religious commonalities—may have progressively used the already locally operative ethnonym as a self-denomination emphasizing their collective identity. In this way Nagô also came to designate the Yoruba-based lingua franca spoken throughout the nineteenth century by Africans and their descendants in Bahia. Given this situation, it is possible that non-Yoruba people, either Africans or Creoles, learned the

Nagô language, and by this means became identified as such.[14] Yet beneath the inclusive Nagô unity, within their inner social circles Africans preserved the ethnonyms of their lands of origin, such as Oyo, Egba, Ijexá, and so on, thus contributing to the formation of a multiple and relational system of ethnic identification.

In any case, collective identities were articulated and expressed by means of participation in institutionalized forms of social organization. Brazilian "African nations," like Angola, Jeje, and Nagô, defined their social boundaries in a dialogical relationship, valuing particular cultural features to establish differences between them. This contrastive and often competitive dynamic favoring ethnic identities found fertile ground in institutions such as work crews (cantos), Catholic brotherhoods and their feasts (folias), secular drumming-dancing gatherings (batuques), and African-derived religious congregations (candomblés).[15]

Space limitations do not permit an examination of all these forms of collective organization, and so I concentrate on the last. Suffice it to say that the division of the batuques into nations was especially significant in the first half of the nineteenth century, and was even supported and encouraged by certain sectors of the dominant class. The Bahian governor Conde dos Arcos, for example, allowed slaves to celebrate their feasts as a way of mitigating their distress, but also to stimulate animosity between different ethnic groups in order to prevent their potential subversive union in revolts.[16]

If the Jeje, Angola, and Nagô ethnic identities found a means of expression and differentiation in secular ritual forms like the batuques, it was probably in African-derived religious practices where these identities took on a critical function. Continuing with the African tradition whereby collective identity was built around the worship of particular spiritual entities, in Brazil, too, despite the disintegration of kinship corporations (or perhaps because of it), religious activities allowed for the reshaping of new communal identities.

By the mid-eighteenth century it is probable that the Angola, Jeje, and other West African groups like the Courana had already set the basis for the future institutionalization of Candomblé, promoting the organization of religious congregations in domestic and, most important, extra-domestic spheres.[17] As I have argued elsewhere, the latter form of religious organization—going beyond the mere healing and oracular activities and involving an *ecclesiastical* structure with fixed shrines, a priesthood hierarchy, and complex processes of initiation— may have been greatly influenced by the Jeje religious experts who had previous experience in the organization of such convents or "mystical schools." A logical inference from this hypothesis is that when the Nagô arrived in Brazil in the late eighteenth and early nineteenth centuries, despite sharing with the Jeje similar forms of religious worship, they may already have found an incipient form of religious institutionalization involving the cult of multiple deities within the same temple, as well as serial forms of ritual performance.[18] It is to be noted that this argument stands in contrast to the contemporary oral tradition, which claims that the first candomblé in Salvador was the Ilê Iya Nassô or Engenho Velho of the Nagô-Ketu nation.[19]

The record indicates a number of religious cult groups in the early nineteenth century, and, if our argument is correct, we could further speculate that, despite the massive demographic superiority of the Nagô from 1820 on, the Jeje religious traditions were critical points of reference in the organization of ritual practice. This seems to be confirmed by the available historical data from the 1860s, as well as by contemporary linguistic ethnographic evidence. For instance, to this day, in houses that claim to be "pure Nagô," the names to designate the members of the initiation group (*dofona, dafonitinha, gamo, gamotinha*, etc.), the initiation room (*hunco*), the shrine's room (*peji*), the drums (*hun*), and other central ritual features are Jeje terminology (i.e., of Gbe linguistic origin). That these elements form a part of the "deep structure" of the cult points toward critical agency by the Jeje in the founding of the institution of Candomblé.[20]

Available copies of the satirical journal *O Alabama* cover the period from 1863 to 1871. The journal was published in Salvador by pro-abolitionist African descendants who launched a systematic campaign against Candomblé. Despite its strong ideological bias, *O Alabama* documented names of participants, locations of terreiros, African terminology, and various feasts and religious activities that were sometimes witnessed by the journalists, who provided quasiethnographic descriptions. This rich data make it clear that by 1860 Candomblé had already attained the stage of institutionalization with levels of ritual and social complexity very similar to those of today.

These data, while often referring to Africans involved in candomblés, give no indication at all that the terreiros were identified with particular nations. Yet a quantitative linguistic analysis of its African terminology indicates a similar number of Jeje and Nagô terms, suggesting a Jeje-Nagô religious equilibrium, if not a slight Jeje-dominance. For instance, "vudum" was the common term to designate the African deities. The most famous term today, the Yoruba word "orixá," only appears in the composite term "babaloixa," a title to designate the high priest. References to specific deities also indicate a relative equilibrium between voduns and orixás.[21]

Furthermore, taking into account the ethnic origin of Candomblé leaders (when reported) and the contemporary identification of the nation of some terreiros mentioned in *O Alabama*—such as the Gantois (Nagô), Bogum (Jeje), or Batefolha (Congo-Angola)—a similar quantitative equilibrium between Nagô and Jeje cult houses is found, if not, once again, a slight predominance of the Jeje over the Nagô. Other examples could be added, but the main point is that, despite the significant demographic and cultural presence of the Nagô in midnineteenth-century Afro-Bahian society, within the institution of Candomblé there is no clear evidence that they exerted a particular dominance or had more social visibility than other nations, at least until 1870. This case would also demonstrate how cultural influence is not necessarily related to demographics.

The First Stage of the "Nagôization" Process: The Late Nineteenth Century

Only at the end of the nineteenth century can the emergence and visibility of the Nagô tradition in Candomblé be identified. In his posthumous work, *Os africanos no Brasil*, Rodrigues acknowledged that at the start of his studies he was not able to differentiate between the Jeje and Nagô mythologies given their "intimate fusion." Nonetheless, he concluded, "Today the Ewe [Jeje] mythology is dominated by the Yoruba one." Following Ellis, he explains the assimilation of the Jeje culture by the Nagô in terms of the latter's linguistic dominance and the "more complex and elevated" nature of the Nagô religious beliefs. While the evolutionist argument is seriously questionable, the perception of a supremacy of the Nagô tradition over the Jeje (and implicitly over all other nations) was reproduced by Edison Carneiro and Artur Ramos in the 1930s and 1940s and persists to this day.[22]

As will be discussed below, authors like Beatriz Gois Dantas have argued that the Nagô prestige was mainly owing to the work of intellectuals who concentrated their research exclusively on cult houses of this nation. But why did the intellectuals approach the Nagô houses in the first place? Nina Rodrigues indeed conducted his research in the house of Gantois (Ilê Iyá Omin Axé Iyamassé) but, as reported in *O Alabama*, this terreiro (then known as Moinho) was already quite well known by the late 1860s. Decades later, in 1896, still led by her African founder, *tia* Julia, and her daughter, Pulcheria, Gantois continued to garner the attention of the Afro-Bahian community with feasts that attracted enormous crowds.[23]

Thus Gantois's reputation had already been established well before Rodrigues started his research, which may have been one of the reasons why he approached it in the first place. His focus on this Nagô congregation probably minimized his perception of the internal diversity of Candomblé in the same way that, when studying the work crews (*cantos*), he focused on the African ones, ignoring the Creole ones. Yet it seems unlikely that an attentive observer like Rodrigues would not have noticed the use of the term "vudum" if it was still widely used in the religious community as it appears to have been in the 1860s. This suggests that a significant change took place between 1870 and 1895, finally propelling Nagô referents—such as the term "orixá," for instance—to the foreground.

The first stage of what I call the Nagôization process in Candomblé cannot be explained as the result of a single cause. Rather, it must be understood in the context of a complex interaction of a plurality of factors that can only be tentatively explored here. The agency of the Nagô cult groups and the charisma of their leaders should be noted as a first possible vector. For instance, in mentioning the Jeje vodun Loko, Rodrigues comments that "some black Nagô tried to correct me about the name Lôco . . . saying it was just a Creole corruption of the true name Irôco."[24] In *O Alabama* all references to this important tree deity appear under the Jeje version, Lôco, but by the end of the century the Nagô practitioners themselves are imposing their own Yoruba version, dismissing the traditional Jeje name as just a "Creole corruption." This shows that an ethnocentric Nagô "purification" in opposition to "Creole corruption" was already under way, and also demonstrates how the agency of the Nagô practitioners may have been instrumental in their social-religious promotion.

The effect of individual charisma on religious change has not been sufficiently stressed. Within the relatively small Afro-Bahian religious community, strong characters like Pulcheria, Martiniano Eliseu do Bomfim, Aninha, and others were able to emerge as leaders whose words and actions—whether traditional or innovative—might have been readily followed or taken as models to imitate. Their idiosyncrasies of character, together with their ability to mobilize a wide social network, greatly contributed to the prestige of their cult houses, and, consequently, the ritual practices of terreiros like Gantois began to serve as models for many other cult houses emerging in the post-Abolition period.

As documented by local newspapers, between 1896 and 1905 there seems to have been a significant increase of new candomblés.[25] The perception of religious activity as a means of social upward mobility for blacks in as tumultuous a period as post-Abolition may partially explain this growth. Most of these new cult houses were founded by Creole women and not male Africans as had been the tendency in previous decades. This gender shift in leadership does not seem to be linked to the Nagôization process, except that Candomblé's moment of expansion coincided with the emergence of the Nagô prestige, hence contributing to the mimetic replication and diffusion of Nagô ritual patterns.

What circumstances would have favored the awareness of a Nagô identity and subsequent efforts to legitimate its "superiority" against concurrent traditions perceived as "Creole corruption"? The gender shift may not have been critical, but the long-established African-Creole antagonism seems to have been important. By the end of the century there were still a few African terreiros, as suggested by an old African woman who told Rodrigues she did not dance in the Gantois because it was of "gente da terra" [i.e., Creole and mulatto], whereas her terreiro was of "gente da costa" [i.e., Africans].[26] In fact, Gantois, founded by Africans, had become increasingly Creole. One can hypothesize that precisely because of this, as African terreiros began to disappear, the claims of African identity by terreiros like Gantois increased, as African religious practices began to be seen as more efficacious than the discriminated Creole ones. But why was the Nagô tradition the one to gain such a privileged position? This may be related to a particular idea of Africa taking shape precisely at that moment.

Following Paul Gilroy's lead, Lorand Matory has looked at the transnational construction of black identities in Brazil. Examining the nineteenth-century black Atlantic network of communication, he has noted that "at the British-dominated crossroads of African / African-American interaction, the Yoruba acquired a highly-publicized reputation for superiority to other Africans. This reputation for superiority was useful in the 1880s and 1890s, as the bourgeois black

Lagosians faced new forms of economic disadvantage and racial discrimination." Taking into account this transnational Yoruba ethnogenesis, Matory further argues that values of black racial and religious purity associated with contemporary Candomblé "seem to be rooted in the racial and cultural nationalism of the Lagosian renaissance in the 1890s" and that "much that appears to 'survive' of African religion in the Americas is in fact shaped by an African cultural politics that long postdated the slave trade."[27]

Ethnographic and historical data provide ground to relativize Matory's thesis, showing how the legacy of African religious practices during the slave trade period, together with the local agency of Creole descendants, had a major role in creating and reshaping ethnic-religious identities within Candomblé. However, as Matory suggests, it is also possible that late-nineteenth-century trans-Atlantic cultural exchanges had some influence on this process.

The trans-Atlantic communication between Bahia and the Mina Coast had been under way since the late eighteenth century but increased after 1835, with hundreds of African returnees settling along the Mina Coast each year, many of them in Lagos, contributing to the above-mentioned Yoruba renaissance, and others regularly traveling and doing business between both shores. In this context, it is probable that the disputes between English and French colonial powers in the 1880s and 1890s, each promoting new local ethnic identities—like Yoruba and Djedje in Nigeria and Dahomey, respectively—may have had some resonance for the Afro-Bahian community.[28] This influence might have been particularly fruitful in the area of religion where a long-established, latent ethnic-ritual division provided fertile ground for "nationalistic" revivals. It should be noted that Lagos was the most common ship destination during this period; it thus follows logically that it was more likely that news would be brought from the Yoruba cultural area than from other regions. It is also worth noting for our subsequent argument that the city of Ketu, after being destroyed by the Dahomeans in 1883 and 1886, was only reconstructed in 1896, and that news from these events may have reached Bahia at that time.

In this context, the factual or imagined trips of religious experts to Africa—acquiring "authentic" esoteric knowledge and thus recovering a "tradition" that had been lost during the traumatic experience of slavery—constituted symbolic cultural capital that greatly increased their social prestige, religious efficacy, and power. The journey back to the origins became a central narrative element in the myth of foundation of the "oldest candomblé of Brazil," the Ilê Iyá Nassô or Engenho Velho. Pierre Veger collected oral testimonies stating that Iyá Nassô—one of the founders of the terreiro—together with her spiritual daughter, Marcelina da Silva (Obá Tossi), and the latter's biological daughter, Magdalena, traveled to Africa and spent seven years in Ketu. They then returned to Bahia accompanied by the African *babalawo* Rodolfo Martins the Andrade (Bamboxé) and Magdalena's three newborn children.

According to Bastide's version, Iyá Nassô arrived in Bahia as a free person to found the candomblé in the 1830s; Obá Tossi also arrived as a free person but returned to Ketu for seven years before assuming leadership of the terreiro after Iyá Nassô's death. Despite the possible and yet undocumented factual reality behind these contradictory narratives, the mythical character of these journeys is apparent. They legitimate the myth of foundation of the Engenho Velho by reinforcing the idea of direct contact with "pure" African sources while stressing the free status of its actors.[29]

The case of Martiniano Eliseu do Bomfim is probably the other most well known example of a "trans-Atlantic religious expert" and has been widely commented on in Afro-Brazilian studies. In interviews by Pierson in the years 1935–37, Martiniano stated that he had lived in Lagos between 1875 and 1886, and subsequently made two shorter trips as well. In West Africa he became initiated as *babalawo*, and after his return to Bahia he became an informant of Rodrigues, thus reinforcing the researcher's already Nagô-oriented gaze. Martiniano helped his close friend *mãe* Aninha to found Axé Opô Afonjá in 1910, and to establish the ministers of Xangô in 1937, when he was already famous and well respected. His charisma, religious zeal, and Yoruba "purism" made him an early advocate of the re-Africanization of Candomblé or, more precisely, a critical agent of its Nagôization.[30]

Summarizing, the first stage of the Nagôization of Candomblé seems to be the result of a complex series of interrelated factors favoring the visibility and prestige of a small number of cult houses. The late nineteenth century seems to establish the conceptual basis for a notion of Africa as the original *locus* of a "tradition" that had to be recovered, reinventing continuities in order to overcome a "disrupted past." This African idealization also constituted an alternative to, and reaction against, the growing assimilationist Creole culture. Synchronized with the heightening of Yoruba cultural supremacy in the black Atlantic world, this process of re-Africanization emerged effectively as one of Nagôization and within some sectors of the religious community it may also have been perceived as a strategy to achieve black political empowerment.

Nagô "Purity" against Caboclo "Mixture" and the Role of Intellectuals

If in the late nineteenth century there were already some signs of the myth of African purity associated with a selected number of terreiros, by the 1930s that myth had been consolidated and somehow made "official." In 1937 the Second Afro-Brazilian Congress was held in Salvador, with both intellectuals and significant members of the Candomblé priesthood participating. This event was significant as a strong statement in favor of religious freedom and social recognition for Candomblé as a whole, while also sanctioning the traditionalism and social visibility of a few Nagô-Ketu houses. In this second stage of the Nagôization process, the late-nineteenth-century African-Creole ethnic antagonism seems to transform into an Orixá-Caboclo religious antagonism discriminating against the latter as a "mixed" cult. Concurrently the influence of intellectuals in the internal dynamic of Candomblé began to be significant.

The 1920s and early 1930s are remembered as a period of strong police repression of Candomblé. It was during the late 1920s, for instance, that the legendary and feared police chief Pedrito was in office. Local newspapers report regular interventions in various terreiros denouncing their "barbarous" and "uncivilized" practices. Significantly most of the terreiros suffering from this repression were non-Nagô and headed by men, while there are no reports at all of assaults on the main Nagô-Ketu traditional houses.[31]

Following a long-established tradition dating back to the nineteenth century, Candomblé priests and priestesses maintained regular contacts and sometimes intimate relationships with the political elite. As Lima notes, these strategies should be analyzed from the perspective of an "ideology of prestige." Mãe Aninha had contacts with the Brazilian president Getúlio Vargas and knew Osvaldo Aranha, chief of the Civil House, as well as other ministers and diplomats. Bernardinho of Batefolha was a close friend of Juracy Magalhães, who was governor of Bahia between 1934 and 1937, and instrumental in creating a political climate relatively favorable to Candomblé.[32]

By 1936 this political tolerance resulted in a significant positive shift in media representation of Candomblé. This change anticipated the occurrence, in January 1937, of the Second Afro-Brazilian Congress, organized by Edison Carneiro and Aydano do Couto Ferraz, and presided over by Martiniano Eliseu do Bomfim. Before the conference Carneiro published in the Estado da Bahia several informative articles and interviews with priests like Martiniano, Jubiabá, Joãozinho da Goméia, and Manoel Paim. Live Candomblé music was played by Joãozinho da Goméia and his filhas-de-santo at a local radio station with "Nagô, Bantu and Caboclo" songs. The Congress program included visits to the three main Nagô-Ketu terreiros, Engenho Velho, Gantois, and Axé Opô Afonjá, to the terreiro of Procópio, and a public ceremony in the house of Joãozinho da Goméia. In following months local papers announced the public feasts in the Nagô-Ketu candomblés Gantois and Engenho Velho, "the oldest and purest candomblés of Bahia" [my emphasis], as well as those of the house of Alaketu.[33]

In subsequent reports, whether critical or supportive of Candomblé, whenever ethnic referents appeared they were always Nagô, Yoruba, or, for the first time, Ketu.[34] Hence, despite Carneiro's effort to include representatives of various tendencies, the Congress came to reinforce the Nagô visibility and to further consolidate the supremacy of the three traditional houses: Engenho Velho, Gantois, and Opô Afonjá.

In order to guarantee and secure the religious freedom of Candomblé supported by the Afro-Brazilian Congress, in September 1937 Carneiro managed to organize and found the União das Seitas Afro-Brasileiras (Union of Afro-Brazilian Sects), which would replace the police in controlling religious activities. The União was inaugurated with formal support from governor Juracy Magalhães and included sixty-seven terreiros out of an estimated one hundred existing at that time. According to Bastide, the União signaled what Couto Ferraz then already called "the return to Africa," unifying the traditional houses in search of the African "primitive purity of the cults," to the detriment and exclusion of syncretic practices, particularly those involving caboclos.[35]

While attending the Congress in 1937, composer Camargo Guarnieri collected 152 Candomblé ritual songs. Of these, 46 were described as Ketu, Jeje, or Ijexá, 14 were Angola-Congo, and 92 were categorized as Caboclo. The large number of caboclo songs may be indicative of the importance of the caboclo worship at that time, and may also explain why its cult, which had been growing since the late nineteenth century, was perceived as a menace. Pierson's interviews clearly indicate the discrimination against and even scorn for the new Caboclo houses by several orthodox priests, who denounced the caboclo cult as "mixed nonsense" or "imitators" deprived of any tradition. Lima also mentions the discrimination against the new terreiros of the 1930s "called 'clandestinos' by the old priests and priestesses in their ethnocentric severity." It should be noted that it was during this period that *mãe* Aninha stressed the Nagô purity of her house.[36]

Candomblé experts indeed have a critical sense for differentiating what they judge "certo" (authentic, true) from what they label "errado," "deturpado," or "misturado" (wrong, modified, mixed). These criteria rely mostly on formal aspects of the religious practice rather than on significant differences of beliefs. In a competitive religious market, constantly evaluated and judged is the opportunity and efficacy of the practice, and implicitly the knowledge or spiritual power of its agents. It is the structural and formal orders of the praxis that become the target of criticism among experts. In that sense, mediated by informal gossip (*fofoca*), disputes between experts in matters of ritual orthodoxy form one of the main arenas for establishing difference and identity.

As we have seen, the practices of a particular cult group are legitimized in terms of an alleged African cultural heritage transmitted by previous generations through initiation and spiritual genealogy. When this historical past is absent, an important mechanism in legitimizing new houses involves the recruitment or fostering of a senior member of a prestigious house who, with the necessary esoteric knowledge, assumes an important hierarchical position in the new congregation. Alternatively religious knowledge is said to be "inspired" by the spiritual entities themselves, which usually translates as idiosyncratic imitation of prestigious models. By these means, despite formal accusations of "unorthodoxy," strategic alliances are established, and ritual values and practices are replicated and perpetuated. Ultimately the micro-politics of religious congregations are always based on simultaneous alignment with a few allied terreiros and the ancestors from which the knowledge was inherited, and a parallel differentiation (or disqualification) of concurrent religious groups.

In this dialogic dynamic, the concept of purity—understood as fidelity to an African cultural heritage perpetuated through generations without change— becomes an important category in the discourse of Candomblé participants. Although any historic analysis of religious practices would reveal this concept of static continuity to be merely an ideal or a myth, it must be admitted that many religious experts seriously believe in it and have difficulty in acknowledging change, at least when dealing with their own practices. In that sense, the notion of purity appears to have a double finality or dimension, one internal and the other external.

On the one hand, it serves to establish boundaries of identity (articulated in the discourse of nations and ritual orthodoxies) and to privilege the "old" and "traditional" vis à vis the "new" and "modern" (i.e., the African orixá versus the Brazilian caboclo). At the same time it presupposes hierarchies of spiritual power (axé, força). The purer the ritual tradition, the greater its religious efficacy will be; the ultimate value of purity is in legitimizing and reinforcing power status *within* the religious community. This is the internal dimension.

On the other hand, there is also an external dimension that goes beyond the religious community into the wider social order. Here the discourse of African purity, articulated by the most prestigious terreiros, serves to legitimate and reinforce the social and political power of these religious communities as emblematic representatives of the Afro-Brazilian community as a whole. It is in this domain that the discourse of the imagined African purity and African nations acquires a real political dimension, and it is in this realm that the discussion about the influence of intellectuals on Candomblé becomes relevant.

Certainly scholars have used the concept of purity in analyzing Candomblé, particularly in association with the Nagô terreiros. Beginning in the 1930s, and especially from the 1970s on, their publications have circulated widely among cult groups, contributing to reinforcing Nagô visibility and prestige. Rodrigues, Ramos, Carneiro, Pierson, Bastide, Verger, and Elbein dos Santos, to name only the most well known authors, conducted their major research in the three main Nagô-Ketu terreiros (i.e., Engenho Velho, Gantois, and Opô Afonjá) and projected the image of these houses as the most faithful survival of the African tradition in Brazil, to the detriment of the cults of other nations that were perceived as syncretic. This imagined Nagô-Ketu purity was identified with positive ideas of cultural resistance and permanence, whereas the syncretism of other cults was implicitly associated with negative ideas of cultural assimilation and change. The main question is to understand how researchers interpreted and absorbed an ongoing dynamic within Candomblé that revolved around purity, how they transformed this emic value into an analytical category, and how this new external objectifying category was reinternalized within Candomblé.

The myth of purity first began to be criticized in the 1970s with the work of Lapassade and Luz, who began to recognize the importance of Macumba and Quimbanda, but it emerged more significantly in the 1980s with the works of Beatriz Gois Dantas, Peter Fry, and Patricia Birman.[37] These authors argued that the obsession to identify "Africanisms" in the Brazilian cults and the subsequent valorization of the Nagô purity was mainly a scholarly construction of researchers and anthropologists. Dantas further suggested that this intellectual construction of the Nagô "as a true religion, in contrast with Bantu magic/

sorcery," concealed the interests of the white Euro-Brazilian elites and that it disguised a subtle form of domination. According to Dantas, the white elites, while promoting the recognition of the Brazilian African heritage (thus favoring an apparent idea of "racial democracy" as conceived by Freyre), would pursue two main objectives. On the one hand, they would try to "clean" the African religion of its most dangerous aspects. Nagô purity is often associated with a denial of black magic practices, criticism of the increasing professionalism of religious experts, and, in some cases, certain ideas of "matriarchy," which implicitly disqualify male or homosexual priesthood. On the other hand, the stress on African purity would "exoticize" Afro-Brazilian culture and would also implicitly promote the establishment of a "cultural ghetto," which would deprive its social agents of a real insertion and participation in the wide national society.[38]

Subsequently Dantas was severely criticized by several authors for overemphasizing the role played by intellectuals in the construction of the Nagô purity myth and for ignoring the agency of the religious participants themselves.[39] The historical dynamic of Candomblé cannot be reduced to the influence of external factors, and even if these factors do exist they do not themselves justify or determine the whole process. Some of the examples mentioned above clearly confirm the internal agency or active role of participants: Martiniano Eliseu do Bomfim was advocating for the preservation of African-Yoruba practices and values since the beginning of the century, and in the 1930s there was a serious internal debate among priests with the purity of the African-derived cults confronting the "mixture" of the caboclo cults. Mãe Aninha may have read the works of Carneiro, but surely her religious activities were not modified by these readings nor was her discourse on Nagô purity modeled on them.

My impression is that in the 1930s a sector of the Candomblé leadership perceived ties to intellectuals as one more strategy in securing their position and prestige, and they seized the opportunity. Their previously internal debate on African purity was reproduced by intellectuals in a new public discourse that placed Candomblé within the wider society, praising purity and traditionalism and equating them with cultural resistance. The associated "Nagô-centrism" resulting from this process privileging African purity could only be welcomed by the already hegemonic traditional houses. Candomblé practitioners and Afro-Brazilian social subjects once more demonstrated their own agency, appropriating and transforming the "cultural" discourse of intellectuals into their own discourse of political resistance and black identity, and this takes us a few decades forward.

The "Anti-Syncretism Crusade," Political Resistance, and the Locus of Tradition

The prestige achieved by Nagô-Ketu terreiros such as Engenho Velho, Gantois, and Opô Afonjá contributed to the formation of an ideal of ritual purity and to the creation of an ideal model of religious behavior.[40] This generated a cascading mirror effect, and many cult houses began to self-identify as belonging to the Nagô or Ketu nation, regardless of any spiritual affiliation with the three above-mentioned terreiros. In 1937 the União registered ten Ketu, one Alaketu, one Yorubá, and one Nagô among the total sixty-seven cult houses, and even though some contemporaries thought that there were fewer than ten Ketu terreiros, they did not surpass 20 percent.[41] By 1969 the Nagô-Ketu houses comprised 35 percent of the total surveyed.[42] The gradual increase continued, and by 1998 they comprised 56 percent.[43] Although these figures should be taken with caution, that there was a progressive growth in the proportion of self-denominated Nagô-Ketu cult groups is clear. Also worth noting is that, beginning in the 1930s, Ketu, the name of a particular Yoruba kingdom, became a synonym or even a substitute for the Nagô ethnonym, at least in Salvador.

As far as I know, the Ketu ethnonym does not appear in the slave trade record and, contrary to the views of authors such as Verger, Africans from this kingdom might have been scarce.[44] The first historical evidence of a Dahomean slave raid in the Ketu kingdom dates from 1789, but no more than two hundred captives would have been exported as slaves. Subsequent historically documented raids in Ketu's neighboring villages date only from 1858 and 1860. In 1878 there was a first Yoruba incursion into the capital, while the most important Dahomean invasion and its subsequent destruction—when the city's priesthood could have been enslaved—only occurred in 1883 and 1886, respectively, hence postdating the end of the trans-Atlantic trade. Also, as noted by Lima, Iyá Nassô was not a personal name but was the title (oiê) of the Xangô high priestess in the Oyo kingdom court.[45] These facts pose serious questions regarding the Ketu origin of the founders of the Ilê Iyá Nassô and raise the possibility of this origin having been forged at a later stage.

Interestingly, Pierson mentions "queito" as being a dialect Aninha learned from her parents, different from the Nagô that she learned in the Engenho Velho.[46] We have already suggested the late-nineteenth-century trans-Atlantic communication network as a possible context for the popularization of Ketu in Bahia. Could it also have been related to the foundation of Aninha's Axé Opô Afonjá in 1910? Oral testimonies indicate that in the Recôncavo area surrounding Salvador, the Ketu liturgy was only introduced in the 1930s, whereas earlier there was a distinct Nagô tradition different from that known in the capital.[47]

In any case, in the 1960s Bastide confirms a continuing *"movement of purification* within the candomblés against the degradation of the macumba."[48] The antagonism indicated by Couto Ferraz in the 1930s in relation to the Caboclos now continued opposing the pure candomblés of Bahia to the Macumba of Rio and the emerging Umbanda. As further evidence of the Nagôization process, this was the time when the first cult houses began to ritually change their nation to the Nagô-Ketu liturgy (*troca de axé*).[49]

The travels between Africa and Bahia in the 1950s and 1960s by French photographer Pierre Verger, who was closely tied to *mãe* Senhora (high priestess of the Axé Opô Afonjá), continued to consolidate the Yoruba referents as emblems of African purity. In 1952, for instance, he brought from Nigeria a *xere* and an *edu ara* (emblems of Xangô) and a letter from the king of Oyo investing *mãe* Senhora with the title of Iyá Nassô. Subsequently, in 1967, Deoscóredes Maximiliano dos Santos (Mestre Didi), son of *mãe* Senhora, traveled to Dahomey with his wife, Juana Elbein dos Santos. The couple was introduced by Verger to the king of Ketu, and when Mestre Didi recited his oriki (lineage praise verse) he was recognized as a descendant of the Asipá, "one of the seven families founders of the Ketu kingdom."[50] Other intellectuals and priestesses from Salvador, such as Olga de Alaketu, also a "descendant of the Arô royal family of Ketu,"[51] and more recently *pai* Balbino Daniel de Paula and *mãe* Stella de Azevedo Santos (present high priestess of the Axé Opô Afonjá) have continued with the long-established tradition of trans-Atlantic journeys. By these means, the Nagô-Ketu identity continued to consolidate its already high prestige as the most authentic African tradition.

In 1959 the first Yoruba language classes were taught at the Center for African and Oriental Studies (CEAO) of the Federal University of Bahia, and from 1965 throughout the 1970s these courses were regularly offered. In 1974 the university inaugurated an exchange program with several African countries, thus facilitating the arrival of Yoruba teachers and students. From 1976 on, courses in Yoruba and Afro-Brazilian culture, often involving the learning of the Ifá divination system, were held in Rio de Janeiro, and starting in 1977 the University of São Paulo began to follow this lead, offering courses on Yoruba culture and language. These courses were frequently attended by Candomblé priests and priestesses who, besides learning the meaning of religious songs, also wanted access to esoteric knowledge, attributing to their African teachers a religious status which they sometimes did not have. The appearance of "impostor" African priest-teachers taking advantage of the naïf Brazilian fascination for anything African seems to have been more acute in the southern cities than in Salvador.[52]

Coinciding with a new moment of social recognition for Candomblé, the 1970s mark the beginning of a third phase in the Nagôization process, although this process would be better understood as continuous rather than fragmented. On the one hand, the Bahian political establishment seemed to realize the value of black culture as an exportable commodity that could contribute to shaping an image of Bahia that would appeal to the national and international tourism market. Recycling the representations of Bahian black culture projected since the 1940s by artists like Jorge Amado, Dorival Caymmi, Pierre Verger, and Carybe, institutions like Bahiatursa (the official Bahian tourism agency) began to promote Salvador as a "mystic" city and Candomblé as a tourist attraction and "exotic" spectacle. Newspapers such as *A Tarde* also began to announce regularly the feasts of several terreiros, among them the "most pure" and traditional Nagô-Ketu ones.

On the other hand, influenced by the civil rights movement in the United States, the 1970s saw a significant growth of black political organization with the founding of the Movimento Negro Unificado (MNU) and other associations like the Afro-centric carnival group Ilê Aye. The formation of a racially defined black ethnic identity found in Candomblé a rich source of cultural referents and dignified icons to guarantee the necessary unity for achieving the political goals of black empowerment and social equality. The notion of an African religious purity may have started as part of the internal dynamics of the religious community to establish legitimacy. However, since the 1970s the black movement played an active role in its articulation and dissemination, inserting it within a wider concept of an imagined Africa, emblematic of black identity and black pride. The elite cult groups, already self-conscious of their African purity, were logically more successful in attracting the attention of black activists seeking emblems of differentiated identity. Consequently the Yoruba-Nagô religious complex was once more reified, and terreiros like Gantois and Axé Opô Afonjá, and their leadership, emerged as visible political representatives of the Afro-Brazilian community as a whole.

In sync with North American pan-Africanist ideology, Brazilian black activism fought against white hegemony and racial discrimination, while its most radical wing promoted ideas of political and cultural separatism. It is in this ideological context that the anti-syncretism movement in Afro-American religions emerged, both in the United States and Brazil. This trend argued for the necessity of separation between African deities and Catholic saints whose blending was perceived as the legacy of white acculturation and the period of slavery. In Brazil these ideas were galvanized around the SECNEB (Sociedade de Estudos da Cultura Negra no Brasil), founded in 1974 by the couple Juana Elbeim and Deoscóredes Maximiliano dos Santos with the participation of other significant black intellectuals.[53]

The SECNEB was responsible for the organization, in 1981, of the first Conference of the Tradition of Orixá Culture (COMTOC) held in Ilê Ifé (Nigeria) and gathering together the African and African diaspora priesthood. During the second COMTOC, held in 1983 in Salvador, *mãe* Stella, high priestess of the Axé Opô Afonjá, declared herself in favor of removing Catholic imagery from the terreiros, and became the most visible advocate of the re-Africanization movement. Julio Braga refers to this "crusade against syncretism" as a search for the "Nagô hegemony."[54]

This "crusade" or "act of decolonization" against Catholicism is an indication of the relative autonomy of Afro-Brazilian discourse and practice, and questions once more Dantas's hypothesis which sees in the construction of a Nagô purity the machination of the white Euro-Brazilian elite. Instead, the re-Africanization process could be interpreted as a counteracculturation movement (similar to messianic or fundamentalist movements praising a return to the origins) occurring when cultural transformation is sufficiently advanced to impede any pure and simple re-creation of the original culture. Counteracculturation, far from being the return to the origins that it would like to be, is just another type of cultural change. It does not regenerate the old but creates the new. As stated by Bastide, the discourse of continuity between African and Afro-Brazilian religious traditions results from an ideology of compensation that tends to place value on a rooting in the past to counterbalance real rupture and discontinuity.[55]

The last two decades have seen Candomblé's final transformation into a "universal religion" open to anyone regardless of color, gender, or social class. This change has led to a series of inner tensions and contradictions. While some terreiros, most often from Rio and São Paulo, found in the re-Africanization movement—involving Yoruba courses, readings of African religious ethnographies, and the establishment of direct links with Africa—a way to claim "authenticity" and to legitimize their practices, the old Nagô-Ketu houses claimed that the "true tradition" was to be found in Bahia. *Mãe* Stella, for instance, despite advocating for the anti-syncretism crusade and having been in Africa a couple of times, claimed, in a conference held in São Paulo in 1987, that "our roots are here [i.e., Bahia]. Going to Africa is just a fashion."[56]

The debate about the true locus of tradition, whether in Africa or Bahia, which in fact expresses a struggle for leadership, was somehow parallel to the one going on in the United States since the 1970s. There, the usually white santeros exiled from Cuba considered their Afro-Cuban heritage of Regla Ocha the true tradition ("la tradición"), while the American Yoruba movement or Yoruba Reversionism, epitomized by Oba Ofuntola and his Oyotundji community, by means of direct links with Africa vindicating their black racial identity and fighting against Santería's syncretism, pretended to re-create a Yoruba society in rural South Carolina.[57] This antagonism between "Afro-centrics" and "diaspora-centrics" seems also to have been at the base of the schism which divided the organizers of the conferences about the orixá tradition (COMTOC).

What is worth retaining for our argument is that, despite the antagonisms, both trends privileged the Yoruba culture as the expression of African purity. For Afro-centrics, Africa was identified exclusively with Yorubaland, particularly Ilê Ifé, whereas diaspora-centrics, in alliance with intellectuals, promoted the Nagô-Ketu traditional houses as the hegemonic model. In Brazil INTECAB (Instituto Nacional da Tradicão e Cultura Afro-Brasileira), founded in 1987, although including representatives of all nations of Candomblé and promoting a certain ecumenism under the maxim of "unity within diversity," nevertheless considered the Nagô-Ketu tradition as the model to which the less African-oriented cult groups should eventually aspire.

In any event it is important to note that neither the Nagô-centered ecumenism of the INTECAB led by the Santos couple nor the anti-syncretism movement favored by *mãe* Stella is a unanimous position within Candomblé or, for that matter, within the Nagô cult groups themselves. *Mãe* Stella's crusade against syncretism found significant resistance from other traditional terreiros who claimed that Catholic saints were part of their cultural heritage, and from the INTECAB, which argued that the caboclo worship was legitimate since these entities were the original "owners of the land."[58] In fact, what these different trends make evident is a continuous struggle for leadership, not only against the prosperous Afro-centric terreiros of the southern cities but also within the Afro-Bahian religious field itself.

Similarly the alignment of traditional candomblés with the political agenda of black activists (i.e., affirmation of ethnic identity, promotion of social activities in the terreiros, and policies against racism) is not unanimous. There is an increasing interest among certain cult groups in promoting community-oriented social action because, besides its moral significance, it is perceived as a way to gain both visibility and material resources from public funding bodies. An increasing number of young black activists and intellectuals have also become initiated, blurring the boundaries between internal and external social actors and favoring this political shift. However, this tendency does not spare the more conservative and less politically aware religious discourse of another important sector of practitioners.

Therefore, despite internal power struggles and the increasing pluralism of interests within Candomblé, the Nagô-Ketu hegemony remains unaltered. Some Nagô practitioners may deny the idea of an imposed dominance proclaiming the existence of a tolerant ecumenism, yet this is typically the attitude expected from hegemonic powers. Members of cult groups belonging to other nations like the Angola or Jeje may feel a certain uneasiness when faced with the existing Nagô-centrism although they may not express it overtly. If we do not dare to speak of a Nagô-Ketu hegemony in contemporary Candomblé, we must at least recognize that its supremacy has been historically constructed.

In this chapter I have tried to examine this intricate Nagôization process in the longue durée, suggesting that there are not univocal explanations and that the process involved a plurality of interrelated social factors as well as the agency of internal and external human actors. In a first stage, corresponding to the post-Abolition period, the long-established and local African-Creole antagonism was resignified in the religious field as one of contrast between purity and corruption. This process coincided with a decreasing presence of Africans in Bahia and with an increasing racialization of social relationships that favored a new black identity associated with an idealized image of Africa. Synchronized with the heightening of Yoruba cultural supremacy in the black Atlantic world, this process of re-Africanization emerged effectively in Candomblé as one of Nagôization that favored the visibility and prestige of a small number of cult houses claiming the Nagô-Ketu ethnic-religious identity.

In this initial stage the agency of the Nagô practitioners has been emphasized. Yet in the 1930s, corresponding with the second Nagôization stage and coinciding with the social recognition of Candomblé as a valuable national heritage, the intervention of intellectuals was critical in using the emic concept of purity as an analytical category that came to reinforce the status and authority of the already famous Nagô houses. In a third stage, dating from the 1970s on, the re-Africanization and anti-syncretism movements acquired overt political meaning, dividing the religious community into a diversity of often conflicting interests. In this dynamic the image of Africa, variously used to legitimate religious authority and leadership, has been persistently identified with Yorubaland reifying once more the Nagô supremacy. Hence the ambitions and struggles of the Nagô congregations gradually contributed to establishing a religious elite that, using, and aligning with, the interests of intellectuals and black activism, has secured its power for more than a century. Yet the visibility of this minority, despite its pervasive influence, should not lull us into forgetting the significant, if less highly acclaimed, contributions of other less visible groups.

Notes

1. Each of the three main nations is divided in subcategories related to specific African "lands" or "provinces." Nagô comprises Nagô-Ketu, Nagô-Ijexá, and Efon. The Jeje—ethnonym by which enslaved peoples from the Gbe-speaking area were known in Bahia from the eighteenth century on—differentiate between Jeje-Mahi, Jeje-Savalu, and Jeje-Mudubi. The Angola nation also includes the Congo. As discussed below, many cult houses self-identify as belonging to a combination of nations (i.e., Ketu-Angola, Jeje-Angola-Caboclo, etc.).

2. Following Hounkpati B. C. Capo, *Comparative Phonology of Gbe* (Berlin: Foris, 1991), I use the term "Gbe" to refer to the linguistically related Fon, Gun, Aïzo, Mahi, Hueda, Hula, Ouatchi, Adja, Ouemenu, Agonli, Ewe, Gen, and affiliated peoples occupying the southern regions of modern Togo and Republique du Benin and usually referred to in the literature as Adja-Ewe.

3. Author's translation. Donald Pierson, *Brancos e Prêtos na Bahia: Estudo de contato racial* (São Paulo: Editora Nacional, 1971), 319.

4. The term "terreiro," literally a piece of land, designates the cult house and, by implication, the cult group. In this chapter, as a synonym of that term, I also use "candomblé" in lowercase, whereas "Candomblé," with a capital letter, refers to the religious institution as a whole.

5. Vivaldo da Costa Lima, "A família-de-santo nos Candomblés Jeje-Nagôs da Bahia: Um estudo de relações intra-grupais" (master's thesis, UFBa, Salvador, 1977), 20–21.

6. Vivaldo da Costa Lima, "Os obás de Xangô," *Afro-Ásia* 2–3 (June–December 1966): 5–36; Júlio Braga, *Na Gamela do Feitiço, Repressão e Resistência nos Candomblés da Bahia* (Salvador: EDUFBa, 1995), 47–48; Stefania Capone, *La quête de l'Afrique dans le candomblé. Pouvoir et tradition au Brésil* (Paris: Karthala, 1999), 260–67.

7. Sidney Mintz, *Caribbean Transformations* (New York: Columbia University Press, 1989 [1974]), 14; as cited in Stephan Palmié, "Against Syncretism: 'Africanizing' and 'Cubanizing' Discourses in North American Òrìsà Worship," *Counterworks* (1993): 93.

8. Jean-Baptiste Labat, *Voyage du Chevalier des Marchais en Guinée, isles voisines et à Cayenne, fait en 1725, 1726 et 1727*, 4 vols. (Paris: Chez Saugrain, Quay de Gefvres, à la Croix Blanche, 1730), 2:125–26.

9. Paul Mercier, "Notice sur le peuplement Yoruba au Dahomey-Togo," *Études Dahoméennes* 4 (1950): 30; Robert S. Smith, *Kingdoms of the Yoruba*, 3rd ed. (London: James Currey, 1988), 55, 70–71; Lima, "A família," 16. For a detailed analysis on the origins of the term "Nagô," see Robin Law, "Ethnicity and the Slave Trade:

'Lucumi' and 'Nago' as Ethnonyms in West Africa," *History in Africa* 24 (1997): 205–19.

10. John Duncan, *Travels in Western Africa in 1845 and 1846, Comprising a Journey from Whydah, through the Kingdom of Dahomey, to Adofoodia, in the Interior* (London: Richard Bentley, 1967 [1847]), 41, 192–200; Pierre Verger, *Notes sur le culte des Orisa et Vodun, à Bahia, la Baie de tous les Saints, au Brésil et à l'ancienne Côte des Esclaves en Afrique* (Dakar: IFAN, 1957), 97; Henri Labouret and Paul Rivet, *Le Royaume d'Arda et son Évangélisation au XVIIe siècle* (Paris: Travaux et Mémoires de l'Institut d'Ethnologie, 1929); R. P. B. Segurola, *Dictionnaire Fon-Français* (Cotonou: Procure de l'Archidiocèse, 1963); Smith, *Kingdoms of the Yoruba*, 59; Celestin Dako, personal communication, Abomey, 1995.

11. Gerhard Kubik, *Angolan Traits in Black Music, Games and Dances of Brazil: A Study of African Cultural Extensions Overseas* (Lisbon: Junta de Investigações Científica do Ultramar, Centro de Antropologia Cultural, 1979), 10.

12. Inventories, boxes 1–70, Colonial-Judicial Section, Arquivo Regional de Cachoeira.

13. Carlos Ott, "O Negro Bahiano," *Les Afro-Americains* (Dakar: IFAN, 1952), 141–53; Maria Inês Côrtes Oliveira, "Retrouver une identité: jeux sociaux des africains de Bahia vers 1790–1890" (Ph.D. thesis, Université de Paris–Sorbonne, 1992). Considering the total slave population for the period from 1830 to 1850, the Nagô comprised 36 percent (Maria José de Souza Andrade, "A mão-de-obra escrava em Salvador, de 1811 a 1860; um estudo de História Quantitativa" (master's thesis, UFBa, Salvador, 1975), appendix, table 4. For a detailed analysis on the Nagô slave population in nineteenth-century Bahia, see João José Reis and Beatriz Gallotti Mamigonian, "Nagô and Mina: The Yoruba Diaspora in Brazil," chapter 5 in this volume.

14. For example, in the police and judiciary documentation of the Malê revolt in Salvador in 1835, there are a couple of instances of Jeje Africans who opt to self-identify as Nagô. Regardless of possible errors by the transcriber, this recurrent ambiguity suggests a certain fluidity of ethnic identifications and the possibility that the Nagô label may have operated as an umbrella term, providing minority groups the chance to align with the most visible, numerous, and powerful group ("Devassa do levante de escravos ocorrido em Salvador em 1835," *Anais do Arquivo Público do Estado da Bahia* 40 [1971]: 57; 53 [1996]: 59).

15. The earliest-known written document in which the term "candomblé" appears relates to an Angolan slave, Antonio, who was described by a militia captain in 1807 as "president of the candomblé terreiro" ["presidente do terreiro dos candombleis"] (João José Reis, "Candomblé in Nineteenth-Century Bahia: Priests, Followers, Clients," in *Rethinking the African Diaspora: The Making of a Black Atlantic World in the Bight of Benin and Brazil*, ed. Kristin Mann and Edna Bay [London: Frank Cass, 2001]). "Candomblé" is probably a Bantu-derived term suggesting the importance of Central African groups in the formation of the religious institution. For a discussion on its etymology, see Mary C. Karasch, *A vida dos escravos no Rio de Janeiro 1808–1850*, 2nd ed. (São Paulo: Companhia das Letras, 2000), 573.

16. Nina Rodrigues, *Os africanos no Brasil* (São Paulo: Companhia Editora Nacional, 1977 [1906]), 156. For an interesting document describing an 1809 *batuque* divided into several African "nations," see Rachel Elizabeth Harding, *A Refuge in Thunder: Candomblé and Alternative Spaces of Blackness* (Bloomington: Indiana University Press, 2000), 188–89.

17. See, for example, Luiz Mott, "Acotundá—raízes setecentistas do sincretismo re-

ligioso afro-brasileiro," *Revista do Museu Paulista* 31 (1986): 124–47; João José Reis, "Magia Jeje na Bahia: A Invasão do Calundu do Pasto de Cachoeira, 1785," *Revista Brasileira de História* 8, no. 16 (March–August 1988): 57–81, 233–49.

18. Luis Nicolau Parés, "Transformations of the Sea and Thunder Voduns in the Gbe-Speaking Area and in the Bahian Jeje Candomblé," in *Africa and the Americas: Interconnections through the Slave Trade*, ed. J. Curto and R. Soulodre (Trenton, N.J.: Africa World Press, forthcoming).

19. The date of the founding of the Ilê Iyá Nassô is uncertain. Some authors speculate that it could be the end of the eighteenth century, while a more conservative hypothesis suggests the early decades of the nineteenth century. Regardless, oral traditions and Afro-Brazilian studies have regularly insisted on this "myth of origin" of Candomblé that attributes to the Ilê Iyá Nassô the privileged role of "the oldest terreiro in Brazil." Gantois and Axé Opô Afonjá were founded in 1849 and 1910, respectively, by initiates of this "original" cult house.

20. Lima, "A família," 72–73; Yeda Pessoa de Castro, "Língua e nação de candomblé," *África* 4 (1981): 75; Braga, *Na Gamela*, 38–39, 56.

21. *O Alabama*, 1863–71. I have analyzed in detail the *O Alabama* data in Luis Nicolau Parés, "Do Lado do Jeje: História e Ritual do Vodun na Bahia" (Rio de Janeiro: Pallas, forthcoming). Contrary to my results, Reis's analysis of the same data suggests a slight Nagô predominance, possibly because he used other nineteenth-century sources besides *O Alabama* (Reis, "Candomblé in Nineteenth-Century Bahia"). In any case, the difference is little and the relative equal proportion is of more concern.

22. Rodrigues, *Os africanos*, 230–31; Edison Carneiro, *Religiões Negras e Negros Bantos* (Rio de Janeiro: Editora Civilização Brasileira S.A., 1991 [1936–37]), 33; Artur Ramos, introdução to *A casa das Minas. Culto dos voduns Jeje no Maranhão* by Nunes Pereira (Petrópolis: Vozes, 1979 [1947]), 13. For more contemporary authors, see, for example, Pierre Verger, *Orixás. Deuses iorubás na África e no Novo Mundo* (Salvador: Corrupio, 1981); Juana Elbeim dos Santos, *Os Nàgo e a Morte: Pàde, Àsésé e o Culto Égun na Bahia* (Petrópolis: Vozes, 1986).

23. *O Alabama*, 4 January 1868; 29 December 1870; 31 December 1870; and 24 November 1871. Among other activities, the Moinho congregation organized a "devotion" for Nossa Senhora da Conceição, together with a feast for a "Mãe d'Agoa" (probably Oxum) in December, and the feast of the new yam in November (*Diario de Notícias*, 5 October 1896; as cited in Rodrigues, *Os africanos*, 239).

24. Rodrigues, *Os africanos*, 231.

25. Ibid., 240–45.

26. "O seu terreiro era de gente da Costa (africanos) e ficava no bairro de Santo Antônio; que o terreiro do Gantois era terreiro de gente da terra (creoulos e mulatas)" (Nina Rodrigues, *O animismo fetichista dos negros baianos* (Rio de Janeiro: Civilização Brasileira, 1935 [1896]), 171.

27. J. Lorand Matory, "Afro-Atlantic Culture: On the Live Dialogue between Africa and the Americas," available online at http://www.africana.com/tt_669.htm

28. J. Lorand Matory, "Jeje: Repensando Nações e Transnacionalismo," *Mana* 5 (April 1999): 64.

29. Edison Carneiro, *Candomblés da Bahia* (Salvador: Ediouro, 1985 [1948]), 48; Verger, *Orixás*, 28–29; Roger Bastide, *Sociología de la Religión* (Madrid: Ediciones Jucar, 1986 [1960]), 323; Capone, *La quête*, 248–50. Capone (250) also attributes a character of myth of foundation to the alleged journey to Africa of Marcos Teodoro Pimentel,

founder of the first egun cult in the Itaparica island (Bahia). Jeje oral tradition also claims that Ludovina Pessoa, the "first" priestess founder of the Jeje nation, traveled each year to Africa (Parés, *Do lado do Jeje*).

30. Pierson, *Brancos e Prêtos na Bahia*, 278 –79; Vivaldo da Costa Lima and Waldir Freitas Oliveira, eds., *Cartas de Edison Carneiro a Artur Ramos* (São Paulo: Corrupio, 1987), 45–53; Braga, *Na Gamela*, 37–58; Capone, *La quête*, 250–52. In the Arquivo Público do Estado da Bahia, using the books registering the arrival of passengers into the Port of Salvador, I identified the arrival from Lagos of an Eleseo do Bomfim (freed African) in 26 September 1878 (book 1) and the arrival from Rio de Janeiro of an Elizio do Bomfim (freed, single, worker, fifty-six years old) in 27 October 1880 (book 3), and an Elizeo do Bomfim (businessman, forty years old) in 18 November 1880 (book 3). Also, in the 1880s Joaquim Francisco Devodê Branco (1856–1924), a freed Mahi, resident in Lagos with business in Porto Novo, made regular trips between the two coasts. He was a close friend of *mãe* Aninha and godfather of *mãe* Senhora, Aninha's successor in the Opô Afonjá (Lorand J. Matory, *Black Atlantic Religion: Tradition, Trans-nationalism, and Matriarchy in the Brazilian Candomblé* [Princeton, N.J.: Princeton University Press, forthcoming]).

31. Angela E. Lühning, "'Acabe com este santo, Pedrito vem aí . . .' mito e realidade da perseguição policial ao Candomblé baiano entre 1920 e 1942," *Revista USP* 28 (December 1995–February 1996): 194–220. See also Braga, *Na Gamela*.

32. Lima and Oliveira, *Cartas*, 61, 92, 153.

33. *Estado da Bahia*, 12 December 1936; 11, 13 January 1937; 24, 26 May 1937; as cited in Lühning, "Acabe."

34. For instance, Calmon wrote about the "danger of valorising in front of foreign audiences the Nagô tune from the samba terreiros" [O perigo de "valorizar-se perante plateas estrangeiras" a toada Nagô dos "terreiros de samba"] (*Estado da Bahia*, 8 July 1939). A writer from São Paulo attending a ceremony in the Axé Opô Afonjá reported: "Our thought is transported to the land of *Yoruba* where Xangô was king. It seems we are seeing the big king among the 12 members of his counsel: the obás . . . a perfect parliament of the *Quetô* nation" [my translation] (Domingos Laurito, Salvador, 30 September 1940; as cited in Lühning, "Acabe").

35. Lima and Oliveira, *Cartas*, 152–53; Carneiro, *Candomblés*, 44– 45; Bastide, *Sociología*, 330; cf. A. de Couto Ferraz, "Volte à África," *Revista do Arquivo Municipal de São Paulo* 54 (1939): 175–78.

36. Angela E. Lühning, "O compositor Mozart Camargo Guarnieri e o 2 Congresso afro-brasileiro em Salvador, 1937 (homenagem póstuma)," in *Ritmos em Trânsito. Sócio-Antropologia da Música Baiana*, ed. L. Sansone and J. Teles dos Santos, 59 –72 (São Paulo-Salvador: Dynamis Ed. and A Cor da Bahia, 1998), 66; Pierson, *Brancos e Prêtos na Bahia*, 305; Lima and Oliveira, *Cartas*, 42.

37. Marco Aurélio Luz and Georges Lapassade, *O Segredo da Macumba* (Rio de Janeiro: Paz e Terra, 1972); Beatriz Góis Dantas, *Vovó Nagô e Papai Branco. Usos e abusos da África no Brasil*, 2nd ed. (Rio de Janeiro: Edições Graal, 1988); idem, "Pureza e Poder no Mundo dos Candomblés," in *Candomblé: Desvendando Identidades*, ed. C. E. M. de Moura (São Paulo: EMW Ed., 1987), 121–28; Peter Fry, "Reflexões sobre a II Conferência Mundial da Tradição dos Orixás e Cultura. De um Observador não Participante," *Comunicações do ISER* 8, no. 3 (1984): 37– 45; Patrícia Birman, "Feitiço, Carrego e Olho Grande, os males do Brasil são. Estudo de um centro Umbandista numa favela do Rio de Janeiro" (master's thesis, Museu Nacional, PPGAS, Rio de Janeiro, 1980).

38. Dantas, "Pureza," 125; idem, *Vovó Nagô*, 200, 205, 208 –209, 213. For the dis-

qualification of male and homosexual priesthood, see Carneiro, *Candomblés*, 96–98; and Ruth Landes, "A Cult Matriarchate and Male Homosexuality," *Journal of Abnormal and Social Psychology* 35, no. 3 (1940): 386–97.

39. See, among others, Renato da Silveira, "Pragmatismo e milagres de fé no Extremo Ocidente," in *Escravidão e Invenção da Liberdade. Estudos sobre o negro no Brasil*, ed. João José Reis (São Paulo: Editora Brasiliense, 1988), 191; Ordep Serra, *Águas do Rei* (Petrópolis: Vozes, 1995), 48–65; and Sergio Ferretti, *Repensando o Sincretismo* (São Paulo: EDUSP, 1995), 64–70.

40. Lima, "A família," 23, 26.

41. Carneiro, *Candomblés*, 45.

42. Results of the research project on the Candomblés of Salvador directed by Vivaldo da Costa Lima, CEAO, 1960–69. As cited in Jocélio Teles dos Santos, *O dono da terra (O caboclo nos candomblés da Bahia)* (Salvador: Editora Sarah Letras, 1995), 21.

43. Luiz Mott and Marcelo Cerqueira, eds., *As religiões Afro-Brasileiras na luta contra a Aids* (Salvador: Editora Centro Baiano Anti-Aids, 1998), 13.

44. Pierre Verger, *Notícias da Bahia — 1850* (Salvador: Corrupio, 1999 [1981]), 230. For a critique of Verger's valorization of the Ketu, see Lima, "A família," 22–24.

45. Archibald Dalzel, *The History of Dahomey, an Inland Kingdom of Africa* (London: Frank Cass, 1967 [1793]), 202; Édouard Dunglas, "Contribution à l'histoire du Moyen-Dahomey (Royaumes d'Abomey, de Kétou et de Ouidah)," *Etudes Dahoméennes* 19 (1957): 39, 133, 152; Lima, "A família," 24–25. See also Stefania Capone, "Regards contemporains sur les premiers candomblés à Salvador de Bahia," in *Modenités transversals citoyenneté, politique et religion*, ed. Abel Kouvouama and Dominique Cochart, 47–72 (Paris: Editions Paari, 2003), 47–72.

46. Pierson, *Brancos e Prêtos na Bahia*, 306, 318.

47. Luiza Frankelina da Rocha, Cachoeira, interview, 25 June 1999. Manoel Cirqueira de Amorim, alias Nezinho da Mangabeira, a priest linked to the Gantois, was responsible for the Ketu expansion in the Recôncavo.

48. Bastide, *Sociología*, 330.

49. Joãozinho da Gomeia, a famous priest from the 1930s, changed the nation of his terreiro from Angola to Ketu with the collaboration of *mãe* Menininha from the Gantois in 1958–60 (Capone, *La quête*, 280).

50. Deoscóredes Maximiliano dos Santos, *História de um terreiro Nagô: crônica histórica* (São Paulo: Carthago and Forte, 1994), 18–19, 36. For a critique of the Asipá liaison see Capone, *La quête*, 257–58.

51. Lima, "A família," 28.

52. Vagner Gonçalves da Silva, *Orixás da Metrópole* (Petrópolis: Vozes, 1995), 261–71; Capone, *La quête*, 272–84.

53. Capone, *La quête*, 288.

54. Silva, *Orixás da Metrópole*, 269; Capone, *La quête*, 271–72; Braga, *Na Gamela*, 38.

55. Roger Bastide, "Continuité et discontinuité des societés et des cultures afro-américaines," *Bastiana* 13–14 (January–July 1996 [1970]): 78.

56. Silva, *Orixás da Metrópole*, 278.

57. Palmié, "Against Syncretism," 73–94.

58. Capone, *La quête*, 291, 294; Serra, *Águas do Rei*, 63–64.

CHAPTER ELEVEN

Santería in Cuba: Tradition and Transformation

Christine Ayorinde

Cuban Santería, also known as the "Regla de Ocha" (the rule or law of the orisha), is an example of how cultural and religious forms that are identifiably Yoruba have not only survived but have flourished in a new environment. Anthropologist William Bascom's research in Nigeria and Cuba in the 1930s and 1940s prompted him to suggest that Yorubas could go to the New World to learn about their religion.[1] This chapter describes some of the features of Santería that illustrate continuity but also the changes that make it a distinctively Cuban form. These changes reflect the challenges of transmission over space and time, societal constraints on practice, and the encounter with other cultures. It is important to note, however, that it is not only elements of ritual, language, and material culture that can be identified as Yoruba but also the *processes* by which the Regla de Ocha was able to successfully incorporate new cultural elements and capture new audiences. Although Christianity and Islam appear to have displaced the orishas in West Africa, it would be a mistake to attribute their expansion in the Americas solely to the effects of the middle passage. Recent studies of the orisha cults demonstrate how their incorporative, decentralized, and flexible nature made them eminently suitable for transmission and growth.[2]

The Regla de Ocha was originally the religion of the people who became known as Lucumí in the Spanish American colonies.[3] They carried with them their deities, called orishas or, in Cuba, orichas. Although Africans grouped under the Lucumí ethnonym are recorded from the first half of the seventeenth century, the majority arrived in the nineteenth century at the height of the sugar boom. Mortality rates were extremely high, and it was cheaper to replace slaves than to breed them.[4] The Lucumí were sent mainly to plantations in

209

the Havana-Matanzas region on the western side of the island. Their arrival late in the trade explains the overwhelming Yoruba influence on Cuban cultural and religious forms, though it is often also attributed to their presumed cultural superiority.[5]

The processes that shaped the Regla de Ocha and other Afro-Cuban religious practices began on the plantations and in the cabildos de nación, also called cabildos de africanos. These were civil institutions that helped Africans to adapt to their new environment by providing practical assistance, a decent burial for the dead, and the gathering of funds to buy freedom for slaves.[6] During the colonial period Africans were encouraged to congregate in cabildos divided along ethnic lines in order to prevent their uniting against the regime. This division facilitated the preservation and reconstitution of their cultural and religious practices. At times the persistence of these perturbed both religious and secular authorities. Public parades were prohibited, and the more overtly African dances and dirges were no longer allowed at funerals. The apparent religious syncretism was also an area of concern. One disposition stated that blacks would not be allowed to raise altars to the Catholic saints "for the dances in keeping with the customs of their country."[7]

By the late nineteenth century, during the period of the abolition of slavery and the wars of independence against Spain, the policy changed from one of maintaining cultural divisions to facilitating the assimilation of the former slave population. The cabildos were seen as anachronistic. The dances, masquerades, and other customs were regarded as vestiges of slavery, inappropriate and undesirable in a modernizing nation. Yet despite efforts to eradicate cultural (and sometimes also biological) Africanity, instead of fading away it spread among all sectors of the population. The religious traditions forged in the cabildos were carried on in the ilé ocha (house[s] of the oricha), ethnically heterogeneous cult groups where blacks, mulattoes, and whites could assume a Lucumí identity through initiation.

In addition to historical data about the Lucumí communities in Cuba, the information we have about the process of reconstitution of the orisha cults is found largely, but not exclusively, in oral accounts transmitted from generation to generation of practitioners. These tell of renowned "iyalochas" (cult priestesses) and "babalochas" (cult priests) who established ritual lineages or "ramas" that continue to the present day.[8] At some point there was an exchange of ritual knowledge between the priests and priestesses of orisha cults that had been independent of one another in Yorubaland, and this led to their merging into the Regla de Ocha.[9] This compression accounts for some of the main differences between Cuban and West African practice discussed in this chapter.

It is not known how many orishas are worshiped in Africa, despite estimates ranging from mythical figures such as 401 to 1,444. Surveys of specific towns show that a finite number of cults are important for inhabitants.[10] In Cuba most sources suggest that between 20 and 25 orichas are worshiped, with perhaps around 15 being the most popular. That some orichas mentioned in myths no longer have active cults indicates diminishing knowledge of their rituals, although in some cases societal conditions have made particular orichas less relevant.[11] This is true for those related to certain economic activities, for example, Oricha Oko (farming) became less important in a plantation slavery society. In some cases their function was modified, as with Ochosi who protects hunters in Africa, and in Cuba is appealed to by anyone in trouble with the law. Jails are called "ilé ochosi" by practitioners.[12]

Cosmological orichas, such as Obatalá, the creator of mankind and Orula (Orunmila), the deity associated with the Ifá oracle or divination system, remain important though they are not necessarily the most popular orichas. Also prominent is Eleggúa (Eshu-Elegbara), the messenger of the gods, who is invoked at the beginning and end of all Santería ceremonies. The most widely revered, however, are those connected with aspects of daily life: motherhood, love, wealth, health, and sex. These orichas—Yemayá (Yemoja), Changó (Shango), and Ochún (Oshun)—are also commonly worshiped throughout Yorubaland.[13] In Cuba their functions may be modified: Yemayá is associated with the sea rather than with the river Niger. Ochún, the orisha of the Oshun River, became the goddess of all fresh water. This reflects their adaptation to a new geography but, in the case of Yemayá, also shows how the semantic space occupied by one oricha, the African sea deity Olokun, has been gradually subsumed by the cult of another.

This adaptation or transfer of the characteristics and functions of orichas is not just a Cuban development, however. Karin Barber's study of the anthropology of Yoruba oral literature and culture, in particular "orikì òrìsà" (praise poems attributed to the gods), indicates that overlapping and inconsistency of Yoruba spiritual beings is the norm in West Africa. There is a tendency to merge orishas that have regional variants, to split off the separate aspects of a single orisha, or to share the same attributes among different orisha.[14] The "caminos" (literally, "roads") or avatars of the orichas perform a similar function in Cuba, namely, they ensure the flexibility and adaptability of the system of worship.

For example, Obatalá, an orisha with numerous regional manifestations in Yorubaland, has a profusion of Cuban caminos, each having different characteristics. One set of Obatalás is portrayed as old and usually female or androgynous: Obatalá Achó, Ochabí, Orishalá, Osakunún, and Baba Funké. There are even older Obatalás who are represented as men, for example, Obatalá Alabuché, Alámoreré, and Alayé. These are called the "owners of the world" and are sometimes confused with Olofi, the Supreme Deity. Another set of caminos relates to a warrior Obatalá. One of these, Obatalá Ayagguna, resembles Changó and has similar attributes: a sword, a horse, and a castle. In this way, caminos can reflect personalities quite distinct from the dominant identity of the oricha. Ochún is a prostitute in one camino, Yeyé Cari, and a wise old woman in another, Ibú Kolé.[15] Yemayá Asesú is violent and stormy, like the sea, while Yemayá Awoyó is calm and motherly. A particular camino of an oricha may have a relationship with another oricha that is not shared by the other caminos. For example, Oggún Areré is a friend of Changó, whereas Oggún Alagguede is his enemy. Santería ritual reflects the multiple representations of orichas as devotees are initiated into only one camino of an oricha, each with its own attributes, taboos, and requirements.

In some cases, a camino can serve to link an oricha more closely to the Cuban environment. In addition to Ogun's African-derived representations as iron-worker (Oggún Alagguede or Alawedde) and warrior (Oggún Arere), he is also a cane cutter (Oggún Laibé and Obaniyé). The historical deity and third Alaafin of Oyo, Changó, has a "Chinese" camino called Changó Sanfancón or San Fan Kung. A myth tells how the inveterate traveler visited a land where the people were "small and yellow with slanting eyes" and was himself transformed into a "chino" (Chinese). When Changó returned to his homeland, only Orula recognized him in the guise of Sanfancón and returned him to his original form.[16]

The process of merging into the the Regla de Ocha did not, as might have been expected, create a more coherent pantheon by bringing order to deities who were in separate cults in Africa. An examination of Cuban mythology and practitioners' statements indicates that inconsistency in relations between orichas has also traveled across the Atlantic. For example, Yemayá is the wife of ten different orichas, and both the mother and daughter of Olokun and the sister and mother of Ochún.[17] There was already flexibility within the existing structures that allowed for the reconstitution of separate orisha cults, where possible, and for these to retain their African historical references and fields of experience or else to acquire others more relevant to their new environment. Regional variants need not necessarily be discarded but could be retained and aggregated to a ruling version of the oricha. The "pataki(n)es" (in Yoruba [hereafter, Y.]: "pataki," "important") or myths serve to reflect and underpin the developing relationships between the orichas and locate them in both a Cuban and African context.

Ritual and Practice

Physical evidence of the merging of separate orisha cults is seen in the way that shrines to a number of orichas are normally all kept together in one room of the ilé ocha, normally also the home of a babalocha / iyalocha. This contrasts with African and Brazilian practice where a shrine to each orisha occupies a separate space. The "otanes," stones embodying the oricha's "aché" or spiritual power, are placed in covered china soup tureens called "soperas." Eleggúa is kept behind the door or in a cupboard. Oggún, represented by iron objects, lives in a cauldron, and Changó's sacred thunderstones are stored in a "batea" (wooden vessel) on top of a "pilón" (upturned mortar). The soperas are usually placed in a "canastillera," a type of sideboard, which may have doors so that the sacred items can be hidden from view. Devotees call on the orichas by shaking maracas or "acheré" for Changó and Yemayá and ringing bells or "agogo" for Obatalá and Ochún.

One aspect of African practice was affected by the disruption of family lineages by the middle passage: the inheritance of ritual roles and responsibilities within a family.[18] In Cuba, in order to become the devotee of a particular oricha one normally has to become initiated into his or her cult. The merging of separate cults into the Regla de Ocha is reflected in the way that, while only one oricha is ever made on the head ("asentado"), devotees can also have ritual relationships with other orichas. These are received at different initiations offering increasing levels of protection from negative forces, the progressive acquisition of religious knowledge, or when required for particular ritual roles.

Some devotees simply receive the "collares" or "elekes" (Y. "ìlekè," "beads"), a set of beaded necklaces, color-coded to represent different orichas and their own personal Eleggúa. The initiate receives necklaces of different colors representing four or six orichas (Eleggúa, Ochún, Obatalá, Changó, Yemayá, and possibly Oyá if the person is not a child of Yemayá or Changó).[19] The next stage is to receive the "guerreros" (warriors), so called because Eleggúa, Oggún, Ochosi, and Osun will "fight" to protect a person, something that became increasingly important in the conditions of a slavery society.[20] Other orichas, called "oricha de adimú," such as Olokun, Odua, Inle, and the Ibeji, may be received when determined by divination. For example, receiving Olokun, the deity of the depths of the sea, is believed to give the person greater stability.

It is suggested to some devotees that they enter into a deeper relationship with one oricha and take an initiation called "asiento"[21] or "kariocha" (to make oricha). This is the most important and hermetic ritual, during which an oricha, determined or confirmed by divination, is made on the initiate's head. Not all the orichas worshiped in Cuba may be "asentados." Explanations given are that some orichas are too powerful to fit in the head or simply that their rituals have been forgotten. In such cases the oricha is made indirectly through another, related oricha. Thus, for Olokun, Yemayá is made on the head at the asiento.

As in Africa, this initiation represents the ultimate relationship with an oricha. It reinforces the "orí" or spiritual head, enabling a person to realize their full potential, but it is not essential for every devotee. The initiate is regarded as the child of the oricha ("omó oricha") and the oricha is called the "dueño de la cabeza" (owner of the head). As part of the asiento ritual a number of other orichas, called the "santos de fundamento," are also given to the devotee. These include Changó, Obatalá, Ochún, Yemayá, and Oyá, unless one of them is made on the head, in which case the remaining four will be received. The giving of additional orichas at this initiation differs from both African and Brazilian practice.

The rituals inside the "igbodu"[22] (Y. "igbó odù") or "cuarto de santo" (room of the saint) during the asiento are forbidden to non-initiates. They apparently resemble that of "adosu" in West Africa where incisions are made on the scalp of the devotee. In Cuba these marks are now painted on the head, though small incisions are made to insert substances. It has been suggested that the Yoruba concept of sacred kingship is reenacted in the asiento ceremony, also called "coronación" (crowning). The "iyawó" (new initiate, Y. "ìyawó," "bride, spouse") is said to be "crowned" with the oricha and sits on a throne.[23]

One example of an initiation that is required for a particular ritual role is the "pinaldo" or "cuchillo," or "knife of Oggún." This authorizes babalocha to sacrifice four-legged animals. The equivalent for babalawos (Ifá diviners) is called "wanaldo." Iyalochas (priestesses) may receive the knife but cannot perform sacrifices of these animals. A babalocha who has pinaldo is known as an "oriaté." He acts as the master of ceremonies at rituals, and needs to know the norms and rites of all orichas that are made on the head or received. He is also an expert "diloggún" diviner or "italero."[24]

Many devotees extend their range of ritual obligations (and protection) by becoming initiated into the cult of Ifá. The "abofaca"[25] or "mano de Orula" (hand of Orunmila) (for men) and the "icofá" (for women) are initiations that may be taken after receiving the collares. As well as offering spiritual protection and having a beneficial effect on health, this indicates whether a man should continue in the cult of Ifá to become a babalawo (Ifá divination priest, literally "father of secrets"). The male devotee receives nineteen "ikines" or one hand of palm nuts. Women receive one or two *ikines* and may go no further into the Regla de Ifá as only men can become babalawos. The outward sign of these initiations is a green and yellow bracelet called an "idé."

Initiations are costly and most people take them in the hope of improving their material and psychological circumstances. When I inquired as to why they did so, many informants named health as their reason. Other motives included professional success, help with legal or emotional problems, money, and love. In Africa devotees similarly petition orishas for children, wealth, health, and long life.[26] What seems to have become less important in Cuba are children. This may be the result of the slavery past when enslaved mothers were reluctant to bear children, or it could indicate a more recent trend toward smaller families. To some extent, ritual descent can be a substitute for this. "Santeros / Santeras" who have initiated others are called the "padrino" or "madrina" (godfather, godmother), and the initiates are their "ahijados" or godchildren.

Efficacy is part of the appeal. As Ricardo Guerra, the babalawo, remarked: "People no longer want miracles, they want solutions."[27] This is one reason why many people were and are attracted to Santería, even though, until recently, it was not considered socially respectable and the practice was discouraged by the regime. Devotees are able to control unseen forces with the assistance of the orichas and the "egun" (ancestors), whose favor is gained by making offerings or a sacrifice, called "feeding" the orichas. They hope to gain material as well as spiritual compensation, and believe that the costs of their devotion will be repaid.[28] Rituals or ceremonies are performed to offer praise or thanks to an oricha and when specified by divination. Each "oloricha" (person who has undergone the asiento initiation [Y. "olórìsa"]) is also supposed to celebrate their "cumpleaños en el santo" (birthday in the saint). This is an annual commemoration of the day when they made the asiento and should be as lavish as their means will allow.

Rituals begin with a "moyuba" (Y. "ijuba," "to salute with ritual respect") to pay homage to Olofin and the ancestors—both ritual and biological. Several generations of iyalochas, babalochas, and babalawos are mentioned by name. Then the orichas are called down, beginning with Eleggguá as befits his role as opener of paths, followed by Oggún, who in rituals involving sacrifice is said to eat first, as the knife receives the blood of the animal, and Ochosi (the three guerreros), followed by Oricha Oko, Inle, Obatalá, Dadá, Oggué, Agayú, Ibeyi, Changó, Yemayá, Ochún, and Orula.

The liturgy is called "oro" or "oru" (Y. "òrò," "words") and consists of drumming and singing led by an "akpuón" or lead singer while devotees sing and dance around in a circle. Musical instruments are modeled on African originals. The most sacred drums, called "tambores de fundamento," are consecrated batá drums. These may be played in Cuba at ceremonies for all the orichas, not just Changó, with whose cult they are associated in Africa.[29] In fact, periodic banning of drums by the authorities meant that they were sometimes modified to give them a less "African" appearance or replaced by other instruments such as "güiros" (gourd instruments) or "cajones" (box drums).

The songs or chants of the oro are called "suyeres" and are in Lucumí. They praise the orichas or refer to phases in their lives. As each oricha is called down, the dance resembles a performance or pantomime of aspects of their personalities. Changó can be warrior-like or erotic, brandishing his axe or "oche" (Y. "os.é") or flirting with bystanders. Yemayá moves in a stately fashion like the waves of the sea. Ochún is flirtatious and laughs a lot. After the orichas have been greeted in succession, their "toques" (drum rhythms) can be used to "bring them down." At ceremonies a person may become possessed by an oricha. He or she is called *elegún* or *caballo* (mount, horse).[30] During the trance they will assume the characteristics of that oricha. For example, a frail elderly woman may stride around like the warrior Changó and perform prodigious feats of endurance. Spiritual power or "aché" (Y. "a.se") is received during ritual encounters.

Aché is also released from the substances and plants used in healing and ritual work. "Osainismo" or herbal knowledge, reflecting the specialty of the herbalist or doctor oricha Osaín, is a very important element of practice. The "ewé" (Y. "ewé," "sacred plants") are collected in "el monte" (forest, "the bush"). They may be used for herbal remedies and in the preparation of sacrifices. Substitution of some animals and plants used in rituals was necessary in the transfer to a new environment, and devotees sought out equivalents among the Cuban flora and fauna. Sometimes substitution has a more recent origin, as when postrevolutionary rationing restricted the availability of livestock. This increased the cost of sacrificial animals, and, as result, the types of sacrifice required became less specific or birds replaced four-legged animals.

Divination Systems

A very important element of religious practice is divination. Using shells or pieces of coconut, figures are cast and interpreted to shed light on a specific problem or to determine a person's destiny. The most highly regarded divination system is performed by babalawos, male diviners initiated into the cult of the oricha Ifá, also called Orúnmila or Orula. Divination is an attractive feature as it offers a sense of control. Devotees are told what their problem is and what they must do to solve it. It is also essential for communicating with the orichas and finding out their requirements.

There have been some adaptations to the systems which are known as "los oráculos" (oracles) in Cuba. "Obí," kola nut or four-cowry divination, is commonly called "los cocos" because pieces of coconut have replaced these. The pieces are thrown to produce five possible results, depending on how many of the white concave or brown convex sides are showing. As in all the divination systems, the combinations or figures produced are called "letras." Although it is the simplest form, obí is believed to be effective and is sometimes used by babalawos for less complex divination.

In diloggún, or sixteen-cowry divination, the "odu" or letras are determined by the number of shells facing upward with the serrated mouth showing. Evidence of the amalgamation of separate oricha cults is the way that each letra is associated with a varying and changeable number of orichas who may speak through the oracle, including Orula. In African "owó merindinlogun" only the presiding deity of the particular cult will speak, and only Orunmila ever speaks in Ifá divination. Yet, despite Orula's appearance in diloggún, the letras 13 to 16 can only be read by a babalawo.[31] This restriction is supported by myths. In one, Yemayá is learning the diloggún but at a certain point is told that she has acquired enough information. Another tells of how Orula taught Ochún how to divine but that she did not have time to learn all the letras. This indicates how the extended role of diloggún divination in Cuba, a change that potentially gives greater power to the women who head cultic groups, has been tempered by sustaining the concept of male-only access to the most secret knowledge. Also, and in contrast to Brazil, priestesses are excluded from some of the higher ritual roles within the Regla de Ocha by either the oriaté or the babalawo.

Another Cuban innovation is that diloggún has apparently been made more complex to resemble Ifá, as casting is sometimes done to obtain combined figures or "mellis" (Y. "méjì," "couple") (5–5 = Oche Melli) and combinations of letras (3–8 Ogundá Elleunle, 8–3 Elleunle Ogundá). This appears to contradict Bascom's claim that the relative simplicity of "owó merindinlogun" (which in Africa does not have combined figures) accounts for its greater importance in the Americas.[32] It suggests an attempt to upgrade diloggún as a replacement for Ifá. This is surprising as Cuba appears to be unique in the diaspora in having preserved the Ifá divination system to the present day. As in Africa, either a divining chain, "ekuele" / "okpele" (Y. "òpelè") or the "ikines" (palm nuts) are used to produce the "odu" / "oddun" or figure. Specific information relating to the oddun is gathered using "igbo" to determine whether the path is "iré" (good) or "osogbo" / "osobo" (bad). There are variations in the order and naming of odus or figures in different regions of Africa, Brazil, and Cuba.[33]

One explanation for the changes to diloggún may lie in the fact that, although Ifá has retained its position as the most prestigious divination system, it is not always seen as the most efficacious. Aside from Orula, a number of orichas are believed to be gifted diviners. Cuban myths even make Changó the first owner of the Ifá divining tray or, in some cases, both Elegguá and Changó.[34] I have been unable to find this myth in West African material and, like other features of Santería, it appears to suggest an Oyo-centrism, or predominance of Oyo ritual forms following large-scale imports from that region late in the slave trade.[35]

For important divination, Cuban practitioners may choose either diloggún or Ifá. However, Ifá is believed to be more reliable for determining which oricha a devotee should have made on the head at asiento. This is because, unlike the orichas who may fight for possession of a head, Orula, the deity of Ifá, cannot be asentado and is therefore impartial. Nevertheless, on the third day of the asiento, called the Día del Itá, diloggún divination is used to reveal the "itá" or personal narrative of the iyawó.[36] This lists the predictions and the "ewos" (taboos) that must be observed throughout his or her life. It also names the specific caminos of the orichas to be received and the Lucumí name of the iyawó. A "mano" (hand, set) of cowries for the oricha made on the head and one for each of those received are given to the iyawó.[37]

The development in the relationship between Ifá and the Regla de Ocha in Cuba is also apparent in the way ritual roles and responsibilities may be allocated to either babalocha or babalawos. This varies between cult houses. In some, divination for certain rituals and the killing of four-legged animals must be performed by babalawos, whereas in others they are traditionally done by oriatés. However, the most hermetic ritual of the Regla de Ocha—the asiento— is closed to babalawos unless they have also been initiated into ocha. Most babalawos in Cuba now tend to do so as it extends their ritual repertoire and enhances their prestige.[38] It is not clear why certain ritual roles within the Regla de Ocha have come to be performed by Ifá priests, who in Africa deal solely with the cult of the orisha Orunmila and only offer divination to members of other cults. It may indicate an extension of the hegemony of Ifá in the diaspora, or quite the opposite, as in the past there were relatively few Cuban babalawos. Bascom estimated around two hundred when he did his research in the late 1940s. Not all ilé ocha rely on the services of babalawos, and the extension of diloggún also suggests that santeros often dispensed with their services as diviners. In any case, there seems to be no consensus among practitioners as to whether the Regla de Ifá has remained a separate cult from the regla de ocha or whether they have fused into the Regla de Ocha–Ifá. Competition between the two also revolves around questions of orthodoxy. Most babalawos claim that the Regla de Ifá is more "African" and that the Regla de Ocha is more syncretic and therefore less orthodox. Omotoso Eluyemi, the Apena of Ife, apparently supported this view on his visit to Cuba in 1987 when he referred to the babalawos as the guardians of the ritual aspect of Yoruba culture.[39]

Yoruba Subgroups

As mentioned above, in Cuban Santería a number of elements specific to the cult of Shango, the Alaafin or king of Oyo, have intruded into the rituals of all orichas. These include the kingly crown, the mortar, and batá drums. Despite this, cult groups identified as belonging to other Yoruba subgroups are still found in the city and province of Matanzas, which, to some degree, has withstood the tendency toward homogenization found in Havana practice. The Cabildo Iyessá Moddú San Juan Bautista, founded on 24 June 1845, has as its patron the oricha Oggún Arere.[40] Its name and patron oricha reveal origins among the Ijesha people of northeastern Yorubaland. One major difference between this and other ilé ocha is that the orichas can only be inherited. They are called "santos parados."[41] Any cabildo member who does not belong to the actual, as opposed to the ritual, family must be initiated in another ilé ocha. Other points of differentiation may be found in the "osainismo," ritual language, dances, and musical instruments.[42]

There are also two important houses that have preserved traditions described as Egguado that derive from the Egbado Yoruba. These have ceremonies for the egun and masks called "máscaras" or "caretas." The Egguado house of Fermina Gómez held feasts in honor of Olokun until 1957.[43] The Iyesá and the Egguado houses are regarded as "specialist clinics" for problems beyond the expertise of other santeros. The Iyesá house is the highest authority for rituals of Ochún and Oggún.[44] The heads of these prestigious houses are women.[45] There are also, according to Israel Moliner, what he called southern Yoruba or Ibadan houses called "sangá," in Unión de Reyes and Limonar in Matanzas Province.[46] The main variant is that a gourd called an "agwe" or "agbé" (Y. "agbè," "gourd") is used as the main ceremonial instrument. A closer study of these variants would yield important information about patterns of migration and shed further light on the process of merging or reconciliation of Yoruba regional forms in Cuba.

Orichas, Catholic Saints, and Religious Syncretism

Most accounts of African-derived religions in the diaspora tend to focus on the syncretism with Roman Catholicism. This means that they often overlook the other developments detailed above. However, it is evident that the orisha cults entered into competition not only with other orishas or regional variants of themselves but also with the Catholic saints. Often slaves were forced to conceal African gods and rituals behind a "mask" of saints and Catholic feast-days in order to escape religious persecution. But as Herskovits pointed out, Africans in the Americas also identified structural similarities between their religions and Roman Catholicism. The saints' cults and advocations of the Virgin Mary of folk Catholicism had already incorporated pre-Christian practices such as promises, votive offerings, and the supplication of divine intervention in material or affective problems. Like the orichas, they were conceived less as intermediaries to a Supreme Deity and more as objects of devotion in themselves.[47]

The most visible signs of "syncretism" are the correspondences drawn between oricha and santo. These derive in many cases from hagiography and religious lithographs. In Brazil Ogum, the orisha of iron and war, is matched with Saint George who carries a sword, whereas in Cuba Ogún is commonly linked with Saint Peter who holds an iron key. Curiously Changó, the oricha who is polygamous in Nigeria and a womanizer in Cuba, is linked to the virgin Santa Bárbara. Yet an examination of the saint's legend reveals the logic behind this: Santa Bárbara chose martyrdom, and her father was struck dead by lightning as a punishment for killing her when she refused to give up her Christian faith. Catholic lithographs depict Santa Bárbara wearing a red cloak and crown, and carrying a sword. Her connection with royalty and valor identifies her with the Alaafin of Oyo, among whose attributes are the color red, a sword, and a lightning stone.

Any concern devotees might have about the gender disparity between the male oricha and the female Catholic saint is neatly dealt with in a "patakín" (narrative) telling how, on one occasion, while fleeing his enemies, Changó borrowed a dress or a red cloak from Oyá. When they come looking for him, she introduces him as her sister, Barbara, and sends them off in another direction. In Africa there is also a female representation of Changó. Male Shango possession priests in Oyo cross-dress and wear their hair in braids.[48] This also traveled to Cuba, as formerly "omó-Changó" (men initiated into the cult of Changó) used to wear "a little pigtail like the Chinese."[49] Also when Changó descends during possession trance, although his mounts may adopt military poses, they sometimes speak in effeminate tones.

The relationship between santo and oricha has sometimes resulted in a transfer of qualities from one to the other. One such case is Sòpònnón who, in Africa, both spreads and cures smallpox. In Cuba, where he is commonly known as Babalú Ayé, he is the patron of those with skin diseases like his counterpart Saint Lazarus and is petitioned mainly for healing. His shrine stands beside a former leper hospital. Close by is a sanatorium for Aids victims, founded by the revolutionary government. This reflects, consciously or otherwise, Babalú Ayé's more recent incarnation as the patron of those suffering from the Aids epidemic.

In other cases the Catholic saint is altered through the link with the oricha.

The Virgin of Regla, a town across the bay from Havana, has been transformed into a black virgin because of her identification with Yemayá. The patron saint of Cuba, the Virgen de la Caridad (Virgin of Charity), whose cult is centered on the former copper mining town of El Cobre in the eastern region, was originally the Virgin of Illescas near Madrid. The Spanish virgin became matched with Ochún some time in the last century and began to be represented as a mulata and was commonly dressed in yellow, the color associated with the oricha.

It is important to note that, although the terms "oricha" and "santo" are used interchangeably, this does not necessarily reflect a fusion of the two in the minds of devotees. Often they see only the qualities of the oricha. Conversely, for those who are already Catholic, the use of Catholic images and concepts helps to explain Santería in already familiar terms. The nature of the relationship has been much debated by scholars; what seems likely is that every practitioner will have their own particular conception. Many, though not all, santeros display images of the Catholic saints among their ritual objects, but the orichas are represented by the otanes (stones) that embody their aché (spiritual power). Separate ritual contexts and approaches are recognized and maintained: Catholic statues in a church or in the house receive flowers and candles whereas the otanes are fed with blood and herbs.

According to Bascom, the otanes are the Cuban equivalent of the Yoruba "iponri," the material object representing the power of the deity. Bascom believed that these became more important in Cuba, reflecting a shift not toward a fusion with Catholic beliefs but toward a greater emphasis on the distinctive features of the African religion.[50] By the same token, while it might have been expected that orisha worship, incorporating elements from Christianity, would have moved closer to monotheism, this has not been the case. While such claims have been made for Brazilian Candomblé, in Santería Olofin remains a "deus otiosus": "He lives in a remote place. . . . He does not come down into the world," according to an informant of Lydia Cabrera.[51] However, the names of the supreme deity, which in Africa reflect different aspects of Olodumare, in Cuba show the influence of the concept of the Catholic Holy Trinity. Thus Olodumare is God the Father; Olofi is his son, Jesus Christ; and Olorun is the Holy Spirit.[52]

On the other hand, a number of Catholic elements have remained visible in Santería practice despite the relatively weak influence of the Church in Cuba owing to a history of anti-clericalism as well as the 1959 Marxist-Leninist revolution. In most cult groups baptism is a prerequisite for initiation into the Regla de Ocha. As part of the ritual, the initiate should also visit a Roman Catholic Church, which they call the "ilé Olofi." Annual celebrations in honor of Changó take place on the eve of 4 December, the feast of Saint Barbara, his Catholic counterpart. There is an important pilgrimage to the sanctuary outside Havana of Saint Lazarus, whose oricha equivalent is Babalú Ayé, on the eve of 17 December. Although the main rituals in honor of the orichas are held in the ilé ocha (cult houses), practices that stemmed from a need for concealment have become enshrined in tradition. This explains why they persist even when there is no longer a need to hide the orichas behind a "mask" of Catholicism.

The other important point, of course, is that the incorporation of external elements did not always occur for reasons of persecution. Orisha worship in Africa developed in an environment where traditional culture was a base from which to appropriate new cultures. This incorporativeness is also a feature of its Cuban variant. The environment in which slaves and their descendants survived included not only Roman Catholicism but other African-derived practices: the "reglas congas" or "palo monte" of western Central African origin, and the Abakúa secret society from the Calabar region of Nigeria, as well as Cubanized forms of Kardecan spiritism. Today it is common for individuals to take initiations into or participate in several religious practices in keeping with the (perfectly Yoruba) perception that "two powers can destroy one enemy."[53] Palo monte and the Regla de Ocha serve complementary ritual purposes as some believe palo has extremely wide-ranging "magical" powers.

Some scholars in the diaspora have assumed that the ancestor cult was lost, unlike the oricha cults, which continued because they were not dependent on kinship systems destroyed by the middle passage and slavery.[54] However, in Santería, the importance of giving recognition to the dead is encapsulated in the saying "Ikú lo bi osha" or "el muerto pare al santo," which means "the dead person gives birth to the oricha." Since the early part of the nineteenth century, spiritism has offered additional cult possibilities for dealing with the dead. Many santeros have a little altar to the spirits called a "bóveda espiritual" (spiritual vault). This is normally a small table covered by a white cloth on which seven glasses of water, a crucifix, and candles are placed, along with other offerings. Many santeros perform "misas espirituales" (spiritual masses, séances) at which invocations to the dead are made. Oyá, who is the oricha of cemeteries in Cuba, will sometimes refer devotees to the practice of spiritism and palo, both of which specialize in ritual work with the dead. The Ifá verses reflect the model of incorporativeness established in Africa.[55] They mention Christianity and Islam, but also palo, spiritism, freemasonry, and other practices, sometimes proscribing them and sometimes recommending them. In Havana some predict a fusion of popular religious practices into something resembling Brazilian "umbanda." Yet ritual spaces for each practice are normally kept separate. Some santeros and babalawos also attempt to minimize the intrusion of elements they perceive as extraneous by claiming that in the most important rituals, such as the asiento, everything is of Yoruba origin or that the divination systems are less "syncretic" than other ritual elements.

Another result of the encounters between cultures is that Yoruba forms have become the model for other Afro-Cuban cults. The "mpungus" (deities) of palo monte have assimilated characteristics of the orichas, including their equivalence to the Catholic saints: Nsasi Siete Rayos–Changó–Saint Barbara; Madre de Agua–Yemayá–Virgin of Regla. The position allocated to Lucumí traditions is also reflected in a hierarchy of initiation, with the highest position accorded to the Regla de Ifá. For example, if you want to initiate into both the palo monte and the Regla de Ocha you must take the palo initiation first. The reason is because once you have had the oricha seated on the head, you cannot subsequently be "rayado en palo" (become initiated into palo monte by having small incisions made on the body) as that would be a retrograde step, forbidden by the oricha.

The Written Oral Tradition

Although much sacred knowledge is still transmitted orally, with prayers, songs, and ritual practices learned by repetition and observation, there is also a profusion of religious texts. This is perhaps an inevitable development in a society where greater authority is attributed to the written word, and the time available for oral transmission is limited by other obligations. Like other aspects of Santería, this, too, has a parallel in Africa.[56] For the Regla de Ocha there are two main types: "libretas" (notebooks) and "manuales" (manuals).[57] The libretas, intended primarily for individual use, are often handwritten exercise books. Rather than replacing oral transmission, they are intended mainly to act as a personal, mnemonic resource.[58] The manuales are aimed at a wider audience. They list the figures of the diloggún divination system and their accompanying narratives, called "patakines" or "historias." The myths fall into a number of categories; they can be cosmogonic, or relate to the caminos of the orichas or their taboos. Some are very close to the African originals, for example, the myth of Elegbara wearing a two-sided black-and-white hat has an almost identical Cuban equivalent in which Eleggúa wears a red-and-white outfit. Other myths follow the Yoruba style, but the characters and themes correspond to Cuban Creole life.

There are also extensive collections of Ifá divination texts. The *Tratado de Oddun de Ifá* is a treatise listing what practitioners refer to as the "theology" or "doctrine" contained in each sign or "oddun." The predictions or advice are listed in volumes called *Dice Ifá* (Ifá says).[59] These reveal the application of ancient wisdom to contemporary problems in form of advice, precautions, and recommendations, dos and don'ts to be followed. While some babalawos refer to texts during a divination session, others will not. The texts serve as an aide-mémoire or they provide additional material or a path through an oddun that a babalawo does not know in detail. Because of the reduced possibilities for long periods of apprenticeship in Cuba, there is no requirement for babalawos to memorize huge numbers of Ifá verses before initiation.

Although thus far no one has attempted a sustained study of these texts, Bascom found correspondences in the Ejiogbe verses for Cuba and Nigeria.[60] The Cuban Ifá corpus is in Spanish prose although some verses, called "suyeres," are in Lucumí, as are the names of some of the "ebó" (sacrifices). Whereas the African Ifá corpus appears not to display a thematic or affective quality for each odu, nor a systematic ordering of the verses, the existence of a written corpus has facilitated attempts by Cuban babalawos to structure the material. Each oddun has particular themes associated with it. These relate to four spheres: the human body, the religious system, social relationships, and nature.

Literacy is clearly an important factor in the transmission and preservation of knowledge that might otherwise have been lost and, in Cuba, is sanctioned by Ifá itself.[61] However, some practitioners oppose an overreliance on textual transmission. Transcribing the "rezos" (prayers) has meant that the tonality of the Lucumí ritual language, preserved to some extent by oral transmission in traditional houses, is being lost. Literacy, as well as commercial recordings of songs and prayers, is also threatening the adaptive and incorporative nature of a nontext-based belief system, a factor that had ensured its successful transmission.

The vitality of Yoruba traditions in Cuba, as elsewhere in the Americas, clearly demonstrates the ability of the orishas to "travel well," as Soyinka observed.[62] Not only have they managed to adapt to a new environment, they have also survived attempts over the centuries to eradicate or marginalize Afro-Cuban cultural and religious practices. One extreme example being the "brujería" (witchcraft) scares in the 1910s and 1920s, when practitioners who were commonly known as "brujos" (sorcerers, witchdoctors) were falsely linked with crimes such as the abduction and murder of white children for ritual purposes. This fanned an apparent battle between civilization and "African barbarism." It drove the Afro-Cuban religions further underground, and also led some to despise and reject the cultural heritage of their forefathers. However, it was also in the 1920s that some elements of Afro-Cuban culture began to be used to denote national distinctiveness.[63]

Yet the problem remained that while at the level of discourse, "mestizaje" or racial mixing is often celebrated as a defining, positive feature of "Cubanía" (Cuban-ness), there is an unequal evaluation of the different ingredients in the mixture. Cultural diversity has tended to be proscribed within certain parameters. When they were not actively suppressed, there was an assumption that progress and education would eventually uproot the Afro-Cuban religious forms, leaving only the purely aesthetic elements to be assimilated into the national culture. They would survive as national folklore rather than as living religions. After 1959 the revolutionary cultural policy carried on the project of making Afro-Cuban forms "respectable" by attempting to divorce the mythology, music, and dance from the associated religious practice.[64] Confiscated ritual items were placed in museums, rescued before they inevitably disappeared with the construction of a new society. As at earlier periods in history, studies of what were called the "syncretic cults" linked practitioners with the criminal underworld or suggested that they might display psychological disorders.

It is only in recent years that the status of Santería is becoming elevated because of a willingness by the leadership to accommodate all religions, and also because of the continued expansion of the Afro-Cuban practices. In 1987 the "Ooni" or king of Ile-Ife, the cradle of the Yoruba, was invited to visit Cuba by a state body, the Cuban Institute of Friendship with the Peoples (ICAP). The visit raised awareness among practitioners of Santería that there were institutions in Nigeria to which Cubans could look for support and authentication of their ritual practices. Indeed, the Ooni made a number of declarations to that effect, calling for the establishment of a Yoruba "templo" (church, temple) and for a Yoruba congress to be held in Havana. Subsequently, at the International Workshop on Yoruba Culture in 1992, a proposal for the "Yorubización" (Yorubization) of Santería was made.[65] This advocated emphasizing the African roots of Santería and recovering orthodoxy in ritual through a return to the liturgy of the Nigerian orisha cults and the Ifá corpus. Syncretic (Roman Catholic and spiritist) elements were to be eliminated from the practice. The term "Regla de Ocha–Ifá" would replace "Santería," and "babalocha/iyalocha" would be used instead of "santera/santero." Orichas were no longer to be referred to by the names of Catholic saints. Along with a reappropriation of Yoruba history and language, there were calls for the Regla de Ocha–Ifá to be ruled by the dictates of the Ooni. This was backed by the Yoruba Cultural Association, founded in 1991, which has since proclaimed itself the recognized perpetuator of Yoruba tradition under the jurisdiction of Ile-Ife. Partly funded by the Ministry of Culture, its cultural center with a museum of the orichas occupies an impressive building in downtown Havana.

For many ocha practitioners, recourse to African practice is part of a recovery process that aims to complete or deepen and extend ritual knowledge. Some believe that rites were distorted and deviations occurred because the ritual knowledge of their forebears was lost either in transmission from Africa or over the centuries in Cuba. Nigerian texts are sometimes used for comparative purposes and to fill in perceived lacunae in Cuban practice. The search for greater orthodoxy also reflects a need to rehabilitate what till now were denigrated as syncretic and therefore mongrel forms, inferior to the "universal religions." Attempts at institutionalizing the practice and creating a uniform doctrinal and liturgical system are part of a rehabilitation process. Of course, this brings with it the danger of freezing religion in an imaginary "authentic" past, stifling the dynamism that has ensured its successful re-creation in the diaspora.

Recourse to Africa may also be used to uphold rather than to question the legitimacy of Cuban practice. Both the Ooni and the Yoruba scholar Wande Abimbola confirmed that Cubans had maintained the "línea directa del secreto" (direct line of the secret). For many, Cuban Santería with its Catholic elements is no less orthodox than Yoruba orisha cults in Africa. While they acknowledge and respect continuity, practitioners feel themselves to be the owners and co-creators of a religion.[66] They acknowledge that Santería thrives precisely because it is not static. Gaps or variants in Cuban practice may not necessarily imply that it is simply a deficient version of an original. According to Babalawo Orestes Calzadilla: "the *how* [i.e., ritual elements and practices] was faithfully transmitted down the generations by imitative repetition, what is sometimes missing is an understanding of *why* things are done in a certain way." An unnecessarily circuitous route may be required to reach the desired end result, but the efficacy is not diminished.[67] In fact, the defense for the existing Cuban version of orisha worship often rests on the view that if it works, why change it. Ritual items unknown in Africa such as tobacco, cakes to celebrate "cumpleaños en el santo" (birthday in the saint), and "soperas" are examples of what Cuban tradition deems necessary for efficacy.[68] If ilé ocha attract members, as is indeed the case, this indicates that they are successful.

There has been a visible increase in religious practice on the island since the early 1990s following the removal of support from Eastern Europe, which compelled the government to consider its own form of liberalization in response to worsening economic conditions. As elsewhere in the diaspora, the changing official response toward African-derived religious expressions is leading to their emergence from a position of marginality. Now not only Afro-Cuban cultural practices but also the religions are increasingly acknowledged to be part of the patrimony. Santería is being hailed by many as the national religion of Cuba. It has developed from being the religion of Yorubas into the symbol of a "mestizo" (mixed) nation.

Cultural nationalists, like some santeros, stress that "la Santería cubana" is a cultural form whose fruits are more important than its roots. Cultural and religious syncretism is seen not merely as a survival strategy but as a process of exchange that has nourished the national identity.[69] Perhaps the ultimate marker of the successful transplantation of Yoruba cultural and religious elements is not only their re-creation in a new environment but also the possibility for their transformation. Whether they choose to look to Africa for affirmation, either of religious and cultural practices or of a diasporic identity, many Cubans, including the leadership, are acknowledging the centrality of Santería to the expression of Cubanía.

Notes

The author would like to acknowledge the financial support of the Arts and Humanities Research Board of the British Academy and the UNESCO Nigerian Hinterland Project.

1. William Bascom, "La religion africaine au Nouveau Monde," in *Les religions africaines traditionnelles*, 119–27 (Paris: Éditions du Seuil, 1965), 127. The Yoruba traditional religion was thought to have little chance of recovering from its relegation to the status of "bush religion" linked with rulers whose powers were displaced by modern government. See Ulli Beier, "Ancient African Religions and the Modern World," *Présence Africaine* 13, no. 41 (1962): 43; and idem, *The Return of the Gods: The Sacred Art of Susanne Wenger* (Cambridge: Cambridge University Press, 1975), 14, 56 ff. Of

course, the rulers became Christians and Muslims and have transformed old ritual structures into a "civic" ideology of modern-traditional kingship.

2. See, especially, the work of Karin Barber, "How Man Makes God in West Africa: Yoruba Attitudes towards the Òrìsà." *Africa* 51, no. 3 (1981): 724–45. See idem, "Oríkì, Women and the Proliferation and Merging of Òrìsà," *Africa* 60, no. 3 (1990): 313–37, on the self-contained and portable nature of the orisha cults in Nigeria; and Margaret Thompson Drewal, *Yoruba Ritual: Performers, Play, Agency* (Bloomington: Indiana University Press, 1992), on the improvisatory nature of Yoruba ritual. See also J. Lorand Matory, *Sex and the Empire That Is No More: Gender and the Politics of Metaphor in Oyo Yoruba Religion* (Minneapolis: University of Minnesota Press, 1994); J. D. Y. Peel, "A Comparative Analysis of Ogun in Precolonial Yorubaland," in *Africa's Ogun: Old World and New*, ed. Sandra T. Barnes (Bloomington: Indiana University Press, 1997), 263–89.

3. The ethnographer and criminologist Fernando Ortiz was the first Cuban to assign a Yoruba origin to the Lucumí practices in his 1906 work, *Los negros brujos*. For a comprehensive listing of Lucumí generic labels as applied to Yoruba subgroups and non-Yoruba groups in Cuba, see Rafael L. López Valdés, "Notas para el estudio etnohistórico de los esclavos lucumí en Cuba," in *Estudios Afro-cubanos*, ed. Lázara Menéndez, 4 vols. (Havana: Universidad de la Habana, 1990), 2:342. For a detailed discussion of the origin of the name Lucumí, see Robin Law, "Ethnicity and the Slave Trade: 'Lucumi' and 'Nago' as Ethnonyms in West Africa," *History in Africa* 24 (1997): 205–19.

4. Imports from the Bight of Benin, and specifically from Oyo, rose overall in the 1850s to the 1870s. See David Eltis and David Richardson, "West Africa and the Transatlantic Slave Trade: New Evidence of Long-Run Trends," *Slavery and Abolition* 18, no. 1 (April 1997): 21. Whereas in the seventeenth and eighteenth centuries the Oyo captured slaves either by raiding neighbors such as the Mahi or by purchasing them from the North, by around 1810–20 the military weakness of Oyo and the disruption of northern trade routes meant that the European demand for slaves had to be satisfied from within Oyo itself. See Robin Law, *The Oyo Empire, c. 1600–c. 1836: A West African Imperialism in the Era of the Atlantic Slave Trade* (Oxford: Clarendon, 1977), 306 ff.

5. "In the natural struggle between the African religions, the religion of the Yorubas or *nagos* triumphed in Cuba as in Brazil" (Fernando Ortiz, *Los negros brujos* [Havana: Ciencias Sociales, 1995 (1906)], 67; "the Lucumí were the best of Africa" (Lydia Cabrera, *El Monte* [Havana: SI-MAR, 1996 (1954)], 21; the Swedish traveler Frederika Bremer referred to the Lucumí as belonging to one of the most noble races of Africa (*Cartas desde Cuba* [Havana: Fundación Fernando Ortiz, 2002 (1851)], 101).

6. See also Philip A. Howard, *Changing History: Afro-Cuban Cabildos and Societies of Color in the Nineteenth Century* (Baton Rouge: Louisiana State University Press, 1998).

7. See Fernando Ortiz, *Los cabildos afrocubanos* (Havana: Ciencias Sociales, 1992 [1921]), 9.

8. See Nicolás Valentín Angarica, *Manual de Orihate: Religión Lucumí* (n.p, 1955), 22; and Cabrera, *El Monte*, 113.

9. There was a similar tendency in Africa: Beier noted that a decline in the number of worshipers, and the fact that orisha were becoming homeless when old priests died, meant that integration and exchange between cult groups in Oshogbo was necessary to ensure their survival (*Return of the Gods*, 14, 56–57, 62).

10. See Andrew Apter, *Black Critics and Kings: The Hermeneutics of Power in Yoruba Society* (Chicago: University of Chicago Press, 1992); and Barber, "Oríkì," 313–37.

11. Yoruba orisha cults are kept in existence by the attention of humans. See Barber, "How Man Makes God in West Africa," 724, 740. In Africa, too, rapid social change obliterated some of the fields of experience with which the cults concerned themselves. See Robin Horton, "African Conversion," *Africa* 41, no. 2 (1971): 86. Barnes notes that the capacity of a cult to survive or to expand depended on the meanings attached to a particular deity, and its ability to capture and communicate a part of the human experience (Sandra T. Barnes, "The Many Faces of Ogun: Introduction to the First Edition," in Barnes, *Africa's Ogun*, 18–20).

12. In western Ekiti his functions have been usurped by Ogun, and Oshosi becomes a healer and protector against witchcraft (Peel, "A Comparative Analysis," 277).

13. Israel Moliner, interview with author, Matanzas, 12 February 1997; Peel, "A Comparative Analysis."

14. See Barber, "Oriki."

15. In Yorubaland she is sometimes a concubine and sometimes a wise woman. See Beier, *Return of the Gods*, 36.

16. Israel Moliner, "Patakines. Vol. 3 (Del ciclo Shangó)" (typescript). This camino reflects the incorporation of cultural elements brought to Cuba by Chinese indentured laborers. From the late 1840s until the early 1870s they provided an alternative labor supply as British demands for abolition of the slave trade were making it increasingly difficult and raising costs. See Rebecca J. Scott, *Slave Emancipation in Cuba: The Transition to Free Labor, 1860–1899* (Princeton, N.J.: Princeton University Press, 1985).

17. See Rosa María Lahaye Guerra and Rubén Zardoya Loureda, *Yemayá a través de sus Mitos* (Havana: Editorial de Ciencias Sociales, 1996).

18. In West Africa, Yoruba religious practice depends on descent and divination, the former ensuring continuity and the latter opening up the system. See Margaret Thompson Drewal and Henry John Drewal, *Gelede: Art and Female Power among the Yoruba* (Bloomington: Indiana University Press, 1990), 247.

19. This is because Oyá will "fight with" these orichas.

20. Eleggúa is an essential oricha in Cuba and has many caminos. He protects both the home and his owner. In Africa the *osun* is the staff of the babalawo. See Robert F. Thompson, *Flash of the Spirit: African and Afro-American Art and Philosophy* (New York: Vintage, 1984), 44 ff.; and J. Olumide Lucas, *The Religion of the Yorubas* (Lagos: CMS, 1948), 168. In Cuba there is some debate as to whether Osun is an oricha. It represents the life of the owner and is regarded as the messenger of Olofi or as the guardian of Obatalá.

21. The most common meaning of *asiento* is "seat," thus referring to the throne on which the *iyawó* sits. It also means a pact or contract, which, in effect, it is, between oricha and devotee.

22. *Igbó odù* is the sacred space associated with the Ifá divination cult in Africa.

23. See Barber, "Oriki," and William Bascom, *Sixteen Cowries: Yoruba Divination from Africa to the New World* (Bloomington: Indiana University Press, 1993), for descriptions of West African initiations; and see Cabrera, *El Monte*, 253, for the Cuban ritual. It resembles the Shango initiation in West Africa, which condenses major symbolic forms of Oyo royal sovereignty whereby the *oba* or king becomes the bride of the god. See J. Lorand Matory, "Government by Seduction: History and the Tropes of

Mounting in Oyo-Yoruba Religion," in *Modernity and Its Malcontents*, ed. J. and J. Comaroff (Chicago: University of Chicago Press, 1993), 66.

24. *Oriaté* is a Cuban title without African antecedents. For a discussion of the emergence of this role in Cuba, see David H. Brown, "Garden in the Machine: Afro-Cuban Sacred Art and Performance in Urban New Jersey and New York" (Ph.D. dissertation, Yale University, 1989), 94.

25. In Yoruba: *owò òkàn Ifá*, "first hand of Ifá."

26. See Barber, "Oriki," 735.

27. Babalawo Ricardo Guerra, interview, Lawton, Havana, 21 January 1997.

28. This is also the case in Africa. See Barber, "How Man Makes God in West Africa," 735.

29. The drummers must also be consecrated. They are known as *olú batá* or *olú aña* after Aña, the deity of the drum (named after the *aayán* tree from which Chango hanged himself). A batá ensemble consists of three drums, called *iyá*, *itótele*, and *okónkolo* in decreasing order of size.

30. In Oyo possession priests are called elégùn and the term ".e.sin" (mount, horse) is used. See Matory, *Sex and the Empire*.

31. The literature on *owo merindinlogun* in West Africa suggests that diviners also seemed unwilling to read odus above 12. See Bascom, *Sixteen Cowries*, 782.

32. See ibid., 3.

33. For a listing, see ibid., 775 ff.

34. See Rómulo Lachatañeré, *El sistema religioso de los Afrocubanos* (Havana: Ciencias Sociales, 17); and Angarica, *Manual*, 54.

35. This also reflects the centralizing influence of the Oyo Empire and the way that, after its fall, the dispersal of refugees spread the Shango cult throughout Yorubaland. See Elizabeth Isichei, *A History of African Societies to 1870* (Cambridge: Cambridge University Press, 1997), 78. According to Peel's survey of CMS documents, Shango and Ifá were the most popular orishas of late-nineteenth-century Yorubaland. Shango priests intruded into areas of specialization of other orishas ("A Comparative Analysis," 279).

36. Cf. Margaret Thompson Drewal's description of the third day of Ifá rituals, called ìta Ifá, when divination is used to check the progress of the initiates, in her "Embodied Practice / Embodied History: Mastery of Metaphor in the Performances of Diviner Kolawole Ositola," in *The Yoruba Artist: New Theoretical Perspectives on African Arts*, ed. Roland Abiodun, Henry John Drewal, and J. Pemberton (Washington, D.C.: Smithsonian, 1994), 171–90.

37. A *mano* has eighteen or twenty-one (for Elegguá) shells, of which sixteen are used for a reading, and the rest, called *adeles* (Y. *adèlé*, "deputy"), are set aside. The mano of Elegguá is used most frequently as he is the master of communication.

38. A babalawo who has also had an oricha made on his head is called an *oluwo* or *olúo*. The ocha initiation must be performed first. He also has *wanaldo* or the Ifá version of the knife of Oggún which allows him to perform sacrifices of four-legged animals. In Africa the *olu awo* is the highest grade of babalawo and head of all babalawos in Oyo (see William Bascom, *Ifá Divination: Communication between Gods and Men in West Africa*, 2nd ed. [Bloomington: Indiana University Press, 1991], 83) or in Ede, the senior title holder of the Ogboni society (Ulli Beier, *A Year of Sacred Festivals in One Yoruba Town* [Lagos: Nigeria Magazine, 1959], 9).

39. "Yoruba Culture Is Alive in Cuba," *Granma Weekly Review*, 5 June 1987.

40. Formerly Iyesá houses were also found in Havana and Las Villas. See Rogelio Martínez Furé, *Diálogos Imaginarios* (Havana: Arte y Literatura, 1979), 139; Israel Moliner, interview, Matanzas, 12 February 1997.

41. Literally, "motionless or standing saints" (Moliner, interview).

42. See Furé, *Diálogos*, 153.

43. Formerly there was an Egguado house in Havana, that of Guillermo Castro in Guanabacoa, that specialized in Yemayá rituals (Lázaro Vidal, personal communication, Havana, October 1996). See also Fernando Ortiz, *Los bailes y el teatro de los negros en el folklore de Cuba* (Havana: Letras Cubanas, 1981 [1951]), 512. Drewal and Drewal compare the Olokun feasts to the Gelede cults of the Lagos and Egbado areas (*Gelede*, 184, 242).

44. In Nigeria Ogun is associated with Ilesha. See Peel, "A Comparative Analysis."

45. Moliner, interview.

46. See López Valdés, "Notas para el estudio," 342; possibly Lucumí sagá or chagá (Egba).

47. Melville J. Herskovits, "African Gods and Catholic Saints in New World Negro Belief," *American Anthropologist* 39 (1937): 635–43.

48. See Matory, "Government by Seduction: History and the Tropes of 'Mounting' in Oyo-Yoruba Religion," in *Modernity and Its Malcontents*, ed. John Comaroff and Jean Comaroff (Chicago: University of Chicago Press, 1993), 76. The gender of particular orishas is not always consistent in West Africa. See Barber, "Oríki," 313. On the female representation of Shango where he is a latecomer to communities that already have a male thunder deity, see Peel, "Ogun in Precolonial Yorubaland," 275–76, 285 n. 52.

49. Cabrera, *El monte*, 262; Lachatañeré, *Sistema religioso*, 99, 117.

50. William Bascom, "The Focus of Cuban Santería," *Southwestern Journal of Anthropology* 6, no. 1 (1950): 64–68.

51. Cabrera, *El monte*, 71.

52. For a discussion of the names of the Supreme Deity in Africa, see Bolaji Idowu, *Olodumare: God in Yoruba Belief* (London: Longman, 1962).

53. Lachatañeré, *El sistema*, 116.

54. See Roger Bastide, *The African Religions of Brazil: Toward a Sociology of the Interpenetration of Civilizations* (Baltimore: The Johns Hopkins University Press, 1978 [1960]). The *egun* in Cuba are not masquerades, although there is evidence of the past existence of both *egúngún* and Gelede masquerades in Cuba. See Ortiz, *Los bailes y el teatro*, 347.

55. See Karin Barber, "Discursive Strategies in the Texts of Ifá and in the 'Holy Book of Odù' of the African Church of Orunmila," in *Self-assertion and Brokerage: Early Cultural Nationalism in West Africa*, ed. P. F. de Moraes Farias and K. Barber (Birmingham: Centre of West African Studies, 1990); and Matory, *Sex and the Empire*.

56. See Barber, "Discursive Strategies," on the Ìwé Odù Mím.6 (Holy Book of Odu), which arranged Ifá texts into a Bible equivalent. This was intended to demonstrate that indigenous modes of worship are capable of developing along lines equal to the world religions.

57. Some libretas have extensive Lucumí-Spanish vocabularies listing the names of animals, items used in rituals, and so forth, sometimes incorporating material from the Oxford University Press English-Yoruba dictionary and Spanish translations of anthropological texts on the Yoruba. See Jesús Guanche and Argeliers León, "Integración y

desintegración de los cultos sincréticos de origen africano en Cuba," *Revolución y Cultura* (April 1979): 17; Furé, *Diálogos*, 212.

58. Argeliers León, "Un caso de tradición oral escrita," *Islas* 39/40 (1971): 141–51.

59. The first Dice Ifá was produced in the 1940s by Pedro Arango. He was a son of Oggún and had taken some Ifá initiations, although he was not, in fact, a babalawo. He is credited with giving a structure and organization to the Ifá predictions. He also wrote a *manual de santero*. See Pedro Arango, "Manual de Santería de Pedro Arango," in *Estudios afrocubanos: Selección de lecturas*, ed. Lázara Menéndez, 4:129–344. Some of his observations suggest that he may have spent time in Dahomey and Nigeria.

60. See William Bascom, "Two Forms of Afro-Cuban Divination," in *Acculturation in the Americas*. Proceedings of the Twenty-Ninth International Congress of Americanists, ed. Sol Tax (Chicago: University of Chicago Press, 1952), 2:169–79.

61. As a story from the odu Erdibre/Oddibre (Odi Ogbe) recounts:

Story:

Olofin went to give three blessings to Oddibre and said to him: "Wherever you may go say: 'I have peace, I have security, I have prosperity.'" Afterwards Olofin said to him: "Write it down so that you don't forget it." Erdibre replied: "No, I don't need to . . . I never forget anything." Time passed and war came to the land. Oddibre was forced to flee and he went to other lands, but, forgetting what Olofin had said to him, he said: "I do not have peace, I do not have security, I do not have prosperity," so no one wanted to help him and he had a very difficult time. He remembered that Olofin had told him to write it down and because of his pride he did not do so and thus had a hard time. After some time he heard that there was peace in his native land and he returned there. When he arrived he knelt down and asked for forgiveness for disobeying him. Olofin said: "Very well, I forgive you, but from now on you must make a note of everything that you hear so as not to forget it. To Iban Echu."

Here originated that babalawos write down the patakines of Ifá to keep and study them at opportune moments.

(Source: Ofún Yemiló, *Documentos para la historia de Osha-Ifá en Cuba: tratado enciclopédico de caminos*, Odi, Regla 1997)

62. Wole Soyinka, *Myth, Literature, and the African World* (Cambridge: Cambridge University Press, 1992), 1.

63. See Vera Kutzinski, *Sugar's Secrets: Race and the Erotics of Cuban Nationalism* (Charlottesville: University Press of Virginia, 1993), chap. 5.

64. Cf. West African attempts to culturalize religion by secularizing traditional rituals (J. D. Y. Peel, "Review Article. Historicity and Pluralism in Some Recent Studies of Yoruba Religion," *Africa* 64, no. 1 (1994): 150–66.

65. The workshop was reported in *Granma International*, "The Freedom of Worship and Respect for All Religious Traditions," 14 June 1992, 4.

66. Lázara Menéndez, interview, Havana, 5 February 1997.

67. Orestes Calzadilla, interview, Havana, 18 April 1998.

68. Lázara Menéndez Vázquez, "Un cake para Obatalá?" *Temas* 4 (October–December 1995): 38–51.

69. See Jesús Guanche, "Santería cubana e identidad cultural," *Revolución y Cultura* (March–April 1996): 43–46; Miguel Barnet, "La hora de Yemayá," *Gaceta de Cuba* (1996): 48–50.

CHAPTER TWELVE

From Gbe to Yoruba: Ethnic Change and the Mina Nation in Rio de Janeiro

Mariza de Carvalho Soares

The Mina People in Rio de Janeiro

In Rio de Janeiro different African ethnic groups were hidden under the category "Mina" in the eighteenth and nineteenth centuries. This classification gives a false sense of continuity to a social and ethnic process that was, in fact, extremely flexible over time. In Brazil most slaves identified as Mina came from the Bight of Benin, having been brought there from Ouidah, Lagos, and other ports. In the eighteenth century the term "Mina" basically referred to Gbe-speaking peoples, but during the nineteenth century the term also included Yoruba-speaking peoples, who by then were in the great majority. This study focuses on both the Yoruba and Gbe peoples and on their role within the Mina of Rio de Janeiro.[1] Gbe and Yoruba are not usual terms in the Brazilian historiography. In Brazil the usual name for Yoruba-speaking peoples is Nagô (especially in Bahia) or Mina, as a generic name. Yoruba and Gbe are categories taken from the linguistic context that offer an operational classification of the different peoples of the Bight of Benin.

According to Mary Karasch, the ethnic composition of the African population in Rio de Janeiro consisted of various African groups, including Mina, which in the Brazilian context were referred to as "nações" (nations). The Mina nation in Rio de Janeiro has been analyzed in a former work of mine.[2] The present chapter reviews the information on the subject for the nineteenth century but demonstrates that people who were referred to as Mina were also present in the eighteenth century. A careful analysis of the eighteenth and nineteenth centuries suggests that the meaning of this term changed over time. During the eighteenth century the Gbe peoples (Fon, Ewe, Mahi, Allada, and others) who were brought to Brazil were largely sent to Bahia, but some also went to Rio de Janeiro, and from both places to Minas Gerais. The question here is to elucidate when the Yoruba reached Rio, and when they became visible in the city.

Most of the Yoruba in Rio de Janeiro arrived there from Bahia in the early nineteenth century and joined an existing community of people identified as Mina. As is well known, the Yoruba were concentrated in Bahia, migrating to Rio de Janeiro, the capital of the newly independent empire since 1822. In Rio the Yoruba were called Mina. By the second half of the nineteenth century, however, they had come to form a majority because of continued migration from Bahia.

This investigation of the Mina in Rio de Janeiro goes against a major trend, which focuses largely on the "Bantu" origins of the African local slave population. Hence this study suggests that the movement of Africans to Rio was more complicated than previously recognized. While the major Atlantic routes did involve two axes, one from the Bight of Benin to Bahia and the other from Angola to Rio de Janeiro, such an approach overlooks the minor but important migration from the Bight of Benin to Rio and from Angola to Bahia.[3]

A first point to be discussed is terminology. As Robin Law has observed, the words "Yoruba," "Nagô," and "Lucumí" have been used in different ways, in both Africa and the Americas, depending on place and time. The term "Lucumí" was used as early as the sixteenth and seventeenth centuries, whereas Nagô appears only in the eighteenth century. Also, the word "Lucumí" was more frequently used in Spanish America, while the Portuguese, French, and English tended to use the word "Nagô." Law also found no reference to the word earlier than the mid-eighteenth century. According to Parés, the word "Nagô" first appears in Bahia in 1734.[4]

One way to measure the relative importance of Gbe and Yoruba in Rio is by comparing information from local documentation about the Mina with information about the slave trade from the Bight of Benin to Rio and to Bahia. Unfortunately, given the large gaps in the available documentation to Brazil, and especially to Rio de Janeiro, it is impossible to resolve the issue in this way.[5] An additional problem is that many slaves who arrived in Bahia were actually reshipped to Rio de Janeiro. The transfer of those slaves is not included in the voyage database. According to oral tradition and several biographies, the Yoruba began to be recognized as a representative ethnic community in Rio de Janeiro in the 1830s, when the Gbe were still the majority among the Mina. Yet, by the 1850s, the Yoruba had already become the major group. The second half of the nineteenth century witnessed the growth of a strong new Yoruba ethnic community composed of Catholics, orisha worshipers, and Muslims, religious divisions that apparently did not weaken ethnic identification. In effect, the process of ethnic change allowed the Yoruba to appropriate a category that at one time referred almost exclusively to Gbe-speaking peoples and, in fact, was a term that served as an umbrella to include many people.

Ethnic Origins of African-Born Slaves in Eighteenth-Century Rio de Janeiro

At the beginning of the seventeenth century the population of Rio de Janeiro numbered about 3,850 people: 750 Portuguese, 100 Africans, and 3,000 Indians and people of mixed descent. An epidemic in the year 1613 decimated the Indian population, which led to the request for African slaves.[6] In 1699 the Portuguese Crown officially opened commercial relations between Rio de Janeiro and the Mina Coast that had already been trading regularly with Bahia since 1670. There is little information about the origins of these slaves. The baptismal records for slaves of Irajá (1704–1708), a rural Parish in Rio de Janeiro, includes 222 slaves, 14 of children with African mothers whose identities are given. Ten of the mothers were referred to as Guiné, three as Mina, and one as Fula. The records also include the baptisms of 7 African adults: 4 female Mina, 2 male Mina, and 1 female Loango, as well as 1 Mina child.[7] Hence it is clear that some Mina were already in Rio de Janeiro by the end of the seventeenth century.

Moreover, the trade from West Africa to Rio continued into the early eighteenth century. The Portuguese Crown had underestimated the importance of gold as a source of wealth in the early eighteenth century, and instead the Overseas Council tried to enforce agricultural development in Brazil. As a result, there was no formal commercial network providing the gold mines of Minas Gerais with African slaves. The gap was filled by independent traders, all of them working without regular contracts. After 1699 the traders received authorization, called "licenças avulsas," for each voyage. This system supplied small numbers of slaves for each mine, paid for in gold. As D. Rodrigo Costa, the governor of Brazil, complained to the king of Portugal in 1703, traders from Rio de Janeiro were sending ships to buy slaves in the Bight of Benin with gold that should have been forwarded as tax to Portugal.[8]

From 1651 to 1675 the slave trade from Ouidah to the Americas totaled 133,400 people. For the years 1701 to 1725 this figure reached 374,400 people. For the same period the trade of Yoruba-speaking peoples to Brazil reached 93,000 slaves, averaging 3,720 slaves a year.[9] Relying on the observations of D'Elbée and Labat, Patrick Manning has shown that most slaves exported from the Bight of Benin to Mexico in this period were Gbe-speaking and not Yoruba-speaking.[10]

For the eighteenth century there is considerable evidence for Mina who were primarily Gbe speakers in Rio de Janeiro. There were Mina in the Black Brotherhood of Santo Elesbão and Santa Efigênia, founded in 1740. A Mahi Congregation was established within this brotherhood in 1762. The document on which this information is based was written in c. 1786 and records a dialogue between two Mahi men who mention their African origins and describe their lives in Rio de Janeiro. One of these men, Francisco Alves de Souza, became the "king" of Mahi in the 1780s, when the dialogue was written.[11] According to Francisco, "in 1748 when I arrived in this capital coming from the city of Bahia, I found this Congregation or Corporation of Black Mina of different nations from that Coast, such as Dagomê, Maquii, Ionno, Agolin, [and] Sabarû."[12] These are to be identified as Dahomey, Mahi, Oyo, Agonli, and Savalou, or from Dassa. At that time they were all called "Mina," or "Black Mina," having in common the "língua geral da Mina," which appears to have been a Gbe language.[13] The Brotherhood of Santo Elesbão and Santa Efigênia also included Africans from Cape Verde, Mozambique, and São Tomé. In building the church between 1746 and 1754 they demonstrated their ability to save enough money for its construction.[14] Moreover, at least some of these Mina had achieved their freedom in 1740. Usually these Mina declared in their wills the amount that they had paid for their emancipation. Allowing time to accumulate such savings, it is likely that they had arrived as early as the 1720s, or earlier still. It has been estimated that between 1711 and 1730 the Bight of Benin exported 351,700 slaves to the Americas, and it is clear that some of these people ended up in Rio.[15] Slaves were usually baptized on arrival, since masters had about six months to do so. It appears that the peak of arrivals from the Bight of Benin in Rio de Janeiro occurred in the 1720s, and most probably around 1722–24.

Until 1751 the city of Rio de Janeiro had two "freguesias" or parishes. From 1718 to 1733 the Freguesia of Sé registered the baptism of 1,074 Mina, all of whom were at least twelve years old, considered adults as follows: 1718 (57), 1719 (64), 1720 (50), 1721 (95), 1722 (107), 1723 (73), 1724 (125), 1725 (79), 1726 (96), 1727 (89), 1728 (80), 1729 (29), 1730 (51), 1731 (37), 1732 (20), and 1733 (22, until August).[16] It is likely that these people were enslaved during the Dahomean conquest of Allada (1724) and Ouidah (1727).[17] For example, Pedro Costa, who became king of the Mina, was baptized in September 1727. He had been bought and baptized by the Desembargador Ouvidor Geral do Rio de Janeiro, Manoel da Costa Mimozo. Whether he was from Dahomey, Allada, Ouidah, or elsewhere, we may never know.[18]

What deserves special attention is that Francisco refers to Yoruba as well as to various Gbe groups. His term "Iono" or "Ionno" appears to refer to Oyo, apparently following French usage of the term for Oyo. For example, the Mahi were called "Maquinos," which resembles the French term, "Mahinous"; also the French referred to the Iono as "Ayonous," and Nagô as "Nagonous."[19] The general term for Yoruba, "Nagô," appears in the early eighteenth century, derived from Anagô, a subsection of the Yoruba who lived east of the Weme River, and was the generic term for those who spoke Yoruba among the Fon and other Gbe speakers, but this term was not used in Rio then. The presence of Oyo in Rio de Janeiro during the first half of the eighteenth century was probably related to the expansion of the kingdom of Dahomey.[20]

The connection between the Portuguese/Brazilian slave trade and the French slave trade has been largely overlooked. As Manning has shown, there were some Yoruba sent to the Americas in this period, and some of these probably were taken to Brazil. The French trade expanded in 1701–25 from approximately 5,100 to 25,200 in 1726–50. These numbers may point to the possibility of a temporary transference of slaves from the French route to Brazil during the second half of the 1720s.[21] In 1723 the Portuguese Crown created the Companhia da Costa da África, usually known as Corisco Company, at the behest of a Frenchman named Jean Dansaint.[22] The Company was to build a fort in the river Anges and on Corisco Island on the coast of Gabon, and was to trade for fifteen years in slaves and other goods, but in fact Dansaint appears to have traded elsewhere. The Corisco Company clashed with the interests of the Dutch Company of the Indies and also with the interests of the Bahian merchants who often traded with them. According to Verger, the Corisco Company was trading to Rio before 1725, and we may assume before 1723, and the Company kept on after 1725. However, Dansaint apparently did not abide by the terms of the Portuguese license. As a result of his irregular business in West Africa, Jean Dansaint was convicted of violating the terms and was imprisoned in Portugal. It is clear, however, that during this period slaves were being transferred from Bahia to Rio and Minas Gerais. A volume for registering slave passports (1718–29) mentions at least one lot of slaves that was the property of the "Companhia da Africa."[23] It is likely that the interconnection of the Portuguese and French slave trades explains Brazilian usage of French terms for slaves brought from the Bight of Benin at that time.

According to Francisco, there were Yoruba in Rio de Janeiro, and they shared with the Gbe speakers the responsibilities and benefits of Mina membership in the Catholic Brotherhood of Santo Elesbão.[24] The presence of the Mina in Rio de Janeiro shows that circumstances such as political alliances, shared religion, and common resources may have provided elements of cohesion necessary to bring different ethnic groups together to forge a common identity. Such groups were organized in captivity, creating liaisons that brought different ethnic groups together, although it can be assumed that they kept some distinctions. The Mina nation therefore should be considered a "more inclusive" identification, which I have previously argued and as has been noted by Lovejoy.[25] The brotherhoods and other places where Africans congregated facilitated the organization of the Mina nation, transforming Mina nationality into a strong and genuine social identity resting on a shared African background. This social identity would ultimately survive slavery, enduring until the twentieth century.

Ethnic Origins of African-Born Slaves in Nineteenth-Century Rio de Janeiro

From 1795 to 1811, according to Manolo Florentino, about 3.0 percent of slave arrivals at Rio de Janeiro came from West Africa. At mid-century (1830–1852), according to Mary Karasch, a small proportion of the slave trade to Rio de Janeiro was also from West Africa (79.7% from West-Central Africa, 17.0% from East Africa, 1.5% from West Africa, and 0.9% of unknown origin).[26] The trade is usually understood to mean the route from Africa directly to Salvador or to Rio de Janeiro and does not allow for the transference of slaves from Salvador to Rio de Janeiro, and hence the internal trade almost certainly meant that there were even more West Africans in Rio.

This presence is reflected in the slave records of baptism for the Parish of São José (1802–1821), which contains 5,909 records, including 397 from the Bight of Benin. Of these, 236 were Mina (including 95 women), 38 Calabar (including 12 women), and 2 were Hausa women, called "Ussa."[27] The majority of these baptisms were in 1810–14. As in the 1700s, the slave trade between Rio de Janeiro and the Bight of Benin seems to have supplied Rio de Janeiro, only then it was the need for labor in the gold mines, and in the early nineteenth century it was because of the establishment of the Portuguese Crown in Rio. Similarly, 69 African-born slaves were shipped from Bahia to Rio de Janeiro in 1835, 59 of whom were Yoruba.[28] The numbers are small, but they were there. The 1849 census indicates that 66.4 percent of the slave population in Rio de Janeiro was born in Africa. From 1833 to 1849 a total of 1,735 African slaves were buried at the Santa Casa da Misericórdia; among them were 110 West Africans, 85 identified as Mina and 2 as Nagô.[29] Although they constituted only a small proportion of the different African nations, the Mina people were well known in the city. This visibility had been clear since the eighteenth century.

In the mid-nineteenth century Thomas Ewbank, an American in Rio in 1846, commented on the various African nations. In addition to Congo, Angola, Mina, and Mozambique, he also mentioned "Ashantee," who were unusual for Rio.[30] Unfortunately this and other reports provide general impressions that prevent more certain identification of ethnicities. Sometimes there are pictorial representations and photographs that require careful analysis. Such is the case regarding the collections of Jean Baptiste Debret, Johann Moritz Rugendas, Christiano Jr., and Francis de Castelnau, as well as the woodcuts in Agassiz's study, among others. According to Castelnau (who was in Bahia in 1848), the Nagô people made up "nine-tenths" of the slaves in Bahia and were easily recognized by their facial scarifications. Rugendas identified similar scarifications between 1818 and 1825. Debret, who was in Brazil during the same period (1816–31), shows scarifications in his drawings, but these may not be Yoruba scarifications but rather Gbe. Castelnau's depiction is based on a Nagô man in Bahia, while Rugendas (who visited Rio, Bahia, and many other places) does not indicate where he met the Mina woman he recorded. Debret, however, stayed solely in Rio de Janeiro, and most of the Africans he portrayed were from there.[31]

At the Church of Santa Efigênia, authorizations for burial and two volumes of records on the affiliation of new members of the brotherhood reveal a strong Mina presence, as observed above. The authorizations show a total of 428 burials from 1832 to 1850,[32] with 218 men and 210 women distributed as follows: 126 adults, 125 children up to twelve years of age, and 177 for whom no age is given. From this total I focus on the 147 African-born: 85 males (including 44 male Mina), and 62 females (including 28 female Mina). Beyond the diversity of the Africans buried in the Church of Santa Efigênia, however, the records show a clear social line separating the Mina from the others. Of 42 male slaves, 15 are listed as Mina and 27 are not; of 30 female slaves, only 7 are Mina and the other 23 are not. At the same time, of 17 freed males, 13 are identified as Mina and only 4 are not; of 20 freed females, 14 are Mina and 6 are not. These figures reveal that Mina were the most important group in terms of numbers as well as social standing.[33]

Although one might suppose that the composition of the Mina population of Rio de Janeiro should have been similar to that of Bahia, the port of arrival for almost all ships from the Bight of Benin, transplanted Africans adopted different organizational strategies in each city. In Bahia the Yoruba were called Nagô, but those in Rio de Janeiro were usually called Mina. There are occasional uses of the term "Nagô" in Rio, such as among the burials of the Church of Santa Efigênia that included two males so identified. But most were simply called "Mina" without further reference. For the period from 1843 to 1900 the books of affiliation refer to 609 males and 335 females, a total of 944 affiliations. These figures break down as follows: a total of 199 records refer to Africans, and these included 94 Mina; 15 Congo; 13 each Cabinda and Benguela; 11 Mozambique; 7 Calabar; 2 each Rebolo, Inhambane, and Moange; and 1 each Monjolo, Tapa, Cassange, Cape Verde, and Mumbolo. Twenty-three were registered simply as Africans. Once again, for unknown reasons, among 94 Mina (59 males and 35 females), 4 males are identified as Jeje, 1 as Nagô, and 1 as Mahi.[34]

The great majority of the documents that mention African "nations" in Rio de Janeiro suggest that there was a clear strategy to make use of Mina identity as an umbrella. Information on Mina prisoners in the 1820s seems to corroborate this thesis. A list of African prisoners from 1826 to 1829 indicates that 11 percent of the African prisoners came from West Africa, including Mina (7%) and Nagô (4%).[35] The presence of some imprisoned Nagô in the 1820s suggests that they were coming from Bahia before the Muslim revolt in 1835. Second, the recognition of two separate groups in the 1820s makes it clear that the Nagô were different from the Gbe, reinforcing the idea that the use of the name "Mina" for Nagô and Gbe was a local strategy peculiar to Rio.

In 1830 the municipality of Rio de Janeiro adopted an urban policy that relied on a new legal code. One of the priorities was public health, which meant regulations of the poor quarters located in the Freguesia of Santissimo Sacramento, next to the churches and residences of black people. At that time orisha worshipers attended religious houses variously called Zungu, Batuque, and Candomblé, the last name prevailing in the twentieth century. The persecution of these houses, which were considered places of disorder and rebellion, was a goal of the municipal code.[36] These places allowed Africans to be together to practice religion, but also to eat, dance, and organize themselves in many activities, including work and protection against persecution.[37] The municipal code was intended to regulate these activities and was directed especially against African-born networks, and particularly against the Mina. In 1835 the chief of police investigated several houses where Mina people congregated. They were looking for a man whose name is not given but who was a religious leader of the Mina.[38] Unfortunately we do not know if he was Gbe or Yoruba.

The Muslim uprising in Bahia in 1835 was a major factor that influenced the movement of people to Rio and also partially explains why the term "Mina" was used as an umbrella to incorporate people who might want to hide other identities, such as being Muslim. The Rio authorities moved against any type of organized network based on African ethnicity, and because of the uprising attempted to suppress the Muslim community, and indeed anyone who was considered a threat to authority.[39] For example, the Yoruba woman Luiza Mahin, who moved from Bahia to Rio in 1837,[40] was arrested the following year in a "casa de dar fortuna" (fortune-teller's house) with some "malungu"[41] and was kept in prison for a time, and then disappeared. Thirty years later her son, the black abolitionist Luís Gama, went to Rio looking for her. Interestingly he inquired about her among the Mina. This report is important not only for Luiza's biography but also because it elucidates how, thirty years after those events, the Mina community still kept alive the memory of a woman who had lived among them for less than two years.[42]

With the end of the Atlantic slave trade in 1850, fewer African-born slaves arrived in Brazil, cutting the principal link whereby people renewed their ties with Africa. The 1850s marked the turning point for the Yoruba in Rio de Janeiro. Once they formed the majority of those identified as Mina, their identity as Nagô was still hidden under the Mina umbrella. The description of Rio de Janeiro by Elizabeth Agassiz, the wife of the famous naturalist Louis Agassiz, demonstrates this shift. Agassiz stayed in Rio during the years 1865–66. Observing some groups of Mina, she noted that women were more "commonly employed as venders of fruit and vegetables than as house-servants." She described their attire as consisting of "a high muslin turban, and a long, bright-colored shawl." Some of "these negroes are Mohammedans, and are said to remain faithful to their prophet, though surrounded by the observances of the Catholic Church."[43]

In fact, some of the Yoruba moving from Bahia in the wake of the 1835 uprising were Muslims who had reason to leave. Some Mina women had been freed and were distinguished by their headscarf, which was a common feature of Yoruba dress as well as that of Muslims. An Ottoman visitor to Rio in 1865 observed this community, although he did not identify the people as Yoruba or Mina. However, he remained in Brazil and interacted with the Muslims for almost two years, and he spent his time teaching and reforming the religious practices of the community.[44] As Alberto da Costa e Silva has demonstrated, it was possible to buy copies of the Qur'an that were imported from France in Rio de Janeiro in the mid-nineteenth century, and almost certainly these were intended for this community.[45]

Thus the identity as Mina incorporated distinct ethnic and religious features, including those associated with Gbe and Yoruba peoples, no matter their religion, whether Christianity, orisha worship, or Islam. Agassiz's observations also confirm Ewbank's comments from 1846 that "young Minas" were among those African street venders "reputed to be the smartest." In reference to the "lavadeiras" (laundresses), he noted that some are Mina women, "as evinced by their superior forms and attentions to attire. If others are naked to the waist, these are seldom."[46] These street venders and washerwomen were apparently not members of the brotherhood of the Church of Santa Efigênia. Details on employment of women in the church include two lavadeiras, nine "domésticas" (servants), and 11 "costureiras" (dressmakers), none of whom were Mina. There is no mention of street venders, suggesting that such women were probably Yoruba who were not in the brotherhood. These women probably had religious links with the orisha houses or with the Muslim community. The same appears to be the case for men. Among the twenty-one different occupations mentioned for men in the church, those relating to the port, customhouse, and shipping are not present.[47]

The apparent contradiction between the information about the presence of Mina in the Church of Santa Efigênia and the travel reports of Mina in the city as a whole suggests that most Yoruba had other religious and social networks. The church itself appears to have remained the domain of Gbe and not Yoruba. As in West Africa, the Gbe groups were not associated with Islam. Those coming from Bahia who were identified as Mina were not all Yoruba. At least some were Hausa. As the case of Luiza Mahin demonstrates, many Yoruba were not Catholics. As her son reports, she had never been baptized but remained an "infiel" (infidel).[48] While the Mina identity had been associated primarily with Gbe, by the mid-nineteenth century the Yoruba had come to be characterized as such as a way to distinguish them from the far more numerous people whose origins were from Angola and other parts of West-Central Africa.

Yoruba Ethnicity and Religion in Rio de Janeiro

The end of the Atlantic slave trade coincided with the return migration of freed Africans to the continent of their birth. Through their commercial activities some people were able to save money and thereby return to Africa, and, if they could not go, their children might be able to. This return movement reinforced ethnic ties, even though slavery itself continued in Brazil until 1888. By this time there is no doubt that the great majority of those identified in Rio as Mina were, in fact, Yoruba, and they were associated with orisha houses and the remnant community of Islam and in some way to the Catholic Church.

239

We do not know who all these people were, but they silently consolidated a Yoruba identity inside the African community that eventually became associated with Candomblé. Those who attended these houses increasingly were the children of the African-born. Despite these explicit associations to Mina, these orisha houses accepted people of any background. When initiated, adepts were given Yoruba names that were used both in ritual situations and in everyday life.[49]

The new generation included such individuals as the founders of the Ketu Candomblé, João Alabá,[50] who died in 1926; Cipriano Abedé,[51] who died in 1933; and Benzinho Bamboxê,[52] who died a few years later.[53] All three died at an advanced age, suggesting that they had been born in the mid-nineteenth century, if not earlier. Moreover, there was a Muslim leader known as "Alikali" in 1904, who was the successor to earlier Muslim leaders. The Muslims called the orisha worshipers "auauadó-chum," and the orisha worshipers called Muslims "malês," but they were all related by language, which was Yoruba. In 1904 the journalist Paulo Barreto (1881–1921), who was known as João do Rio, visited many of these houses. His articles provide an excellent description of the life of the Yoruba-speaking peoples in Rio de Janeiro at the turn of the twentieth century.[54]

Two orisha houses deserve special attention: the house of Guaiaku Rozenda[55] and the house of Cipriano Abedé.[56] According to oral tradition, Guaiaku Rozenda (d. 1930s) was a free woman whose title "Guaiaku" suggests that she was of Gbe origin. She arrived in Rio de Janeiro during the 1850s. Presently, her house is considered the oldest Jeje Candomblé in Rio de Janeiro, but in fact this is unlikely since there were probably earlier houses that had disappeared. Nonetheless, hers was the last Gbe house to be founded. After her death she was replaced by Adelaide, who was given the title "Mejitó." In Bahia the title "Guaiaku" refers to a "Nagô-vodum" tradition that mixed Yoruba and Gbe elements, and the title "Mejitó" is specifically related to Mahi tradition.[57] As argued by Luis Nicolau Parés, this blurring of tradition suggests that in Bahia, Gbe and Yoruba combined different religious traditions within the same house.[58] The same appears to have been the case in Rio.

In another street not far from Rozenda's house was the house of Cipriano Abedé (1829–1933), one of the most famous orisha worship leaders in Rio de Janeiro who was certainly Yoruba in origin. The overseer of this house ("yalorixá" in Yoruba and "mãe-de-santo" in Portuguese) was a black woman called Oiá Bomin. She was one of Cipriano Abedé's wives. Though not his first wife, she was charged with the religious affairs of the house.[59] The existence of this kind of position reinforces the information that Abedé actually occupied a special position as babalaô (the one who knows how to unveil the destiny) and babalossain (the one who knows the secrets of the sacred plants). He is thought to have died at the age of 104. Early in his life he had lived in Lagos and could speak both Yoruba and English. He is thought to have come from Bahia, where he had attended Casa Branca do Engenho Velho, credited with being the oldest Nagô house in Salvador and being of Oyo and Ketu origin. He also had an important position in the Brotherhood of Rosário as well as in the Church of Santa Efigênia. First mentioned in an anonymous letter to the police in 1898, his house in Rio is specifically identified with Ketu, and at that time he was well known as a sorcerer.[60] Like Rozenda, it is claimed that he had never been a slave and was not descended from slaves.[61] By the early twentieth century there were at least two other houses associated with Ketu in Rio. These included the houses of the Benzinho Bamboxê and João Alabá. Although all three houses had close ties to the Candomblé of Bahia, they were not associated with Oyo, as were the Nagô houses in Bahia.

The Muslims among the Yoruba in Rio lived in the same neighborhood on the streets of São Diogo, Barão de São Félix, Hospício, Núncio, da América, and others, where the Candomblé houses were located. They were under leaders known as "alufá" (Muslim cleric) and had judges known as "alikaly." These Muslims used Arabic greetings and participated in public ceremonies in Muslim attire that included a white "abadá" (a long flowing gown) and a red "filá" (fez). Although they lived in the city, they organized ceremonies that included riding horses in the suburbs at the initiation of their "lemanos" or imams. Seventy years after the Muslim uprising they no longer had to hide their allegiance to Islam as they had to do in the aftermath of the uprising in 1835.[62]

In a series of articles published between 1904 and 1908, the journalist João do Rio noted that a portion of this Mina community could speak "eubá." This appears to be the first reference to the use of Yoruba as a language in Brazil, or at least in Rio. His guide was Antônio, a black man who spoke Yoruba and had lived in Lagos. According to Antônio, the Yoruba of Rio de Janeiro could be classified into two groups, orisha worshipers and Muslims. The first group was led by various babalorixá (the leader of the orisha houses), the second by the lemano, the imam who supervised the mosque on a street called Barão de São Felix.[63] According to Antônio, the Yoruba-speaking Mina taught their children to speak Yoruba and, if they could afford to do so, even sent them to Lagos for their education. As Antonio informed João do Rio, "whoever can speak Yoruba (Eubá) can cross over from Africa and live among the blacks of Rio."[64]

João do Rio understood that there was something more than a common language that kept these Mina together, because the community included orisha worshipers and Muslims. Besides language they also shared what he called "external customs" which he did not specify. The community was concentrated in a neighborhood behind the port where many of them worked.[65] The orisha houses and the mosque were important as religious sites and as places to socialize.

Among the Yoruba speakers was another Antônio, whose African name was Adeoiê. He was also known as Antônio Mina. João do Rio mentions him as a babalorixá but Agenor Miranda regards him as a sorcerer, who never had a "house." It is his Christian name, Antônio Mina, which follows the rule for baptism of Africans in Brazil, that suggests he was African-born. Following oral information from Agenor Miranda, Antônio Mina disappeared between 1915 and

1920. From 1906 to 1915 Antônio was jailed at least three times, for disorder and drunkenness. He was last arrested in 1915, a date that coincides with his disappearance.[66] Another memorable character was "Assumano Henrique Mina do Brasil," who died in the 1930s. In Rio Muslims were called "mussu-rumim" (in Bahia, "malê"). He was probably the last Muslim of this African community. His father was Muhammad Salim, and his mother, a Brazilian-born, was Fatima Faustina Mina do Brazil. His name provided him an identity and also revealed his diverse ancestry.[67]

Though belonging to different religious traditions, Guaiaku Rozenda (Gbe-orisha worshiper), Assumano (Muslim), and Adeoyé (Yoruba-orisha worshiper) were all related in some way to the end of the use of Mina to describe this community in Rio de Janeiro. They were also connected to the genesis of the religious community of Ketu, which at that time was presided over by Cipriano Abedé, João Alabá, and Benzinho Bamboxé. All of them died in the 1930s.[68]

The Gbe tradition vanished, as did the first Yoruba houses. It is not even certain where the mosque was located.[69] The deaths of the various religious leaders in the 1930s establish a clear break with the past. Until then the term "Mina" had significance as an ethnic label, but after the 1930s the new houses that were founded were clearly no longer related to ethnicity but rather to religious identity. From then on, orisha worshipers referred to their African background but they no longer maintained clear ties with Yorubaland itself, as memories of the linkage had faded. Nevertheless, the Ketu Candomblé continued to function in Rio, and from that time to the present all people initiated into Candomblé are referred to by the origin of their African nation, for example, "children of the Angola nation," "children of the Jeje nation," and "children of the Ketu nation," but, in fact, anyone could join.

The history of the Yoruba people in Rio de Janeiro is full of gaps, misunderstandings, and changes that make their study risky business for historians and anthropologists. The objective of this chapter was to demonstrate that ethnic identification changed over time, which was partly related to politics and partly to memory of the African homeland. It is likely that additional research will uncover new sources, and especially that comparative research with Yoruba in other parts of the Americas and in Africa will add significantly to our understanding of the process of ethnic identification and religious change within the context of the wider Atlantic world.

Notes

The present research is supported by a grant from the Ministério da Educação/ CAPES of Brazil and by the Social Sciences and Humanities Research Council of Canada through the Tubman Centre. I am indebted to Vanderbilt University, and especially Jane Landers, for receiving me as a visiting scholar. I wish to thank Juliana Barreto Farias, who assisted me in Rio de Janeiro. I am especially grateful to Paul Lovejoy and João José Reis for their valuable suggestions to the final version of this chapter.

1. Nations are not ethnic groups but "provenance groups," broader categories of identification that recover ethnic groups. See Mariza de Carvalho Soares, *Devotos da cor. Identidade étnica, religiosidade e escravidão no Rio de Janeiro, século XVIII* (Rio de Janeiro: Civilização Brasileira, 2000), chap. 3.

2. Mary C. Karasch, *Slave Life in Rio de Janeiro, 1808–1850* (Princeton, N.J.: Princeton University Press, 1987); Carvalho Soares, *Devotos da cor*; Carlos Eugênio Líbano Soares, *A negregada instituição. Os capoeiras na corte imperial, 1850–1890* (Rio de Janeiro: Acess, 1999); idem, *A capoeira escrava e outras tradições rebeldes no Rio de Janeiro, 1808–1850* (Campinas: Unicamp, 2001).

3. On the slave trade between West Africa and Brazil, see Pierre Verger, *Flux et reflux de la traite de nègres entre le Golf de Benin et Bahia de Todos os Santos du XVIIe au XIXe siècle* (The Hague: Mouton, 1968); Manolo G. Florentino, *Em costas negras. Uma história do tráfico de escravos entre a África e o Rio de Janeiro (séculos XVIII e XIX)* (São Paulo: Companhia das letras, 2002).

4. Robin Law, "Ethnicity and the Slave Trade: 'Lucumi' and 'Nago' as Ethnonyms in West Africa," *History in Africa* 24 (1997): 208; Luis Nicolau Parés, "The 'Nagôization' Process in Bahian Candomblé," chapter 10 in this volume.

5. David Eltis et al., *The Trans-Atlantic Slave Trade: A Database on CD-ROM* (Cambridge: Cambridge University Press, 1999).

6. Delgado de Carvalho, *História da cidade do Rio de Janeiro*, 2nd ed. (Rio de Janeiro: Prefeitura da Cidade do Rio de Janeiro / Secretaria Municipal de Cultura / DGDIC, 1994), 32; José de Souza Azevedo Pizarro Araújo, *Memórias históricas do Rio de Janeiro*, 10 vols. (Rio de Janeiro: Imprensa Nacional, 1948), 2:239–41.

7. Bartolomeu Homem d'El Rei Pinto, "Livro de batismo dos pretos pertencentes a Paróquia de Irajá," *Anais da Biblioteca Nacional* 108 (1988): 129–73.

8. Letter of D. Rodrigo Costa, the Portuguese Governor in Brazil (1702–1705), 29 June 1703, in Verger, *Flux et reflux*, 47.

9. David Eltis, "The Diaspora of Yoruba Speakers, 1650–1865: Dimensions and Implications," chapter 2 in this volume. See Table 2.3, "Estimated Departures of Slaves from Ports in the Bight of Benin by Quarter Century, 1650–1865"; and Table 2.5, "Preferred Series of Departures of Yoruba-Speaking Captives from Africa and Their Destinations in the Americas by Quarter Century, 1651–1867."

10. Aja (15), Calabar (6), Fon (12), Allada (7), Ouidah (7), Popo (6), and Oyo (1). See Patrick Manning, "The Slave Trade in the Bight of Benin, 1690–1890," in *The Uncommon Market: Essays in the Economic History of the Atlantic Slave Trade*, ed. Henry A. Gemery and Jan S. Hogendorn (New York: Academic Press, 1979), pp. 125–29.

11. Francisco wrote the dialogue in Portuguese, with a few words in the Gbe language. For further information, see Mariza de Carvalho Soares, "Apreço e imitação no diálogo do gentio convertido," *Ipotesi. Revista de Estudos Literários* 4, no. 1 (2000): 111–23.

12. Biblioteca Nacional, Rio de Janeiro, "Regra ou estatutos pormodo de hûm diálogo onde, se dá notícias das Caridades e Sufragaçoens das Almas que uzam os prettos Minnas, com seus Nancionaes no Estado do Brazil, expecialmente no Rio de Janeiro, por onde se hao de regerem e gôvernarem fora de todo o abuzo gentilico e supersticiozo; composto por Françîsco Alvês de Souza pretto e natural do Reino de Makim, hûm dos mais exçelentes e potentados daqûela ôriunda Costa da Minna," BN(MA) 9, 3, 11. About the Mahi Congregation, see Mariza de Carvalho Soares, *Devotos da cor*, 21–22, chap. 6.

13. *Obra Nova de Língua Geral de Mina de António da Costa Peixoto. Manuscrito da Biblioteca Pública de Évora e da Biblioteca Nacional de Lisboa. Publicado e apresentado por Luís Silveira e acompanhado de comentário filológico de Edmundo Correia Lopes* (Lisboa: Agência Geral das Colónias, 1945). In Brazil, during the eighteenth century, the "língua geral de Mina" is the Brazilian name for the Gbe languages. For further explanation, see Carvalho Soares, *Devotos da cor*, chap. 6.

14. Arquivo da Irmandade de Santo Elesbão e Santa Efigênia, Rio de Janeiro, Compromisso da Irmandade de Santo Elesbão e Santa Efigênia, 1740–1767.

15. See Paul Lovejoy, *A escravidão na África. Uma história de suas transformações* (Rio de Janeiro: Civilização Brasileira, 2002), 96.

16. Arquivo da Cúria Metropolitana do Rio de Janeiro, Rio de Janeiro, Livros de Batismo de Escravos da Freguesia da Sé, 1718–1726, 1726–1733.

17. For this chronology, see Robin Law, *History of Ouidah*, forthcoming.

18. Pedro is mentioned in two documents: his record of baptism and the dialogue. See Arquivo da Cúria Metropolitana do Rio de Janeiro, Rio de Janeiro, Livro de Batismo de escravos da Freguesia da Sé. Rio de Janeiro, 1726–1733, 12 September 1727, fl. 38; Biblioteca Nacional, Rio de Janeiro, "Regra ou estatutos," BN(MA) 9, 3, 11 fl. 22.

19. About the spelling of Fon words, see Law, "Ethnicity and the Slave Trade," 212. For French orthography of the African names, see Paul Hazoumé, *Doguicimi* (Paris: G-P Maisonneuve et Larose, 1978). About the Oyo in Africa, see Robin Law, *The Oyo Empire, c. 1600–c. 1836: A West African Imperialism in the Era of the Atlantic Slave Trade* (Oxford: Clarendon, 1977).

20. Paul Lovejoy, "The Yoruba Factor in the Trans-Atlantic Slave Trade," chapter 3 in this volume; Robin Law, *The Slave Coast of West África, 1550–1750: The Impact of the Atlantic Slave Trade on an African Society* (Oxford: Clarendon, 1991).

21. Manning, "The Slave Trade in the Bight of Benin."

22. The board of directors of the Corisco Company included Jean Dansaint, Noël Houssaye, Bartholomeo Miguel Vienne, Manoel Domingos do Paço, Francisco Nonez da Cruz, and Lourenço Pereira (Verger, *Flux et reflux*, 75–76, 92–94). In the Slave Voyage Database he is listed as "Jean Danssainct," the captain of the slave ship *Reine*, which left Nantes in 1713. The ship took slaves from the Bight of Benin to Rio de Janeiro and Bahia (Eltis et al., *The Trans-Atlantic Slave Trade*, record number 30038).

23. A volume of passports for slaves lists about 19,500 slaves sent from Bahia to Minas Gerais in this period (Arquivo Público Estado da Bahia, Salvador, Livro de Passaportes e Guias, 1718–1729, doc. 248).

24. In Cuba the Araras (Allada) are considered "a sort of Lucumis" (Law, "Ethnicity and the Slave Trade," 207).

25. Paul Lovejoy, "Enslaved Africans in the Diaspora, " in *Identity in the Shadow of Slavery*, ed. Paul Lovejoy (London: Continuum, 2000), 11.

26. Florentino, *Em costas negras*, 79; Karasch, *Slave Life in Rio de Janeiro*, 25.

27. Arquivo da Cúria Metropolitana do Rio de Janeiro, Rio de Janeiro, Livro de Batismo de escravos, Freguesia de São José, 1802–1821. I would like to thank Roberto Guedes for sending me his personal database. I emphasize the attention to the presence of two Hausa women. On Hausa in Brazil, see Paul Lovejoy, "Jihad e escravidão: as origens dos escravos muçulmanos da Bahia," *Topoi* (Rio de Janeiro) 1 (2000): 11–44.

28. Karasch, *Slave Life in Rio de Janeiro*, 52. On Mina in this period, see Líbano Soares, *A capoeira escrava*.

29. Karasch presents four ships from Calabar, twenty-one from Dahomey, two from

Mina (from Cape Mount to Cape Lopez), thirty from Nigeria, and five from Ilha do Príncipe, reaching a total of sixty-two ships between 1830 and 1852. For burials, the others were twenty from Calabar, one from Cape Verde, one from Cameron, and one from Hausa (Karasch, *Slave Life in Rio de Janeiro*, 25, 8, 12, 371).

30. Thomas Ewbank, *Life in Brazil; or, A Journal of a Visit to the Land of the Cocoa and the Palm* (New York: Harper and Brothers, 1856), 111, 94, 114.

31. Francis de Castelnau, *Reseignement sur l'Afrique Centrale et sur une nation d'hommes a queue que s'y trouvait d'après le rapport des nègres du Soudan, esclaves a Bahia* (Paris: P. Bertrand, Librarie-Editeur, 1851), 26; Jean Baptiste Debret, *Viagem pitoresca e histórica ao Brasil*, commentary by Sergio Milliet (São Paulo: Livraria Martins, 1940), plates 22, 36; Johann Moritz Rugendas, *Viagem através do Brasil* (São Paulo: Itatiaia / USP, 1979), plate 2ª; div. plate 10.

32. These burial permissions do not represent the total number of burials in the period. The 428 records are being considered as a random sample that may induce errors. The cemetery was closed in 1850.

33. The 147 Africans buried in the Church of Santa Efigênia include 72 Mina (44 males and 28 females), 12 Calabar, 4 Congo, 9 Angola, 8 Cabinda, 19 Benguela, 6 Rebolo, 3 Calange, 1 Monjolo, 1 Inhanbane, 8 Mozambique, and 4 said Africans (Arquivo da Irmandade de Santo Elesbão e Santa Efigênia, Rio de Janeiro, Collection of authorization for burials, 1832–1850).

34. Arquivo da Irmandade de Santo Elesbão e Santa Efigênia, Rio de Janeiro, Collection of authorization for burials, 1832–1850; Livros de registro de entrada de irmãos e irmãs para os anos de 1843–1900.

35. Soares, *A capoeira escrava*, 600.

36. *Código de Posturas da Ilustríssima Câmara Municipal do Rio de Janeiro* (Rio de Janeiro: Typographia Imperial e Nacional, 1930). On zungus, see Carlos Eugênio Líbano Soares, *Zungu: rumor de muitas vozes* (Rio de Janeiro: Arquivo Público de Estado do Rio de Janeiro, 1998).

37. On African ethnic religious houses in Minas Gerais in the eighteenth century, see Luis Mott, "Acotundá: raízes setecentistas do sincretismo religiosos afro-brasileiro," in *Escravidão, homosexualidade e demonologia* (São Paulo: Ícone Editora, 1988); also in later-eighteenth-century Louisiana, slaves called Mina had ethnic organizations with houses used for "balls." During one of these balls they organized a rebellion. See Gwendolyn Midlo Hall, *Africans in Colonial Louisiana: The Development of Afro-Creole Culture in the Eighteenth Century* (Baton Rouge: Louisiana State University Press, 1992), 317–42.

38. Arquivo Nacional, Rio de Janeiro, "Correspondência reservada recebida pela Repartição de Polícia," 1833–1840, códice 334.

39. See João José Reis, *Slave Rebellion in Brazil: The Muslim Uprising of 1835 in Bahia*, trans. Arthur Brakel (Baltimore: The Johns Hopkins University Press, 1993).

40. Mahin is one of the main Yoruba groups of the Ondo division (Darryl Forde, *The Yoruba-Speaking People of South-Western Nigeria* (London: International African Institute, 1951). I would like to thank Alberto da Costa e Silva and Olatunji Ojo for this information.

41. "Malungu" is what Africans in Brazil called other Africans who shared the same ship during the middle passage. See Robert Slenes, "'Malungu ngoma vem!': África coberta e descoberta do Brasil," *Revista da USP*, no. 12 (December 1991–February 1992): 48–67.

42. Luis Gama, "Luis Gama's letter to Lúcio de Mendonça," published in English in *Negro de Corpo e Alma* (São Paulo: Fundação Bienal de São Paulo, 2000), 180–83.

43. Louis and Elizabeth Agassiz, *A Journey in Brazil* (New York: Praeger, 1969), 83–85.

44. Abd al-Rahmān al-Bagdādï, *The Amusement of the Foreigner* (1865), trans. Yacine Daddi Addoun and Renée Soulodre–La France. Harriet Tubman Resource Centre on the African Diaspora, SHADD, www.yorku.ca/nhp/shadd/index.htm

45. Alberto da Costa e Silva, "Buying and Selling Korans in Nineteenth-Century Rio de Janeiro," *Slavery and Abolition* 22, no. 1 (April 2001): 83–90.

46. Ewbank, *Life in Brazil*, 94, 114.

47. Arquivo da Irmandade de Santo Elesbão e Santa Efigênia, Rio de Janeiro, Livros de registro de entrada de irmãos e irmãs para os anos de 1843–1900. Men who worked in the customs were called "carregadores de cangalhas." They were depicted many times, including by Debret, who specify that usually this was a job for Africans, not necessarily Mina (Debret, *Viagem pitoresca e histórica ao Brasil*, plates 22, 36).

48. Gama, "Luis Gama's letter to Lúcio de Mendonça," 180–83.

49. Oral information from Agenor Miranda Rocha.

50. "Alabá" is considered a Yoruba word the specific meaning of which I could not identify. Supposedly João Alabá was born in Brazil. He had a house in Rua Barão de São Felix and was well known among the rich people of the city, having many followers who attended to his house.

51. The name "Abedé" is a reference to the personal orisha of Cipriano, called "Ogun Abedé" in Brazil. Abedé in the Brazilian Nagô-Ketu Candomblé is considered a "quality" or subsession of Ogun. On the orisha Ogun in Africa and Brazil, see Pierre Verger, *Orixás: Deuses iorubás na África e no Novo Mundo* (São Paulo: Corrupio, 1981).

52. Benzinho Bamboxê, also known by the name Felisberto Souza, was a Babalossain in Bahia who moved to Rio de Janeiro on an uncertain date. He was a member of the Bamboxê family, who were well known in both Bahia and Africa.

53. Interview with Agenor Miranda Rocha, ninety-six years old, a Brazilian of Nagô-Ketu Candomblé who was a ritual son of Abedé. The interviews he gave me were used as a basis for his book *Os candomblés antigos do Rio de Janeiro. A nação de Ketu: origens, ritos e crenças* (Rio de Janeiro: Top Books, 1994).

54. João do Rio [Paulo Barreto], "No mundo dos feitiços. Os feiticeiros," in *As religiões no Rio* (Rio de Janeiro: Nova Aguilar, 1976).

55. According to Agenor Miranda Rocha, Rozenda was a daughter of the vodum Bessen. On vodun houses of Bahia, see Luis Nicolau Parés, "Transformations of the Sea and Thunder Voduns in the Gbe-Speaking Area and in the Bahian Jeje Candomblé," in *Enslaving Connections: Africa and Brazil during the Era of the Slave Trade*, 3 vols. (Toronto: York University, 2000), 2:1–30.

56. The first title indicates one who is charged with Ifá divination and the second with the care of sacred plants.

57. I wish to thank Luis Nicolau Parés for this information.

58. Luis Nicolau Parés, "Do Lado do Jeje. História e Ritual do Vodun na Bahia," unpublished paper.

59. Interview with Agenor Miranda Rocha.

60. See Rocha, *Os candomblés antigos do Rio de Janeiro*; Yvonne Maggie, *Medo do feitiço: relações entre magia e poder no Brasil* (Rio de Janeiro: Arquivo Nacional, 1992), 31; Rio, *As religiões do Rio*, 35.

61. Many of those important leaders were there. But there are few reports from the oral tradition about specific events, and most of these are actually based on a doubtful reconstruction of the ethnic past, having been collected by various people working on the history of samba and not by historians researching slavery or ethnicity. Since the end of the 1970s, and especially during the 1980s, some publications about the history of samba in Rio de Janeiro shaped a particular interpretation about Africans in Rio de Janeiro, referring basically to Mina people. See the collection edited by Fundação Nacional de Arte-FUNARTE; see also the documentation of Corisco Filmes with many interviews; the documentation of the Museu de Imagem e do Som-MIS, and other personal archives such as those of Marília Barbosa, Hermínio Bello de Carvalho, and others.

62. Rio, *As religiões do Rio.*

63. Little work has been done on the history of the Ketu Candomblé in Rio de Janeiro. For Muslims, see João Baptista M. Vargens and Nei Lopes, *Islamismo e negritude: da África ao Brasil, da Idade Média aos nossos dias* (Rio de Janeiro: Setor de Estudos Árabes Faculdade de Letras, UFRJ, 1982); see also da Costa e Silva, "Buying and Selling Korans," 84–90.

64. Rio, *As religiões do Rio,* 19.

65. See Roberto Moura, *Tia ciata e a pequena África no Brasil,* 2nd ed. (Rio de Janeiro: Municipal de Cultura, Turismo e Esportes, 1995).

66. Arquivo Nacional, Rio de Janeiro, Processos do Código Penal, 1890–1940, Processo Crime n. 175 (1906); n. 648 (1912); n. 811 (1915).

67. "Assumano" is the Brazilian version for Uthman (Arabic). The name is also written Osumanu (Hausa) and Sumanu (Yoruba). The proximity with the Hausa spelling may mean that his father was a Hausa. His name follows the Muslim rule that when the father has more than one woman, the son should receive his mother's family name. I wish to thank Bashir Salau for this information. Unlike Yoruba names, Muslim names do not provide enough information to distinguish African Muslims from Brazilian-born Muslims. Some of these names were Alikali (the lemano), Abubaca Caolho (actually Abubacar; Caolho is a Brazilian nickname for people who are blind in one eye), João Mussê, and Luis Sanin (actually Sani). See Rio, *As religiões do Rio.* I wish to thank João José Reis, and especially Paul Lovejoy, who provided me with the necessary information and emphasized the importance of considering the meaning of Muslim names while trying to identify the biographies of Muslim slaves.

68. Assumano is mentioned in many oral reports. He went to jail in 1927. His trial provides important information to his biography (Arquivo Nacional, Rio de Janeiro, Processos do Código Penal, 1890–1940, Processo Crime no. 261 [1927]). From 1890 to 1940 the Brazilian Penal Code authorized imprisonment of anyone suspected of practicing medicine illegally. Most black religious leaders were jailed during this period, including Antônio Mina and Assumano. These trials are a precious source to construct not only biographies but also a complete religious network. See Juliana Barreto Farias, "Crenças e religiosidades cotidianas. Práticas culturais e religiosidades afro-brasileiras no Rio de Janeiro (1870s–1930s)," unpublished paper, 2002.

69. Alberto da Costa e Silva, "Buying and Selling Korans," 86.

247

CHAPTER THIRTEEN

Yoruba Family, Gender, and Kinship Roles in New World Slavery

Kevin Roberts

Studying Yoruba family and kinship within the context of the Yoruba diaspora connects three major historiographies that speak too little to one another.
First, examining the manner in which Yoruba family structures and kinship ideologies were transformed during the era of New World slavery necessarily builds
on the voluminous studies of slave families in the Atlantic World. Second, in
order to assess which New World societies are worthy of inclusion in a study on
Yoruba kinship, one must rely on historians' lively debate of the trans-Atlantic
slave trade and of Africa, both of which have come to rely increasingly on the
use of databases to make their arguments more precise. Finally, the corpus of
literature that has become increasingly reliant on the second thread—the study
not just of African origins and New World destinations but also the ways in
which African peoples enslaved in the New World altered and were forced to
alter their cultural traditions and identities—forms the theoretical grounding
for my approach to understanding Yoruba kinship throughout the Yoruba
diaspora.[1]

By looking at Yoruba family and kinship as the point of convergence of these
three rich threads in recent scholarship, this chapter posits that modern scholars can find evidence of major Yoruba kinship structures in specific New World
societies to which a critical number of ethnic Yoruba were sold. But the aim
of the chapter is not simply to revisit the well-tread debates over African cultural "survivals" and the "stability" of black slave families. Rather, in examining societies where Yoruba comprised a major proportion of the slave population, and consequently, therefore, influenced the cultural traditions that
emerged during the assimilation of so many different African peoples, as well
as societies where Yoruba were notable minorities within the slave population,

this chapter demonstrates the factors that were crucial to the emergence of Yoruba family forms and cultural traditions. Most centrally I argue that Yoruba in the New World preserved in altered form their central practices of extended family, fictive kinship, and even gender roles in some cases while also continuing to emphasize communal activities such as garden plots in which all members of the kin network participated.[2]

Studies of slave families and kinship systems in the New World have waned in recent years, given the explosion of compelling examinations on these subjects in the 1970s. Studying slave families was sparked by then policy analyst Daniel P. Moynihan, whose government report *The Negro Family* caused great consternation, not only among black political activists but also sociologists and historians. For historians of the family and of slavery, Moynihan's reliance on E. Franklin Frazier's study *The Negro Family in the United States,* and frequent citing of Stanley Elkins's work *Slavery: A Problem in American Institutional and Intellectual Life* ushered in a new direction in scholarship. The magnum opus of this field, Herbert Gutman's *The Black Family in Slavery and Freedom,* itself sparked a spate of studies of slave families not only in the United States but throughout the New World.[3]

Though varying degrees of agreement exist among scholars, the consensus is that African and African-descended slaves were able to maintain some modicum of African kinship systems in their New World environs. Nonetheless, the extent to which African agency was responsible for this remains unresolved because of the paucity of direct evidence. Philip Morgan's recent suggestion that "perhaps the compatibility of homeland beliefs and the imperatives of slavery combined to produce these behavioral patterns" seems closest to the mark in emphasizing the combination of forces responsible for the ultimate contours of slave family structures and kinship.[4] That such a combination did exist is certain, for evidence of the ability of slaves to mitigate the rigors of enslavement is voluminous. In 1786 one Virginian thought that the Yoruba's "cheerful nature, a jocular disposition, wit and humor and playfulness, . . . and readiness to oblige, went a long way to insure a slave against ill-treatment."[5]

Though the issue of agency is unlikely to be resolved definitively, the recent momentum in slave culture studies has been aided by increasing specificity of the origins and destinations of slaves. This development, in turn, has led to the possibility of positing new questions regarding family structure, function, and ideology among specific African peoples who were sold into New World slavery. With a substantial proportion of trans-Atlantic slave traffic being comprised of peoples from the Bight of Benin, as the chapters in this volume by Eltis and Lovejoy demonstrate, the specific cultures within this dispersal are logical places to start this new direction in slave family and culture scholarship.[6]

Few African cultures are better case studies for this convergence of historiographies than the Yoruba. Like most cultures, the Yoruba sold into New World slavery became numerically dominant in certain societies and less so in others. In particular, as indicated elsewhere in this volume, the Yoruba and Yoruba culture were wholly influential on the development of an assimilated slave culture and identity in societies such as Brazil, Cuba, and Saint Domingue, and were one of a handful of influential African cultures in Jamaica and Trinidad. In addition, the Yoruba were the majority of repatriates to Sierra Leone and a significant proportion of the population of Liberia. Thus, by concentrating on slave family scholarship on these societies where the Yoruba were culturally influential, one can best determine the similarities and differences between kinship practices in Yorubaland and those in the New World.

By also examining those societies where the Yoruba were important but not dominant, one might also assess the influence of the Yoruba in spite of being outnumbered by peoples from other cultures. One would reasonably expect that enslaved people from African cultures that were not numerically dominant in a given place would be less influential in the creation either of specific identities or an assimilated slave culture. Nonetheless, the Yoruba appear to have been influential beyond their numbers in many societies throughout the New World, mainly because specific aspects of their worldview were effective binding forces for peoples of disparate African cultures. Yoruba ideology of kinship, emphasis on extended kin, and centrality of family not only fit well with the traditions of most other West and West-Central African cultures but were also successful means of ameliorating the effects of being enslaved. By examining first the major contours of these kinship practices in Yorubaland, and then moving on to assess their constants and changes in specific New World societies, this chapter will demonstrate the centrality of the Yoruba notion of kinship to the cultural vibrancy of Yoruba- and African-based culture in the New World.

Family and Kinship in Yorubaland

The era of the trans-Atlantic slave trade was one in which Yorubaland was fraught with internal strife that led to a constant supply of slaves for European traders. Barring the unusual practice of selling a member of one's own ethnic group into slavery, the various subgroups of the Yoruba, as well as nearby enemies, caused the Yoruba to be one of the most numerous African ethnicities in the New World during the late eighteenth and nineteenth centuries. In spite of these wars, and in some cases because of them, Yorubaland rose to become a region filled with powerful leaders and an intricate sociopolitical organization that itself inherently relied on an intricate system of kinship.

The Yoruba practiced patrilineal descent and were, especially compared to some other West African cultures whose members were sold to New World slave owners, a patriarchal society. Upon marriage, a woman moved to her husband's home, which was usually located in a village comprised of his kin members. The close physical grouping of dwellings and extended kin members emphasized the everyday importance of an extended kin network, something that would carry over into New World enslavement. The congregation of nuclear households within the extended kinship network led to a melding of the terms "family" and "kin."[7]

Aside from the important functions of extended kin in socializing children, extended family groups in Yorubaland had the equally important economic function of farming land owned by the group. Corporate ownership of land, as well as communal work on the land, helped to integrate both nuclear family units and the extended kin group, as well as to integrate the social, cultural, and economic functions of kinship. Even in nonagricultural enterprises, such as smelting, Yoruba extended kin families were the predominant economic labor force in the region.[8] The practice of work crews under New World slavery, which slave owners often divided according to kin groups, continued, in slightly altered form, to be a prominent Yoruba and West African practice.[9]

Within this corporate arrangement were definite divisions of labor according to gender. While men participated in the farming of the group's land, women took part in a communitywide system of weaving. Explaining this aspect of Yoruba life, G. J. Afolabi Ojo notes, "Before European contact was established, every woman, assisted by her daughters, ginned, carded and spun. To ensure a steady and adequate supply of thread for dyeing and weaving, there was a system by which all the women in an extended family contributed a definite length of yarn every market day."[10] Though New World enslavement altered these practices, enslaved Yoruba nonetheless were able to preserve some aspects of this gendered division of labor; that slave owners also saw the benefit of dividing work groups according to sex also reinforced the continuation of such traditions.

Compared to other West African cultures whose members comprised a significant proportion of African slaves in the New World, the Yoruba, because of their gendered labor traditions, were ironically best suited to withstand the pressures of being enslaved. In comparing the patrilineal and patriarchal societies of the Igbo, Hausa, and Yoruba, Carolyne Dennis explained, "The opportunities for women to participate in other economic activities such as manufacturing and trade varied from one society to another. They were probably greatest in Yoruba society in which the responsibility of a woman to provide for her family was interpreted as meaning [to provide] the material resources for such care."[11] Under enslavement, in which families were frequently broken apart and in which husband and wife often lived on separate estates, the cultural traditions of women as material providers served as bulwarks of families and extended kin networks.

Though most attention on family and kinship upheaval should rightly be placed on New World slave societies, similar processes occurred in Yorubaland itself. This development was especially prominent starting in the early 1830s, when the jihad of the Sokoto caliphate accelerated the collapse of the long-standing Oyo kingdom. While many scholars have focused on the political effects and religious motivations for this long-term disintegration of the Oyo kingdom, the process also had monumental effects on Yoruba kinship practices. Noting the effects of the Oyo collapse, historian S. A. Akintoye argues, "Probably more than ever before, the nineteenth century witnessed a great deal of mixing of Yoruba peoples. Fragments of the various Yoruba subgroups were thrown all over the Yoruba homeland, most getting absorbed into their new homes."[12] The massive dispersal of Yoruba during this time led to an ethnic mixing not unlike the consequences of the slave trade, and therefore similar in result to family relations. This process undoubtedly led to a similar emphasis on fictive kin relations, an emphasis that superseded even the common practice of that prior to the early nineteenth century.[13]

Brazil

The result of the jihad in the 1840s in Yorubaland was the creation of a tremendous number of non-Muslim slave migrants from the region. With the slave trade closed in most New World societies by this time, the vast majority of Yoruba sold from the region to the New World during this era ended up in Brazil and Cuba, two regions where Yoruba culture had already achieved a permanent foothold in slave cultures.[14] Forced migrants from Yorubaland comprised significant proportions of the Brazilian slave population during the late eighteenth and nineteenth centuries. Known in Brazil as "Nagô," the Yoruba placed their mark on studies of specific African ethnicities and on the study of African Islam in the Americas with their role in the 1835 rebellion in Bahia.[15]

Though some scholars have focused on the ethnic and religious questions surrounding the role of these Yoruba peoples in the Bahia uprising, an entirely different group of scholars has focused on slave families in Brazil. Unfortunately neither body of literature speaks to the other, specifically in assessing how cultural institutions—whether nuclear families, extended kin networks, or the numerous lay sodalities throughout Brazil—affected the development of the necessary collective identity required of the 1835 rebellion or others.[16]

More recent scholarship has focused on some aspects of slave life that go beyond the nuclear family and stability argument, though still not connected with the level of origin / destination specificity that scholars could attempt to exact. Alida Metcalf, for example, demonstrates that slave marriages and slave women's fertility rates were much higher than has been commonly argued in reference to Brazil. As Herbert Gutman argued about slaves in the United States, the major force negatively affecting the ability of slaves in Brazil to marry was the death of their master. Nonetheless, Metcalf argues, on large estates nuclear families were more the rule than not in Santana de Parnaíba (near São Paulo), and on smaller estates matrifocality predominated.[17] Although the evidence used by scholars of slave families to examine the structure of slave families does not always allow for precise identifications of specific African ethnicities, the prevalence of extended kin networks and the important role of women—not to

252

mention gendered divisions of labor—favored the reinforced nature of Yoruba kinship in the Americas.

As with the vagaries of slave family structure, either through the actions of masters or agency of slaves or, more likely, a combination of the two, Brazil had certain institutional structures that helped to reinvigorate African tendencies. One such institution was the Roman Catholic Church, which in both theological and social terms provided the Yoruba and other Africans the means by which important aspects of their lives, such as kinship, could prevail. Moreover, the Catholic sacrament of baptism preserved the ever-more-important Yoruba tradition of fictive kin. With slaves playing active roles in the selection of godparents—and with some godparents serving as sponsors for numerous baptized slaves—the act of baptism and godparentage both enlarged the extended kin network and provided semiautonomy for some slaves.[18]

In addition to the theological source for fictive kinship that Catholic sacraments provided, black lay sodalities, associations sponsored by the Church, provided Yoruba and other African slaves in Brazil with a powerful means of emphasizing the communalism so prevalent in Yorubaland.[19] These vibrant associations and the membership they attracted are testaments to the diverse strategies that Africans and their descendants used to carve out social and cultural space for themselves, even if the means for accomplishing that aim were white-sponsored. Mieko Nishida explains, "No matter how strongly African-born slaves had initially reacted against forced conversion to Christianity, they soon found it beneficial to belong to lay sodalities for their daily survival in slave society."[20] In accommodating, at least publicly, the wishes of their owners, slaves often inverted whites' goals of social control by using the same institutions for their own ends. Black lay sodalities constituted one tremendously effectual example of this phenomenon.[21]

Though many Yoruba apparently joined the Angolan sodalities and therefore appropriated the ascendant identity of "Angolan" in spite of their real ethnic background, by the mid-eighteenth century Yorubas had established the sodality of Our Lady of the Good Death in Salvador, Bahia.[22] The collective identity forged through these sodalities relied on a combination of African emphasis on the extended family, the increasingly important practice (under slavery) of fictive kin, and, of course, the existing institutionalism of the Roman Catholic Church in Brazil. Seemingly, then, the debate is no longer about "agency," "stability," or even "survival" but rather the innovative manner in which Yoruba and their descendants used New World institutions to further their own. The subsequent development of Candomblé festivals is equally symbolic of the cultural, religious, and kinship syncretism exacted by Nagôs in Brazil.[23]

Thus Yoruba in Brazil found some needs of the slave regime ironically in tandem with their own traditions of family relations, gendered divisions of labor, fictive kinship, and extended kin networks. Using institutions such as the Roman Catholic Church to further their aim of emphasizing their "Yoruba-ness" in their new, syncretic identities, the Yoruba succeeded in establishing a New World version of Yoruba culture in this nation with so many others of their own and related cultures.

The Caribbean

As with Brazil, Yoruba people dominated the populations and culture of slaves throughout the region. In particular, the colonies of Cuba, Jamaica, Trinidad, and St. Domingue were particularly important destinations for the Yoruba. Not surprisingly one can find hints of Yoruba kinship ties there.

As in Brazil, the development of associations in Cuba not only perpetuated certain African ethnicities and identities but also serve as examples of the type of community built by peoples to whom the extended family was so important. The "cabildos de nación," or Afro-Cuban mutual aid societies, emerged during the eighteenth century and were originally sponsored by the Catholic Church. Eventually these associations became more secular than religious, and after slavery were still vessels of Afro-Cuban culture and religion. In some cabildos de nación members not only preserved the same communalism as their counterparts did in the sodalities of Brazil, but they even enjoyed the Africa-like community ownership of property, even slaves. Most notably, however, members viewed the cabildo membership as family: numerous examples exist of Cuban slaves commenting on their "family," "kin," and "relatives," all of whom were not blood relatives but were simply members of the association.[24]

Unlike most regions in the New World, Cuba has not received the same attention from scholars interested in the structure of slave households. Recent examinations of the slave trade and slavery in Cuba, however, reveal demographic statistics that suggest the existence of strong nuclear families. In particular, the large size of sugar and tobacco plantations, as it would indicate elsewhere in the Americas and the Caribbean, seems to suggest that Afro-Cuban slaves enjoyed the same form of family organization as did their counterparts in other slave societies. Regardless, until more work is done in probate records and sacramental records of the Catholic Church in Cuba, ascertaining Cuba's similarities or differences in reference to this main thread of slave family scholarship will have to be postponed. In the interim, that the Yoruba, or "Lucumí" were such important components of the Cuban slave population, both numerically and culturally, and that their communitarian ideal was preserved by the cabildos de nación in cities and by large slaveholdings on plantations, will be sufficient evidence of the expanding Yoruba kinship ideology in the Yoruba diaspora.[25]

The dearth of scholarship on slave families in Cuba is especially frustrating given the virtual surplus of studies on the subject about nearby British Caribbean colonies. Yoruba slaves were much less numerous in the British Caribbean (and in the British trade in general), but some parts of that region provide historians with the best evidence for family structure in general, which may, of course, be transferred to places where Yoruba were more numerous. In particular, historian Barry Higman has shown that in Trinidad, in 1813, the family patterns between African-born and Creole slaves were significant. Interestingly, Higman argues that Creoles were much more likely to live in mother-headed households, whereas the nuclear family unit predominated among African-born parents; perhaps, as Higman notes, the nuclear family, which was only the norm for the Congos, was "seen by most of the African-born merely as the essential building-block of extended or polygynous family types rooted in lineage and locality."[26] The preponderance of African-born slaves marrying someone not of their own ethnicity led to the rapid assimilation of cultures, which in turn built large extended kin networks, especially for Africans and their children. Apparently, then, specific ethnicity was not an important factor in the specific kinship structures favored by Africans in Trinidad, though the common ideas — extended kin networks on large plantations, nuclear family households in rural areas, and matrifocality in the towns—were certainly a function of Africans and their descendants building a variety of kinship strategies that best maneuvered through the situation at hand.[27]

In that sense, then, Yoruba kinship practices, because they were so similar to those of neighboring peoples who also were sold into slavery, were able to persevere even in societies where the Yoruba comprised a tiny percentage of the slave population. Other practices central to Yoruba life—communal preparation of food, exogamous marriage within extended kin groups, community gardens and yards, and the practice of market days dominated by women—all were prevalent parts of slave family life throughout the British Caribbean.[28]

In order for the aforementioned practices to be feasible, slaves throughout the New World had to be living fairly close together, either all on one large plantation or in the same vicinity. The physical layout of the slave quarter, as well as the individual cabins themselves, suggests an arrangement not unlike the patrilineal villages so prominent in Yorubaland during the trans-Atlantic slave trade. Some dwellings even represented the communal nature of Yoruba and other West African peoples, either in their round architecture, large fireplace, or communal kitchen and dining areas.[29]

When slaves could not reinforce their kinship ideologies with the architecture of their dwellings or with the physical layout of the quarter, they relied on one realm where the master appeared to have control but in reality had very little: the naming of children. Conceivably, even in the total absence of kin members in one location—whether that meant spread across a single plantation or across many—Yoruba- and other West African–descended slaves used naming practices to secure intangibly what they could not do physically.[30]

Another intangible but powerful strategy associated with kinship ideology of the Yoruba was the practice, most often by women, of melding Yoruba religion with Christianity.[31] That belief system in Yorubaland manifested itself in every society in which the Yoruba predominated numerically. Candomblé in

Brazil, Santería in Cuba, and even the Congo-based but Yoruba-influenced voodoo in Haiti and Louisiana were affected by the original practices of the Yoruba and their combination with Catholicism. Almost exclusively the realm of females, practitioners of the three major forms of West African religion in the New World traded the "real" political and economic power they possessed in Yorubaland for what whites perceived to be even more powerful.

As in Brazil, Yoruba in the Caribbean succeeded in establishing a New World identity that was based more on their native culture than the pressures of enslavement might lead one to realize. In both regions Catholicism provided the Yoruba with an institutional structure that they used to appropriate physical and cultural space, both of which led to the vibrant, Yoruba-based identities of "Nagô" and "Lucumí." Without better evidence from Cuba that would allow for rich slave family studies as scholars have crafted in reference to Brazil, the role of the Yoruba in forging nuclear families and extended kin networks in Cuba will remain unknown. That the Yoruba succeeded in building an identity, a language, and a musical form distinctly their own, however, indicates that whenever scholars do initiate family studies in Cuba, they will find similar results in the Yoruba-dominated slave population.

Although one could presumably use any major West African culture as a case study for kinship ideology among slaves in the New World, the Yoruba are a compelling example for historians. Well-known practices in their homeland, vibrant cultural traditions, and highly visible ethnic identities in almost all societies in which they were sold provide much evidence for assessing the success of the Yoruba and their descendants born in the New World in using Yoruba traditions to strategize their survival of the challenges of enslavement. Among the many notable kinship practices of the Yoruba, the centrality of the extended kin network, the well-defined gender roles in work, the physical layout of the village, and the communal activities all appear to have been central parts of the daily existence and survival strategies of enslaved Yoruba. Just as music, folklore, and religious traditions were transferred and then altered by the Yoruba, their kinship ideologies and practices made the transition from the Old World to the New less harrowing than it otherwise would have been.

Notes

1. For slave families, see Herbert Gutman, *The Black Family in Slavery and Freedom, 1750–1925* (New York: Pantheon, 1976); Barry W. Higman, *Slave Populations of the British Caribbean, 1807–1834* (Baltimore: The Johns Hopkins University Press, 1984); Larry E. Hudson Jr., *To Have and to Hold: Slave Work and Family Life in Antebellum South Carolina* (Athens: University of Georgia Press, 1997); Ann Patton Malone, *Sweet Chariot: Slave Family and Household Structure in Nineteenth-Century Louisiana* (Chapel Hill: University of North Carolina Press, 1992); Alida Metcalf, *Family and Frontier in Colonial Brazil* (Berkeley: University of California Press, 1992). For

slave-trade and African origins literature, see David Eltis, *The Rise of African Slavery in the Americas* (Cambridge: Cambridge University Press, 2000); Paul Lovejoy, *Transformations in Slavery: A History of Slavery in Africa*, 2nd ed. (Cambridge: Cambridge University Press, 2000 [1983]); Joseph C. Miller, *The Way of Death: Merchant Capitalism and the Angolan Slave Trade, 1730–1830* (Madison: University of Wisconsin Press, 1988); and John Thornton, *Africa and Africans in the Making of the Atlantic World, 1400–1800* (Cambridge: Cambridge University Press, 1998). For databases, see David Eltis et al., *The Trans-Atlantic Slave Trade: A Database on CD-ROM* (Cambridge: Cambridge University Press, 1999); and Gwendolyn Midlo Hall, *Afro-Louisiana History and Genealogy Database* (Baton Rouge: Louisiana State University Press, 2000). Also see the website of the Harriet Tubman Research Centre at York University, Canada, http://www.yorku.ca/nhp/index2.htm. For cultural issues, see Michael A. Gomez, *Exchanging Our Country Marks: The Transformation of African Identities in the Colonial and Antebellum South* (Chapel Hill: University of North Carolina Press, 1998); Gwendolyn Midlo Hall, *Africans in Colonial Louisiana: The Development of Afro-Creole Culture in the Eighteenth Century* (Baton Rouge: Louisiana State University Press, 1992); and Sidney Mintz and Richard Price, *The Birth of African American Culture: An Anthropological Perspective* (Boston: Beacon, 1992 [1976]).

2. For an overview of Yoruba kinship customs and economic organization, see Samuel Johnson, *The History of the Yorubas: From the Earliest Times to the Beginning of the British Protectorate* (London: Routledge and Kegan Paul, 1966 [1921]), esp. 98–140; Peter C. Lloyd, "Divorce among the Yoruba," *American Anthropologist* 70, no. 1 (February 1968): 67–81; Kristin Mann, "Marriage Choices among the Educated African Elite in Lagos Colony, 1880–1915," *The International Journal of African Historical Studies* 14, no. 2 (1981): 201–28.

3. Daniel P. Moynihan, *The Negro Family: The Case for National Action* (Washington, D.C.: Office of Policy Planning Research, U.S. Department of Labor, 1965); E. Franklin Frazier, *The Negro Family in the United States* (Chicago: University of Chicago Press, 1966 [1939]); Stanley Elkins, *Slavery: A Problem in American Institutional and Intellectual Life* (Chicago: University of Chicago Press, 1959); Gutman, *The Black Family*.

4. Philip D. Morgan, *Slave Counterpoint: Black Culture in the Eighteenth-Century Chesapeake and Lowcountry* (Chapel Hill: University of North Carolina Press, for the Omohundro Institute of Early American History and Culture, 1998), 553.

5. John Pryor, *Virginia Gazette or American Advertiser*, 10 May 1786, quoted in Morgan, *Slave Counterpoint*, 608.

6. See Thornton, *Africa and Africans*, 304; David Richardson, "Slave Exports from West and West-Central Africa, 1700–1810: New Estimates of Volume and Distribution," *Journal of African History* 30 (1989): 10.

7. Jack Goody, *Comparative Studies in Kinship* (Stanford, Calif.: Stanford University Press, 1969), 165–67; Toyin Falola, *Culture and Customs of Nigeria* (Westport, Conn.: Greenwood, 2001), 117–21; G. J. Afolabi Ojo, *Yoruba Culture: A Geographical Analysis* (London: University of London Press, 1966), 132.

8. Ojo, *Yoruba Culture*, 56, 97.

9. For one example of this practice, see "Notes on Work Crews, 1858–66," in William J. Massie Papers, Center for American History, University of Texas at Austin.

10. Ojo, *Yoruba Culture*, 84.

11. Carolyne Dennis, "Women and the State in Nigeria: The Case of the Federal

Military Government, 1984–1985," in *Women, State, and Ideology: Studies from Africa and Asia*, ed. Haleh Afshar, 1–23 (London: Macmillan, 1987), 14.

12. S. A. Akintoye, *Revolution and Power Politics in Yorubaland, 1840–1893: Ibadan Expansion and the Rise of Ekiti Parapo* (London: Longman, 1971), xviii.

13. On the impact of this political upheaval on kinship systems and gender practices, see J. Lorand Matory, *Sex and the Empire That Is No More: Gender and the Politics of Metaphor in Òyó Yoruba Religion* (Minneapolis: University of Minnesota Press, 1994), 13–15.

14. On this wave of Yoruba slaves from Yorubaland to Brazil and Cuba, see Peter Morton-Williams, "The Yoruba Kingdom of Oyo," in *West African Kingdoms in the Nineteenth Century*, ed. Daryll Forde and P. M. Kaberry, 27–49 (London: Oxford University Press, 1967), 42–43.

15. For an excellent treatment of the origins of "Nagô," see Robin Law, "Ethnicity and the Slave Trade: 'Lucumi' and 'Nago' as Ethonyms in West Africa," *History in Africa* 24 (1997): 205–19. For the 1835 rebellion in Bahia and the role played by Nagô, see João José Reis, *Slave Rebellion in Brazil: The Muslim Uprising of 1835 in Bahia*, trans. Arthur Brakel (Baltimore: The Johns Hopkins University Press, 1993), 93–104, 124.

16. The scholarship on the slave family in Brazil is expansive. Among many fine studies, see Richard Graham, "Slave Families of a Rural Estate in Colonial Brazil," *Journal of Social History* 9 (1976): 382–402; Eni de Mesquita Samara, "A familia negra no brasil," *Revista de História* 120 (1989): 27–44; Robert Slenes, "Lares negros, olhares broncos: histórias de familia escrava no seculo XIX," *Revista Brasileira de História* 8 (1988): 89–103.

17. Alida Metcalf, "Searching for the Slave Family in Colonial Brazil: A Reconstruction from São Paulo," *Journal of Family History* 16 (1991): 283–97.

18. Ibid., 292; Stephen Gudeman and Stuart B. Schwartz, "Cleansing Original Sin: Godparenthood and the Baptism of Slaves in Eighteenth-Century Bahia," in *Kinship Ideology and Practice in Latin America*, ed. Raymond T. Smith, 35–58 (Chapel Hill: University of North Carolina Press, 1984). An excellent recent study of godparentage in New Orleans offers scholars of Afro-Catholicism in any New World slave society a model for understanding the central role that slaves, and women in particular, had in godparenting. See Emily Clark and Virginia Meacham Gould, "The Feminine Face of Afro-Catholicism in New Orleans, 1727–1852," *William and Mary Quarterly* 59 (April 2002): 409–48.

19. The literature on black sodalities in Brazil is large and impressive. For example, see Manoel S. Cardozo, "The Lay Brotherhoods of Colonial Brazil," *Catholic Historical Review* 33 (1947): 12–30; Patricia A. Mulvey, "The Black Lay Brotherhoods of Colonial Brazil" (Ph.D. dissertation, City College of New York, 1976); Julita Scarano, "Black Brotherhoods: Integration or Contradiction?" *Luso Brazilian Review* 16 (1979): 1–17; A. J. R. Russell-Wood, "Black and Mulatto Brotherhoods in Colonial Brazil: A Study in Collective Behavior," *Hispanic American Historical Review* 54, no. 4 (1974): 567–602.

20. Mieko Nishida, "From Ethnicity to Race and Gender: Transformations of Black Lay Sodalities in Salvador, Brazil," *Journal of Social History* 32 (1998): 330.

21. Obviously accommodation within resistance has a rich historiography. For what remains the standard in this field, see Eugene Genovese, *Roll, Jordan, Roll: The World the Slaves Made*, 2nd ed. (New York: Vintage, 1976), 597–98.

22. Nishida, "From Ethnicity," 332.

23. Ibid., 335.

24. Matt D. Childs, "The Aponte Rebellion of 1812 and the Transformation of Cuban Society: Race, Slavery, and Freedom in the Atlantic World" (Ph.D. dissertation, University of Texas at Austin, 2001), chap. 6. For these examples of members viewing other members as kin, see 284–85. See also Philip A. Howard, *Afro-Cuban Cabildos and Societies of Color in the Nineteenth Century* (Baton Rouge: Louisiana State University Press, 1998); Fernando Ortiz, *Los cabildos y la fiesta afrocubanos del Día de Reyes* (Havana: Ciencias Sociales, 1992 [1921]).

25. See Laird Bergad, *Cuban Rural Society in the Nineteenth Century: The Social and Economic History of Monoculture in Matanzas* (Princeton, N.J.: Princeton University Press, 1990), 77.

26. Barry W. Higman, "African and Creole Slave Family Patterns in Trinidad," *Journal of Family History* 3 (1978): 171.

27. Ibid., 176–77.

28. On these practices in Yorubaland, see Ojo, *Yoruba Culture*, 148; Richard Edward Dennett, *Nigerian Studies; or, The Religious and Political System of the Yoruba* (London: Frank Cass, 1968 [1910]), 175–82. On these practices in the British Caribbean, see Michael Craton, "Changing Patterns of Slave Families in the British West Indies," *Journal of Interdisciplinary History* 10 (Summer 1979): 1–35; Eugene Genovese, *Roll, Jordan, Roll*, 535–37; Roderick A. McDonald, *The Economy and Material Culture of Slaves: Goods and Chattels on the Sugar Plantations of Jamaica and Louisiana* (Baton Rouge: Louisiana State University Press, 1993).

29. John Michael Vlach, *Back of the Big House: The Architecture of Plantation Slavery* (Chapel Hill: University of North Carolina Press, 1993), 12, 23–24, 85–86, 165–66, 187–88, 190–91, 247.

30. An excellent recent analysis of slave naming is Jerome S. Handler and JoAnn Jacoby, "Slave Names and Naming in Barbados," *William and Mary Quarterly* 53 (1996): 685–726. See also F. Niyi Akinnaso, "Traditional Yoruba Names and the Transmission of Cultural Knowledge," *Names* 31 (1983): 139–58; Cheryll Ann Cody, "Naming, Kinship, and Estate Dispersal: Notes on Slave Family Life on a South Carolina Plantation, 1786 to 1833," *William and Mary Quarterly* 39 (1982): 192–211; idem, "There Was No 'Absalom' on the Ball Plantations: Slave-Naming Practices in the South Carolina Low Country, 1720–1865," *American Historical Review* 92 (1987): 563–96; Barry W. Higman, "Terms for Kin in the British West Indian Slave Community: Differing Perceptions of Masters and Slaves," in Smith, *Kinship Ideology*, 59–81.

31. Dennett, *Nigerian Studies*, 32, 33.

CHAPTER FOURTEEN

Revolution and Religion:
Yoruba Sacred Music in Socialist Cuba

Robin Moore

> When the revolution triumphed and the study of the African roots of our culture
> began, many like me felt very happy, truly happy. But we soon noticed that some-
> thing was lacking, or at least that what was being done represented only a single
> perspective. They were viewing our religions like something that was pure tradition,
> something that was in the process of dying out, something that would become part
> of history and memory over time. . . . The revolution helped bring the legends of our
> gods to the theater, studied our music and dances more earnestly. Something that
> earlier had been viewed as insignificant was seen as important. But many had to keep
> their beliefs and their personal faith secret, their ideas, hide their religious necklaces.
>
> —*Enrique Hernández Armenteros*

Those who study the arts as a pan-cultural phenomenon have long recognized the close ties between music and religious activity. Virtually all religions
incorporate sound in some form into worship: from Gregorian chant and Bach
toccatas to the bamboo flutes of Mevlevi Sufis and Buddhist meditation bells,
ritual sounds are endlessly diverse. Chanting and singing are especially prominent as a means of communicating with the divine in nearly every culture. It
is interesting to speculate as to why music has such importance in these settings and exactly what it contributes. Music appears to help mark the boundaries between the everyday and the exceptional, to foster a strong sense of community among participants, to evoke powerful emotional responses, and, in

some cases, to contribute to altered states of consciousness. Many religions, including Cuban Santería, recognize instruments themselves as sources of divine power. Their believers consecrate them, ritually feed them with animal sacrifices, and view them as a primary way to communicate with ancestors and deities.

Music and dance are more central to Yoruba religion than to many others, including Catholicism. The "orichas" (deities) themselves are said to love music so much that they rarely resist the chance to visit worshipers personally when summoned by songs and drum rhythms dedicated to them.[1] Some describe the activities surrounding Santería and related religions as a form of choreographic rather than verbal liturgy, but the musical component of worship is at least as important as the kinesthetic; the most common vernacular name for religious events of this nature, for instance, is "toque" or "tambor," literally a musical / rhythmic performance or "drumming." The repertoire associated with Yoruba religious expression is extensive, consisting in many cases of intricate percussive sequences played in strict ritual order, mimetic body movement, vocal and instrumental improvisation, and hundreds of responsorial songs with texts primarily in Yoruba languages. This rich folkloric heritage is a powerful form of individual as well as group expression. African cultures have served as the "fuente viva" (life source)—to quote Miguel Barnet's term—that feeds many innovations in commercial music making, much as black gospel has influenced blues, rhythm and blues, and soul in the United States. The artistic forms associated with Santería represent some of the most sophisticated and engaging manifestations of Cuban national culture.

The adoption of Marxist philosophy by Cuba's leadership in 1961 soon resulted in tension between the state and the people over religious activity. The state's position toward religion is officially neutral, ostensibly involving neither attempts to "stimulate, support, or aid any religious group" nor efforts to impede such activities.[2] Communist Party doctrine guarantees citizens the right to profess and devote themselves to any religion of their choosing as long as it does not incorporate antirevolutionary ideology.[3] Yet, in practice, socialist leaders intervened vigorously to suppress religions from the first years of the revolution. Although under Batista a majority of Cubans described themselves as Christian or participated in Santería or did both, by 1976 only 2 percent of the population openly professed such views.[4] Bias against religious belief on the part of the state resulted in the disappearance of most devotion from public view for decades. The Cuban leadership reacted to religion in ways similar to their counterparts in Eastern Europe,[5] monitoring and regulating the expression of believers even in private homes and branding many forms of religious folklore superstitious nonsense.

This chapter describes specific ways that religious music, especially that of Yoruba groups, has been affected by socialist doctrine through the years. It discusses religious repertoire performed in the 1960s, and early conflicts between revolutionaries and religious practitioners. It considers the harshest moments of repression and then the gradual movement toward greater tolerance. Finally, it describes the explosion in religious music performance following policy changes of the Fourth Party Congress in 1991. Analysis focuses on the ambivalence of policy makers toward sacred music for many years. On one hand, the government supported devotional music of all kinds as an important cultural legacy, part of Cuba's unique heritage. On the other hand, they believed that religion was a form of false consciousness, misguided and unfounded, an impediment to social progress. Militant publications reserved their harshest criticism for Santería, Palo, Espiritismo, and Abakuá ritual, believed to be especially primitive religions of the uneducated. These conflicting views—nationalism versus militant atheism or cultural racism or both—led to a wide variety of contradictory actions through the years.

Religion and Music in the Prerevolutionary Period

Serious racial tensions existed in prerevolutionary Cuba that affected cultural life in many ways and continued to do so during the socialist period. The early twentieth century witnessed brutal campaigns to suppress Yoruba and other forms of African cultural heritage in the name of progress.[6] With the abolition of slavery (1886) and the founding of the new Republic (1902) came a desire on the part of the leadership to modernize their nation and to divest it of what they considered a shameful African legacy. In this context very few Cubans, black or white, demonstrated an interest in the study of Yoruba culture. The few who did frequently left the country, as they found audiences abroad more receptive to their work. Painter Wifredo Lam (1902–1982) eventually established himself in Spain; Lydia Cabrera wrote and published her first work, *Cuentos negros,* in Paris. Composers Amadeo Roldán (1900–1939) and Alejandro García Caturla (1906–1940) consistently debuted and performed Yoruba-influenced works outside Cuba rather than at home.

Religion featured prominently in the discourse of those preoccupied by the legacy of slavery but only as a pretext for repression. During most of the prerevolutionary period, middle-class Cuban society did not refer to African-derived "religion" at all, but rather only to "brujería," or witchcraft. Ernesto Chávez Alvarez, in 1991, documented half a dozen well-publicized cases that occurred between 1900 and the 1920s in which practitioners of Santería were falsely accused of crimes associated with devotional events. María Teresa Vélez's *Drumming for the Gods* (2000) describes the surprisingly antagonistic environment confronting believers in Matanzas during the 1940s and 1950s. She notes that inspector José Claro directed his police force to persecute members of Yoruba religions, confiscate their instruments, and jail them if they continued to perform in ceremonies.[7] Most members of middle-class society, although they had no firsthand exposure, considered African-derived religion savage in the extreme.[8] Eugenio Matibag confirms that, in the prevailing bourgeois opinion prior to 1959, Yoruba culture represented "a stage of barbarity" that the republic would eventually outgrow.[9]

Despite the negative views of African-derived religion before 1959, musical and verbal references to sacred acts in commercial recordings of the era are surprisingly frequent. Little sacred drumming or singing itself—little traditional folklore of any kind—was recorded in Cuba prior to 1959, apparently because foreign-based and later Cuban-based record labels did not believe them worthy of interest. Yet, in stylized form, references to Yoruba and other religions—Congo, Dahomey, Efik—appear constantly in many different genres because the working-class blacks involved with them dominated popular music performance. Commercial music with religious themes first gained popularity during the "afrocubanismo" period, serving as markers of local and national identity.[10] Songs as European-sounding as the Rodrigo Prats bolero "Una rosa de Francia" include ritual greetings to Yemayá and Ifá in the Antonio Machín version from 1932.[11] María Teresa Vera's recording of Ignacio Piñeiro's "En la alta sociedad" from 1925 is one of dozens to include Abakuá terminology: "obón" or king, "iyamba" or chief priest, "yuanza" or ritual consultant, and "eribó" or sacred drum,[12] as does Piñeiro's "Lindo yambú" from 1934.[13] This tendency became even more marked in the 1940s and 1950s. Arsenio Rodríguez included African-derived vocabulary in his "conjunto" songs to such an extent that the uninitiated have difficulty understanding their meaning.[14] Many white as well as black performers established their careers by composing and recording popular music with lyrics or melodies or both taken from Yoruba liturgy, for example, Rita Montaner, Miguelito Valdés, Merceditas Valdés, Celina González and Reutilio Domínguez, Noro Morales, Facundo Rivero, Celia Cruz, and others.[15] Many more were heavily involved in Santería privately, although they chose not to manifest their knowledge of religious song, for example, Ignacio Villa (Bola de Nieve), Enrique Jorrín, and Benny Moré.[16]

"Religious pop" of the 1950s meant very different things to different social groups in Cuba. For practitioners, the inclusion of African-derived terminology represented the only means by which they could publicly allude to their beliefs without risking harassment. For middle-class listeners unsympathetic to such beliefs, religious references were in part unintelligible and in part tolerated as a means of referencing "colorful" elements of local folklore. The contradictions surrounding this repertoire cannot be stated strongly enough: while Cuban commercial music of the Batista era constantly alluded to Afrocuban religions, much of the public remained largely (or totally) ignorant of the substance of ceremonies themselves, their traditional chants, drumming patterns, and dances, and the religious ideology that informed them. In fact, many Cubans know little about them even today. Fernando Ortiz and others made efforts beginning in the late 1930s to stage public concerts of Afrocuban religious music and dance, but the presentations were poorly attended and eventually ended.[17] Cuban radio of the 1950s disseminated very little folkloric music of any kind with the exception of some *punto* and other secular string pieces.

> In Cuba of the 1950s there was a very strong middle class consisting of bankers, telephone company employees, those in the electrical union, in commerce. Middle-class housewives listened avidly to radio soap operas and had the money to buy the products advertised on the air. As a result, their tastes dictated much of the programming. If you played them a traditional African chant they wouldn't listen to it. On the contrary, they would revile it because they believed it was something evil . . . they viewed it as obscurantism, backward, something perpetuated by illiterate blacks.[18]

Nowhere was Cuba's ongoing cultural war over Yoruba influences more aggressively negotiated than in the realm of music. At the same time that the José Claros of the 1950s continued to persecute practitioners of Santería, performers made ever bolder attempts to incorporate devotional songs into their recordings, and with fewer stylistic changes. The Panart Santero LP from approximately 1954, an important landmark in this sense, featured singers Merceditas Valdés, Celia Cruz, Caridad Suárez, and "batá" drumming led by Jesús Pérez.[19] Although arranged with four-part choral accompaniment and other concessions to European aesthetics, the record was one of the first to include sacred drumming sequences and traditional Yoruba chants in their entirety. It features "toques" (consecrated rhythms) and praise songs to Changó, Babalú Aye, Ochún, Obatalá, Elegguá, Ogún, and Ochosi, for instance, as well as "rezos" (less strictly rhythmic praise songs over drumming) to Yemayá, Changó, and other deities. At roughly the same time, dance groups like the Sonora Matancera experimented with the use of batás as part of dance compositions.[20] Radio station CMBL (Radio Cadena Suaritos) and the Communist Party station Mil Diez played an important role in the dissemination of these progressive commercial recordings by featuring the artists mentioned above, and others.

> There were . . . two radio stations, Radio Suaritos and La Mil Diez, where . . . for the feast of La Mercedes, La Caridad, San Lázaro, and Santa Bárbara, they would bring drums to the station and give toques for those "santos" [saints, deities] and you could hear them on the radio.[21]

Composer Obdulio Morales represents a central figure in the dissemination of stylized Afrocuban religious music during the prerevolutionary years, as does CMBL station owner and disc jockey Laureano Suárez. In 1943 Morales created the Sociedad Folklórica de Cuba and shortly thereafter, with Suárez's support, began organizing broadcasts of music with religious themes once a week from 7:00 to 8:00 P.M.[22] The program apparently began—as do Santería ceremonies—with "oru seco"[23] rhythms on batá drums dedicated to Elegguá. Many devotees received the program enthusiastically; one interviewee from Havana notes that his community never missed a show. "Everyone danced, from the very first toque to the last."[24] In Matanzas, the religious community seems to have been more reticent to accept the broadcasts, however. Radio Cadena Suaritos continued broadcasting through the early 1960s, at which time the station was nationalized and officials decided to suspend the show.

The New Socialist Government and Religion

The policy of Cuba's socialist government toward religion is difficult to characterize in general terms. This is true because discrepancies exist between the official position of the Party and the lived experiences of many citizens, and because the experiences of individuals themselves often have little in common. All believers have suffered some persecution through the years, but the degree of its severity and the forms in which it has manifested itself differ. Socialists' predisposition to discourage religion derives from Marx's view that it was essentially a sham, an invention of the weak and misguided in search of comfort. "Man makes religion, religion does not make man. . . . Religion is the sigh of the oppressed creature, the heart of a heartless world, just as it is the spirit of a spiritless situation. It is the opium of the people."[25] Interestingly, not all intellectuals influenced by Marx concurred with him on this issue. Several, including William Morris and Franz Mehring, came close to dedicating their lives to religious ends.[26] The tone of Marx's own work often has a quasi-religious feel, guided and propelled as it was by the loftiest of intentions. Marx effectively elevated the human spirit itself to the center of his own secular religion, believing it capable of any goal if properly educated and nurtured.

A large number of practicing Protestants, Catholics, and Santería devotees joined in the struggle against Batista in the 1950s. This fact makes clear that the eventual positions adopted by Castro and his leadership against religion represent a narrowing of revolutionary policies that were initially more inclusive, or at least less well defined. Bishop Pérez Serantes of Santiago, a close personal friend of Castro, interceded to spare his life after the Moncada attack.[27] Father Guillermo Sardinas rose to the rank of *Comandante* in the rebel army.[28] José Antonio Echeverría, prominent in the urban resistance, also participated in a Catholic student organization.[29] Perhaps the most prominent example in terms of involvement in African-derived religions is longtime union activist and Communist Party member Lázaro Peña, a Santero and child of Obatalá.[30] René Vallejo, Fidel Castro's personal doctor, was a practicing Santero and Espiritista (believer in spiritualism).[31] Granma survivor Juan Almeida, one of the few Afrocuban leaders of the rebel army, is said to have kept an altar devoted to Changó in his house until members of the Central Committee persuaded him to remove it.[32] Celia Sánchez, Castro's personal secretary, frequently visited babalaos for guidance and support.[33] Many other Santeros fought in the Sierra Maestra and elsewhere in support of revolution. They frequently saw no contradiction between their religious views and the goals of the socialist state.[34]

Most of the revolutionary government's earliest conflicts with the religious community involved problems with Catholics rather than members of Yoruba religion, for various reasons. Catholic institutions were more hierarchical and centrally organized; as a result, their elders could make grand pronouncements on the part of multiple congregations and represented more of a potential threat. Cardinal Manuel Arteaga of Havana, one of the Church's most prominent spokesmen, had a close personal friendship with Batista and demonstrated only tepid support for rebel leaders from the outset.[35] Most priests in Cuba came from Spain, controlled at the time by Franco, and tended to have conservative, right-wing political views.[36] They voiced open hostility to communist doctrine even before Castro officially allied himself with the Soviet Union. Additionally, those attending Catholic churches tended to be wealthier, middle-class professionals and elites (especially women) living in urban areas. This group had the least to gain from socialist political reforms and were the first to become agitated by them.[37] Professionals generally sent their children to private parochial schools and resented the nationalization of all such institutions in 1961. As a result of all these factors, Catholics became a thorn in the side of revolutionaries almost from the start and biased the leadership against religious activity.[38]

The largely white, middle-class revolutionary leadership also did not approve of African-derived religions, but they viewed them differently from Christian institutions. Perhaps most important, whereas they associated Catholicism with the rich, they recognized Santería and related practices as genuinely popular. Santería played an important role in the lives of the working classes, especially blacks, precisely the people the revolution intended to help through their new social programs. In addition, Afrocuban houses of worship functioned autonomously and had no central leadership on a national level that might pose a political threat. For these reasons, Santería worshipers experienced little persecution during the early 1960s, very possibly less than they had under Batista. Evidence suggests that Castro and his supporters actually made attempts to associate the new government, in the minds of the public, with African religions in order to increase popular support for the government. The colors red and black on the flag of the July 26 movement, for instance, are also associated with the oricha, or Yoruba deity, Elegguá. Just as Elegguá opens spiritual pathways, revolutionaries seem to have suggested with this symbol that the Moncada attack opened new political and social paths, and that African deities were directly involved in the process. On 8 January 1959, during one of Castro's first public speeches, someone arranged to have doves fly over Castro's head and for one dove to land on his shoulder.[39] Since doves and the color white are associated with the oricha Obatalá, this had special significance for believers as well. Manipulation of religious imagery in this way brings to mind Haitian dictator François "Papa Doc" Duvalier and his government's use of Vodun symbolism.[40] Castro's approach tended to be more subtle, however, perhaps in an attempt not to alienate the middle classes who disapproved of African culture.

The period extending from 1959 through the mid-1960s gave rise to a profusion of Afrocuban religious performance, as well as "high" art compositions inspired by religious folklore. The scope of this activity had no precedent in Cuban history and is a testament to the spirit of cultural freedom existing at the time. Yoruba religious music had been performed for centuries, of course, but almost never in public. While the government did not organize most of the new ensembles devoting themselves to this repertoire, or pay them (at least initially), it also did not discourage or persecute the performers as authorities had done during the Republic. Thus members of the Afrocuban community, with some justification, seem to have believed that they themselves and their cultural forms had achieved a greater level of respect under the new leadership. Incorporating themselves into the Amateurs' movement, their grass-roots ensembles created a strong national presence.[41] No formal statistics have been published on the numbers of Afrocuban groups established at this time, but in Santiago alone seven troupes appeared, each comprising approximately thirty members.[42] They performed music and dance associated with Santería, Vodun ceremony, Congo rites, espiritismo,[43] and Abakuá music, in addition to secular pieces. Felipe García Villamil affirms that similar groups emerged throughout the Matanzas and Havana provinces.[44] By the late 1960s many performers had attained official status as cultural workers and earned salaries higher than the ones they received as manual laborers.[45]

To a greater extent than supporting the performance of religious folklore by amateur groups, the socialist government encouraged conservatory-trained artists to incorporate elements of religious folklore into their works. Oil paintings by René Portocarrero (1912–1986) depicting "diablito" dancers, that is, masked dancers symbolizing African ancestor spirits, and by Manuel Mendive (1944–) with Santería iconography represent some of the most influential visual creations of the period. Building on the work of Wifredo Lam and others, these individuals fused elements of folk religion with neo-Expressionistic techniques as a means of representing a modernist nationalism.[46] Musical and choreographic works of a similar nature appeared at the same time, largely in productions of the newly created Teatro Nacional under the direction of Isabel Monal. Established in 1959, the National Theater played a central role in the cultural activities of the early revolution. It consisted of five departments devoted to modern classical music, modern dance, theater, choral activities, and folklore, respectively.[47] Of these, the departments of modern dance under Ramiro Guerra and of folklore under Argeliers León (1918–1991) made significant use of religious music. It should be noted that León, Guerra, and others had been involved in similar activities during the 1950s as well; the two collaborated in 1952, for instance, to produce a ballet sketch called *Toque* with original music by León himself.[48] Nevertheless, their new prominence as policy makers and the increasing numbers of presentations for which they were responsible underscore the greater support for the staging of religious folklore in the early 1960s.

Most cultural histories within Cuba discuss the seminars organized by León on Afrocuban religions in conjunction with his work in the National Theater. Although of undeniably high quality, their scope and impact have been exaggerated. The lectures began in October 1960 and lasted through May 1961, and were designed to support academically the development of African-derived musical presentations on stage.[49] León conceived of his lectures as a means of educating younger researchers about Afrocuban religion and culture. He hoped that the dissemination of such information would help to combat the ignorance and fear of this subject still demonstrated by many.[50] Partly because of limited interest, and partly because acceptance into the classes required León's personal invitation, participation was minimal; any given session had only three to seven individuals in attendance.[51] However, some of the most respected academics in the country offered lectures as part of these events, including León himself, his wife María Teresa Linares, ethnologists Isaac Barreal and Alberto Pedro, historian Manuel Moreno Fraginals, and German anthropologist Peter Neumann. Although the seminars lasted only a short time, they did much to prepare future generations of folklorists: Miguel Barnet, Rogelio Martínez Furé, Eugenio Fernández, and other well-known authors took part and gained valuable training. Indeed, it is unfortunate that the lectures were not more widely disseminated, were not repeated in later years, and never became a permanent part of university offerings in Havana or elsewhere.

A review of program notes from the archives of the National Theater provides examples of the sorts of activities presented there under León's guidance. Some of the earliest sketches seem to have involved the staging of afrocubanismo art music in conjunction with stylized folkloric dance choreographed by Ramiro Guerra. Amadeo Roldán's "Milagro de Anaquillé" was one of the pieces presented in this way, featuring costumed appearances by figures from nineteenth-century folklore: the "negro curro," the "mulata del rumbo," "diablito" dancers, and a "mayoral" or plantation overseer with his slaves. Later events tended to be more academically oriented. A concert entitled "Bembé" took place on 5 May 1960 with religious drumming by Jesús Pérez and singing by Lázaro Ros, among others. "Congos reales," produced on 18 November 1961 under the guidance of León and Martínez Furé, re-created nineteenth-century style "tango-congo" processional music from colonial "cabildos," which are social organizations based on distinct African ethnicities. "Yimbula: Fiesta de Paleros" premiered on 29 November 1961. It included sacred music and dance of Bantu origin associated with "Palo Monte" and attempted to re-create the ceremony onstage. The accompanying liner notes are impressive, detailing the fundamental beliefs of the religion, the instruments and rhythms used in worship, the sacred vestments employed, and accompanying dances. Chants of ritual salutation to "open" the altar and to greet particular deities began the event and were followed by less formal music and dance: a "baile de maní" and "toque de garabatos."

Less easy to document than the rigorous nature of the National Theater presentations at this time is public reaction to such events. Given the strong bias against Afrocuban religions on the part of many professionals, attendance of the shows was undoubtedly reduced, consisting of practitioners themselves and the few interested academics and students. The concerts were not televised or heavily promoted in the media, limiting their impact. Within the Afrocuban religious community itself, considerable ambivalence toward staged religious folklore seems to have emerged as well. Because their ceremonies had been persecuted for many years, worshipers often preferred that the specific details of rituals be kept secret. In some cases drummers who performed sacred music on stage were physically threatened, accused of betraying other members of their house of worship; this was especially true of public Abakuá demonstrations such as those organized by the National Folklore Troupe in 1964.[52] In time, the community learned to accept educational activity of this kind, but performers continued to walk a fine line between allegiance to their religious community, on the one hand, and to the state and its cultural goals on the other.

Increasing Intolerance of All Religious Activity

Beginning in the later 1960s the relative freedom of religious and artistic expression associated with the early revolutionary period began to disappear. In its reorganized schools and in official publications, the state advocated the renunciation of religion and the adoption of what it referred to as "scientific atheism."[53] Party documents from that time on recognized among the ideological goals of the country that of universally "overcoming" religious beliefs through scientific-materialist education and "elevating" the cultural level of the workers.[54] Thus, although the official position of the government since the early 1970s had been to allow freedom of religious expression,[55] in practice it tended to suppress religions of all types. Dedication on the part of the state to proving the fallacies of religion lasted through the late 1980s. Such efforts manifested themselves in multiple ways: in the realm of education, through training in work centers, and through interventions of a more personal level in homes and neighborhoods.

A few examples suffice to illustrate the government's well-documented policy toward religion, and its effects. As mentioned, news about religious issues disappeared from the mass media starting in 1961.[56] Beginning in the late 1960s anyone openly professing a faith could not be a member of the Communist Party, an affiliation extremely beneficial to one's educational opportunities and career. The same applied to membership in trade unions.[57] Educational centers barred members of religious groups from professions such as psychology, philosophy, and political science entirely.[58] Religion became taboo as a topic

269

of academic investigation even among those who did not profess a faith themselves.[59] Job application forms ("planillas de trabajo") regularly asked applicants if they had religious beliefs and denied them prominent positions if they answered yes.[60] By dressing in ceremonial white, shaving one's head for ritual purposes, or wearing sacred "collares" (necklaces), Santería devotees ran the risk of serious professional consequences. In terms of access to new housing, cars, appliances, and a host of related concerns, the preference given to Party members and atheist revolutionaries meant that religious beliefs could not be admitted openly.

Campaigns to inculcate negative views toward religion were especially apparent among the young. The state forbade the baptism of children or their initiation into Santería, ordering the police to intervene in some cases to forcibly remove them from ceremonial contexts.[61] In primary and secondary schools instructors allowed no discussion of religious subject matter other than to deride it as worthless or backward.[62] Revolutionary summer camps sponsored by the Unión de Jóvenes Comunistas represented an important venue for the dissemination of such ideas as well.[63] Older practitioners might be allowed to continue their religious involvement relatively undisturbed, but the government intervened to stop children and young adults from doing so in order to ensure a gradual decline in the numbers of the faithful.

Enrique Hernández Armenteros suggests that the government should be held accountable for the theft of the public face and voice of religion that existed prior to 1959.[64] In addition to these many structural impediments to religious activity, other more random and vicious acts were taken against believers by individuals. These actions represented non-sanctioned activity, that is, they were neither advocated nor condoned by authorities but were tolerated. Many overzealous socialists, hoping to prove their commitment to the revolutionary agenda, acted with unnecessary cruelty to religious practitioners.[65] Some harassed neighbors for keeping Yoruba artifacts in their homes. In some cases the overzealous took it upon themselves to tear down altars, throw "cazuelas" or "guerrero" statues[66] into the street, deface iconography or buildings, and destroy religious instruments.[67]

Such attitudes help to explain why research on religious folklore has progressed little beyond the writings of Fernando Ortiz, Lydia Cabrera, and Rómulo Lachatañeré from the 1950s. The year 1964 saw the publication of León's *Del canto y el tiempo* based on seminars at the National Theater. It is an important work but is only an overview, intended as an introduction to Cuban folk music with an emphasis on African-derived repertoire. *Actas del folklore*, the official journal of folklorists at the National Theater, published insightful studies on religious traditions beginning in January 1961, but stopped suddenly the following year. The journal briefly allowed Afrocuban authors themselves to write on religious and cultural history, often for the first time, but its distribution and readership were severely limited from the outset.[68] Articles of a similar nature appeared in *Etnología y Folklore* at the beginning of 1966 under the auspices of the Academy of Sciences, but the journal ceased publication shortly thereafter, in 1969.[69] Issues appearing prior to 1968 contained more religious essays than later volumes. Examples from the early years include an analysis of Abakuá ritual by Rafael López Valdés[70] and of sacred Bantu/Palo vocabulary by Lydia González Huguet and Jean René Baudry.[71] In later volumes the analysis of Afrocuban themes remained central but became more historical and secular. Topics tended to revolve around social or demographic trends, often those of the nineteenth century, for example, abolition and its immediate social effects or colonial maroon activity, and demonstrated less concern for religious expression.

Between 1968 and 1975 very little of substance appeared in print or on LPs related to Afrocuban religions or religious music. Publications that did allude to the subject increasingly expressed condescending attitudes toward the rituals or referred openly to the ways that revolutionary policy intended to hinder their perpetuation. León and other progressive members of the academic community, despite their commitment to the revolution, met with growing resistance to attempting to continue research on religious music. León himself apparently lost his job in the Academy of Sciences over this issue.[72] The entire careers of individuals involved in sacred ritual have been ruined as a result of the state's disinterest in the subject, as in the case of Teodoro Díaz Fabelo (1916–1970?).[73] To the extent that such research continued, involvement with religious practitioners revolved around attempts to manipulate or modify their behavior rather than to valorize it. Even today, detailed studies of Santería's extensive song and dance repertoire have yet to be undertaken. Recordings of religious folklore, though common once again since the 1980s, still rarely include extended transcriptions of melodies or lyrics or detailed explanations of the ceremonial context. Rogelio Martínez Furé suggests that the Party refused to support publications of this type because they believed that its dissemination might result in the unnecessary perpetuation of undesirable beliefs.[74]

Negative comments about Afrocuban religions in Party documents tend to fuse multiple and often discrepant critiques into a single voice. Some derive from Marxist doctrine; others are based on thinly veiled racial prejudices that manifest themselves in the new government essentially in the same way they did in earlier times. One of the most common justifications for the suppression of religion, of course, was the assertion that it represented a form of false consciousness. Publications frequently refer to "the ludicrous beliefs of the enslaved" during the colony and to the fact that they constituted, among other things, a "refuge for the oppressed, a sterile hope, elemental opium and cane alcohol used to anesthetize their suffering and to mentally escape from their real circumstances."[75] Folklorist Miguel Barnet—one of the more prominent students in León's seminars from the early 1960s—described Afrocuban religions in terms of a refuge, a helmet donned by men living in inhuman conditions who would otherwise be unable to make sense of their fate.[76] However picturesque or engaging they believed religious folklore to be from an aesthetic point of view, these observers ultimately denounced such expression as an ideological fetter tying one to the past, an obstruction to the creation of the "hombre nuevo," or new socialist citizen.[77] Similarly, Jesús Guanche described the principal motivations of religious belief as "ignorance," "obscurantism," and "intellectual underdevelopment."[78] He and others asserted that faith in supernatural beings would simply disappear as a result of higher levels of education among the public.[79] This belief, as we shall see, was entirely unfounded.

According to the leadership, Afrocuban religion derived from primitive modes of thought tied to prehistoric Africa. Party members argued through the 1980s that the views of santeros represented an "earlier stage" of thinking that had no place in revolutionary Cuba.[80] Distinguished scholars, even some from the Afrocuban community, described the belief system surrounding Santería as the "remainders of yesterday."[81] Party militants derided the religion as less sophisticated than Christianity, based as it was on the use of crude symbols and ritual acts rather than on abstract ideas.[82] They similarly attacked Abakuá and Palo ceremony as misguided, confused, backward, uncultured, and submerged in myths of "antediluvian" origin.[83] Guanche referred to those involved in Santería as "limited in their physical and intellectual faculties," adding that when men and women "manage to supersede this phase of prehistory . . . they will stop being dependent subjects of supernatural beings . . . created out of ignorance or fear."[84] These views bear an eerie resemblance to racist commentary in the works of Cuban scholars from the turn of the twentieth century.[85]

Other, more outlandish critiques of Afrocuban religion are found in government publications, although it is unclear to what extent they represented the leadership or only the views of particular individuals. Representatives of the Ministry of Education, as part of their campaign against "delinquency" of all sorts, singled out Yoruba religion as a central factor contributing to it.[86] Some described Santería as a "pathological" influence, and others accused religious elders of utilizing the faithful to organize criminal acts.[87] Still others (a surprising number) suggested that belief in Afrocuban religion should be considered a symptom of mental disorder. Angel Bustamonte argued that participation in Yoruba religious ceremonies contributed to psychological illness.[88] Contributors to *El Militante Comunista* described believers as "completely dominated by their neuroses."[89] Guanche, in his essay "Psychic Disorders" ("Los trastornos psíquicos"), also characterized Santería as a disease and believers as paranoids: "Syncretic beliefs, and particularly Santería . . . present symptomatic modalities that make the patient [sic] appear to be a real *schizophrenic*, along with manifesting *hysterical, dissociative reactions*." The term "schizophrenic" is defined in a footnote as "a grave, morbid process characterized by mental incoherence and disassociative thought."[90] Not surprisingly, the same authors frequently called for the elimination of Afrocuban religion in the name of the wellbeing of Cuban society.

These absurd, nonsensical beliefs that defy common sense continue to exist among us, are trying to perpetuate themselves in the middle of our Socialist Revolution. They keep numerous persons enslaved, challenge our sense of education and culture, destroy homes, deform lives, and for all these reasons constitute a painful reminder that much remains to be done.[91]

Many Afrocubans opposed what they saw as a growing intolerance for their beliefs and traditional arts in the mid-1960s. It appeared to many as if Marxist doctrine was being used as an excuse to root out cultural practices of which the white/Hispanic leadership did not approve. Of course, they had few options for public dissent given that all media remained in the hands of the government, and that few blacks and mulattoes occupied positions of authority. Figures who might have voiced such opinions—Juan René Betancourt, Walterio Carbonell, Carlos Moore—had either been driven into exile, publicly humiliated, or otherwise silenced. Writing from abroad, Carlos Moore was one of the first to criticize the socialist government's insensitivity to Afrocuban culture. His scathing attacks may be overstated, but they raise important concerns.

> First comes the silence; second comes the effort to distort the rôle blacks have played in the formation of a true Cuban consciousness and the liberation of Cuba from Spanish colonialism . . . third comes the affirmation that [Afrocuban] religions are "the opium of the people" and thus incompatible with a socialist revolution; fourth comes the branding of them as counter-revolutionary, and the grave has been opened to bury an entire culture. . . . Yes, of course our religions have "entered into conflict with the revolution" for the simple reason that what white "revolutionaries" are intending to destroy are the values, customs, habits, creeds, and culture that constitute the essence of the Afrocuban nation, as an indispensable prerequisite to their objective of turning Cuba and its inhabitants into a [culturally] white nation.[92]

Despite the oppressive nature of political policy for many years, Afrocuban religious events continued to take place much as they had during the capitalist era. Most participants denied their beliefs in order to get a job or obtain permission for studies at the university, yet they continued to practice. The revolution, in this sense, pressured them to adopt a hypocritical stance toward their faith[93] but did not necessarily hinder their involvement. The fact that much Santería worship is conducted in private homes helped devotees maintain it in an often hostile environment.[94] Believers had managed to keep their events secret since at least the mid-nineteenth century and knew how to organize discreet gatherings. In additional, government authority did not always extend into the marginal neighborhoods that constituted the primary centers of Afrocuban religious activity. In Pogolotti, Manglar, Atarés, and other sectors of Havana, national policy did not affect the lives of inhabitants as quickly or to the same extent as in Vedado or Marianao, for instance.

The Suppression of Sacred Music

With the hardening of government policy toward religion in the late 1960s the presentations of religious folklore went into decline. The sorts of concerts promoted by Argeliers León during the early years of the National Theater did not disappear overnight but became less frequent and lost their prominence in national cultural planning.[95] Publications from the Folklore and Ethnology Institute dwindled in the 1970s, as did those of independent scholars. The National Folklore Troupe managed to record their music and perform it on national television only rarely at this time. But religious folklore never disappeared from public view entirely. The state continued to support many grass-roots ensembles that performed religious repertoire within their own communities, often as part of events in neighborhood Casas de Cultura. Modern dance troupes based at the Escuela Nacional de Arte (ENA) incorporated some sacred movements into their choreographies and often performed with traditional drummers such as Justo Pedrito, himself a founding member of the Conjunto Folklórico Nacional. Students who pursued university degrees in the humanities at the University of Havana (admittedly a small number)[96] had at least some exposure to Afrocuban religious philosophy through the writings of Ortiz, Cabrera, and others. Beginning in the late 1970s percussion students at the ENA began to receive limited instruction on batá drums, "chéqueres" (a Yoruban shaker instrument), and other sacred instruments during their final years of study.[97]

It is difficult to interpret a government policy that actively supported the performance of Afrocuban religious folklore in particular settings, and yet that allowed few publications on African-derived traditions and suppressed the religions themselves. Tomás Fernández Robaina has explained this apparent contradiction by suggesting that while policy makers believed Afrocuban religions to be undesirable, they nevertheless recognized that the music and dance associated with them had aesthetic value and thus chose to authorize their incorporation into some school curricula. Afrocuban arts also represented a populist symbol of nationhood and thus had positive connotations as a marker of localness or "cubanidad." The support of dances and drumming associated with Santería, therefore, has not been an implicit statement in support of religion, but rather a statement in support of a secularized, and thus "purified," national culture. In the words of the Communist Party platform, socialist educators felt that cultural manifestations — music, dance, musical instruments, and so on — should be assimilated into educational programs, while "divesting themselves of mystical elements, so that the utilization of their essences does not serve to maintain customs and practices alien to scientific truth."[98]

As part of their campaign to discourage Yoruba religions, the Party attempted to restrict the numbers of sacred gatherings taking place. Castro himself is said to have disliked drumming and to have taken an active part in some early restrictions.[99] By the mid-1960s officials required celebrants to apply for a special permit in order to hold a "toque de santo" (a religious event involving drumming, dance, and song), acquired either through the newly created Bureau of Religion (part of the Ministry of the Interior), a police station, or one's local Comité Defensa de la Revolución.[100] Applications involved submitting forms thirty days in advance with a list of all participants, information on how much money was to be charged by the drummers and singers, a photo of the person, if any, "making his or her saint," and an explanation of why one wanted to hold the ceremony. Presentation of the application did not ensure that permission for the ceremony would be granted by any means, especially if children or adolescents were involved, and, in any case, complicated preparations. Officials might deny the petitions outright, visit worshipers in an attempt to convince them not to participate, or severely restrict the time allowed for the ceremony. Abakuá groups often suffered regulations of an even more intrusive nature: Helio Orovio remembers that "plantes" (ceremonial Abakuá events) became virtually impossible for years after Castro came to power.[101] Felipe García Villamil describes his fear of being jailed in the 1970s even for making replicas of Abakuá drums for tourists.[102] Of course, many devotees continued to plan toques without government consent, often with minimal consequences.

Authorities maintained strict limits for many years on the quantity of religious music performed on the radio and television. To this day they have never created a program devoted exclusively to traditional religious song despite its widespread popularity and the expansiveness of the repertoire.[103] By contrast, many secular styles ("nueva trova," dance repertoire, "música guajira") have been featured in this way. A few radio shows occasionally air Afrocuban liturgical music,[104] but they are the exception rather than the rule. Even in the new millennium most of this music has only just begun to enter the commercial sphere, at least within Cuba. Television programmers have occasionally invited Afrocuban groups such as Yoruba Andabo or the now deceased Merceditas Valdés to perform in recent years, but asked them as often as not to perform stylized "afros" or secular pieces rather than religious folklore. Again, these policies result in part from the biases of Marxist philosophy but also from the fundamental ambivalence over African-derived culture, as well as outright cultural ignorance. Much of the political leadership has never attended a toque; the music and dance associated with it remain totally unintelligible and uninteresting, even offensive to them.

Through the late 1980s officials from the state music label EGREM forbade performers from including references to Santería in their compositions.[105] Well-known pieces written before the revolution such as "Que viva Changó" disappeared from the airwaves or were lyrically altered; the piece mentioned here was re-recorded as "Que viva Fidel" on at least one occasion![106] Representatives from the Ministry of Culture forbade this song's primary interpreter, Celina González, from singing the original even during live shows,[107] restricting her to secular "campesino" (Cuban country music) material. For decades they refused her permission to travel outside the country, despite her support of the Castro leadership, apparently fearing that she would take royalty payments waiting for her in the United States and opt for exile. Merceditas Valdés, who collaborated closely with Fernando Ortiz in the 1950s and had similarly built her career performing the music of Santería, found herself unable to perform this music publicly for decades.[108]

During the periods of greatest intolerance the police occasionally arrested some worshipers for organizing their ceremonies without government consent. More often they forcibly confiscated musical instruments and other possessions of prominent spiritual leaders who had died. Items owned by Arcadio, the famous santero from Guanabacoa, were taken from his family in this manner. Most of his artifacts eventually ended up in the Museum of Guanabacoa where they remain to this day, although others have been stolen or were lost.[109] In other cases the state banned traditional Yoruba celebrations outright, as in the case of an important annual ritual in Matanzas meant to prepare the community spiritually for the sugar harvest.[110] Beyond government policy, the acts of individuals have resulted in abuses within various communities. One especially tragic example is that of the temple of San Juan Bautista in Matanzas, one of the oldest centers of Yoruba religion on the island. When the last of the older generation of worshipers there died, revolutionary youth from Havana entered the building and destroyed everything inside, including "tambores yuka" (drums derived from Congolese ethnic groups), batá drums from the nineteenth century, and sacred sculpture.[111] Acts of this nature, and the overall climate of religious intolerance, led to the exodus of many believers during the Mariel boat lift of 1980. Drummer Felipe García Villamil chose to leave Cuba at that time after being threatened with a four-year prison term for religious involvement if he decided to stay.[112]

Rectification: Greater Tolerance for Religious Music

Beginning in the mid-1970s the intolerant stance of the government toward religion and related music began to soften. During the initial years such changes were minor and did not improve the day-to-day conditions of believers perceptibly. Nevertheless, over time they gradually resulted in less belligerent official pronouncements and practices. The role played by the Catholic Church and by Liberation Theology in progressive movements within Central America had a positive impact on Party policy in this sense. The example of Oscar Romero and other pro-Sandinista priests in Nicaragua, especially, proved that belief in God was not inherently in conflict with Marxist values and could actually be a tool of insurgents.[113] Cuba's military involvement in Africa, beginning with Che Guevara's excursions to Algeria in 1964 and ending with participation in the Angolan civil war in the 1970s and 1980s, also helped to develop greater sensitivity on the part of Cuba's leadership toward sub-Saharan culture. From the start, the heightened contact with Africa stimulated new research among Cubans and conferences that included the participation of West African academics.[114] By the end of the 1970s more than three hundred thousand Cubans had already been active combatants either in Angola or Ethiopia[115] and had returned with a new appreciation for cultural forms that had long been stigmatized in the Caribbean.

Early manifestations of policy changes in the realm of music included increased support for the use of sacred instruments in secular contexts. In the mid-1970s adventurous dance bands such as Irakere and the Orquesta Elio Revé began experimenting with the use of sacred batá drum rhythms in secular music.[116] In 1980 the government established a Center for Investigation and Development of Cuban Music (CIDMUC) in Havana, a much more dynamic agency than the Institute of Ethnology and Folklore. CIDMUC specialized for years in field recordings of predominantly Afrocuban sacred events and within a few years had released more recordings of these events than had ever been attempted before or since the revolution. While at times demonstrating a somewhat condescending attitude toward their object of study—publications did not always valorize the religious practices they documented—the work of CIDMUC scholars represented an important achievement.[117]

The qualified liberalization of government attitudes toward religion applied to Christians and practitioners of African religions alike, a fact noted by Havana's Archbishop Jaime Ortega in the mid-1980s.[118] In 1984 Castro met with the Reverend Jesse Jackson and publicly visited a Methodist church with him. In 1987 he permitted a series of interviews by the priest Frei Betto that resulted in the best-selling book *Fidel and Religion*. During the conversations with Betto, Castro modified his earlier criticisms of the Catholic Church and attempted rapprochement. In 1987 the government opened the Casa de Africa in Havana, the first institution in Cuba devoted to the promotion of African culture. In June of the same year the Instituto Cubano de Amistad con los Pueblos (ICAP), or the Cuban Institute of Friendship with Nations, invited Alaiyeluwa Oba Okunade Sijuwade Olubuse II, the supreme representative of Yoruba religion in Nigeria, to Cuba for a five-day visit.[119] Culture Minister Armando Hart, Castro himself, and other members of the Central Committee came to greet him personally.[120] Members of the Afrocuban community noted that his presence meant a great deal to santeros but also that the subject of African religions continued to inspire controversy among the general public.

> There were many who didn't like [the coverage that African spirituality received at that time]. They continued to view Santería, Palo, and Abakuá religions as a "black thing," something associated with degenerates, the superstitious, something to be rejected, forgotten. It was great that [Okunade] received attention in the press, the radio, and television. But, after the king left, the subject of religion disappeared; nothing more was spoken or said about it.[121]

The increased tolerance of government leaders for religious folklore manifested itself in the realm of publications during the 1980s. In his 1983 book, *La fuente viva*, Miguel Barnet devoted considerable attention to national syncretic religions and described them, at least at times, as manifesting a "revolutionary" spirit rather than only misguided or delusional views.[122] The follow-ing year the government re-released Argeliers León's 1964 musical study fore-grounding Afrocuban traditions under the new title Del canto y el tiempo. These works were the first to discuss religious folklore positively, or at least neutrally, in nearly twenty years. They were followed by Maria Elena Vinueza's Presen-cia arará en la música folklórica de Matanzas.[123] The latter is typical of the period for while it is well researched and does much to valorize religious drum-ming and song, at the same time it criticizes the religions themselves.[124] Two years later Letras Cubanas published Ramiro Guerra's Teatralización del folk-lore y otros ensayos.[125] This work is significant for having been published by an Afrocuban choreographer who worked closely with the National Folklore Troupe. It includes useful information about African-influenced traditions from various parts of the island but sidesteps the question of whether the religions themselves constitute a positive component of Cuban culture.

The conflicted nature of these academic studies has its corollary in popular song; one especially telling example is Papá Eleguá by Elio Revé (1930–1997) and his "charanga" (a dance band featuring flute and violins as its primary melodic instruments) composed around 1984. Revé, a black Cuban and a mem-ber of the Communist Party, was one of many who kept his religious involve-ment hidden for years in order to ingratiate himself with the political estab-lishment. In the piece mentioned he simultaneously associates himself with Santería and Palo through the inclusion of ritual terminology—"Yalorddé" (a name for an incarnation of the goddess Ochún), "irá" (Yoruba for good, posi-tive), and kimbisa (a specific form of Palo)—and suggests that religion in gen-eral is nothing but meaningless superstition. Such contradictions are typical of discourse during this period. Despite his attempt to make the song more ac-ceptable through the inclusion of Marxist critiques, representatives of EGREM refused to record it for nearly a decade.

Papá Eleguá by Elio Revé

La religión, la religión	Religion, religion
Es la concepción limitada de los hombres	Is a limited conception of mankind
Los hombres, al verse imposibilitados	Men, unable to explain
ante los fenómenos que crean la naturaleza	The phenomena created by nature
tuvieron que crear sus propios dioses . . .	Have had to create their own gods . . .

(Source: Papá Eleguá. EGREM CD #0078. Havana: EGREM, 1993.)

Noting the more liberal attitudes toward religion in the late 1980s, some musicians began experimenting with the incorporation of additional Yoruba elements into their compositions. The group Síntesis, led by husband and wife Carlos and Ele Alfonso, stands out in this regard. It was one of the first to fuse entire traditional ritual chants in Yoruba languages, often performed by singers from the religious community, with rock music played on electric bass, guitar, keyboard, and percussion. The Alfonsos collaborated closely on their recordings with singer Lázaro Ros, soliciting his advice on vocal performance style and sometimes inviting him to sing with them. The repertoire of the group from the late 1980s and 1990s is striking for the origins of many chants, often taken from obscure sources. Their compositions can be heard on the albums *Ancestros, Ancestros II,* and *Olorun para todos*.[126] In the wake of such experiments and the recognition that expression of this nature would be tolerated, religion once again surfaced as a central theme in the songs of many commercial groups. In contrast to the often ambivalent responses to the presentation of religious song in the National Theater of the 1960s, the public's reactions to the Síntesis repertoire were overwhelmingly positive. This reflects the fact that its primary audience was younger and more open to experimentation, as well as that "religious rock" did not compromise ritual secrets in the same way that León and the National Folklore Troupe potentially had done.

In the first years following the collapse of the Soviet Union, Yoruba religion reestablished itself in the lives of Cubans to a surprising extent, far surpassing the tentative developments of earlier years. This religious "boom," as it is often described on the island, brought virtually all facets of devotion into public view. Many observers attribute it at least in part to the onset of economic crisis; the liberalization of policies toward religion seems to have been a calculated move taken in order to assure the continued support for socialism among blacks during periods of severe food shortages.[127] Of course all forms of religion, including Christianity, attracted more followers as life became difficult and the future uncertain, and as the state proved unable to fulfill its role as provider with any degree of effectiveness. Adopting an overtly religious lifestyle also constituted a way of manifesting one's dissatisfaction with past government dogmatism. Natalia Bolívar[128] views Cubans' mass involvement with religion in the 1990s at least partly in this way, a rejection of twenty-five years of overzealous vigilance and regulation of spiritual life. Similar trends in other postsocialist countries lend credence to her position. The surprising degree of tolerance for religious folklore in the 1990s may also result from the need to attract foreign investment and loan money. Groups such as the European Union have consistently linked economic aid to improvements in human rights, including freedom of religious expression. Officials recognize the potential profits to be made, in any case, both from the sale of music recordings influenced by Santería and by folklore tourism workshops in which foreigners pay to take drumming and dance classes. Both have increased exponentially in recent years.

In about 1990 documentaries on Afrocuban religions began to appear with greater regularity on television, and recordings of music with religious themes received more representation on the radio. Officials gave spokesmen of the Catholic Church access to the media on some religious holidays,[129] and singer Celina González managed to record and distribute a new version of "Que viva Changó" for the first time in more than twenty years.[130] In 1991 the Union of Cuban Writers and Artists (UNEAC) published *Los orichas en Cuba*, the first book specifically discussing the belief system of Santería in decades.[131] It was released at roughly the same time as Lázara Menéndez's four-volume *Estudios afrocubanos* series (1990) with significant religious content, Lino Neira Betancourt's *Como suena un tambor arará* (1991), and Tomás Fernández Robaina's *Hablen paleros y santeros* (1994) documenting the experience of santeros during the revolution. This last work is especially noteworthy in that it includes practitioners' own comments about their communities.

The government permitted the creation of a Yoruba cultural society in the early 1990s, loosely uniting members of religious houses across the island for the first time since the 1950s, and the Academy of Sciences sponsored an international workshop dedicated to Yoruba culture.[132] As of this period it became acceptable for Santería initiates to walk in the streets wearing ritual vestments and necklaces. Those abroad with an interest in African religions visited Cuba to consult openly with spiritual leaders.[133] Perhaps most important, during the Fourth Party Congress of October 1991 the political leadership began to allow religious individuals into the Communist Party. José Felipe Carneado, the chief of the Office of Religious Affairs (a working group of the Central Committee), is said to have spearheaded this policy change as well as the cessation of all de facto discrimination based on religious affiliation; other advocates included historian Eusebio Leal and writer Cintio Vitier.[134] Members of all religious groups now freely identify their affiliations. In terms of Santería this state of affairs has no precedent in Cuba's entire history.

The profusion of new popular music recordings influenced in some way by Santería is understandable, given that Afrocubans represent a majority of contemporary performers and that they tend to live in neighborhoods where African religious traditions remained strong. Albums with religious content produced since the early 1990s typically fuse sacred folklore with secular music, as in the case of Síntesis's *Ancestros* or Elio Revé's *Papá Eleguá*. They combine lyrical descriptions of Santería ceremony, Yoruba terminology, and sacred melodies and fragments of *batá* rhythms with a dance beat. One of the first pieces to incorporate material of this nature and receive widespread airplay was "Yo voy a pedir pa' tí" by Adalberto Álvarez in 1991.[135] It begins with a traditional chant to Ochún, harmonized and superimposed over sounds of ocean waves. Álvarez was viewed as daring at the time because of his decision to mention his spiritual godparents by name,[136] openly acknowledging his personal involvement with Santería.[137] "Yo voy a pedir pa' tí" was a tremendous hit and inspired similar compositions by Dan Den, Los Van Van, Isaac Delgado, and others.[138] Between 1992 and 1996 references to religion in dance music became more prevalent than virtually any other theme, effectively dominating commercial repertoire.[139] In many cases bands that had never recorded music with religious subject matter began to do so at that time. Numerous CD anthologies appeared using religious references as a central marketing ploy. A few years after the onset of the boom in stylized religious recordings, traditional Afrocuban religious (and secular) folklore itself began to appear in increasing quantities. Artists involved in devotional repertoire who had been unable to record suddenly had new opportunities to make videos and CDs, and to perform for tourists within the country or abroad.[140]

The social revolution spearheaded by Fidel Castro and Che Guevara had overtly moralist, perhaps even quasi-religious, associations from the beginning. Theirs was in many respects a crusade on behalf of the downtrodden, the forsaken, and the exploited. Through ongoing campaigns to build new schools and hospitals, to provide work for the unemployed, to foster adult literacy, to retrain prostitutes, and to provide universal health and retirement care, the goals of the revolutionary leadership parallel those of established charities and religious institutions. Some describe the leadership as promoting Marxist ideals with the same utter dedication that one might pursue a religious war.[141] Musicians supportive of the socialist state such as Pedro Izquierdo have gone as far as likening Castro to "a materialized Jesus Christ" because of his sacrifices and struggles on the part of the working classes.[142]

In light of their common goals, it is striking that revolutionaries have at times been in such direct conflict with religious groups. Conflicts with Christians surfaced early on, in part because of the close ties between the Catholic Church and elite Cubans, generally antagonistic to socialism, and in part because of the strong presence of Spanish priests allied with Franco's right-wing dictatorship. Tensions with Yoruba religious groups surfaced somewhat later, derived from long-standing prejudices in white, middle-class Cuban society against African-derived culture and aggravated further by Marxist philosophy. The experiences of believers have varied widely through the years, but most suffered some form of persecution through at least the late 1980s. This most often consisted of losing educational or job opportunities. Through the mid-1980s government spokesmen often maintained that Afrocuban religion was on the decline in Cuba and that the "deep well" represented by such confused beliefs was finally going dry.[143] No official recognition exists of these abuses, let alone an apology for them or for the fact that, for decades, religious influences were purged almost completely from social and musical life.

Since the late 1980s conditions for worshipers, and for those interested in religious folklore, have improved dramatically. The ranks of Christian organizations have swelled, owing in part to political changes and in part to their support from aid groups abroad. In 1997 Cubans celebrated their first official Christmas in twenty-nine years with the government's blessing.[144] Some religious festivities are once again considered "national heritage"; government-funded centers are beginning to publish information on their histories and manifestations. Many members of Afrocuban religions now earn their living by performing or teaching ritual drumming, song, and dance to visitors. Few restrictions limit the recording of religious songs in traditional or stylized forms. Some have suggested that in Cuba of the new millennium the "religion problem" has been solved.[145] Believers interviewed by Tomás Fernández Robaina, including one who self-identified as a "santero-espiritista-palero-católico-militante" (!), considered herself totally integrated into the revolutionary process.[146] One might suggest, nevertheless, that religion and religious music, especially derived from Africa, remain controversial. On the one hand, they are now accepted as a component of the nation's heritage. On the other, many continue to view popular religions as "false consciousness" and even as degenerate. Government presses have yet to produce compilations of Afrocuban religious repertoire or even sheet music of individual songs, despite the efforts of prominent practitioners. Yoruba or Congolese chants have not yet been consistently integrated into study at national art schools, and no specific institution exists where the tradition might be perpetuated and disseminated more widely.[147]

On a broader level, constraints remain on all religious expression. Performance ensembles and representatives of religious groups have no direct access to the media, appearing on television, for instance, only at the invitation of state representatives. They cannot freely publish or circulate printed material for themselves and their communities, even of a nonpolitical nature.[148] The police still officially require permits in order for casas de santo to schedule a toque, and the events must generally end by 9 p.m.[149] In many ways it seems that "no god can accept a competitor,"[150] and that the Party reserves that role for itself. But if the "secular myth"[151] of the revolution has, until recently, replaced that of the Catholic saints and orichas, it may be that their reappearance in song over the past decade suggests that a more balanced and equitable future for all Cubans is near.

Notes

1. Katherine J. Hagedorn, "Anatomía del Proceso Folklórico: The 'Folkloricization' of Afro-Cuban Religious Performance in Cuba" (Ph.D. dissertation, Brown University, 1995), 189.

2. Ministerio de Educación, *Memorias: Congreso nacional de educatión y cultura* (Havana: Ministerio de Educación, 1971), 201.

3. Partido Comunista de Cuba, *Plataforma programática del Partido Comunista de Cuba: Tesis y resolución* (Havana: Ciencias Sociales, 1978), 101.

4. Harvey Cox, introduction to *Fidel and Religion*, ed. Fidel Castro and Frei Betto (New York: Simon and Schuster, 1987), 2, 4.

5. Katherine Verdery, "Theorizing Socialism: A Prologue to the 'Transition,'" *American Ethnologist* 18, no. 3 (August 1991): 434; Timothy Rice, *May It Fill Your Soul: Experiencing Bulgarian Music* (Chicago: University of Chicago Press, 1994), 171.

6. Walterio Carbonell, *Crítica: Cómo surgió la cultura nacional* (Havana: Ediciones Yaka, 1961).

7. Hugh Thomas, *Cuba: The Pursuit of Freedom* (New York: Harper and Row, 1971), 851. Thomas notes that Batista, a mulatto, was generally more supportive of Santería during the 1940s and 1950s than the socialist leaders who later forced him from power, and that he even gave financial support to prominent "casas de santo" in the Havana area. While this may be true, Villamil's testimony suggests that the president's personal views and actions did not prevent widespread persecution of African religions.

8. Carbonell, *Crítica*, 108.

9. Eugenio Matibag, *Afro-Cuban Religious Experience: Cultural Reflections in Narrative* (Gainesville: University Press of Florida, 1990), 228.

10. Robin D. Moore, *Nationalizing Blackness: Afrocubanismo and Artistic Revolution in Havana, 1920–1940* (Pittsburgh: University of Pittsburgh Press, 1997).

11. Natalia Bolívar, interview by the author, 7 October 1996. Bolívar indicates that the terms appearing include "iborere," the greeting for Ifá, and "akolona silaguao," corresponding to Yemayá.

12. Bolívar, interview.

13. For additional information on the recording of "En la alta sociedad," see Jorge Calderón González, *Maria Teresa Vera* (Havana: Letras Cubanas, 1986), 52–53. African-derived terminology in "Lindo yambú" as interpreted by Natalia Bolívar includes "masa como indilisamba" (run, mulatto), "masamba me lo sambuye" (corn that we ritually offer), "gamba" (sun), and "jubilanga" (in drunkenness and joy). A reissue of the original version of "Lindo yambú" is available on Piñeiro (1992). See Ignacio Piñeiro, *Ignacio Piñeiro and his Septeto Nacional*, Tumbao Cuban Classics CD TCD-019.

14. The culmination of religious references in Rodríguez's recordings comes on the album *Quindembo* from 1964 in which verbal references to his Congolese background blend with Santería chants performed instrumentally on the "tres" (a folkloric string instrument) (David García, personal communication to the author).

15. A good introduction to this sort of material can be found in Isabel Castellanos, *Elegua quiere tambó: cosmovisión religiosa afrocubana en las canciones populares* (Cali, Colombia: Departamento de Publicaciones, Universidad del Valle, 1983).

16. Fernández, *Hablen paleros y santeros*, 71.

17. The very first of these took place in the Teatro Campoamor. It was entitled "La música sagrada de los negros yorubas en Cuba" (Rogelio Martínez Furé, *El Conjunto folklórico de Cuba: XX aniversario (1962–1982), apuntes cronológicos* (Havana: Ministerio de Cultura, 1982), 3.

18. Cristóbal Sosa, interview by the author, 12 November 1997.

19. Cristóbal Díaz Ayala, *Música cubana del areíto a la nueva trova* (Miami: Ediciones Universal, 1981), 238; Panart LD-2060.

20. Helio Orovio, personal communication to the author.

21. García Villamil quoted in María Teresa Vélez, *Drumming for the Gods: The Life and Times of Felipe Garcia Villamil, Santero, Palero, and Abakua* (Philadelphia: Temple University Press, 2000), 80. Cristóbal Díaz Ayala, in a personal communication to the author, disputes Villamil's assertion that Mil Diez played an important role in the dissemination of popular music with religious themes. He notes that it was one of the most popular stations in Havana but suggests that it did little for religious music in particular.

22. Martínez Furé, *El Conjunto folklórico de Cuba*, 20; Jorge Prieto, personal communication to the author.

23. Formal religious events in Santería begin with a complex instrumental drum rhythm cycle known as "oru seco" or "oru del igbodu." This is eventually followed by the "oru cantado" or "oru del eyá aránla," accompanied by song and dance.

24. Fernández, *Hablen paleros y santeros*, 19.

25. Karl Marx and Friedrich Engels, *The Marx-Engels Reader*, ed. R. Tucker (New York: Norton, 1978), 53–54.

26. Maynard Solomon, ed., *Marxism and Art: Essays Classic and Contemporary* (New York: Knopf, 1973), 84, 99.

27. Thomas, *Cuba: The Pursuit of Freedom*, 1129.

28. Jean Stubbs, *Cuba: The Test of Time* (London: Latin American Bureau, 1989), 74.

29. Ernesto Cardenal, *In Cuba*, trans. D. Walsh (New York: New Directions, 1974), 79.

30. María Teresa Vélez, "The Trade of an Afrocuban Religious Drummer: Felipe Garcia Villamil" (Ph.D. dissertation, Wesleyan University, 1996), 95.

31. Cristóbal Sosa, personal communication to the author.

32. Carlos Alberto Montaner, *Fidel Castro y la revolución cubana* (Barcelona: Plaza y Janes, S.A., 1985), 138.

33. Ibid.

34. Fernández, *Hablen paleros y santeros*, 8–9, 20.

35. Fidel Castro and Frei Betto, eds., *Fidel and Religion*, 177.

36. Cox, introduction, 24.

37. Thomas, *Cuba: Pursuit of Freedom*, 1127.

38. Conflicts of a similar but less severe nature developed early on between Protestant groups and the revolutionary leadership. This was especially true of Jehovah's Witnesses because of their creed of nonviolence and their refusal to incorporate themselves into many new social projects (Sosa, interview).

39. Andrés Oppenheimer, *Castro's Final Hour: The Secret Story behind the Coming Downfall of Communist Cuba* (New York: Simon and Schuster, 1992), 344.

40. Gage Averill, *A Day for the Hunter, a Day for the Prey: Popular Music and Power in Haiti* (Chicago: University of Chicago Press, 1997), 73.

41. The large numbers of Afrocuban performers appearing at this time may result in part from attempts to diversify the Cuban economy during the early years of the revolution. Many religious drummers, singers, and dancers were involved in sugar production; as these jobs became more difficult to secure, they searched for other options (Vélez, *Drumming for the Gods*, 69).

42. José Millet and Rafael Brea, *Grupos folklóricos de Santiago de Cuba* (Santiago de Cuba: Oriente, 1989), 92–118.

43. "Espiritismo" is not necessarily considered an "Afrocuban" form of religious expression. As Reinaldo Román (2002) has noted, variations of the practice exist that contain differing degrees of influence from African religious beliefs. "Espiritismo de mesa" or "table spiritism" (also known as "scientific spiritism") is a practice that developed from Allan Kardec's writings of the 1850s and 1860s. It is essentially European in origin and involves séances, that is, communication with spirits while sitting around a table. "*Espiritismo de cordón*" or "cordon spiritism" is more closely associated with syncretic folk religions of various sorts. Its name derives from the fact that practitioners form a circle or cordon of dancers holding one another's hands during worship. "Espiritismo cruzao" or "mixed spiritism" contains overt elements from Congo-derived religions.

44. Vélez, "Trade of an Afrocuban Religious Drummer," 77.

45. Vélez, *Drumming for the Gods*, 75.

46. Tomás Fernández Robaina, personal communication to the author, suggests that Mendive's work was influenced both by the writings of Franz Fanon as well as leaders of the civil rights movement in the United States.

47. Hagedorn notes that all departments eventually grew and played an even more significant role in national culture. The music department, led by composer Carlos Fariñas, developed into the National Symphony Orchestra; the modern dance department eventually became an independent modern performance ensemble; the choir, under Serafín Pro, was eventually transformed into the National Polyphonic Chorus; and Léon's folklore group bifurcated into the Institute of Ethnology and Folklore (a research center) and the National Folklore Troupe (dedicated to performance) (Hagedorn, "Anatomía del Proceso Folklórico," 220).

48. Díaz Ayala, *Musica Cubana*, 313.

49. Argeliers León, "El instituto de etnología y folklore de la academia de ciencias de Cuba," *Etnología y Folklore* 1 (1966): 12.

50. Hagedorn, "Anatomía del Proceso Folklórico," 225.

51. Katherine Hagedorn, personal communication to the author.

52. Vélez, *Drumming for the Gods*, 81.

53. This view appears in *El Militante Comunista* (January 1968): 43, as one example.

54. Partido Comunista de Cuba, *Plataforma programática*, 98.

55. Ministerio de Educación, *Memorias*, 201.

56. María Elena Vinueza, personal communication to the author.

57. Fernández Robaina, *Hablen paleros y santeros*, 36.

58. Sosa, interview; Cardenal, *In Cuba*, 22, 142.

59. The rigidity of university curricula and of academic investigation in this sense appears to be partly the result of the creation of a separate Centro de Investigaciones Socio-Religiosas, staffed by loyal Party members. Only individuals at this center were authorized to pursue such matters.

60. A picture of a typical "planilla" can be found in Juan Clark, *Cuba: Mito y realidad. Testimonios de un pueblo* (Miami: Saeta Ediciones, 1992). Cristóbal Sosa (interview, 1997) notes that, as an unwritten rule, the directors of virtually all work centers tended to be Party militants. These individuals usually held rather hard-line views toward religion that, in many cases, exceeded in severity the Central Committee guidelines for the treatment of believers (Lázaro Ros, personal communication to the author).

61. Ariana Orujuela, personal communication to the author.

62. Alexis Esquivel, personal communication to the author.

63. Linares in Hagedorn, "Anatomía del Proceso Folklórico," 232.

64. Fernández, *Hablen paleros y santeros*, 88–89.

65. Vinueza, personal communication to the author.

66. Symbolic items associated with Santería.

67. Orujuela, personal communication to the author.

68. Examples of work published by Afrocuban authors in *Actas del folklore* include that of Rómulo Lachatañeré (1909–1951) on slave ethnicity in the nineteenth century (March 1961), studies of the "cabildos de nación" by poet Marcelino Arozarena (1912–) in the same issue; and Elisa Tamanes's "Antecedentes históricos de las tumbas francesas," *Actas del folklore* (September 1961). Alberto Pedro is another important Afrocuban author represented in the journal.

69. The Instituto de Etnología y Folklore had already existed for a decade, having been created by the new government's Law 994.

70. This article appears in *Etnología y Folklore* 2 (July–December 1966). Cristóbal Díaz Ayala (personal communication) notes that López Valdés requested asylum in Puerto Rico many years ago and now works as a professor in the Instituto de Estudios Avanzados del Caribe in San Juan, directed by Ricardo Alegría.

71. *Etnología y Folklore* 3 (January–June 1967).

72. Zoila Lapique Becali, personal communication to the author.

73. Díaz Fabelo, who began his work as an assistant to Fernando Ortiz, was totally marginalized during what would have been the most productive years of his professional life. His only significant works published in Cuba are *Lengua de santeros* from 1956—a book he himself paid to have published—and *Olorún*, which appeared in 1960 with the help of León at the National Theater. Díaz Fabelo's frustration over the lack of support for his work eventually led to his defection to Venezuela (Lázara Menéndez, personal communication to the author). His unpublished manuscripts, many of which are available at the National Library, include: "Análisis y evaluación cultural de las letras del Diloggún" (1967), 151 pp.; "Los caracoles" (1967), 291 pp.; "Introducción al estudio de las culturas afrocubanas," "El poblamiento" (1969); and "Cómo se tira y lee el coco" (1969), 74 pp. Other works the author managed to have published by UNESCO but that never became well known on the island include "Diccionario de yerbas y palos rituales, medicinales y el alimenticios en el uso por los afrocubanos" (1969), 369 pp.; "La escritura de los abakuá" (1971), 263 pp.; "Diccionario de la cultura conga residual en Cuba," 2 vols. (1972); and "Los negros cimarrones de Cuba" (1974), 31 pp.

74. Rogelio Martínez Furé, personal communication to the author.

75. This quote comes from EMC, "Trabajo político: Boletín de organización del PCC-FAR" año 2, no. 4 (December 1968): 49. The article is signed "EMC."

76. Miguel Barnet, *La fuente viva* (Havana: Letras Cubanas, 1983), 143.

77. Unsigned article in *El Militante Comunista* (December 1968): 41.

78. Jesús Guanche, *Procesos etnocultures de Cuba* (Havana: Letras Cubanas, 1983), 450–51.

79. The López Valdés article mentioned above is one of many others containing critiques of this nature (López Valdés, "La sociedad secreta 'Abakuá' en un grupo de obreros portuarios," *Etnología y Folklore* 2 [July–December 1966]: 5–26). Commentary of this nature, even by practitioners themselves, is included in Robaina, *Hablen paleros y santeros*, 48. During the early years of the revolution, many decided to bring all their canastilleros, soperas, and other ritual items to museums, or to break them as a gesture of solidarity with government policy.

80. Tomás Fernández Robaina and Walterio Carbonell, personal communication to the author.

81. Deschamps Chapeaux in Matibag, *Afro-Cuban Religious Experience*, 242. Pedro Deschamps Chapeaux was an Afrocuban historian who specialized in nineteenth-century history. A number of black and mulatto scholars derided African-derived religions in their publications at times out of genuine conviction or because they felt compelled to conform to the views of the leadership. Preeminent scholar Rogelio Martínez Furé confided to me that he saw no contradiction between devoting his life to the support of Afrocuban arts and challenging racist attitudes, on the one hand, while taking issue with practices in the black community that he viewed as sexist, homophobic, or otherwise misguided (personal communication to the author).

82. Consider the following unsigned quote translated from *El Militante Comunista* (October 1968): ". . . a religion is primitive if it has not even begun to elaborate abstractions but rather works directly with objects and subjects. Here is one example: secretions from the eyes of a bird with penetrating eyesight used to augment the clairvoyance of human eyes. To us the idea is revolting, yet for primitive minds it is logical" (85).

83. Reference to congo/palo religion can be found in an unsigned article from *El Militante Comunista* (November 1968): 24–25. An unsigned article on abakuá groups in the same publication is entitled "La sociedad secreta abakuá" (44). Elsewhere a writer for *El Militante Comunista* described all Afrocuban religions as "sumamente arcaica [absolutely archaic]" (December 1968: 39).

84. Guanche, *Procesos etnoculturales de Cuba*, 400.

85. Matibag, *Afro-Cuban Religious Experience*, 247; Robin D. Moore, "Representations of Afrocuban Expressive Culture in the Writings of Fernando Ortiz," *Latin American Music Review* 15, no. 1 (spring/summer 1994): 32–54.

86. Ministerio de Educación, *Memorias*, 202.

87. Gayle L. McGarrity, "Race, Culture, and Social Change in Contemporary Cuba," in *Cuba in Transition: Crisis and Transformation*, ed. Sandor Halebsky and John M. Kirk (Boulder, Colo.: Westview, 1992), 199; and *El Militante Comunista* (November 1968): 24–25, 47.

88. José Angel Bustamonte, "Influencia de algunos factores culturales en nuestros cuadros psiquiátricos," *Etnología folklore* no. 7 (January–June 1969): 75–84.

89. *El Militante Comunista* (January 1968): 45.

90. Guanche, *Procesos etnoculturales de Cuba*, 396, 397–99; quote at 398.

91. *El Militante Comunista* (November 1968): 25. Compare these comments with those used in the 1910s and 1920s in Cuba to justify the persecution of the same practices (Moore, *Nationalizing Blackness*, 29–31).

92. Carlos Moore, "Cuba: The Untold Story," *Présence Africaine: Cultural Review of the Negro World* 24 (English edition), no. 52 (1964): 222.

93. Robaina, *Hablen paleros y santeros*, 36.

94. Hagedorn, "Anatomía del Proceso Folklórico," 191.

95. One of the last public concerts for years of religious repertoire that I know of took place on 3 May 1970 in the National Library. The concert, organized by Rogelio Martínez Furé, included sacred songs of Yoruba, Bantu, and Dahomeyan origin as well as batá drumming by Jesús Pérez, Ricardo Caraballo, and Bárbaro Valdés. Nancy Morejón, reviewing the recital shortly afterward, observed that, since Ortiz's presentations of Afrocuban religious music in the late 1930s, few similar events had followed (Nancy Morejón, "Cantos africanos de Cuba," *Revista de la Biblioteca Nacional "Jose Martí"* 12, no. 2 (May–August 1970): 173–75). Lázaro Ros took part in a similar though slightly less "traditional" performance in 1973, singing as guest artist with the Matanzas Symphony Orchestra ("Ito Iban Echu, Sacred Yoruba Music of Cuba," Los Muñequitos de Matanzas. Qbadisc compact disc QB 9022).

96. Professor Lázara Menéndez suggested to me that the university typically admitted only three or four students a year into the Arts and Letters or Humanities majors.

97. Tomás Jimeno, interview by the author.

98. Partido Comunista de Cuba, *Selección de Documentos del I y II Congresos del Partido Comunista de Cuba* (Havana: Editora Política, 1982).

99. Carlos Moore, *Castro, the Blacks, and Africa* (Los Angeles: University of California, Center for Afro-American Studies, 1988), 100.

100. Matibag, *Afro-Cuban Religious Experience*, 230.

101. Orovio, personal communication to the author.

102. María Teresa Vélez, "Drumming for the Gods: The Life and Times of Felipe García Villamil" (unpublished manuscript), 88.

103. Sosa, personal communication to the author.

104. These included broadcasts under the direction of Alberto Faya and Vladimir Zamora with an eclectic or educational focus or both.

105. Bolívar, personal communication to the author.

106. A recording of the transformed piece is included on a disc by José Luis Rupérez, ed., *Album de la revolución*, Cuba Soul compact disc, no ID number (Madrid: Cuba Siglo XXI Music, Inc., 2000).

107. Orovio, personal communication to the author.

108. The first opportunity Valdés had to record religious music in the socialist period came in the 1980s with the release of *Aché* I, II, and III. See Merceditas Valdéz, *Ache*. EGREM cassette C-230.

109. Fernández, *Hablen paleros y santeros*, 64.

110. Vinueza, personal communication to the author.

111. Ibid.

112. Vélez, "Drumming for the Gods: Villamil," 95.

113. Cardenal, *In Cuba*, 102; Cox, introduction, 176.

114. *Etnología y folklore* 2 (July–December 1966): final pages; 6 (July–December 1968): 106.

115. Marifeli Pérez-Stable, *The Cuban Revolution: Origins, Course, and Legacy* (New York: Oxford University Press, 1993), 176.

116. Orovio, personal communication to the author.

117. The most well known of CIDMUC's field recordings is its nine-volume *Antología de la Música Afrocubana*. The set includes examples of "bembé" music (informal Yoruba devotional music), Dahomeyan-derived "arará" ceremony, batá drumming, "música iyesá," and other sacred styles. Many of the field recordings from which these LPs date are from the 1970s, but they did not appear in commercial form at that time. Cristóbal Díaz Ayala notes that volume 1 of the series first appeared in Mexico in 1980 on the label Nueva Cultura Latinoamericana in collaboration with the Cuban Academy of Sciences.

118. Cox, introduction, 25.

119. ICAP typically devotes its energies to forging closer cultural and political ties between Cuba and other developing countries.

120. Matibag, *Afro-Cuban Religious Experience*, 232.

121. Fernández Robaina, *Hablen paleros y santeros*, 90.

122. Barnet, *La fuente viva*, 146.

123. Maria Elena Vinueza, *Presencia arará en la música folklórica de Matanzas* (Havana: Casa de las Américas, 1989).

124. Ibid., 51, 55. Vinueza describes Dahomeyan beliefs as "obscurantism" resulting from a lack of formal education. She refers to the arará community as if it were an antiquated survival from the past and emphasizes that the goal of Marxism is to eradicate religion (55).

125. Ramiro Guerra, *Teatralización del folklore y otros ensayos* (Havana: Letras Cubanas), 1989.

126. Carlos Alfonso et al., "Olorun para todos," Lázaro Ros con Grupo Mezcla. EGREM LP #LD-4662; Carlos Alfonso et al., "Ancestros," Qbadisc CD 9001; Carlos Alfonso et al., "Ancestros II," Qbadisc CD 9015. These are the citations for discs currently available in the United States. The first important album by this group, *Ancestros*, appeared in 1987 (Ned Sublette, personal communication to the author). Sublette notes additionally that an earlier incarnation of the Síntesis band, named Tema IV, released a record a few years before *Ancestros* that included a few of the same pieces. The appearance of *Ancestros*, however, represented the most definitive moment in the popularization of "religious pop."

127. Alexis Esquivel, personal communication to the author.

128. Natalia Bolívar, personal communication to the author.

129. Internal documents from Radio Habana Cuba (RHC), for instance, indicate that on 31 March 1991 a program dedicated to the celebration of Holy Week aired on that station. Speakers included Raúl Suárez Ramos, president of the Ecumenical Council of Cuba, Reverend Arnaldo Mirando, president of the Nazarene Church, and Joel Ajo, bishop of the Methodist Church. It should be noted that RHC is a short-wave station intended primarily for listeners abroad.

130. Oppenheimer, *Castro's Final Hour*, 343.

131. Observers note that Bolívar's publication contained nothing new and, in reality, was nothing more than a condensed reproduction of writings on the orichas by Fernando Ortiz and others during the pre-Castro years. Nevertheless, that it appeared at all is significant.

132. Fernández, *Hablen paleros y santeros*, 2.

133. The practice of charging foreigners to "make their saints" has become common, helping the religious community economically but bringing unpleasant tensions into ritual contexts.

134. A disposition of the Party the following year made the change official; see *CubaINFO* 4, no. 8 (21 July 1992), for a summary of this document.

135. Adalberto Álvarez, *Adalberto Álvarez y su son*, P.O.W Records. Sony Discos PWK 83563.

136. He mentions his "padrina," for instance, mentioning her public name (Rosa Zayas) as well as her religious name (Oché Elogüe).

137. Orovio, personal communication to the author.

138. Example of specific pieces by these and other artists include "Maferefú Obatalá" and "La reina de Ifé" by Pachito Alonso y su Kini Kini, "Viejo Lázaro" by Dan Den, "Babalú Ayé" by Kiki Korona, "Santa palabra" by NG La Banda, "Soy todo," "Hierbero, ven" and "Ay, Dios ampárame" by Los Van Van. The Caribe Productions CD *Despójate* from 1994 contains many of these songs.

139. David Calzado, in a personal communication to the author, notes that in more recent years the subject of religion has been somewhat less prominent. The topic began to be perceived as overused, and the market for such material saturated.

140. Examples of the countless releases of traditional religious song and drumming that have appeared since the mid-1990s include Lázaro Ros, *Olorun 1*, EGREM CD #0013; the CIDMUC ed., *Sacred Rythms of Cuban Santería*, Smithsonian Folkways compilation, CD SFCD40419; the Los Muñequitos de Matanzas, *Ito Iban Echu*, Qbadisc compact disk QB 9022; and Justo Pelladito et al., *Chants et rythmes afrocubaines*, AIMP and VDE-Galo. VDE-Gallo compact disk CD 959.

141. Manuel Vázquez Montalbán, *Ydios entró en la Habana* (Madrid: Aguilar, 1998).

142. Pedro Izquierdo, "Detrás de la música, esta música," *Trabajadores*, 4 April 1990 (archives, Instituto Cubano de Radio y Televisión).

143. Miguel Barnet's exact comment, in this case discussing African-derived religions, is as follows: "In Cuba it is evident that cults like Santería have been losing their preeminence since the first years after the triumph of the revolution. Our new society . . . creates life incentives that permit human perspectives to open up and rid themselves of religious structures. . . . Deities will occupy in the near future the place that the Greek and Roman pantheons hold. They will be figures of legend. . . . The well of African religions in Cuba . . . is drying up day by day" (*La fuente viva*, 196).

144. *CubaINFO* 10, no. 2 (1997): 7.

145. Calzado, personal communication to the author.

146. Robaina, *Hablen paleros y santeros*, 37.

147. Lázaro Ros himself, along with his manager, discussed these issues with me in 1996. They had lobbied for some time for the creation of musical compilations of sacred chants as well as for their inclusion in curricula, without success. It would seem that the government is much more willing to accept studies of religious music by nonparticipants than by those personally involved.

148. Spokespersons for the Catholic Church voiced this concern in their famous underground document of 1993; although conditions have improved since that time, many issues have yet to be addressed.

149. Lázaro Ros and Valdés, personal communication to the author.

150. Ference Féher, Agnes Heller, and György Márkus, eds., *Dictatorship over Needs: An Analysis of Soviet Societies* (New York: Basil Blackwell, 1983), 199.

151. Matibag, *Afro-Cuban Religious Experience*, 246.

CHAPTER FIFTEEN

Reclaiming the Past:
Yoruba Elements in African American Arts

Babatunde Lawal

The term "African American" indicates a synthesis of two traditions, the African and the American. Like the latter—a cluster of European, Amerindian, and other traditions—the African component comprises bits and pieces from different parts of the motherland. Over time, the African fragments have meshed so much with one another and with the American cluster that it is often difficult to trace their origin to specific ethnic groups in Africa. This chapter examines the historical, social, cultural, and ideological dynamics resulting in the carry-over, retention, loss, reclamation, and reinterpretation of Yoruba cultural and artistic elements in African American arts.[1] "Yoruba element," as used here, has a double connotation. On the one hand, it refers to cultural and artistic items transmitted to North America during the Atlantic slave trade by Yoruba-born or Yoruba-influenced African-born captives from present-day southwestern Nigeria, the Republic of Benin, and Togo. On the other, it designates a more recent revival of Yoruba traditions by American artists of African descent in their attempt to reclaim their African ancestral legacy and, in the process, negotiate new, black-specific identities for individual or collective empowerment.

The Yoruba

Numbering more than twenty-five million people today, the Yoruba live in present-day Nigeria, Benin, and Togo in West Africa. Although united by a common language and culture, they are divided into many independent kingdoms, each headed by a king. Abundant natural resources enabled them to develop one of the most advanced cultures in sub-Saharan Africa. By the beginning of the second millennium A.D., Ile-Ife, their most sacred city, had become a major urban center with highly sophisticated religious, social, and political institutions. The ancient arts of Ile-Ife include extremely naturalistic terra-cotta and bronze sculptures dated between the eleventh and sixteenth centuries A.D., hinting at an era of economic prosperity and intense cultural activities. Archaeological research in the city has yielded important data now being used to reconstruct its past.[2] Other important Yoruba kingdoms are Ketu, Sabe, Ohori, Anago, Igbomina, Ijebu, Ijesa, Ekiti, Ondo, Akoko, Owo, Egba, Egbado, and Oyo. Because the latter (Oyo) was located in the northern grassland and near the Niger River, it was able to participate in the trans-Saharan trade between West and North Africa. It soon developed economically and militarily to become the most powerful kingdom between the sixteenth and early nineteenth centuries, controlling a vast empire that included some non-Yoruba groups.

Indigenous Yoruba religion centers on a belief in a Supreme Being (Olodumare), the creator of the universe and the generator of the vital principle called *ase* that sustains the universe. After completing the act of creation, the Supreme Being reportedly delegated the responsibility of administering the earth to a number of divinities called *orisa* who mediate between him and humanity. Each *orisa* embodies an *ase*, associated with a natural or cultural phenomenon. Thus Obatala personifies creativity; Ile personifies the nurturing earth; Yemoja personifies motherhood; Osanyin, herbal medicine; Ogun, iron tools, warfare, and bravery; Sango (or Shango), the thunderstorm and social justice; Osun, fertility and beauty; Oya, the tornado; and Ifa, clairvoyance and wisdom. Esu Elegbara is the divine messenger, associated with fate and dynamism. The ultimate goal of Yoruba religion is to secure the benevolence and spiritual protection of Olodumare and the *orisa* in the human quest for peace and happiness on earth.

Art looms large in Yoruba culture because it is inseparable from life. According to the Yoruba creation myth, the archetypal human image was molded from clay by Obatala, the creativity deity, after which the Supreme Being infused it with a life force called "èmí." The human body, being a work of art, thus contains a special power, inspiring and sustaining the creativity manifest in the visual and performing arts. From the decoration of architecture and utilitarian objects to communicate taste or high status, to the use of dress, sculpture, leatherworks, beaded objects, and ritual emblems for social, political, and religious purposes, art is used by the Yoruba not only to mediate between the human and spirit worlds but also to enrich the quality of life and celebrate the joy of living.

From Yoruba "Ijuba"
to the African American "Juba" Dance

Since there was no systematic head count, the exact number of Yoruba captives in the Americas during the trans-Atlantic slave trade cannot be ascertained. But most scholars put the number between one and two million, although many of them were taken to the Caribbean and South America (see the chapters in this volume by David Eltis and Paul Lovejoy). Ethnic identification of slaves in North America is made much more difficult by the fact that they were sometimes classified according to their port of embarkation. Thus scores of Yoruba captives were listed, along with the Ewe and Fon, as coming from the Bight of Benin, the coastal area corresponding to present-day Togo, Republic of Benin, and southwestern Nigeria.[3] This Bight of Benin group constituted about 28 percent of the African population of colonial Louisiana between 1760 and 1800.[4] The slave records indicate that many North American slave owners considered the Yoruba captives (then identified as Nago, Popo, and Whydahs)[5] as the most ideal and esteemed of all slaves because "they were lusty and industrious and . . . submissive."[6] They were reported to be "very polite and civilized, most respectful of superiors before whom they immediately fell on their knees and kissed the earth while thrice clapping their hands."[7] Hence some Yoruba served as house servants and artisans, while less submissive slaves from other parts of Africa were made to work in the fields.

A watercolor painting in the collection of the Abby Aldrich Rockefeller Folk Art Center, Williamsburg, Virginia, titled *The Old Plantation,* is often cited as one of the earliest visual records of Yoruba presence in North America (Fig.15.1).[8] Believed to have been produced by an unidentified South Carolina artist between the late eighteenth and early nineteenth centuries, the painting features three dancers—two females (with pieces of cloth) and a male, wearing a head tie and holding a stick. There are two musicians—one is playing a bowl-shaped single-membrane drum, and the other a stringed instrument. The audience consists of seven people; among them is a man wearing a head tie. The scene is thought to represent a Yoruba ceremony partly because the dance of the figures resembles that of the Yoruba, and partly because the drum looks like the Yoruba bowl-shaped drum ("gudugudu"), and the stringed instrument like the Yoruba lute ("molo").[9]

Striking as the Yoruba parallels might be, however, there is as yet no satisfactory explanation for the stick dance and the male head ties which, as Beatrix Rumford and Carolyn Weekley rightly observe, "apparently have a significance tied to the dance."[10] Second, both the bowl-shaped drum and lute are not exclusive to the Yoruba; they are found among the Hausa of present-day northern Nigeria as well. There is a consensus among musicologists that the Yoruba borrowed the two instruments from the Hausa (their northern neighbors) who have identical names for the instruments: "kutunku" for the bowl-shaped drum, and "molo" for the lute.[11] And given the extensive influence of Islamic music on the Hausa, they, in turn, would seem to have adopted the two instruments from the Arabs and Berbers with whom they have had contact for several centuries. The origin of the stringed instrument in other parts of West Africa is often traced to the same groups—the Arabs and Berbers—who dominated the trans-Saharan trade from the early decades of the Christian era to the late sixteenth century.[12] Of course, a wide variety of lutes and bowl-shaped drums abound in different parts of Africa, and it is difficult, if not impossible, to trace all of them to Islamic influence.

**Fig. 15.1. Unidentified artist, *The Old Plantation*, probably South Carolina.
Water color on paper, 1790–1800; 12" × 18".**
The Abby Aldrich Rockefeller Folk Art Center, Williamsburg, Virginia.

Nonetheless, it is significant that some of the men in *The Old Plantation* painting wear head ties—dress accessories not normally associated in indigenous African cultures with men, but rather with women. These head ties, especially those worn by the gudugudu player and the man standing on the extreme (viewer's) left of the painting, recall the turban or the Arabic "kaffiyeh" which had become popular in the West African savannah as early as the thirteenth century when some Muslims in the area (including the kings of Ancient Mali) went on pilgrimage to Mecca. Thus it is likely that these men are Muslims, given that many enslaved Muslims were transported to North America in the eighteenth and early nineteenth centuries. One of them, Ayuba Suleiman Diallo (known by the slave name Job Ben Solomon), was brought to Maryland from the Gambia in 1731. An engraving published in the *Gentleman's Magazine* of 1750 shows him wearing a turban.[13] Nor did his fellow Muslims in South Carolina abandon their faith; they "continued to observe the prayers and devotions of Islam as best as they could."[14] Even those Muslims who converted to Christianity, such as Omar Ibn Said—who had traveled to Mecca before his enslavement—continued to write in Arabic.[15]

It is plausible, therefore, that this painting has more to do with the Hausa, Fulani, or other Africans who had been exposed to Islam much earlier than the Yoruba among whom Islam did not make any significant inroad until the early nineteenth century. Yet, all things considered, the dancing style of the

294

two women in the painting is so close to that of the Yoruba that the women appear to hail from that culture, despite their new European outfit. As Robert Farris Thompson has observed:

> I was to see this very action many times in Yorubaland in the 1960s and 1970s: women dancing, swinging suddenly close to the earth, showing off youth and flexibility, dancing a strip of cloth held before their bodies as a final fillip of design. They are dancing a cloth while dancing the dance.[16]

A photograph taken by musicologist Darius Thieme in the Yoruba village of Isundunrin in the 1960s corroborates Thompson's observation (Figure 15.2).[17] It shows a woman "dancing a strip of cloth" in front of an orchestra that includes a musician playing a bowl-shaped drum similar to the one in the Old Plantation painting. Another photograph taken by Michel Huet in the 1970s features two female Gelede masks performing a similar dance.[18] The strip of cloth they are holding is called "oja" (baby sash). Though normally used by Yoruba mothers to secure a child to the back, the oja may also be employed in rituals aimed at insuring fertility and asking the "orisa" (deities) to protect humanity, just as the oja firmly secures a child on its mother's back.[19] At times Yoruba women may use a head tie ("gele") or shoulder cloth ("iborun") to usher in a guest of honor to the dance arena, dancing backward in front of the person and holding the cloth in the same way as shown in this watercolor painting. They may occasionally spread the cloth on the ground for the honoree to walk or dance on. This is called "iyesi" (red carpet treatment). In return, the honoree drops gifts or money on the pieces of cloth to thank these admirers for their public demonstration of affection. It is conceivable, then, that the man dancing in the painting is the honoree, using what appears to be his walking stick to respond to the motion of the cloth being "danced" by the two women in front of him. Unfortunately there is no clue as to what the celebration is all about. Nor do we know why he wears a scarf. However, that some elements in the painting can easily be identified with Yoruba traditions whereas others cannot may very well indicate that the scene includes not only the Yoruba but other Africans who were obliged by the circumstances of slavery to synthesize different African as well as foreign traditions in the New World.[20]

The Yoruba contribution to this cultural synthesis in North America is evident in the "juba," a dance characterized by intensive body movements and intricate footwork. In Wilmington, North Carolina, for example, the dance is said to have been popularized by the "Guinea Negroes," who "had retained many of the ideas and traditions of their native land."[21] They entertained the public during the Christmas season. Edward Warren provides an eyewitness account from the early nineteenth century:

> The leading character is the "ragman," whose "get up" consists in a costume of rags, so arranged that one end of each hangs loose and dangles; two great ox horns, attached to the skin of a racoon, which is drawn over the head and face,

Fig. 15.2. Yoruba Dundun Orchestra, Isundunrin Village, Nigeria, 1967.
Note the musician *(second from left)* playing the gudugudu bowl-shaped drum
and the woman *(far left)* dancing with a piece of cloth.
Photo by Darius Thieme.

leaving apertures only for the eyes and mouth; sandals of the skin of some wild "varmint"; several cow and sheep bells or strings of dried goats' horns hanging about their shoulders, and so arranged as to jingle at every movement; and a short stick of seasoned wood, carried in his hands.

The second part is taken by the best looking darkey of the place, who wears no disguise, but is simply arrayed in what they call his "Sunday-go-to-meeting suit," and carries in his hand a small bowl or tin cup, while the other parts are appropriated by some half a dozen fellows, each arrayed fantastically in ribbons, rags, and feathers, and bearing between them several so-called musical instruments or "gumba boxes," which consist of wooden frames covered over with tanned sheep skins. They are usually followed by a motley crowd of all ages, dressed in ordinary working clothes. . . .

Having thus given you an idea of the characters I will describe the performance as I first saw it at the "Lake." Coming up to the front door of the "great house," the musicians commenced to beat their gumba boxes violently, while characters No. 1 and No. 2 entered upon a dance of the most extraordinary character—a combination of bodily contortions, flings, kicks, gyrations, and antics of every imaginable description, seemingly acting as partners, and yet each try to excel the other in the variety and grotesqueness of his movements. At the same time No. 2 led off with a song of a strange, monotonous cadence, which seemed extemporized for the occasion, and run somewhat in this wise:

"My massa am a white man, juba!
Old missus am a lady, juba!
De children am de honey-pods, Juba! juba!
Krimas come but once a year, juba!
Juba! juba! O, ye juba! . . ."

After singing a verse or two, No. 2 moved up to the master, with his hat in one hand and a tin cup in the other, to receive the expected "quarter," and, while making the lowest obeisance, shouted: "May de good Lord bless old massa and missus, and all de young massas, juba!"[22]

Although the juba dance was popular all over the Americas (as part of the John Kunering / Jonkonnu Christmas masquerade),[23] its exact origin and the meaning of the term "juba" are obscure. One legend claims that the term once referred to the leftover food placed in a big container that enslaved Africans shared with livestock. But this legend does not fully explain how leftover food came to be associated with the juba dance. The current assumption is that the dance originated among the Bantu slaves and that the term "juba" probably derives from the Central African (Bantu) words "giouba," "nguba," "ginguba," or "diuba" which mean, respectively, "peanut," "the hour," "the sun," and "to pat or to beat time."[24] Although this is possible, it should be noted that the term also occurs among the Akan of Cote d'Ivoire, Ghana, and Togo where it refers to a female born on a Monday. But it is not associated with a dance in these cultures. Among the Yoruba of Nigeria and the Republic of Benin, on the other hand, the term means homage or obeisance,[25] and often refers to the gesture or dance accompanying it. The association of the Wilmington juba dance with "obeisance" is therefore significant: not only does it tally with the Yoruba meaning of the term, it also recalls the preference for Yoruba slaves in North America who, as noted earlier, were reputed for their "submissiveness" and "politeness." Indeed, the term "juba," along with its variations like "jiba," "yuba," and "moyuba" ("paying obeisance"), features prominently in songs, dances, and religious ceremonies associated with Yoruba captives and their descendants in the Caribbean and Brazil.[26] It is worth mentioning that there is an "Ijuba Shrine" (said to be one of the oldest) in Trinidad dedicated to Ogun, the Yoruba deity of iron tools, weapons, and warfare. According to Candice Goucher, "The dance steps of Ogun devotees as seen in African-Caribbean orisha ceremonies in Trinidad and Tobago are also preserved in the most traditional carnival sailor dance today."[27]

Another aspect of the Wilmington juba dance that suggests a Yoruba origin is the "costume of rags, so arranged that one end of each hangs loose and dangles." As Sterling Stuckey rightly observes, this configuration reminds one of the "Egungun" ancestral mask of the Yoruba that the Dahomeans (Fon) and related groups might have introduced to North Carolina.[28] One account of the dancers mentions the presence of masked men dressed like women—in "strips of cloth of gay colors sewn to their usual garments and producing an effect of exotic grotesquerie."[29] This is reminiscent of the Gelede, a Yoruba masque dedicated to the spiritual powers of women. As a result, the Gelede mask, worn by men, often represents a female, and the costume consists of "multicolored female headwraps and baby sashes . . . tied round the body."[30]

A characteristic feature of the juba dance in the Caribbean and the United States is its emphasis on foot stamping and vigorous body movements.[31] This is also present in the Gelede dance. For example, the Gelede mask, called "Efe,"

at the beginning of his performance, breaks into incantatory chants . . . to superior powers. This . . . is called "ijuba," the paying of homage. . . . His dances consist of masculine strides, quick dramatic turns, rhythmic staccato foot patterns and stamping, vigorous swinging of the arms. . . . Efe makes a brisk roundabout turn to make his panel of headties swirl and flutter, stamping his feet on the ground to maintain his equilibrium.[32]

Equally relevant here is Edward Warren's observation that the costumes of the Wilmington juba dancers included "sheep bells or strings of dried goats' horns . . . [that] jingle at every movement." These may very well be a substitute for the metal anklet ("iku") of the Gelede mask that jingles rhythmically during the dance, amplifying the "staccato foot patterns."[33] Thus, could the Yoruba slaves have originated or popularized the term "juba" in spite of the Creolized nature of the dance associated with it? In Brazil and the Caribbean, Yoruba and Bantu (especially Kongo) religious and cultural elements are known to have reinforced each other because of the fundamental similarities in their constituent elements.[34] The juba dance does seem to be yet another example of this cultural convergence.[35] It is hoped that future research will cast more light on the subject.[36]

The Yoruba Contributions to the Shotgun House

A common sight in many areas of the Deep South, the shotgun house is widely regarded as one of the most prominent African American contributions to the North American landscape (Fig. 15.3). It is so called because of the passage or hallway that leads from the front to the back door, so that a bullet fired through the entrance would travel unimpeded through the back door (Fig. 15.4). Others liken this "thoroughfare" effect to peeping through the barrel of a shotgun. A typical shotgun house has a front porch and a gable roof. It is about one room in width and about three or four rooms long. Although the interior is often partitioned into rooms, each room does not have a door.

Most scholars agree that the shotgun house was introduced to the Deep South (particularly Louisiana, the Carolinas, and Alabama) in the late eighteenth or early nineteenth century by African captives and free blacks / Creoles from Haiti and Cuba.[37] John M. Vlach, the leading authority on the subject, identifies Haiti as the cradle of this architectural type in the Caribbean and North America since some of the oldest examples have been found there. According to him, despite the fact that the Arawak Indians of rural Haiti are known to have constructed similar houses before the beginning of the trans-Atlantic slave trade, what eventually became known as the shotgun house is a synthesis of Arawak and African architectural traditions, benefiting from French building and woodwork techniques.[38] In other words, the first black captives in Haiti, on finding the indigenous Arawak house similar to theirs, adopted and modified it into something close to what they had left behind in Africa. The modification seemed to have occurred in the late eighteenth century when most of the African captives in rural Haiti came from the Bight of Benin.[39] The area was not only controlled by the Yoruba kingdom of Oyo, but many of the slaves exported from there were either Nagô (another name for the Yoruba) or kindred groups such as the Fon, Egun, Arada, Adja, or Ewe.[40]

Although structures similar to the shotgun house exist in many parts of sub-Saharan Africa, some of the most advanced forms are to be found among the Yoruba and related groups such as the Edo and Fon. The Yoruba examples are constructed either as single, gabled-roof units with porches or as a complex, comprising four or more units. Called "agbo-ile" (compound), each complex is occupied by an extended family and has an "impluviate" courtyard and elaborate verandahs sometimes adorned with carved posts (Fig. 15.5).[41] A comparison of the principal elements of the shotgun house (such as the front porch, the gable roof, and the open interior space) with Yoruba architecture reveals important similarities. As Vlach observed in the course of his fieldwork in Nigeria:

> The most shared feature is the reliance on the rectangular two-room module. The Yoruba 10' × 20' unit coincides closely with the 10' × 21' rural shotgun of Haiti. Vertical dimensions are also similar so that wall heights commonly range between six and eight feet in both Haitian and African houses. The Yoruba house

Fig. 15.3. "Shotgun Houses." Mobile, Alabama, 1937.
Photo, collection of the U.S. Library of Congress, Washington, D.C.

thus contains the spatial features of the shotgun. While the aspect of orientation is variable in Yoruba architecture, it does happen that the two-room house will have its gable facing the front like Haitian shotgun houses. In such cases all that is required to convert the Yoruba hut into a morphologically completed shotgun is a shift of the doorway. In the Yoruba house, as in the shotgun, one passes first through a parlor before entering the bedroom; room function does not need to be shifted. Since the two-room house is a working unit in Yoruba architecture that is intended to be elongated, compressed, and reordered into different building types, the movement of a doorway or the shift of a parallel to a perpendicular alignment is an expected kind of change. Such modifications occasionally occur in the African context, and thus the Haitian shotgun may be considered a product of continuing process of African architectural modification. Haitian houses certainly include in their design the same spatial preferences that are found in West Africa. The rural shotgun thus retained a core of African expectation while satisfying plantation owners' need for slave quarters, and so there was a meeting of priority and preference.[42]

In short, as Vlach points out, the closeness of the Haitian shotgun house to indigenous Yoruba architectural design suggests ancient links, if not a genetic relationship.[43] This is not to say that this structure is exclusive to the Yoruba. It is also found among other groups in West, Central, and Equatorial Africa who conceivably might equally well have contributed to its develop-

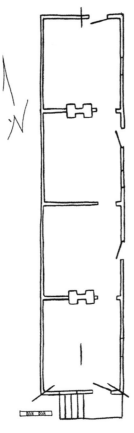

Fig. 15.4. Floor plan of a typical shotgun house, frame construction.
New Orleans.
Drawing after J. M. Vlach.

ment in Haiti and elsewhere in the Americas. Yet the possibility of a major contribution by the Yoruba (and related groups from the Bight of Benin) remains very strong and is corroborated by the fact that the shotgun house was equally popular in neighboring nineteenth-century Cuba where Yoruba captives (sometimes identified as Lucumí)[44] constituted the majority. In fact, the Cuban market was so overflooded with Bight of Benin slaves that some of them were constantly smuggled into mainland America long after the 1808 law prohibiting fresh imports.[45] For example, even though Spain ceded Florida to the United States in 1819, many Africans with facial marks could still be found in the state as late as the 1830s.[46] Needless to say, many Yoruba subgroups, in the past, wore facial marks by which they were identified in Cuban and Brazilian slave markets. Incidentally one Lucumí (Yoruba) slave interviewed in

301

Fig. 15.5. Front view of the Seru Family compound, Ile-Ife, Nigeria,
February 1974. Since the early twentieth century, the thatched roof and carved
posts of big compounds (*agbo ile*) such as this one have been replaced with
corrugated iron sheets and mud pillars plastered with cement.
Photo by John Michael Vlach (from "Affecting Architecture of the Yoruba,"
African Arts 10, no. 1 [1976], fig. 12).

Florida in the 1850s remarked that "he had been smuggled hither from Cuba
several years ago."[47]

That the Yoruba contributed significantly to the development of the shotgun
house can also be inferred from the prominence of Yoruba deities ("orisa") in
such African-inspired religions as Vodou (Haiti, Louisiana, and the Dominican
Republic), Santería (Cuba), and Candomblé (Brazil). The Yoruba deity of the
crossroads and divine messenger, Esu Elegba, links all these religions, known as
"Lebat" in nineteenth-century Louisiana,[48] "Legba" in Haiti, "Leggua" in Cuba,
and "Exu" in Brazil. By and large, while its beginnings in the American Deep
South are difficult to trace, the shotgun house became very popular and assumed
a distinctive form in the early nineteenth century, as many slaves, free black Creoles, and other immigrants from Cuba, Haiti, and the Dominican Republic
settled in New Orleans and other major cities such as Charleston and Mobile.[49]

Transformations in the Visual Arts

The shotgun house has survived to the present day in many parts of the
Deep South for two main reasons. First, the slave masters allowed African captives to build them; second, the houses are inexpensive and suitable for the

hot climate.[50] The slave masters discouraged the production of traditional African art partly because of its association with religion—which they regarded as pagan—and partly because its conceptual approach was mistaken for a failed attempt to imitate nature. Nevertheless, some slaves did produce works in the African style either for private rituals or secret ceremonies involving other Africans.[51]

In Florida the Seminoles are known to have sheltered runaway African slaves in the eighteenth and early nineteenth centuries when that part of North America was colonized and exploited by the British, Spanish, and French. Some of the refugees continued with their African traditions, creating shrines for reconnecting with their ancestors. Others adopted Amerindian dresses and customs, and even married Seminoles.[52] By the second decade of the nineteenth century dramatic changes occurred in Seminole beadwork. The vogue for new beaded items such as a shoulder pouch or bandoleer bag can easily be traced to the influence of European settlers.[53] But the appearance of irregular patterns and asymmetrical compositions as well as certain filled-in designs on some of the bandoleer bags cannot. Nor can one find convincing precedents in Seminole beadwork or that of any contiguous Amerindian groups. Since these new characteristics are more typical of African beadwork, Marcilene Wittmer, Dorothy Downs, Thomas Larose, and other scholars have suggested that they might have been introduced by blacks, given their large number among the Seminole in the 1820s and 1830s.[54] Many of the new arrivals were from the Bight of Benin.[55] Indeed, one bandoleer bag features a black figure in trousers not normally worn by the Seminoles at this time.[56] Some of the diamond motifs in Seminole beadwork are comparable to those found in the Kongo culture of the present-day Democratic Republic of Congo. However, a good majority of the symbols, colors, styles, and techniques associated with the changes in Seminole beadwork can easily be matched with Yoruba beadwork (Fig. 15.6).[57] Can these parallels be taken as evidence of Yoruba influence on Seminole beadwork? The possibility cannot be ruled out altogether. For at the time the changes occurred the Yoruba constituted a sizeable part of the slave population in Florida,[58] many of them, as mentioned earlier, having been illegally imported from Cuba. Moreover, the Yoruba have a rich and ancient tradition of beadwork the antiquity of which is attested by the beaded dress of some of the Ife brass and terra-cotta figures, which date to the early part of the second millennium of the Christian era.[59]

By the mid-nineteenth century the Euro-American devaluation of African art had led black artists such as Robert Scott Duncanson (1821–1872), Patrick Reason (1816–1898), Edward Mitchell Bannister (1826–1901), Mary Edmonia Lewis (1845–1911), and Henry Ossawa Tanner (1859–1937) to acquire the necessary skills in academic realism. This move disconnected the artists from their African heritage in the visual arts, relating them more and more to the European tradition. It was not until the Harlem Renaissance of the 1920s and 1930s that formally trained American artists of African descent began to re-

Fig. 15.6. Top row: Motifs from the beaded
shoulder bags (bandoleer) of the Seminoles.
From Dorothy Downs, *Art of the Florida Seminole and Miccosukee Indians* (Gainesville: University
Press of Florida, 1995), fig. 6.2. Reprinted with permission of the University Press of Florida.
Bottom row: Motifs from Yoruba beadworks and decorated panels.
Line drawings by Babatunde Lawal (for examples of works with these motifs,
see Drewal and Mason, *Beads, Body and Soul* (1998) and Lawal, *The Gelede Spectacle* (1996).

connect with their artistic heritage—thanks to the efforts of the African American art critic and philosopher Alain Locke, who drew the attention of black artists to the influence of African sculpture on modern European art, advising them to seek inspiration from their ancestral legacy instead of aping the naturalism of pre-twentieth-century Europe.[60] In response, some black artists stylized their forms in the African manner. Others created compositions with African themes.

Resurrecting the Orisa in North America

One of the first African American intellectuals to involve the orisa in a theatrical performance was W.E.B. Du Bois (1868–1963). A member of the Board of Governors of the National Emancipation Exposition of New York, Du Bois wrote an opera in 1913 entitled *The Star of Ethiopia*. It commemorated the fiftieth anniversary of the Emancipation Proclamation of 1863. Aimed at inspiring fellow blacks to rediscover themselves, to reclaim their cultural heritage, and then to fight for total freedom, the opera synthesized characters and artistic elements from different parts of Africa and the black world. As Freda Scott notes:

Du Bois started the first of several drafts of *The Star of Ethiopia* in 1911. At first he called the work *The Jewel of Ethiopia: A Masque in Episodes* (there were six in the first draft). Since the masque is more allegorical than commemorative, he began with a scene in which Shango, the God of Thunder, gives the Jewel of Freedom to Ethiopia in return for her soul. The jewel finally reaches the United States after being lost and found several times. There the foundation stones of Labor, Wealth, Justice, Beauty, Education, and Truth are laid and the jewel is finally ensconced on a Pillar of Light and placed on this foundation. . . . The thirteen leading characters included Queen of Sheba, Nat Turner, Toussaint L'Ouverture, and Mohammed Askia.[61]

As mentioned earlier, the Yoruba deity Sango is associated not only with the thunderstorm but also with retributive and social justice. That Du Bois included the deity among the thirteen leading characters in The Star of Ethiopia reveals his awareness of Sango's potential as an instrument for empowering the African American struggle for social justice and cultural emancipation. He probably encountered Sango in the course of his avid collection of materials on African history and culture or as a result of his interactions with African Americans who had migrated to the United States from the Caribbean where many of the Yoruba orisa had survived in various forms. However, the orisa did not attract public attention in the United States until the 1940s when more immigrants arrived from the Caribbean (especially from Cuba and Puerto Rico), bringing with them the African-inspired religion called Santería, that is, the worship of the orisa in the guise of Roman Catholic saints.[62] Soon the intricate music and dances associated with orisa worship caught the attention of Katherine Durnham, the famous African American choreographer. She employed some of the new arrivals in her dance company, and also organized monthly concerts featuring Cuban orchestras that played Yoruba-influenced music. In 1947 the jazz trumpeter and bebop maestro, Dizzy Gillespie, collaborated with the Cuban conga drummer Chano Pozo in recording sessions during which Chano sang Yoruba songs in honor of Yemoja, the Yoruba personification of motherhood.[63] In Dizzy Gillespie's words:

> Chano taught us all the multirhythm; we learned from the master. . . . He'd teach us some of those Cuban chants and things like that. . . . You have different ones, the Nanigo, the Arara, the Santo (music of the Yoruba *orisha*) and several others, and they each have their own rhythm. . . . They are all of African derivation.[64]

Such collaborations between African Americans and Afro-Cubans generated a lot of interest in musical circles, culminating in Cubop Jazz, which sometimes included bata rhythm, Sango's sacred music (see Figure 15.11 below). The jazz drummer Mongo Santamaria is credited with staging the first public concert of orisa music in 1956 at the Palladium Night Club in New York.[65] The concert was dedicated to Sango whose name was already familiar to American theater audiences through Katherine Durnham's dance-drama Carib Song staged in New York in 1945.[66] One of the first African American converts to Santería was Walter Eugene King (b. 1928), a graphic artist and member of the Katherine Durnham Dance Company, who was at that time searching for African alternatives to Christianity and Islam. King traveled to Matanzas, Cuba, in 1959, where he was initiated and became a priest of Obatala, the Yoruba creativity deity.

The early 1960s marked a turning point in the African American experience. A combination of events such as the emergence of independent African states, the intensification of black nationalism in the United States, as well as the struggle there for desegregation, equal opportunity, and cultural emancipation, encouraged many blacks to identify more closely with their motherland. The creation of the Peace Corps and Operation Crossroads programs, coupled with the availability of travel grants, enabled many African Americans to visit Africa. Some did so as a kind of homecoming. Others traveled and lived in Africa for some time either to conduct research or simply to have a firsthand experience of their cultural heritage which they had only learned about till then in the ethnographic literature. The creation of African and black studies programs in American universities offered a unique opportunity for blacks who could not leave the United States to deepen their knowledge of Africa and its cultural traditions. One consequence of the new development is that some African Americans abandoned the Christian faith and converted to Islam or indigenous African religions.

In 1960 Walter Eugene King established a Yoruba temple in Harlem, New York, and began converting fellow blacks to orisa religion. He broke with the Cuban tradition of worshiping the orisa in the guise of Christian saints, restoring to the deities their original Yoruba identity and calling the reformed religion Orisa-Vodou, instead of Santería. He did away with the Christian images of Catholic saints used by Afro-Cubans to represent the orisa on altars, replacing them with sculptures in the Yoruba style. Being an artist himself, he carved some of the altar sculptures dedicated to the orisa in the Yoruba temple. He also introduced the performance of Egungun masks which the Yoruba use to signify the souls of deceased ancestors returning to the physical world to interact with living descendants (Fig. 15.7). He opened a fashion store in Harlem that popularized among blacks the wearing of African dresses, especially the Yoruba "agbada," "dansiki," "fila," "buba," "iro," and "gele," which soon became symbols of black nationalism and the black quest for cultural redemption.[67] Some blacks adopted Yoruba names. King himself changed his name to Efuntola Oseijiman Adefunmi. In 1970 he founded the Oyotunji Village in South Carolina, which has since become a Mecca for Yoruba religion, art, and culture in the United States. The village, influenced by Yoruba architectural design (Fig. 15.8), is headed by Adefunmi who wears a beaded crown like a Yoruba king. Since 1972 he has visited Yorubaland several times, and he speaks the Yoruba language. Admittedly, as Mikelle Smith Omari aptly observes, the revival of Yoruba traditions at Oyotunji Village cannot be traced directly to

Fig. 15.7. "Egungun mask from Oyotunji Village (Sheldon,
South Carolina) performing in Richmond, Virginia, 1998."
Photo by Babatunde Lawal.

Fig. 15.8. "Inside Oyotunji Village." Sheldon, South Carolina, 1997.
Note the Yoruba architectural design. Compare with Fig. 15.5.
Photo by Loria King.

"survivals of slave cultures" as in Brazil, Cuba, Haiti, and other parts of the Caribbean.[68] This point is also reflected in the eclectic nature of the revival which incorporates ancient Egyptian, Fon, Edo, and Asante elements.[69] Yet, according to a resident of the village, the experiment constitutes an act of reclamation and reintegration of a lost and found heritage that has been of tremendous therapeutic value to thousands of African Americans at critical periods in their struggle for survival in North America.

Many American cities now have a growing population of orisa devotees or individuals who identify with the Yoruba tradition and use its tenets to enrich their lives. The number of botanicas (shops selling herbs and orisa-related goods) has increased over the years. Some of the goods are imported from Yorubaland, Brazil, and the Caribbean; others, including Yoruba-looking images and beadwork, are made in the United States (Fig. 15.9).[70] There is a general belief, however, that materials and images from Yorubaland are more effective ritually. This partly explains why members of the Yemoja Descendants Society of New York (Egbe Yemoja), founded in 1988, traveled to Ibadan (Nigeria) in 1990 to commission a special image of the goddess for use in its rituals.[71] In short, shrines for the orisa combine Yoruba- and American-made images and ritual furniture.

308

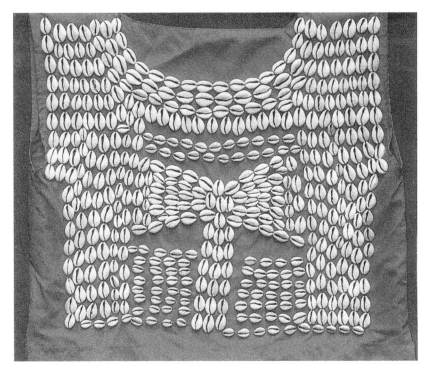

Fig. 15.9. Stephanie Weaver, *Sango Shirt, with Cowrie Shells and Thunder-Ax Motif.* Brooklyn, New York, mixed media, 1994.
Photo by John Mason.

Invoking the Orisa in Word and Image

Given their association with salvation, dynamism, and retributive justice, the orisa inspired new plays, poems, and art forms during the civil rights struggle of the 1960s and 1970s, and they continue to do so today. In the following excerpt from the play *The Slave Ship* (1967) by Amiri Baraka (formerly Leroi Jones), black captives invoke the orisa during the middle passage:

WOMAN 1. Oooooooooo, Obatala!
WOMAN 2. Shango!
. . . .
MAN 1. Shango, Obatala, make your lightning, beat the inside bright with paths for your people. Beat. Beat. Beat.

(Drums come up, but they are walls and floors being beaten. Chains rattled. Chains rattled. Drag the chains.)
. . . .
MAN 2. Fukwididila! Fukwididila! Fukwididila! Fuck you, Orisha!

309

God! Where you be? Where you now, Black God? Help me.
I be a strong warrior, and no woman. And I strain against these chains!
But you must help me, Orisha. Obatala![72]

The invocation of the Yoruba orisa for divine intervention in *The Slave Ship*
reverses previous dependence of enslaved and oppressed blacks on the Christian God:

O my Lord delivered Daniel
O why not deliver me too?[73]

That dependence resulted in the metaphorical expectation of a black "Moses"
to lead the disenfranchised to the Promised Land, just as the biblical Moses led
the "Children of Israel" out of Egyptian bondage.[74] The above scene from *The
Slave Ship*, therefore, has two major implications. First, it recalls the traumatic
experience of the middle passage, so that the present generation can learn from
and correct some of the social injustices of the past with a view to bettering the
future for African Americans. Second, it draws attention to the fact that the leaders of successful slave revolts (such as Haitian Toussaint L'Ouverture and Amistad's Cinque) had an abiding faith in their own ability to fight for freedom before resorting to charms, the orisa, and Vodou.[75] This point resonates in the
passage "I be a strong warrior, . . . But you must help me, Orisha. Obatala." In
other words—and as the saying goes—"God helps those who help themselves."

The playwright Barbara Ann Teer, the founder of the National Black Theater of Harlem (NBT), also involved the orisa in many of her plays. In the 1970s
she took members of her troupe to Nigeria to deepen their understanding of
African, especially Yoruba, drama. While in Nigeria members of the NBT collaborated with local dramatists.[76]

According to Teer, the orisa tradition has been a powerful instrument that
reconnects the African American playwright with his or her past, while at the
same time serving as an effective agency of inspiration and liberation:

. . . Orisha arise
I am changeless / Arise / Imperishable / Arise
By nature I am pure
Of whom shall I be afraid?
Ogun[77] bring down your mighty army, Orisha, Orisha
Free us from mental bondage, break these chains
Now move swiftly Oya[78] into our communities
Like a hurricane cut through our thought forms of pain
Uproot the negativity in our families
Fill our ghettos Obatala[79] with a new force of white light
Orisha send down your rainbow colors
Send down your rainbow sound
Shango descend like thunder
Oshun[80] bring down your heavy rain

Fill our hearts with your love and compassion
Orisha free our mind of these Western chains.[81]

Audre Lorde's 1970 poem entitled "The Winds of Orisha" makes a similar point:

... Impatient legends speak through my flesh
changing this earth's formation
spreading
I become myself an incantation
dark raucous characters
leaping back and forth across bland pages
Mother Yemaja raises her breasts to begin my labor
near water
the beautiful Oshun and I lie down together
in the heat of her body's truth
my voice comes stronger
Shango will be my brother roaring out of the sea
earth shakes our darkness
swelling into each other
warning winds announce us living
as Oya, Oya my sister my daughter
destroys the crust of the tidy beaches
and Eshu's Black laughter
turns up the neat sleeping sand.[82]

In this poem Audre Lorde finds herself undergoing a rite of passage. She has been transformed at once into a spirit medium and "an incantation," becoming an embodiment of what the Yoruba traditionally describe as "ase"—the enabling force with which the orisa manifest their power and presence that can then be harnessed for the human good or for opening new windows of opportunity for the disadvantaged.[83]

A better understanding of the history and significance of African art has enabled contemporary African American visual artists to utilize orisa images and symbols in a more meaningful way.[84] Hale Woodruff was one of the first African American visual artists to invoke Sango in his works. In 1951 he completed six murals entitled *Art of the Negro* for the Trevor-Arnett Library, Atlanta (now Clark-Atlanta) University, Atlanta, Georgia. One of the murals, "Native Forms," is dominated by a figure surmounted by a double-axe, alluding to Sango's divine presence and protective power. The figure is flanked (on the left) by dancing masks, representing spirit beings and ancestors and (on the right) by warriors carrying shields, spears, and double-weapons. Below the central "Sango" figure are representations of black artists at work and examples of ancient African art—all aimed at inspiring contemporary African American artists to strive for the same high level of creativity as their African ancestors.[85] A review of the works produced during the Black Arts movement of the 1960s and 1970s reveals different but related invocations of Sango to empower the quest for social justice. Take, for instance, the mixed media painting entitled *Sango* (1969) by Ademola Olugebefola, formerly Bedwick Thomas (Fig. 15.10). Here the artist transforms Sango's double-axe thunder wand into a female figure discharging fire from the head, as if invoking Sango's wrath (from the African side of the Atlantic) on those who maltreat or discriminate against fellow human beings. The fire atop the figure is fueled by roots deeply embedded in the female figure's body, metaphorically connecting Africa to the Americas. The painting recalls the *Ethiopian Manifesto,* published in 1829 by Robert Alexander Young, warning slave owners of divine intervention.[86]

The use of orisa motifs is more complex in Jeff Donaldson's 1971 painting entitled *Victory in the Valley of Esu* (Fig. 15.11). It features a black couple, the artist's parents, who had instilled in him right from childhood the resolve to fight for social justice, a resolve signified by the Sango ritual double-axe staff held by his father. In front of the couple is the "Black Star," a symbol of the African American quest for cultural, political, and spiritual emancipation. The eye in the center of the star mirrors the image of another black couple—Mr. and Mrs. Edwin Lexie of Washington, D.C., who had successfully challenged an arbitrary attempt by the city authorities to acquire their residential property for public use.[87] Thus the Sango ritual double-axe staff in the painting also emblematizes the Lexies' victorious struggle for equity. The eye motif, on the other hand, denotes the protective watch of Esu Elegba, the dynamic gatekeeper and the catalytic agent of fate and the crossroads.[88] Like Sango, Esu Elegba champions the cause of the oppressed, bringing help to the helpless and hope to the hopeless, providing the checks and balances crucial to the maintenance of the social order.[89]

The 1960s also witnessed the emergence of the feminist movement when women staged public protests against gender discrimination. Before then, the black female had been stereotyped as the docile Aunt Jemima, the housemaid logo for selling a popular pancake mix. Jeff Donaldson's watercolor painting *Wives of Shango* (1968) challenges this stereotype.[90] The painting features three black ladies sporting bushy "Afros" and bullet belts, recalling Oya (left), Oba (center), and Osun (right), the Yoruba goddesses of tornado, tranquility, and beauty/fertility, respectively. These Yoruba goddess are revered as dynamic female role models whose powers complement those of the male orisa. Through them, Donaldson reminds us of the contributions made by black female heroes to the African American struggle for racial and gender equality—black female heroes such as Harriet Tubman, Sojourner Truth, Maggie Walker, Rosa Parks, and Angela Davis.

Muneer Bahauddeen's public monument, entitled *Orisha Wall,* is one of the boldest sculptural invocations of the African ancestral past on the American landscape. Located on the median strip of 55th Street between Lake Park and Kenwood Avenues in Chicago, Illinois, the monument was commissioned in 1987 by Chicago's Hyde Park Chamber of Commerce. Made of concrete

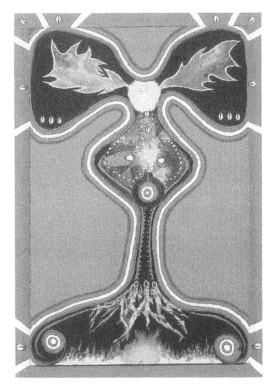

Fig. 15.10. Ademola Olugebefola (formerly
Thomas Bedwick), *Shango*, mixed media, 1969.
Private collection. Photo by Babatunde Lawal.

and multicolored tiles, it is about ten feet high and fourteen feet wide. Although
it represents six of the principal Yoruba orisa, namely, Sango (thunderstorm deity), Obatala (creativity deity), Ogun (metal and warfare deity), Esu Elegba (divine messenger), Oya (tornado goddess), and Osun (fertility and beauty goddess), the sculpture consists of only two figures, a male and female. The male
figure (in the rear), with red colors, represents Sango, the thunderstorm deity.
One side of the female figure (in the front holding a fan) has pink and reddish
colors to signify Oya, the tornado goddess. The other side of this female figure
has amber green and gold colors that allude to Osun, the fertility and beauty
goddess. Obatala, Ogun, and Esu Elegba are represented by three other colors.[91] Another public monument dedicated to Sango is a ceramic mosaic at the
110th Street Station, Lexington Avenue Subway, New York City Transit (Fig.
15.12). It is entitled *Fire: A Saturday on 110th Street*. Created by Manuel Vega
in 1996, the mosaic depicts a priest with Sango ritual staff, dancing to the in-
vigorating rhythm of bata, the sacred music of Sango. As noted earlier, bata
music featured prominently in New York's Cubop Jazz of the 1950s and 1960s.[92]

Fig. 15.11. Jeff Donaldson, *Victory in the
Valley of Eshu*, Gouache, 1971, 36" × 26".
Courtesy of the artist.

In short, by glorifying the image of the orisa in such highly urbanized and industrialized cities as Chicago and New York City, Bahauddeen and Vega proclaim their relevance to the struggle for survival in the technological age. Sango's association with fire (lightning), and, by extension, dynamic energy, resonates in these two monuments because of the emphasis on ceramic tile, which is made by firing clay.

By and large, while African American creative expression cannot be divorced from its North American ambience, the fact remains that the African ancestral legacy in the visual and performing arts has continued to nourish and revitalize it. The contribution of Yoruba aesthetics to this revitalization has been immense. It has enabled many African American artists to relate their creativity more meaningfully to individual life situations and to the social, economic, and ideological forces impacting the black experience in the United States. By digging deeper into their African past, these artists have developed a new self-confidence in their innate ability to excel and find their bearing and new identities in a technology-driven era with its increasing complexities.

Fig. 15.12. Manuel Vega, *Fire: A Saturday on 110th Street.*
Mosaic, 1996. 110th Street Station,
Lexington Avenue Subway, New York City.
Photo by Babatunde Lawal.

At the turn of the century W.E.B. Du Bois described the black American as an individual with a "double consciousness," reflecting the fact of being an African and American at the same time. In his words, that individual has "two souls, two thoughts, two unreconciled strivings; two warring ideals in one dark body."[93] The increasing adaptation of the African cultural and artistic heritage to the black experience in the United States has enabled many African American artists to take giant steps toward the reconciliation of this "double consciousness." By trying to synthesize the African with the American, these artists are beginning to forge a truly African American identity.

Notes

This chapter is a revised and much-expanded version of a public lecture entitled "African American Art: The Yoruba Connection" first given at the University of Alaska, Anchorage, 25 March 1998. I wish to thank Professor Charles E. Licka for the invitation to give the lecture. I am also grateful to Marcilene Wittmer, Thomas Larose, and Tolagbe Ogunleye for making available to me copies of their publications and unpublished conference papers on African influences on Seminole bead/patchwork and Yoruba presence in Florida. Lastly, special thanks to the anonymous readers of the preliminary draft of this chapter for their insightful comments.

1. Being a tonal language, Yoruba is normally transcribed with marks above or beneath certain consonants or vowels to facilitate pronunciation. This cannot be done in this chapter for some technical reasons. However, the author has tried as much as possible to follow the orthography commonly used in Yoruba literature and linguistics, eliminating the "h" that is often used to indicate the "sh" sound in the Anglicized transcription of such words as "Ase," "Esu," "Orisa," "Osun," "Sango," and so on. The only exception is when Anglicized transcriptions appear in quoted passages.

2. For details, see Frank Willet, *Ife in the History of West African Sculpture* (London: Thames and Hudson, 1967); G. J. Afolabi Ojo, *Yoruba Culture: A Geographical Analysis* (London: University of London Press, 1967).

3. Philip D. Curtin, *The Atlantic Slave Trade, A Census* (Madison: University of Wisconsin Press, 1969), 201–203.

4. Gwendolyn M. Hall, *Africans in Colonial Louisiana: The Development of Afro-Creole Culture in the Eighteenth Century* (Baton Rouge: Louisiana State University Press, 1992), 402–404.

5. Before the nineteenth century the subgroups that now constitute the Yoruba identified themselves by different names such as Oyo, Egba, Egbado, Ijebu, Ijesa, Ife, Ketu, and so on. The name Yoruba at first referred only to the Oyo subgroup before it was later applied to all the others who share a common language and culture.

6. Ulrich B. Phillips, *Life and Labor in the Old South* (Boston: Little, Brown, 1929), 190.

7. Michael Mullin, *Africa in America: Slave Acculturation and Resistance in the American South and the British Caribbean, 1736–1831* (Urbana: University of Illinois Press, 1992), 285–86. See also Thomas Astley, ed., *A New General Collection of Voyages and Travels*, 4 vols. (London: printed for T. Asley, 1745–47). It is necessary here to shed some light on the alleged "submissiveness" and "politeness" of the enslaved Yoruba. According to a popular Yoruba proverb, "Until you have a sword in your hand, don't confront the person who killed your father!" (*Bi owo eni ko ba te eeku ada, a ki I bere iku ti o pa baba eni*). See J. O. Ajibola, *Owe Yoruba* (Oxford: Oxford University Press, 1947), 14. In other words, diplomacy pays; if you cannot defend yourself successfully, do not challenge your adversaries, especially in antebellum North America where brutal force was used in crushing slave revolts. But in other places, as in nineteenth-century Cuba, where they were known as Lucumi and had the means to challenge the system, the Yoruba turned out to be "the most rebellious and courageous slaves." See Esteban Montejo, *The Autography of a Runaway Slave* (New York: Pantheon, 1976), 37–38; quoted in George Brandon, *Santeria from Africa to the New World: The Dead Sell Memories* (Bloomington: Indiana University Press, 1993), 57. For the contribution of Yoruba captives to slave revolts in other parts of the New World, see John H. H. Clarke, "Some Neglected Aspects of Yoruba Culture in the Americas and in the Caribbean," in *The Proceedings of the Conference on Yoruba Civilization*, ed. Isaac A. Akinjogbin and G. O. Ekemode (Ile-Ife, Nigeria: Department of History, University of Ife, 1976), 2:607–12.

8. Illustrated and discussed in Judith W. Chase, *Afro-American Art and Craft* (New York: Van Nostrand Reinhold, 1971), 52; Elisa Honig Fine, *The Afro-American Artist: A Search for Identity* (New York: Holt, Rinehart and Winston, 1973), 11; Beatrix T. Rumford and Carolyn J. Weekley, *Treasures of American Art from the Abby Aldrich Rocke-*

feller Folk Art Center (Boston: Little, Brown, 1989), 98, and plate 68; and Maria Franklin, "Early Black Spirituality and the Cultural Strategy of Protective Symbolism: Evidence from Art and Archaeology," in *African Impact on the Material Culture of the Americas: Conference Proceedings, Diggs Gallery at Winston-Salem State University,* Museum on Early Southern Decorative Arts, Winston-Salem, 30 May–2 June 1996, 9.

9. Chase, *Afro-American Art and Craft,* 52; and Rumford and Weekley, *Treasures of American Art,* 98, 104, and plate 68.

10. Rumford and Weekley, *Treasures of American Art,* 98.

11. See Darius L. Thieme, "A Descriptive Catalogue of Yoruba Musical Instruments" (Ph.D. dissertation, Catholic University of America, Washington, D.C., 1969), 14; Akin Euba, *Yoruba Drumming: The Dundun Tradition* (Bayreuth, Germany: Bayreuth African Studies Series, 1990), 56; and Oyetunji Mustapha, "A Literary Appraisal of Sakara: A Yoruba Traditional Form of Music," in *Yoruba Oral Tradition: Poetry in Music, Dance, and Drama,* ed. Wande Abimbola, 517–49 (Ile-Ife, Nigeria: Department of African Languages and Literatures, University of Ife, 1975), 518–19.

12. See, for instance, Jacqueline C. Djedje, "The Fulbe Fiddle in the Gambia: A Symbol of Identity," in *Turn Up the Volume! A Celebration of African Music,* ed. Jacqueline C. Djedje, 98–113 (Los Angeles: University of California Museum of Cultural History, 1999), 105.

13. Philip D. Curtin, "Ayuba Suleiman of Bondu," in *Africa Remembered: Narratives by West Africans from the Era of the Slave Trade,* ed. Philip D. Curtin, 17–59 (Madison: University of Wisconsin Press, 1967), 53.

14. Albert J. Raboteau, *African American Religion* (New York: Oxford University Press, 1999), 54.

15. Ibid.

16. Robert F. Thompson, "African Art in Motion," in *Art from Africa: Long Steps Never Broke a Back,* ed. Pamela McClusky, 17–60 (Princeton, N.J.: Princeton University Press, 2002), 17.

17. Darius L. Thieme, "Style in Yoruba Music," *Ibadan, A Journal Published at the University of Ibadan* 24 (1967): 37, fig. 4. Figure 15.2 of this chapter depicts a Yoruba musician playing a stringed instrument similar to the one in *Old Plantation.*

18. Illustrated in Michel Huet, *The Dances of Africa* (New York: Harry N. Abrams, 1996), 134.

19. For more information on the significance of the baby sash ("oja") among the Yoruba, see Babatunde Lawal, *The Gelede Spectacle: Art, Gender, and Social Harmony in an African Culture* (Seattle: University of Washington Press, 1996), 184–86.

20. A painting at the Mint Museum of Art, Charlotte, North Carolina, is similar in form, style, and content to the one in the Abby Aldrich Rockefeller Folk Art Center. (It is illustrated in Franklin, "Early Black Spirituality," 9.) Believed to have been executed at a later date, possibly in the early nineteenth century, the Mint Museum painting has six instead of twelve figures, performing the very same dance against the same background. The two musicians have been separated. The man dancing with the stick in the first picture now holds a piece of cloth, facing only one female dancer instead of two. In the center of the picture is a frog. The relationship between the two paintings is yet to be clarified.

21. Edward Warren, *A Doctor's Experience in Three Continents* (Baltimore: Cushings and Bailey, 1885), 200.

22. Ibid., 201–202.

23. For a survey, see Judith Bettelheim, "Jonkonnu and Other Christmas Masquer-

ades," in *Caribbean Festival Arts: Each and Every Bit of Difference*, ed. John W. Nunley and Judith Bettelheim (Seattle: University of Washington Press, 1988), 39–83.

24. For a review of the literature, see Beverly J. Robinson, "Africanisms and the Study of Folklore," in *Africanisms in American Culture*, ed. Joseph E. Holloway, 211–24 (Bloomington: Indiana University Press, 1990), 215–17. See also Winifred Kellersberger Vass, *The Bantu Speaking Heritage of the United States* (Los Angeles: Center for Afro-American Studies, University of California at Los Angeles, 1979), 110; and Marshall Stearns and Jean Stearns, *Jazz Dance: The Story of American Vernacular Dance* (New York: Da Capo, 1994), 27–29.

25. Samuel Crowther, *A Dictionary of the Yoruba Language* (London: Oxford University Press, 1950), 135.

26. The Cuban variation of juba is "yuba," as in "moyuba." The latter can be etymologized as "mo" = I; "yuba" = pay respect/homage. In the Cuban Yoruba-influenced Santería religion, it refers to the invocation to the "orisa" (Yoruba deities). See Migene González-Wippler, *The Santería Experience* (New York: Original, 1982), 40, 52. In Trinidad, the terms "juba" and "jiba" are used interchangeably by people of Yoruba ancestry to mean "homage." See Maureen Warner-Lewis, *Yoruba Songs of Trinidad with Translations* (London: Karnak House, 1994), 23, 37.

27. Candice Goucher, "African-Caribbean Metal Technology: Forging Cultural Survivals in the Atlantic World," in *African Sites: Archaeology in the Caribbean*, ed. Jay B. Haviser (Princeton, N.J.: Markus Wiener, 1998), 156.

28. Sterling Stuckey, *Slave Culture: Nationalist Theory and the Foundations of Black America* (New York: Oxford University Press, 1987), 68–69. The Fon of Dahomey were once dominated by the Yoruba and thus assimilated many aspects of Yoruba culture.

29. Dougald MacMillan, "John Kuners," *Journal of American Folk-lore* 39 (January–March 1926): 54–55.

30. Lawal, *The Gelede Spectacle*, 173, plates 6.1–6.12. Being a popular seaport, Wilmington is said to be "in close touch" with Nassau and the Bahamas (see MacMillan, "John Kuners," 55). And given the prominence of Yoruba cultural influence in the Caribbean, the Wilmington-Caribbean connection further reinforces the possibility that the dance witnessed by Edward Warren contained some Yoruba elements, even if all the dancers might not have come from only one African ethnic group.

31. Marian H. Winter, "Juba and American Minstrelsy," in *Chronicles of the American Dance*, ed. Paul Magriel (New York: Henry Holt, 1948), 40.

32. Benedict M. Ibitokun, *Dance as Ritual Drama and Entertainment in the Gelede of the Ketu-Yoruba Subgroups in West Africa* (Ile-Ife, Nigeria: Obafemi Awolowo, 1993), 105, 113. For other accounts of the Ijuba, especially the circular dance of the Efe chorus, see Peggy Harper, "The Role of the Dance in the Gelede Ceremonies of the Village of Ijio," *Odu, A Journal of West African Studies* 4 (1970): 67–94; Henry John Drewal and Margaret Thompson Drewal, *Gelede: Art and Female Power among the Yoruba* (Bloomington: Indiana University Press, 1983); and Lawal, *The Gelede Spectacle*, 118, 125.

33. For details, see Lawal, *The Gelede Spectacle*, 187–88.

34. Robert Farris Thompson, "Recapturing Heaven's Glamour: Afro-Caribbean Festivalizing Arts," in *Caribbean Festival Arts: Each and Every Bit of Difference*, ed. John W. Nunley and Judith Bettelheim (Seattle: University of Washington Press, 1988), 20. See also Michael A. Gomez, *Exchanging Our Country Marks: The Transformation of African Identities in the Colonial and Antebellum South* (Chapel Hill: University of North Carolina Press, 1998), 55.

35. In the 1840s William Henry Lane, from Providence, Rhode Island, became the most popular juba dancer in the United States and was nicknamed "Master Juba." In 1846 he traveled to London where he performed before packed halls. He died in London in 1852. See Edward Thorpe, *Black Dance* (Woodstock, N.Y.: Overlook, 1990), 42–44.

36. Other African-derived but Creolized dances performed by slaves included the Ring Shout, Buzzard Lope, Bamboula, Pas-ma-la, and Calenda. For a survey, see Richard A. Long, *The Black Tradition in American Dance* (New York: Rizzoli, 1989); Thorpe, *Black Dance*; and Langston Hughes and Milton Meltzer, *Black Magic: A Pictorial History of the African American in the Performing Arts* (New York: Da Capo, 1990). See also Babatunde Lawal, "The African Heritage of African American Art and Performance," in *Black Theatre: Ritual Performance in the African Diaspora*, ed. Paul C. Harrison, Victor L. Walker, and Gus Edwards (Philadelphia: Temple University Press, 2002), 45–47.

37. John M. Vlach, *The Afro-American Tradition in the Decorative Arts* (Athens: University of Georgia Press, 1980), 125–26.

38. Ibid.; and idem, "The Shotgun House: An African Architectural Legacy, Part II," *Pioneer America* 8, no. 1 (1976): 47–56, 57–60. See also Sharon F. Patton, *African-American Art* (New York: Oxford University Press, 1998), p. 59.

39. Vlach, *The Afro-American Tradition*, 125.

40. Philip D. Curtin, *The Atlantic Slave Trade: A Census* (Madison: University of Wisonsin Press, 1969), 192–96, 201–202, 227.

41. For more on Yoruba architecture, see G. J. Afolabi Ojo, *Yoruba Culture: A Geographical Analysis* (London: University of London Press, 1966); Z. R. Dmochowski, *An Introduction to Nigerian Traditional Architecture* (London: Ethnographica [in association with the National Commission for Museums and Monuments], 1990), vol. 2; and John M. Vlach, "The Affecting Architecture of the Yoruba," *African Arts* 10, no. 1 (1976): 48–53.

42. John M. Vlach, *By the Work of Their Hands: Studies in Afro-American Folklife* (Charlottesville: University of Virginia Press, 1991), 207.

43. Ibid.

44. This term derives from the Yoruba "oluku mi," meaning "my friend or associate."

45. See Richard L. Hall, "African Religious Retentions in Florida," in *Africanisms in American Cultures*, ed. Joseph E. Holloway (Bloomington: Indiana University Press, 1990), 103. For other cases, see Dorothy Dodd, "The Schooner Emperor: An Incident of the Illegal Trade in Florida," *Florida Historical Quarterly* 13 (January 1935): 117–28.

46. See Hall, "African Religious Retentions in Florida," 103.

47. Ibid; quoting Fredrika Bremer, *The Homes of the New World: Impressions of America*, trans. from the Swedish by Mary Howitt (London: Arthur Hall, Virtle, 1853), 289–90.

In the 1830s and 1840s there were sharp disagreements between free blacks in North America as to whether to participate in the "Back to Africa" program of the white-controlled American Colonization Society that encouraged the resettlement of free blacks in Liberia. Dr. Martin Robison Delany, the famous black medical doctor and civil rights activist, was one of those who opposed the program on the grounds that it had a hidden agenda aimed at depriving the enslaved blacks of the informed and dynamic leadership required to set them free. He later changed his mind partly because of the excruciating hardships encountered by many free blacks and partly after reading, among other works, Reverend Thomas J. Bowen's *Adventures and Missionary Labors . . . in the Interior of Africa from 1849 to 1856*, released in 1857 by the Southern Baptist Publication Society, Charleston. In it, Reverend Bowen gave an impressive account of his missionary work among the Yoruba, thus persuading Dr. Delany to support the idea of a possible immigration to Africa. He visited Yorubaland in 1859 and acquired parcels of land on behalf of the National Emigration Convention of Colored Men (NECCM). Chances are that the choice of Yorubaland as one of the possible sites for resettling American blacks might also have been influenced by the presence of many Yoruba-born slaves and free blacks in North America at the time. In fact, there is a rumor that Dr. Delany's maternal grandfather was known as "Shango," implying that he was a Yoruba prince from Oyo (see Victor Ullman, *Martin Delany: The Beginnings of Black Nationalism* [Boston: Beacon, 1971], 4). At any rate, the NECCM's project was later overtaken by the American Civil War (1861–1865) during which Dr. Delany served as an army major and surgeon. For more information on the NECCM's settlement project, see Martin R. Delany, *Official Report of the Niger Valley Exploring Party* (New York: Thomas Hamilton, 1861); and Robert Campbell, *Pilgrimage to My Motherland: An Account of a Journey among the Egba and Yorubas of Central Africa* (Philadelphia, 1861; privately published).

48. George W. Cable, *The Grandissimes* (New York: Sagamore, 1898), 85, 167; quoted in Melville J. Herskovits, *The Myth of the Negro Past* (Boston: Beacon, 1958 [1941]), 246. An image of Esu Elegba from New Orleans is illustrated in Jim Haskins, *Voodoo and Hoodoo: The Craft as Revealed by Traditional Practitioners* (New York: Scarborough House, 1978), 105.

49. Patton, *African American Art*, p. 59.

50. Ibid.

51. A carved drum seized from slaves in colonial Virginia in the seventeenth century is in the Akan style, while the so-called Afro-Carolinian and Afro-Georgian face vessels display physiognomic features that recall the "minkisi" carved figures of the Kongo. Other examples include carved altar figures, spoons, and walking sticks with snake motifs. For illustrations, see *Georgia Writers' Project, Drums and Shadows: Survival Studies among the Georgia Coastal Negroes* (Athens: University of Georgia Press, 1940), plates I–IV; and Vlach, *The Afro-American Tradition in Decorative Arts*. Many aspects of the African style seem to have survived in African American vernacular or self-taught art. For details, see Babatunde Lawal, "African Roots, American Branches: Tradition and Transformation in African American Self-Taught Art," in *Souls Grown Deep: African American Vernacular Art from the South*, ed. William Arnett and Paul Arnett (Atlanta: Tinwood Books, in association with the Schomburg Center for Research in Black Cultures, 2000), 30– 49.

52. See Tolagbe Ogunleye, "The Self-Emancipated Africans of Florida: Pan-African Nationalists in the 'New World,'" *Journal of Black Studies* 27, no. 1 (1996): 27; and Daniel F. Littlefield, *Africans and Seminoles: From Removal to Emancipation* (Westport, Conn.: Greenwood, 1977).

53. However, these shoulder bags are decorated with uniquely American Indian designs, though the adoption of European beading techniques is apparent.

54. See Dorothy Downs, *Art of the Florida Seminoles and Miccosukee Indians* (Gainesville: University Press of Florida, 1995), 155–56; Marciline Wittmer, "African Influences on Seminole Indian Patchwork," *Southeastern College Art Conference Review* 11 (1989): 269–75; Dorothy Downs, "Possible African Influence on the Art of the

Florida Seminoles," in *African Impact on the Material Culture of the Americas: Conference Proceedings, Diggs Gallery at Winston-Salem State University* (Winston-Salem: Museum of Early Southern Decorative Arts, 1996): 1–10; and Thomas Larose, "African Influence on Seminole Beadwork," paper presented at the Twelfth Triennial Symposium of the Arts Council of the African Studies Association, St. Thomas, U.S. Virgin Islands, 25–29 April 2001.

55. See Larose, "African Influences on Seminole Beadwork," quoting Curtin, *The Atlantic Slave Trade*, 235– 64.

56. Illustrated and discussed in Downs, *Art of the Florida Seminoles and Miccosukee Indians*, 166 – 67, and color plate 24. Also discussed in Larose, "African Influences on Seminoles Beadwork."

57. These comparisons are well made in Thomas Larose's unpublished conference paper.

58. Larose, "African Influences on Seminole Beadwork," 6–7; citing Curtin, *The Atlantic Slave Trade*, 235– 64. See also Tolagbe M. Ogunleye, "*Aroko* and *Ogede:* Yoruba Arts as Resistance to Enslavement Stratagems in Florida in the 18th and 19th Centuries," paper presented at the Conference on Yoruba Culture and Ethics held at the University of California, Los Angeles, February 1999.

59. For illustrations, see Frank Willett, *Ife in the History of West African Art* (London: Thames and Hudson, 1967); William Fagg, *Yoruba Beadwork* (New York: Rizzoli, 1980); and Henry J. Drewal and John Mason, *Beads, Body, and Soul: Art and Light in the Yoruba Universe* (Los Angeles: Fowler Museum of Cultural History, 1998).

60. Alain Locke, "The Legacy of the Ancestral Arts," in *The New Negro*, ed. Alain Locke (New York: Atheneum, 1968), 254– 67.

61. Freda M. Scott, "*The Star of Ethiopia:* A Contribution toward the Development of Black Drama and Theatre in the Harlem Renaissance," in *The Harlem Renaissance: Revaluations*, ed. Singh Amritjit, William S. Shiver, and Stanley Brodwin (New York: Garland, 1989), 259.

62. Marta Moreno Vega, "The Yoruba Orisha Tradition Comes to New York," *African American Review* 29, no. 2 (1995): 210–12. Pancho Mora (whose Yoruba name is Ifa Morote) is widely believed to be the first Afro-Cuban to be publicly associated with orisa worship in the United States. He arrived in 1946. See George Brandon, *Santeria from Africa to the New World: The Dead Sell Memories* (Bloomington: Indiana University Press, 1993), 106.

63. Robert F. Thompson, "The Three Warriors: Atlantic Altars of Esu, Ogun, and Osoosi," in *The Yoruba Artist: New Theoretical Perspectives on African Art*, ed. Rowland Abiodun, Henry Drewal, and John Pemberton (Washington, D.C.: Smithsonian Institution Press, 1994), 227.

64. Dizzy Gillespie (with Al Fraser), *To Be, or Not to Bop* (Garden City, N.Y.: Doubleday, 1979), 319; quoted in Vega, "The Yoruba Orisha Tradition Comes to New York," 202–203.

65. Vega, "The Yoruba Orisha Tradition Comes to New York," 202–203.

66. Long, *The Black Tradition in American Dance*, 72–73. Note that in 1936, however, Momodu Johnson and Norman Coker, two Yoruba residents of New York, staged a play in the city called *Bassa Moona* (Land of love). Sponsored by the Federal Theatre Project, the play was set in Lagos, Nigeria, and some of the actors spoke Yoruba. See K. K. Martin, "America's First African Dance Theatre," *Odu: A Journal of West African Studies*, n.s. 11 (January 1975): 123–24.

67. Carl M. Hunt, *Oyotunji Village: The Yoruba Movement in America* (Washington, D.C.: University Press of America, 1979), 28.

68. Mikelle Smith Omari, "Completing the Circle: Notes on African Art, Society, and Religion in Oyotunji, South Carolina," *African Arts* 24, no. 3 (1991): 67.

69. Ibid.

70. See, for example, John Mason, "Yoruba Beadwork in the Americas," in *Beads, Body and Soul: Art and Light in the Yoruba Universe*, ed. Henry J. Drewal and John Mason (Los Angeles: University of California Fowler Museum of Cultural History, 1998), 87–177.

71. John Mason, *Olookun: Owners of Rivers and Seas* (New York: Yoruba Theological Archministry, 1996), 70.

72. Amiri Baraka (Leroi Jones), *The Motion of History, and Other Plays* (New York: William Morrow, 1978), 133–34.

73. Raboteau, *African American Religion*, 53. For a collection of African American prayers from the earliest period to the 1990s, see James M. Washington, ed., *Conversations with God: Two Centuries of Prayers by African Americans* (New York: HarperCollins, 1994).

74. Hence the popular slave spiritual: "Canaan land is the land for me / And let God's Saints come in / There was a wicked man / He kept them children in Egypt land / Canaan land is the land for me / And let God's saints come in / God did say to Moses one day / Say, Moses, go to Egyptland / And tell him to let my people go / Canaan land is the land for me / And let God's saints come in." See Albert J. Raboteau, "African-Americans, Exodus, and the American Israel," in *African American Christianity*, ed. Paul E. Johnson (Berkeley: University of California Press, 1994), 1. See also Babatunde Lawal, "Anticipating Ethiopia's Rise to Glory: Rereading James Hampton's *Throne of the Third Heaven of the Nations Millennium General Assembly*," in *Souls Grown Deep: African American Vernacular Art of the South*, ed. William Arnett and Paul Arnett, 2 vols. (Atlanta: Tinwood, 2001), 2:98–103.

75. Toussaint L'Ouverture led the slave revolt that resulted in Haitian independence in 1804. In 1839 Cinque, whose African name was Sengbe Pieh, spearheaded the successful mutiny aboard the Spanish slave ship *Amistad* during its voyage from Havana to Puerto Principe in Cuba. Cinque and his colleagues were enslaved in Sierra Leone and brought to Havana in a different ship. After being sold, they were transferred to the *Amistad*.

76. Mance Williams, *Black Theatre in the 1960s and 1970s: A Historical-Critical Analysis of the Movement* (Wesport, Conn.: Greenwood, 1985), 52–53

77. Ogun is the deity of iron tools, weapons, and warfare.

78. Oya is the tornado goddess.

79. Obatala is the creativity deity.

80. Osun is the goddess of fertility and beauty.

81. Barbara Ann Teer, "The African American Experience: Needed a New Mythology," in *Proceedings of the First World Conference on Orisa Tradition, Ile-Ife, Nigeria, 1–7 June 1981* (Ile-Ife, Nigeria: Department of African Languages and Literatures, University of Ife, 1981), 210, 235–36.

82. Audre Lorde, *Undersong: Chosen Poems Old and New*, rev. ed. (New York: Norton, 1992), 93.

83. For a discussion of orisa motifs in the works of the famous African American

playwright and Pulitzer Prize winner August Wilson, see Sandra Richards, "Yoruba Gods on the American Stage: August Wilson's 'Joe Turner's Come and Gone,'" *Research in African Literatures* 30, no. 4 (1999): 93–105.

84. African American artists who visited Yorubaland between the 1950s and 1970s include Elton Fax, John Biggers, Jacob Lawrence, James Lewis, Carrol Sims, Lois Mailou Jones, David C. Driskell, Jeff Donaldson, and Charles Searles. Since then, several others have been there for longer periods, doing fieldwork or serving as visiting professors in educational institutions.

85. M. Akua McDaniel, "Reexamining Hale Woodruff's Talladega College and Atlanta University Murals," *International Review of African American Art* 12, no. 4 (1995): 5–17. One of the preliminary sketches for "Native Forms," now in the Bellevue Gallery, Trenton, New Jersey, is dated 1941. See Halima Taha, *Collecting African American Art: Works on Paper and Canvas* (New York: Crown, 1998), 146.

86. Robert A. Young, *The Ethiopian Manifesto: Issued in Defense of the Black Man's Rights in the Scale of Universal Freedom* (New York: Robert A. Young, 1829); cited in Wilson J. Moses, ed., *Classical Black Nationalism: From the American Revolution to Marcus Garvey* (New York: New York University Press, 1996), 60–67.

87. See Moyo Okediji, *The Shattered Gourd: Yoruba Forms in Twentieth Century American Art* (Seattle: University of Washington Press, 2003), 104, 192 n. 31.

88. For more on Esu, see John Pemberton, "Eshu-Elegba: The Yoruba Trickster God," *African Arts* 9, no. 1 (1975): 20–27, 66–70, 90–91; and Babatunde Lawal, "Aworan: The Self and Its Metaphysical Other in Yoruba Art," *The Art Bulletin: A Quarterly Published by the College Art Association* 83, no. 3 (2001): 501–502.

89. For the implications of Esu Elegba in African American literature, see Henry L. Gates, *The Signifying Monkey: A Theory of Afro-American Literary Criticism* (New York: Oxford University Press, 1988); and Femi Euba, "Legba and the Politics of Metaphysics: The Trickster in Black Drama," in *Black Theater: Ritual Performance in the African Diaspora*, ed. Paul C. Harrison, Victor L. Walker, and Gus Edwards (Philadelphia: Temple University Press, 2002), 167–80.

90. For an illustration, see Kay Brown, "The Emergence of Black Women Artists: The 1970s, New York," *The International Review of African American Art* 15, no. 1 (1998): 52.

91. For more details, see Mark Glinski, "Orisha Wall," *The International Review of African American Art* 9, no. 3 (1991): 33–47.

92. It is pertinent at this juncture to mention the contributions to African American music by Yoruba musicians such as Babatunde Olatunji, Fela Anikulapo-Kuti, and Solomon Ilori. The famous jazz tenor saxophonist John Coltrane was a close friend of Babatunde Olatunji, who had a cultural center in Harlem, New York, in the 1960s. John Coltrane visited the cultural center and interacted closely with Olatunji, seeking inspiration from his music. See Richard Turner, "John Coltrane: A Biographical Sketch," *The Black Perspective in Music* 3, no. 1 (1975): 10. Fela visited the United States several times in the 1960s and 1970s, collaborating with eminent jazz musicians such as Roy Ayres, who also visited Nigeria and played with Fela in his nightclub, "Kalakuta Republic." In the 1970s Solomon Ilori led an orchestra in the United States that popularized Yoruba music. The orchestra consisted of Yoruba and African American musicians. See John S. Roberts, *Black Music of Two Worlds: African, Caribbean, Latin, and African American Traditions*, 2nd rev. ed. (London: Schirmer, 1998), 255–56;

Michael E. Veal, *Fela: The Life and Times of an African Musical Icon* (Philadelphia: Temple University Press, 2000), 258–59; and Trevor Schoonmaker, ed., *Black President: The Art and Legacy of Fela Anikulapo Kuti* (New York: New Museum of Contemporary Art, 2003).

93. William E. B. Du Bois, *The Souls of Black Folk* (Greenwich, Conn.: Fawcett, 1903), 3.

CHAPTER SIXTEEN

"Yorubaisms" in African American "Speech" Patterns

Augustine H. Agwuele

> Some of these thoughts of mine have seen the light before in other guises.
>
> —*W.E.B. Du Bois*

The collective intellect, achievement, and memory of any civilization or group of people can only be shared and transmitted from one generation to the other through the superlative capacity of mankind to hear and make those meaningful sounds that make up a language. When people especially from aural civilization are displaced, they carry their culture with them in their languages and unfold them in the new place. Thus the language, in a sense, is a summary of their communal and individual consciousness and subconsciousness, the synopsis of their existence and experience, the accomplishment of the previous generations, their values, and their worldview, which by nature are irrepressible. Yoruba in the diaspora bequeaths to the continent of America a rich linguistic legacy that permeates many facets of the society. This legacy is the fulcrum and the cornerstone, to a greater or lesser extent, of many (linguistic) practices found among African descendants of America both historically and currently.

This chapter explicates the linguistic legacy of Yoruba in the Americas from two perspectives: by enumerating some Yoruba linguistic features found in some languages of America[1] and by demonstrating how some of these linguistic features impact sections of American social life. The final section of the chapter is a tentative report from an ongoing ethnographic study of a Yoruba community based in Austin, Texas. Brief mention is made of some of the ways Yoruba language is employed by these African American Yoruba who are re-creating a Yoruba lifestyle in the New World. The chapter notes in passing that the present-day "American Yoruba" profit from greater contact with Nigerian Yoruba and "baba-alawos" (priests), and from pilgrimages and trainings in Yorubaland. Finally, the chapter submits that contemporary "American Yoruba" is a syncretism of religion and lifestyle that is responsible for the slowly emerging speech pattern that Aina Olomo, a Yoruba priestess, has termed "Yorubabonics."

Background

Several groups of people and cultures were taken from Africa and brought to the Americas. Many of these transplanted people have participated in shaping the Americas. Similar to other people and cultures like the Congos, East Africans, or indentured servants from Great Britain, Yoruba cultural practices, traditional religion, and language have exerted profound influences in the New World. Yoruba is one of the most researched subjects among many diaspora scholars. It remains one of the most widely taught African languages in American universities, and one of the most versatile cultural and belief systems found in the Western world. Yoruba language, religion, and culture are prominent in African studies across America.[2] The Reverend Samuel Johnson, in 1921, characterized the West African Yoruba as a nation.[3] According to Matory, since the nineteenth century the Yoruba nation has risen above all other Afro-Latin nations: "it is preeminent in size, wealth, grandeur, and international prestige, it is studied, written about, and imitated far more than any other, not only by believers but by anthropologists, art historians, novelists, and literary critics."[4]

The "nation" of Yoruba is an umbrella term that defines people of different countries outside Africa who profess the religion of divinities cum divination and ancestral worship, and who accept Yorubaland as their provenance. These include the Xango, Umbanda, and Candomblé worshipers in Brazil; the Lucumí and Santería worshipers in Cuba, Trinidad, and the United States; and the Nagôs of Haiti. The nationhood consists of shared religious persuasion, the mode of worship, which often includes trance, sacrifice, divination, and the idea of "ori" [spiritual head] mutual ancestors, a shared history, and a common language, namely, Yoruba, and recently "Yorubabonics."

Several factors responsible for the dominance of Yoruba have been identified in the literature. These include their numerical strength at transplantation to America, their resilience and tenacity in preserving their cultural heritage in spite of the separation from their homeland, and the cruel fate they were exposed to in the Americas. For instance, the Yoruba were considered one of the chief tribal groupings in Trinidad, according to the testimony of Joseph Lewis to the Royal Franchise Commission in 1888 and according to Garcia-Zamor,[5] and they are the most influential group in Brazil and Cuba. Some scholars have argued that they possessed a more organized priesthood with a more highly evolved and therefore more complex mythology of Yoruba religious practice. Others posited that the enslaved Yoruba were of high social status that included priests who were conscious of their institutions and were firmly attached to the precepts of their religion.[6] Although there is no consensus among scholars on this issue, one cannot overlook an important factor, that is, their unity and social status, which may have especially, and uniquely, positioned them to be influential.

Their unity and personal traits as a distinct ethnic and cultural group endeared the Yoruba to their slave owners. Commenting on them, De Verteuil said, "the Yarrabas deserve particular notice, . . . they are a fine race . . . their houses neat, comfortable and kept in perfect order within. In character they are generally honest, and in disposition proud, and even haughty." According to Gamble in 1910, "The Yarrabas dwell in cluster, co-operate with one another . . . and are apt in learning languages,"[7] and, most important, as a result of these qualities, and the fact that they were considered less rebellious than other races, it is not surprising that they were the preferred ethnic group as domestic servants and artisans.[8] Hence their daily contact with the Europeans placed them in a favorable position, as the closest or probably the first recipients of European languages, to imprint the form of speech that developed within the slave community, which perhaps is the precursor to contemporary African American languages,[9] with unmistakable phonological and syntactical structure of their native tongue. Hence it follows that the Yoruba language likely played a decisive role in shaping the development of early slavery speech and culture, which invariably continued to some degree and in various forms in the Americas of today. This chapter offers some linguistic and cultural practices found within mainstream American culture that are probably the result of Yoruba influence.

Early Slavery Condition / Interaction

The new social network and linguistics system that were forged through the macro-institutional interaction as found within each plantation (Plantation Creole) and the micro-institutional interaction between the Africans and the Europeans (West African Coast) resulted in a unique linguistic and social system that bears, to a varying extent, aspects of the many West African cultures. Much as it is reasonable to argue that only those African habits that are prevalent and common to all the groups have the greatest chance of survival in the New World, it is not altogether difficult to note, however, that certain groups will exert greater influence than others. The Yoruba, as one of the dominant groups, indisputably play a considerable role in the linguistic legacy of Africa to the present Americas. This chapter, then, not only accepts and leans on the extensive work of such scholars as Frances Herskovits, Lorenzo D. Turner, and Ian Hancock, among many, but shares their conviction that considerable elements of Africanisms, through slavery, are retained and continued in several aspects of the lives of African Americans, in spite of their acculturation. Although this chapter focuses on the influence of Yoruba (Yorubaisms) in particular, it nevertheless implicates African influence in general.

For this exposition, this chapter maintains that Africanisms, to quote the *American Heritage Dictionary*, are "a characteristically African cultural feature, such as a belief or custom. 2. A linguistic feature of an African language occurring in a non-African language."[10] We expect Africanisms to continue in the various languages of African Americans, even if only out of one simple conviction: that, except for complete annihilation, no amount of repression, enslavement, or punishment is enough to cause any group of people socially and geographically displaced to completely lose their language. Some basic features of their language will survive, regardless of the extent of syncretism with other languages. The languages of continental America evince some non-European features that have considerable affinity with West African languages, including Yoruba. This affinity transcends chance occurrence, leaving the antagonist with the onerous task of disproving the West African roots of these features.

More evidence for accepting the survival of Africanisms in America are the common but peculiar traits and characteristics found in the speech of the black communities across America. Scholars have examined the speech forms of some communities that became homes to dispersed slaves, such as Liberia, Sierra Leone, South America, the Caribbean, and Canada, and found them to share basic linguistic elements. Some of these shared elements are peculiar features of African American vernacular English that various researchers have identified as having African roots. Essentially my position in this chapter is that there are multifarious influences on the language and culture of America, and although it might be difficult to point to any one particular all-influential source, a denial of the participation of Yoruba, given its advantageous position, would appear strange in the face of the more-than-chance resemblances between the linguistic system of Yoruba and those of the Atlantic Creoles and African American languages and practices, including African American English. What follows are examples in support of this assertion.

Fragments of Yoruba Language in the Americas

Yoruba is no longer a language of communication in most parts of America. In Trinidad, Tobago, Cuba, Brazil, and the United States, the use of the Yoruba language, or whatever remains of it, is largely confined to special purposes, one of them religious activities. Nevertheless, fragments of the Yoruba language have survived in the Americas. There are some dying pockets of speakers in Jamaica, Trinidad, Brazil, and Cuba. In these cases the phonology and structural forms of the Yoruba language are preserved, the grammar simplified, and the lexicon largely reduced, since it is no longer actively used and acquired as a first language by children.

Here I turn to some of those Yoruba traits that are observed in the forms of speech found in the Americas. Examples are taken from the English-speaking Americas to allow for proper comparison with the form of English found among the Nigerian Yoruba. The scholar Martha Baudet, based on her analysis of structural parallels found in four West African languages (Twi, Ewe, Yoruba, and Igbo), concluded that "there [are] considerable similarities in syntactic patterns between the Caribbean Creoles and West African languages, and substantial support is given to the hypothesis that Creole is expected to exhibit those grammatical features common to all languages that provided grammatical input."[11] Given this, let us consider evidence found in the phonetics.

Phonetics is that branch of linguistics that studies human speech sounds. It seeks to identify what these sounds are and how they form patterns, and to formulate general laws concerning the production and perception of these sounds. The following examples from the phonetics of some languages of the Americas show their relatedness to, and affirm, their African / Yoruba influences.

Jamaican Creole (JC) replaces fricatives (sounds like f, s, v, and th) of English-based lexical items with either stop consonants or affricated stops. Thus $[\theta] > [t]$: "nothing" becomes "notin," "method" becomes "metod"; $[ð] > [d]$: for instance, "father" becomes "fada," "them" becomes "dem," and "there" is pronounced "dere"; and occasionally [s] or [ʃ] interchanges in replacing [t ʃ]: "which" or "wish" becomes "wis." The phones that are replaced correspond to those absent in the West African substrates, including Yoruba and Twi, and the pattern of replacement tallies with what obtains in West African English-based Pidgins and Creoles.[12]

The oral vowel systems of most African American speech forms, that is, Saramaccan, Jamaican, Guyanese, and Gullah, are similar. They mostly consist of seven vowels, with a back-front distinction rather than a three-way distinction with a central vowel. When compared to the vowel system of Yoruba, a greater affinity not found in the various colonial forms of English during their emergence becomes apparent.[13]

Yoruba		Gullah	
i	u	i	u
e	o	e	o
ɛ	ɔ	ɛ	ɔ
a		a	

In addition to these there are nasal vowels such as ĩ, ã, and ũ.

Phonology, similar to phonetics, is the science of speech sounds. It deals with the permissible arrangement of speech sounds and their interactions in a language. What follows is an illustration of some phonological features of American languages that are owing to Yoruba influence. An essential and distinguishing characteristic of African American speech is its tonal contours that owe directly to Africa if not to Yoruba. Whereas English and other European languages are classified as intonational languages, Yoruba and African American languages make use of tone to mark semantic difference. For instance, depending on the tone, the negation particle "ko" (not) as used in the phrase "ko lo" (not go) could either mean "she/he did not go" or "let him/her go" or "moved away" (residency). The use of tone to create changes in meaning is absent in European languages of the Americas, yet it permeates such languages as Saramaccan, Jamaican, Guyanese, and Trinidadian, among others, spoken, for instance, by African descendants:

"dem kya kuk"   "they can cook"
"dem kya kuk"   "they can't cook"[14]

The tones found in African American languages are both lexical and grammatical, and are present to varying degrees. Suzanne Sylvain reported grammatical tone for Haiti,[15] and Carter reported two tones for Trinidad and Guyanese.[16] Jamaica has three tonal systems: high, low, and mid-tone. Saramaccan has two lexical tones, high and low, as well as contour tones that co-occur with vowel length when there is a shift of pitch through the duration of the vowel length.[17] Yoruba, proposed here as the source of the tones in these languages, has three tones analogous to Jamaican. The Yoruba tones function similarly to the Haitian, Trinidadian, Saramaccan, and Guyanese tones. Again, the argument is that as long as these tonal traits, otherwise not attested in European speech forms, are specifically African, they are part of Yoruba's influence on the American languages.

Another vestige of Yoruba found in the Americas has to do with the syllable shape. The peculiar and predominant (C) VCV,[18] that is, open syllable structure, or one closed by a nasal consonant, and the lack of consonant cluster other than those that are nasal + stop clearly are traceable to the Kwa language family to which Yoruba belongs. The avoidance of consonant cluster, especially in word initial and word final syllable, must have resulted from the efforts of the enslaved Africans to impose their own phonology on the various European languages that were dominant in the various plantations to which they were transplanted. For instance, a close examination of Yoruba speakers of English and of Pidgin English in Nigeria reveals that closed syllable structures are avoided. Clusters of consonants are either broken up through epenthesis or deletion. For instance, we have "buredi" and "fulawa" for bread and flower, and "srongi" / "siron(gi)" for strong. Lisa Green, in her discussion of consonant cluster reduction for African American English (AAE), gave the following examples: "tes" (test), "des" (desk), "han" (hand), and "contac" (contact), and noted that, for

Africologists who lean toward West African origins of AAE, "speakers have such pronunciations, not because the final consonant sound is deleted in some environments, but because the languages from which AAE descended do not have final consonant clusters."[19] This same pattern is attested in Jamaican, Saramaccan, and Gullah, among others. The argument here is that the structural discrepancy vis-à-vis European languages simply attests to the influence of the substrates (Yoruba, among others), if not a direct retention of the structure of the substrates.

Beyond these mere surface equivalences, Alleyne has shown that there exists a form restructuring of English and other words in Afro-American dialects, in accordance with a basic (C) V structure that obeys the rules of vowel harmony as found in West Africa languages.[20] The operation of vowel harmony in Saramaccan and Sranan is modeled after the rules of the Yoruba vowel system. Thus we have a prevalent system where tense and lax vowels do not co-occur. The phonetic and phonological features mentioned above are pervasive and are either specific or general to many of the languages of the West Indies, Latin America, and some of North America.

Syntax has to do with the subconscious but active grammar in the mind of any speaker through which they construct correct and acceptable sentences within their linguistic community. Consider the use of "dem" associative as plural marker. This practice especially prevalent in Caribbean English–based Creole parallels similar usage among Nigerian Yoruba speakers and speakers of West African Pidgin English. Using Nigerian Pidgin English (NPE) to exemplify West African Pidgin English, one divides speakers according to their level of education and place of residence.[21] This division owes to the lexicon of the speakers and the innovation in their speech. Consider plurality, for example; generally nouns appear in their singular or bare forms, with plurality designated morphosyntactically or pragmatically. The most common morphosyntactical form of plural marking is the use of "dem" associative. This occurs in Jamaican and Gullah postnominally, for example, "luku o, one tausand soja$_i$, dem$_i$ dey kom"[22] (look, one thousand soldiers are coming), and prepositionally in Saramaccan and Sranan, for example, "dem$_i$ pikin$_i$ dey kom" (the children are coming). Both versions occur in NPE, Krio, and Guyanese. The point here is that speakers of forms of English with Yoruba influence do not mark plural with "s," so phrases like "the pikins" or "one thousand soldiers" are rare borrowings or recent innovations.

Attested innovations result from infiltration or the borrowing of "s" plural marker from Standard English by educated speakers. Such usage then finds its way into the syntax; however, where it occurs, it is accompanied by a lack of concord between the verb and the object, hence one hears a sentence such as "The people / the Children / We was home," which is the pattern that appears in Yoruba.

Another Yoruba syntactic feature found in the Americas is the use of non-gender third-person singular pronouns (him or her) and the use of "am" or

"-um" for the third person regardless of gender and number. For instance, "a gi am im book" (I give him / her their / his / her book) or "a gi am book" (I give him / her the books). Note again the lack of plural for "book" and the absence of the definite article.

There is also the use of the undifferentiated Creole pronoun "him, dem, and me," undifferentiated in that these same pronominal forms are employed to show subject, object, and sometimes possession. For instance, in "dem dey house" (they are at home), "dem" is used as the subject; in "dat na dem book" (that is/are their book[s]), "dem" occurs as possessor; and in "him/me talk say" (He/I said), him/me occur as subject.

There is also the use of "bin" for marking an action that is in the past without a complete differentiation between perfect and past. Consider the following:

JMC: We ben a nyam-an' we a drink, too
SRA: We ben de nyang-en' we de dringe, too.
WAP: We bin de chop-an' we de dring, too.[23]

Finally, there are some choice of word forms and sentence constructions that are found in African American speech that would sound rather strange to English ears, which, however, mirror perfectly their equivalent rendition in Yoruba; for instance, "I come see say" (I came to realize, or it dawned on me) is a word-for-word translation of the Yoruba sentence "mo wa ri wipe" (I come see say). Another example is the Yoruba phrase "mo wa lati ri," which occurs in its literal form in Afro-American English, for example, in Gullah as "I come for to see" (I came in order to see). The Gullah and Jamaican Creole sentence "go bring am come" could have only stemmed from the Yoruba syntax "lo mu u wa." These examples are made to substantiate the point that it takes an African influence, in general, and a Yoruba one, in particular, to generate such syntax.

Further illustration of the influence of Yoruba includes serialization of verbs and events. Serial verbs refer to the use of more than one verb to express complex events that might require only one verb in standard American English; essentially there is a sequence of verbs without any overt element connecting them. The verbs in a serial construction share a common subject in the surface structure, and the second verb furthers the intention of the first. For instance, "o ba mi se ere" ([s]he meet / aid / support me make game). In standard English, the sentence reads "(s)he played with me." Constructions of this kind, that is, where events are broken into their narrative components, are found in Ebonics, Jamaican, Gullah, Sranan, and other African American speech patterns. Consider the following examples:

"I hear tell you went home." (Ebonics)[24]
"I hear that you went home."
"An di people gadda roun tune een to er soun." (Jamaican)
"And the people gathered round and tuned in to her sound."

"Dɛm də caəm ɟi dɪ ɲaɲ pipl." (Gullah)
"They carry it to [literally, give] the young people."[25]

Underlying these examples is the same narrative style. The speaker describes each action that makes up the event, using one verb at a time. The underlying assumption of an utterance like "we played together" is made explicit in the Yoruba sentence "(S)he joined me, (s)he played, with me." Another example of a serial construction is the following:

"Yu a man dat e pai dji." (That man is paying for you.)
However, the literal translation is as follows:
"You, that man is paying give."[26]

Lastly, with respect to comparative constructions, Baudet gave the following examples to illustrate similarities among the Creoles and West African languages:

Yoruba	loye ju mi lo
	Intelligent surpass (ju . . . lo) me
	"more intelligent than I"
Gullah	tɒl pas mi
	"taller than I"
Martinican Creole	grã pase fĩ mwẽ
	"older than my girl"
Sranan	pasá tén lítri
	"more than ten liters"[27]

The few syntactic features pointed out above follow the general line of argumentation that this chapter adopts; that is, to the extent that these features, as well as others mentioned throughout the chapter, are specific to those languages that are identified with the speech of African Americans regardless of their lexifier languages, and to the extent that these features find no parallel with any linguistics system of any Euro-American language, but follow patterns found in Yoruba language and among Yoruba speakers, then it goes without much ado that this similarity, no matter how superficial, transcends a chance occurrence.

Word Lists

Of the 30 African languages that Turner listed as having contributed a total of 3,328 words to the Gullah language,[28] Yoruba alone accounts for 788 words. Turner lists the words alphabetically; under the letter "A," for example, are words such as "abashe," Nigerian Yoruba (NY): "agabase" (the work of a laborer); "agogo," NY: "agogo" (bell); "akasa," NY: "akara" (corn meal);

"alamisha," NY: "alamisi" (Thursday); "awu," NY: "ewu" (dress); "apara," NY: "apara" (jest); "awusa," NY: "ewusa" (walnut); "ayedele," NY: "ayo(dele)" (joy). Out of the 33 entries under "A," 16 are identifiable to me as Yoruba words. Similarly, out of the total of 4,870 personal names, from 33 African languages also found in Gullah, Yoruba is responsible for 775 names, that is, 16 percent. (These numbers are given to illustrate the undeniable presence of African / Yoruba among contemporary American Creoles, "for some such as Saramac-can, they constitute a fifth or more of the total lexicon; outside of their oc-currence in specialized semantic domains, they only account for 2% and 4% of everyday working vocabulary. This is true, for example, for Krio, Jamaican, Belizean, Gullah, Kittitian, Vincentian and most others.")[29] These names, as it will soon be illustrated, serve the purpose of reinforcing the African iden-tity of the bearers; they show their spiritual patronage and also uphold their sense of community.

Werner-Lewis gives an inventory of Yoruba names across categories. "One category of such Yoruba names is called 'amutorunwa,' names a child brings from heaven."[30] Examples are "Aina," "Ajayi," "Ojo," and so on; these names describe the physical conditions that surrounded the birth of the child so named. Another category is "abiso," and that includes names given at birth as well as other names the child might acquire in life. These usually reflect the circum-stances prevalent at the home of the child or the child's life achievements. Names falling into these categories are found among African Americans, but it is not clear if these names have the same representation in America as they do in Africa. For instance, at the "ile" (home, or community) where I conducted the ethnographic study, some of the people's names include "Aina," "Omi," "Alalade," and "Olu," to name only a few.

Social Influences

Another glaring area where Yoruba has left its definite and indelible presence on the African American linguistic pattern is in the sphere of kinesthesia. This is a strong cultural trait or feature that distinguishes Africans and their descen-dants from other inhabitants of America. A cursory observation of blacks during any social interaction will reveal a peculiar confluence of linguistic expressions that transcends sounds and rhythm, and includes distinctive gestures, liveliness, and fascinating external modes of discourse. Speech, in this context, becomes performance, such that the discourse is infused with physical actions to the ex-tent of "supplanting the words not only for succinctness but also for cogency and clarity in transition of meaning."[31] This enacted mode of speech has become known as "shout'n," a phenomenon that has been mentioned and studied for over a century.[32] Shout'n refers to the performative acts of dancing, singing, clap-ping, and, in fact, gesticulating, which started first as part of the ritual practices of African Americans and has continued in various forms among practitioners of West African traditional religion, namely, Sango worshipers of Trinidad, Candomblé adherents of Brazil, Santeríans of Cuba, and those of Lucumí persuasion in the United States. It is an emotional explosion, responsive to rhythms.[33] The physical manifestation of "shout" includes singing, drumming, and spiritual possession. Beyond this, currently observable peculiar gestures and an animated manner of conversation among African Americans are rooted in shout.

The phenomenon of "shout" is of West African origin, and it connotes celebration, joy, and praiseful jubilation. Mary Zeigler correctly illustrated the etymology and connected it with the Yoruba word "we" as it occurs in the sentence "A fe lo we ile Mary." The Yoruba verb "we" translates into English as "wash" and is found in Nigerian English. Thus the sentence literally means, "We want to go and wash Mary's house."[34] However, "wash," in this context, bears as much affinity to water and soap as the word "shower" in the phrase "have a baby shower" bears to bathing. The actual meaning of the Yoruba sentence, then, translates into "We want to go and celebrate, proclaim with joy, laughter, and singing the accomplishment of Mary." Seen in this light, the term "shout" is only homophonous to the English word "shout," meaning holler.

Of greater significance, however, is that "shout" "is a communication structure that consists of a combination of objects or events and its meaning."[35] Hence it is a manner of speech that bears a peculiar message interpretable only to those who share this language. Spiritually it conveys and signals, among other things, the presence of the spirit in one. Thus, during Christian services, the "sermon nearly always rises to a pitch of exaltation at which ordinary prose accent, intonation, word-order are too tame to express the streaming emotion within; the sermon becomes a cry, a poem, an improvisation; it is intoned with melodious energy . . . that it becomes an orgy of figures and metaphors sobbed or shouted out."[36] It is also, for most, an outlet for the mixture of joy, pain, and confusion. Shout then is a linguistic route, through which enslaved Africans and their descendants escape the immediate hostility and endure their pain. It is a collective joyful worship experience and a means of communing or participating with the ancestors. To this day this has continued as a way of life, and it underlies the much acclaimed passion for music, sense of tact, and rhythmic speech pattern of African Americans.[37]

The verbal devices of the African churches that involve a call-response between preacher and audience, for instance, the "Amen, preach it, I hear you," are all part of the culture of shout. This culture is not limited to religious experiences or music or conversations on the street corner; in fact, one probable extension of this culture into everyday life is often heard when people call in to a radio program to send a "shout out" to their friends; this may, in fact, be lexicalization in progress.

Folktales from Africa

Another essential part of the linguistic legacy of Yoruba found in the African diaspora includes folktales and songs. Tales and storytelling are a vital and vibrant part of Yoruba life. Traditional Yoruba lore is used to teach morals and to convey values. For the Afro-Americans, storytelling is an important part of continuing their African past. The very particular types of tale that are of concern here are those that have their origins in Yorubaland. These include tales from the enslaved that feature African animal trickster figures and exhibit motifs peculiar to Africa. Lawrence Levine has explored some of these tales.[38] William Bascom, persuaded that African tale types were to be found in America, compiled several of such tales across the American continent.

One such tale is Oba's ear, which is more of a sacred Yoruba myth about a Yoruba goddess, Osun, who, out of love for her husband, Sango, cuts off her ear and cooks it in porridge, so that Sango's love for her will intensify. But Sango, after eating the porridge and discovering that one of Osun's ears is missing, and that in fact it was fed to him, becomes irate and leaves her. Osun, unable to bear the pain of her loss, weeps so much that her tears become the river Osun, of which she is the goddess.[39] Bascom collected several versions of this tale in French, Spanish, Portuguese, and Yoruba, and translated them. Versions of this same story can be found in Brazil and Cuba, and also among the Nigerian Yoruba.

Another such tale is "Dogs Rescue Master in Tree Refuge." It is known in the Cape Verde Islands, the southern part of the United States, the Bahamas, the Dominican Republic, Puerto Rico, and Guyana. Several versions of this tale, with minor variations, can be found throughout Africa, but, given its preponderance among the Yoruba, the likelihood is that it came with the enslaved Yoruba to the New World. Basically this tale deals with three dogs that rescue their master, the hunter, from the hands of a witch, who could turn herself into a snake or teeth. One of the dogs kills the witch, the second laps the blood, and the third cleans up the spot. Yet another popular tale of this kind is the Brer Rabbit story, first written by Emily Harvey.[40] One can still hear it being told in the evening in several Yoruba households in Nigeria.

These types of plot, motif, the use of animal characters, and the manner of narration have continued among African Americans despite their adaptation to the New World. For example, in teaching the importance of obligation and friendship, a tale is told about a frog trapped in a deep well who begs a rattlesnake for help. The frog promises to reward the rattlesnake if the snake helps him. When he is saved, the frog refuses to fulfill his obligation. Shortly afterward they meet in the woods, and the rattlesnake grabs him. "Yas, I pay yer!!! Yas, I pay yer!! Yas, I pay yer!" the frog cries, but "as Grawg tell dat rattlesnake chaw him up." Another story is told to teach contentment and to accept one's identity with pride: One time Buh Wolf ax Buh Rabbit, "How come you got such a short tail?" — "'Cause Gawd put it on, an' he didn' mean fur me to have any long tail."[41] Essentially all these didactic tales cover several aspects of life and circumstances and are dished out as a warning, and as an exhortation, in accordance with each situation, and, beyond that, they are a means of fostering communal living.

Lifestyle

The discussion so far has concentrated on the diachronic influence of Yoruba in the Americas. The remainder of the chapter focuses on contemporary American Yoruba as it is unfolding in North America. Examples are from an ongoing ethnographic study with a Yoruba community in Austin, Texas. The choice of this particular ile was influenced by both personal association and convenience. However, one could not have chosen a "better" ile to observe. The priestess Aina Olomo is a spiritual activist with three decades in the orisa traditions. She was initiated into the Cuban tradition of Lucumí in the United States, in the Bronx. Her viewpoint is a compilation of her experiences in the African diaspora with the santeros of the East Coast, the traditionalists of Oyotunji Village, South Carolina, the culturally diverse community of South Florida, and the orisa people of Nigeria, Panama, Puerto Rico, and Trinidad. She has conducted women's right-of-passage groups, worked on racial sensitivity workshops, and trained police officers on ethical interaction with orisa communities. She was appointed special adviser to Osogbo's Cultural and Heritage Council of Chiefs in Nigeria. She is a practitioner of the third generation from the house of Olokun Sanya Awopeju, and is among those championing the documentation of the otherwise aural-based traditional practice. She is the author of *Core of Fire: A Guide to Yoruba Spiritual Activism.* This ile could thus be seen as representative of the contemporary Yoruba communities in the United States. A particular implication of the discussion in the following section is that the Americas did not remain a passive receptor of Yoruba influences; rather, the continent continued its own development within its own sociocultural contexts.

Beyond the features of Yoruba found in the vernaculars of African Americans, Yoruba has become a way of life for many. These Americans (both European and African Americans) define their personhood based on Yoruba conceptions, and find emotional and cultural anchorage in the history and cultural practices of Yoruba. This new wave of pan-Yoruba identity is increasingly being realized in practical terms, in the form of "ile" or "home." The ile is a community of people who have accepted Yoruba traditional religion, cultural practices, and language as a way of life. The cohesiveness found at the homes is reminiscent of the unity observed among the enslaved Yoruba.

At the ile in Austin daily existence unfolds as it would in a Yoruba community. Organized like the "agbo-ile" or "compound," this ile consists of a "Yeye," the priestess (mother), and her children (members). The family relationship is not biological, although it does not preclude it; it is, however, based on a remarkable bond that is as pure and real as it is spiritual. Among themselves members go by their Yoruba names. While some maintain these names at all times, others revert to their birth names once outside the ile. The Yoruba names that they have are mostly anthroponyms. Members receive these names after consulting with the deity that directs their "ori" or "spiritual head." Each name also reflects the characters of the individual's patron deity. Members' names include Omiosun (Osun is the primary deity), Sangobiyi (Sango), Omiyemi, Alalade, Aina, Efunsalewa, Egbegbenga, and so on. Efunsalewa, a female name in Nigeria, is a male's name at the ile. Also, Aina is not an anthroponym; it is one of the so-called amutorunwa, which is given to a female child born with the umbilical cord about her neck. However, the circumstance of birth was not always the basis for this name in this situation.

Yoruba customs are observed at the ile. The day begins with the Yeye pouring libation to the ancestors. Life decisions are made only after proper divination. Furthermore, the Yoruba custom of salutation whereby females kneel and males prostrate is practiced. Spiritual seniority, as against the African Yoruba preference for age and social attainment, is observed in the chain of command. Courtesy is expressed in Yoruba; "thank you" becomes "e se o" or "adupe"; goodbye is "odaabo"; and "welcome" is expressed as "ekaabo." At night "odaaro" is said instead of good-night, and when libation is poured to the ancestors, or when words of wisdom are spoken, and counsel given, "ase" or "may it be so" is spoken in chorus. Although conversations are carried out in English, they are heavily interspersed with Yoruba words and koine.

Outside the ile, the personal lives of adherents are equally guided by the Yoruba lifestyle and language. For instance, during lunch with a devotee outside the ile, grace was said before the meal. Although announced as grace, it was not the Christian art of grace, but rather it was thanksgiving rendered in Yoruba. On another occasion, while visiting with another practitioner, I observed that personal questions were rendered in Yoruba: "Tani yen?" (Who is that?), "Kilode?" (What is the matter?), "Ki loruko e?" (What's your name?), and "Se o ti gbo?" (Did you understand?).

The Legacy of Yoruba in Liturgy

Certain vital aspects in the worship of orisha, whether it is known as Santería in Cuba, Candomblé in Brazil, or Lucumí in the United States, are mainly facilitated through the Yoruba language. The elaborate process of initiation, for instance, involves rituals whose efficacy depends on "awo" (secret knowledge) and Yoruba incantations. The orisha that govern the worshiper's "ori" (fate) are mostly believed to be accessible through praises and encomiums that then become potent and fruitful when rendered in the powerful oral language of awo. "Ebo" (sacrifices) and other commemorative ceremonies made in honor of a particular orisha may only be performed under the auspices of one with a priestly training, that is, one who has knowledge of the rites, one who knows the ethos and is able to speak with the ancestors; this is in order that supplications, litigations, and any other form of entreating the deities for interventions will be sanctioned. Burial rites, marriage rites, naming ceremonies, consecration of houses, and so forth all require carefully made rituals offered in the Yoruba language, or else the gods will be offended and might exert vengeance.

The Yoruba language keeps open the line of communication with deities and ancestors. Even when worshipers have lost the correct tones of the lyrics and supplications to the orisha, they are still diligent in maintaining and passing them on to the next generation in order to maintain their mystical power and to keep away strangers. This special religious role further underscores the tenacity and continuity of the Yoruba language in the Americas.

Yorubabonics

One fascinating development that will interest any social linguist is the form of speech that is being fashioned out of the religious practices and relationship with native African Yoruba people. Aina Olomo has named this function-orientated speech Yorubabonics.[42]

As mentioned, religious practices such as Santería, Lucumí, Orisha, and Ifa are directly based on the Yoruba belief system. Integral parts of these religious practices include ceremonies and rituals whose efficacy is contingent on Yoruba incantations, chanting, and songs. These religious practices, reinforced by communal existence such as that in the iles, have become a repository of (archaic) Yoruba language, and also "a locus classical in the study of memory, retention and continuity."[43] More recently it has become an influential mechanism for linguistics transmission and a place of interaction between native Nigerian Yoruba and American Yoruba practitioners.

Through this interaction a form of pidgin or fragmentary Yoruba has arisen that is mostly employed during religious services and, more recently, in conversation. Yorubabonics is an umbrella term for that negotiated form of Yoruba language that is found among African American Yoruba adherents in America. The speakers, usually adults, have in their liturgy and repertoire an atrophied form of Yoruba. The recent influx of Nigerian Yoruba practitioners and the resident Nigerian Babaalawo at the iles (e.g., Oyotunji Village, New York, and Atlanta) has allowed for a greater interaction between American and African Yoruba. Americans who desire a greater affinity with the Yoruba life are picking up more Yoruba lexicons and are incorporating them directly into their speech. Another impetus comes from the increasing number of Americans going on pilgrimages and for spiritual training in Yoruba cities in Nigeria. These individuals, having been immersed in the Yoruba language in Nigeria, try to maintain it after their return to America by means of formal language classes.

Yorubabonics is arguably the product of historical and synchronous events. The diachronic events lay in the initial attempt of uprooted Africans to maintain a cultural and historical connection with the "utopic" West Africa, as a means of escaping the immediate pain of slavery. This psychological connection may have been furthered by their diasporic descendants, probably as a spiritual consciousness and cultural renaissance in response to their having been linguistically, and culturally, marginalized in the New World. The contemporary event may be psychological. Chances are that contemporary African Americans, especially the orisha devotees who, on seeing themselves as partly Yoruba, hold the Yoruba language and practices as their heritage, will therefore linguistically define themselves as such. Should this initial trend continue—in other words, should the ile continue to grow across the country, and should cooperation with the Nigeria Yoruba persist—this linguistic process may become a useful source of information on the course of language development.

Instances of Yorubabonics

Initiation to orisha exemplifies a religious circumstance where Yorubabonics could be observed.[44] Ending a weeklong initiation process at the ile in Austin is a festive day called the Throne Day. It is a day of feasting, drumming, dancing, and rejoicing with the new initiate, called "iyaawo" or "novitiate." Dressed in her sacred regalia, wearing a crown and veil, the iyaawo is presented to friends, family, and devotees. The use of "iyáawo" (high priestess) for a new initiate instead of "ìyàwó" (bride) is an example of Yorubabonics. During this presentation only Yoruba songs are allowed. Each song is offered to a particular deity and is accompanied by specific dance steps. The songs reveal the personality of the particular deity, eulogize their deeds, warn of their taboos, and exhort adherence to their commands. More important is the eulogy. Each one says prayers to his or her ancestors; people are observed to eulogize the deeds of their American ancestors, including activists, leaders, and people who have positively contributed to the course of African Americans. Calling their spirits means narrating their deeds. An admixture of Yoruba and English is used.

The following is one of the many songs rendered at the initiation. Some of these songs were comprehensible to native Yoruba speakers, and others were lexically and intonationally difficult to parse.

Yenmonja Yemonja olodo
"Yemonja, Yemonja, the owner of the river"
Yenmonja Yenmonja iya mi olodo
"Yemonja, Yemonja, my mother, the owner of the river"
Yenmomja Yenmonja Yenmonja olodo
"Yemonja, Yemonja, Yemonja, the owner of the river"
Yenmonja iyami asesun olodo
"Yemonja, the source of the river"

340

The saying of grace is another illustration of Yorubabonics: prayer before meals exemplifies one of those social practices that are now facilitated through the mother tongue. One Yoruba adherent uttered the following prayer as we sat down to lunch:

E se ori	Thank you for ori (spiritual head)
E se owo	Thank you for finance
E se inu	Thank you for the stomach
E se o nje	Thank you for the meal
Mo dupe olodumare	I am grateful to you Olodumare

Though some of the tones were off, the prayer is perfectly comprehensible to native Yoruba speakers.

In addition to the place of Yoruba language in the life of the people, Yoruba has become a vehicle for emotive expressions. For most Yoruba Americans, their joys and woes find appropriate expression, or the highest channel of expression, through the ancestral language. Warner-Lewis reported on an informant in Trinidad, who, when ill in the hospital, was asked what was the matter by his son, to which the man "burst into a song expressive of the joy at being visited by his own children":

Arálé ni	Relatives inquire
Sé ni mo ma jí ire	Whether I indeed woke well
Sé ni mo ma jí ire	Whether I indeed woke well
Kò sé bí abímo ni	(But) it cannot be the same as if my own children ask.[45]

Warner-Lewis also reported that the same subject, on another occasion, used "Yoruba song as a means of maintaining steady work rhythm and also of distracting his mind from the awareness of arduous physical activity":

Ojónkpéré	We are all together
Sáwé ojúdè	Cut the grass outside
Sáwé ojúdè	Cut the grass outside.[46]

I observed this same phenomenon among some practitioners of Yoruba in Texas during their yard cleaning at the ile; also, when a member returned home safely after traveling outside the country, the individual was met with joyful songs and thanksgiving in the Yoruba language. Aside from these examples and the occasional expression of a Yoruba proverb, however, I did not observe a complete conversation in Yoruba. Of course, most Yoruba words have acquired a different meaning in the New World. "Odunde," currently said in Nigeria in advent of Christmas, in the New World is used to denote the celebration attached to the end of the iyawo's mandatory one-year training. In Yorubaland there is the phrase "oriki orile" (the praise, or history of a dynasty), which is replaced in the New World with "Orikiile" (The history of the family). "Osesede" literally means a newcomer, but it is used at the ile to denote an adherent at the initial stage of spiritual training.

Also noteworthy is that at the ile members do not only speak in English but insert as many Yoruba words as possible. For instance:

"Mustafa wanbi" (Mustafa come here)
"We need mariwo for the ebo, se o ye?" (We need palm-frond for the sacrifice, understand?)

Many spiritual duties are carried out strictly in Yoruba, and it is this speech form, together with its peculiar phonology and semantics, that is referred to as Yorubabonics. This speech form, regardless of its grammatical deviation from Nigerian Yoruba, serves a greater purpose than merely as a means of communication or conversation. It can be seen as a unity of culture, identity, and faith, and it is carried forth and maintained by a linguistic expression that transcends the momentary geopolitical boundary in the American continent.

As shown in this chapter, Yoruba has influenced the Americas both linguistically and socially. Much of the current contemporary way of life in the Americas is also based on Yoruba beliefs. Yoruba is no longer a foreign or distant culture. Rather, it has taken root in the Americas, producing new Yoruba people who are conscious of their history and whose experiences have shaped their worldview in a unique fashion. Finally, the Yoruba language is no longer merely a religious language but is increasingly being used as a means of communication.

Notes

I am highly indebted to Lisa Green for her invaluable comments and advice on earlier and later drafts of this chapter. I received helpful suggestions and support from Ian Hancock, I thank Joni Jones for introducing me to the African American Yoruba community in Austin, and I am very grateful to Yeye Olomo for supplying me with useful information. I thank the people of "ile" Olokun Sanya Awopeju for welcoming me into their midst. None of these people is responsible for any error or conclusion in this chapter.

1. Owing to language constraints, most examples will come from the English-speaking Americas, but the claims will be valid for non-English-speaking sections of the Americas. It should also be noted that this paper is primarily concerned with "African American" speech forms, and by that is meant those speech forms found in America since the slave trade that are a result of the contact between Africans and various European languages that are their lexifiers.

2. Yoruba has a huge number of practitioners, but because of the history of repression and other sociopolitical factors of the New World, adherents have had to submerge within the mainstream culture in order to survive. Hence proper and accurate documentation is difficult to obtain in the usual way. In an interview with Aina Olomo, she said that

in 1987, while training police officers on ethical interactions with orisa communities, there were forty-three thousand documented Yoruba in Dade County, Florida, alone. Facts concerning the Yoruba are largely, and essentially, still oral in nature and must be thus obtained. Also, as further evidence of the spread of Yoruba, Yoruba communities from fifty-seven countries registered for the "Eighth Ifa Orisa World Conference" (6 July 2003, in Cuba). Beyond this there are organized annual pilgrimages to Osogbo, Oyo, and Ede from the American continent.

3. Samuel Johnson, *The History of the Yorubas: From the Earliest Times to the Beginning of the British Protectorate* (London: Routledge and Kegan Paul, 1966 [1921]).

4. Lorand J. Matory, "The English Professors of Brazil: On the Diasporic Roots of the Yorùbá Nation," *Comparative Studies in Society and History* 41, no. 1 (January 1999): 76.

5. Jean-Claude Garcia-Zamor, "Social Mobility of Negroes in Brazil," *Journal of Inter-American Studies* 12, no. 2 (April 1970): 243.

6. Matory, "The English Professors of Brazil," 77.

7. Louis Antoine Aime de Verteuil, *Three Essays on the Cultivation of Sugar Cane in Trinidad . . .* (Port of Spain: Printed at the Standard's Office, 1858), 175. Quoted in Maureen Werner-Lewis, *Trinidad Yoruba: From Mother Tongue to Memory* (Tuscaloosa: University of Alabama Press, 1996), 31.

8. J. E. Holloway, ed., *Africanisms in American Culture* (Bloomington: Indiana University Press, 1990), 12.

9. I acknowledge that this is a hotly debated issue, and since it is outside the scope of this chapter I will not participate in it. However, within the various substrate hypotheses, African influence on American speech has been effectively established since described in Salikoko S. Mufwene, ed., *Africanisms in Afro-American Language* (Athens: University of Georgia Press, 1993).

10. *The American Heritage Dictionary of the English Language*, 4th ed. (Boston: Houghton Mifflin, 2000).

11. Martha Baudet, "Identifying the African Grammatical Base of the Caribbean Creoles: A Typological Approach," in *Historicity and Variation in Creole Studies*, ed. Arnold R. Highfield and Albert Valdman (Ann Arbor: Karoma, 1981), 115.

12. Genevieve Escure, "Decreolization in a Creole Continuum: Belize," in Highfield and Valdman, *Historicity and Variation in Creole Studies*, for similar data on Belize.

13. Note that apparent deviations among these languages are a consequence of separate developments and pressure from the dominant languages of their surroundings (Ian Hancock, "Creole Language Provenance and the African Component," in Mufwene, *Africanism in Afro-American Language*, 182–91). For a complete treatment of Gullah vowels, see D. L. Turner, *Africanisms in the Gullah Dialects* (Chicago: University of Chicago Press, 1963).

14. Mervyn C. Alleyne, *Comparative Afro-American: A Historical Comparative Study of English-Based Afro-American Dialects of the New World* (Ann Arbor: Karoma, 1980), 74.

15. Suzanne M. Sylvain, *Le Creole Haitian: Morphologie et Syntaxe* (Port-au-Prince, Wetteren: Imprimerie de Meester, 1936).

16. H. Carter, "Suprasegmentals in Guyanese: Some African Comparisons," in *Pidgin and Creole Languages: Essays in Memory of John E. Reinecke*, ed. G. Gilbert (Honolulu: University of Hawaii Press, 1987), 221.

17. Alleyne, *Comparative Afro-American*, 67.

18. C stands for consonant, and V for vowel.

19. Lisa J. Green, *African American English: A Linguistic Introduction* (Cambridge: Cambridge University Press, 2002), 107 ff.

20. Alleyne, *Comparative Afro-American*, 94.

21. Despite this division, code switching is common, the only difference being that highly educated people include standard lexical items in their speech and sometimes mark tense. Note also that black English users in the United States are not exclusively identified by educational level; code switching is equally a common practice.

22. The subscript, as used here, only shows that "dem" refers to soldier.

23. William A. Stewart, "Continuity and Change in American Negro Dialects," in *Perspectives on Black English*, ed. J. Dillard (The Hague: Mouton, 1975), 245. JMC = Jamaican, SRA = Sranan, and WAP = West African Pidgin.

24. Holloway, *Africanisms*, 28.

25. David Sutcliffe and John Figueroa, *System in Black Language* (Philadelphia: Multilingual Matters, 1992), 45.

26. Alleyne, *Comparative Afro-American*, 94.

27. Baudet, "Identifying the African Grammatical Base of the Caribbean Creoles," 111.

28. Turner, *Africanisms in the Gullah Dialect*.

29. Hancock, "Creole Language Provenance and the African Component," 85.

30. Werner-Lewis, *Trinidad Yoruba*, 75.

31. Mary B. Zeigler, "Something to Shout About," in *Sociocultural and Historical Context of African American English*, ed. S. L. Lanehart (Amsterdam: John Benjamins, 2001), 172.

32. Zora N. Hurston, in her article "Shouting," which discussed this phenomenon in a religious setting, writes, "There is little doubt that shouting is a survival of the African 'possession' by the gods. In Africa it is sacred to the priesthood and acolytes, in America it has become generalized" ("Shouting," in *Negro: An Anthology*, ed. Nancy Cunard [New York: Ungar, 1970], 34).

33. Ibid.

34. Zeigler, "Something to Shout About," 175.

35. Ibid., 32.

36. J. A. Harrison, "Negro English," in Dillard, *Perspectives on Black English*, 145.

37. By no means am I suggesting that every black exhibits these traits, nor do I claim that African and European Americans do not share any of these kinesics or nonverbal communication skills. Yet one recognizes that the separation and exclusion of blacks for hundreds of years during slavery also led to the development of peculiar and distinctive traits. At the same time, years of separation of blacks from Africa, and of interaction with others in the New World, have definitely produced new patterns, more traceable to West African culture than to any European culture.

38. Lawrence W. Levine, *Black Culture and Black Consciousness: Afro-American Folk Thought from Slavery to Freedom* (New York: Oxford University Press, 1977), 81–133.

39. William Bascom, "Oba's Ear: A Yoruba Myth in Cuba and Brazil," *Research in African Literature* 7 (1976): 149–65.

40. Emily N. Harvey, "A Brer Rabbit Story," *Journal of American Folklore* 32 (1919): 443–44.

41. Levine, *Black Culture and Black Consciousness*, 93.

42. There is great tonal and intonational disparity between Yorubabonics and Niger-

ian Yoruba. The spelling of words deviates from those of Nigerian Yoruba, and the labiove-lar consonants are not simultaneously realized. Sometimes they are realized sequentially or as a single phone. Yorubabonics shares some phonological features of pidgin.

43. Matory, "The English Professors of Brazil," 1.

44. Without the permission of the priestess, I cannot report on the speech from the religious sessions. Hence my limited examples will concentrate on lexical items heard in normal conversations.

45. Maureen Warner-Lewis, *Trinidad Yoruba: From Mother Tongue to Memory* (Tuscaloosa: University of Alabama Press, 1996), 59.

46. Ibid.

IV

THE RETURN
TO YORUBALAND

CHAPTER SEVENTEEN

Yoruba Liberated Slaves
Who Returned to West Africa

Robin Law

The creation of a Yoruba diaspora in the Americas through the Atlantic slave trade is dealt with elsewhere in this volume. Enslaved Yoruba were sufficiently numerous in trans-Atlantic slave populations to remain visible as a distinct linguistic and cultural group, most often known in the Americas (in Brazil, for example) as "Nagô" but in Spanish colonies (including Cuba) as "Lucumí." Although Yoruba slaves were carried across the Atlantic from as early as the sixteenth century, the slave trade out of Yorubaland reached its greatest scale in the early nineteenth century, when it was fed by the outbreak of the devastating series of intra-Yoruba wars that began with the extension of the Sokoto jihad into the region from 1817 on, and then spread into southern Yorubaland from the 1820s on; this development was also connected to the emergence of Lagos as the principal port of embarkation of slaves within the "Slave Coast" (or Bight of Benin), overshadowing the previously dominant port of Ouidah, in the kingdom of Dahomey, to the west. By this time the directional flow of enslaved Africans was affected by the legal banning of the slave trade, and was largely restricted to those territories where this abolition proved most difficult to enforce, namely, Brazil and Cuba. The Yoruba element was especially prominent in the slave population of Brazil, and more particularly in the province of Bahia. In Salvador, the capital of Bahia, Nagô comprised nearly 30 percent of African-born slaves, and played the leading role in the great slave rebellion there in 1835.[1] In Cuba, Lucumí slaves represented a smaller but still significant proportion, around 9 percent.[2]

As a direct consequence of their prominence among the victims of the Atlantic slave trade in this period, Yoruba were also prominent in reverse diasporas of "repatriates," persons of African birth or descent who, having been freed from slavery, returned to resettle in their natal or ancestral communities. The best-known example is the movement from the British colony of Freetown, Sierra Leone, settled with persons liberated from illegal slave ships intercepted by the British navy, some of whom began to make their way home to Yorubaland from the late 1830s.[3] But this return migration of Sierra Leoneans (or "Saros") was paralleled and indeed preceded by a similar movement of persons who had actually been slaves in the Americas but had bought or otherwise obtained their freedom there. This re-emigration came mainly from Brazil, but there was also a smaller movement of ex-slaves back to Africa from Cuba;[4] in West Africa, however, such Cuban returnees were generally absorbed into the larger Brazilian community, rather than retaining a distinct identity. This reflected not only the preeminence of Brazil and Cuba as destinations for the trans-Atlantic slave trade in this period but also the greater facility for slaves to obtain their freedom in these places, compared to elsewhere in the Americas. In Bahia in the 1830s, for example, free blacks and mulattoes were more numerous than slaves; although it was easier for locally born ("Creole") slaves to obtain freedom than for those born in Africa, around one-fifth of African-born Bahians were free.[5] In Cuba down to the 1870s, manumissions of slaves, normally through self-purchase, represented about one-fifth of all recorded slave sales.[6]

Brazilian settlers in Africa were generally known as "Aguda," a term that, when first attested in contemporary records in the mid-eighteenth century in use among slaves in Brazil originating from the Dahomey area, designated Brazil, as opposed to Portugal;[7] but in West Africa in the nineteenth century its reference was national or linguistic rather than geographical, applied to Portuguese in general, including Brazilians, rather than to Brazilians as distinct from Portuguese. Its origin is unknown.[8] The term "Aguda" included Portuguese and Brazilians of European as well as African descent, but an alternative term, "Maro" (or, in Yoruba, "Amaro"), seems to have been used more specifically of the African-born ex-slaves. This latter usage apparently derived from the interior, where "Maro" was a name sometimes given to the quarters of a town occupied by foreign (usually Muslim) merchants, for example, in Nikki.[9]

Former slaves from Brazil settled at various places on the West African coast, including Accra on the Gold Coast (Ghana), where they were known as "Tabon," which is said to derive from the Portuguese phrase "'tabon," (all's well).[10] However, the main concentration of Brazilian settlement was farther east, along the Bight of Benin, corresponding to modern Togo, Benin, and western Nigeria. The most substantial research on the Brazilian diaspora to West Africa has focused on the Benin area;[11] the Nigerian section of the coast, including the Yoruba homeland, has been relatively neglected.[12]

Although the Brazilian diaspora to West Africa is commonly perceived as a specifically nineteenth-century phenomenon, it should be stressed that persons of African birth or descent had been returning to resettle in Africa already during the seventeenth and eighteenth centuries. In the 1650s and 1660s the king of Allada, the dominant kingdom on the Slave Coast prior to the rise of Dahomey, had a Portuguese-speaking interpreter called Mattéo Lopes, a professed Christian, who in 1670 undertook a diplomatic mission to the court of King Louis XIV in France; he was described as being "of Portuguese nationality," which suggests that he was an immigrant (or re-emigrant) rather than locally born. Likewise in Hueda, the kingdom which included the principal coastal "port" of Ouidah, in 1694 the king had in his service a "Portuguese Negro," also a Christian, called João Fernandes, who served as his gunner and physician.[13] It is not specified where Lopes and Fernandes came from, and it may well have been the island of São Tomé rather than Brazil; nor are their specific African origins recorded. Similarly, in the eighteenth century, several prominent slave traders on the Bight of Benin were returned ex-slaves, from Brazil and elsewhere, including some who were born in Africa. An early example was João de Oliveira, taken as a slave in his childhood originally to Pernambuco but later resident in Bahia, who returned to Africa as a trader around 1733 and retired back to Bahia in 1770. He was credited with opening, at his own cost, two new ports for the Portuguese slave trade, Porto-Novo and Lagos. Documents relating to Oliveira describe him merely as being born in Africa (or the "Costa da Mina," meaning the Gold Coast, but, in Portuguese usage, including the Bight of Benin). However, a description of his facial scarifications— three lines on each of his cheeks—suggests that he may well have been Yoruba, these corresponding to the "abaja" marks distinctive of the Oyo and some related groups.[14] A leading slave trader at Porto-Novo in the 1780s named Pierre, who also served as secretary to the king, was also an ex-slave, formerly owned by a French ship's captain and educated in France; he is said to have been Hausa in origin, but it was noted that he spoke Yoruba ("Eyeo," i.e., Oyo) as well as Hausa and French, which evidently facilitated his dealings with merchants from Oyo who brought slaves for sale at the coast.[15]

A much larger-scale re-emigration from Brazil to Africa occurred in the nineteenth century, however, beginning in the 1830s. This was part of a more general process of the creation and consolidation of a resident Brazilian community on the coast of the Bight of Benin, initially at Ouidah but later spreading into other coastal towns of the region, which reflected the predominance of Brazil as a market for the trans-Atlantic slave trade in this period.[16] The leading figures in this Brazilian community were substantial slave traders: most notably Francisco Felix de Souza (d. 1849), who arrived on the coast around 1800 and traded at Badagry, Ouidah, and Little Popo (Anécho) before settling permanently in 1820 at Ouidah, where he became commercial agent to the king of Dahomey; Domingos José Martins (d. 1864), who was initially prominent in the slave trade at Lagos but established himself at Porto-Novo in 1846; Joaquim d'Almeida (d. 1857), who traded mainly at Agoué, west of Ouidah, where he eventually settled permanently in 1845; and Francisco José de Medeiros (d. 1875), who was actually from Madeira rather than Brazil, who settled at Agoué in the late 1850s but moved to Ouidah in the 1860s.[17] Such traders married locally (generally polygamously), fathering families by their African wives which remained prominent after their deaths, in many cases to the present day. Although the coastal towns where they settled belonged to different African states, they retained a sense of common identity that transcended local political boundaries, reflecting not only their continued use of the Portuguese language but also the facility of communication afforded by the system of lagoons which, in this region, run parallel to the coast, providing an almost continuously navigable waterway from Little Popo in the west to Lagos and beyond in the east. Brazilian settlers in the Bight of Benin often moved their residence among ports along the lagoon, as has been seen, or maintained multiple residences simultaneously, so that their descendants became scattered all along the coast. This transnational dimension has indeed remained characteristic of "Brazilian" families to the present day, crossing modern political boundaries between Nigeria, Benin, and Togo, as they earlier did those of previous African states.[18]

Some of the Brazilian slave traders in the Bight of Benin in this period were themselves ex-slaves of African origin, the wealthiest instance being Joaquim d'Almeida, who was born in Mahi, north of Dahomey. More generally former slaves who re-emigrated to West Africa were attracted to settle in towns where there were substantial Brazilian merchants already established, who could offer them protection and to whom they commonly attached themselves in relations of clientage. Although individual ex-slaves had returned to Africa earlier, large-scale re-emigration began in the aftermath of the great Bahia slave rebellion of 1835, which the local authorities blamed on the influence of the free black population, and which was followed by the deportation of many suspected of complicity in it or regarded as a potential threat.[19] The re-emigration then continued on a voluntary basis, however, throughout the rest of the nineteenth century, from a variety of motives, including commercial opportunities as well as nostalgia for their home country (including some retiring to Africa in their old age) and perhaps also the increasing hostility and discrimination facing free blacks in Brazil. Initially the re-emigrants traveled mostly as passengers on ships trading between Brazil and Africa, ironically including many that were engaged in the continuing slave trade; even after the end of the slave trade to Brazil in 1850, regular shipping contacts continued, since there remained a demand in Africa for Brazilian products such as rum and tobacco, and, conversely, a market in Brazil for African products such as palm oil, kola nuts, and African cloth. After the establishment of a regular steamship service from Liverpool to Lagos in 1852, however, many came via England. Over the whole of the nineteenth century it is estimated that the total number of Brazilian re-emigrants to West Africa was between three thousand and four thousand;[20] the size of the Brazilian community in West Africa was, of course, much larger than this, including their families by local marriages, and also slaves and free clients incorporated into their households, who might come to identify themselves as "Brazilian" even though they had never left Africa.

The ex-slaves who returned to West Africa came from a variety of origins in Africa, including Mahi, "Atakpa" (Nupe), Hausa, and "Kaniké" (Borno), as well as "Nagô" (Yoruba). However, the Yoruba were the most numerous, reflecting their numerical preeminence among enslaved Africans in Bahia, and perhaps also the particular suspicion attached to Yoruba in the aftermath of the 1835 slave rebellion, in which Yoruba slaves and freedmen took the leading role. The concentration of re-emigrant settlement in the Bight of Benin presumably reflected not only the dominant pattern of seaborne communication, and hence of shipping opportunities, between Bahia and Africa, but also the desire of many of the re-emigrants to return to their own specific countries of origin, rather than merely to Africa in general. Nevertheless, not all of the re-emigrants chose or were able to return to their home communities. Brazilian resettlement was in general concentrated in the coastal towns rather than in the interior, and many re-emigrants of Yoruba origin settled in non-Yoruba communities to the west, especially in Agoué, Ouidah, and Porto-Novo in what is today the Republic of Benin.

Brazilian Settlement in Benin: Ouidah, Agoué, and Porto-Novo

On the coast of Benin the main focus of Brazilian resettlement was initially Ouidah, the port of the kingdom of Dahomey and the principal center for the Atlantic trade in the region of the Slave Coast prior to the rise of Lagos. In the immediate aftermath of the 1835 slave rebellion in Bahia, as part of the deportation of those suspected of involvement, the provincial authorities there chartered a ship to deliver two hundred free Africans to Ouidah.[21] Local tradition in the town likewise recalls the arrival of a party of liberated Africans on a particular ship, who were welcomed by the locally established Brazilian slave merchant Francisco Felix de Souza, and given land on which to settle, in what became known as the Maro quarter.[22] In contemporary sources the Brazilian repatriate community in Ouidah was first noted, in 1845, by the Scottish explorer John Duncan, who observed that, in addition to the "real Portuguese" resident in the town, there were "numerous" former slaves from Brazil, who had obtained their freedom either by purchase or by returning as servants to slave dealers. Duncan understood that "many" of them had left Brazil after being "concerned in an attempted revolution among the slaves there," referring evidently to the Bahia uprising of 1835. The British naval officer Frederick Forbes in 1849–50 also alludes to "liberated Africans" living in Ouidah, including some from Brazil as well as from Sierra Leone, who had purchased their freedom in Brazil, and "many" of whom he said were now themselves engaged in the slave trade.[23] An idea of the size of this repatriate community is provided by the French Catholic Mission established in Ouidah in 1861, which estimated the number of already existing Christians in the town, who were mainly former slaves from Brazil, at six hundred.[24]

Duncan stated that the freed slaves in Ouidah were mainly of "Fulani" (meaning probably Hausa) and Oyo origin; Forbes stated that they were from "Yoruba" (i.e., Oyo) and Borno. The French Roman Catholic mission, which arrived in the 1860s, listed Yoruba ("Nago") with Fon and Portuguese as the "usual languages" in Ouidah; and although this prominence of the Yoruba language was probably due in part to the large numbers of Yoruba slaves held in the town who were imported directly from the interior, it also reflected the predominantly Yoruba origins of the Brazilian repatriates. It was noted of the Brazilians that they "almost always speak Nago and Portuguese, but rarely the local language where it is not Nago, even those born in Ouidah of Nago parents rarely speak the local language."[25] The families that are descended from Brazilian ex-slaves that still reside in the Maro quarter and elsewhere in Ouidah often recall the original African ethnicity of their founders, and, although these include persons from Mahi, Nupe, Hausa, and Borno, many of them are remembered to have been Yoruba. In several cases their particular towns or areas of origin within Yorubaland are indicated. The descendants of Antonio d'Almeida (d. 1890), for example, recall that he was originally from Iseyin, and the family still retains a Yoruba surname, Olufade.[26] The principal local historian of Ouidah, Casimir Agbo, in a book published in 1959, was able to record the praise-names ("oriki") of several Yoruba Brazilian families; in addition to that of Antonio d'Almeida, these include those of the Americo and Villaça families, which recall their origins, respectively, from Iseri and Ijesa.[27]

West of Ouidah a substantial repatriate community also developed in Agoué. According to local tradition, this originated in the reign of Toyi (1835–1844) and therefore probably also derived, in the first instance, from the deportations that followed the 1835 rebellion in Bahia.[28] The French Catholic mission in Ouidah, when it first made contact with Agoué in 1863, estimated that there were already about one hundred Christians there, all repatriates from Brazil, who were "almost all Nago by nationality."[29] But, in the long run, the Brazilian community clearly grew larger than this and was more variegated in its ethnic origins, although the Yoruba element remained the largest. Agoué came to include no fewer than four quarters settled by Brazilian ex-slaves, as well as a "Salo [i.e., Saro]" quarter occupied by repatriates from Sierra Leone. One of these, Zokikomè, "Zoki's [i.e., Joaquim's] quarter," represents the establishment of the slave merchant Joaquim d'Almeida; the names of the other three—Anagakomè (also called Idi-Ata), Fonkome, and Haoussakomè (i.e., the Nago, Fon, and Hausa quarters)—evidently reflect the ethnic origins of the settlers. A list of Agoué families of repatriate ancestry compiled in the 1930s includes forty-six whose ancestors came from Brazil, with an additional five originating from Cuba and seven from Sierra Leone. More than half the Brazilian families were of Yoruba origin: twenty-four, compared to eleven that were Mahi, four Fon, five Hausa, and one each who were Nupe and Bariba (from Borgu); most of the Sierra Leonean families were also Yoruba, but none of the Cuban families were, these being Fon, Mahi, and Hausa.[30]

On the coast east of Ouidah, its principal commercial rival prior to the rise of Lagos was Porto-Novo. Although a non-Yoruba community, this might be regarded as effectively part of the Yoruba homeland, since its role as the principal outlet for the slave trade of the kingdom of Oyo led to the establishment in it of a substantial Yoruba community, founded according to tradition in the second half of the eighteenth century.[31] Porto-Novo also became host to a Brazilian repatriate community, although perhaps rather later than Ouidah and Agoué. By 1884 there were reported to be about one hundred repatriates settled there, most of them from Brazil although some were from Sierra Leone.[32] The leading figure in the Porto-Novo Brazilian community was José Paraíso, who is said to have arrived in West Africa in 1850.[33] He was of Yoruba origin and, according to family tradition, a member of the royal family of Oyo. He seems to have come to Africa not as a freedman but still as a slave, employed as a barber by the leading slave merchant Domingos Martins. On the death of Martins in 1864, however, Paraíso was among his assets seized, by way of inheritance tax, by the king of Porto-Novo, and thereby Paraíso became a "caboceer" (chief) and senior royal adviser. His son, Ignacio Paraíso, in turn became a leading notable (a member of the Conseil d'administration) under French colonial rule.

It may be noted that in Benin the Brazilian repatriates generally remained settled in the coastal towns rather than returning to their home communities in the interior. This may have been mainly by necessity, rather than choice; Forbes, in 1850, reported that Brazilian ex-slaves whom he met in Ouidah had originally returned to Africa "in high hopes of reaching their country" but found themselves prevented from so doing and instead confined to Ouidah by the Dahomean authorities.[34] Given the facility of travel along the coastal lagoon, however, it is difficult to believe that anyone determined to get back to their home country could not have done so. In some cases, of course, there proved to be no longer any home to return to; Duncan, in 1845, in the interior north of Dahomey, met a former slave from Bahia, a man originally from Borno, who had returned to Ouidah and from there via Yorubaland to his native town, only to find that it had been "twice destroyed by the enemy, and was chiefly inhabited by strangers from a far country," and he was now on his way back to the coast, with the intention of returning, if possible, to Brazil.[35] But even when returning home was feasible, it was not always attractive, once repatriates had become established in positions of affluence in the coastal towns, which offered commercial opportunities in the rising "legitimate" trade in palm produce as well as in the slave trade, and as agents for European firms for those with insufficient capital to set up as independent merchants who were less readily available in the interior.

Lagos and Its Hinterland

Yoruba repatriates for whom returning home was a priority would presumably choose to go to Lagos rather than to the ports farther west. Lagos ultimately became the location of the largest Brazilian repatriate community, as well as a principal center of Sierra Leonean resettlement.[36] The settlement of Brazilian ex-slaves is said to have begun around 1840.[37] The earliest arrivals did not meet with a warm welcome, as King Kosoko of Lagos (from 1845 to 1851) had reportedly "plundered" their wealth and even executed some who resisted his exactions. In 1847, however, Kosoko is said to have changed his policy, and sent one of his senior chiefs, Oshodi Tapa, on a mission to Brazil to reassure potential emigrants of their security in Lagos. By 1853 there were already about 130 families of "self-emancipated Africans from the Brazils" settled in Lagos, who were said to be "all of them from Yoruba originally, and mostly from the province of Egba."[38]

The establishment of British influence over Lagos after their intervention to depose King Kosoko at the end of 1851, although it led to the expulsion of the leading Brazilian slave traders, otherwise served to encourage Brazilian as well as Sierra Leonean resettlement by providing a more effective framework of security. This was already evident during the period of the British Consulate (1852 to 1861), under which Lagos became effectively a British quasi-protectorate even before its formal annexation as a British colony in 1861. The British authorities also offered positive encouragement to the Brazilians, regarding them, as well as the Sierra Leoneans, as a potential influence for progress in Lagos. The British Consul intervened with the indigenous King Dosunmu, for example, to reduce and finally to abolish a head tax (of ten bags of cowries) that had been imposed on Brazilian settlers.[39] Several further parties of Brazilian re-emigrants arrived during the 1850s, and, in 1855, a group of 48 former slaves from Cuba also arrived, via England, by the steamship service from Liverpool.[40] By 1887 the number of Brazilian repatriates in Lagos was counted at 3,221,[41] and others continued to arrive until the end of the century. These Brazilian repatriates occupied what was termed the "Brazilian quarter" (also called "Portuguese Town" and, in Yoruba, "Popo Aguda" or "Popo 'Maro"), which was separate from the Sierra Leonean quarter centered around Campos Square at the northern end of the still surviving Campos Street, named after a prominent Brazilian; the neighboring Bamgbose and Tokunboh Streets also commemorate Brazilian repatriates of the nineteenth century. In the Lagos press of the late nineteenth century the social activities of the Brazilian community were prominently reported, including a Brazilian Dramatic Company that put on performances for the birthday of the Brazilian Emperor Pedro II in 1880, as well as for the birthday of Queen Victoria in 1882, and also a celebration of the proclamation of the emancipation of slaves in Brazil in 1888.[42]

The Brazilian community in Lagos was predominantly Yoruba in origin, although some repatriates also came from further inland, including Nupe and Hausaland. Unlike the pattern on the western Slave Coast, some Brazilian repatriates who came initially to Lagos went on to resettle in the interior. The British Consul in 1859 noted that "several of the self-emancipated Africans from the Brazils" had shown "great anxiety to return to their former homes" in Yoruba, Nupe, and Hausaland; and he had issued them passports in English and Arabic to facilitate their security.[43] Abeokuta, which was the principal center in the interior of the resettlement of repatriates from Sierra Leone, also attracted some Brazilians. A man called F. Ribeiro (who may have been from a Brazilian family settled in Accra) acted as agent there to the Italian trader Giambattista Scala from 1856 and became a figure of some standing in the Abeokuta commercial community, serving, for example, along with several Sierra Leonean repatriates, in the Abeokuta Road-Improving Society formed in 1859, and the Abeokuta Mercantile Association of 1860. He also served as a representative of the Egba, together with the Sierra Leonean Henry Robbins, in negotiations with the Lagos authorities for peace later in the 1860s.[44] Another Brazilian resident in Abeokuta from the 1860s was Pedro P. Martins, who played a leading role in organizing the supply of arms and providing financial support for the town's war efforts; in 1893 he acted as "friend and advisor to the Chiefs" in the negotiation of the treaty of "friendship" (in effect, of protectorate, although Abeokuta's independence was formally guaranteed) with Britain in 1893, and when Gbadebo became Alake of Abeokuta in 1898, Martins became the king's secretary.[45]

Even when they did not return to settle permanently in the interior, Brazilian repatriates resident in Lagos often maintained an identification with their homelands and championed their interests. Brazilians as well as Sierra Leoneans were active in the "tribal" associations formed in Lagos to mobilize support for the different sides in the intra-Yoruba wars of the period. A Yoruba (i.e., Oyo) National Association formed in 1865 to mediate in the hinterland wars had as one of its vice presidents a Brazilian, Francisco Reis, though all the other prominent members were Saros; by 1886 its members included another Brazilian, Gaspar da Silva.[46] Another, Philippe José Meffre, was prominently active in the Ijesa Association, which in the 1870s became the Lagos Ekitiparapo Society. In 1866 Meffre was among a group of Ijesa repatriates from Lagos who took the opportunity of the reopening of roads after the end of the Ijaye War to make a visit to their homeland, and found themselves arrested as suspected spies at Ibadan on their return journey to the coast. In 1882 Meffre served, together with the Sierra Leonean Joseph Haastrup, as a delegate of the Lagos governor to sound out the willingness of the Ijesa to make peace with Ibadan. In the peace negotiations of 1886 the governor's representative, the Sierra Leonean clergyman Charles Phillips, found his efforts at pacification opposed by a "special messenger" from the Lagos Ekitiparapo Society, named Abeh, who was "a Brazilian Creole, a carpenter by trade."[47]

Christianity and Islam

In their commercial and political activities, the Brazilian repatriates largely replicated or supplemented those of the Sierra Leoneans, rather than playing a distinctive role. They also contributed a range of craft skills learned in Brazil. The numerical prominence of such craftsmen among the repatriates reflected the fact that skilled work commonly afforded opportunities for independent accumulation and therefore for self-redemption from slavery. Brazilian carpenters and masons, in particular, had a lasting impact on architectural style in the coastal towns of the region, where many of the principal buildings in the nineteenth and early twentieth centuries were built by repatriate craftsmen from Brazil, and in Brazilian style.[48] Such "Afro-Brazilian" buildings notably included the major religious buildings, churches, and mosques.

The Brazilians also made a distinctive contribution in the sphere of religion through their association with the Roman Catholic Church. Whereas the Sierra Leoneans generally adhered to English-speaking missions, the Anglican Church Missionary Society, and the Methodists, the Brazilians were mainly Catholics, having been baptized into the Roman Catholic Church in Brazil. Their Catholicism was admittedly often superficial, and many reverted to their ancestral African religion, or combined it with Christianity, after their return to Africa. Philippe Meffre, for example, practiced as an Ifa diviner (until he was converted to the Protestant version of Christianity by the Church Missionary Society [CMS]).[49] The French missionaries who arrived in the 1860s were highly critical of the Brazilians' understanding and practice of Christianity (including the descendants of white Brazilians, such as the de Souzas, as well as the African-born returned slaves), stigmatizing them as living "exactly like pagans for the most part," practicing polygamy and a syncretistic religion, "a monstrous amalgam of paganism, Christianity, and fetishist superstitions."[50] But Christian baptism nevertheless remained an important badge of Brazilian identity in West Africa.

The Brazilian repatriates were, in fact, the effective pioneers of Roman Catholicism in coastal Benin and Nigeria prior to the establishment of any organized missions. In Agoué, for example, the first Catholic chapel was built in the 1830s by a liberated female slave from Brazil, and Joaquim d'Almeida in 1845 built a second chapel, for which he brought the necessary furnishings from Brazil, including even church bells.[51] In Lagos, in 1853, the "white and black Portuguese and Brazilians" set up a "Roman Catholic cross" to mark the prospective site of a Catholic Church, to the annoyance of the CMS missionaries who had lately arrived there. Further, a former slave from Bahia called "Pa" Antonio established a Roman Catholic chapel and conducted nonsacramental services prior to the arrival of the first ordained Catholic missionary in 1863.[52]

An official Roman Catholic Church was established in the region in 1844, when the Portuguese fort in Ouidah, which had been abandoned when the slave trade became illegal, was reoccupied; its personnel, supplied from São Tomé, included a priest to act as chaplain of the chapel in the fort.[53] These Portuguese priests conducted weekly masses and performed baptisms in Ouidah, and also periodically visited Agoué to the west. They saw their function not as the evangelization of local pagans but as the provision of religious services to the existing Roman Catholic population, including the returned ex-slaves as well as the locally settled freeborn Brazilian merchants and their families. In 1861 an explicitly missionary body arrived, in the form of the Société des Missions Africaines (SMA) of Lyon, which established itself first in Ouidah, and from there visited Agoué, Porto-Novo, and Lagos.[54] However, prior to the establishment of colonial rule, the Catholic mission in practice had a negligible impact in winning converts, and also served basically to cater to the preexisting Catholic community represented by the Brazilians. The dependence of the mission on the Brazilians is shown by the fact that it found itself obliged to use the Portuguese language to communicate with its congregation. On its first arrival in Ouidah in 1861, the head of the mission, Francesco Borghero (who was actually himself Italian), knowing no Portuguese, preached in Spanish in order to make himself understood.[55] Further, the mission's schools initially used Portuguese rather than French as their language of instruction.

Not all the Brazilian repatriates who returned to Africa were Christians, however. The enslaved population in Bahia included a significant element of Muslims, including many Yoruba as well as Hausa and other northerners, and some who were converted to Islam by fellow slaves in Brazil itself; Muslims in Bahia were known as "Male," which is the usual Yoruba (and also Fon) term. The slave rebellion of 1835 had been associated specifically with Muslims, and presumably, therefore, Muslims were especially liable to deportation in its aftermath. Muslims from Brazil played a significant role in the establishment of Islam in the coastal towns of Bénin.[56] In Ouidah, local tradition confirms that a section of the Brazilian ex-slaves who settled in the Maro quarter were Muslims, who were the first Muslims in the town and built the first mosque; Muslims from the interior (mainly Hausa) arrived only later, under French colonial rule, and settled in a separate quarter, called Zongo. The first Imam of Ouidah, Baba Onioubon, was a repatriate from Brazil and a Yoruba in origin, from the town of Ofa. Later Imams were Yoruba, Hausa, and from Borno, and were also from within the Brazilian community.[57] Likewise in Agoué, the Yoruba quarter, Anagokomè, and the Hausa quarter, Haoussakomè, included some Muslim settlers, and both had mosques. The first Imam of Agoué, Saidou, was a Yoruba freed slave from Brazil, and leadership within the Muslim community remained with the Yoruba until 1915, when it passed to the Imam of the Hausa mosque.[58]

In Porto-Novo and Lagos, Brazilian Muslims played a lesser role, since in these places Islam had already been introduced, directly from the interior, before the Brazilian re-emigration in the 1830s. In Porto-Novo, however, individual Brazilians were prominent in the Muslim community, notably José Paraïso, whose Muslim name was Abubakar. He is said to have been converted to Islam in Brazil, and tradition among his descendants nowadays holds that he was involved in the slave rebellion of 1835.[59] However, in West Africa he is said to have initially concealed his faith, publicly professing Catholic Christianity, and declared himself openly as a Muslim only after he entered the service of the king of Porto-Novo after 1864. José Paraïso, and later his son Ignacio (whose Muslim name was Sule Nunassu), operated as the effective political leaders of the Porto-Novo Muslims. A schism within the Muslim community, which began in 1911, was in part a challenge to the authority of the Paraïsos, and reflected a division between Brazilians and Yoruba from the interior.[60] In Lagos, too, some of the Brazilian repatriates were Muslims and erected their own mosques, such as the Salvador Mosque (named after its Brazilian patron) on Bamgbose Street.[61]

Roman Catholicism in these places also retains identifiably Brazilian features, notably the prominence of the festival of Nosso Senhor de Bonfim (in January), derived from Bahia, and the associated carnival masquerade of Buriyan, modeled on the Brazilian "bumba-meu-boï," at which songs in Portuguese are still sung. It may also be argued that Brazilian religious practice contributed to a tradition of religious tolerance, or peaceful coexistence, with, for example, many Brazilian families having Christian and Muslim branches, and even Brazilian Muslims commonly having children baptized in the Catholic Church, as well as often also practicing traditional cults—which remain strongly influential in the region to the present day.[62]

Yoruba Ethnogenesis

It may also be suggested that the Brazilian repatriate community played some role in the emergence of a collective Yoruba identity. It is well established that the Yoruba as a self-conscious ethnic group ("tribe" or "nation") are a recent phenomenon (if not perhaps quite an "invention"). The actual name "Yoruba" originally designated the Oyo specifically, rather than the peoples nowadays called Yoruba in general, who had no generic name for themselves before the nineteenth century. A sense of common ethnicity first arose in the diaspora rather than in the homeland. According to the conventional view, this occurred initially among the liberated slaves settled in Freetown, Sierra Leone (where the generic term most in currency was "Aku," though "Yoruba" was also used), and was fed back into the Yoruba homeland through the re-emigration of "Saros" from the late 1830s on.[63] As an explanation of the process of Yoruba ethnogenesis, however, this account seems incomplete. What is missing, I suggest, is the trans-Atlantic dimension. A sense of pan-ethnic identity had emerged even earlier among Yoruba-speaking slaves in the Americas, where they first began to employ a common collective name for themselves. However, the name was not "Yoruba" (or "Aku," as initially in Freetown), but "Nagô" or, in Cuba, "Lucumí," both of which were ethnonyms (or toponyms) that existed in West Africa in a restricted sense, applied only to particular subgroups of the Yoruba, but were generalized in the Americas to designate the entire linguistic group.[64] Given the large scale of re-emigration of Yoruba ex-slaves to West Africa, there is every likelihood that the enlarged ethnic identity that had emerged in Brazil was fed back into West Africa. As has been seen, returned slaves from Brazil retained a sense of identification with their African communities of birth or ancestry, as well as a sense of their collective Brazilian identity; although the primary loyalty of Yoruba repatriates was in some contexts to particular states or communities (as in the "tribal" politics of Lagos) rather than to the Yoruba "nation," a sense of generic "Nago" identity evidently also persisted. To the present day, for example, families of Brazilian origin in Ouidah will define themselves as Nagô, as well as Brazilian.

Moreover, during the nineteenth century, and indeed into the next, there was regular communication, which must have facilitated the exchange of ideas and information, as well as of commodities and people, between Brazil and Yorubaland. As Lorand Matory has argued, in order to properly understand the intellectual history of the Yoruba, including the construction of Yoruba ethnicity on both sides of the Atlantic, they have to be conceptualized as a "trans-Atlantic nation."[65] The Brazilian input into the process of Yoruba ethnogenesis is illustrated by the fact (easily overlooked by Nigerian, and more generally Anglophone, scholarship) that in francophone usage, in Benin, it was "Nagô" rather than "Yoruba" that was adopted as the preferred ethnic name; and in its generic, as opposed to its original more restricted application, this seems likely to represent a borrowing from Brazilian usage. The term "Nagô" was established in francophone usage in the first instance through its adoption by the French Roman Catholic missionaries, which in turn reflected the close association that developed, as noted above, between the French mission and the Brazilian community in this region.

The Yoruba former slaves who returned from Brazil and Cuba to resettle in West Africa represented a numerically tiny group—a few thousand—in relation to the population of the Yoruba homeland, but they nevertheless played a very important role in Yoruba history during the nineteenth century (and indeed beyond), parallel to that of the better-known reverse diaspora of Yoruba repatriates from Sierra Leone. Like the Sierra Leoneans, the Brazilians functioned as critical intermediaries between indigenous African communities and the growing penetration of European influence, in the spheres of religion and politics, as well as commerce, and in the consequent redefinition of Yoruba culture and identity. The activities and influence of the Brazilians, moreover, did not merely replicate those of the Sierra Leoneans but made a distinctive contribution, especially in the sphere of architecture and in relation to the spread of Roman Catholic Christianity and Islam, the legacy of which remains visible to the present day.

Notes

1. João José Reis, *Slave Rebellion in Brazil: The Muslim Uprising of 1835 in Bahia*, trans. Arthur Brakel (Baltimore: The Johns Hopkins University Press, 1993).
2. Laird W. Bergad, Figlésias García, and María del Carmen Barcia, *The Cuban Slave Market, 1790–1880* (Cambridge: Cambridge University Press, 1995), 72.
3. See, esp., Jean Herskovits Kopytoff, *A Preface to Modern Nigeria: The "Sierra Leonians" in Yoruba, 1830–1890* (Madison: University of Wisconsin Press, 1965).
4. The Cuban re-emigration has been little studied, but see Rodolfo Sarracino, *Los que volvieron a África* (Havana: Ciencias Sociales, 1988).
5. Reis, *Slave Rebellion*, 4–6. For freedpersons in Bahia, see also Maria Inês Côrtes de Oliveira, *O Liberto: o seu mundo e os outros: Salvador, 1790–1890* (Salvador, Bahia: Corrupio, 1988).
6. Bergad, Garcia, and Carmen Barcia, *Cuban Slave Market*, 128.
7. Antonio da Costa Peixoto, Luis Silveira, and Edmundo Correia Lopes, eds., *Obra nova de lingua geral de Mina de António da Costa Peixoto* (Lisbon: República Portuguesa, Ministério das Colônias, Divisão de Publicações e Biblioteca, Agência Geral das Colônias, 1945), 20. The vocabulary is of Gun, the language of Porto-Novo and Badagry.
8. The suggestion commonly made that it derives from Ajudá, the Portuguese form of the name Ouidah, is improbable on both linguistic and historical grounds.
9. The suggestion sometimes made that "Amaro" derives from "America" is certainly incorrect.
10. John Parker, *Making the Town: Ga State and Society in Early Colonial Accra* (Oxford: James Currey, 2000), 14–16.
11. See, especially, Jerry Michael Turner, "Les Brésiliens: The Impact of Former Brazilian Slaves upon Dahomey" (Ph.D. dissertation, Boston University, 1975); Milton Gurán, *Agudás: os "brasileiros" do Bénim* (Rio de Janeiro: Editora Nova Fronteira, 1999).
12. Some references to Brazilians, however, are made in Herskovits, *Preface to Modern Nigeria*. See also Pierre Verger, *Trade Relations between the Bight of Benin and Bahia, 17th to 19th Centuries* (Ibadan, Nigeria: Ibadan University Press, 1976), chap. 16.
13. Robin Law, "Religion, Trade, and Politics on the 'Slave Coast': Roman Catholic Missions in Allada and Whydah in the Seventeenth Century," *Journal of Religion in Africa* 21 (1991): 42–77.
14. Pierre Verger, *Os libertos: sete caminhos na liberdade de escravos da Bahía no século XIX* (Salvador, Bahia: Corrupio Fundação Cultural, Estado da Bahia, 1992), 9–13, with texts of original documents, 101–106.
15. John Adams, *Remarks on the Country Extending from Cape Palmas to the River Congo* (London: G. & W. B. Whittaker, 1823), 82–84.
16. See, generally, Robin Law and Kristin Mann, "West Africa in the Atlantic Community: The Case of the Slave Coast," *William and Mary Quarterly*, 3rd series, 56 (1999): 307–34; and, for the specific case of Ouidah, see Robin Law, "The Evolution of the Brazilian Community in Ouidah," *Slavery and Abolition* 22, no. 1 (April 2000): 22–41.
17. See David Ross, "The First Chacha of Whydah: Francisco Felix de Souza," *Odu*

2 (1969): 19–28; and idem, "The Career of Domingo Martinez in the Bight of Benin, 1833–64," *Journal of African History* 6 (1965): 79–90; Robin Law, "A carreira de Francisco Felix de Souza na Africa occidental (1800–1849)," *Topoi: Revista de História* (Rio de Janeiro) 2 (2001): 9–39; Verger, *Os libertos*, 43–48 (for d'Almeida); Turner, "Les Brésiliens," 126–27 (on de Medeiros).

18. This coastwise dimension of Brazilian activities and identity is well brought out in the historical novel by António Olinto, *A Casa de Aqua* (Rio de Janeiro, 1969); English translation: *The Water House* (London: Rex Collings, 1970).

19. Reis, *Slave Rebellion*, 207–208, 220–22.

20. Turner, "Les Brésiliens," 77–78, 85.

21. Reis, *Slave Rebellion*, 220.

22. See traditions of the founding of the Maro quarter in "Note historique sur Ouidah par l'Administrateur Gavoy (1913)," *Etudes dahoméennes* 13 (1955): 69–70; "Ouidah: organisation du commandement" (document of 1917, by the French administrator Reynier), *Mémoires du Bénin* 2 (1993): 44–46. The dates given (1812 by Gavoy, 1829 by Reynier) are clearly incorrect.

23. John Duncan, *Travels in Western Africa in 1845 and 1846, Comprising a Journey from Whydah, through the Kingdom of Dahomey, to Adofoodia, in the Interior* (London: Richard Bentley, 1847), i, 138, 185, 201–202; F. E. Forbes, *Dahomey and the Dahomans; Being the Journals of Two Missions to the King of Dahomey, and Residence at His Capital, in the Year 1849 and 1850* (London: Longman, Brown, Green, and Longmans, 1851), ii, 71–72.

24. Francesco Borghero, "Relation sur l'établissement des missions dans le Vicariat apostolique du Dahomé," 3 December 1863, in *Journal de Francesco Borghero, premier missionnaire du Dahomey 1861–1865*, ed. Renzo Mandirola and Yves Morel (Paris: Karthala, 1997), 280. Although some of these Brazilian Christians were freeborn immigrants rather than ex-slaves, some of the ex-slaves were not Christian.

25. Borghero, *Journal*, 48; idem, "Relation," 251.

26. Verger, *Os libertos*, 48–53.

27. Casimir Agbo, *Histoire de Ouidah du XVIe au XIXe siècle* (Avignon: Les Presses Universelles, 1959), 276–77, 279, 295.

28. See, especially, traditions collected in the 1930s and 1940s in Régina Byll-Cataria, ed., *Histoire d'Agoué (République du Bénin) par le Révérend Père Isidore Pélofy* (Leipzig: University of Leipzig, 2002); see also Silke Strickrodt, "'Afro-Brazilians' of the Western Slave Coast in the Nineteenth Century," ed. José C. Curto and Paul E. Lovejoy (New York: Humanity Books, 2004).

29. Borghero, *Journal*, 123.

30. Byll-Cataria, *Histoire d'Agoué*, 31–32.

31. Adolphe Akindélé and Cyrille Aguessy, *Contribution à l'étude de l'histoire de l'ancien royaume de Porto-Novo* (Dakar: IFAN, 1953), 71, 73.

32. Verger, *Trade Relations*, 543.

33. Verger, *Os libertos*, 34–41.

34. Forbes, *Dahomey*, ii, 72.

35. Duncan, *Travels*, ii, 177.

36. See, especially, Lisa A. Lindsay, "'To Return to the Bosom of Their Fatherland': Brazilian Immigrants in Nineteenth-Century Lagos," *Slavery and Abolition* 15 (1994): 22–50. Some references can also be found in general works on Lagos: Spencer H. Brown, "A History of the People of Lagos, 1850–1886" (Ph.D. dissertation, Northwestern Uni-

versity, 1964); Patrick Cole, *Modern and Traditional Elites in the Politics of Lagos* (Cambridge: Cambridge University Press, 1975); Michael J. Echeruo, *Victorian Lagos: Aspects of Nineteenth Century Lagos Life* (London: Macmillan, 1977); Robert Smith, *The Lagos Consulate, 1851–1861* (London: Macmillan, 1978).

37. According to the account of Governor Moloney of Lagos, dated 20 July 1887 (quoted in Verger, *Trade Relations*, 553).

38. United Kingdom Parliamentary Papers: Correspondence Relating to the Slave Trade, 1853–54, Class B, no. 56, Consul Campbell, Lagos, 28 December 1853.

39. Ibid., 1857–58, Class B, no. 11, Campbell, 5 June 1857.

40. See "Cuban Slaves in England," *Anti-Slavery Reporter* 2, no. 10 (October 1854): 234.

41. Lindsay, "'To Return to the Bosom of Their Fatherland,'" 27.

42. Verger, *Trade Relations*, 557.

43. Ibid., 549.

44. Borghero, *Journal*, 165 ff.; UK Parliamentary Papers, Slave Trade 1860, Class B, no. 9, Consul Brand, Lagos, 1 December 1859; 1861, Class B, no. 22, Acting Consul Hand, Lagos, 13 August 1860; Ajayi Kolawole Ajisafe, *History of Abeokuta*, 2nd ed. (Abeokuta: Fola Bookshops, 1964), 113; Saburi O. Biobaku, *The Egba and Their Neighbours, 1842–1872*, 2nd ed. (Ibadan, Nigeria: Ibadan University Press, 1991 [1957]), 76.

45. Ajisafe, *History of Abeokuta*, 111, 124, 135, 147, 153.

46. Brown, "History of the People of Lagos," 192–93.

47. Samuel Johnson, *The History of the Yorubas: From the Earliest Times to the Beginning of the British Protectorate*, 2nd ed. (Lagos, 1937), 369–70, 467, 534.

48. On "Afro-Brazilian" architecture more generally, see Manuela and Marianno Carneiro da Cunha, *From Slave Quarters to Town Houses: Brazilian Architecture in Nigeria and the People's Republic of Bénin* (São Paulo: Nobel, 1985).

49. Herskovits, *Preface to Modern Nigeria*, 368 n. 121.

50. Borghero, *Journal*, 46.

51. Pélofy, *Histoire d'Agoué*, 7.

52. Smith, *Lagos Consulate*, 39; Turner, "Les Brésiliens," 169–74.

53. Augusto Sarmento, *Portugal no Dahomé* (Lisbon: Livraria Tavares Cardoso, 1891), 61.

54. For the SMA mission, see, especially, Christiane Roussé-Grosseau, *Mission catholique et choc des modèles culturels en Afrique: l'exemple du Dahomey (1861–1928)* (Paris: L'Harmattan, 1992).

55. Borghero, *Journal*, 46.

56. See, especially, P. Marty, "Etudes sur l'Islam au Dahomey, Livre 1: Le Bas Dahomey," 2 parts, *Revue du monde musulman* 60 (1925): 109–88; 61 (1926): 75–146; see also Robin Law, "Islam in Dahomey: A Case Study of the Introduction and Influence of Islam in a Peripheral Area of West Africa," *Scottish Journal of Religious Studies* 9, no. 2 (1986): 50–64.

57. Marty, "Etudes sur l'Islam," part 2, 103–104; Reynier, "Ouidah," 44–45.

58. Pélofy, *Histoire d'Agoué*, 7; Marty, "Etudes sur l'Islam," part 2, 113–14.

59. Interview with Urbain Karim da Silva, Porto-Novo, September 1994.

60. Marty, "Etudes sur l'Islam," part 1, 164–80; and documents published in "L'Islam au Dahomey: les musulmans de Porto-Novo," *Mémoires du Bénin* 3 (1994): 45–81.

61. T. G. O. Gbadamosi, *The Growth of Islam among the Yoruba, 1841–1908* (London: Longman, 1978), 28, 30.

62. Olabiyi Babalola Yai, "The Identity, Contributions, and Ideology of the Aguda (Afro-Brazilians) on the Gulf of Benin: A Reinterpretation," *Slavery and Abolition* 22, no. 1 (2001): 72–82.

63. On Yoruba ethnogenesis, see especially J. D. Y. Peel, *Religious Encounter and the Making of the Yoruba* (Bloomington: Indiana University Press, 2000); see also Robin Law, "Local Amateur Scholarship in the Construction of Yoruba Ethnicity, 1880–1914," in *Ethnicity in Africa: Roots, Meanings, and Interpretations,* ed. Louise de la Gorgendière, Kenneth King, and Sarah Vaughan, 55–90 (Edinburgh: Centre of African Studies, University of Edinburgh, 1996).

64. Robin Law, "Ethnicity and the Slave Trade: 'Lucumi' and 'Nago' as Ethnonyms in West Africa," *History in Africa* 24 (1997): 205–19.

65. J. Lorand Matory, "The English Professors of Brazil: On the Diasporic Roots of the Yorùbá Nation," *Comparative Studies in Society and History* 41, no. 1 (January 1999): 72–103.

CHAPTER EIGHTEEN

The Yoruba Diaspora in Sierra Leone's Krio Society

C. Magbaily Fyle

The term "African diaspora" that emerged in the middle of the twentieth century was, according to historians T. R. Patterson and R. D. Kelly, intended to "emphasize unifying experiences of African peoples dispersed by the slave trade."[1] Wherever such peoples are dispersed, the essence of a diaspora is "in large measure contingent on a diasporic identity that links the constituent parts of that diaspora to a homeland," in this case with the African continent. Thus while the diaspora idea generally relates to a wide dispersal of peoples of African origin throughout the world, a key element in any diaspora is the creation and survival of a diasporic consciousness. For Patterson and Kelly, this involves a constant "construction and reproduction of diasporic identities" similar to what Stuart Hall describes as a perpetual re-shaping of identity.[2] Hall also reminds us that the construction of an African diasporic identity does not occur in isolation but rather is implicitly complicated by "broader socioeconomic, cultural and political developments of a given historical moment." It is in essence an issue of a constantly shifting identity, always related to the homeland.

Viewed from a more restricted focus, these issues of identity and homeland relate squarely to the emergence of diasporas within Africa itself, although studies of the African diaspora have more generally disregarded this conceptualization.[3] The diaspora and homeland here would relate to different parts of the large continent of Africa, as well as to issues of intervening influences from outside the continent such as the Atlantic slave trade and the role of returnees from the Americas.

This is the basis of this chapter's discussion of a Yoruba diaspora in Sierra Leone in relation to the growth of an urban culture. The issue of an urban culture with basic similarities across the continent has been generally treated with respect to isolated elements of that culture such as music, education, or religion.[4] There is a greater need to study the intricate complexities of a fusion of all these elements into a single mass.

The emergence of a new ethnicity in the form of Krio society in Freetown, the capital of Sierra Leone by the end of the nineteenth century, was a result of a concatenation of factors from different directions. Typically, as with the growth of an urban bourgeoisie under colonial rule, the dominant element of the new culture, the factor that set the standard for advancement and status, was Western culture. With Krio culture, however, the base African element came from different ethnic groups from across West Africa, as a result of British naval activity in West Africa against the Atlantic slave trade. The welter of African ethnicity that fused with a largely British overlay to give Krio culture had a dominant African strain, that of the Yoruba from present-day Nigeria. This prevailing Yoruba ethnicity therefore fostered a prominent Yoruba flavor in Krio culture. There has been quite a controversy among scholars about the name of this new ethnicity in Sierra Leone, whether it is called "Creole," as predominant in the literature, or "Krio," as the people refer to themselves when speaking their own language, a conclusion supported by evidence from the Yoruba language. We will visit this controversy later in this discussion.

Compared to the Yoruba diaspora in Brazil,[5] for example, it would have been easier by reason of proximity for the Yoruba in Freetown to maintain a constant link with their homeland in present-day Nigeria. This factor would have encouraged a vibrant reinforcement of the Yoruba element in Freetown society from the 1840s. As Krio society emerged by the end of the nineteenth century, older groups and identities began to give in to a new perception of themselves as Krio. There was a strong reluctance on the part of vocal elements in this new mix to relinquish their identity, which ensured that the numerically stronger Yoruba in the Freetown community held on to their own culture for a more extended period. Krio society emerged, however, dominated by Western and then Yoruba cultural elements such as food patterns and anthroponymy, while the Yoruba had also significantly influenced other ethnic groups surrounding Freetown, particularly the Temne.

The Freetown Experiment

The colony of Sierra Leone started as a Province of Freedom, a spillover from the philanthropic efforts of a few British citizens.[6] A few hundred former slaves in England were transported to the Sierra Leone peninsula to start a new settlement on land negotiated from the local Temne chiefs at Romarong.[7] Although this early settlement failed, it was refounded with the new name of "Freetown" in 1792 with about a thousand freed slaves from Nova Scotia. These latter had fought against their slave masters in the American colonies on the invitation of the British. When the British lost the war, the "loyal blacks,"[8] who were thus liberated by fighting for the British, were taken to Nova Scotia in Canada, which was still a British colony. The bitter cold and unfulfilled promises of land made these African Americans welcome the evacuation to Sierra Leone. These "Nova Scotians," as they came to be called in Sierra Leone historiography, were joined in 1800 by another group of freed blacks, the Maroons from Jamaica, who were moved to Nova Scotia from Jamaica where they were a threat to British authority. They were finally sent to Sierra Leone.[9] These three groups formed the early "settlers" in the new colony of Sierra Leone, taken over by the British government in 1808 from the Sierra Leone Company that had been running it.

These three groups themselves represent a diaspora of returned blacks from the Americas who started living in Freetown, striving to maintain identities separate from one another and from the surrounding local inhabitants to whom they felt superior because of their Western background.[10]

The Anti–Slave Trade Patrols and the Liberated Africans

In the beginning years of the nineteenth century the British navy started plying the West African waters to intercept slave ships still conducting the illegal slave trade. The victims found onboard such ships were set free in Freetown, a good reason for the British takeover of the Sierra Leone colony in 1808. These newly freed blacks came from all along West Africa, from Senegal to the Congo. They had once been captured and put onboard ships as slaves and then recaptured by the British navy. They were therefore called "Recaptives" or "Liberated Africans." Among these Liberated Africans could be found a large number of cultures in West Africa. A German linguist, Sigismond Koelle, testified to this when he published his *Polyglotta Africana* in 1854, based on a painstaking study he did of vocabulary among the Liberated Africans. Among languages spoken by the Liberated Africans, Koelle identified more than two hundred African languages extant between Mozambique and Senegal.[11] This brought in a very rich linguistic and cultural background that was later to feed into the new Krio culture.

The Aku Element

There was a very rapid increase in the Yoruba group among the Liberated African population in the 1820s. This was a result of the wars of succession accompanying the fall of the Oyo Empire beginning at the end of the eighteenth century.[12] One of these wars, described by the Recaptives as the "Owu War," occurred in 1821.[13] As was the case, for different reasons, regarding wars in West Africa at the time, such conflagrations were fueled by the demand for slaves at the coast and the incessant supply of firearms. Many of the victims of the Owu War were captured and sold to slavers bound for the Atlantic crossing. Since the British navy was particularly active on the West African coast at this time, a number of these slave ships were intercepted and the slaves onboard liberated in Freetown. Thus, by the end of the 1820s, the Yoruba decidedly outnumbered all other Liberated African groups. The Yoruba were regarded in the colony as "Aku," a term derived from a Yoruba greeting—"akushɛ."[14] As the population of Liberated Africans increased, they were settled in newly created villages around the colony. The largest of these villages—Hastings, Waterloo, and Benguema—were predominantly peopled by the Aku.[15]

The Aku accompanied their numerical preponderance with enterprise, and this gradually led to their dominance, first among the Liberated Africans, but by the 1840s noticeably among the earlier settlers, too. These earlier Nova Scotians had at first regarded the Maroons as inferior. By the end of the 1820s that distinction was fading. Nova Scotians and Maroons then came to be regarded as "Settlers" as against the "Liberated Africans" whom the Settlers now regarded as "krut" (unpolished). The Aku were known for sticking together as a separate community, practicing and holding on to their Yoruba traditions in the face of the dominant Westernizing influence of the Nova Scotians and the colonial government. As their numbers were rapidly reinforced by new Recaptives, the Aku organized together economically and socially, and this solidarity began to bear fruit.

The Aku would join together in business ventures, for example, and outbid others in public auction of goods from condemned slave trade vessels. Socially they acted as a distinct community and elected their first "king," at the latest by the mid-1820s. The Aku king was recognized by the colonial governor[16] who needed such assistance in the administration of the colony. Supervised by the king, the Aku passed laws obeyed by all Aku on pain of being ostracized by the rest of the community. For example, those who did not obey such laws were not accorded traditional burial rites, a consequence all Aku feared.

This first Aku king, Thomas Will, was among the wealthiest in the colony. Like other leading Aku, colony members were buying up prized property in the center of Freetown, against the vehement protest of the Settlers who considered that area their territorial preserve.[17] As observed by A. B. C. Sibthorpe, an indigenous historian writing in the 1860s: "The Akus [were] the most prominent of the improved Liberated Africans" by the 1840s.[18]

Freetown society, by the 1840s, had become dominated both economically and culturally by the Aku. Their numbers, their unity, and their economic prosperity ensured that the Aku earned the Settlers' respect. Some of the Nova Scotians returned to America in disgust. A number of Maroons resisted this change by leaving their rental property empty and losing income rather than renting the property to Aku peoples. But as the numbers of Settlers dwindled through lack of reinforcement and disdainful attitudes, the Aku thrived. By the 1850s the Settlers were grudgingly beginning to accept Aku dominance as a fact of life, and this contributed to breaking down the barriers between Settlers and Liberated Africans.

Westernization

All these developments were acted out under the watchful eyes of the British colonial rulers who provided the dominant cultural overlay for all the Africans in the colony. Aku or non-Aku were socialized into a predominantly Christian and Western schooling paradigm. Missionaries were active in the new villages supported by the colonial government. Standards of acceptability were set by the dominant colonial system. As Christopher Fyfe relates, "Recaptives were forbidden to wear Muslim gowns."[19] A good number of the Aku were Muslims before they arrived in Freetown. Their practice of Islam was contested by the colonial system; one governor, in the 1830s, showed his disgust of the Muslim Aku. When the Aku built a mosque at Fourah Bay outside Freetown, they were attempting to maintain an identity as Muslims separate from their Fula co-religionists. The governor of the colony,

> Doherty, refused to believe they had been converted in their Yoruba homeland. . . . He presumed them won over by (the neighboring) Fula, whose successful propagation of their polygamous faith seemed to him subversive of the Christian principles the Colony was founded to propagate. . . . In 1839 the Police pulled down the Foulah Town mosque. Doherty, without directly opposing, took the opportunity of proposing to the Colonial Office that he move the recaptive Muslims away from Freetown and pass an ordinance to expel aliens.[20]

The Settlers and some Recaptives, jealous of the Aku, supported the governor in these moves. But this did not deter the Aku. It merely represented a declaration of values by the controlling force, the colonial governor, which the African subjects had to follow, by and large, or face at times unsavory consequences. Thus Aku and other Recaptives experienced a dynamic above their own group squabbles against which they had little power to fight. The entire Settler and Liberated African community in Freetown was consequently being indoctrinated into a Western, Christian influence with all the trappings of Western culture that came with it, providing the other side of the emergent Krio culture.

The resilience of the Aku, however, largely served to maintain a strong African, mainly Yoruba, element in Krio culture as is shown in the food, dress, language, and religious and naming patterns of the Krio. But before this development formalized, the Aku community was experiencing internal acculturation processes of its own. The question of Aku identity, by the mid-nineteenth century, has posed some problem for historians. Fyfe rightly comments that in Freetown the term "Aku" was "loosely applied to those from countries adjacent to Yorubaland."[21] Indeed, this process of acculturation has occurred in many societies where a dominant majority culturally absorbs those more closely associated with it. In this case, the close association was diasporic, having been transferred from physical proximity in their place of origin to virtual assimilation in their new diasporic setting. Thus these ethnic groups that emanated from original homes adjoining the Yoruba in Nigeria became associated with the relatively large Yoruba diaspora in Freetown. One of the Yoruba kings, John Macauley, who took office in 1840, was of Hausa origin. He was evidently enculturated to become Yoruba, and his nickname, "atakpa" (kicker), was Yoruba.

Thus, while the concept of "becoming Aku" was definitely a socializing process in the mid-nineteenth century, it might be an exaggeration to assume that all the Africans who became part of Krio society were known as Aku in the colony.[22] It is clear that the term "Aku," up to the late nineteenth century, was not synonymous with what became "Krio" as some scholars would imply, and that Aku was differentiated from other ethnic groups in the colony right down to the end of the nineteenth century. Even with the first census in the colony in April 1891, it was indicated that half the thirty thousand people living in Freetown were Liberated Africans, the majority Aku and Ibo.[23] The discrimination provided between Aku and Ibo in this census clearly indicates that Liberated Africans were not all regarded as Aku.

Aku Return to the Original Homeland

By 1840 the prosperity won by the Aku began to find expression in their desire to return to their original homeland. This started with the first boat bought jointly by three Aku for the purpose of the first expedition to Yorubaland of sixty-seven Aku in April 1839. This movement was not initiated nor particularly supported by the colonial government, even though the Aku repeatedly called on the government to support them.[24]

The initial destination of these Aku was the Yoruba town of Badagry. A couple of freed Hausa from Trinidad on their way to Badagry had passed through Freetown and stimulated the interest of the Freetown Aku to relocate to this town. Successive Aku joint or individual ventures bought ships and started transporting Racaptive Aku from Freetown to Badagry, hardly discouraged by the initial lukewarm reception they received there. Thus, as Fyfe comments, within three or four years of the first venture, "several hundred" Aku had returned to Yoruba country in Nigeria.[25]

While Badagry was their original destination, they began moving to the Egba heartland at Abeokuta starting in 1842. They were welcomed there, and Abeokuta soon became the predominant place of choice for returning Aku. The Church Missionary Society (CMS) soon acceded to the urgings of the Aku and agreed to open a mission in Abeokuta. A white missionary, Henry Townsend, was the first to be sent there since he was given free passage by the Aku who owned the ship he traveled on. Townsend was accompanied by another Aku Christian leader named Andrew Wilhelm, whose passage was paid for by his Aku Church members at the predominantly Aku village of Hastings. Wilhelm was so satisfied with his trip to Abeokuta that he returned to Hastings and easily persuaded a large group of Aku there to return home to Abeokuta.

Abeokuta soon became the center of a CMS mission station in Yorubaland. This town's development as a Christian center was largely owing to the labors of Ajayi Crowther, a liberated Yoruba slave.[26] Crowther had accompanied a British expedition to the Niger River and, at his urging, was sent to Britain to study religion and was ordained a priest in 1843. He returned to Freetown and ministered to Aku at their church in the east end of Freetown. Crowther preached sermons in Yoruba at this church to the delight of the Aku congregation. This so thrilled the Yoruba that even the Aku Muslim headman asked his Muslim Aku community to attend the church and enjoy the Yoruba culture expressed in the Christian element.[27]

Identity among the Aku

These activities demonstrate a remarkable sense of identity among the Aku that transcended religious specificities. That identity was now an Aku identity, not particularly Yoruba although it had a Yoruba base. These Aku had lived in Freetown for a couple of decades since the early 1820s. While Aku children born in Freetown by the mid-nineteenth century grew up speaking predominantly Yoruba and retained cultural elements like face marks,[28] they had been born into a society that was slowly blending Yoruba values with a new culture. Many had been given Western names that they continued to carry. They were socialized in Western schools, with Christian missionary effort that carried a distinctly European flavor. As mentioned earlier, they had assimilated peripheral groups from their area of origin around present-day Nigeria. All these factors were molding a new Aku identity.

That was why Crowther's missionary preaching in Yoruba was very welcome. Even the Muslim Aku were now being socialized in terms of an Islamic culture away from their original milieu. They now associated mostly with the Fula Muslims in Freetown, forced to adopt Islamic reinforcement from this source to counter the predominantly Christianizing influence of the colonial system. For advanced Islamic training, they were sending their children to Futa Jalon, the "Mecca" of Fula Muslims in this region of Africa. From all fronts, the Aku were being socialized into a new culture while they determinedly stuck to their Yoruba base. This new identity was expressed when the Aku of Freetown began raising money to build a "Freetown Church" in Abeokuta.[29] They did not identify it as a Yoruba church, for they were now people of Freetown, largely of Yoruba descent, and though becoming Westernized, were proudly touting a strong leaning toward Yoruba culture.

Emergent Krio Society

By the end of the nineteenth century a new Krio culture was emerging that embraced Nova Scotians, Maroons, and Liberated Africans, Aku or otherwise. Nova Scotians at first had regarded Maroons as inferior, since initially the Maroons had been the group least influenced by Western culture and had continued to practice elements of their African heritage, such as polygyny, when they returned to Sierra Leone in 1800.[30] As Nova Scotians and Maroons faced the alarmingly growing number of Liberated Africans, they began to close ranks and to regard the latter as inferior. I could hear my own grandmother hurling what was considered an abusive slur, such as "you liberated, far-fetched"!

By the 1850s the success of the Liberated Africans, particularly the Aku, at first disillusioned the Nova Scotians and Maroons. As they would have put it at the time, it was intolerable for them to endure these "nouveau riche" Liberated Africans lording it over "cultured" Nova Scotians and Maroons. Writing in the 1860s, the native Sierra Leonean historian Sibthorpe neatly summed up the situation by mid-century:

> The Nova Scotians saw with chagrin and envy themselves sinking into oblivion, and the "captives" as they styled them, rising into influence and power. Instead of competing with these whom they deemed their inferiors, the Nova Scotians, with a few exceptions withdrew from the field of industry in disgust, some transporting themselves back to America.[31]

The "few exceptions" among the Nova Scotians and Maroons led the way to integration, for, by the last quarter of the nineteenth century, Nova Scotians and Maroons were no longer objecting to their sons and daughters marrying Liberated African children.

The use of the term "Krio" in reference to this new culture has stirred quite a discussion among historians, with Sierra Leone Krio scholars insisting that the term derived from the Yoruba "akiriyo," meaning those who go about paying visits.[32] Gibril Cole, a Muslim Krio scholar, delves deeper into the etymology of the term "Krio." He posits,

> The word *Krio* could be traced to the Yoruba verb "*kiri*" (to trade). Among the Yoruba, it was customary for potential buyers to enquire from traders "*kilo'on Kiri?*" (What are you selling?). In Sierra Leone, the word *Akiriyo* was used initially to refer to the Yoruba Liberated Africans who went from place to place selling their wares in the rural villages outside Freetown. According to oral tradition, the name was initially used as an "*oki*" (or nickname) for petty traders in the village settlements by fellow Yoruba. However, in time, other non-Yoruba Liberated Africans began to use the name as a generic referent for all Yoruba Liberated Africans, especially as their penchant for commerce became even

more commonplace. The term *Akiriyo* has evolved over the years to *Kiriyo*, and finally to its present form Krio.[33]

The Krio linguist Clifford Fyle insists about the Krio language that "linguistically, words borrowed from English do not lose a final 'l' sound in Krio pronunciation."[34] Therefore, contrary to what Western linguists have insisted, the word "Krio" could not have come from the English "Creole," any more than the Krio word "adu" would have come from the English "how do" rather than from the Yoruba greeting term "adukpe," as these same linguists had claimed. Paul Hair, an English historian of Sierra Leone, has more recently been insisting that, because of the historical and scholarly antecedent of the term "Creole," with historical evidence dating to the seventeenth century, the name of this Sierra Leone people must have been derived from "Creole."[35]

There is no particular reason to conclude that the seventeenth-century antecedent would have lingered until the late nineteenth century. There was no structure or system that could have served to preserve the use of this term over that period. It could have been preserved in any of the local languages just as the Temne term "ɔpotho," meaning "whiteman," derived from the word "Portuguese," the first white people to have contact with the coastal Temne.[36] There is no hint of such preservation in any form. If, on the other hand, the Nova Scotians had been familiar with the term "Creole" in any form before they came to the colony, this would have showed up in one form or the other in the available evidence. There is no trace of this in oral or written sources.

Interestingly, Paul Hair's view is supported by many Krio people who would pour scorn on the interpretation of Krio scholars. One needs to trace this attitude to the beginnings of the colony, when Nova Scotians regarded everyone else as inferior and uncultured. Thus a "Western"-derived interpretation of the term "Krio" was more "dignified" to the Krio people than one coming from this same "inferior" Yoruba culture.

The evidence is unequivocal that the term "Krio" was initially applied to the descendants of Liberated Africans, most of whom were Aku. As John Peterson comments, "originally, to have been a Creole meant that one was a child of Liberated African parents."[37] This would strengthen the argument for the derivation of the term "Krio" from the Yoruba "akiriyo." Peterson argues that the greatest objectors to the application of the term "Krio" to themselves were the descendants of Nova Scotians and Maroons.[38]

The Nova Scotians and Maroons, who considered themselves more Westernized and therefore superior to the Liberated Africans, resented being identified by an appellation generally applied to the latter. In spite of their vehement objections, sometimes expressed in print, the term "Krio," by the early twentieth century, came to be applied to all Westernized Africans in Freetown.[39]

The Liberated Africans, particularly the Aku, also doggedly held on to their Yoruba culture to the very end of the century, but this was succumbing to a larger Krio identity by that time. The last Aku king, I. B. Pratt, carried influence until his death in 1880. The kingship was not filled after Pratt's death. When some determined Aku attempted to revive it in 1891, they strove to relate the revival not only to Aku but to all Freetown peoples,[40] a clear indication of their recognition of the emergent Krio society embracing not only Aku but others. That the plan failed and was ridiculed by educated and vocal Krio of all backgrounds was additional testimony to the growing acceptance of all Africans in the colony as belonging to a single Krio identity.

The Yoruba in Krio Culture

The Krio culture that was clearly evident by the early twentieth century was a blend of Western and African, predominantly Yoruba culture of the Aku. The Western element was significantly British, although aspects of American culture brought by the Nova Scotians remained. Thus, for example, Freetown high society would dance the "Charleston" at respectable ballroom events.[41]

The British aspect predominated, however, with the unfortunate element, common in colonial rule in Africa, of teaching Africans that their own cultural values were worthless or at best inferior, while Western culture was lauded as superior in every respect. It was possible to implant this attitude among the Krio people, as the dominant colonial government had the resources and control, and insisted on condemning African culture in the colony, sometimes by legislation. The Nova Scotians, too, had imbibed similar attitudes through slavery in America and therefore also believed that the Western culture they came with to the Sierra Leone colony was unquestionably superior to African values. Thus one aspect of Krio culture, the Western element, was hegemonic, laden with prejudice and a near intolerance of other African cultures.

It is with this derived attitude that the Krio regarded the African element in their new culture. However, since there was a strong Aku element in Krio society that had earlier experienced rejection by Nova Scotians and Maroons, there had been a tendency among the Aku to react by clinging to their Yoruba-based culture. The Aku therefore ensured that Krio culture retained a strong Yoruba element in language, food, anthroponymy, and other factors that even the highly Westernized and Christianized of the Krio found it difficult to easily disregard. The Krio would then readily practice the African part of their culture but would want to speak "more proudly" of the Western elements—the Church, the Masonic lodge, and Western dress, food, and music—and would quickly slip into speaking English or throwing in English sentences in their speech, no matter how quaint the style.[42]

Krio Language

One of the most telling areas of the Yoruba in Krio culture is the Krio language. While the Krio language is dominated by an English-derived vocabulary, perhaps a quarter of the Krio words are from Yoruba. With the dominant position of the British at the colony and Britain's hegemonic insistence on the superiority of its own values, the preponderance of the English-based vocabulary in Krio is readily explained. Yoruba, the largest ethnic group in the colony, were the next strongest influence on vocabulary. Krio words of Yoruba origin, like their English counterpart, adopted meanings not exactly determined by those languages of origin. For instance, while Yoruba would say "oko" to mean husband, in Krio the term "oko" is only used to refer to the bridegroom at a wedding ceremony. Krio would say "odukoko" to describe a large ditch, dangerous when flooded by rain, whereas, in Yoruba, "odukoko" means "a large pot." Further, the Yoruba "akpari," a yam head, means a bald person in Krio. Not just words but whole phrases were carried from Yoruba into Krio. A Krio phrase like "a je-o" (please accept this price I am offering you) or "shegbu ma shegbu" (we know it is no good, but let us try to deal with it) became part of normal speech in Krio.

The juxtaposition of Yoruba, other African words, and English-derived words in the Krio language meant that Yoruba and other African words were sometimes used as synonyms of English counterparts to express disdain, disapproval, or contempt. A good example is the word "dance," used in Krio with much the same meaning as in English. In Krio, however, the Yoruba word for dance, "sire," means dancing in a rather wild and unrespectable way, with a similar attitude of facetiousness attached to the Yoruba word "rokoto," which means, in Krio, "shaking the hips vigorously while dancing."[43]

Food and Associated Cultural Patterns

A predominant area of Yoruba influence in Krio culture is related to cultural matters surrounding food.[44] One such event in Krio is the "awujo" feast. The word in Yoruba refers to "an assembly of persons." In Krio, an "awujo" is a "ceremonial feasting for the dead in remembrance of them or to secure their cooperation and blessing on an important family occasion (e.g., a wedding, the possession of a new house)."[45] An "awujo" is usually made at specified periods after a death, the most popular being the "foti de" (fortieth day). This occurs forty days after a funeral has taken place.

Specific types of dishes are done for the "awujo," especially the beans dish, made with black-eyed peas and palm oil in the Yoruba fashion, served with fried plantain, sweet potato, and "akara," also made out of crushed black-eyed peas. Incidentally black-eyed peas are used for other snacks such as "abobo" and "olèlè," both Yoruba foods also usually served at the "awujo" but also eaten commonly in Freetown.

Another important dish at the "awujo" is the "fufu ɛn bitas." The "fufu" is made out of crushed cassava and is cooked like mashed potatoes. This is accompanied by the "bitas," named from "bitter leaves," a base vegetable that normally has a bitter taste that is removed by crushing and washing the vegetable. A small amount of the bitter leaves is used and blended with a much larger quantity of another "plasas" (vegetable used to prepare soup dishes). The predominant "plasas" can be one or two types drawn from a number of options. Examples of this variety are most popularly "bologi" but also possibly "ogumo" or "ajefawo," all directly Yoruba-introduced vegetables.

Another "plasas" dish for the "awujo" is the "krenkren," a slimy vegetable used for the sauce, but sometimes boiled separately from the "alakpa," that is, the rest of the soup, to better retain its green property. "Alakpa" and boiled "krenkren" are then blended together when the meal is consumed. This variant of the "krenkren" is called the "obiata." There are other types of foods among the Krio that emanate from Yoruba traditions. Crushed corn is used to cook a pap called "ogi" and a snack called "agidi."

It has been necessary to dwell at some length on an identification of these dishes and methods of preparation in order to demonstrate that the "awujo" and the food system associated with it are derived from Yoruba traditions. Krio of all persuasion, from those who believe that they are superior to others, to the meek and humble, practice the "awujo" tradition. While most Krio would extol Western foods like the French salad or ham and bacon treats, because of the perceived prestige associated with Western elements, they would all go back to basic African foods for everyday consumption.

Esoteric Clubs

The Yoruba introduced into Krio culture esoteric organizations that are still prominent among Krio people. These are the "oje" and hunters societies. These societies are described here as esoteric since the majority of their activities are decidedly kept secret from the uninitiated. There is a public element involved, whereby members hold public masquerades accompanying a masked dancer, either in a field or a clearing or dancing through the streets of Freetown.

One way of keeping the bulk of the activities of these organizations away from the general public is through the use of an esoteric language, unfamiliar to the rest of the population. Thus, when the public masquerades take place, these organizations conduct their activities in the Yoruba language.[46] The general public can only follow the songs through the syllables uttered, but becomes familiar with commands and single Yoruba words in the discourse, words such as "igberi" (uninitiated), "gbada" (stay), "fakuŋ" (wearing Egungun costumes), "Iyaode" (senior woman in a hunting society), and so on.[47]

This practice of using an esoteric language is not uncommon within secret society organizations in Sierra Leone, for it has been noted that, among the Mende ethnic group in Sierra Leone, the female secret society called the Sande uses songs and words in the neighboring Temne language, and the reverse is done in the Temne Bundo society.[48]

377

The "ojɛ" organization was more prevalent among Muslim Krio in the east end of Freetown. These Muslims related more readily with their co-religionists of other ethnic groups who migrated to Freetown from polities beyond the Sierra Leone colony and settled mostly in the same general area as the Muslim Krio. Consequently the "ojɛ" society spread to other Muslim groups, notably the Temne.[49] Hunters societies in Freetown still maintain the Yoruba tradition, with a strong emphasis on the use of herbs and hunting for meat in the forested areas especially to commemorate the wedding or death of a member or a major public event. Krio of all social levels have increasingly grown to identify with these societies in the more recent past, getting beyond the Western stigma, which many upper-class Krio shared, of belonging to "heathenish" groups.

Naming Ceremony and Names

A number of other Krio cultural practices are directly derived from Yoruba. The "komojade" ceremony of the Krio carries a similar meaning as the Yoruba "ako konjade"—the naming ceremony of a child. The "komojade," done a few days after birth, differs from the Christian christening ceremony among the Krio people. The christening ceremony is also performed a few months later, after the "komojade." The Krio regard the "komojade" as "pul na do" (taking out of doors), a ceremony in which the new baby is taken outside for the first time, as many births at first took place at home. The baby is literally introduced to its immediate surroundings by an elderly female after prayers are said by the local pastor or by an elderly relative. The child would already have been named and the naming formalized at the christening. Among the Muslim Krio, "komojade" still retains the feature of a naming ceremony, and no christening ceremony follows.

Among the Christian Krio, children are given names reflecting the blend of Western and African values in Krio culture. Children receive a first name, usually referred to as a "Christian name," which is invariably a Western name. A second name, an "os nem" (literally, "house name"), is also given. This is the name the individual comes to be called by friends and relations and in informal settings. Some of these "os nem" come from Ibo, Akan, or Hausa cultures, reflecting the varied background of the Krio. The overwhelming majority of "os nem," however, are Yoruba. Names like Ayodele, Iyatunde, Babashola, Ekundayo, Abiodun, Iyalode, and a host of others are common fare among the Krio.

Krio people shorten Yoruba names in their own fashion, however. They do not follow any principles of the Yoruba language by which each name has a meaning, and breaking up words usually conforms to related principles. The Krio pay little attention to the meanings of names and, when they shorten the names, the abbreviations are incomprehensible to Yoruba people. The name

"Omolara," for example, is shortened in Krio to "Omo." This is uncharacteristic of the Yoruba who would rather say "Molara," thereby rendering an intelligible part of the meaning of the name "my children are my kith and kin." Another example is the name "Modukpɛ" which the Yoruba would abbreviate to "Dukpe," meaning "I gave thanks," whereas the Krio would use "Modu," a name the Yoruba could not understand. By the late twentieth century Krio culture had varied "os nem" to a considerable degree so that the preponderance of Yoruba "os nem" is no longer as remarkable.

The issue of altered forms of Yoruba names among the Krio people raises the question of transformation in diasporic cultures. Patterson and Kelley address this quite succinctly in their discussion of the processes of cultural change as Africans were forcibly taken across the Atlantic into the diaspora in the Americas.[50] Matters of "proper" retention of cultural forms would essentially be irrelevant, as culture is a dynamic on which various indeterminate factors in the process of migration have an impact. End products are often at variance with original copies, and even those products eternally mutate into newer forms, with sometimes dangerously unrecognizable complexities.

Esusu

Another Krio institution that was fairly common among ethnic groups in southern Nigeria and was undoubtedly introduced into Krio by the Yoruba is the thrift and savings club called "esusu" (also "osusu").[51] In this method of savings, friends, relatives, or co-workers come together in a defined group and at a specified period, usually at the end of the calendar month, and each deposits a fixed amount into a fund that is harvested at the same time by one of the group members. Assuming, then, that there are twelve members, once a year each will receive the amount he or she invests multiplied by twelve. "Esusu" has spread widely in Sierra Leone and, to the present day, remains an attractive savings mechanism for people who may have cogent reasons to distrust a bank.

This chapter has attempted to identify the major elements of Krio culture derived from Yoruba traditions, elements such as food, anthroponymy, and popular culture which are sometimes glossed over in discussions of cultural hybridization. A host of other items basically define the African aspect of Krio culture. Significantly, the chapter has also explored the use of ethnicity in power relations between the early Settlers and the Recaptives, all of which melted away as the economic fortunes of the Recaptives raised their status in relation to the Settlers with whom they had merged, thus giving rise to Krio society. As noted earlier, Krio people have always tended to emphasize their identity in terms of the Western elements of their culture, relegating the African aspects to a less prominent place, although practicing the latter as vigorously as the former. This attitude is quite prevalent in urban African cultures,[52] although "public" denial of the practice of some African values, such as indigenous religious beliefs, persists.

In the past couple of decades public acceptance has increasingly come to include certain aspects of African values in African urban culture. A reorientation of identity among urban Africans, including the Krio, is therefore in progress. Thus, in the process delineated here, one experiences the development of Krio culture as a formulation and reformulation of identity based on overlapping influences from various directions, yet preserving a base identity, significantly Yoruba in this case.

Notes

1. T. R. Patterson and R. D. Kelley, "Unfinished Migrations: Reflections on the African Diaspora and the Making of the Modern World," *African Studies Review* 43, no. 1 (2000): 14.

2. Stuart Hall, "Cultural Identity and Diaspora," in *Colonial Discourse and Post-Colonial Theory*, ed. Patrick Williams and Laura Chrisman (New York: Columbia University Press, 1994), 392–403.

3. For a geographic concentration of diaspora studies on areas outside Africa, see Paul Gilroy, *The Black Atlantic: Modernity and Double Consciousness* (Cambridge, Mass.: Harvard University Press, 1993); J. E. Harris, ed., *Global Dimensions of the African Diaspora* (Washington, D.C.: Howard University Press, 1982); Isidore Okpehwo, Carole Boyce-Davies, and Ali A. Mazrui, eds., *The African Diaspora: African Origins and New World Identities* (Bloomington: Indiana University Press, 1998); and Michael L. Conniff and Thomas J. Davis, *Africans in the Americas: A History of the Black Diaspora* (New York: St. Martin's, 1994).

4. For example, S. H. Martin, "Music in Urban East Africa: Five Genres in Dar es Salaam," *Journal of African Studies* 9, no. 3 (1982): 155–63; E. S. Kinney, "Urban West African Music and Dance," *African Urban Notes* 5, no. 4 (1970): 3–10; Philip Foster, *Education and Social Change in Ghana* (London: Routledge, 1965); and M. Glélé, *Religion, culture et politique en Afrique noire* (Paris: Economica, 1981).

5. See, e.g., Abdias do Nascimento, *Africans in Brazil: A Pan African Perspective* (Trenton, N.J.: Third World Press, 1992).

6. John Peterson, *Province of Freedom: A History of Sierra Leone, 1787–1870* (Evanston, Ill.: Northwestern University Press, 1969). For a qualification of this concept, see Mavis Campbell, *Back to Africa: George Ross and the Maroons—From Nova Scotia to Sierra Leone* (Trenton, N.J.: Africa World Press, 1993).

7. A. B. C. Sibthorpe, *History of Sierra Leone*, 4th ed. (New York: Humanities, 1970), 7.

8. J. Walker, *The Black Loyalists: The Search for a Promised Land in Nova Scotia and Sierra Leone, 1783–1830* (New York: Africana, 1976).

9. Nemata Blyden, *West Indians in West Africa: 1808–1880: The African Diaspora in Reverse* (Rochester, N.Y.: University of Rochester Press, 2000).

10. Tom Schick, *Behold the Promised Land! A History of Sierra Leone and Liberia* (Madison: University of Wisconsin Press, 1977).

11. S. W. Koelle, *Polyglotta Africana* (London: Church Missionary Society, 1854).

12. A. Akinjogbin, ed., *War and Peace in Yorubaland, 1793–1893* (Ibadan, Nigeria: Heinemann Educational Press, 1998), 409.

13. Christopher Fyfe, *A History of Sierra Leone* (London: Oxford University Press, 1962), 156; Sibthorpe, *Sierra Leone*; Akinjogbin, *Yorubaland*.

14. Fyfe, *History*, 170, cites evidence from an 1828 publication to support this. However, it is widely known in Freetown among Krio people that the term came from the very common greeting "akushe O" or "okushe O." Thus, in literary works, these people are represented as "Aku," whereas in more general speech they are called "Oku."

15. Fyfe, *History*, 233.

16. Ibid.

17. Ibid., 204–205.

18. Sibthorpe, *Sierra Leone*, 57.

19. Fyfe, *History*, 187.

20. Ibid., 215.

21. Ibid., 170.

22. Barbara Harrell-Bond, Allen M. Howard, and David E. Skinner, *Community Leadership and the Transformation of Freetown (1870–1976)* (The Hague: Mouton, 1978), 106.

23. Sibthorpe, *Sierra Leone*, 112.

24. Fyfe, *History*, 212.

25. Ibid., 213.

26. Sibthorpe, *Sierra Leone*, 61. See also J. F. Ade Ajayi, *Christian Missions in Nigeria: The Making of a New Elite* (London: Longmans, 1965).

27. Fyfe, *History*, 236.

28. Ibid., 292.

29. Ibid., 236.

30. Ibid., 88.

31. Sibthorpe, *Sierra Leone*, 50.

32. A. J. G. Wyse, *The Krios of Sierra Leone* (London: Hurst, 1989).

33. Gibril Rashid Cole, "Embracing Islam and African Traditions in a British Colony: The Muslim Krios of Sierra Leone, 1787–1910" (Ph.D. dissertation, University of California, Los Angeles, 2000), 10.

34. Clifford N. Fyle, "Language Krio," *BBC Focus on Africa Magazine* 3, no. 3 (1992): 15–18.

35. P. E. H. Hair, "Aspects of the Prehistory of Freetown and 'Creoledom,'" *History in Africa* 25 (1998): 112.

36. A. K. Turay, personal communication, late 1970s.

37. J. Peterson, "The Sierra Leone Creole: A Reappraisal," in *Freetown: A Symposium*, ed. C. Fyfe and E. D. Jones (Freetown: Sierra Leone University Press, 1968), 101.

38. Ibid., 102

39. A. J. G. Wyse, "On Misunderstandings Arising from the Use of the Term 'Creole' in the Literature on Sierra Leone," *Africa* 49, no. 4 (1979): 405–15; Wyse was reacting to a piece by D. E. Skinner and B. Harrell-Bond, "Misunderstandings Arising from the Use of the Term 'Creole' in the Literature on Sierra Leone," *Africa* 47, no. 3 (1977): 305–19.

40. Fyfe, *History*, 497.

41. Personal communication, the late Ojumiri Cole, several occasions in the 1970s.

42. Clifford N. Fyle, "Official and Unofficial Attitudes and Policy towards Krio as the Main Lingua Franca in Sierra Leone," in *African Languages, Development and the State*, ed. Richard Fardon and Graham Furniss (London: Routledge, 1994), 48 – 49.

43. Clifford N. Fyle and Eldred D. Jones, *Krio-English Dictionary* (New York: Oxford University Press, 1980), 1. The Yoruba derivation of names and terms on the next few pages comes from this source. The Yoruba words are not readily identified in some Yoruba dictionaries as some of them are archaic.

44. This discussion of Yoruba food and related cultural patterns comes from oral interviews conducted by the author.

45. Fyle and Jones, *Krio-English Dictionary*, 18.

46. Helga Kreutzinger, *The Eri Devils in Freetown, Sierra Leone* (Vienna: Osterreichische Ethnologische Gesellschaft, 1966), 30–39.

47. Ibid., 35.

48. A. K. Turay, "Loan Words in Temne" (Ph.D. dissertation, University of London, 1972).

49. Kreutzinger, *Eri Devils*, 42.

50. Patterson and Kelly, "Unfinished Migrations," 14–19.

51. For a discussion of the "esusu" club, see Shirley Ardener, "The Comparative Study of Rotating Credit Association," *Journal of the Anthropological Institute* 94, no. 2 (1964): 201–29.

52. Clifford N. Fyle, "Contemporary African Urban Culture, Indigenous Religious Beliefs, and Issues of African Identity in the Diaspora," in *Ghana in Africa and the World: Essays in Honor of Adu Boahen*, ed. Toyin Falola (Trenton, N.J.: Africa World Press, 2003), 391– 408.

CHAPTER NINETEEN

Liberated Slaves and Islam
in Nineteenth-Century West Africa

Gibril R. Cole

Much of the literature on the nineteenth-century communities established by Africans liberated from the scourge of slavery and the trans-Atlantic slave trade has tended to portray these communities as if they were exclusively Christian entities. The narrative on the African settlements along the coast of West Africa following the abolition acts promulgated by the British Parliament in 1807 and 1833, respectively, has certainly privileged the role and impact of Victorian English Christian values on the ex-slave communities. Without question, Christian influence on the Yoruba in the diaspora supersedes that of Islam, at least in the eyes of many scholars. Hence we know more of the role, and religious and cultural influences, of such groups as the Church Missionary Society (CMS), the Wesleyans, and other evangelical missionary groups from Europe. And thus attention has been concentrated almost exclusively on the resultant impact of the students of the mission societies, most notably Bishop Samuel Adjai Crowther and other members of the Niger Mission.

The prevailing paradigm may have been owing to the influence of European colonial and evangelical officials who sought to convince their superiors in Europe that their proselytizing endeavors in Africa had had unequivocal impact on their African charges. Thus, as early as 1834, Governor Octavius Temple was reporting to the Colonial Office in London that the colony government in Sierra Leone was in control of "a nation of free Black Christians."[1] Temple's claim was an obvious exaggeration. Nonetheless, subsequent writers have almost invariably concentrated on the Christian presence in the liberated slave communities of nineteenth-century West Africa.

The colony of Freetown was the main settlement of freed slaves taken from Yorubaland in the nineteenth century. The colony government that assumed control of the settlement in 1808 consistently sought to create a Christian society out of the manumitted Africans. The increasing number of liberated slaves arriving in the colony in the 1820s, mostly from Yorubaland, encouraged the colonial officials to create an evangelical base in Sierra Leone where African lay preachers would be trained and dispatched to other parts of West Africa and beyond to spread European Christian values. To this end, the colony government and evangelical missionaries cooperated closely in overseeing the activities of the liberated slaves. This close coordination of religio-political activities resulted in the majority of liberated slaves being converted to the Christian faith.

However, a sizeable proportion of the Yoruba ex-slaves elected to retain their Islamic faith, which they had contacted prior to their captivity, and subsequently many more opted for Islam in spite of the entreaties and the social and political pressures they had to undergo within the colony. This connection between the liberated slaves and Islam is, without question, a new area that should command our attention.

The Collapse of Old Oyo, the Owu War, and the Sierra Leone Colony

The Sierra Leone Colony, which was established as a settlement of freed slaves in 1787, originally was composed of groups of ex-slaves from England and the southern United States (known as the "Black Poor"); the so-called Nova Scotians, that is, Maroons from Jamaica and other freed slaves and military pensioners from the West Indies, and the Liberated Africans.

The most populous of these demographic groups in nineteenth-century Sierra Leone were the Liberated Africans. The latter, unlike the earlier groups, were originally referred to as Recaptives (because they had been recaptured from slave ships bound for the Americas) who were set free in Freetown by the British West African Squadron. The earliest Liberated African groups had very few of the various subcultural groups such as the Oyo, Ketu, Egbado, Egba, Ijebu, Owu, Ife, Ibadan, and so on, who came to constitute the Yoruba.[2] By the 1820s, however, the population of Yoruba peoples had increased exponentially and eventually came to constitute the predominant demographic group in Sierra Leone. By 1831 the majority of the inhabitants of the Liberated African settlements in the rural villages outside Freetown, such as Hastings and Waterloo, were of Yoruba origin.[3] This increased presence of the Yoruba subcultural groups was primarily owing to the collapse of Old Oyo and the outbreak of the Owu War in 1821. The resultant social instability following the disintegration of the Oyo Kingdom saw the dispersal of many people from what was till then "the most thickly populated part of Yorubaland before 1800."[4] Many of those moving out of Old Oyo eventually became involved in the Owu War.

The Owu War itself has been characterized as "the signal for the general disruption of the Yoruba Country."[5] According to Ade Ajayi, the Owu War was largely a contest for dominance of trade, especially in the area of Apomu.[6] With the collapse of Old Oyo, Owu felt militarily strong enough to extend its control over what was in reality Ife territory. The war began "as a contest for the market town of Apomu which Oyo, Ife, Ijebu, and Owu traders used to frequent." Saburi Biobaku suggests that the Owu debacle should be seen against the background of the Islamic jihad and trans-Atlantic slave trade.[7] The collapse of Oyo made possible the conditions that facilitated the kidnappings and removal of people from society. The Fulani jihad effectively served to assist the slave traders in enslaving many members of society.

The Owu War had a severe impact on the entire Yorubaland in casualties and brought a significant demographic change to the region. As war created an opportunity for slave traders, thousands of people were consequently taken prisoners and then sold to slave buyers who placed them onboard ships bound for the Americas. A significant number of those taken into slavery were eventually recaptured by the British anti–slave trade naval squadron and relocated to Sierra Leone.

Many of the Yoruba who were resettled in Sierra Leone were Muslims. Islam had begun to make inroads in Yoruba towns such as Oyo, Ikoyi, Ogbomoso, Iseyin, Iwo, and Kuwo even before the collapse of the Oyo Kingdom.[8] Despite their limited number, Muslims in Oyo, for instance, succeeded in acquiring prestige status in society as warriors and long-distance traders. The Fulani jihad and the emergent Islamic preeminence in Ilorin thus led to the conversion of many Yoruba to Islam. Once in Sierra Leone, the liberated slaves retained their Islamic faith in spite of the earnest efforts of the European Christian evangelists in the colony to convert them to Christianity. The efforts of the Christian missionaries were made even more difficult by the growing influence of Muslim Fula and Mandinka clerics in Freetown and colony villages such as Hastings and Waterloo.[9] This growing influence of Islamic clergymen and scholars by the mid-1820s came to be perceived by the colonial administration as a real threat to the development of Christianity in the colony. Governor Charles Turner observed in a memo to Whitehall in 1824 that the presence of Muslims undermined the express purpose for the very existence of the colony, that is, "the introduction of the blessings of Christianity and Civilization to Africa."[10] The Christian missionaries were prepared to address the question of the growing Islamic presence through cooperation with the colony government.

Yoruba Muslims and Colony Government Opposition

The perceived threat to the growth of Christianity by the presence of Muslims in the colony led the colonial state to adopt a decidedly anti-Islamic attitude. The efforts of the colony government in this regard were specifically directed against the Yoruba Liberated Africans who had chosen to follow the

Islamic faith. By 1826 the colony government had identified a clear target in a group of Muslims who were opposed not only to conversion to Christianity but also to the manual labor and strict disciplinary measures enforced by the village managers (who were also CMS missionaries). In an attempt to avoid manual labor and the stringent daily orders of the village managers, and desiring to adhere to their Islamic faith and Yoruba cultural traditions, a group of Liberated African Muslims decided to remove themselves from the supervision of the CMS village managers. They relocated a few miles northeast of the village of Waterloo, settling in an area known as Cobolo, along the Ribbie River.[11]

The decision to relocate to Cobolo was perceived as a deliberate defiance of colonial policy by the authorities in the villages as well as in Freetown. The Reverend Godfrey Wilhem, rector and superintendent of Waterloo, reported to Freetown that the Muslims of Waterloo were about to lay siege to the village. Reverend Wilhem ordered a hastily assembled village militia to arrest every Muslim Oku (as Yoruba Liberated Africans were called).[12] Subsequently thirteen Yoruba Muslims found in possession of cutlasses in their homes were apprehended and transferred to Hastings.[13] Reverend Wilhem had become very frustrated with the Muslims at Waterloo, having made little headway in his proselytizing efforts among them. The Yoruba Muslims likewise did not hide their resentment of the Christian missionaries' presence in their rural villages, and consequently made life quite unpleasant for the missionaries. As the representative of the colony administration, Reverend Wilhem suffered much disapproval and resentment from the village inhabitants, and he was eventually removed from Waterloo.

Wilhem's recall from Waterloo coincided with the inauguration of the administration of Lieutenant Colonel Alexander Findlay in Freetown in 1830. Findlay's administration ushered in a period of close military supervision of the colony. Superintendents were replaced by managers who were expected to enforce the edicts of the new governor with swiftness and vigor. Findlay made it clear that he was not about to allow the Muslims and other non-Christian inhabitants of the villages, especially worshipers of Sango (the Yoruba god of thunder), to undermine the efforts of the Christian proselytizers in the colony. Among his very first edicts upon assuming control of the colony administration was a restriction placed on the free movement of people. The governor further instructed his managers to "use every endeavour to make the Liberated Africans under your control appreciate the blessings which attend a careful use of their time."[14]

Findlay's Attitude toward Yoruba Muslims

Findlay did not allow himself enough time to have a firm grasp of the local situation in the rural villages before carrying out decisions that were bound to have a significant impact on the political and religious landscape. Having already ordered his village managers to restrict the movement of Liberated Africans, Findlay issued further orders in August 1830 forbidding the worship of what he described as idols. Two years later he formalized these instructions with an order-in-council that sought to put the Yoruba Liberated Africans on notice that the new administration was going to adopt even sterner measures to curtail their religious and cultural activities.[15] A month after Findlay's order-in-council was promulgated, the Yoruba Liberated Africans who had been arrested for allegedly plotting to besiege the rural villages were sentenced to imprisonment.

Meanwhile, the issue of slavery and the slave trade subsequently came to be used by the colony government to justify its repression of the agitation by Yoruba Muslims in the villages. The senior official of the Liberated African Department, Thomas Cole, announced that the Oku Muslims who had relocated to Cobolo from Waterloo had been prevailed upon by their co-religionists outside the colony, who were primarily interested in the slave trade. Cole maintained that these outside forces were in reality only interested in inducing the Yoruba ex-slaves to move "beyond the reach of the jurisdiction of this colony" in order to re-enslave them.[16] Cole further noted that "three of the discontented Ackoos (Ogubah, Odohoo, and Joko) . . . [had confessed] that they are of the Mahomedan faith in their own country."[17]

Notwithstanding the insistence of the Muslims that they were already converted to Islam in their areas of origin, the colony government believed that the Yoruba Muslims had been profoundly influenced by the presence of increasing numbers of Muslim scribes and traders from the interior of Sierra Leone within the colony villages. The colony of Freetown itself started experiencing an influx of Muslim traders and preachers from the interior not long after the settlement of the first batch of freed slaves. By the early nineteenth century Muslim Fula, Mandinka, and Soso traders were becoming an essential part of the growing trade relations between Freetown and the interior states. Muslim traders, scholars, and farm producers thus sought to take advantage of their increasing contact with the colony.[18] Many Fula scribes had taken up residence in Freetown by 1819, and established reliable and credible business reputations as cattle traders, meat suppliers, blacksmiths, and leather workers.[19] The Muslim migrant traders from the interior subsequently had a significant impact on their co-religionists in Freetown and the rural villages of the colony. Indeed, the Fula, Mandinka, and Soso did not limit their contact with the Yoruba ex-slaves to trade relations alone but increasingly engaged in proselytizing activities within the villages.

Consequently the Liberated African Department advised the colony governor to prohibit the presence of Muslim scribes in the rural villages. In the meantime, Yoruba Muslims quietly continued to resist the efforts of the authorities to limit their freedom of religious worship. In spite of government instructions to the contrary, the Yoruba Liberated African Muslims continued to adhere to their faith, including the donning of Muslim robes. Findlay concluded that the only way to curb the growing influence of Islam on the Yoruba community was by apprehending and prosecuting the Muslims who had left the colony's jurisdiction. He therefore instructed the assistant superintendent of the Liberated African Department to seek the assistance of the chief of the neighboring Plantain Islands, Thomas Caulker, in apprehending and repatriating to Freetown "a number of Liberated Africans of the Mahomedan persuasion."[20] In a bid to convince his superiors at Whitehall of the propriety of his actions, Findlay reported that the Muslims were poised to attack the colony, and he informed the colonial office that he was about to "adopt the most rigid measures with a view to bringing these offenders to punishment."[21] In addition to rounding up the Yoruba Muslims, Findlay also proscribed the wearing of Muslim gowns in the villages and in Freetown.

Cobolo War and Treason Trial

The apparent purpose of the Yoruba Muslims in leaving the jurisdiction of the colony was the pursuit of their religious obligations, and to escape what they perceived as oppressive measures taken by village managers. Findlay was convinced, therefore, that it was necessary to take further action beyond the political measures he had already adopted toward the Yoruba Muslims. So on 13 November 1832 he dispatched a militia group to arrest the Muslims at Cobolo. The governor announced that he had received a report that "a large party of Ackoos" was in the process of launching an attack on the village of Waterloo, and that fellow Yoruba compatriots were expected to join them.[22]

Not very confident of the capacity of his militia to carry out his orders effectively, Findlay mobilized the police forces of Waterloo and Hastings to back up the militia, purportedly to ensure that the entire group of Muslims be apprehended and returned to the colony. The troops sent to Cobolo, however, were well armed and evidently prepared for war, and were given detailed instructions regarding their objective. The manager of Hastings village, John Dougherty, was chosen to lead the militia, assisted by the manager of Waterloo, John Hazeley, who also led a contingent of troops from his village.

Hazeley's forces met with stiff resistance outside Cobolo, and his panic-stricken troops retreated in an undisciplined manner. The obviously chagrined leader of the colony forces, Dougherty, suggested that Hazely and his troops were cowards as he recalled seeing no Muslims in pursuit of the fleeing militiamen. However, two of the troops reportedly suffered severe injuries, "one by a blow from a cutlass on the head, the other with an arrow on the cheek."[23] As a result of the initial losses of the militia troops, Findlay thought it necessary that the colony forces be supplemented with a fresh batch of troops from Freetown. He decided to send in the navy to the Ribbie River up the Sierra Leone peninsula.

A British naval contingent under the command of Colonel Islington was given orders to move up the Ribbie and provide assistance to the militia forces. Islington was further instructed to make it quite clear to the militiamen from Hastings and Waterloo that they risked being summarily executed if they attempted to flee from the battlefront. In addition to Islington's forces, Findlay also instructed the British frigate, HMS *Charybdis*, then in the Freetown Harbor, to go to the Ribbie as well. The commander of the *Charybdis*, Lieutenant Crawford, was ordered to postpone his impending trip to Bathurst, the Gambia, and provide assistance in the war against the Yoruba Muslims at Cobolo. The naval forces were expected to attack the Muslim Liberated Africans from the rear or cut off their retreat should they attempt to cross the Ribbie.

It is not exactly clear from available sources how the war itself was conducted once the colony forces entered Cobolo. The leader of the colony troops, Dougherty, reported seeing no one in the village when his troops entered. It was later determined that the Yoruba Muslims had already been defeated by the neighboring Loko before the colony troops arrived.[24] The governor later informed the colonial office in London that the Liberated Africans who were captured would be punished for their participation in the rebellion. Findlay asserted that the evidence garnered from an examination of the imprisoned Muslims provided ample proof of a "deep concerted rebellious plan laid by the Mahomedan Ackoos." According to Findlay, the Yoruba Muslims were intent on "killing all the Whitemen" in the colony.[25] He informed Whitehall of his decision to prosecute for high treason the surviving leaders of the Liberated African Muslims.

Treason Trial

The governor was extremely confident that his justice department could successfully prosecute the accused Liberated Africans in the colony court. However, Findlay's assertion that the evidence gathered by his colony lawyers would unmistakably point to a planned siege seems to have had little, if any, legal basis. The weakness of the colony administration's case against the Yoruba Muslims became apparent very early in the ensuing treason trial in Freetown. On New Year's Day, 1833, the acting chief justice of the Supreme Court of Sierra Leone, Michael Melville, began proceedings in what became a watershed case in the constitutional history of the colony.

On trial for treason before Justice Melville were William Cole (1), William Cole (2), George Cole (1), and George Cole (2). All gave their occupations as laborers. Each faced five counts of treason. The government's case against the Muslims was grounded on the charge that they had acted in a disloyal manner against the authority of the British monarch.[26] The accused Muslims had no legal representation of their own, so Chief Justice Melville appointed William Henry Savage, a lawyer of mixed European and African heritage, as the defense counsel.

Savage questioned the colony administration's ability to legally prosecute the Muslims for having participated in an activity that had taken place outside the geographical boundaries of the colony of Sierra Leone. Cobolo, Savage pointed out, was clearly outside the jurisdiction of the colony, and therefore the court could not legally try the Muslims.[27] The chief justice agreed with the argument of the defense counsel and thus acquitted the accused persons.

Findlay was not prepared to accept the verdict of the Supreme Court. He ordered the Muslim Liberated Africans tried a second time, only to see them acquitted again after the jury found no evidence supporting the charges that the accused had murdered members of the militia. The case was much undermined by the prosecution's main witness, who conceded under cross-examination that he could not prove that any of the Muslims on trial were implicated in a plot to attack the colony. Findlay was adamant about trying the Muslims a third time, this time having them charged with piracy since their war with the colony militia had been fought near the Ribbie River. He was eventually dissuaded by his own prosecuting team that, since the act of piracy can only occur on the high seas, it would be legally impossible to convict the accused men of piracy, for the Ribbie can hardly be classified as an ocean.[28]

The acquittal of the Yoruba accused of treason may have served to enhance the confidence and resolve of the Muslim Liberated Africans. Rather than remain restricted to the rural villages, groups of Muslims frequently trekked to Freetown from Waterloo and the surrounding villages in order to attend prayer services at Yardie in Freetown.[29] The frequency of these treks and the evident difficulty involved in making the twenty-mile journey between Freetown and Waterloo on foot led many to stay close to their place of worship for extended periods. It was in order to alleviate this evident difficulty that the Muslims made entreaties to their legal counsel, William Savage, who owned several parcels of land in the area. Savage had lived in the colony for a number of years and had served in several capacities in addition to being a legal advocate. Thus, by the 1820s, he had become a successful import-export merchant and landowner in Freetown. Following his successful representation of the Yoruba Muslims after Cobolo, Savage, having suffered from racial prejudice himself in the colony establishment, identified with the Liberated African Muslims. He later became the legal champion of those whom he perceived as victims of political and religious persecution.

Hence, in 1833, when the Muslims needed a place to stay, Savage was able and quite willing to offer them a portion of his real estate holdings at Fourah Bay. The grant of land to the Muslims was largely the result of the relentless efforts on the part of the leaders of the Yoruba Liberated Africans, including Mohammed Yadalieu, Sumanu Othman Ajibode, and Mohammed Badamasie.[30] By 1836 a significant number of the Muslim Liberated Africans had taken up residence at Fourah Bay, even though many more continued to maintain domiciles in the rural villages and made the long trek to Freetown on Fridays for juma'a prayers.

Meanwhile, with the number of Muslims from the Liberated African villages increasing at Fourah Bay, some began to move west to live and study the Qur'an under the tutelage of their Fula co-religionists at Fula Town. The Liberated Africans subsequently outnumbered their Fula hosts but retained the name of the community in honor of their religious mentors.

The Church, the Colonial State, and Yoruba Muslims

With the establishment of distinctive Muslim communities at Fourah Bay and Fula Town dominated by Liberated Africans of Yoruba heritage, Islam continued to flourish in the colony much to the chagrin of the European colonial and religious officials. The evangelical officials of the Church Missionary Society found their work increasingly less exciting as a result of the growth of a high-profile Muslim community within the colony. The church and the colonial state were thus faced with an interesting dilemma: how were they to attain the agenda of constructing a Christian society based on Victorian English values with a growing body of Muslims within the colony population? What type of policy should the colonial state adopt toward these Muslims?

With the European missionaries increasingly frustrated in their proselytizing efforts because of the unwillingness of Yoruba Liberated African Muslims to renounce their faith, the colony government was called on to become more actively involved in the efforts to curb the Islamic presence. On 13 January 1839 the European agents of the CMS sent a petition to Governor Richard Doherty denouncing the growth of Islam and advocating active governmental action in suppressing the religion. Doherty subsequently asked for the opinion of the African lay preachers with regard to the Islamic presence within the Liberated African society. The lay preachers responded that Islam and the Sharia writ regarding matrimony were "contrary and inconsistent to the law of God and the common usage and custom of this colony."[31]

With the European and African clergymen clearly against the Islamic presence within the freed slave community, Doherty felt assured of official support in Freetown and from Whitehall in pursuing a policy of strict containment of Islam in the colony. Doherty, like his predecessors, was not persuaded by the assertion of the Yoruba Muslims that they had contacted Islam prior to their arrival in Freetown, and instead believed that the Fula and other Muslim preachers were somehow responsible for what he considered an Islamic subversion of the colonial state. On 18 March 1839 he notified the Secretary of State for the Colonies that there was evidence of Islamic subversion of the colony government. He informed Whitehall "of a somewhat new and curious problem for bringing to the test our principles of religious tolerance."[32]

Doherty proposed to his superiors in London to remedy the Islamic threat by dispossessing the Muslim Liberated Africans of their mosques and homes, on the ground that these structures were constructed on Crown Land. He believed that the immediate effect of confiscating the land occupied by the Muslims would be the displacement of these people from the colony and their relocation either to some remote district of the colony or beyond its geographical limits. Such an action was clearly extra-legal, especially because the colony government had never contested the ownership of the land by William Savage. The governor himself was certainly aware of the legal implications of his proposed remedy. He therefore advised the Secretary of State that the colonial state should exercise caution in its attempt to eject the liberated slaves who had embraced Islam from land which they had occupied uncontested for many years. Doherty pointed out that the removal of some Liberated Africans merely because they had embraced Islam "seems to me nothing less than persecution."[33] Nonetheless, the governor was not about to let constitutional nicety stand in the way. In order to avoid transgressing the letter of the law, Doherty chose instead to compromise the spirit of the law. He thus proposed to the Secretary of State for the Colonies that the Muslims be removed not on the ground that they had embraced Islam and thereby rejected Christianity, which he conceded would be tantamount to religious persecution, but on the more convenient and legally pliable ground that they were bad tenants.[34] Doherty informed London that while the paperwork was being prepared to eject the liberated slaves from the colony, he had put those at Fula Town on notice by having their mosque burned down by some police officers who had "recently waited upon me and signified their willingness to meet my wishes."[35] The governor later attributed the fire to police error.

With their mosque at Fula Town destroyed, and facing impending eviction from their domiciles at Fourah Bay, the Liberated African Muslims resolved to move out of the colony rather than renounce their faith. But they were not about to leave without making their position known. Thus on 21 June 1839 the inhabitants of Fourah Bay sent a letter to Governor Doherty expressing disapproval of the government's policy against them.

Describing themselves as dutiful and loyal Liberated African subjects of the British monarch, they acknowledged receipt of the governor's notice of eviction and expressed sorrow on this "melancholy mandate" which specified that they vacate their homes within a period of five months but should cease worshiping in their mosque in less than a week. They maintained that Doherty's actions were prejudicial, and rejected his opinion of them as "a set of idle, lazy people." On the contrary, they informed the governor that they were a working-class people comprising sawyers, carpenters, blacksmiths, tailors, hawkers, traders, laborers, and farmers.[36] They further reminded Doherty that his predecessors had not challenged their occupation of the land and, more important, "never disputed Mr. Savage's right to the said property during his lifetime." They also maintained that Doherty's predecessor, Governor Campbell, had even encouraged them to build a mosque prior to his departure for England.

The Liberated African Muslims directly disputed Doherty's assertion that they were converted to Islam only after their arrival in the colony. Quite the reverse, they insisted that they were already Muslims in Yorubaland before their resettlement in Freetown. They implored Doherty, therefore, to refrain from compelling them to "renounce that faith which is so deeply rooted and sunk in their minds."

By an odd twist of fate, Doherty was recalled to London before he could carry out his decision against the inhabitants of Fourah Bay and Fula Town. His replacement at the governor's office, Sir John Jeremie, who arrived in the colony in October 1840, advised the Secretary of State against expulsion of the Yoruba Muslims and allowed the rebuilding of the mosque at Fula Town. Much to the disappointment of the Christian missionaries, Jeremie took a very different and dispassionate view of the perceived Muslim threat to Christian civilization. One missionary who was quite uncomfortable with the presence of Muslims in the colony population was the Reverend Samuel Adjai Crowther.

Reverend Adjai Crowther and Yoruba Muslims

Reverend Adjai Crowther, the leading evangelist in the CMS mission for most of the first half of the nineteenth century, was immensely grateful to the British for having rescued him from slavery. The young Adjai arrived in the colony in 1822, and was baptized in 1825 and renamed Samuel Crowther, "after the Vicar of Christ Church, Newgate."[37] Ade Ajayi describes the new Christian convert of 1825 as "an industrious, intelligent, humble young man, the type beloved by missionaries." He was subsequently ordained a minister in the Church Missionary Society in 1843 after graduating from divinity school in Islington, England. He returned to Freetown shortly after.[38]

Reverend Crowther, upon his return to the colony, decided that part of his primary evangelical obligations was the conversion of his Yoruba compatriots who were Muslims to Christianity. With the colony administration less hostile to the presence of Muslims in the colony, the Christians became more aggressive in their quest to Christianize the Muslims and traditionalists, all of whom they classified as heathens. Despite their different religious beliefs, however, the Yoruba Muslims were quite proud of Reverend Crowther, whom they also considered one of their own. In his well-maintained journal, Crowther recalled being very moved by the gesture of the Imam of the Fourah Bay jamaat who, on learning of Crowther's impending move to the Niger delta, sent a delegation to Crowther's residence at Bathurst village on 17 December 1843 to visit the reverend and "to ask after my health, and to learn for certainty whether I was going to the Yoruba country."[39]

A day after the visit of the Fourah Bay Muslims to his Bathurst residence, Crowther made a reciprocal visit to the home of the Imam of the Fourah Bay jamaat, whom he recalled speaking to him in fluent Yoruba. Crowther preached to the Imam and others who were present of the blessings of Christianity, and attempted to convince his hosts about "the importance of surrendering to the religion of the Whiteman's Bible, because it leads the sure way to happiness."[40] Crowther noted that, on an earlier occasion, he had given a copy of the Arabic version of the Bible to the Imam of Fourah Bay. He informed the latter that he had been instructed by the London Committee of the CMS to translate the Bible into the Yoruba language so "that the people may be able to read this book for themselves in their own tongue."

Reverend Crowther maintained that he was always careful not to object to the embracing of Islam by Liberated Africans, but "endeavoured to show them the great blessings Christianity bestows on mankind whenever it is embraced." He noted that the reaction of the Muslims to his role of CMS evangelist was rather interesting. He reported that they were quite proud of the fact that their "countryman" was a minister of the Church of England. He was disappointed, however, that the Yoruba Muslims were adamant about retaining allegiance to their faith.

On 8 January 1844 Reverend Crowther notified the Imam of Fourah Bay of his impending inaugural Yoruba service at the Mission Church in Freetown, and invited the Muslims to attend. Crowther suggested that the Yoruba Muslims attend especially because they would hear the Christian doctrine interpreted in their own language, thus removing whatever reservations they may have entertained about Christianity.

The Yoruba community of Fourah Bay sent a delegation to the service, which Crowther noted "brought a large number of people together, Yorubas, Igbos, Calabars, etc. to witness the reading and preaching [of] the gospel of Christ in a native language in an English Church." Because the Muslims had observed, at one of their meetings with Crowther, that the Islamic and Christian faiths were essentially the same except for the question of the relationship of Jesus Christ to God, Crowther's sermon for the service was taken from verse 35, chapter 1, of St. Luke.[41] He noted in his journal that the main point of his sermon was "Ohung Ohwoh ti aobih mi inoh reh li aomokhe li ommoh olorung" (That holy thing which shall be born of thee shall be called the Son of God).

At subsequent services Reverend Crowther took direct aim at several aspects of life in the colony. One other group that bore the brunt of Crowther's admonition was that of the adherents of Sango, the Yoruba deity of thunder and lightning. The members of this group had consistently rejected the proselytizing efforts of both Christians and Muslims. On 23 February 1844 he visited the place of worship of the Sango adherents and proceeded to question their beliefs. Consequently Crowther was confronted by disdainful worshipers who pointed out the perceived hypocrisy of Christians "who were the greatest adulterers that could be met in the whole colony."[42] Crowther reported feeling quite mortified when the Sango believers pointed out that the habit of Christians to claim, during Church services, that they could literally see God was ludicrous, and he noted that he had "to hold my tongue," because "the charges were true."

The Reverend Crowther was generally disappointed by the reluctance of his Muslim and Sango compatriots to convert to Christianity. He was further offended by the unwillingness of both the Muslims and Sango adherents to cease doing any type of manual work on Sunday, the Christian Sabbath. While he did not cease preaching to the Muslims and the Sango worshipers, he did not report any success in changing their respective faiths. It appears that Christians, Muslims, and those clinging to traditional forms of religious worship within the Yoruba community in the colony had become entrenched in their respective belief systems. And they were evidently prepared to make room for religious plurality. Their common Yoruba cultural heritage, they seemed to have concluded by the second half of the nineteenth century, was not to be sacrificed at the altar of religion.

The colonial state itself, by 1853, was not in a position to pursue a consistent policy of aggressive anti-Islamism. The colony's growing trade relations with the interior states were becoming ever more contingent upon cordial relations with the Yoruba Muslims who were becoming increasingly important in maintaining contact with the mostly Islamic states of the interior. Consequently the colonial state felt compelled by purely economic reasons to adopt what was tantamount to an ambivalent policy regarding Islam and the Muslims in colonial Freetown.

Liberated African Muslims and Colony Trade with Interior States

Cognizant of the role of the Muslims in the increasing trade with the interior states, the colony administration sought to discourage open antagonism toward Muslims in Freetown and the colony villages. While assuring the Christian missions of continued government support, the administration was slowly making an effort to recruit some Muslims into the colonial civil service. On 16 December 1872 Mohammed Sanusi, a Yoruba Muslim, was appointed to the post of Arabic Writer in the Native Affairs Department.[43] Sanusi's role was very crucial to the relations between the colony administration and the Muslim traders from the interior. As Arabic Writer, he was delegated the added responsibility of Assistant to the Government Interpreter, in which position he became the official liaison between Freetown and the interior states.

The increasingly prominent role of Liberated African Muslims in the colony served to enhance the trade with the hinterland. By 1879 trade missions or "caravans" from the interior had increased significantly. The Government Interpreter reported that "1,176 Caravans" arrived in Freetown from the interior during the first quarter of that year.[44] Among the items of trade featuring prominently at this time were ivory and gold. The gold reaching Freetown between 1878 and 1879 originated from Segu and Buré; merchants from such places as Dinguiray and Kankan transported articles like shea butter, calabashes, and fine cotton country cloth.[45]

Increased trade between Freetown and the interior was further facilitated by the Yoruba Muslims who made the journey to the hinterland sometimes on small boats along the northern rivers. By the end of 1886 many of these colony-based traders were actively making available to the Freetown markets such commodities as India rubber, palm kernels/oil, benneseeds, cattle, gold, beeswax, rice, and hides.[46] Success in the interior trade allowed the Liberated African Muslims to cast their entrepreneurial eyes even further afield. Many were quite interested in venturing into trade in the Gambia, Senegal, and the colony of Lagos where others had already established contact.

Many of the Liberated African Muslims by the 1890s had become an integral part of the trade with the coastal communities of West Africa, primarily the Gambia, Senegal, and Nigeria. Indeed, many of the freed Yoruba slaves had been embarking on trade missions along the coast from as early as the 1830s. Motivated by a desire to attain economic success like their predecessors, some purchased slave vessels condemned by the Mixed Commission Courts in Freetown and went on trade sojourns to several places along the coast. While many were of the Christian faith, others retained their Islamic faith and still others continued to worship Sango.[47]

In the Gambia and Senegal the Muslim traders from Freetown engaged in the kola trade. Large quantities of kolanuts would normally be purchased in Freetown and then sold at a fairly high rate in the Gambia.[48] Taking advantage of their contacts with fellow Muslims in the Gambia, the Oku Marabous (as the Yoruba Muslims were referred to in the Gambia and Senegal) also traded in such sundry goods as leather, palm oil, pepper, shea butter, yams, beans, fufu, dried fish, and oysters in both the Gambia and Senegal.[49] Having successfully marketed their wares, they purchased sizeable quantities of such items as baskets, calabashes, candles, haberdashery, iron pots, goats, sheep, and other trade goods for sale at Freetown and the Sierra Leone interior.[50] Although the Muslim traders were mostly men, several were women who engaged largely in the trade in dried fish, kola, fufu, agidi, ogiri, egusi, and olele.[51] Many of the male traders married into local families in such places as Bathurst and Georgetown in the Gambia, and Dakar, St. Louis, and Kaolak in Senegal. They thereby established strong social bonds with the local Wolof, Sarakule, and Mandinka peoples. By the turn of the century these social contacts had helped to solidify the place of Oku-Marabous in the local communities, many becoming dominant in what would later become a thriving seasonal trade in sheep between Freetown and the Senegambia region. But it was in Nigeria where many more were to find significant success.

Saro Muslims in Nigeria

The great majority of traders from the population of liberated slaves of Freetown who traded along the coast of West Africa went to various parts of what is today southern Nigeria. Many of the Christians, Muslims, and those who still clung to traditional forms of religious worship demonstrated an active interest in the growing import-export trade that was emerging between Freetown and Lagos and its environs. Many in the Muslim community of Liberated Africans in Freetown had long been convinced, like other liberated slaves of Yoruba heritage, that not only could they return home again but that they could also tap into what they perceived to be a thriving economy in Yorubaland. The first group of traders had reached Badagry by the late 1830s. However, some of the "Saro" (as the Liberated Africans became known in Nigeria) immigrant traders seem to have been preparing for this eventuality much earlier. Yoruba ex-slaves reportedly used part of their newfound wealth to purchase condemned slave ships with the aim of eventually sailing to Lagos. Osoba and Harry Johnson were two of the first liberated slaves to have purchased these vessels. The former used his ship, named *Nancy*, to relocate his entire household to Lagos.[52] Encouraged by the success of the earlier returnees, several of the leading members of the Liberated African community pooled their resources to purchase a ship, which they loaded with a myriad of trade goods and about forty passengers, and left Freetown for Badagry. The news of the warm reception accorded the Saro traders in Egba country stimulated further interest in the emergent trade. Many expressed a desire to go to Abeokuta for the purpose of trade or simply to return to their area of origin. The evident success of the earlier groups encouraged the leader of the Liberated Africans (or Oku king), Thomas Will, to petition the Colony administration in Freetown for official permission to establish a settlement at Badagry.[53] While the colony government was reluctant to endorse the move to Badagry, many of the liberated slaves, of all creeds, continued to pursue sojourns in Badagry.

Others chose to risk their lives and venture into the interior in spite of the instability in the region generated by the activities of Ijebu and Ibadan forces in the area. The Egba, under the leadership of Shodeke, eventually gained control of Ijebu and Ibadan, thereby bringing a semblance of social stability to the region. Abeokuta, meanwhile, continued to grow in size, with Oyo, Ife, and Ijebu refugees swelling the population.[54] It was the news of this bustling interior cosmopolitan environment that may have motivated the Saro at Badagry to venture into the uncertainty of the interior roads that led to Abeokuta. Once the first group succeeded in getting through to Abeokuta, others became brave enough to follow in their wake, usually arriving to warm receptions. The Muslim liberated slaves arrived in Abeokuta and soon became part of a small but growing and significant Islamic community.

The Egba leader, Shodeke, was quite cognizant of the Islamic presence in what was as yet a society dominated by adherents of non-Islamic traditional religious groups. He was also not averse to the presence of new Christian immigrants from Freetown, Bahia, and Cuba,[55] even though he was probably aware of the potential for tension between the religious traditionalists and the new monotheistic faiths. Indeed, the Muslims and Christians were to suffer some amount of religious persecution by the mid-nineteenth century: the Muslim mosques were destroyed, and Christians were prohibited from holding church services.[56] Nonetheless, by 1851, the liberated slave population in Abeokuta had increased considerably.

Muslim and Christian leaders in Freetown came to see the movement to Nigeria as essential to the success of their respective religious agendas. The African clergy of the Niger mission were eventually displaced by the European evangelists of the CMS, but the Muslim Liberated Africans were unimpeded in their own movement to Badagry, Abeokuta, and Lagos. Some of the leading Muslim Saro who had found success in trade in Badagry, Abeokuta, and Lagos helped to erect the first concrete mosques in these places. One of the more prominent of the Muslim Saro traders was Mohammed Shitta, whose leadership role and benevolence became universally known within Yorubaland and beyond.

Mohammed Shitta

Born at Waterloo to Liberated African parents who had been taken into slavery from Badagry, Shitta accompanied his parents home at a young age in 1844. Before returning to Badagry, his father had risen to religious and political prominence in Freetown, where he was the Imam of the Fourah Bay jamaat.[57] The elder Shitta died in 1849. His death appears to have motivated the already enterprising and ambitious Mohammed Shitta, who decided to relocate to Lagos. He was finally able to convince the rest of the family to move out of Badagry and to make a new life for themselves in the more exciting and relatively thriving larger town, where there was a growing Saro community.

Shitta entered the kola trade while also engaging in the buying and selling of various other commodities, including cotton cloth, hides, egusi, and gum copal. By 1864 he was in control of a thriving business for which he traveled between Lagos and the upper Niger delta and Sierra Leone. By 1869 he was settled semi-permanently in the upper Niger, letting his brother, Yusuf, and other family members run the Lagos end of his business.

Until his death in 1895 Shitta devoted his enormous wealth to the development of the Muslim communities of Lagos, Badagry, and Freetown. He built what was described, upon its completion, as "a magnificent mosque" at Lagos that was formally opened with great fanfare on 5 July 1894. As part of the opening ceremonies Shitta was given the title of "Bey" by the Sultan of the Ottoman Empire, and henceforth became known as Mohammed Shitta Bey in the Muslim communities of Sierra Leone and Nigeria.[58] Shitta also made significant financial contributions toward the construction of the mosques at Fourah Bay and Fula Town in Freetown Colony in the 1890s. Thus, when news of his demise reached Freetown by telegraph on 4 July 1895, the *Sierra Leone Weekly News* reported a gloomy atmosphere within the community of liberated slaves and their progeny in Freetown, Muslims and Christians alike.

Shitta Bey was perhaps the most widely known of the Liberated African Muslims who prospered in trade in Yorubaland. Yet he was only one of many within the community of liberated slaves who ventured to seek a fortune in trade outside Sierra Leone colony. Many more traveled back and forth between Lagos and Freetown, and in the process helped to solidify the cultural bonds between these societies. With their success in trade, many of the leading merchants sought and gained leading positions within the Muslim community and the jamaat. The tensions that had existed between the traditionalists and the followers of Islam and Christianity in Abeokuta and Badagry would eventually appear within the Muslim communities of Fourah Bay and Fula Town.

Fissure at Fourah Bay: Islam and Yoruba Culture

Having gained the right to maintain their own Islamic communities within the colony, many of the Muslim leaders sought to have Islam serve as the sole guide of every aspect of community life. From the social and political institutions of their communities to the cultural aspects of communal living, the religion of Islam was to be a living force influencing the outlook of the people of Fourah Bay and Fula Town. Yet, notwithstanding such a strong presence, Islam had to coexist with an equally strong influence of Yoruba cultural institutions. A notable feature of the interaction of religion and Yoruba culture within the Muslim Liberated African communities was not just the syncretic nature of religious and social life but the tensions that existed between Islam and Yoruba traditional culture. A major consequence of this encounter was the friction and eventual breakup of the Fourah Bay jamaat into two distinct factions in the 1870s.

While the Muslim Krio had spent a significant period of time resisting the efforts of Christian missionaries and the colonial state to stamp out Islam and certain aspects of Yoruba culture, many in this liberated slave society had to contend with Islamic purists in their midst who also perceived certain cultural practices as anathema to Islamic precepts. The historical feud at Fourah Bay was thus borne out of fundamental differences between those, on the one hand, who believed that there was no legitimate place for some Yoruba cultural forms in an Islamic community and those, on the other, who faithfully adhered to Islamic faith but did not necessarily perceive their community as a theocracy. To the latter, the Islamic Sharia was not to be an overwhelming force in their daily lives. Although the Sharia was regarded as relevant to the community with regard to marriage, personal and communal disputes, inheritance, and certain political issues, many in the community did not feel obligated to renounce or discard their Yoruba traditions and customary ceremonies in order to be good Muslims. They saw no contradiction between maintaining their Islamic faith and embracing customs that, they maintained, had been passed on to them by their forefathers.

The growth of Islamic orthodoxy among some of the leaders of the community and the unwillingness of many to disengage themselves from such Yoruba cultural societies as the Egugu, Ogunuko, Gelede, and Keri-Keri eventually contributed to the breakup of the jamaat into two factions—Tamba and Jama. The most important source of the fissure centered around the question of ownership of the plot of land on which the central mosque, Jami-ul-atiq, was built. However, the breakup itself may have been motivated by political disagreement within the mosque regarding the position of the Imam, an issue dating back to the 1850s.

By the late 1870s and 1880s the conflict over the place and role of the most resilient of these secret societies, the Egugu (or Orjeh), had become a major factor in the feud leading to the breakup at Fourah Bay. The Reverend Adjai Crowther observed that the Egugu may have been introduced to Yorubaland by the Nupe,[59] and was later transplanted to the colony villages of Waterloo and Hastings by the liberated slaves. Many Islamic scholars at Fourah Bay did not approve of the secretive nature of the Egugu, nor of the elaborate rituals supposedly required for membership. The more conservative Tamba faction advocated a more doctrinaire Islam, and thus questioned the continued membership in the Egugu of many within the leadership of the mosque. While they recognized the Yoruba origins of the society, they steadfastly maintained that the Egugu was un-Islamic in its nature and practices.

Although the land issue was eventually addressed in the first of a series of legal cases adjudicated in 1893, the struggle continued between adherents of orthodox Islam and those who were inclined to maintain their Yoruba cultural institutions. The liberated slaves who had contacted Islam prior to their being captured and sold into slavery in their Yoruba cultural milieu succeeded in maintaining their Islamic faith within a colony envisaged to be an exclusive Christian entity from which the gospel of Jesus Christ was to be disseminated across the African continent. As much as their Islamic faith turned out to be quite resilient in the face of continued efforts by the colonial and evangelical officials to Christianize and "civilize" them, the liberated slaves from Yorubaland, who had helped form what by the turn of the century had come to be known as Krio Society, still have managed to retain much of their Yoruba heritage to this day.

Notes

1. See Christopher Fyfe, "Reform in West Africa: The Abolition of the Slave Trade," in *History of West Africa*, vol. 1, ed. J. F. Ade Ajayi and Michael Crowder (London: Longman, 1974), 30–56.

2. J. F. Ade Ajayi, *Christian Missions in Nigeria: The Making of a New Elite* (Evanston, Ill.: Northwestern University Press, 1969), 25; see also idem, "The Aftermath of the Fall of Old Òyó," in Ajayi and Crowder, *History of West Africa*, 2:129–66; and Christopher Fyfe, *Sierra Leone Inheritance* (London: Oxford University Press, 1964), 149.

3. Gibril R. Cole, "Embracing Islam and African traditions in a British Colony: The Muslim Krios of Sierra Leone, 1787–1910" (Ph.D. dissertation, University of California, Los Angeles, 2000), 95.

4. Ajayi, "The Aftermath of the Fall of Old Òyó, 145.

5. Saburi O. Biobaku, *The Egba and Their Neigbours, 1842–1872* (Ibadan, Nigeria: Ibadan University Press, 1991), 13.

6. Ajayi, "The Aftermath of the Fall of Old Òyó."

7. Biobaku, *The Egba and Their Neigbours,* 13; see also J. F. Ade Ajayi, "Samuel Adjai Crowther of Oyo," in *Africa Remembered,* ed Philip D. Curtin (Madison: University of Wisconsin Press, 1967).

8. Ajayi, "The Aftermath of the Fall of Old Òyó," 142.

9. CO 267/204, Report of Governor Pine, enclosed in despatch no. 88, 27 October 1848, Public Record Office (hereafter, PRO).

10. CO 267/60, Turner to Bathurst, 20 September 1824, PRO.

11. CO 267/118, Treason Indictment, J. W. Cole, Colonial Secretary, Freetown, 3 January 1833, PRO.

12. John Peterson, *Province of Freedom: A History of Sierra Leone, 1787–1870* (Evanston, Ill.: Northwestern University Press, 1969), 212. The name "Oku" was a reference to the Yoruba ex-slaves' traditional form of greeting, "oku-o." I am grateful to Professor Ade Ajayi for this information.

13. Ibid., 213.

14. Liberated African Department, T. Cole to J. Auguin, Freetown, 1 April 1831, Sierra Leone Archives (hereafter, SLA).

15. CO 267/119, Order-in-Council, Executive Council Chamber, Freetown, Sierra Leone, 24 October 1832, PRO.

16. Liberated African Letter Book, 1830–31, Liberated African Department, 11 September 1830, SLA.

17. Ibid.

18. See Alusine Jalloh and David Skinner, eds., *Islam and Trade in Sierra Leone* (Trenton, N.J.: Africa World Press, 1997); see also J. S. Trimigham and Christopher Fyfe, "The Early Expansion of Islam in Sierra Leone," *Sierra Leone Bulletin of Religion* 2 (December 1960): 37; David Skinner, "Islam and Trade in Sierra Leone in the Nineteenth Century" (Ph.D. dissertation, University of California, Berkeley, 1971); S. A. Alharazim, "The Origins and Progress of Islam in Sierra Leone," *Sierra Leone Studies* 21 (January 1939): 13–26.

19. Christopher Fyfe, *A History of Sierra Leone* (London: Oxford University Press, 1962), 149.

20. F. Campbell to T. Caulker, Liberated African Letter Book, 1831–34, no. 5, 21 October 1832, Freetown, SLA.

21. Findlay to Viscount Goderich, 15 May 1833, Liberated African Letter Book, SLA.

22. C. B. Jones to J. Dougherty, 12 November 1832, Liberated African Letter Book, 1832, SLA.

23. CO 267/118, Enclosure no. 4, Findlay to R. W. Hay, 14 January 1833, PRO.

24. Findlay to Goderich, 15 May 1833, Liberated African Letter Book, SLA; see also Peterson, *Province of Freedom,* 215; Fyfe, *A History of Sierra Leone,* 187.

25. CO 267/118, Findlay to Hay, 15 May 1833, PRO.

26. "Examination of Ackoo Rebels," enclosure no. 4, Findlay to Hay, 14 January 1833, PRO.

27. Peterson, *Province of Freedom*, 216–17; Fyfe, *A History of Sierra Leone*, 187.

28. Ibid.

29. See Alharazim, "The Origins and Progress of Islam in Sierra Leone," 13–26; see also Gibril R. Cole, "Krio Muslim Society of Freetown: A Case Study on Fourah Bay and Foulah Town" (B.A. [Hons] dissertation, Fourah Bay College, 1979). Yardie is the name of the domicile of Alfa Yadalieu Savage, first Imam of Fourah Bay.

30. B. B. Ibrahim, "Fourah Bay—The First Hundred Years, 1836–1936," pamphlet presented at the launching of the Fourah Bay Community Foundation, 11 April 1993. Several of the leaders at Fourah Bay, including Imam Yadalieu and Mohammed Badamasie, added Savage to their name, perhaps as a tribute to their benefactor.

31. CO 267/154, Doherty to Russell, enclosure no. 2, 4 December 1839, PRO.

32. Ibid., enclosure no. 77.

33. Ibid.

34. Ibid.

35. Ibid.

36. Ibid., enclosure no. 4.

37. For a detailed study of the Reverend (later Bishop) Samuel Adjai Crowther's life and impact on Christianity in West Africa, see Ajayi, *Christian Missions in Nigeria*; Emmanuel Ayankanmi Ayandele, *The Missionary Impact on Modern Nigeria, 1842–1914: A Political and Social Analysis* (London: Longman, 1966).

38. CA1/079/0, Rev. Crowther's Report, Bathurst, 18 December 1843, CMS Archives, Birmingham (hereafter, CMS).

39. Ibid.

40. CA1/079/11a, Rev. Crowther's journal for the quarter ending 25 March 1844, CMS. All subsequent quotes of Rev. Crowther are from Crowther's journal for the quarter ending 25 March 1844, except where otherwise indicated.

41. Ibid.

42. Ibid.

43. Sierra Leone Blue Book, 1879, SLA.

44. Document labeled "Miscellaneous," Aborigines no. 54, Caravans from Interior, 2 April 1879, SLA.

45. T. G. Lawson to Government House, Miscellaneous, Freetown, 7 April 1879, SLA.

46. Miscellaneous no. A 142/8G, Lawson to Parkes, 10 November 1886, SLA.

47. Ajayi, *History of West Africa*, 156–57.

48. I am grateful to Professor Allen Howard of Rutgers University for graciously providing me with a transcript of an interview done with Oku Muslim traders in Aberdeen Village (Freetown Colony) in 1968; see also Allen Howard, "Islam and Trade in Sierra Leone," in Jalloh and Skinner, *Islam and Trade in Sierra Leone*, 21–63.

49. Sierra Leone Blue Book, 1894, SLA.

50. Ibid., 1900, SLA.

51. Ramatoulie O. Othman, *A Cherished Heritage: Tracing the Roots of the Oku-Marabou, Early 19th to Mid-20th Century* (Serrekunda, the Gambia: Edward Francis Small Printing Press, 1999), 16–17.

52. Biobaku, *The Egba and Their Neigbours*, 25.

53. Fyfe, *A History of Sierra Leone*, 212.

54. Biobaku, *The Egba and Their Neigbours*, 23–24.

55. Ajayi, *History of West Africa*, 157.

56. Biobaku, *The Egba and Their Neigbours*, 35.

57. *Sierra Leone Weekly News* 9, no. 45 (6 July 1895): 5, in the British Library, Colindale, England.

58. Ibid.

59. CA1/079/12, Bishop Crowther's journal for the quarter ending 25 June 1844, CMS. For a discussion of the Egugu in the Nigerian context, see Wole Soyinka, *Ake: The Years of Childhood* (New York: Vintage International, 1989).

Bibliography

Archival Collections

Bahamas—Nassau

The National Archives of the Bahamas

Brazil—Bahia

Arquivo Público do Estado da Bahia
    Legislativa. Abaixo-assinados
    Livros de Registros do Tabelião
    Livro de Registros de Testamentos

Arquivo Regional de Cachoeira
    Inventories

Brazil—Rio de Contas

Arquivo Municipal de Rio de Contas
    Matrícula Seg. do Ano de 1848

Brazil—Rio de Janeiro

Arquivo da Cúria Metropolitana do Rio de Janeiro
    Livros de Batismo de Escravos da Freguesia da Sé

Arquivo da irmandade de Santo Elesbão e Santa Efigênia
    Collection of Authorization for Burials

Compromisso da Irmandade de Santo Elesbão e Santa Efigênia
Livro de registro de entrada de irmãos

Arquivo Nacional
Correspondência reservada recebida pela Repartição de Polícia
Processos do Código Penal

Biblioteca Nacional

Cuba—Havana

Archivo Nacional de Cuba, Havana
Asuntos Políticos
Gobierno Superior Civil

Costa Rica—San José

Archivo Metropolitana de la Curia de San José
Archivo Nacional de Costa Rica, San José

Nigeria—Kaduna

Nigerian National Archives Kaduna

Sierra Leone—Freetown

Sierra Leone Archives

Spain—Madrid

Archivo Histórico Nacional
Estado
Ultramar

Spain—Seville

Archivo General de Indias

United Kingdom

British Library, Colindale, England

Church Missionary Society Archives, University of Birmingham

Public Records Office, Kew, England
Colonial Office
Foreign Office

United States

University of Texas at Austin
Center for American History, William J. Massie Papers
Nettie Lee Benson Latin American Collection

Published Primary Sources

Abd al-Rahmān al-Bagdādi. *The Amusement of the Foreigner* (1865). Translated by Yacind Daddi Addoun and Renée Soulodre –La France. Harriet Tubman Resource Centre on the African Diaspora, SHADD, www.yorku.ca/nhp/shadd/index.htm

Adams, John. *Remarks on the Country Extending from Cape Palmas to the River Congo.* London: G. & W. B. Whittaker, 1823.

Agassiz, Louis, and Elizabeth Cabot Cary. *A Journey in Brazil.* New York: Praeger, 1969.

Aime de Verteuil, Louis Antoine. *Three Essays on the Cultivation of Sugar Cane in Trinidad* . . . Port of Spain: Printed at the Standard's Office, 1858.

Ajayi, J. F. Ade. "Samuel Ajayi Crowther of Oyo." In *Africa Remembered: Narratives by West Africans from the Era of the Slave Trade,* ed. Philip D. Curtin, 289–316. 2nd ed. Prospect Heights, Ill.: Waveland, 1997 [1967].

Alfonso, Carlos, et al. *Ancestros.* Qbadisc CD 9001. New York: Qbadisc, 1992. Originally released in 1987 on an LP of the same name, EGREM LD- 4432.

———. *Ancestros II.* Qbadisc CD 9015. New York: Qbadisc, 1993.

———. *En los limites del barrio.* Artcolor CD #1A-501-36031 A. Canada: Arcolor, 1995.

———. *Olorum para todos.* Lázaro Ros con Grupo Mexcla. Havana: EGREM LP #LD-4662, 1991.

Álvarez, Adalberto. *Adalberto Álvarez y su son.* Sony Discos PWK 83563. Miami Beach, Florida: POW Records, 1999.

Araújo, José de Souza Azevedo Pizarro. *Memórias históricas do Rio de Janeiro.* 9 vols. Rio de Janeiro: Imprensa Nacional, 1948.

Astley, Thomas, ed. *A New General Collection of Voyages and Travels.* London: Printed for T. Astley, 1745–1747.

Bachiller y Morales, Antonio. *Los Negros.* Barcelona: Gorgas y compañía, n.d.

Bowen, Thomas J. *Central Africa: Adventures and Missionary Labors* . . . *in the Interior of Africa from 1849 to 1856.* Charleston: Southern Baptist Publication Society, 1857.

Bremer, Frederika. *Cartas desde Cuba.* Havana: Fundación Fernando Ortiz, 2002 [1851].

———. *The Homes of the New World: Impressions of America.* Translated from the Swedish by Mary Howitt. London: Arthur Hall, Virtle, 1853.

Byll-Cataria, Regina, ed. *Histoire d'Agoué (République du Bénin) par le Révérend Père Isidore Pélofy.* Leipzig: University of Leipzig, 2002.

Campbell, Robert. *Pilgrimage to My Motherland: An Account of a Journey among the Egba and Yorubas of Central Africa.* Philadelphia: T. Hamilton, 1861.

Castelnau, Francis de. *Reseignements sur L'Afrique Centrale et sur une nation d'hommes à queue qui s'y trouvait d'aprés le rapport des négres du Soudan, esclaves à Bahia.* Paris: P. Betrand, Librarie-Editeur, 1851.

Castro, Terezinha, ed. *História documental do Brasil.* São Paulo: Record, 1969.

CIDMUC, ed. *Sacred Rhythms of Cuban Santería.* Smithsonian Folkways compact disc #SFCD40419. Washington, D.C.: Smithsonian Institution, 1995.

Clapperton, Hugh. *Journal of a Second Expedition into the Interior of Africa, from the Bight of Benin to Soccatoo.* London: Cass, 1966 [1829].

Código de Posturas da Ilustríssima Câmara Municipal do Rio de Janeiro. Rio de Janeiro: Typographia Imperial e Nacional, 1930.

Creswell, Nicholas. *The Journal of Nicholas Creswell, 1774–1777.* New York: Kennikat, 1924.

Crowther, Samuel, and John Taylor. *The Gospel on the Banks of the Niger: Journals and Notices of the Native Missionaries Accompanying the Niger Expedition of 1857–1859.* London: Dawsons, 1859.

"Cuban Slaves in England." *Anti-Slavery Reporter* 2, no. 10 (October 1854): 234.

Curtin, Philip A., ed. *Africa Remembered: Narratives by West Africans from the Era of the Slave Trade.* Prospect Heights, Ill.: Waveland, 1997.

Dalzel, Archibald. *The History of Dahomey, an Inland Kingdom of Africa.* London: Frank Cass, 1967.

Debret, Jean Baptiste. *Viagem pitoresca e histórica ao Brasil.* Commentary by Sergio Milliet. São Paulo: Livraria Martins, 1940.

Delany, Martin R. *Official Report of the Niger Valley Exploring Party.* New York: Thomas Hamilton, 1861.

"Devassa do levante de escravos ocorrido em Salvador em 1835." *Anais do Arquivo Público do Estado da Bahia* 38 (1988): 1–142.

———. *Anais do Arquivo Público do Estado da Bahia* 40 (1971).

———. *Anais do Arquivo Público do Estado da Bahia* 53 (1996).

Duncan, John. *Travels in Western Africa in 1845 and 1846, Comprising a Journey from Whydah, through the Kingdom of Dahomey, to Adofoodia, in the Interior.* London: Richard Bentley, 1967 [1847].

Ellis, Alfred. *The Yoruba-Speaking Peoples.* Oosterhout: Anthropological Publications, 1966 [1894].

Ewbank, Thomas. *Life in Brazil; or, A Journal of a Visit to the Land of the Cocoa and the Palm.* New York: Harper and Brothers, 1856.

Forbes, Frederick E. *Dahomey and the Dahomans; Being the Journals of Two Missions to the King of Dahomey, and Residence at His Capital, in the Year 1849 and 1850.* London: Longman, Brown, Green, and Longmans, 1851.

Formell, Juan y Los Van Van. *Te pone la cabeza mala.* Metro Blue CD 7243-8-21307-2-7. Madrid: EMI-ODESON, S.A., 1997.

Fry, Peter. "Reflexões sobre a II Conferência Mundial da Tradição dos Orixás e Cultura. De um Observador Não Participante." *Comunicações do ISER* 8, no. 3 (1984): 34–45.

Gillespie, Dizzy (with Al Fraser). *To Be, or Not to Bop.* Garden City, N.Y.: Doubleday, 1979.

Gilroy, Paul. *The Black Atlantic: Modernity and Double Consciousness.* Cambridge, Mass.: Harvard University Press, 1993.

Grant, Gov. Lewis. *Governour's Dispatches, 1827–1831.* Nassau, Bahamas: Department of Archives, n.d.

Hazoumé, Paul. *Doguicimi.* Paris: G-P Maisonneuve et Larose, 1978.

"Informe sobre la Provincia de Costa Rica presentado por el Ingeniero Don Luis Diez Navarro al Capitán General De Guatemala Don Tomás de Rivera y Santa Cruz. Año de 1744." *Revista de los Archivos Nacionales* 3 (1939): 579–600.

Justesen, Ole, ed. *Danish Documents concerning the History of Ghana.* Forthcoming.

Koelle, S. W. *Polyglotta Africana.* London: Church Missionary Society, 1854.

Labat, Jean-Baptiste. *Voyage du Chevalier des Marchais en Guinée, isles voisines et à Cayenne, fait en 1725, 1726 et 1727.* 4 vols. Paris: Chez Saugrain, Quay de Gefvres, a la Croix Blanche, 1730.

Lander, Richard, ed. *Records of Captain Clapperton's Last Expedition to Africa.* 2 vols. London: Cass, 1967 [1830].

Lewis, Maureen Warner. *Yoruba Songs of Trinidad.* London: Karnak House, 1994.

Montejo, Esteban. *The Autobiography of a Runaway Slave.* New York: Pantheon, 1976.

Muñequitos de Matanzas, Los. *Ito Iban Echu: Sacred Yoruba Music of Cuba.* Qbadisc compact disc QB 9022. New York: Qbadisc, 1996.

"Note Historique Sur Ouidah Par L'Administrateur Gavoy (1913)." *Etudes dahoméennes* 13 (1955): 69–70.

Olawoyin, J. S. *My Political Reminiscences: 1948–1983.* Ikeja, Nigeria: John West, 1993.

"Ouidah: Organisation du Commandement." *Mémoires du Bénin* 2 (1993): 44–46.

Partido Comunista de Cuba. *Plataforma programática del Partido Comunista de Cuba: Tesis y resolución.* Havana: Editorial de Ciencias Sociales, 1978.

———. *Selección de documentos del I y II Congresos del Partido Comunista de Cuba.* Havana: Editora Política, 1982.

———. *Tesis y Resoluciones: Primer Congreso del Partido Comunista de Cuba.* Havana: Departamento de Orientación Revolucionaria del Comité Central del Partido Comunista de Cuba, 1976.

"Pedimento del Procurador Sindico de Cartago al Cabildo para que reciba el Cacao como Moneda en la compra de toda clases Víveres y otros artículos de comercio. Año de 1703." *Revista de los Archivos Nacionales* 1 (1937): 590–99.

Peixoto, Antonio da Costa. *Obra nova de língua G. de Mina traduzida, ao nosso idioma . . . anno de 1741.* Lisboa: Agência Geral dos Colónias, 1945.

Peixoto, Antonio da Costa, Luis Silveira, and Edmundo Correia Lopes, eds. *Obra nova de língua geral de Mina de Antonio da Costa Peixoto.* Lisbon: República Portuguesa, Ministério das Colónias, Divisão de Publicações e Biblioteca, Agência Geral das Colónias, 1945.

Pelladito, Justo, et al. *Cuba. Afroamérica. Chants et rythmes afrocubaines.* VDE-Gallo compact disc CD-959. Lausanne, Switzerland: AIMP& VDE-Gallo, 1997.

Phillips, U. B. *Life and Labor in the Old South.* Boston: Little, Brown, 1929.

Piñeiro, Ignacio. *Ignacio Piñeiro and His Septeto Nacional.* Tumbao Cuban Classics CD TCD-019. Spain: Camarillo Music, 1992.

Pinto, Bartolomeu Homem d'el Rei. *Livro de Batismo dos Pretos pertencentes a paróquia de Irajá.* Rio de Janeiro: Biblioteca Nacional, 1988.

Revé, Elio. *Papá Eleguá.* EGREM CD #0078. Havana: EGREM, 1993.

Rio, João do (Paulo Barreto). *As religiões no Rio.* Rio de Janeiro: Nova Aguilar, 1976.

Rocha, Agenor Miranda. *Os candomblés antigos do Rio de Janeiro. A nação de Ketu: origens, ritos e crenças.* Rio de Janeiro: Top Books, 1994.

Ros, Lázaro. *Asoyí. Cantos arará.* OK Records CD-9476. Havana: Caribe Productions, 1995.

———. *Olorun 1.* EGREM CD #0013. Havana (Canada): EGREM, 1992.

Rugendas, Johann Moritz. *Viagem pitoresca através do Brasil.* São Paulo: Itatiaia / USP, 1979.

Saco, José Antonio. *Historia de la esclavitud: Desde los tiempos mas remotos hasta nuestros días.* 6 vols. Havana: Editorial "Alfa," 1937.

Sagra, Ramón de la. *Cuba en 1860, o sea cuadro de sus adelantos en la población, la agricultura, el comercio y las rentas públicas. Suplemento a la primera parte de la historia política y natural de la isla de Cuba.* Paris: L. Hachette, 1863.

"Si dispone que el cacao corra en la Provincia de Costa Rica para la Compra de Víveres por no habar en ella Moneda de Plata. Año de 1709." *Revista de los Archivos Nacionales* 1 (1937): 600–603.

Simmons, William H. *Notices of East Florida.* A facsimile reproduction of the 1822 edition. Bicentennial Floridiana Facsimile series. Gainesville: University Press of Florida, 1973.

Spix, J. B. von, and C. F. P. von Martius. *Viagem pelo Brasil.* Rio de Janeiro: Imprensa Nacional, 1938.

Tucker, Miss Sarah. *Abbeokuta; or, Sunrise within the Tropics: An Outline of the Origin and Progress of the Yoruba Mission.* London: James Nisbet, 1853.

Valdés, Jesús "Chucho." *Indestructible.* P.O.W. Records compact disc #PWK 83558. Miami Beach, Florida: Sony, 1999.

——. *Irakere.* Vol. 1: *Selección de éxitos, 1973–1978.* Aréito cassette #C-4003. Havana: EGREM, n.d.

Valdés, Merceditas. *Ache.* EGREM cassette C-230. Recorded in Santiago de Cuba, 1985. Havana: EGREM, 1992.

——. *Cantos afrocubanos: Merceditas Valdés con los tambores de Jesús Pérez.* Aréito cassette C-224. Havana: EGREM, 1995.

Vandeleur, Seymour. *Campaigning on the Upper Nile and Niger.* London: Methuen, 1898.

Verger, Pierre. *Notícias da Bahia—1850.* Salvador: Corrupio, 1999 [1981].

Warren, Edward. *A Doctor's Experiences in Three Continents.* Baltimore, Md.: Cushings and Bailey, 1885.

Washington, James M., ed. *Conversations with God: Two Centuries of Prayers by African Americans.* New York: HarperCollins, 1994.

Secondary Sources

Abimbola, Wande, ed. *Ifá Divination Poetry.* New York: Nok, 1977.

Adderley, Roseanne Marion. "New Negroes from Africa: Culture and Community among Liberated Africans in the Bahamas and Trinidad, 1810–1900." Ph.D. dissertation, University of Pennsylvania, 1996.

Adediran, Biodun. *The Frontier States of Western Yorùbáland, circa 1600–1889: State Formation and Political Growth in an Ethnic Frontier Zone.* Ibadan, Nigeria: French Institute for Research in Africa, 1994.

——. "Yoruba Ethnic Groups or a Yoruba Ethnic Group? A Review of the Problem of Ethnic Identification." *África: Revista do Centro de Estudos Africanos da Universidade de São Paulo, Brazil* 7 (1984): 57–70.

Agbo, Casimir. *Histoire de Ouidah du XVIe au XXe siècle.* Avignon: Les Presses Universelles, 1959.

Aguilar Bulgarelli, Oscar R. *La esclavitud negra en Costa Rica: Origen de la oligarquía económica y política nacional.* San José: Progreso Editora, 1997.

Aguirre Beltrán, Gonzalo. *La población negra de México, 1519–1810: Estudio etno-histórico.* México: Fondo de Cultura Económica, 1972.

Ajayi, J. F. Ade. "The Aftermath of the Fall of Old Òyó." In *History of West Africa,* ed. J. F. Ade Ajayi and Michael Crowder, 2:129–66. New York: Columbia University Press, 1972.

———. *Christian Missions in Nigeria, 1841–1891: The Making of a New Elite.* London: Longmans, 1965.

Ajayi, J. F. Ade, and Robert Smith. *Yoruba Warfare in the Nineteenth Century.* Ibadan, Nigeria: Ibadan University Press, 1971.

Ajibola, J. O. *Owe Yoruba.* Oxford: Oxford University Press, 1947.

Ajisafe, Ajayi Kolawole. *History of Abeokuta.* Abeokuta: Fola Bookshops, 1964.

Akindélé, Adolphe, and Cyrille Aguessy. *Contribution à l'étude de l'histoire de l'ancien royaume de Porto-Novo.* Dakar: IFAN, 1953.

Akinjogbin, A., ed. *War and Peace in Yorubaland, 1793–1893.* Ibadan, Nigeria: Heinemann Educational Press, 1998.

Akinnaso, F. Niyi. "Traditional Yoruba Names and the Transmission of Cultural Knowledge." *Names* 31 (1983): 139–58.

Akintoye, S. A. *Revolution and Power Politics in Yorubaland, 1840–1893: Ibadan Expansion and the Rise of Ekiti Parapo.* London: Longman, 1971.

Akinyele, I. B. *Iwe Itan Ibadan, Iwo, Ikirun ati Osogbo.* Ibadan, Nigeria: Ibadan University Press, 1911 (?).

Alharazim, S. A. "The Origins and Progress of Islam in Sierra Leone." *Sierra Leone Studies* 21 (1939): 13–26.

Alleyne, Mervyn C. *Comparative Afro-American: A Historical Comparative Study of English-Based Afro-American Dialects of the New World.* Ann Arbor: Karoma, 1980.

Andrade, Maria José de Souza. *A mão-de-obra escrava em Salvador de 1811 a 1860.* São Paulo: Corrupio, 1988.

Angarica, Nicolás Valentín. "El 'Lucumí' al Alcance de Todos." In *Estudios Afro-Cubanos: Selección de Lecturas,* ed. Lázara Menéndez. Havana: Universidad de la Habana, 1990.

———. *Manual de Orihaté: Religión Lucumí.* N.p., 1955.

Apter, Andrew. "Atinga Revisited: Yoruba Witchcraft and the Cocoa Economy, 1950–1951." In *Modernity and Its Malcontents: Ritual and Power in Postcolonial Africa,* ed. Jean Comaroff and John L. Comaroff. Chicago: University of Chicago Press, 1993.

———. *Black Critics and Kings: The Hermeneutics of Power in Yoruba Society.* Chicago: University of Chicago Press, 1992.

Arango, Pedro. "Manual de santería de Pedro Arango." In *Estudios afrocubanos: Selección de lecturas,* ed. Lázara Menéndez, 4:129–344. Havana: Universidad de la Habana, 1990.

Ardener, Shirley. "The Comparative Study of Rotating Credit Association." *Journal of the Royal Anthropological Institute of Great Britain and Ireland* 94, no. 2 (1964): 201–29.

Argüelles Mederos, Aníbal, and Ileana Hodge Limonta. *Los llamados cultos sincréticos y el espiritismo: Estudio monográfico sobre su significación social en la sociedad Cubana contemporánea.* Havana: Editorial Academia, 1991.

Aróstegui, Natalia Bolívar. *Los Orishas en Cuba.* Havana: Ediciones Unión, 1990.

Asiegbu, Johnson U. *Slavery and the Politics of Liberation, 1787–1861: A Study of Liberated African Emigration and British Anti-Slavery Policy.* New York: Africana, 1969.

Asiwaju, A. I. "Dynamics of Yoruba Studies." In *Studies in Yoruba History and Culture: Essays in Honour of Professor S.O.I. Biobaku,* ed. G. O. Olusanya, 26–41. Ibadan, Nigeria: Ibadan University Press, 1983.

Askari, Eva K. "The Social Organization of the Owe." *African Notes* 2, no. 3 (1964–65): 9–12.

Astley, Thomas, ed. *A New General Collection of Voyages and Travels.* 4 vols. London, 1745–47.

Averill, Gage. *A Day for the Hunter, a Day for the Prey: Popular Music and Power in Haiti.* Chicago: University of Chicago Press, 1997.

Awolalu, J. Omosade. *Yoruba Beliefs and Sacrificial Rites.* London: Longman, 1979.

Ayandele, Emmanuel Ayankanmi. *The Missionary Impact on Modern Nigeria, 1842–1914: A Political and Social Analysis.* London: Longman, 1966.

Babayemi, S. O. *The Fall and Rise of Oyo c. 1706–1905: A Study in The Traditional Culture of an African Polity.* Lagos: Lichfield Nigeria, 1990.

Babbitt, Milton. "Who Cares If You Listen." *High Fidelity* 8 (1958): 39.

Baraka, Amiri. *The Motion of History and Other Plays.* New York: William Morrow, 1978.

Barber, Karin. "How Man Makes God in West Africa: Yoruba Attitudes towards the Òrìsà." *Africa* 51, no. 3 (1981): 724–45.

———. "Oríkì, Women and the Proliferation and Merging of Òrìsà." *Africa* 60, no. 3 (1990): 313–37.

Barickman, B. J. *A Bahian Counterpoint: Sugar, Tobacco, Cassava, and Slavery in the Recôncavo, 1780–1860.* Stanford, Calif.: Stanford University Press, 1998.

Barnes, Sandra T., and Paula Girshick Ben-Amos. "Ogun, the Empire Builder." In *Africa's Ogun: Old World and New,* ed. Sandra T. Barnes, 39–64. Bloomington: Indiana University Press, 1997.

Barnet, Miguel. *La fuente viva.* Havana: Letras Cubanas, 1983.

———. "La hora de Yemayá." *Gaceta de Cuba* 34 (1996): 48–50.

Barreal, Isaac. "Tendencias sincréticas de los cultos populares en Cuba." *Etnología y Folklore* 1 (1966): 17–24.

Bascom, William. "The Focus of Cuban Santería." *Southwestern Journal of Anthropology* 6, no. 1 (1950): 64–68.

———. *Ifá Divination: Communication between Gods and Men in West Africa.* 2nd ed. Bloomington: Indiana University Press, 1991.

———. "Oba's Ear: A Yoruba Myth in Cuba and Brazil." *Research in African Literature* 7 (1976): 149–65.

———. "La religion africaine au Nouveau Monde." In *Les religions africaines traditionnelles,* 119–37. Paris: Éditions du Seuil, 1965.

———. *Sixteen Cowries: Yoruba Divination from Africa to the New World.* Bloomington: Indiana University Press, 1993.

———. "Two Forms of Afro-Cuban Divination." In *Acculturation in the Americas,* ed. Sol Tax. New York: Cooper Square, 1952.

———. *The Yoruba of Southwestern Nigeria.* New York: Holt, Rinehart, and Winston, 1969.

Bastide, Roger. *African Civilizations in the New World.* New York: Harper and Row, 1971.

———. *The African Religions of Brazil: Toward a Sociology of the Interpenetration of Civilizations.* Baltimore: The Johns Hopkins University Press, 1978 [1960].

———. "Continuité et discontinuité des sociétés et des cultures afro-américains." *Bastiana* 13–14 (January–July 1996 [1970]): 77–88.

———. *As Religiões Africanas no Brasil.* São Paulo: Pioneira, 1971.

———. *Sociología de la Religión.* Madrid: Ediciones Jucar, 1986 [1960].

Baudet, Martha. "Identifying the African Grammatical Base of the Caribbean Creoles:

A Typological Approach." In *Historicity and Variations in Creole Studies*, ed. A. Highfield and A. Valdman. Ann Arbor: Karoma, 1981.

Bearden, Romare, and Harry Henderson. *A History of African-American Artists from 1792 to the Present*. New York: Pantheon, 1993.

Beier, Ulli. "Ancient African Religions and the Modern World." *Présence Africaine* 13, no. 41 (1962): 38–45.

———. *The Return of the Gods: The Sacred Art of Susanne Wenger*. Cambridge: Cambridge University Press, 1975.

———. *A Year of Sacred Festivals in One Yoruba Town*. Lagos: Nigeria Magazine, 1959.

Belasco, Bernard I. *The Entrepreneur as Culture Hero: Preadaptations in Nigerian Economic Development*. New York: Praeger, 1980.

Bergad, Laird W. *Cuban Rural Society in the Nineteenth Century: The Social and Economic History of Monoculture in Matanzas*. Princeton, N.J.: Princeton University Press, 1990.

Bergad, Laird W., Fe Iglésias García, and María del Carmen Barcia. *The Cuban Slave Market, 1790–1880*. Cambridge: Cambridge University Press, 1995.

Bethell, Leslie. *The Abolition of the Brazilian Slave Trade: Britain, Brazil, and the Slave Trade Question, 1807–1869*. Cambridge: Cambridge University Press, 1970.

Bettelheim, Judith. "Jonkonnu and Other Christmas Masquerades." In *Caribbean Festival Arts: Each and Every Bit of Difference*, ed. John W. Nunley and Judith Bettelheim, 17–29. Seattle: University of Washington Press, 1988.

Biobaku, Saburi O. *The Egba and Their Neighbours, 1842–1872*. Ibadan, Nigeria: Ibadan University Press, 1991 [1957].

Birman, Patricia. "Feitiço, Carrego e Olho Grande, os males do Brasil São. Estudo de um centro Umbandista numa favela do Rio de Janeiro." Master's thesis, Museu Nacional, PPGAS, Rio de Janeiro, 1980.

Bisnauth, Dale. *History of Religions in the Caribbean*. Trenton, N.J.: Africa World Press, 1996.

Blassingame, John W. *The Slave Community*. New York: Oxford University Press, 1976 [1972].

Blum, Denise. "Cuban Youth and Revolutionary Values: Alla en la lucha." Ph.D. dissertation, University of Texas at Austin, 2002.

Blyden, Nemata. *West Indians in West Africa: 1808–1880: The African Diaspora in Reverse*. Rochester, N.Y.: University of Rochester Press, 2000.

Borghero, Francesco. "Relation sur l'établissement des missions dans le Vicariat apostolique du Dahomé, 3 December 1863." In *Journal de Francesco Borghero, premier missionnaire du Dahomey, 1861–1865*, ed. Renzo Mandirola and Yves Morel. Paris: Karthala, 1997.

Bowser, Frederick P. *The African Slave in Colonial Peru, 1524–1650*. Stanford, Calif.: Stanford University Press, 1974.

Boxer, C. R. *A idade de ouro do Brasil (Dores de crescimento de uma sociedade colonial)*. São Paulo: Companhia Editôra Nacional, 1969.

Braga, Júlio. *Na Gamela do Feitiço, Repressão e Resistência nos Candomblés da Bahia*. Salvador: EDUFBA, 1995.

Brandon, George. *Santeria from Africa to the New World: The Dead Sell Memories*. Bloomington: Indiana University Press, 1993.

Bretas, Marcos Luiz. *Ordem na cidade: o exercício cotidiano da autoridade Policial no Rio de Janeiro*. Rio de Janeiro: Rocco, 1997.

413

Brown, David H. "Garden in the Machine: Afro-Cuban Sacred Art and Performance in Urban New Jersey and New York." Ph.D. dissertation, Yale University, 1989.

Brown, Kay. "The Emergence of Black Women Artists: The 1970s, New York." *International Review of African American Art* 15, no. 1 (1998): 45–52.

Brown, Spencer H. "A History of the People of Lagos, 1850–1886." Ph.D. dissertation, Northwestern University, 1964.

Bustamonte, José Angel. "Influencia de algunos factores culturales en nuestros cuadros psiquiátricos," *Etnología folklore* no. 7 (January–June 1969): 75–84.

Cable, George W. *The Grandissimes: A Story of Creole Life.* New York: Sagamore, 1898.

Cabrera, Lydia. *Anagó: vocabulario Lucumí (el Yoruba que se habla en Cuba).* Miami: Cabrera y Rojas, 1970.

——. *El Monte.* Havana: Ed. SI-MAR, 1996.

Cáceres, Rina. "Costa Rica, en la frontera del comercio de esclavos africanos." *Reflexiones* (Facultad de Ciencias Sociales, Universidad de Costa Rica), no. 65 (December 1997): 3–14.

——. *Negros, mulatos, esclavos y libertos en la Costa Rica del siglo XVII.* México: Instituto Panamericana de Geografía e Historia, 2000.

Calderón González, Jorge. *María Teresa Vera.* Havana: Letras Cubanas, 1986.

Campbell, Mavis. *Back to Africa: George Ross and the Maroons — From Nova Scotia to Sierra Leone.* Trenton, N.J.: Africa World Press, 1993.

Campbell, Robert. *Pilgrimage to My Motherland: An Account of a Journey among the Egba and Yorubas of Central Africa.* Philadelphia, 1861. Privately published.

Canet, Carlos. *Lucumí: Religión de los Yorubas en Cuba.* Miami: Editorial A.I.P., 1973.

Capo, Hounkpati B. C. *Comparative Phonology of Gbe.* Berlin: Foris, 1991.

Capone, Stefania. *La quête de l'Afrique dans le candomblé. Pouvoir et tradition au Brésil.* Paris: Karthala, 1999.

——. "Regards contemporains sur les premiers candomblés à Salvador de Bahia." In *Modernités transversals citoyenneté, politique et religion,* ed. Abel Kouvouama and Dominique Cochart, 47–72. Paris: Editions Paari, 2003.

Carbonell, Walterio. *Critica: como surgió la cultura nacional.* Havana: Ediciones Yaka, 1961.

Cardenal, Ernesto. *In Cuba.* New York: New Directions, 1974.

Cardozo, Manoel S. "The Lay Brotherhoods of Colonial Brazil." *Catholic Historical Review* 33 (1947): 12–30.

Carneiro da Cunha, Manuela. *Negros, estrangeiros: Os escravos libertos e a sua volta à África.* São Paulo: Brasiliense, 1985.

Carneiro da Cunha, Manuela, and Marianno Carneiro da Cunha. *From Slave Quarters to Town Houses: Brazilian Architecture in Nigeria and the People's Republic of Benin.* São Paulo: Nobel, 1985.

Carneiro, Edison. *Candomblés da Bahia.* Salvador: Ediouro, 1985 [1948].

——. *Religiões Negras e Negros Bantos.* Rio de Janeiro: Editora Civilização Brasileira, 1991 [1936–37].

Carroll, Patrick J. *Blacks in Colonial Veracruz: Race, Ethnicity, and Regional Development.* Austin: University of Texas Press, 1991.

Carter, H. "Suprasegmentals in Guyanese: Some African Comparisons." In *Pidgin and Creole Languages: Essays in Memory of John E. Reinecke,* ed. G. Gilbert. Honolulu: University of Hawaii Press, 1987.

Carvalho, Delgado de. *História da cidade do Rio de Janeiro*. Rio de Janeiro: Prefeitura da Cidade do Rio de Janeiro / Secretaria Municipal de Cultura / DGDIC, 1988.

Cash, Philip, Shirley Gordon, and Gail Saunders. *Sources of Bahamian History*. London: Macmillan, 1991.

Castellanos, Isabel. *Elegua quiere tambó: cosmovisión religiosa afrocubana en las canciones populares*. Cali, Colombia: Departamento de Publicaciones, Universidad del Valle, 1983.

Castellanos, Jorge, and Isabel Castellanos. *Cultura Afro-Cubana: El negro en Cuba, 1492–1844*. Vol. 1. Miami: Ediciones Universal, 1988.

———. *Cultura Afro-Cubana: Las religiones y las lenguas*. Vol. 3. Miami: Ediciones Universal, 1992.

———. "The Geographic, Ethnologic, and Linguistic Roots of Black Cubans." *Cuban Studies* 17 (1987): 95–110.

Castro, Fidel, and Frei Betto. *Fidel and Religion*. New York: Simon and Schuster, 1987.

Castro, Hebe M. M. *Das cores do silêncio. Os significados da liberdade no sudeste escravista. Brasil séc XIX*. Rio de Janeiro: Arquivo Nacional, 1995.

Castro, Yeda Pessoa de. "Língua e nação de candomblé." *África* 4 (1981): 57–77.

Chalhoub, Sidney. *Visões de liberdade: uma história das últimas décadas da escravidão na corte*. São Paulo: Companhia das Letras, 1990.

Chambers, Doublas B. "Tracing Igbo into the African Diaspora." In *Identity in the Shadow of Slavery*, ed. Paul Lovejoy. London: Continuum, 2000.

Chase, Judith W. *Afro-American Art and Craft*. New York: Van Nostrand Reinhold, 1971.

Chávez Álvarez, Ernest. *El Crimen de la niña Cecilia. La brujería en Cuba como fenómeno social (1902–1925)*. Havana: Editorial de Ciencias Sociales, 1991.

Childs, Matt. "The Aponte Rebellion of 1812 and the Transformation of Cuban Society: Race, Slavery, and Freedom in the Atlantic World." Ph.D. dissertation, University of Texas at Austin, 2001.

———. "Pathways to African Ethnicity in the Americas: African National Associations in Cuba during Slavery." In *Sources and Methods in African History: Spoken, Written, Unearthed*, ed. Toyin Falola and Christian Jennings, 118–44. Rochester, N.Y.: University of Rochester Press, 2003.

Clark, Emily, and Virginia Meacham Gould. "The Feminine Face of Afro-Catholicism in New Orleans, 1727–1852." *William and Mary Quarterly* 59 (2002): 409–48.

Clark, Juan. *Cuba: Mito y realidad. Testimonios de un pueblo*. Miami: Saeta Ediciones, 1992.

Clarke, John H. "Some Neglected Aspects of Yoruba Culture in the Americas and in the Caribbean." In *The Proceedings of the Conference on Yoruba Civilization*, ed. Isaac A. Akinjogbin and G. O. Ekemode, 2:607–12. Ile-Ife, Nigeria: University of Ife, Department of History, 1976.

Cody, Cheryll Ann. "Naming, Kinship, and Estate Dispersal: Notes on Slave Family Life on a South Carolina Plantation, 1786 to 1833." *William and Mary Quarterly* 39 (1982): 192–211.

———. "There Was No 'Absalom' on the Ball Plantations: Slave-Naming Practices in the South Carolina Low Country, 1720–1865." *American Historical Review* 92 (1987): 563–96.

Cole, Gibril R. "Embracing Islam and African Traditions in a British Colony: The Muslim Krios of Sierra Leone, 1787–1910." Ph.D. dissertation, University of California, Los Angeles, 2000.

415

———. "Krio Muslim Society of Freetown: A Case Study on Fourah Bay and Foulah Town." B.A. (Hons) dissertation, Fourah Bay College, 1979.

Cole, Patrick. *Modern and Traditional Elites in the Politics of Lagos*. Cambridge: Cambridge University Press, 1975.

Collinwood, Dean W. "The Bahamas in Social Transition." In *Modern Bahamian Society*, ed. Dean W. Collinwood and Steve Dodge, 3–26. Parkersburg, Iowa: Caribbean Books, 1989.

Colmenares, Germán. *Popayán: Una sociedad esclavista, 1600–1800*. Medellín, Colombia: La Carreta, 1979.

Commonwealth of the Bahamas. "An Account of All Cotton Plantations in the Bahamas." In *The Bahamas in the Age of Revolution, 1775–1848*. Nassau, Bahamas: Department of Archives, Ministry of Education, 1989.

———. *Aspects of Slavery Part II: A Booklet to Commemorate the 150th Anniversary of the Abolition of Slavery*. Nassau, Bahamas: Department of Archives, Ministry of Education, 1984.

Conniff, Michael L., and Thomas J. Davis. *Africans in the Americas: A History of the Black Diaspora*. New York: St. Martin's, 1994.

Côrtes de Oliveira, Maria Inês. *O liberto: o seu mundo e os outros: Salvador, 1790–1890*. Salvador: Corrupio, 1988.

———. "Quem eram os 'negros da guiné'? A origem dos africanos na Bahia." *Afro-Ásia* 19/20 (1997): 53–63.

———. "Retrouver une identité: jeux sociaux des Africains de Bahia (Vers 1750–Vers 1890)." Ph.D. dissertation, Université de Paris–Sorbonne, 1992.

Cox, Harvey. Introduction to *Fidel and Religion*, ed. Fidel Castro and Frei Betto, 11–27. New York: Simon and Schuster, 1987.

Crahan, Margaret E., and Franklin W. Knight. *Africa and the Caribbean: The Legacies of a Link*. Baltimore, Md.: The Johns Hopkins University Press, 1979.

Craton, Michael. "Changing Patterns of Slave Families in the British West Indies." *Journal of Interdisciplinary History* 10 (1979): 1–35.

———. *Testing the Chains: Resistance to Slavery in the British West Indies*. Ithaca, N.Y.: Cornell University Press, 1982.

Craton, Michael, and Gail Saunders. *Islanders in the Stream: A History of the Bahamian People*. Vol. 1: *From the Aboriginal Times to the End of Slavery*. Athens: University of Georgia Press, 1992.

Crowder, Michael. *The Story of Nigeria*. London: Faber and Faber, 1973.

Crowther, Samuel A. *Dictionary of the Yoruba Language*. London: Oxford University Press, 1950.

Crozier, D. H., R. M. Blench, and Keir Hansford. *An Index of Nigerian Languages*. Dallas: Summer Institute of Linguistics, 1992.

Curtin, Philip D. *The Atlantic Slave Trade: A Census*. Madison: University of Wisconsin Press, 1969.

———. "Ayuba Suleiman of Bondu." In *Africa Remembered: Narratives by West Africans from the Era of the Slave Trade*, ed. Philip D. Curtin, 17–59. Madison: University of Wisconsin Press, 1967.

———. "From Guesses to Calculations." In *The Atlantic Slave Trade*, ed. David Northup. Lexington: Heath, 1994.

Dalton, Harlon. *Racial Healing: Confronting the Fear between Blacks and Whites*. New York: Doubleday, 1995.

Daniel, Yvonne. *Rumba, Dance, and Social Change in Contemporary Cuba.* Bloomington: Indiana University Press, 1995.

Danmole, Hakeem Olumide. "The Frontier Emirate: A History of Islam in Ilorin." Ph.D. dissertation, Center of West African Studies, University of Birmingham, U.K., 1980.

Dantas, Beatriz Góis. "Pureza e poder no mundo dos Candomblés." In *Candomblé: Desvendando identidades,* ed. Carlos Eugênio Marcondes de Moura, 121–27. São Paulo: EMW Ed., 1987.

———. *Vovó Nagô e Papai Branco. Usos e abusos da África no Brasil.* 2nd ed. Rio de Janeiro: Edições Graal, 1988.

Debien, Gabriel. "Les origines des esclaves aux Antilles." *Bulletin de l'Institut d'Afrique Noire* sèr. B, 23 (1961): 363–87; 24 (1962): 1–41; 25 (1963): 1–38, 215–66.

Dennett, Richard Edward. *Nigerian Studies; or, The Religious and Political System of the Yoruba.* London: Frank Cass, 1968 [1910].

Dennis, Carolyne. "Women and the State in Nigeria: The Case of the Federal Military Government, 1984–1985." In *Women, State, and Ideology: Studies from Africa and Asia,* ed. Haleh Afshar, 13–27. London: Macmillan, 1987.

Deschamps Chapeaux, Pedro. *El negro en la economía habanera del siglo XIX.* Havana: Unión de Escritores y Artistas de Cuba, 1971.

———. *Los cimarrones urbanos.* Havana: Editorial de Ciencias Sociales, 1983.

Desmangles, Leslie Gérald. *The Faces of the Gods: Vodou and Roman Catholicism in Haiti.* Chapel Hill: University of North Carolina Press, 1992.

Díaz Ayala, Cristóbal. *Cuando salí de la Habana, 1898–1997. Cien años de música Cubana por el mundo.* San Juan, Puerto Rico: Fundación Musicalia, 1998.

———. "Intercambios, diásporas, fusiones." *Encuentro de la cultura Cubana* 15 (1999): 86–95.

———. "La música Cubana como producto exportable." Presented at the Cuban Research Institute Conference at Florida International University, 2002.

———. *Música cubana del areyto a la nueva trova.* Miami: Ediciones Universal, 1981.

Díaz Fabelo, Teodoro. "Análisis y evaluación cultural de las letras del Diloggun." Unpublished manuscript. Biblioteca Nacional José Martí, 1967.

———. *Diccionario de la lengua conga residual en Cuba.* UNESCO Library, 1972.

———. *Diccionario de yerbas y palos rituales, medicinales, y el alimenticios en el uso por los Afrocubanos.* UNESCO Library, 1969.

———. *El Poblamiento.* Unpublished manuscript. Biblioteca Nacional José Martí, 1969.

———. *La escritura de los Abakua.* UNESCO Library, 1971.

———. *Introducción al estudio de las culturas Afrocubanas.* Unpublished manuscript. Biblioteca Nacional José Martí, 1969.

———. *Lengua de Santeros.* Havana: Vanity, 1956.

———. *Los caracoles.* Unpublished manuscript. Biblioteca Nacional José Martí, 1967.

———. *Los Negros cimarrones de Cuba.* UNESCO Library, 1974.

———. *Olórun.* Havana: Teatro Nacional, 1960.

Diaz, Juan Gonzalez. "El cabildo congo de nueva paz a sociedad africana virgin de regal." *Revista de la Biblioteca Nacional José Marti* 2 (1992): 37–54.

Díaz, María Elena. "Rethinking Tradition and Identity: The Virgin of Charity of El Cobre." In *Cuba, the Elusive Nation: Interpretations of National Identity,* ed. Damían J. Fernández and Madeline Cármara Betancourt, 43–59. Gainesville: University Press of Florida, 2000.

Dillard, J., ed. *Perspectives on Black English.* The Hague: Mouton, 1975.

Djedje, Jacqueline C. "The Fulbe Fiddle in the Gambia: A Symbol of Identity." In *Turn Up the Volume! A Celebration of African Music,* ed. Jacqueline C. Djedje, 98–113. Los Angeles: University of California at Los Angeles, Fowler Museum of Cultural History, 1999.

Dmochowski, Z. R. *An Introduction to Nigerian Traditional Architecture.* London: Ethnographica (in association with the National Commission for Museums and Monuments), 1990.

Dodd, Dorothy. "The Schooner Emperor: An Incident of the Illegal Trade in Florida." *Florida Historical Quarterly,* 13 (January 1935): 117–28.

Dominguez, Virginia R. "The Marketing of Heritage." *American Ethnologist* 13, no. 3 (1986): 546–55.

Doortmont, Michael R. "The Invention of the Yorubas: Regional and Pan-African Nationalism versus Ethnic Provincialism." In *Self-Assertion and Brokerage: Early Cultural Nationalism in West Africa,* ed. P. F. de Moraes Farias and K. Barber, 101–108. Birmingham: Center for West African Studies, University of Birmingham, 1990.

Downs, Dorothy. *Art of the Florida Seminoles and Miccosukee Indians.* Gainesville: University Press of Florida, 1995.

———. "Possible African Influence on the Art of the Florida Seminoles." In *African Impact on the Material Culture of the Americas: Conference Proceedings, Diggs Gallery at Winston-Salem State University.* Winston-Salem: Museum of Early Southern Decorative Arts, 1998.

Drewal, Henry John. "Art or Accident: Yòrúba Body Artists and Their Deity Ògun." In *Africa's Ogun: Old World and New,* ed. Sandra T. Barnes, 235–60. Bloomington: Indiana University Press, 1997.

Drewal, Margaret Thompson. "Embodied Practice/Embodied History: Mastery of Metaphor in the Performances of Diviner Kolawole Ositola." In *The Yoruba Artist: New Theoretical Perspectives on African Arts,* ed. Roland Abiodun, Henry John Drewal, and J. Pemberton, 171–92. Washington D.C.: Smithsonian, 1994.

———. *Yoruba Ritual: Performers, Play, Agency.* Bloomington: Indiana University Press, 1992.

Drewal, Henry J., and John Mason. *Beads, Body, and Soul: Art and Light in the Yoruba Universe.* Los Angeles: Fowler Museum of Cultural History, 1998.

Drewal, Henry John, and Margaret Thompson Drewal. *Gelede: Art and Female Power among the Yoruba.* Bloomington: Indiana University Press, 1983.

Driskell, David C. *Two Centuries of Black American Art.* New York: Knopf, 1976.

Du Bois, W. E. B. *The Negro.* New York: Oxford University Press, 1970 [1915].

———. *The Souls of Black Folks.* New York: Allograph, 1968 [1903].

———. *The Supression of the African Slave Trade to the United States of America, 1638–1870.* Baton Rouge: Louisiana State University Press, 1969.

Dunglas, Édouard. "Contribution à l'histoire du Moyen-Dahomey (Royaumes d'Abomey, de Kétou et de Ouidah)." *Etudes Dahoméennes* 19 (1957): 19–74.

Dupigny, E. G. M. *Gazetteer of Nupe Province.* London: Waterlow, 1920.

Echeruo, Michael J. C. "An African Diaspora: The Ontological Project." In *The African Diaspora: African Origins and New World Identities,* ed. Isidore Okpewho, Carole Boyce Davies, and Ali A. Mazuri, 3–18. Bloomington: Indiana University Press, 1999.

———. *Victorian Lagos: Aspects of Nineteenth Century Lagos Life.* London: Macmillan, 1977.

Elkins, Stanley. *Slavery: A Problem in American Institutional and Intellectual Life*. Chicago: University of Chicago Press, 1959.

Eltis, David. *Economic Growth and the Ending of the Transatlantic Slave Trade*. New York: Oxford University Press, 1987.

———. "The Export of Slaves from Africa, 1821–1843." *Journal of Economic History* 37 (1977): 409–33.

———. "Fluctuations in Sex and Age Ratios in the Transatlantic Slave Trade, 1663–1864." *Economic History Review* 46 (1993): 308–23.

———. "Free and Coerced Migrations from the Old World to the New." In *Coerced and Free Migration: Global Perspectives*, ed. David Eltis, 34–74. Stanford, Calif.: Stanford University Press, 2002.

———. "Nutritional Trends in Africa and the Americas: Heights of Africans, 1819–1839." *Journal of Interdisciplinary History* 22 (1982): 453–75.

———. *The Rise of African Slavery in the Americas*. Cambridge: Cambridge University Press, 2000.

———. "The Slave Trade in Nineteenth-Century Nigeria." In *Studies in the Nineteenth-Century Economic History of Nigeria*, ed. Toyin Falola and Ann O'Hear, 85–96. Madison: African Studies Program, University of Wisconsin, 1998.

———. "Welfare Trends among the Yoruba at the Beginning of the Nineteenth Century: The Anthropometric Evidence." *Journal of Economic History* 50 (1990): 521–40.

Eltis, David, and Stanley Engerman, "Fluctuations in the Age and Sex Ratios of Slaves in the Nineteenth-Century Transatlantic Slave Traffic." *Slavery and Abolition* 7 (1986).

Eltis, David, and David Richardson. "West Africa and the Transatlantic Slave Trade: New Evidence of Long-Run Trends." In *Routes to Slavery: Direction, Ethnicity, and Mortality in the Transatlantic Slave Trade*, ed. David Eltis and David Richardson, 16–35. London: Frank Cass, 1997.

Eltis, David, and Stanley Engerman. "Was the Slave Trade Dominated by Men?" *Journal of Interdisciplinary History* 23 (1992): 237–57.

Eltis, David, David Richardson, and Stephen Behrendt. *The Atlantic Slave Trade: A New Census*. Cambridge: Cambridge University Press, forthcoming.

Eltis, David, Paul Lovejoy, and David Richardson. "Ports of the Slave Trade: An Atlantic-Wide Perspective, 1676–1832." In *The Ports of the Slave Trade (Bights of Benin and Biafra)*, ed. Robin Law and Silke Strikrodt, 12–34. Stirling, U.K.: Centre of Commonwealth Studies, University of Stirling, 1999.

Eltis, David, Stephen Behrendt, David Richardson, and Herbert S. Klein. *The Trans-Atlantic Slave Trade: A Database on CD-ROM*. Cambridge: Cambridge University Press, 1999.

Eneas, Cleveland W. *Bain Town*. Nassau, Bahamas: Timpaul, 1976.

Epstein, Dena J. *Sinful Tunes and Spirituals: Black Folk Music to the Civil War*. Chicago: University of Illinois Press, 1977.

Escure, Genevieve. "Decreolization in a Creole Continuum: Belize." In *Historicity and Variations in Creole Studies*, ed. A. Highfield and A. Valdman. Ann Arbor: Karoma, 1981.

Euba, Akin. *Yoruba Drumming: The Dùndún Tradition*. Bayreuth, Germany: Bayreuth African Studies Series, 1990.

Euba, Femi. "Legba and the Politics of Metaphysics: The Trickster in Black Drama." In

Black Theatre: Ritual Performance in the African Diaspora, ed. Paul C. Harrison, Victor L. Walker, and Gus Edwards, 167–80. Philadelphia: Temple University Press, 2002.

Fabre, Geneviève. "African-American Commemorative Celebrations in the Nineteenth Century." In *History and Memory in African-American Culture*, ed. Genevieve Fabre and Robert O'Meally, 72–91. New York: Oxford University Press, 1994.

Fagg, William. *Yoruba Beadwork: Art of Nigeria*. New York: Rizzoli, 1980.

Falola, Toyin. *Culture and Customs of Nigeria*. Westport, Conn.: Greenwood, 2001.

——. "The End of Slavery among the Yoruba." *Slavery and Abolition* 19, no. 2 (1998): 232–49.

——. "Power Relations and Social Interactions among Ibadan Slaves, 1850–1900." *African Economic History* 16 (1987): 95–114.

——. "Slavery and Pawnship in the Yoruba Economy of the Nineteenth Century." In *Unfree Labour in the Development of the Atlantic World*, ed. Paul E. Lovejoy and Nicholas Rogers, 221–45. London: Frank Cass, 1994.

——. "The Yoruba Wars of the Nineteenth Century." In *Yoruba Historiography*, ed. idem, 135–45. Madison, Wis.: African Studies Program, 1991.

Falola, Toyin, and Akanmu Adebayo. *Culture, Politics, and Money among the Yoruba*. New Brunswick, N.J.: Transaction, 2000.

Falola, Toyin, and G. O. Oguntomisin. *Yoruba Warlords of the Nineteenth Century*. Trenton, N.J.: Africa World Press, 2001.

Farias, Juliana Barreto. "Crenças e religiosidades cotidanas. Práticas culturais e religiosidades afro-brasileiras no Rio de Janeiro (1870s–1930s)." Unpublished paper, 2002.

Farias, P. F. de Moraes, and K. Barber, eds. *Self-Assertion and Brokerage: Early Cultural Nationalism in West Africa*. Birmingham, U.K.: Center for West African Studies, University of Birmingham, 1990.

Fehér, Férenc, Agnes Heller, and György Márkus, eds. *Dictatorship over Needs: An Analysis of Soviet Societies*. New York: Basil Blackwell, 1983.

Fernández, León, ed. *Asentamientos, hacienda y gobierno*. San José: Editorial Costa Rica, 1976.

Fernández Robaina, Tómas. *Bibliografía de temas Afrocubanos*. Havana: Biblioteca Nacional José Martí, 1985.

——. *El Negro en Cuba, 1902–1958: Apuntes para la historia de la lucha contra la discriminación racial*. Havana: Editorial de Ciencias Sociales, 1994.

——. *Hablen paleros y santeros*. Havana: Editorial de Ciencias Sociales, 1994.

——. *Recuerdos secretos de dos mujeres públicas*. Habana: Letras Cubanas, 1983.

Ferraz, A. de Couto. "Volte à África." *Revista do Arquivo Municipal de São Paulo* 54 (1939): 175–78.

Ferreira dos Reis, Isabel Cristina. *Histórias de vida familiar e afetiva de escravos na Bahia do século XIX*. Salvador: Centro de Estudos Baianos/UFBA, 2001.

Ferrer, Ada. *Insurgent Cuba: Race, Nation, and Revolution, 1868–1898*. Chapel Hill: University of North Carolina Press, 1999.

Ferretti, Sergio Figueiredo. *Repensando o sincretismo*. São Paulo: EDUSP, 1995.

Fick, Carolyn E. *The Making of Haiti: The Saint Domingue Revolution from Below*. Knoxville: University of Tennessee Press, 1990.

Fine, Elisa Honig. *The Afro-American Artist: A Search for Identity*. New York: Holt, Rinehart and Winston, 1973.

Florentino, Manolo. "Alforria e etnicidade no Rio de Janeiro oitocentista: Notas de pesquisa." *Topói* 5 (2002): 9–40.

———. *Em costas negras. Uma história do tráfico atlântico de escravos entre a África e o Rio de Janeiro (séculos XVIII e XIX)*. Rio de Janeiro: Arquivo Nacional, 1995.

Fonseca, Elizabeth C. "El cultivo de la caña de azúcar en el Valle Central de Costa Rica: Época Colonial." In *Costa Rica Colonial*, ed. Luis F. Sibaja, 79–104. San José: Ediciones Guayacán, 1989.

Forde, Darryl. *The Yoruba-Speaking People of South-Western Nigeria*. London: International African Institute, 1951.

Foster, Philip. *Education and Social Change in Ghana*. London: Routledge, 1965.

Foster, Robert J. "Marketing National Cultures in the Global Ecumene." *Annual Review of Anthropology* 20 (1991): 235–60.

Fraginals, Manuel Moreno. *El Ingenio: Complejo económico social cubano del azúcar*. 3 vols. Havana: Editorial de Ciencias Sociales, 1978.

Franco, José Luciano. *Afroamérica*. Havana: Junta Nacional de Arqueología y Etnología, 1961.

———. *La Conspiración de Aponte de 1812*. Havana: Publicaciones del Archivo Nacional, 1963.

Franklin, Maria. "Early Black Spirituality and the Cultural Strategy of Protective Symbolism: Evidence from Art and Archaeology." In *African Impact on the Material Culture of the Americas: Conference Proceedings, Diggs Gallery at Winston-Salem State University*. Museum on Early Southern Decorative Arts, Winston-Salem, 30 May–2 June, 1996.

Frazier, E. Franklin. *The Negro Family in the United States*. Chicago: University of Chicago Press, 1966 [1939].

Freyre, Gilberto. *The Masters and the Slaves: A Study in the Development of Brazilian Civilization*. Translated by Samuel Putnam. New York: Knopf, 1946.

The Freeman. May 1888. Newsletter in the Bahamas National Archives.

Fuente García, Alejandro de la. "Esclavos africanos en la Habana: Zonas de Procedencia y denominaciones étnicas, 1570–1699." *Revista Española de Antropología Americana* 20 (1990): 135–60.

Fyfe, Christopher. *A History of Sierra Leone*. London: Oxford University Press, 1962.

———. "Reform in West Africa: The Abolition of the Slave Trade." In *History of West Africa*, vol. 2, ed. J. F. Ade Ajayi and Michael Crowder, 2:30–56. London: Longman, 1974.

———. *Sierra Leone Inheritance*. London: Oxford University Press, 1964.

Fyle, C. Magbaily. "Contemporary African Urban Culture, Indigenous Religious Beliefs, and Issues of African Identity in the Diaspora." In *Ghana in Africa and the World: Essays in Honor of Adu Boahen*, ed. Toyin Falola, 391–406. Trenton, N.J.: Africa World Press, 2003.

———. "Language Krio." *BBC Focus on Africa Magazine* 3, no. 3 (1992): 15–18.

———. "Official and Unofficial Attitudes and Policy towards Krio as the Main Lingua Franca in Sierra Leone." In *African Languages in Development and the State*, ed. R. Fardon and G. Furniss, 44–54. London: Routledge, 1994.

Fyle, Clifford M., and Eldred D. Jones. *Krio-English Dictionary*. New York: Oxford University Press, 1980.

Gama, Luis. "Luis Gama's letter to Lúcio de Mendonça." Published in English in *Negro de Corpo e Alma*. São Paulo: Fundação Bienal de São Paulo, 2000.

Garcia-Zamor, Jean-Claude. "Social Mobility of Negroes in Brazil." *Journal of Inter-American Studies* 12, no. 2 (April 1970).

Garret, Romeo B. "African Survivals in American Culture." *Journal of Negro History* 51, no. 4 (1966).

Gates, Henry L. *The Signifying Monkey: A Theory of Afro-American Literary Criticism.* New York: Oxford University Press, 1988.

Gbadamosi, T. G. O. *The Growth of Islam among the Yoruba, 1841–1908.* London: Longman, 1978.

Geggus, David Patrick. "The Demographic Composition of the French Caribbean Slave Trade." In *Proceedings of the Thirteenth and Fourteenth Meetings of the French Colonial History Society,* ed. P. Boucher, 14–30. Lanham, Md.: University Press of America, 1990.

———. "Marronage, Vodou, and the Saint Domingue Slave Revolt of 1791." *Proceedings of the Annual Meeting of the French Colonial Historical Society* 15 (1992): 22–35.

———. "Sex Ratio, Age, and Ethnicity in the Atlantic Slave Trade: Data from French Shipping and Plantation Records." *Journal of African History* 30, no. 1 (1989): 23–45.

———. "Slavery, War, and Revolution in the Greater Caribbean, 1789–1815." In *A Turbulent Time: The French Revolution and the Greater Caribbean,* ed. David Barry Gaspar and David Patrick Geggus. Bloomington: Indiana University Press, 1997.

———. "Sugar and Coffee Cultivation in Saint Domingue and the Shaping of the Slave Labor Force." In *Cultivation and Culture: Labor and the Shaping of Slave Life in the Americas,* ed. Ira Berlin and Philip Morgan, 73–98. Charlottesville: University of Virginia Press, 1993.

Genovese, Eugene. *Roll, Jordan, Roll: The World the Slaves Made.* New York: Vintage, 1974.

Georgia Writers' Project. *Drums and Shadows: Survival Studies among the Georgia Coastal Negroes.* Athens: University of Georgia Press, 1940.

Gilroy, Paul. *The Black Atlantic: Modernity and Double Consciousness.* Cambridge, Mass.: Harvard University Press, 1993.

Glazier, Stephen D. *Marchin' the Pilgrims Home: Leadership and Decision-Making in an Afro-Caribbean Faith.* Westport, Conn.: Greenwood, 1983.

Glélé, Maurice A. *Religion, culture et politique en Afrique noire.* Paris: Economica, 1981.

Glinski, Mark. "Orisha Wall." *International Review of African American Art* 9, no. 3 (1991): 33–47.

Gomes, Flávio dos Santos, *Histórias de Quilombolas: mocambos e comunidades de senzalas no Rio de Janeiro — século XIX.* Rio de Janeiro: Arquivo Nacional, 1995.

———. "Jogando a rede, revendo as malhas: fugas e fugitivos no Brasil escravista." *Tempo* 1, no. 1 (1996): 67–93.

Gomez, Michael A. *Exchanging Our Country Marks: The Transformation of African Identities in the Colonial and Antebellum South.* Chapel Hill: University of North Carolina Press, 1998.

González-Wippler, Migene. *The Santería Experience.* New York: Original, 1982.

———. *Santería, the Religion: A Legacy of Faith, Rites, and Magic.* New York: Harmony, 1989.

Goody, Jack. *Comparative Studies in Kinship.* Stanford, Calif.: Stanford University Press, 1969.

Goucher, Candice. "African-Caribbean Metal Technology: Forging Cultural Survivals in the Atlantic World." In *African Sites Archaeology in the Caribbean,* ed. Jay B. Haviser, 143–56. Princeton, N.J.: Markus Wiener, 1999.

Goulart, Mauricio. *A escravidão Africana no Brasil: das origens a extinção do tráfico.* São Paulo: Editora Alfa-Omega, 1975.

Gossai, Henchand, and Nathaniel Samuel Murrell, eds. *Religion, Culture, and Tradition in the Caribbean.* New York: St. Martin's, 2000.

Gragg, Larry. "The Pious and the Profane: The Religious Life of Early Barbados Planters." *The Historian* 62 (winter 2000): 264–83.

Graham, Richard. "Slave Families of a Rural Estate in Colonial Brazil." *Journal of Social History* 9 (1976): 382–402.

Green, Lisa J. *African American English: A Linguistic Introduction.* Cambridge: Cambridge University Press, 2002.

Green, William. "The Creolization of Caribbean History: The Emancipation Era and a Critique of Dialectical Analysis." In *Caribbean Freedom: Economy and Society from Emancipation to the Present,* ed. Hilary Beckles and Verene Shepard, 28–41. Princeton, N.J.: Markus Wiener, 1996.

Guanche, Jesús. *Procesos etnoculturales de Cuba.* Havana: Letras Cubanas, 1983.

———. "Santería cubana e identidad cultural." *Revolución y Cultura* (March–April 1996): 43–46.

Guanche, Jesús, and Argeliers León. "Integración y desintegración de los cultos sincréticos de origen africano en Cuba." *Revolución y Cultura* 80 (April 1979): 14–19.

Gudeman, Stephen, and Stuart B. Schwartz. "Cleansing Original Sin: Godparenthood and the Baptism of Slaves in Eighteenth-Century Bahia." In *Kinship Ideology and Practice in Latin America,* ed. Raymond T. Smith, 35–58. Chapel Hill: University of North Carolina Press, 1984.

Gudmundson, Lowell. "Mecanismos de movilidad social para la población de procedencia Africana en Costa Rica colonial: manumisión y mestizaje." In *Estratificación socio-racial y económica de Costa Rica, 1700–1850,* ed. Lowell Gudmundson, 17–78. San José: Editorial Universidad Estatal a Distancia, 1978.

Guerra, Ramiro. *Teatralización del folklore y otros ensayos.* Havana: Letras Cubanas, 1989.

Gurán, Milton. *Agudás: os "brasileiros" do Benim.* Rio de Janeiro: Editora Nova Fronteira, 1999.

Gutman, Herbert. *The Black Family in Slavery and Freedom, 1750–1925.* New York: Pantheon, 1976.

Hackett, Rosalind. "Revitalization in African Traditional Religion." In *African Traditional Religions in Contemporary Society,* ed. J. K. Olupona, 135–48. New York: Paragon, 1991.

Hagedorn, Katherine J. "Anatomía del proceso folklórico: The 'Folkloricization' of Afro-Cuban Religious Performance in Cuba." Ph.D. dissertation, Brown University, 1995.

———. *Divine Utterances: The Performance of Afro-Cuban Santería.* Washington, D.C.: Smithsonian Institution Press, 2001.

Hair, P. E. H. "Aspects of the Prehistory of Freetown and 'Creoledom.'" *History in Africa* 25 (1998): 111–18.

Hall, Gwendolyn Midlo. "African Ethnicities and the Meanings of 'Mina.'" In *The Transatlantic Dimensions of Slaving,* ed. Paul E. Lovejoy and David Trotman, 65–81. London: Continuum, 2002.

———. *Africans in Colonial Louisiana: The Development of Afro-Creole Culture in the Eighteenth Century.* Baton Rouge: Louisiana State University Press, 1992.

———. *Afro-Louisiana History and Genealogy Database*. Baton Rouge: Louisiana State University Press, 2000.

Hall, Richard L. "African Religious Retentions in Florida." In *Africanisms in American Cultures*, ed. Joseph Holloway, 98–118. Bloomington: Indiana University Press, 1990.

Hall, Stuart. "Cultural Identity and Diaspora." In *Colonial Discourse and Post-Colonial Theory*, ed. Patrick Williams and Laura Chrisman, 392–403. Hertfordshire: Harvester Wheatsheaf, 1994.

Hancock, Ian. "Creole Language Provenance and the African Component." In *Africanisms in Afro-American Language Varieties*, ed. Salikoko S. Mufwene. Athens: University of Georgia Press, 1993.

———. "The Domestic Hypothesis, Diffusion, and Componentiality: An Account of Atlantic Anglophone Creole Origin." In *Substrata versus Universals in Creole Genesis*, ed. Pieter Muysken and Norval Smith, 71–102. Amsterdam: John Benjamins, 1986.

———. "A Preliminary Classification of the Anglophone Atlantic Creoles, with Syntactic Data from Thirty-Three Representative Dialects." In *Pidgin and Creole Languages: Essays in Memory of John E. Reinecke*, ed. G. Gilbert, 264–334. Honolulu: University of Hawaii Press, 1987.

Handler, Jerome S., and JoAnn Jacoby. "Slave Names and Naming in Barbados." *William and Mary Quarterly* 53 (1996): 685–728.

Harding, Rachel Elizabeth. *A Refuge in Thunder: Candomblé and Alternative Spaces of Blackness*. Bloomington: Indiana University Press, 2000.

Harper, Peggy. "The Role of Dance in the Gelede Ceremonies of the Village of Ijio." *Odu: A Journal of West African Studies* 4 (1970): 67–94.

Harrell-Bond, Barbara, Allen M. Howard, and David E. Skinner. *Community Leadership and the Transformation of Freetown (1870–1976)*. The Hague: Mouton, 1978.

Harris, J. E., ed. *Global Dimensions of the African Diaspora*. Washington, D.C.: Howard University Press, 1982.

Harrison, Faye V. *Decolonizing Anthropology: Moving Further toward an Anthropology for Liberation*. Washington, D.C.: American Anthropological Association, 1991.

Harrison, J. A. "Negro English." In *Perspectives on Black English*, ed. J. Dillard. The Hague: Mouton, 1975.

Harvey, Emily N. "A Brer Rabbit Story." *Journal of American Folklore* 32 (1919).

Haskins, Jim. *Voodoo and Hoodoo: The Craft as Revealed by Actual Practitioners*. New York: Stein and Day, 1978.

Helg, Aline. *Our Rightful Share: The Afro-Cuban Struggle for Equality, 1886–1912*. Chapel Hill: University of North Carolina Press, 1995.

Helms, Mary W. "Miskito Slaving and Culture Contact: Ethnicity and Opportunity in an Expanding Population." *Journal of Anthropological Research* 39, no. 2 (1983): 179–97.

Henrique Dias Tavares, Luis. *Comércio proibido de escravos*. São Paulo: Ática, CNPq, 1988.

Hermon-Hodge, H. B. *Gazetteer of Ilorin Province*. London: Allen and Unwin, 1929.

Herskovits, Melville J. "Acculturation and the American Negro." *Southwestern Political and Social Science Quarterly* 8 (1927): 211–412.

———. "African Gods and Catholic Saints in New World Negro Belief." *American Anthropologist* 39 (1937): 635–43.

——. *The American Negro: A Study in Racial Crossing.* New York: Knopf, 1928.

——. *Dahomey: An Ancient West African Kingdom.* 2 vols. New York: J. J. Augustin, 1938.

——. *The Myth of the Negro Past.* Boston: Beacon, 1958 [1941].

——. "The Social History of the Negro." In *A Handbook of Social Psychology,* ed. Carl Murchinson. Worcester, Mass.: Clark University Press, 1935.

Herskovits, Melville J., and Frances Herskovits. "Suriname Folk-lore." In *Columbia University Contributions to Anthropology* 27. New York: Columbia University Press, 1936.

Hewitt, Julia Cuervo. "Yoruba Presence in Contemporary Cuban Narrative." Ph.D. dissertation, Vanderbilt University, 1981.

Heywood, Linda, ed. *Central Africans and Cultural Transformations in the African Diaspora.* Cambridge: Cambridge University Press, 2002.

Higginbotham, A. Leon. *In the Matter of Color: Race and the American Legal Process.* Oxford: Oxford University Press, 1978.

Higman, Barry W. "African and Creole Slave Family Patterns in Trinidad." In *Africa and the Caribbean: The Legacies of a Link,* ed. Margaret E. Crahan and Franklin W. Knight (Baltimore: The Johns Hopkins University Press, 1979).

——. *Slave Populations of the British Caribbean, 1807–1834.* Baltimore: The Johns Hopkins University Press, 1984.

——. "Terms for Kin in the British West Indian Slave Community: Differing Perceptions of Masters and Slaves." In *Kinship Ideology and Practice in Latin America,* ed. Raymond T. Smith, 59–81. Chapel Hill: University of North Carolina Press, 1984.

Hogben, S. J., and A. H. M. Kirk-Greene. *The Emirates of Northern Nigeria.* London: Oxford University Press, 1966.

Holloway, Joseph E., and Winifred K. Vass. *The African Heritage of American English.* Bloomington: Indiana University Press, 1993.

Holm, John Alexander. "The Creole English of Nicaragua's Miskito Coast: Its Sociolinguistic History and a Comparative Study of Its Lexicon and Syntax." Ph.D. dissertation, University of London, 1978.

Horton, Robin. "African Conversion." *Africa* 41 (1971): 85–108.

Houk, James T. *Spirits, Blood, and Drums: The Orisha Religion in Trinidad.* Philadelphia: Temple University Press, 1995.

Hountondji, Paulin, ed. *Les savoirs endogènes: Pistes pour une recherche.* Dakar: Codesria, 1994.

Howard, Phillip A. *Changing History: Afro-Cuban Cabildos and Societies of Color in the Nineteenth Century.* Baton Rouge: Louisiana State University Press, 1998.

Howard, Rosalyn. *Black Seminoles in the Bahamas.* Gainesville: University Press of Florida, 2002.

Hudson, Larry E., Jr. *To Have and to Hold: Slave Work and Family Life in Antebellum South Carolina.* Athens: University of Georgia Press, 1997.

Huet, Michel. *The Dances of Africa.* New York: Harry N. Abrams, 1996.

Hughes, Colin P. *Race and Politics in the Bahamas.* New York: St. Martin's, 1981.

Hughes, Langston, and Milton Meltzer. *Black Magic: A Pictorial History of the African American in the Performing Arts.* New York: Da Capo, 1990.

Hunt, Carl M. *Oyotunji Village: The Yoruba Movement in America.* Washington, D.C.: University Press of America, 1979.

Hunwick, John, and Fatima Harrak. *Mi'Raj Al-Su'Ud: Ahmad Baba's Replies on Slavery.* Rabat: Institute of African Studies, 2000.

Hurston, Zora N. "Shouting." In *Negro: An Anthology,* ed. Nancy Cunard. New York: Ungar, 1970.

Íbítókun, Benedict M. *Dance as Ritual Drama and Entertainment in the Gèlèdé of the Kétu-Yorùbá Subgroups in West Africa.* Ilé-Ifè, Nigera: Obafemi Awolowo, 1993.

Idowu, Bolaji. *Olódùmarè: God in Yoruba Belief.* London: Longman, 1962.

Igue, John, and Olabiyi Yai. "The Yoruba-Speaking Peoples of Dahomey and Togo." *Yoruba* 1, no. 1 (1972): 1–29.

Isichei, Elizabeth. *A History of African Societies to 1870.* Cambridge: Cambridge University Press, 1997.

Izquierdo, Pedro. "Detrás de la música, esta música." *Trabajadores,* 4 April 1990. Archives, Instituto Cubano de Radio y Televisión.

Jalloh, Alusine, and David Skinner, eds. *Islam and Trade in Sierra Leone.* Trenton, N.J.: Africa World Press, 1997.

Jimoh, L. A. K. *Ilorin: The Journey So Far.* Ilorin, Nigeria: L. A. K. Jimoh, 1994.

Johnson, Howard. *The Bahamas in Slavery and Freedom.* Kingston, Jamaica: Ian Randle, 1991.

Johnson, Paul C. "Migrating Bodies, Circulating Signs: Brazilian Candomblé, the Garifuna of the Caribbean, and the Category of Indigenous Religions." *History of Religions* 41, no. 4 (2002): 301–27.

Johnson, Samuel. *The History of the Yorubas: From the Earliest Times to the Beginning of the British Protectorate.* London: Routledge and Kegan Paul, 1966 [1921].

Jones, Rhett. "Why Pan-Africanism Failed: Blackness and International Relations." *The Griot* 14, no. 1 (1995): 53–70.

Jules-Rosette, Bennetta W. "Tradition and Continuity in African Religions: The Case of New Religious Movements." In *African Traditional Religions in Contemporary Society,* ed. J. K. Olupona, 149–68. New York: Paragon, 1991.

Karasch, Mary C. "Central Africans in Central Brazil, 1780–1835." In *Central Africans and Cultural Transformations in the African Diaspora,* ed. Linda Heywood, 117–51. Cambridge: Cambridge University Press, 2002.

———. "Guine, Mina, Angola, and Benguela: African and Crioulo Nations in Central Brazil, 1780–1835." In *Enslaving Connections: Changing Cultures of Africa and Brazil during the Era of Slavery,* ed. José C. Curto and Paul E. Lovejoy, 163–84. New York: Humanities Books, 2004.

———. "Os quilombos do ouro na Capitania de Goiás." In *Liberdade por um fio: história dos quilombos no Brasil,* ed. João José Reis and Flávio dos Santos Gomes, 240–62. São Paulo: Companhia das Letras, 1996.

———. *Slave Life in Rio de Janeiro, 1808–1850.* Princeton, N.J.: Princeton University Press, 1987.

———. *A vida dos escravos no Rio de Janeiro 1808–1850.* 2nd ed. São Paulo: Campanhia das Letras, 2000.

Khan, Aisha. "Journey to the Center of the Earth: The Caribbean as Master Symbol." *Cultural Anthropology* 16 (2001): 271–302.

———. "On the 'Right Path': Interpolating Religion in Trinidad." In *Religion, Diaspora, and Cultural Identity: A Reader in the Anglophone Caribbean,* ed. John W. Pulis, 247–76. Amsterdam: Gordon and Breach, 1999.

Kinney, E. S. "Urban West African Music and Dance." *African Urban Notes* 5, no. 4 (1970): 3–10.

Kiple, Kenneth F. *Blacks in Colonial Cuba, 1774–1899.* Gainesville: University Press of Florida, 1976.

Kirk, John M., and Leonardo Padura Fuentes. *Culture and the Cuban Revolution: Conversations in Havana.* Gainesville: University Press of Florida, 2001.

Klein, Herbert S. *The Atlantic Slave Trade.* Cambridge: Cambridge University Press, 1999.

Klein, Herbert S., and Stanley L. Engerman. "A Note on Mortality in the French Slave Trade in the Eighteenth Century." In *The Uncommon Market: Essays in the Economic History of the Slave Trade,* ed. Henry A. Gemery and Jan S. Hogendorn, 261–72. London: Academic Press, 1979.

Knight, Franklin W. "Cuba." In *Neither Slave nor Free: The Freedman of African Descent in the Slave Societies of the New World,* ed. David W. Cohen and Jack P. Greene, 278–308. Baltimore, Md.: The Johns Hopkins University Press, 1972.

Kolapo, Femi J. "The 1858–59 Gbebe CMS Journal of Missionary James Thomas." *History in Africa* 27 (2000): 159–92.

———. "Military Turbulence, Population Displacement and Commerce on a Slaving Frontier of the Sokoto Caliphate: Nupe, c. 1830–1857." Ph.D. dissertation, York University, 1999.

———. "Nineteenth-Century Niger River Trade and the 1844–1862 Aboh Interregnum." *African Economic History* 28 (2001): 1–29.

Kopytoff, Jean Herskovits. *A Preface to Modern Nigeria: The "Sierra Leonians" in Yoruba, 1830–1890.* Madison: University of Wisconsin Press, 1965.

Kreutzinger, Helga. *The Eri Devils in Freetown, Sierra Leone.* Vienna: Österreichische Ethnologische Gesellschaft, 1966.

Kubik, Gerhard. *Angolan Traits in Black Music, Games, and Dances of Brazil: A Study of African Cultural Extensions Overseas.* Lisbon: Junta de Investigações Cientifica do Ultramar, Centro de Antropologia Cultural, 1979.

Kutzinski, Vera. *Sugar's Secrets: Race and the Erotics of Cuban Nationalism.* Charlottesville: University Press of Virginia, 1993.

Labouret, Henri, and Paul Rivet. *Le Royaume D'Arda et son Évangélisation au XVIIe siècle.* Paris: Travaux et Mémoires de l'Institut e'Ethnologie, 1929.

Lachance, Paul F. "The 1809 Immigration of Saint-Domingue Refugees from New Orleans: Reception, Integration, and Impact." *Louisiana History* 29 (1988): 109–41.

Lachatañeré, Rómulo. *El sistema religioso de los Afrocubanas.* Havana: Editorial de Ciencias Sociales, 1992.

Lahaye Guerra, Rosa María, and Ruben Zardoya Loureda. *Yemayá a través de sus mitos.* Havana: Editorial de Ciencias Sociales, 1996.

Landes, Ruth. "A Cult Matriarchate and Male Homosexuality." *Journal of Abnormal and Social Psychology* 35, no. 3 (1940): 386–97.

Larose, Thomas. "African Influences on Seminole Beadwork." Paper presented at the Twelfth Triennial Symposium of the Arts Council of the African Studies Association, St. Thomas, U.S. Virgin Islands, 25–29 April 2001.

Law, Robin. "The Atlantic Slave Trade in Yoruba Historiography." In *Yoruba Historiography,* ed. Toyin Falola, 123–34. Madison, Wis.: African Studies Program, 1991.

———. "Between the Sea and the Lagoons: The Interaction of Maritime and Inland

Navigation on the Pre-Colonial Slave Coast." *Cahiers d'Études Africaines* 29, no. 2 (1989): 209–37.

———. "A carreira de Francisco Felix de Souza na África Ocidental (1800–1849)." *Topoi: Revista de história* 2 (2001): 9–39.

———. "Ethnicity and the Slave Trade: 'Lucumi' and 'Nago' as Ethnonyms in West Africa." *History in Africa* 24 (1997): 205–19.

———. "The Evolution of the Brazilian Community in Ouidah." *Slavery and Abolition* 22, no. 1 (April 2000): 22–41.

———. "The Heritage of the Oduduwa: Traditional History and Political Propaganda among the Yoruba." *Journal of African History* 14, no. 2 (1973): 207–22.

———. "Islam in Dahomey: A Case Study of the Introduction and Influence of Islam in a Peripheral Area of West Africa." *Scottish Journal of Religious Studies* 9, no. 2 (1986): 50–64.

———. *The Kingdom of Allada.* Leiden: Research School CNWS, School of Asian, African, and Amerindian Studies, 1997.

———. "A Lagoonside Port on the Eighteenth Century Slave Coast: The Early History of Badagri." *Canadian Journal of African Studies* 28, no. 1 (1994): 32–59.

———. "Local Amateur Scholarship in the Construction of Yoruba Ethnicity, 1880–1914." In *Ethnicity in Africa: Roots, Meanings, and Implications,* ed. Louise de la Gorgondière, Kenneth King, and Sarah Vaughan. Edinburgh, 55–90. Centre of African Studies, University of Edinburgh, 1996.

———. *Ouidah: The Social History of a West African Slaving "Port," 1727–1892.* Oxford: James Currey, 2004.

———. *The Oyo Empire, c. 1600–c. 1836: A West African Imperialism in the Era of the Atlantic Slave Trade.* Oxford: Clarendon, 1977.

———. "A Pioneer of Yoruba Studies: Moses Lijadu (1862–1926)." In *Studies in Yoruba History and Culture,* ed. G. O. Olusanya, 105–15. Ibadan, Nigeria: Ibadan University Press, 1983.

———. "Religion, Trade, and Politics on the 'Slave Coast': Roman Catholic Missions in Allada and Whydah in the Seventeenth Century." *Journal of Religion in Africa* 21 (1991): 42–77.

———. "Royal Monopoly and Private Enterprise: The Case of Dahomey." *Journal of African History* 18 (1977): 555–77.

———. *The Slave Coast of West Africa, 1550–1750: The Impact of the Atlantic Slave Trade on an African Society.* Oxford: Clarendon, 1991.

———. "Slave-Raiders and Middlemen, Monopolists and Free Traders: The Supply of Slaves for the Atlantic Trade in Dahomey, c. 1715–1850." *Journal of African History* 30 (1989): 45–68.

———, ed. *From Slave Trade to "Legitimate" Commerce.* Cambridge: Cambridge University Press, 1995.

Law, Robin, and Kristin Mann. "West Africa in the Atlantic Community: The Case of the Slave Coast." *William and Mary Quarterly* 56 (1999): 307–34.

Law, Robin, and Silke Strickrodt, eds. *Ports of the Slave Trade (Bights of Benin and Biafra).* Stirling, U.K.: Centre of Commonwealth Studies, University of Stirling, 1999.

Lawal, Babatunde. "The African Heritage of African American Art and Performance." In *Black Theatre: Ritual Performance in the African Diaspora,* ed. Paul C. Harrison, Victor L. Walker, and Gus Edwards, 39–63. Philadelphia: Temple University Press, 2002.

428

——. "African Roots, American Branches: Tradition and Transformation in African American Self-Taught Art." In *Souls Grown Deep: African American Vernacular Art from the South*, ed. William Arnett and Paul Arnett, 1:30–49. Atlanta: Tinwood, in association with the Schomburg Center for Research in Black Cultures, New York, 2000.

——. "Anticipating Ethiopia's Rise to Glory: Rereading James Hampton's *Throne of the Third Heaven of the Nations Millennium General Assembly*." In *Souls Grown Deep: African American Vernacular Art of the South*, ed. William Arnett and Paul Arnett, 2:98–103. Atlanta: Tinwood, 2001.

——. "Aworan: The Self and Its Metaphysical Other in Yoruba Art." *The Art Bulletin: A Quarterly Published by the College Art Association* 83, no. 3 (2001): 498–526.

——. "From Africa to the New World: Art in Yoruba Religion." In *Santería Aesthetics in Contemporary Latin American Art*, ed. Arturo Lindsay, 3–39. Washington, D.C.: Smithsonian Institution Press, 1996.

——. *The Gèlèdé Spectacle: Art, Gender, and Social Harmony in an African Culture*. Seattle: University of Washington Press, 1996.

León, Argeliers. "El folklore: su estudio y recuperación." In *La cultura Cuba socialista*, ed. Ministerio de Cultura, 182–93. Havana: Editorial Arte y letras, 1982.

——. "El instituto de etnología y folklore de la academia de ciencias de Cuba." *Etnología y folklore* 1 (1966): 5–16.

——. "La música como mercancía." In *Musicología en Latinoamérica*, ed. Zoila Gómez García, 406–28. Havana: Editorial Arte y Literatura, 1985.

——. *Música folklórica Cubana*. Havana: Biblioteca Nacional José Martí, 1964.

——. "Música popular de Origen Africano en América Latina." *América indígena: Órgano Oficial del Instituto Indigenista Interamericano* 29 (1969): 627–64.

——. "Un caso de tradición oral escrita." *Islas* 39/40 (1971): 139–51.

Levine, Lawrence W. *Black Culture and Black Consciousness: Afro-American Folk Thought from Slavery to Freedom*. New York: Oxford University Press, 1977.

Lima, Vivaldo da Costa. "A família-de-santo nos Candomblés Jeje-Nagos da Bahia: Um estudo de relações intra-grupais." Master's thesis, Salvador Universidade Federal de Bahia, Brazil, 1977.

——. "Os obás de Xangô." *Afro-Ásia* 2–3 (June–December 1966): 5–36.

Lima, Vivaldo da Costa, and Waldir Freitas Oliveira, eds. *Cartas de Edison Carneiro a Artur Ramos*. São Paulo: Corrupio, 1987.

Lindsay, Lisa A. "'To Return to the Bosom of Their Fatherland': Brazilian Immigrants in Nineteenth-Century Lagos." *Slavery and Abolition* 15 (1994): 22–50.

Littlefield, Daniel F. *Africans and Seminoles: From Removal to Emancipation*. Westport, Conn.: Greenwood, 1977.

Lloyd, Peter C. "Divorce among the Yoruba." *American Anthropologist* 70, no. 1 (February 1968): 67–81.

——. "Political and Social Structure." In *Sources of Yoruba History*, ed. S. O. Biobaku, 205–23. Oxford: Clarendon, 1973.

Lobo Wiejoff, Tatiana, and Mauricio Meléndez Obando. *Negros y blancos: todo mezclado*. San José: Editorial de la Universidad de Costa Rica, 1997.

Locke, Alain. "The Legacy of the Ancestral Arts." In *The New Negro*, ed. Alain Locke, 254–67. New York: Atheneum, 1968.

Long, Richard A. *The Black Tradition in American Dance*. New York: Rizzoli, 1989.

López Valdés, Rafael L. *Componentes Africanos en el etnos Cubano*. Havana: Editorial de Ciencias Sociales, 1985.

———. "Notas para el estudio etnohistórico de los esclavos lucumi de Cuba." *Anales del Caribe* 6 (1986): 54–74.

Lorde, Audre. *Undersong: Chosen Poems Old and New.* Rev. ed. New York: Norton, 1992.

Lovejoy, Paul E. "The African Diaspora: Revisionist Interpretations of Ethnicity, Culture, and Religion under Slavery." *Studies in the World History of Slavery, Abolition, and Emancipation* 2, no. 1 (1997), available at: www2.h-net.msu.edu/~slavery/essays/esy9701love.html

———. "Background to Rebellion: The Origins of Muslim Slaves in Bahia." *Slavery and Abolition* 15, no. 2 (1994): 151–80.

———. "Biography as Source Material: Towards a Biographical Archive of Enslaved Africans." In *Source Material for Studying the Slave Trade and the African Diaspora*, ed. Robin Law, 119–40. Stirling, U.K.: Centre of Commonwealth Studies, 1997.

———. "The Central Sudan and the Atlantic Slave Trade." In *Paths toward the Past: African Historical Essays in Honor of Jan Vansina*, ed. Robert W. Harms, Joseph C. Miller, David S. Newbury, and Michele D. Wagner, 345–70. Atlanta: African Studies Association Press, 1994.

———. *A escravidão na África. Uma história de suas transformações.* Rio de Janeiro: Civilização Brasileira, 2002.

———. "Identifying Enslaved Africans in the African Diaspora." In *Identity in the Shadow of Slavery*, ed. Paul E. Lovejoy, 1–29. London: Continuum, 2000.

———. "Islam, Slavery, and Political Transformation in West Africa: Constraints on the Trans-Atlantic Slave Trade." *Revue française d'histoire d'outre-mer* 89 (2002): 247–82.

———. "Jihad e escravidão: as origens dos escravos muçulmanos da Bahia." *Topoi* (Rio de Janeiro) 1 (2000): 11–44.

———. *Transformations in Slavery: A History of Slavery in Africa.* 2nd ed. Cambridge: Cambridge University Press, 2000 [1983].

———, ed. *Identity in the Shadow of Slavery.* London: Continuum, 2000.

Lovejoy, Paul E., and David Richardson. "The Initial 'Crisis of Adaptation': The Impact of British Abolition on the Atlantic Slave Trade in West Africa, 1808–1820." In *From Slave Trade to "Legitimate" Commerce*, ed. Robin Law, 32–56. Cambridge: Cambridge University Press, 1995.

Lovejoy, Paul E., and David V. Trotman. "Experiencias de vida y expectativas: Nociones africanas sobre la esclavitud y la realidad en América." In *Rutas de la esclavitud en África y América Latina*, ed. Rina Cáceres, 379–404. San José: Editorial de la Universidad de Costa Rica, 2001.

Lucas, Jonathan Olumide. *The Religion of the Yorubas.* Lagos: CMS, 1948.

Lühning, Angela E. "Acabe com este anto, pedrito vem ai . . . mito e realidade da perseguição policial ao Candomblé baiano entre 1920 e 1942." *Revista USP* 28 (1995–96): 194–220.

———. "O compositor Mozart Camargo Guarnieri e o 2 Congresso afro-Brasileiro em Salvador, 1937." In *Ritmos em trânsito. Sócio-antropologia da música Baiana*, ed. L. Sansone and J. Teles dos Santos, 59–72. São Paulo: Dynamis Editorial and Programa a Cor da Bahia, 1998.

Luz, Marco Aurélio, and Georges Lapassade. *O segredo da Macumba.* Rio de Janeiro: Paz e Terra, 1972.

Macgowan, Fiona, and John Gordon, "Introduction (Syncretism)." *Australian Journal of Anthropology* 12, no. 3 (December 2001): 1.

Machado, Maria Helena. *O plano e o pânico. Os movimentos sociais na década da abolição.* Rio de Janeiro: Editora da UFRJ/EDUSP, 1994.

MacLeod, Murdo J. *Spanish Central America: A Socioeconomic History, 1520–1720.* Berkeley: University of California Press, 1973.

MacMillan, John. "John Kuners." *Journal of American Folk-lore* 39 (January–March 1926): 53–57.

Maggie, Yvonne. *Medo do feitiço: relações entre magia e poder no Brasil.* Rio de Janeiro: Arquivo Nacional, 1992.

Malone, Ann Patton. *Sweet Chariot: Slave Family and Household Structure in Nineteenth-Century Louisiana.* Chapel Hill: University of North Carolina Press, 1992.

Mamigonian, Beatriz G. "Do que 'o preto mina' e capaz: etnia e resistência entre africanos livres." *Afro-Asia* 24 (2000): 71–95.

———. "To Be Liberated African in Brazil: Labour and Citizenship in the 19th Century." Ph.D. dissertation, University of Waterloo, 2002.

Mann, Kristin. *The Birth of an African City: Trade, State, and Emancipation in Nineteenth-Century Lagos.* Forthcoming.

———. "Marriage Choices among the Educated African Elite in Lagos Colony, 1880–1915." *The International Journal of African Historical Studies* 14, no. 2 (1981): 201–28.

———. "Owners, Slaves and the Struggle for Labour in the Commercial Transition at Lagos." In *From Slave Trade to Legitimate Commerce: The Commercial Transition in Nineteenth-Century West Africa,* ed. Robin Law, 144–71. Cambridge: Cambridge University Press, 1995.

———. "Shifting Paradigms in the Study of the African Diaspora and of Atlantic History and Culture." *Slavery and Abolition* 22, no. 1 (April 2001): 3–21.

———. "Slave Exports from Lagos, c. 1760–1851." In *Canadian Association of African Studies, Montreal* (1996).

Mann, Kristin, and Edna Bay, eds. *Rethinking the African Diaspora: The Making of a Black Atlantic World in the Bight of Benin and Brazil.* London: Frank Cass, 2001.

Manning, Patrick. "The Slave Trade in the Bight of Benin, 1640–1890." In *The Uncommon Market: Essays in the Economic History of the Atlantic Slave Trade,* ed. Henry A. Gemery and Jan S. Hogendorn, 107–41. New York: Academic Press, 1979.

———. *Slavery, Colonialism, and Economic Growth in Dahomey, 1640–1960.* Cambridge: Cambridge University Press, 1982.

Marrero, Leví, ed. *Cuba: economía y sociedad, del monopolio hacia la libertad comercial (1701–1763).* Madrid: Editorial Playor, 1980.

Martin, K. K. "America's First African Dance Theatre." *Odu: A Journal of West African Studies* 11 (January 1975): 115–28.

Martin, S. H. "Music in Urban East Africa: Five Genres in Dar Es Salaam." *Journal of African Studies* 9, no. 3 (1982): 155–63.

Martinez-Alier, Verena. *Marriage, Class, and Colour in Nineteenth Century Cuba: A Study of Racial Attitudes and Sexual Values in a Slave Society.* Ann Arbor: University of Michigan Press, 1989.

Martinez Furé, Rogelio. *El Conjunto folklórico de Cuba: XX aniversario (1962–1982), apuntos cronológicos.* Havana: Ministerio de Cultura, 1982.

———. *Diálogos Imaginarios.* Havana: Editorial Arte y Literatura, 1979.

———. "A National Cultural Identity? Homogenizing Monomania and the Plural Heritage." In *Afro-Cuban Voices: On Race and Identity in Contemporary Cuba,* ed.

Pedro Pérez Sarduy and Jean Stubbs, 154–61. Gainesville: University Press of Florida, 2000.

Marty, P. "Etudes sur l'Islam au Dahomey, Livre 1: Le bas Dahomey." 2 parts. *Revue du monde musulman* 60 (1925): 109–88; 61 (1925): 75–146.

Marx, Karl, and Friedrich Engels. *The Marx-Engels Reader.* Edited by R. Tucker. New York: Norton, 1978.

Mason, John. *Olóòkun: Owners of Rivers and Seas.* New York: Yorùbá Theological Archministry, 1996.

———. "Yoruba-American Art: New Rivers to Explore." In *The Yoruba Artist: New Theoretical Perspectives on African Art,* ed. Rowland Abiodun, Henry Drewal, and John Pemberton, 241–50. Washington, D.C.: Smithsonian Institution Press, 1994.

———. "Yoruba Beadwork in the Americas." In *Beads, Body, and Soul: Art and Light in the Yoruba Universe,* ed. Henry J. Drewal and John Mason, 87–177. Los Angeles: University of California Fowler Museum of Cultural History, 1998.

Mason, Michael. *Foundations of the Bida Kingdom.* Zaria, Nigeria: Ahmadu Bello University Press, 1981.

———. "The Jihad in the South: An Outline of the Nineteenth Century Nupe Hegemony in North-Eastern Yorubaland and Afenmai." *Journal of the Historical Society of Nigeria* 5, no. 2 (1970): 193–208.

Matibag, Eugenio. *Afro-Cuban Religious Experience: Cultural Reflections in Narrative.* Gainesville: University Press of Florida, 1996.

Matory, J. Lorand. "Afro-Atlantic Culture: On the Live Dialogue between Africa and the Americas." Available online at http://www.africana.com/tt_669.htm

———. *Black Atlantic Religion: Tradition, Trans-nationalism, and Matriarchy in the Brazilian Candomblé.* Princeton, N.J.: Princeton University Press. Forthcoming.

———. "The English Professors of Brazil: On the Diasporic Roots of the Yorùbá Nation." *Comparative Studies in Society and History* 41, no. 1 (January 1999): 72–103.

———. "Government by Seduction: History and the Tropes of Mounting in Oyo-Yoruba Religion." In *Modernity and Its Malcontents,* ed. John Comaroff and Jean Comaroff. Chicago: University of Chicago Press, 1993.

———. "Jeje: repensando nações e transnacionalismo." *Mana* 5 (April 1999): 57–80.

———. *Sex and the Empire That Is No More: Gender and the Politics of Metaphor in Oyo Yoruba Religion.* Minneapolis: University of Minnesota Press, 1994.

Matsuoka, Atsuko, and John Sorenson. *Ghosts and Shadows: Constructions of Identity and Community in an African Diaspora.* Toronto: University of Toronto Press, 2001.

Mattoso, Katia. *Bahia século XIX: uma orovíncia no império.* Rio de Janeiro: Editora Nova Fronteira, 1992.

———. *Être Esclave au Brésil.* Paris: Hachette, 1979.

Maultsby, Portia K. "Influences and Retentions of West African Musical Concepts in U.S. Black Music." *Western Journal of Black Studies* 3 (1979): 198–200.

Mbiti, John. *African Religions and Philosophy.* New York: Praeger, 1969.

McDaniel, M. Akua. "Reexamining Hale Woodruff's Talladega College and Atlanta University Mural." *International Review of African American Art* 12 (1995): 5–17.

McDonald, Roderick A. *The Economy and Material Culture of Slaves: Goods and Chattels on the Sugar Plantations of Jamaica and Louisiana.* Baton Rouge: Louisiana State University Press, 1993.

McGarrity, Gayle L. "Race, Culture, and Social Change in Contemporary Cuba." In

Cuba in Transition, ed. Sandor Halebsky and John M. Kirk, 193–205. Boulder, Colo.: Westview, 1992.

Meléndez, Carlos. "El negro en Costa Rica durante la colonia." In *El negro en Costa Rica* by Carlos Meléndez and Quince Duncan, 11–58. 9th ed. San José: Editorial Costa Rica, 1989 [1972].

Mello e Souza, Marina. *Reis negros no Brasil escravista: História da festa de coroação de Rei Congo*. Belo Horizonte: Ed. UFMG, 2002.

Mello, Marco Antônio Lirio de. *Reviras, batuques e carnavais: a cultura de resistência dos escravos em Pelotas*. Pelotas: UFPel, Editora Universitária, 1994.

Menéndez, Lazára. *Estudios afro-cubanos: selección de lecturas*. 4 vols. Havana: Facultad de Arte y Letras, Universidad de la Habana, 1990–98.

———. "Un cake para Obatalá?" *Temas* 4 (October–December 1995): 38–51.

Mercier, Paul. "The Fon of Dahomey." In *African Worlds: Studies in the Cosmological Ideas and Social Values of African Peoples*, ed. Darryl Forde, 210–34. London: Oxford University Press, 1954.

———. "Notice sur le peuplement Yoruba au Dahomey-Togo." *Études Dahoméennes* 4 (1950): 40–41.

Metcalf, Alida. *Family and Frontier in Colonial Brazil*. Berkeley: University of California Press, 1992.

———. "Searching for the Slave Family in Colonial Brazil: A Reconstruction from São Paulo." *Journal of Family History* 16 (1991): 283–97.

Meyer-Heiselberg, Richard. *Notes from the Liberated African Department in the Archives at Fourah Bay College, Freetown, Sierre Leone*. Uppsala: Scandinavian Institute of African Studies, 1967.

Miller, Joseph C. *The Way of Death: Merchant Capitalism and the Angolan Slave Trade, 1730–1830*. Madison: University of Wisconsin Press, 1988.

Millet, José, and Rafael Brea. *Grupos folklóricos de Santiago de Cuba*. Santiago de Cuba: Editorial Oriente, 1989.

Mills, Kenneth. *Idolatry and Its Enemies: Colonial Andean Religion and Extirpation, 1640–1750*. Princeton, N.J.: Princeton University Press, 1997.

Ministerio de Cuba, ed. *La cultura en Cuba socialista*. Havana: Arte y Letras, 1982.

Ministerio de Educación, ed. *Memorias: Congreso Nacional de Educación y Cultura*. Havana: Ministerio de Educación, 1971.

Mintz, Sidney W. "Africa of Latin America: An Unguarded Reflection." In *Africa in Latin America: Essays on History, Culture, and Socialization*, ed. Manuel Moreno Fraginals, 286–305. New York: Holmes and Meier, 1984.

———. *Caribbean Transformations*. New York: Columbia University Press, 1989 [1974].

Mintz, Sidney W., and Richard Price. *The Birth of African-American Culture: An Anthropological Perspective*. Boston: Beacon, 1992 [1976].

Montaner, Carlos Alberto. "El testamento de Fidel Castro." *El Nuevo Heráld* (2001).

———. *Fidel Castro y la revolución cubana*. Barcelona: Plaza y Janes, S.A., 1985.

Montejo, Esteban. *The Autobiography of a Runaway Slave*. New York: Pantheon, 1976.

Moore, Carlos. *Castro, the Blacks, and Africa*. Los Angeles: University of California, Center for Afro-American Studies, 1988.

———. "Cuba: The Untold Story." *Présence Africaine: Cultural Review of the Negro World* 24 (English edition), no. 52 (1964): 177–229.

Moore, Robin D. *Nationalizing Blackness: Afrocubanismo and Artistic Revolution in Havana, 1920–1940*. Pittsburgh: University of Pittsburgh Press, 1997.

——. "Representations of Afrocuban Expressive Culture in the Writings of Fernando Ortiz." *Latin American Music Review* 15, no. 1 (spring/summer 1994): 32–54.

——. "Salsa and Socialism: Dance Music in Cuba, 1959–1999." In *Situating Salsa: Global Markets and Local Meanings in Latin Popular Music*, ed. Lise Waxer, 51–74. New York: Routledge, 2002.

Morejón, Nancy. "Cantos africanos de Cuba." *Revista de la Biblioteca Nacional "Jose Martí"* 12, no. 2 (May–August 1970): 173–75.

Morgan, Philip D. "The Cultural Implications of the Atlantic Slave Trade: African Regional Origins, American Destinations, and New World Developments." In *Routes to Slavery: Direction, Ethnicity, and Mortality in the Transatlantic Slave Trade*, ed. David Eltis and David Richardson, 122–45. London: Frank Cass, 1997.

——. *Slave Counterpoint: Black Culture in the Eighteenth-Century Chesapeake and Lowcountry*. Chapel Hill: University of North Carolina Press, 1998.

Morton-Williams, Peter. "An Outline of the Cosmology and Cult Organization of the Oyo Yoruba." *Africa* 34 (1964): 243–60.

——. "The Oyo Yoruba and the Atlantic Slave Trade, 1670–1830." *Journal of the Historical Society of Nigeria* 3, no. 1 (December 1964): 25–45.

——. "Two Studies of Ifa Divination. Introduction: The Mode of Divination." *Africa* 36 (1966): 406–31.

——. "The Yoruba Kingdom of Oyo." In *West African Kingdoms in the Nineteenth Century*, ed. Daryll Forde and P. M. Kaberry, 32–69. London: Oxford University Press, 1967.

Moses, Wilson J., ed. *Classical Black Nationalism: From the American Revolution to Marcus Garvey*. New York: New York University Press, 1996.

Mott, Luiz. "'Acotundá'—raízes setecentistas do sincretismo religioso afro-brasileiro." *Revista do Museu Paulista* 31 (1986): 124–47.

——. *Escravidão homossexualidade e demonologia*. São Paulo: Ícone, 1988.

Mott, Luiz, and Marcelo Cerqueira, eds. *As religiões Afro-Brasileiras na luta contra a AIDS*. Salvador: Editora Centro Baiano Anti-AIDS, 1998.

Moura, Roberto. *Tia ciata e a pequena África no Rio de Janeiro*. Rio de Janeiro: Secretaria Municipal da Cultura, 1995.

Moynihan, Daniel P. *The Negro Family: The Case for National Action*. Washington, D.C.: Office of Policy Planning Research, U.S. Department of Labor, 1965.

Mullin, Michael. *Africa in America: Slave Acculturation and Resistance in the American South and British Caribbean, 1736–1831*. Urbana: University of Illinois Press, 1992.

Mulvey, Patricia. "The Black Lay Brotherhoods of Colonial Brazil: A History." Ph.D. dissertation, City University of New York, 1976.

Murphy, Joseph A. "Ritual Systems in Cuban Santería." Ph.D. dissertation, Temple University, 1981.

Murphy, Joseph M. *Santería: African Spirits in America*. Boston: Beacon, 1993.

Murphy, Joseph M., and Mei-Mei Sanford, eds. *Ọ̀ṣun across the Waters: A Yoruba Goddess in Africa and the Americas*. Bloomington: Indiana University Press, 2001.

Murray, David R. *Odious Commerce: Britain, Spain, and the Abolition of the Cuban Slave Trade*. Cambridge: Cambridge University Press, 1980.

Murray, E. J., ed. *Religions of Trinidad and Tobago: A Guide to the History, Beliefs, and Polity of 23 Religious Faiths*. Port of Spain, Trinidad and Tobago: Murray, 1998.

Nascimento, Abdias do. *Africans in Brazil: A Pan African Perspective*. Trenton, N.J.: Third World Press, 1992.

Naveda Chávez-Hita, Adriana. *Esclavos negros en las haciendas azucareras de Córdoba, Veracruz, 1690–1830*. Xalapa, Ver., Mexico: Centro de Investigaciones Históricas, Universidad Veracruzana, 1987.

Neira Betancourt, Lino A. *Como suena un tambor abakuá*. Havana: Editorial Pueblo y Educación, 1991.

Nicholls, David. *Haiti in Caribbean Context: Ethnicity, Economy, and Revolt*. New York: St. Martin's, 1985.

Nishida, Mieko. "From Ethnicity to Race and Gender: Transformations of Black Lay Sodalities in Salvador, Brazil." *Journal of Social History* 32 (1998): 329–48.

———. "Manumission and Ethnicity in Urban Slavery: Salvador, Brazil, 1808–1888." *Hispanic American Historical Review* 73, no. 3 (1993): 361–91.

Nørregård, Georg. *Danish Settlements in West Africa, 1658–1850*. Translated by Sigurd Mammen. Boston: Boston University Press, 1966.

———. "Forliset Ved Nicaragua 1710." *Årbor 1948* (Handels-og Søfartsmuseet pä Kronborg, Helsinger, Denmark), 67–98.

Northrup, David. *Indentured Labor in the Age of Imperialism, 1834–1922*. Cambridge: Cambridge University Press, 1995.

———. *Trade without Rulers: Precolonial Economic Development in Southeastern Nigeria*. Oxford: Clarendon, 1978.

Nunley, John W., and Judith Bettleheim. *Caribbean Festival Arts: Each and Every Bit of Difference*. Seattle: University of Washington Press, 1988.

Nwokeji, G. Ugo, and David Eltis. "Characteristics of Captives Leaving the Cameroons for the Americas." *Journal of African History* 43 (2002): 191–210.

———. "The Roots of the African Diaspora: Methodological Considerations in the Analysis of Names in the Liberated African Registers of Sierra Leone and Havana." *History in Africa* 29 (2002): 365–79.

O'Hear, Ann. "Ilorin as a Slaving and Slave-Trading State." In *Slavery on the Frontiers of Islam*, ed. Paul E. Lovejoy, 55–68. Princeton, N.J.: Markus Wiener, 2004.

———. *Power Relations in Nigeria: Ilorin Slaves and Their Successors*. Rochester, N.Y.: University of Rochester Press, 1997.

———. "The Yoruba and the Peoples of the Niger-Benue Confluence." In *Yoruba Frontiers*, ed. Toyin Falola and Funso S. Afolyan. Forthcoming.

Obeyemi, Ade. "The Sokota *Jihad* and the *O-Kun* Yoruba: A Review." *Journal of the Historical Society of Nigeria* 9, no. 2 (1978): 61–87.

Oduyoye, Mercy A. Foreword to *Decolonizing Theology: A Caribbean Perspective*, ed. Noel L. Erskine, ix–xiv. Trenton, N.J.: Africa World Press, 1998.

Ogunleye, Tolagbe M. "Aroko and Ogede: Yoruba Arts as Resistance to Enslavement Stratagems in Florida in the 18th and 19th Centuries." Paper presented at the conference on Yoruba Culture and Ethics held at University of California, Los Angeles, February 1999.

———. "The Self-Emancipated Africans of Florida: Pan-African Nationalists in the 'New World.'" *Journal of Black Studies* 27, no. 1 (1996): 24–38.

Ojo, G. J. Afolabi. *Yoruba Culture: A Geographical Analysis*. London: University of London Press, 1966.

Okediji, Moyo. *The Shattered Gourd: Yoruba Forms in Twentieth Century American Art*. Seattle: University of Washington Press, 2003.

Okpewho, Isidore, Carole Boyce Davies, and Ali A. Mazrui, eds. *The African Diaspora: African Origins and New World Identities*. Bloomington: Indiana University Press, 1999.

Olawaiye, James Adeyinka. "Yoruba Religious and Social Traditions in Ekiti, Nigeria, and Three Caribbean Countries: Trinidad-Tobago, Guyana, and Belize." Ph.D. dissertation, University of Missouri, Kansas City, 1980.

Olinto, Antônio. *A Casa de Aqua*. Lisbon: Minerva, 1969. English translation: *The Water House* (London: Rex Collings, 1970).

Olomo, Aina. *Core of Fire: A Guide to Yoruba Spiritual Activism*. New York: Athelia, 2002.

Olupona, Jacob K. *African Traditional Religions in Contemporary Society*. New York: Paragon, 1991.

———. *Kingship, Religion, and Ritual in a Nigerian Community: A Phenomenological Study of Ondo-Yoruba Festivals*. Stockholm: Almqvist and Wiksell, 1991.

———. "The Study of Yoruba Religious Tradition in Historical Perspective." *Numen* 1 (1993): 240–73.

Omari, Mikelle Smith. "Completing the Circle: Notes on African Art, Society, and Religion in Oyotunji, South Carolina." *African Arts* 24, no. 3 (1991): 66–75.

Oppenheimer, Andres. *Castro's Final Hour: The Secret Story behind the Coming Downfall of Communist Cuba*. New York: Simon and Schuster, 1992.

Oro, Ari. "Religiões afro-brasileiras do Rio Grande do Sul: passado e presente." *Estudos Afro-Asiáticos*, 24, no. 2 (2002): 345–84.

Oroge, E. Adeniyi. "The Institution of Slavery in Yorubaland with Particular Reference to the Nineteenth Century." Ph.D. dissertation, University of Birmingham, Center of West African Studies, U.K., 1971.

Ortiz, Fernando. *Los bailes y el teatro de los negros en el folklore de Cuba*. Havana: Letras Cubanas, 1981 [1951].

———. "Los cabildos afro-cubanos." *Revista Bimestre Cubana* 16 (January–February 1921): 5–39. Reprint, Havana: Editorial de Ciencias Sociales, 1992.

———. *Los cabildos y la fiesta afrocubanos del Día de Reyes*. Havana: Editorial de Ciencias Sociales, 1992 [1921].

———. *Los negros brujos*. Havana: Editorial de Ciencias Sociales, 1995 [1906].

———. *Los negros esclavos*. Havana: Editorial de Ciencias Sociales, 1975 [1916].

Othman, Ramatoulie O. *A Cherished Heritage: Tracing the Roots of the Oku-Marabou, Early 19th to Mid-20th Century*. Serrekunda, the Gambia: Edward Francis Small, 1999.

Ott, Carlos. "O Negro Bahiano." In *Les Afro-Americains*, ed. Institut français d'Afrique noire, 141–52. Dakar: IFAN, 1952.

Oyetunji Mustapha, Oyetunji. "A Literary Appraisal of Sakara: A Yoruba Traditional Form of Music." In *Yoruba Oral Tradition: Poetry in Music, Dance, and Drama*, ed. Wande Abimbola, 517–49. Ile-Ife, Nigeria: Department of African Languages and Literatures, University of Ife, 1975.

Palmer, Colin A. *Slaves of the White God: Blacks in Mexico, 1570–1650*. Cambridge, Mass.: Harvard University Press, 1976.

Palmié, Stephen. "Against Syncretism: 'Africanizing' and 'Cubanizing' Discourses in North American Òrìsà Worship." *Counterworks* (1993): 73–103.

Paquette, Robert L. *Sugar Is Made with Blood: The Conspiracy of La Escalera and the Conflict between Empires over Slavery in Cuba*. Middletown, Conn.: Wesleyan University Press, 1988.

Parés, Luis Nicolau. "Do lado de jeje: história e ritual do vodun na Bahia." Rio de Janeiro: Pallas, forthcoming.

———. "Transformations of the Sea and Thunder Voduns in the Gbe-Speaking Area and in the Bahian Jeje Candomblé." In *Africa and the Americas: Interconnections during the Slave Trade*, ed. J. Curto and R. Soulodre. Trenton, N.J.: African World Press, forthcoming.

Parker, John. *Making the Town: Ga State and Society in Early Colonial Accra.* Oxford: James Currey, 2000.

Parrinder Geoffrey. *West African Religion: A Study of the Beliefs and Practices of Akan, Ewe, Yoruba, Ibo, and Kindred Peoples.* 2nd ed. New York: Barnes & Noble, 1970.

Patterson, T. R., and R. D. Kelley. "Unfinished Migrations: Reflections on the African Diaspora and the Making of the Modern World." *African Studies Review* 43, no. 1 (2000): 11–45.

Patton, Sharon F. *African-American Art.* New York: Oxford University Press, 1998.

Peel, J. D. Y. "A Comparative Analysis of Ogun in Precolonial Yorubaland." In *Africa's Ogun: Old World and New*, ed. Sandra T. Barnes, 263–89. Bloomington: Indiana University Press, 1997.

———. "The Cultural Work of Yoruba Ethnogenesis." In *History and Ethnicity*, ed. E. Tonkin, M. MacDonald, and M. Chapman, 198–215. London: Routledge and Kegan Paul, 1989.

———. "The Pastor and the Babalawo: The Interaction of Religions in Nineteenth-Century Yorubaland." *Africa* 60 (1990): 338–69.

———. "Religious Change in Yorubaland." *Africa* 37 (1967): 292–306.

———. *Religious Encounter and the Making of the Yoruba.* Bloomington: Indiana University Press, 2000.

———. "Review Article. Historicity and Pluralism in Some Recent Studies of Yoruba Religion." *Africa* 64, no. 1 (1994): 150–66.

———. "Syncretism and Religious Change." *Comparative Studies in Society and History* 10 (1968): 121–41.

Pemberton, John. "Eshu-Elegba: The Yoruba Trickster God." *African Arts* 9, no. 1 (1975): 20–27, 60–70, 90–91.

Pérez-Stable, Marifeli. *The Cuban Revolution: Origins, Course, and Legacy.* New York: Oxford University Press, 1993.

Peterson, John. *Province of Freedom: A History of Sierra Leone, 1787–1870.* Evanston, Ill.: Northwestern University Press, 1969.

———. "The Sierra Leone Creole: A Reappraisal." In *Freetown: A Symposium*, ed. C. Fyfe and E. D. Jones, 100–17. Freetown: Sierra Leone University Press, 1968.

Pierson, Donald. *Brancos e Pretôs na Bahia: Estudo de contato racial.* São Paulo: Editora Nacional, 1971.

Pradel, Lucie. *African Beliefs in the New World.* Trenton, N.J.: Africa World Press, 2000.

Querino, Manuel. *A raça africana no Brasil e seus costumes.* Salvador: Progresso, 1955.

Quirós Vargas de Quesada, Claudia. "Aspectos socioeconómicos de la cuidad del Espíritu Santo de Esparza y su jurisdicción (1574–1878)." Licenciatura thesis, Universidad de Costa Rica, 1976.

Raboteau, Albert J. *African American Religion.* New York: Oxford University Press, 1999.

———. "African-Americans, Exodus, and the American Israel." In *African American Christianity: Essays in History*, ed. Paul E. Johnson, 1–18. Berkeley: University of California Press, 1994.

Richards, Sandra. "Yoruba Gods on the American Stage: August Wilson's 'Joe Turner's Come and Gone.'" *Research in African Literatures* 30, no. 4 (1999): 93–105.

Ramos, Artur. Introdução to *A Casa das Minas. Culto dos vodus jeje no Maranhão*, ed. Nunes Pereira, 11–18. Petrópolis: Vozes, 1979 [1947].

Reis, João José. "Candomblé in Nineteenth-Century Bahia: Priests, Followers, Clients." In *Rethinking the African Diaspora: The Making of a Black Atlantic World in the Bight of Benin and Brazil*, ed. Kristin Mann and Edna Bay, 116–34. London: Frank Cass, 2001.

———. "De olho no canto: Trabalho de rua na Bahia na véspera da abolição." *Afro-Ásia* 24 (2001): 199–242.

———. "Identidade e diversidades étnicas nas irmandades negras no tempo da escravidão." *Tempo* 3 (1997): 7–33.

———. "Magia jeje na Bahia: A invasão do Calundu do Pasto de Cachoeira, 1785." *Revista Brasileira de História* 8, no. 16 (March–August 1988): 57–81, 233–49.

———. "O 'Rol dos Culpados': Notas sobre um documento da rebelião de 1835." *Anais do APEBa* 48 (1985): 119–38.

———. *Rebelião escrava no Brasil: A história do levante dos males na Bahia em 1835 (Nova Edição Revista e Ampliada)*. São Paulo: Companhia das Letras, 2003.

———. "Recôncavo rebelde: Revoltas escravas nos engenhos baianos." *Afro-Ásia* 15 (1992): 121–26.

———. "'The Revolution of the *Ganhadores*': Urban Labour, Ethnicity, and the African Strike of 1857 in Bahia, Brazil." *Journal of Latin American Studies* 29, no. 2 (May 1997): 355–93.

———. *Slave Rebellion in Brazil: The Muslim Uprising of 1835 in Bahia*. Translated by Arthur Brakel. Baltimore: The Johns Hopkins University Press, 1993.

———. "Tambores e Tremores: A festa negra na Bahia na primeira metade do século XIX." In *Carnaval e outras f(r)estas: Ensaios de história social da cultura*, ed. Maria Clementina P. da Cunha, 101–55. São Paulo: Editora da Unicamp, 2002.

Reynolds, Edward D. *Jesuits for the Negro*. New York: America Press, 1949.

Ribas, Olga Roig. *Santería Yoruba: Magia, culto y sabiduría afroamericana*. Madrid: Ediciones Karma 7, 2001.

Ricard, Robert. *The Spiritual Conquest of Mexico: An Essay on the Apostolate and the Evangelizing Methods of the Mendicant Orders in New Spain, 1523–1572*. Berkeley: University of California Press, 1966.

Rice, Timothy. *May It Fill Your Soul: Experiencing Bulgarian Music*. Chicago: University of Chicago Press, 1994.

Richardson, David. "Slave Exports from West and West-Central Africa, 1700–1810: New Estimates of Volume and Distribution." *Journal of African History* 30 (1989): 1–22.

Roberts, John S. *Black Music of Two Worlds: African, Caribbean, Latin, and African American Traditions*. 2nd rev. ed. London: Schirmer, 1998.

Robinson, Beverly. "Africanisms and the Study of Folklore." In *Africanisms in American Culture*, ed. Joseph E. Holloway, 211–24. Bloomington: Indiana University Press, 1990.

Rodríguez, Victoria Eli. "Cuban Music and Black Ethnicity: Historical Considerations." In *Music and Black Ethnicity: The Caribbean and South America*, ed. Gerard Béhague, 91–108. New Brunswick, N.J.: Transaction, 1994.

Rodrigues, Nina. *O animismo fetichista dos negros bahianos*. Rio de Janeiro: Civilização Brasileira, 1935 [1896].

———. *Os africanos no Brasil*. São Paulo: Companhia Editora Nacional, 1977 [1906].

Roig de Leuchsenring, Emilio. "Bailando junto al abismo." *Social* 17 (September 1932): 12–13, 80.

Román, Reinaldo. "The Routes of Cuban Spiritism: Disciplining Man-Gods in Town and Country." Paper presented at the Cuban Research Institute Conference, Florida International University, March 2002.

Romero Vargas, Germán. *Las sociedades del atlántico de Nicaragua en los siglos XVII y XVIII*. Managua: Fondo de Promoción Cultural–BANIC, 1995.

Ross, David. "The Career of Domingo Martinez in the Bight of Benin, 1833–1864." *Journal of African History* 6 (1965): 79–90.

———. "The First Chacha of Whydah: Francisco Felix De Souza." *Odu* 2 (1969): 19–28.

Roussé-Grosseau, Christiane. *Mission catholique et choc des modèles culturels en Afrique: l'exemple du Dahomey, 1861–1928*. Paris: L'Harmattan, 1992.

Rumford, Beatrix T., and Carolyn J. Weekley. *Treasures of American Art from the Abby Aldrich Rockefeller Folk Art Center*. Boston: Little, Brown, 1989.

Rush, Dana Lynn. "Vodun Vortex: Accumulative Arts, Histories, and Religious Consciousnesses along Coastal Benin." Ph.D. dissertation, University of Iowa, 1997.

Russell-Wood, A. J. R. "Black and Mulatto Brotherhoods in Colonial Brazil." *Hispanic American Historical Review* 54, no. 4 (1974): 567–602.

Ryder, A. F. C. *Benin and the Europeans, 1485–1897*. London: Humanities, 1969.

———. "Dutch Trade on the Nigerian Coast during the Seventeenth Century." *Journal of the Historical Society of Nigeria* 3, no. 2 (1965): 195–210.

Sahlins, Marshall. *Historical Metaphors and Mythical Realities: Structure in the Early History of the Sandwich Islands Kingdom*. Ann Arbor: University of Michigan Press, 1981.

Salikoko, S. Mufwene, ed. *Africanisms in Afro-American Language*. Athens: University of Georgia Press, 1933.

Samara, Eni de Mesquita. "A família negra no Brasil." *Revista de História* 120 (1989): 27–44.

Sánchez de Fuentes, Eduardo. "Bailes y canciones." In *Diario de la Marina. Número centenario*, 101–102. Havana: Ucar, García y Cía., 1932.

Sandoval, Alonso de. *Un tratado sobre la esclavitud*. Madrid: Alianza Editorial, 1987 [1627].

Santos, Deoscóredes Maximiliano dos Mestre Didi. *História de um terreiro Nagô: crônica histórica*. São Paulo: Carthago and Forte, 1994.

Santos, Jocélio Teles dos. *O dono da terra (o caboclo nos candomblés da Bahia)*. Salvador: Sarah Letras, 1995.

Santos, Juana Elbeim dos. *Os Nàgô e a Morte: Pàde, Àsésé e o Culto Égun na Bahia*. Petrópolis: Vozes, 1986.

Sarmento, Augusto. *Portugal no Dahomé*. Lisbon: Livraria Tavares Cardoso, 1891.

Sarracino, Rodolfo. *Los que volvieron a África*. Havana: Editorial de Ciencias Sociales, 1988.

Sarup, Madan, and Tasneem Raja. *Identity, Culture, and the Postmodern World*. Edinburgh: Edinburgh University Press, 1998.

Saunders, Gail. "Aspects of Traditional African-Bahamian Culture in the Late 19th and Early 20th Century." *Journal of the Bahamas Historical Society* 17 (October 1995): 2.

———. *Bahamian Loyalists and Their Slaves*. London: Macmillan Education, 1983.

———. *Slavery in the Bahamas, 1648–1838*. Nassau, Bahamas: The Nassau Guardian, 1990 [1985].

Saunders, H. C. *The Other Bahamas*. Nassau, Bahamas: Bodab, 1991.

Scarano, Julita. "Black Brotherhoods: Integration or Contradiction?" *Luso Brazilian Review* 16 (1979): 1–17.

Schick, Tom. *Behold the Promised Land! A History of Sierra Leone and Liberia*. Madison: University of Wisconsin Press, 1977.

Schiltz, Marc. "Yoruba Thunder Deities and Sovereignty: Ara Versus Sango." *Anthropos* 80 (1985): 67–84.

Schoonmaker, Trevor, ed. *Black President: The Art and Legacy of Fela Anikulapo Kuti*. New York: New Museum of Contemporary Art, 2003.

Schuler, Monica. *"Alas, Alas, Kongo": A Social History of Indentured African Immigration into Jamaica, 1841–1865*. Baltimore: The Johns Hopkins University Press, 1980.

Schwartz, Rosalie. *Pleasure Island: Tourism and Temptation in Cuba*. Lincoln: University of Nebraska Press, 1997.

Schwartz, Stuart B. *Sugar Plantations in the Formation of Brazilian Society: Bahia, 1550–1835*. Cambridge: Cambridge University Press, 1985.

Scott, Freda M. *"The Star of Ethiopia: A* Contribution toward the Development of Black Drama and Theatre in the Harlem Renaissance." In *The Harlem Renaissance: Revaluations*, ed. Amritjit Singh, William S. Shiver, and Stanley Brodwin, 257–80. New York: Garland, 1989.

Scott, Rebecca J. *Slave Emancipation in Cuba: The Transition to Free Labor, 1860–1899*. Princeton, N.J.: Princeton University Press, 1985.

Segurola, R. P. B. *Dictionnaire Fon-Français*. Cotonou: Procure de l'Archidiocèse, 1963.

Sharp, William F. *Slavery on the Spanish Frontier: The Columbian Chocó, 1680–1810*. Norman: University of Oklahoma Press, 1976.

Sibthorpe, A. B. C. *The History of Sierra Leone*. 4th ed. New York: Humanities, 1970.

Silva, Alberto da Costa e. "Buying and Selling Korans in Nineteenth-Century Rio de Janeiro." *Slavery and Abolition* 22, no. 1 (April 2001): 83–90.

———. "Sobre a rebelião de 1835 na Bahia." *Revista Brasileira* 8, no. 31 (2002): 9–33.

Silva, Vagner Gonçalves da. *Orixás da Metrópole*. Petropólis: Vozes, 1995.

Silveira, Renato da. "Iya Nassô Oka, Babá Axipá e Bamboxê Obиticô: uma narrativa sobre a fundação do Candomblé da Barroquinha, o mais antigo terreiro Ketu na Bahia." Unpublished paper, 2001.

———. "Pragmatismo e milagres de fé no Extremo Ocidente." In *Escravidão e Invenção da Liberdade. Estudos sobre o negro no Brasil*, ed. João José Reis, 166–97. São Paulo: Editora Brasiliense, 1988.

Simmons, William H. *Notices of East Florida*. A facsimile reproduction of the 1822 edition. Bicentennial Floridiana Facsimile series. Gainesville: University Press of Florida, 1973.

Skinner, David. "Islam and Trade in Sierra Leone in the Nineteenth Century." Ph.D. dissertation, University of California, Berkeley, 1971.

Skinner, D. E., and B. Harrell-Bond. "Misunderstandings Arising from the Use of the Term 'Creole' in the Literature on Sierra Leone." *Africa* 47, no. 3 (1977): 305–19.

Skinner, Elliot, ed. *Peoples and Cultures of Africa*. Garden City, N.Y.: Published for the American Museum of Natural History by Natural History Press, 1973.

Slenes, Robert W. "The Great Porpoise-Skull Strike: Central African Water Spirits and Slave Identity in Early Nineteenth-Century Rio de Janeiro." In *Central Africans and Cultural Transformations in the American Diaspora*, ed. Linda Heywood, 183–208. Cambridge: Cambridge University Press, 2002.

———. "Lares negros, olhares broncos: histórias de família escrava no século XIX." *Revista Brasileira de História* 8 (1988): 89–103.

———. "'Malungu ngoma vem!': África coberta e descoberta do Brasil." *Revista USP* (Universidade de São Paulo, Brazil) 12 (December 1991–February 1992): 48–67.

Smith, Robert S. *Kingdoms of the Yoruba*. 3rd ed. London: James Currey, 1988.

———. *The Lagos Consulate, 1851–1861*. London: Macmillan, 1978.

Soares, Carlos Eugênio Libano. *A capoeira escrava e outras tradições rebeldes no Rio de Janeiro, 1808–1850*. Campinas: Unicamp, 2001.

———. *A negregada instituição. Os capoeiras na corte imperial, 1850–1890*. Rio de Janeiro: Access, 1999.

———. *Zungú: Rumor de muitas vozes*. Rio de Janeiro: Arquivo Público do Estado do Rio de Janeiro, 1998.

Soares, Mariza de Carvalho. "Apreço e imitação no diálogo do gentio convertido." *Ipotesi. Revista de Estudos Literários* 4, no. 1 (2000): 111–23.

———. *Devotos da cor: Identidade étnica, religiosidade e escravidão no Rio de Janeiro, século XVIII*. Rio de Janeiro: Civilização Brasileira, 2000.

———. "The Mahi-Mina in Rio de Janeiro in the 18th Century." Harriet Tubman Seminar, York University, 2001. Unpublished manuscript.

Solomon, Maynard, ed. *Marxism and Art: Essays Classic and Contemporary*. New York: Knopf, 1973.

Solórzano Fonseca, Juan Carlos. "Comercio exterior de la provincia de Costa Rica (1690–1760)." Licenciatura thesis, Universidad Costa Rica, 1977.

Sorensen-Gilmour, Caroline. "Slave-Trading along the Lagoons of South-West Nigeria: The Case of Badagry." In *Ports of the Slave Trade (Bights of Benin and Biafra)*, ed. Robin Law and Silke Strickrodt, 84–95. Stirling, U.K.: Centre of Commonwealth Studies, University of Stirling, 1999.

Southern, Eileen. *The Music of Black Americans: A History*. New York: Norton, 1997.

Soyinka, Wole. *Ake: The Years of Childhood*. New York: Vintage International, 1989.

———. *Myth, Literature, and the African World*. Cambridge: Cambridge University Press, 1992.

Springer, Pearl E. "Orisa and the Spiritual Baptist Religion in Trinidad and Tobago." In *At the Crossroads: African Caribbean Religion and Christianity*, ed. Burton Sankeralli, 85–108. St. James, Trinidad and Tobago: Caribbean Conference of Churches, 1995.

Staudt Moreira, Paulo Roberto. *Faces da liberdade, máscaras do cativeiro*. Porto Alegre: EDIPUCRS, 1996.

Stearns, Marshall, and Jean Stearns. *Jazz Dance: The Story of American Vernacular Dance*. New York: Da Capo, 1994.

Steckel, Richard N., and Richard A. Jensen. "New Evidence on the Causes of Slave and Crew Mortality in the Atlantic Slave Trade." *Journal of Economic History* 46 (1986): 57–77.

Stein, Robert Louis. *The French Slave Trade in the Eighteenth Century: An Old Regime Business*. Madison: University of Wisconsin Press, 1979.

Stewart, William A. "Continuity and Change in American Negro Dialects." In *Perspectives on Black English*, ed. J. Dillard. The Hague: Houton, 1975.

Stone, R. H. *In Africa's Forest and Jungle; or, Six Years among the Yorubans*. London: Anderson and Fernier, 1900.

Strickrodt, Silke. "'Afro-Brazilians' of the Western Slave Coast in the Nineteenth Century." Edited by José C. Curto and Paul E. Lovejoy. New York: Humanity Books, 2004.

Stubbs, Jean. *Cuba: The Test of Time*. London: Latin American Bureau, 1989.

Stuckey, Sterling. *Slave Culture: Nationalist Theory and the Foundations of Black America*. New York: Oxford University Press, 1987.

Surgy, Albert de. *Le système religieux des évhè*. Paris: Éditions L'Harmattan, 1988.

Sutcliffe, David, and John Figueroa. *System in Black Language*. Philadelphia: Multilingual Matters, 1992.

Sylvain, Suzanne M. *Le Creole Haitian: Morphologie et Syntaxe*. Port-au-Prince, Wetteren: Imprimerie de Meester, 1936.

Taha, Halima. *Collecting African American Art: Works on Paper and Canvas*. New York: Crown, 1998.

Taiwo, Olu. "Music, Art, and Movement among the Yoruba." In *Indigenous Religions: A Companion*, ed. Graham Harvey, 173–89. London: Cassell, 2000.

Taylor, William. *Magistrates of the Sacred: Priests and Parishioners in Eighteenth-Century Mexico*. Stanford, Calif.: Stanford University Press, 1996.

Teer, Barbara Ann. "The African American Experience: Needed a New Mythology." In *Proceedings of the First World Conference on Orisa Tradition, Ili-Ife, Nigeria, 1–7 June 1981*. Ile-Ife, Nigeria: Department of African Languages and Literatures, University of Ife, 1981.

Thieme, Darius L. "A Descriptive Catalogue of Yoruba Musical Instruments." Ph.D. dissertation, Catholic University of America, Washington, D.C., 1969.

———. "Style in Yoruba Music." *Ibadan, A Journal Published at the University of Ibadan* 24 (1967): 33–39.

Thomas, Hugh. *Cuba: The Pursuit of Freedom*. New York: Harper and Row, 1971.

Thompson, Robert F. "African Art in Motion." In *Art from Africa: Long Steps Never Broke a Back*, ed. Pamela McClusky, 17–60. Princeton, N.J.: Princeton University Press, 2002.

———. *Face of the Gods: Art and Altars of Africa and the African Americas*. New York: Museum of African Art, 1993.

———. *Flash of the Spirit: African and Afro-American Art and Philosophy*. New York: Vintage, 1984.

———. "Recapturing Heaven's Glamour: Afro-Caribbean Festivalizing Arts." In *Caribbean Festival Arts: Each and Every Bit of Difference*, ed. John W. Nunley and Judith Bettleheim, 17–29. Seattle: University of Washington Press, 1988.

———. "The Three Warriors: Atlantic Altars of Esu, Ogun, and Osoosi." In *The Yoruba Artist: New Theoretical Perspectives on African Art*, ed. Rowland Abiodun, John Henry Drewal, and John Pemberton, 225–39. Washington, D.C.: Smithsonian Institution Press, 1994.

Thompson, Robert F., and Joseph Cornet. *Four Moments of the Sun: Kongo Art in Two Worlds*. Washington, D.C.: National Gallery, 1981.

Thornton, John K. *Africa and Africans in the Making of the Atlantic World, 1400–1800*. 2nd ed. Cambridge: Cambridge University Press, 1998.

Thorpe, Edward. *Black Dance*. Woodstock, N.Y.: Overlook Press, 1990.

Tijani-Serpos, Noureini. "The Postcolonial Condition: The Archeology of African Knowledge—From the Feat of Ogun and Sango to the Postcolonial Creativity of Obatala." *Research in African Literatures* 27, no. 1 (spring 1996): 3–18.

Tinajero, Pablo Tornero. *Crecimiento económico y transformaciones sociales: Esclavos, hacendados y comerciantes en la Cuba colonial (1760–1840)*. Madrid: Ministerio de Trabajo y Seguridad Social, 1996.

Trimigham, J. S., and Christopher Fyfe. "The Early Expansion of Islam in Sierra Leone." *Sierra Leone Bulletin of Religion* 2, no. 2 (December 1960): 33–40.

Trinidade Serra, Ordep. *Águas do Rei*. Petrópolis: Vozes, 1995.

Turay, A. K. "Loan Words in Temne." Ph.D. dissertation, University of London, 1972.

Turner, Lorenzo Dow. *Africanisms in the Gullah Dialect*. Chicago: University of Checago Press, 1949.

Turner, Jerry Michael. "Les Brésiliens: The Impact of Former Brazilian Slaves upon Dahomey." Ph.D. dissertation, Boston University, 1975.

Turner, Richard. "John Coltrane: A Biographical Sketch." *The Black Perspective in Music* 3, no. 1 (1975): 3–16.

Ullman, Victor. *Martin Delany: The Beginnings of Black Nationalism*. Boston: Beacon, 1971.

Ulrich, B. *Life and Labor in the Old South*. Boston: Little, Brown, 1929.

Valdés, Nelson. "Fidel Castro, Charisma, and Santeria: Max Weber Revisited." In *Caribbean Charisma: Reflections on Leadership, Legitimacy, and Populist Politics*, ed. Anton Allahar, 212–41. Boulder, Colo.: Lynne Rienner, 2001.

Vargens, João Baptista M., and Nei Lopes. *Islamismo e negritude: da África ao Brasil, da Idade Média aos nossos dias*. Rio de Janerio: Setor de Estudos Árabes, 1982.

Vass, Winifred K. "The Bantu-Speaking Heritage of the United States." In *Africanisms in American Culture*, ed. Joseph E. Holloway. Bloomington: Indiana University Press, 1990.

Vázquez Montalbán, Manuel. *Y dios entró en la Habana*. Madrid: Aguilar, 1998.

Veal, Michael E. *Fela: The Life and Times of an African Musical Icon*. Philadelphia: Temple University Press, 2000.

Vega, Marta Moreno. "Interlocking African Diaspora Cultures in the Work of Fernando Ortiz." *Journal of Black Studies* 31 (2000): 39–50.

———. "The Yoruba Orisha Tradition Comes to New York City." *African American Review* 29, no. 2 (1995): 201–206.

Vélez, Maria Teresa. *Drumming for the Gods: The Life and Times of Felipe García Villamil, Santero, Palero, and Abakuá*. Philadelphia: Temple University Press, 2000.

———. "The Trade of an Afrocuban Religious Drummer: Felipe Garcia Villamil." Ph.D. dissertation, Wesleyan University, 1996.

Verdery, Katherine. *National Ideology under Socialism: Identity and Cultural Politics in Ceausescu's Romania*. Berkeley: University of California Press, 1991.

———. "Theorizing Socialism: A Prologue to the 'Transition.'" *American Ethnologist* 18, no. 3 (1991): 419–39.

———. *What Was Socialism and What Comes Next?* Princeton, N.J.: Princeton University, 1996.

Verger, Pierre. *Flux et reflux de la traite des nègres entre le golfe de Bénin et Bahia de Todos os Santos du XVIIe au XIXe siècle*. Paris: Mouton, 1968.

———. *Notes sur le culte des Orisa et Vodun, à Bahia, la Baie de tous les Saints, au Brésil et a l'ancienne Cote des Esclaves en Afrique*. Dakar: IFAN, 1957.

———. *Orixás. Deuses iorubás na África e no Novo Mundo*. São Paulo: Corrupio, 1981.

———. *Os libertos: sete caminhos na liberdade de escravos da Bahia no século XIX*. Salvador, Bahia: Corrupio Fundação Cultural, Estado da Bahia, 1992.

———. *Trade Relations between the Bight of Benin and Bahia, 17th to 19th Centuries*. Ibadan, Nigeria: Ibadan University Press, 1976.

Vinueza, Maria Elena. *Presencia arará en la música folklórica de Matanzas.* Havana: Casa de las Américas, 1989.

Vlach, John M. "The Affecting Architecture of the Yoruba." *African Arts* 10, no. 1 (1976): 48–53.

———. *The Afro-American Tradition in the Decorative Arts.* Athens: University of Georgia Press, 1980.

———. *Back of the Big House: The Architecture of Plantation Slavery.* Chapel Hill: University of North Carolina Press, 1993.

———. *By the Work of Their Hands: Studies in Afro-American Folklife.* Charlottesville: University of Virginia Press, 1991.

———. "The Shotgun House: An African Architectural Legacy." *Pioneer America* 8, no. 1 (1976): 47–56 (Part 1); 57–70 (Part 2).

Wafer, Jim, and Hedimo Rodrigues Santana. "Africa in Brazil: Cultural Politics and the Candomble Religion." *Folklore Forum* 23 (1990): 98–114.

Walker, J. *The Black Loyalists: The Search for a Promised Land in Nova Scotia and Sierra Leone, 1783–1830.* New York: Africana, 1976.

Warner-Lewis, Maureen. *Trinidad Yoruba: From Mother Tongue to Memory.* Tuscaloosa: University of Alabama Press, 1996.

———. "Trinidad Yoruba: A Language of Exile." *International Journal of the Sociology of Language* 83 (1990): 9–20.

———. "Trinidad Yoruba: Notes on Survivals." *Caribbean Quarterly* 17, no. 2 (1971): 40–49.

Watson, John Fanning. *Methodist Errors.* Trenton, N.J.: Fenton, 1819.

Westcott, Joan. "The Sculpture and Myths of Eshu-Elegba, the Yoruba Trickster." *Africa* 32 (1962): 336–54.

Willett, Frank. *Ife in the History of West African Sculpture.* London: Thames and Hudson, 1967.

Williams, Mance. *Black Theatre in the 1960s and 1970s: A Historical-Critical Analysis of the Movement.* Westport, Conn.: Greenwood, 1985.

Williams, Patrice. *A Guide to African Villages in New Providence.* Nassau, Bahamas: Department of Archives, 1991 [1979].

Winant, Howard. "Race and Race Theory." *Annual Review of Sociology* 26 (2000): 169–85.

Winter, Marian H. "Juba and American Minstrelsy: From the Shakers to Martha Graham." In *Chronicles of the American Dance*, ed. Paul Magriel. New York: Henry Holt, 1948. Reprint, New York: Da Capo, 1978.

Wittmer, Marciline. "African Influence on Seminole Indian Patchwork." *Southeastern College Art Conference Review* 11 (1989): 269–75.

Wokeck, Marianne. "Irish and German Migration to Eighteenth Century North America." In *Coerced and Free Migration: Global Perspectives*, ed. David Eltis, 152–75. Stanford, Calif.: Stanford University Press, 2002.

Wyse, A. J. G. *The Krios of Sierra Leone.* London: Hurst, 1989.

———. "On Misunderstandings Arising from the Use of the Term 'Creole' in the Literature on Sierra Leone." *Africa* 49, no. 4 (1979): 408–17.

Yai, Olabiyi Babalola. "The Identity, Contributions, and Ideology of the Aguda (Afro-Brazilians) on the Gulf of Benin: A Reinterpretation." *Slavery and Abolition* 22, no. 1 (2001): 72–82.

Yelvington, Kevin A. "The Anthropology of Afro-Latin America and the Caribbean: Diasporic Dimensions." *Annual Review of Anthropology* 30 (2001): 227–60.

Yemiló, Ofún. *Documentos para la historia de Osha-Ifá en Cuba: tratado enciclopédico de caminos, Odi.* Regla, 1997.

Young, Robert A. *The Ethiopian Manifesto: Issued in Defence of the Black Man's Rights in the Scale of Universal Freedom.* New York: Robert A. Young, 1829.

Contributors

Augustine H. Agwuele holds degrees in German, English, and Pedagogy from the Friedrich-Schiller University, Jena, Germany. His research interests include natural language processing, syntax, phonetics, and phonology, and he has contributed chapters to various books.

Christine Ayorinde has a Ph.D. on Afro-Cuban religion from the Centre of West African Studies at the University of Birmingham, U.K. Current and forthcoming publications include chapters in *Identity in the Shadow of Slavery, Control and Resistance in the Century after Emancipation in the Caribbean*, and *Repercussions of the Atlantic Slave Trade: The Interior of the Bight of Benin and the African Diaspora*.

Matt D. Childs is an assistant professor in Caribbean history at Florida State University. He earned his Ph.D. in history from the University of Texas at Austin (2001). He has published articles in the *Journal of Latin American Studies, The Americas, The Historian*, and the *History Workshop Journal*.

Gibril R. Cole holds a Ph.D. from the University of California, Los Angeles, where he currently teaches African history. His scholarly research interests include the development of Krio society of Sierra Leone and the Krio diaspora, the African diaspora, and Islam in the Atlantic world.

David Eltis is the Robert W. Woodruff Professor of History at Emory University in Atlanta. His publications include *Rise of African Slavery in the Americas, The Transatlantic Slave Trade: A Database on CD-ROM*, and several articles in the *Journal of African History, Economic History Review*, and the *Journal of Economic History*. He is the editor of *Coerced and Free Migrations: Global Perspectives* and *Slavery in the Development of the Americas*, and co-editor of the four-volume *Cambridge World History of Slavery*.

Toyin Falola is the Frances Higginbothom Nalle Centennial Professor in History at the University of Texas at Austin. His published works include *Key Events in African History: A Reference Guide, Nationalism and African Intellectuals*, and several edited volumes including *Tradition and Change in Africa* and *African Writers and the Readers*. He is co-editor of the *Journal of African Economic History*, series editor of *Rochester Studies in African History and the Diaspora*, and series editor of the Culture and Customs of Africa.

C. Magbaily Fyle is a professor of African history in the Department of African American and African Studies at Ohio State University. His publications include *The History of Sierra Leone: A Concise Introduction* and the two-volume *Introduction to the History of African Civilization*.

Rosalyn Howard is an assistant professor of anthropology at the University of Central Florida. She specializes in the African diaspora with a focus on the Caribbean region, and in African/Native American relations. Her published works include *Black Seminoles in the Bahamas*.

Robin Law is a professor of African history at the University of Stirling, Scotland. His publications include *The Oyo Empire c. 1600–c.1836* and *The Slave Coast of West Africa, 1550–1750*. He edited *From Slave Trade to "Legitimate" Commerce: The Commercial Transition in Nineteenth-Century West Africa*, and co-edited, with Silke Strickrodt, *Ports of the Slave Trade*.

Babatunde Lawal received his masters and doctorate degrees in art history from Indiana University. He is a professor of African and African American Art in the Department of Art History at Virginia Commonwealth University in Richmond. He is the author of *The Gelede Spectacle: Art, Gender, and Social Harmony in an African Culture*. He is on the editorial boards of the *Art Bulletin, CAA Reviews*, and *Nineteenth Century Art Worldwide*, among others.

Russell Lohse is a Ph.D. candidate in history at the University of Texas at Austin. He is the author of "Slave-Trade Nomenclature and African Ethnicities in the Americas: Evidence from Early Eighteenth-Century Costa Rica," *Slavery and Abolition* 23, no. 3.

Paul E. Lovejoy is a Distinguished Research Professor in the Department of History at York University, Canada, and a Fellow of the Royal Society of Canada. He holds the Canada Research Chair in African Diaspora History and is director of the Harriet Tubman Resource Centre on the African Diaspora at York. He is the author or editor of more than twenty books and has written more than fifty-five articles and chapters in edited books. He is the co-author, with Robin Law, of *The Biography of Mahommah Gardo Baquaqua: His Passage from Slavery to Freedom in Africa and America*.

Beatriz Gallotti Mamigonian is a history professor at Universidade Federal de Santa Catarina. She earned her Ph.D from the University of Waterloo after completing a study exploring the experience of liberated Africans in nineteenth-century Brazil.

Robin Moore received his doctorate in ethnomusicology from the University of Texas at Austin. He is an associate professor in the College of Music at Temple University, Philadelphia. His published work includes *Nationalizing Blackness: Afrocubanismo and Artistic Revolution in Havana, 1920–1940*, as well as articles in the *New Grove Dictionary of Music and Musicians, Ethnomusicology,* and the *Latin American Music Review,* among others.

Ann O'Hear is an independent scholar who works in publishing. For ten years she taught history at Kwara State Polytechnic, Ilorin, Nigeria. She specializes in the history of Ilorin Emirate and the states and peoples of the Niger-Benue confluence, and has published studies of slavery and other forms of dependency, craft industries, and historiography. She is the author of *Power Relations in Nigeria: Ilorin Slaves and Their Successors* and, from 1992 to 2002, was a co-editor of the journal *African Economic History.*

Luis Nicolau Parés has a Ph.D. in Afro-Brazilian religion from the School of Oriental and African Studies, University of London, and is a visiting researcher at the Universidade Federal da Bahia, where he conducts research on Afro-Bahian history and religion. He has authored papers including "The Jeje in Bahian Candomblé and the Tambor de Mina of Maranhão" and "Transformations of the Sea and Thunder Voduns in the Gbe-speaking Area and in the Bahian Jeje Candomblé."

João José Reis is a professor of history at Universidade Federal da Bahia. Two of his books have been translated into English: *Slave Rebellion in Brazil: The 1835 Muslim Uprising in Bahia* and *Death Is a Festival: Funerary Rituals and Popular Rebellion in Nineteenth-Century Brazil.*

Michele Reid, Ph.D., examined in her dissertation the ways that free people of African descent navigated the intricacies of Cuban slave society in the aftermath of the 1844 repression of the Conspiracy of La Escalera until the beginning of the Ten Years' War in 1868. Her research interests include free people of color in the Americas, and the construction and politics of identity, race, gender, and immigration.

Kevin Roberts is an assistant professor of history at New Mexico State University. He earned his Ph.D. in colonial U.S. and Atlantic history at the University of Texas at Austin. With Toyin Falola he is co-editing *The Atlantic World, 1450–2000,* and has published articles on Bambara identity formation in eighteenth- and nineteenth-century Louisiana and on Yoruba kinship practices in the African diaspora.

Mariza de Carvalho Soares is an associate professor in the Department of History and in the Graduate Program of History at the Universidade Federal Fluminense, Niterói/Rio de Janeiro, Brazil. Her published work includes *Devotos da cor. Identidade étnica, religiosidade e escravidão no Rio de Janeiro (século XVIII).* She has also co-edited *A história vai ao cinema.*

Index

www.ingramcontent.com/pod-product-compliance
Ingram Content Group UK Ltd.
Pitfield, Milton Keynes, MK11 3LW, UK
UKHW032013280325
456865UK00007B/108